OVER-THE-COUNTER DERIVATIVE PRODUCTS

OVER-THE-COUNTER DERIVATIVE PRODUCTS

A GUIDE TO BUSINESS AND LEGAL RISK MANAGEMENT AND DOCUMENTATION

ROBERT M. McLAUGHLIN

McGraw-Hill

New York   San Francisco   Washington, D.C.   Auckland   Bogotá
Caracas   Lisbon   London   Madrid   Mexico City   Milan
Montreal   New Delhi   San Juan   Singapore
Sydney   Tokyo   Toronto

Library of Congress Cataloging-in-Publication Data

McLaughlin, Robert M.
    Over-the-counter derivative products : a guide to business and
legal risk management and documentation / by Robert M. McLaughlin.
        p.   cm.
    ISBN 0-7863-1078-2
    1. Derivative securities.   2. Derivative securities—Law and
legislation.   I. Title.
HG6024.A3M396   1998
658.15′5— dc21   98-9513
                                                            CIP

McGraw-Hill

A Division of The McGraw-Hill Companies

1 2 3 4 5 6 7 8 9 0   DOC/DOC   9 0 3 2 1 0 9 8

ISBN 0-7863-1078-2

*The sponsoring editor for this book was Stephen Isaacs, the editing supervisor
was Paul R. Sobel, and the production supervisor was Suzanne W. B. Rapcavage.
It was set in Times Roman by Victoria Khavkina of McGraw-Hill's Professional
Book Group composition unit.*

Printed and bound by R. R. Donnelley & Sons Company.

McGraw-Hill books are available at special quantity discounts to use as premiums
and sales promotions, or for use in corporate training programs. For more information, please write to the Director of Special Sales, McGraw-Hill, 11 West 19th
Street, New York, NY 10011. Or contact your local bookstore.

This book is printed on recycled, acid-free paper containing a
minimum of 50% recycled, de-inked fiber.

For The Angel Gabriella

CONTENTS

The award of the Nobel Prize for Economics in 1997 to Robert C. Merton and Myron Scholes for their pathbreaking work (with the late Fischer Black) in financial engineering signaled the important role of derivatives in the modern economy. Derivatives are not merely a tool for gambling or tax avoidance; they are used by businesses, households, financial institutions, and governments to modify their exposure to risks. For example, using derivative markets, a business can decide which bundle of risks it is willing to tolerate and can shed unwanted exposures. From a public policy perspective, derivatives allow the financial system to support the improvement of the "real economy," by allowing resources and risks to be shared more efficiently. Exchanging risks has grown to become a very large and important activity of business, and the extraordinary volume of derivative transactions attests to this fact.

Because derivatives have come to play an important role in business transactions, business executives and their legal advisers must understand their economics: what derivatives are (or are not), how they work, how they can be used, and how they are priced. In addition, the business executive and lawyer must be fully conversant with the legal, regulatory, and tax rules that apply to derivative contracts. For example, the economic concept of *put-call parity* establishes a relation among the prices of four claims: a riskless bond, a stock, and call and put options written on that stock. Under put-call parity, we can find many functionally equivalent ways to produce the same payout. However, not all of these will be treated equally under legal or tax rules. Managers and lawyers must appreciate these institutional subtleties, and construct the version of the payout that has the most desirable legal properties. At a more defensive level, although derivatives are used to transfer economic risks, if used imprudently they can create legal risks for firms. Thus, alongside the processes of financial innovation and engineering are parallel activities of legal innovation and engineering.

The businessperson or practicing lawyer who seeks to employ derivative transactions profitably must therefore master both the economics and the legal aspects of derivatives. *OTC Derivative Products: A Guide to Business and Legal Risk Management and Documentation* was written for these professionals, to bridge the gap between derivatives law and economics. In building this bridge, Bob McLaughlin could easily have been overwhelmed by the millions of detailed parts or institutional details that must ultimately fit together. Although these details are important, an overall plan is also needed to establish the bridge's general properties. To find the "plan" that sets the overarching framework, McLaughlin turns to the *functional perspective* proposed by Robert C. Merton.

The functional perspective starts with the proposition that there are a few functions that all financial systems must deliver, and these needs are present in all times and in all places. By starting with a consideration of fundamental functions, this way of thinking highlights how a single need can be met through a variety of institutions or products, and can alert practitioners of potential competition arising from very different types of institutions. The specific financial institutions and products that deliver these needs will certainly differ over time and across countries, but these different institutional structures must be considered endogenous rather than exogenous. The institutions and products are not merely given, they are the result of more basic forces, such as technologies, laws and regulations, and prior innovations, which in turn make certain structures efficient ways to deliver a particular function. For example, Merton speaks of the "financial innovation spiral," by which one set of new products makes the development of another feasible, such as Eurodollar futures supporting the development of the swaps business. The functional perspective was designed to help explain the dynamics of institutional change.

Executives and practicing lawyers who must deal with the fast pace of developments in the derivatives markets will appreciate the attraction of the functional perspective. It focuses attention on basic needs or functions, emphasizes the ever-changing nature of the financial landscape, underscores the important role of financial innovation, and alerts us to pay attention to how technological or legal innovations might change the way that institutions or products are structured. In this spirit, *OTC Derivative Products* provides practitioners with an understanding of the functional needs that derivatives serve, how law and regulation have affected—and will continue to affect—the development of and legal status of various derivative products, senior managers' roles in overseeing derivatives activity in their firms, and the legal requirements for documentation, disclosure, and control of derivatives activities.

With its emphasis on both derivatives economics and law, this ambitious book will prove highly useful to a wide range of readers. It seeks to help senior managers, directors and trustees, and practicing attorneys use derivatives to engage in economically sound transactions, while avoiding legal problems. This is no small task, but the potential reward is large. To some observers, legal and regulatory systems have served as impediments to innovation or have only inadvertently stimulated innovation. However, we can also find numerous examples of how lawyers have worked alongside business people to innovate new products and contracts, and better meet their clients' needs. But to work together confidently, businesspeople and lawyers need a heightened appreciation of each other's expertise as well as a common language. *OTC Derivative Products* is an important contribution that will improve this collaboration.

Peter Tufano
Harvard Business School

Panics, in some cases, have their uses; they produce as much good as hurt. Their duration is always short; the mind soon grows through them and acquires a firmer habit than before.

Thomas Paine, The American Crisis; 1776

I wonder if, in a perverse way, the Orange Counties and Barings and P&Gs might not actually be serving to strengthen the longterm outlook for the risk management and derivatives industry.

Robert McKnew, Executive Vice President,
Bank of America, 1995

Nineteen ninety-four, *CFO* magazine's "Year of Derivatives," seared into the public consciousness the risks of financial derivatives. Large losses humbled major financial institutions and public companies; they damaged the portfolios of pension funds, charities, municipalities, and other ostensibly conservative investors. The derivatives crisis lasted over a year and prompted Congressional hearings, legislative proposals, domestic and international regulatory initiatives, and numerous lawsuits. Many people viewed with alarm the prospect that a derivatives disaster at one financial institution might have repercussions that could undermine the stability of the global financial system. Since then, things have changed.

Derivatives markets began a stunning resurgence in 1995. Trading in many poducts soon far exceeded prior record volumes and has since continued to increase steadily. Important new markets are emerging, a premier example of which is that for credit derivatives, which grew to a national amount of $91 billion in the first quarter of 1998—up 379% from 1997's first quarter. Alan Greenspan cites as a primary cause of the current Asian currency crisis the failure of local borrowers to hedge their hard currency exposures, and the OCC is conserned "that only 451 out of some 9000-odd banks are using derivatives to manage risk."[1] Moreover, the law of trust investments is undergoing profound transformation to accommodate "the use of abstractly high-risk investments or techniques (such as futures or option trading) for the purpose of redusing the risk level of the portfolio as a whole." The resurgence has not been universal, however. Markets for some exotic products, particularly highly-leveraged instruments with opaque pricing structures and complex payoff formulas, have vanished. Nobel laureate Merton H. Miller argues that the net result of this phenomenon is salutary, at least from a systemic perspective. It means that the financial system has again demonstrated a healthy ability to rid itself of "toxic waste."*

Yet doubts about derivatives' legitimacy linger. Many observers consider the products intrinsically speculative and harmful. That perception persists and is occasionally sensationalized, despite abundant empirical evidence that, in Miller's words, "derivatives have made the world a safer place, not a more dangerous one. They have made it possible for firms and institutions to deal efficiently and cost effectively with risks and hazards that have plagued them for decades, if not for centuries."[2] The negative perception is hardly new.

Holbrook Working, an economist and scholar of futures markets, long ago attributed "popular suspicion of futures trading . . . (to) a sense of mystery associated with it."[3] That popular suspicion today can be generalized beyond futures to all derivatives, especially over-the-counter (OTC) products. A predictable result of the suspicion of futures has been episodic calls for legislation prohibiting futures trading. As early as 1893, legislation banning all futures trading in the United States only narrowly escaped enactment. Historical parallels to fervent legislative attacks on derivatives in the 1990s readily emerge.

Management's Predicament. Many businesses and investment funds can realize tangible economic benefits by using derivatives to manage unwanted financial risks. Conversely, the failure to use derivatives may place them at a competitive disadvantage. As Peter Tufano of Harvard Business School advises: "Forward-looking managers need to keep abreast of their rivals' successful uses of promising breakthroughs like financial engineering," defined as "the use of derivatives to manage risk and create customized financial instruments."[4]

However, most trustees, directors, senior executives, and legal advisers— all of when comprise this book's principal intended audi-

---

*Miller was referring specifically to "inverse floaters," collateralized mortgage obligations, and other exotic structured notes. As we discuss in Chap. 3, controversy surrounds the question of whether these and other derivatives securities, as opposed to derivatives contracts, are true derivatives.

ence—are also intimately aware of the economic risks of using derivatives. Many senior managers* and lawyers are also concerned about
potential investor backlashes against their firms' use of derivatives, even
if a business or portfolio suffers no derivatives loss. Worse is that antiderivatives sentiment may increase as heightened derivatives disclosure
requirements take effect under new rules adopted by the Securities and
Exchange Commission (SEC). Further, efforts by the Financial
Accounting Standards Board's to tighten eligibility requirements for
"hedge accounting" treatment of derivatives activities may increase the
volatility of reported earnings. Understandably, many senior managers
and business lawyers approach the topic of derivatives with apprehension.

    A Functional Approach. Recognizing that apprehension, this book's
operative assumption is that many senior managers and business lawyers
can benefit from greater familiarity with derivatives' risk management
functions. The products' primary function is easily stated: Derivatives
enable a user to unbundle packages of risks and manage the resulting isolated risk components more precisely and at lower costs than with other
financial instruments. Generally, the phrase "risk management" is understood to refer to risk reduction.[†] Thus, derivatives economic function is
inherently defensive, because they enable users efficiently to reduce their
exposures to isolated, unwanted financial risks.

    Yet familiarity with derivatives' primary function is not enough;
overcoming potent arguments, grounded in modern finance theory,
against derivatives use demands more. Modern finance theory holds that
entity-level risk management can be unnecessary and, if costly, wasteful.
Often investors, through diversification, can more cheaply manage the
relevant financial risks on their own. Therefore, a firm's management
must know how derivatives can be used to reduce risk without duplicat-
ing investors' own risk management activities. In essence, modern
finance theory states that risk management can add value when it either
increases the present value of a firm's expected net cash flows or reduces
the firm's costs of capital. We will explore in detail how firms can use

---

*We will often use phrases such as "senior manager" and "manager" expansively to include any
    executive with express or implied fiduciary duties to her or his firm or investors. The most
    common examples are trustees, directors, and executive officers.
[†]Of course, derivatives can also be used to increase risk exposures. Throughout this book, however,
    we will refer to the management of financial risk using derivatives in its defensive, risk
    reduction sense.

derivatives strategies* to reduce risk and thereby achieve each of those results.

This book also assumes that many senior managers and lawyers can gain from greater awareness of derivatives' legal implications. Doubtless, a few situations exist where senior managers have a legal duty to cause their firms to use derivatives. Yet ongoing changes in law, particularly the law of trust   investments, suggest that many fiduciaries can no longer safety ignore explicit consideration of derivatives' risk management benefits. Nor can they afford to disregard the potential economic efficiencies of using derivatives to structure optimal investment portfolios.

Consider the consequences of derivatives uses that reduce risk but without increasing the present value of expected net cash flows or reducing costs of capital. Many such activities are, under modern finance theory, subject to attack as being unnecessary and possibly wasteful. Certainly any attacks will only intensify if the derivatives produce losses. Finally, directors, trustees, and other senior executives who authorize the use of derivatives must properly supervise approved activities. As law professor Henry T. C. Hu puts it, "such decisions constitute a form of sustained managerial activity that is novel and commercially significant; it is important to learn to do it right."[5]

"Doing it right," both as a legal and a business matter, demands a supervisory level understanding not only of how derivatives can be used to manage risks: it also impels an understanding of how to manage the risks the products themselves introduce. A supervisory level understanding, in turn, requires access to different types of information, many of which are seldom readily accessible. Even with abundant literature responding to derivatives-related legal concerns, and despite the proliferation of technical works on financial engineering, a pronounced gap is evident in today's derivatives materials.

Information Gap. Inspection of extant finance materials on derivatives' risk management reveals that most focus on product mechanics. Thus, many of those materials have "much less clear cut guidance to offer on the logically prior questions of hedging[†] strategy: What sorts of risks

---

*An understanding of those derivatives uses assumes increasing prominence under the new SEC disclosure guidelines. The reason is that reporting entities either are or will soon be required to explain their risk management strategies in their public filings.

†Many academics writing about the use of derivatives to reduce risk use the term "hedging" in a generic sense. As noted below, the functional analysis we adopt treats hedging as merely one of three "pure methods" of risk management; the other two are diversification and insurance.

should be hedged? Should they be hedged partially or fully? What kinds of instruments will best complish the hedging objectives?"[6]

Similarly, Hu finds that "clarity and richness do not exist" in relevant legal analyses.[7] He concludes that "most of the current legal attention paid to the corporate use of derivatives has dealt not with the question of what is to be achieved through their use, but instead with ancillary, second-order questions." Most business lawyers are, for instance, careful to councel corporate clients to observe proper procedures and establish appropriate internal controls before using derivatives. Yet the paucity of formal inquiry into the legally appropriate and logically prior goals of corporate derivatives usage may reflect "a lack of awareness of the true complexity of the question."

Additional uncertainty is created by the law of trust investments. Many state and federal lawmakers are replacing antiquated notions of investment "prudence" with new, demonstrably superior standards responsive to modern investment practices. Still, the new, purportedly fiduciary-friendly trust rules have led some practitioners to opine inauspiciously that "[f]iduciaries will be acting in a realm of uncertainty for some time to come."[8] John Langbien of Yale Law School also stresses that the new rules place "growing pressure on amateur trustees to yield to professionals."[9] Moreover, in jurisdictions that have not adopted the new standards, trustees are subject to outdated rules that constrain their attempts to realize the full benefits of modern investment technology. Thus, although long overdue changes are meant to reform trust investment law, they have created confusion over the legal duties of trustees, portfolio managers, and other investment fiduciaries.

This Book's Goals and Approach. A primary goal of this book is to explain how derivatives enhance a firm's ability to manage risks and to do so from a supervisory level perspective. Yet to be useful, any such explanation must overcome a threshold difficulty. Namely, modern financial markets are dynamic and unstable. They exhibit unending product innovation, rapidly changing forms and identities of financial institutions, and dynamic legal and regulatory strutures. Instability can magnify the complexity of individual products and of the systems and controls needed to deploy the products successfully and to effectively manage their dynamic business and legal risks. Moreover, any approach to risk management that is unresponsive to dynamic market conditions will quickly become obsolete.

To overcome that threshold difficulty, we adopt the "functional analysis" proposed by Nobel laureate Robert C. Merton. As Peter Tufano notes in his Foreword, Merton developed his analysis to explain the dynamics of institutional change within a financial system. He starts from the premise that all financial systems perform a few basic functions that are essentially the same in all economies, regardless of time and place. One of these functions is risk management, by which he means the efficient allocation of risk-bearing throughout an economy. Our focus will be on derivatives' role in performing the risk management function, with the emphasis on risk reduction.

Merton further identifies three "functional subcategories" or methods of reducing risk: hedging, diversification, and insurance. This functional analysis explains the role of both derivatives and functionally similar non-derivatives strategies play in controlling financial risk. Thus, the three methods refer to explicity functions, not particular products or product types. For example, a put options may be used to limit the holder's potential losses from a stock's price decline. That option serves the same economic function as an insurance policy used to protect a holder against loss from the damage or theft of an automobile.

A functional understanding of Merton's three "pure methods" of reducing risk will prove enormously beneficial to any senior manager responsible for business or investment strategy. Likewise, it greatly reduces the number of financial concepts a business lawyer must be conversant with to meaningfully assess derivatives' legal implications. As we discuss, functional analysis quickens one's ability to apprehend the benefits and risks of many otherwise inscrutable products. Consequently, senior managers and lawyers can employ the analysis, for example, to determine whether a specific product complements or detracts from overall competitive strategy. They can also use it to discern the legal implications of a wide range of functionally similar products, whether or not the products are labeled as derivatives.

To better manage derivatives' legal risks, we adapt key principles of Merton's functional analysis to certain important legal concepts. A functional analysis is useful, for example, in exploring the application of fiduciary duties to derivatives activities. The law in this area is unstable, often appearing to be but a jumble of loosely related, fluid, and inconsistent rules. We gain stability by starting from the premise that all fiduciaries serve a few basic functions that are essentially the same across Anglo-Saxon legal systems. At the highest level, those functions imply both decision making and oversight responsibilities.

Our focus is on the responsibilities fiduciary duties create for officers, directors, senior executives, and certain other individuals. To isolate the specific responsibilities, we rely largely on traditional fiduciary analyses, especially those articulated by Professor Tamar Frankel of Boston University School of Law and Victor Brudney, Professor of Law Emeritus of The Harvard Law School and Visiting Professor of Boston College Law School. Our analysis incorporates important insights from modern finance and, within limitations, the "contractarian" approach to fiduciary duties that enrich a traditional analysis.

Building Block Approach. Every derivative, whether a "plain vanilla" product or complex hybrid instrument, can be deconstructed, or "reverse engineered," into a combination of two simple building blocks: forwards and options. Reverse engineering isolates and categorizes a product's distinct risk components using the taxonomy of the two building blocks. Familiarity with that classification scheme makes understanding and comparing the benefits of diverse types of products far easier than it would otherwise be. It also clarifies an understanding of the nature and magnitude of each specific risk. Consequently, the building block approach, on which we rely extensively, gives essential insights into the principal risks of virtually any derivative. And that is just the beginning.

For lawyers, the building block approach is particularly useful in understanding some of the most difficult issues raised by the rash of derivatives litigation in recent years. We will examine, for instance, the Proctor & Gamble litigation and related SEC and Commodity Futures Trading Commission (CFTC) enforcement actions. All of those cases raise difficult jurisdictional issues which, in turn, depend on complex product classifications. Were the products at issue securities within the meaning of state or federal securities laws? Were they commodity futures or options on commodity futures under the Commodity Exchange Act? A building block approach, combined with various insights from modern finance, enhances one's grasp of the economics of the analyses applied to resolve those cases. Equally important, it reveals the strengths and weaknesses of those resolutions and enhances a lawyer's ability to advise clients concerning the implications of those cases for other products and strategies.

Managers and lawyers can use the building block approach not only to improve their knowledge of individual products but also to enhance their understanding of several key relationships. For example, a critical relationship is that between individual products and the risks they are designed to manage. Another involves the economic effects of a product on the overall risks of a business or an investment portfolio.

A Word on Quantitative Methods Quantitative techniques and powerful computer analytics permit isolated risk components to be measured and aggregated across diverse transactions and instruments. Results can then be expressed in summary statistics that capture dominant portfolio risks and categorize them according to the risk taxonomy of the two building blocks. Properly interpreted, summary statistics enable corporate treasurers and investment managers to communicate effectively derivatives' likely impact on a firm or portfolio. For both business and legal purposes, those statistics are valuable aids to directors, trustees, and other senior managers ultimately responsible for supervising their firms' derivatives activities. Summary statistics also inform investors, creditors, regulators, and other interested parties of the impact derivatives have on a firm's or portfolio market value.

Many people approach the subject of derivatives with trepidation, expecting that any attempt to understand the products will require a grasp of higher-order mathematics. Rarely, however, is that so (although a mathematics background is certainly helpful). Most supervisors and legal advisers merely need enough comfort and facility with quantitative techniques to appreciate the techniques' applications and, equally important, limitations.

Quantitative methods largely determine derivatives pricing and are useful in measuring financial risks. Legally, the ability to supervise the application of quantitative techniques provides a rational basis for deciding whether, when, and how to use derivatives. This is important, because manifestly rational decision-making is critical to protecting directors, trustees, and other senior managers from legal liability. Yet quantitative techniques are not infallible, a point sometimes missed by those deeply immersed in the mathematics of derivatives.

A supervisory level understanding concentrates on confirming that appropriate methods have been employed by others responsible for formulating and solving the mathematical problems. The tedious mechanics that often confuse issues, sidetrack discussions, and discourage those responsible for performing complex calculations are seldom supervisory tasks. They are instead almost always delegated to subordinates or outsourced to outside experts and consultants. The supervisor's concern is the logic and strategy embodied in calculations.

Controls; Best Practices. One might view this as a second-generation derivatives book. Its focus is more on the contributions derivatives can make to enhancing firm value, optimizing portfolio structures, and improving competitive strategy, less on what derivatives industry professionals call "best practices." A strategic focus does not detract from the central importance of risk management practices in managing the risks of derivatives or of any other commercially significant activity. To the contrary, it is only possible because by now most executives and lawyers are well aware of the dangers of using derivatives improperly or without first establishing adequate internal controls.

Indeed, an important benefit of the recent derivatives crisis is that it accelerated the evolution of risk management standards and hastened the diffusion of those standards throughout dealer and end user communities. Diverse groups of market participants—some motivated by business prudence, others spurred by regulators and investors—have crafted detailed guidelines (many of which we cite), tailored to the needs of specific constituencies. Portfolio managers and corporate treasurers can now benchmark their policies and procedures for managing derivatives' risks against accepted industry "best practices." And as industry standards continuously improve, market participants should have immediate access to ample informaiton for updating existing systems and procedures.

This book does not attempt to duplicate successful ongoing industry efforts to improve risk management practices. Instead, it focuses on leadership's role in choosing strategy based on a sound understanding of derivatives' economic functions and legal implications. Strategy choices go beyond mandating best practices. They involve decisions concerning what activities an organization will and will not engage in. For most firms, derivatives are beneficial only if a firm's leadership understands how to use the products prudently to enhance or support other strategic objectives.

ORGANIZATION OF THE BOOK

Chapter 1 explores the causes of financial innovation. It shows why the ceaseless innovative process, especially in derivatives markets, quickly renders obsolete any static analysis of derivatives and their risks. To provide analytical stability, we adopt Merton's functional analysis, which includes an explanation of the three "pure methods" of risk management: hedging and diversifying risk, and insuring against loss. Chapters 2 and 3 explain in greater detail the potentially debilitating flaws of a static, definitional approach to derivatives, which convey little information about product risk and return features. As an alternative, they offer a functional approach to analyzing individual products and their interaction with other assets, liabilities, and business activities. Chapter 4 examines how derivatives, by performing their risk management function, can support and enhance a user's overall competitive strategy.

Chapters 5 and 6 turn to efforts by market participants to establish internal systems of derivatives legal risk management. They assert that prevailing definitions of legal risk, with their dominant emphasis on enforceability concerns, afford but a weak conceptual foundation for any such system. Those definitions fail to account for many obvious diffculties that are legal in nature and readily apparent to both skilled practitioners and derivatives novices alike. The failure is important, because an adequate definition of legal risk is essential to establishing a coherent framework of legal risk management. A new definition, in contrast, should be useful to those responsible for legal risk management and therefore who need a robust working definition. These chapters suggest a new functional framework for analyzing the main categories, or building blocks, of derivatives' legal risks. The framework is intuitively appealing, because of its explanatory power. Because any such system, to be effective, must fit the specific and changing needs of its user, these chapters also emphasize analytical stability and flexibility. Critical is that the system must encourage constant monitoring and feedback and be quickly responsive when revisions are needed.

Chapters 7, 8, and 9 discuss the nettlesome topic of market regulation. In the United States, federal securities and commodities regulation is an evolving "patchwork quilt" of statutes, regulations, and judicial and agency decisions premised on imprecise and ambiguous product definitions. As a result, some products may be subject not only to unforeseen but also inconsistent regulation. In practice, definitional interpretations often depends as much on the interpreter—that is, the SEC, the CFTC, a court, or an agency—rather than on any clear, logical anlyses. A lack of international supervisory coordination creates added uncertainty.

To minimize the risk of regulatory surprises, Chaps. 7 and 8 discuss two types of information essential to managers and legal advisers: information about whether a product fits any obvious regulatory categories; that about a product's economic characteristics. Depending on perceived "economic reality," many products that seemingly fit standard definitions remain unregulated; others that do not may, in the view of one or more regulators, warrant regulation. Yet it would be a mistake to overstate the practical uncertainty confronting most products. As in other areas of the law, confusion generated by hard derivatives cases (usually those involving exotic products, egregious conduct, and anachronistic regulation) belies the considerable degree of judicial and regulatory consistency and predictability as to the vast majority of existing OTC products. Thus, armed with useful regulatory information, management will be well positioned to compare the costs and benefits of derivatives solutions with those of alternatives.

Chapter 9 pays close attention to important recent case law, especially the May 1996 Proctor & Gamble decision. Until then, little directly relevant guidance as to the judicial and regulatory treatment of OTC derivatives was available in the United States. That decision was the first published decision by a U.S. court addressing the broad range of legal issues applicable to swaps and swap-related products. It held that certain complex interest rate swaps were not securities under relevant securities laws and were exempt from the exchange-trading requirement of the Commodity Exchange Act. Not surprisingly, the legal conclusions reached by the court are subject to divergent interpretations.

Chapter 10 introduces the role of trustees, directors, and senior executives in derivatives risk management. Particular attention is paid to a difficult dilemma faced by many managers. In particular, new technologies afford them with unprecedented capabilities for ridding their firms of unwanted financial risks and modifying those risks they choose to take. Still, often management is left with no clear set of risk management goals. If so, "using derivatives can be dangerous" and raises legal and business concerns, neither of which can be adequately understood of managed in isolation. Both as a legal and business matter, senior management has ultimate responsibility for choosing risk management strategies and overseeing and monitoring their implementation. Here, functional analysis is particularly useful, because it provides superior analytical tools.

Chapters 11 through 15 state the arguments from modern finance both for and against the use of derivatives by corporations and institutional investors. The arguments address a central paradox for corporate users: that is, while modern finance provides exceptional guidance in determining the mechanics of risk management, it also suggests that much risk management at the corporate level is wasteful. The chapters explain how to increase firm value by enhancing expected future cash flows or decreasing costs of capital. Those chapters also explore the use of derivatives to maximize expected portfolio returns for given levels of risk and to minimize risks needed to generate specified expected returns.

In Chapters 16 and 17 we examine the rapidly evolving legal responsibilities of senior managers concerning the use and nonuse of derivatives. One clear conclusion is that decision to use or not use derivatives, if lacking the requisite due care because they were based on informal, unclear decision making processes, may not only be subject to severe criticism but also give rise to legal liability. Management of firms that have legitimate opportunities to manage the economic risks of their core businesses through derivatives would, therefore, be well advised first to decide clearly on appropriate levels of investment to make in their derivatives risk management practices and capabilities.

Chapter 18 suggests a formal means-ends approach to thinking about risk management. It shows that, aside from being an interesting academic or intellectual puzzle, defining derivatives terminology is essential to any sound risk management system. This Chapter explores a number of related disclosure, documentation, and other business and legal issues. It concludes with some final thoughts on the beneficial role of functional analysis in derivatives law and finance.

Robert M. McLaughlin

ENDNOTES

1. Bill McConnell, "Banks' 1Q Derivatives Revenue At $2.4B High on Asia Hedging," *American Banker* (June 16, 1998) (quoting (emphasis added) Michal L. Brosnan, deputy comptroller for risk evaluation): 2.

2. Preface to Miller, Merton, H., *Merton Miller on Derivatives* (John Wiley & Sons, Inc., 1997).

3. See Chap. 1, *infra.*

4. Peter Tufano, "How Financial Engineering Can Advance Corporate Strategy," *Harvard Business Review* (January-February 1996): 136–146.

5. Henry T. C. Hu, "Behind the Corporate Hedge: Information and the Limits of 'Shareholder Wealth Maximization,'" *Journal of Applied Corporate Finance,* 9(3) (Fall 1996): 39.

6. Kenneth A. Froot, David S. Scharfstein, and Jeremy C. Stein, "Risk Management: Coordinating Corporate Investment and Financing Policies," *Journal of Finance,* 48(5) (December 1993): 1629–1630; see also Dong-Hyun Ahn, Jacob Boudoukh, Matthew Richardson, and Robert F. Whitelaw, "Optimal Risk Management Using Options," *Journal of Finance* (forthcoming; manuscript dated February 1998) ("Only recently have academics begun to study the risk management practices of financial institutions and other corporations. . . . [A]cacemics and practitioners alike have been silent on how to go about *managing* this risk."): 1–2.

7. The Hu quotations in this paragraph are from Henry T. C. Hu, "Hedging Expectations: 'Derivative Reality' and the Law and Finance of the Corporate Objective," *Texas Law Review,* 73 (1995): 985–1040, 1014–1015.

8. Bernard Karol and M. Antoinette Thomas, "Prudent-Investor Rule Demands New Strategies," *American Banker* (March 19, 1996): 6.

9. John H. Langbien, "The Contractarian Basis of the Law of Trusts," *Yale Law Journal,* 105 (December 1995): 625–675, 640.

ACKNOWLEDGMENTS

This book would not have been possible without generous contributions of ideas, time, comments, and information provided, in varying degrees, by the following individuals: Don Chance of Virginia Tech; Lillian Chew, derivatives author and former editor of *Risk* magazine; Denis Forster of Law Offices of Denis M. Foster; Tamar Frankel of Boston University Law School; Michael Gruson of Shearman & Sterling; Gabriella Morizio of Credit Suisse First Boston; Richard Nathan; Maarten Nederlof of Capital Market Risk Advisors; Tom O'Brien of the University of Connecticut; Don Pardew of Columbia Business School; Nassar Saber of Saber Partnership; René Stulz of Ohio State University; Don Thompson of J. P. Morgan; and Peter Tufano of Harvard Business School. To all of these individuals I am grateful. In fairness however, I accept that all errors are solely my responsibility. Furthermore, I readily admit to having no reason to believe any of these individuals (or their institutions) would necessarily agree with or approve of this book in its entirety.

I also want to acknowledge the support of my colleagues at Eaton & Van Winkle and of my legal assistant, Janis Treanor. What began as a minor imposition upon them quickly expanded into, I am sure, a major distraction. For that matter, the distraction was visited upon my clients, too. For their patience I am likewise grateful.

I am much indebted to McGraw-Hill for its patience and, particularly to Stephen Isaacs, my editor, for wielding the essential goad that eventually produced this book. I thank the rest of the staff of McGraw-Hill who worked on this book, especially Paul Sobel, my editing supervisor.

For my wife, and my family, words cannot express my feelings of thankfulness for their extraordinary support and understanding. Only time. I promise.

OVER-THE-COUNTER DERIVATIVE PRODUCTS

CHAPTER 1

Stability Amid Change:
A Functional Approach

The genie is out of the bottle....Unless you think there will be re-regulation and corporate finance will become less sophisticated and the market less volatile, [derivatives are] here to stay.

Wall Street Journal, December 18, 1986
(Quoting an investment banker)

[D]erivatives are a permanent part of the mainstream global financial system.

Nobel Laureate Robert C. Merton
Harvard University, 1996[1]

Modern derivatives markets moved to the forefront of the world economic scene during the late 1970s and early 1980s with the convergence of two powerful, multifaceted forces. The first was a massive increase in *economic uncertainty* in world financial markets. Among the causes of uncertainty were oil shocks, a bear market in stocks, inflationary pressures, and the collapse of the Bretton Woods monetary system. The second force was a *technological revolution* compelled by dramatic advances in three principal areas: "computing technology, telecommunications, and financial engineering, specifically the logic of dynamic replication that underlies the Black-Scholes [option pricing] model and other models of derivatives pricing."[2]

One aspect of the technological revolution that has received little attention in derivatives literature concerns advances in discipline we might consider the legal analog of financial engineering. Professor Peter Tufano of Harvard University's Graduate School of Business Administration calls this discipline "legal engineering."

Tufano uses the term *financial engineering* to describe the use of derivatives to manage risk and create customized financial instruments for solving "classic and vexing business problems." Likewise, we use *legal engineering* here to mean the use of derivatives to solve classic and vexing legal problems. We also use the term to cover the development and application of legal techniques—some old, some new—for solving legal problems raised by derivatives.

The term *legal engineering* suggests a discipline that, as an adjunct of financial engineering, demands of legal advisers an understanding of derivatives' basic economic functions. That same understanding is essential to senior managers—including directors, trustees, executive officers,

1

and public and private sector fund managers. The lawyer or manager who fails to understand those functions is, as Holbrook Working once wrote, "especially vulnerable to the imperfections of basic concepts."[3] Reliance on flawed concepts can quickly undermine any business or investment strategy, regardless of whether derivatives are involved.

Working pioneered the application of empirical research to economics. In the 1920s he began studying markets for agricultural futures, the precursors of many of today's financial derivatives. Steeped in knowledge of statistical methods, he spent nearly five decades analyzing abundant market data that had previously defied rigorous quantitative analysis. His findings prompted the overhaul or rejection of several previously accepted concepts used to explain the economic functions of futures markets. Although his conclusions predate financial derivatives and the development of modern finance by several decades, Working's rich insights clarify many fundamental issues facing modern derivatives markets.

Of immediate concern to him were prevalent misconceptions about the economic functions of futures trading, the most disturbing of which were misapprehensions about *hedging*. Previously, traditional economic discussions considered hedging to be merely a method of avoiding risk by offsetting one financial exposure with an equal but opposite exposure. Working demonstrated that such risk-avoidance hedging—what corporate finance now calls "variance-minimizing" hedging—is merely one of many different types of hedging.

"Multipurpose concept" of hedging   Hedging by commodity merchants, for example, has long been undertaken for many reasons other than merely avoiding risk; after all, merchants "are in business not to avoid risk, but to make money."[4] Consequently, many of their hedging decisions are dictated by their informed assessments of expected price changes. Working viewed these decisions as involving elements of both hedging and *speculation,* with speculation manifesting as decisions *not* to hedge. He found that many handlers of physical commodities routinely engage in "selective" or "discretionary hedging" to avoid losses from expected price declines. When they expect prices to advance, they either do not hedge or hedge less than all their holdings. Manufacturers today often engage in "anticipatory hedging" when they lock in what they deem to be currently favorable costs of future raw materials purchases or satisfactory revenues from future sales of goods. In contrast, manufacturers who expect favorable price changes might reduce the extent of their hedging or not hedge at all.

Finally, Working explains the economics of "carrying charge" hedging,* which he considers a type of arbitrage. A carrying charge hedger simultaneously enters into a pair of joint commodity transactions: one is a purchase of the commodity in the "cash" or "spot" market; the other is a sale of a futures contract. In the futures contract the hedger agrees to sell (i.e., takes a *short* position) the commodity at a price agreed upon upfront, with delivery of and payment for (i.e., *settlement*) the commodity to occur at a later date. The hedger enters into the joint transaction with a high degree of confidence that it will profit from favorable changes in spot/futures price relations. For present purposes, suffice to say that the focus on price relations is pivotal, because carrying charge hedgers do *not* attempt to profit (or avoid loss) by predicting future spot prices. While selective, operational, anticipatory, and carrying charge hedging ordinarily entail some risk-avoidance, any such benefit is merely an incidental, not primary objective.

Working's analyses provide an illuminating backdrop against which to view the role of derivatives in modern financial markets. With the advent of modern finance, derivatives can now be used to manage not only commodity risk but also, to varying degrees, currency, interest rate, equity, credit, and catastrophe risk. As discussed in Chapters 11 through 15, modern finance states arguments both for and against the corporate use of derivatives to increase firm value by enhancing expected future cash flows. Those chapters also explore the use of derivatives to maximize expected portfolio returns for given levels of risk and to minimize risks needed to generate targeted expected returns.

---

*Working's arguments are at the center of a highly publicized debate over the economic logic of the long-term marketing and hedging program of MG Refining and Marketing, Inc. (MGRM), a subsidiary of Metallgesellschaft AG (MG AG). By year-end 1993, the spectacular failure of that program reportedly resulted in $1.3 billion in derivatives-related losses. Merton Miller and Christopher Culp rely on Working's "carrying charge hedging" concept, which we briefly discuss, as the linchpin of their famous argument that MGRM's program was conceptually sound. They assert that the most likely cause of the debacle was a failure of MG AG's management to appreciate the program's logic and the long-term funding commitments it entailed. The opposing arguments are based on theories from corporate finance that are inapposite to a carrying charge program. Under a standard corporatr finance model (as Miller and Culp happily concede) the entire program was flowed from inception. In essence, then, the academic debate is about the model to be used to analyze the program. Different models dictate opposite conclusions concerning the validity of the program's economic logic. See sources cited at *infra,* Chap. 17, note 51.

Hedging v. Speculation   Another of Working's important contributions is that he demonstrated how seemingly obvious distinctions between hedging and speculation can be deceptive. For example, many people who are unfamiliar with futures trading commonly associate it with speculation. In contrast, the merchandising and processing of agricultural commodities is typically thought to be a paradigmatically conservative venture. Working turned the traditional distinction on its head by approaching it from a statistician's perspective. Edward Tufte recently wrote that "The deep, fundamental question in statistical analysis is *Compared with what?*"[5] Working showed that merchants, processors, even farmers and other commodity handlers, depending on their price expectations, routinely seek profits from *not* hedging. By comparing this to its opposite, which is hedging stored supplies, Working could legitimately label the practice of not hedging the "speculative holding" of physical commodities. In other words, many handlers try to profit from anticipated commodity price increases by strategically refraining from hedging.

Substantial empirical and anecdotal evidence shows that the risk management practices Working observed among handlers of agricultural commodities are prevalent today not only in agricultur but also in many other global industries. For example, in a remarkable roundtable discussion shortly after the initial reports of the Orange County crisis, a number of senior treasury officers of major multinational industrial firms gathered to discuss their firms' risk management practices. Included in one panel, moderated by the head of Bank of America's U.S. capital markets group, were representatives of Union Carbide, R. J. Reynolds Tobacco Company, MCI, and Lukens, Inc.[6]

Perhaps most noteworthy about the discussion was that all of the companies represented *actively* manage their primary exposures to commodity prices and currency exchange rates. That result is consistent with the *1995 Wharton/CIBC Wood Gundy Study* of derivatives usage by nonfinancial firms, which found that a sizable majority of derivatives users allow their market *views* to alter the size and timing of their hedging practices. In other words, many firms apparently have found that risk management can add value if it is based on informed decisions about the percentage of those exposures to be hedged. Important, however, is that none of the firms participating in the panel discussion reported using risk management to increase exposures beyond those naturally present in their businesses. Instead, the strategic issue for them was whether to hedge zero or 100% of their exposures, or some percentage in between. That strategy is consistent with other recent survey evidence and the findings of empirical studies.

Generally, the panelists concluded that to hedge either zero or 100% of their exposures expressed a "strong view" of expected commodity prices or exchange rates. In contrast, hedging 50% appeared to be the neutral or naturally conservative posture for a firm that has formed no particular market view. The market views expressed through a hedging program could have a significant strategic impact, especially if they differ radically from those of competitors. Consider, for example, one firm that manufactures stainless steel, 50% of the cost of which is in nickel. That firm must purchase substantial nickel supplies on the open market. If it hedges 100% of anticipated needs while competitors do not hedge at all, and then nickel prices drop significantly, that firm could, because of its hedging activities, realize significantly lower profit margins than its competitors. In such a case, in the words of the RJR spokesperson, a firm's "competitive position could suffer." Of course, the opposite result would occur if nickel prices were to rise.

The often subtle distinctions between hedging and speculation have important business and legal implications today for potential derivatives users who knowingly refrain from managing some or all of their otherwise hedgable risks. As we discuss in later chapters, the failure to hedge, or decision not to hedge, those risks may leave a firm or portfolio exposed to the same economic risks as outright speculation. That unsettling result has encouraged one former CFTC commissioner to ask, "Is failing to hedge a legal virus?" It also prompted *Barron's* to assert provocatively that "imprudent companies...that don't use derivatives....are, on the whole, much riskier than companies that do."[7] Similarly, one observer of the panel discussion mentioned above stated: "It seems to me that if you hedge anything less than 100% of your exposure, you are choosing to take an open position, you are taking a speculative position." The present Asian currency crisis provides a topical illustration of the arguably speculative aspects of decisions not to hedge.

Newspaper accounts suggest that the 1997 rout of the Indonesian rupiah was fueled more by local U.S. dollar borrowing than by outright currency speculation. To avoid high rupiah interest rates of 18% to 20%, many Indonesian firms borrowed dollars at nominally cheaper rates of 9% or 10% and left their dollar liabilities unhedged. Borrowers considered that strategy safe because the Indonesian central bank had expressly linked rupiah exchange rates to the U.S. dollar. "Few executives took seriously the possibility that Bank Indonesia would let the rupiah fall sharply. Even fewer were willing to pay the cost of hedging…to protect against currency collapse."[8] Yet in August 1997 the dollar link broke upon the announcement that the central bank could no longer maintain it. As Alan Greenspan often emphasizes, borrowers' huge implicit bets on exchange rate stability proved the words "many local" disastrous.

The need for a theoretical framework   Foreshadowing the current derivatives debate, Working attributed early "popular suspicion of futures trading…[to] a sense of mystery associated with it."[9] He attributed that mystery in turn to the absence of a theoretical framework for thinking of futures markets as having a legitimate economic purpose. Absent such a framework, farmers, grain elevators, merchants, processors, and others who depended on futures markets had little ability to defend them from criticism. The prevailing view was that futures markets were inherently speculative and little more than glorified casinos. One predictable result has been episodic, mostly unsuccessful calls for legislation prohibiting or severely restricting futures trading. As early as 1893 legislation that would have banned all futures trading in the United States only narrowly escaped enactment. In 1958 a limited attack succeeded when Congress enacted a law prohibiting all futures trading in onions.

To some observers the difficulty of defending futures was puzzling, because copious statistics had long been widely available demonstrating that futures were mainly used for hedging. Nevertheless, as Working understood, those statistics alone were of little avail. According to former Harvard University president James B. Conant, "a theory is only overthrown by a better theory, never merely by contradictory facts."[10] One of Working's major contributions to economics was to provide much of the new theory futures markets then needed—and on which today's derivatives markets rely—to legitimize their continued existence.

Today, popular suspicion of derivatives (and speculation) continues unabated, as do the recurrent calls for additional legislation. Again, ample statistics showing the staggering volume of hedging or, more generally, risk management activity in derivatives markets seem to have done little to dispel that suspicion. If anything, the statistics may seem to magnify the dangers derivatives pose to the financial system.

Yet as the remarks at the beginning of this chapter suggest, derivatives and derivatives markets continue to fulfill their early promise and thrive despite intermittent turmoil. Economists, regulators, market professionals, and tens of thousands of end users worldwide recognize that derivatives play a critical role in modern capital markets. Equally important, many products that might once have offered their users strategic advantages are increasingly becoming strategic necessities.

Still, confusion and misunderstandings abound about the legitimate economic benefits derivatives offer portfolios and firms and their essential functions within the financial system. However, the economic theory needed to explain those benefits and functions is readily available, whether or not adequately publicized or satisfactorily incorporated into applicable law.One main objective of this book is to provide senior managers and their legal advisers with the concepts they need to benefit from that theory and to avoid or dispel unwarranted criticism.

A note on usage   "The term 'derivatives' today is used to refer to a vast array of privately negotiated over-the-counter (OTC) and exchange-traded products."[11] Our topic here is OTC derivatives, which includes any derivative provided by one market participant to another, whether or not actively traded on standardized terms or in a liquid market. Yet an adequate understanding of OTC derivatives necessitates some familiarity with exchange-traded products and their diverse regulatory structures. If nothing else, that familiarity lessens anxiety by suggesting to OTC derivatives users and their legal advisers the kinds of legal issues about which they need *not* be overly concerned.

A FUNCTIONAL APPROACH

Ceaseless product flow, fast-changing forms and identities of financial institutions, and a dynamic legal and regulatory environment seemingly consign derivatives markets to constant instability. Users of derivatives often confront substantial uncertainty as to products, markets, and applicable legal and regulatory regimes. If not properly understood and managed, derivatives like any other important financial product present dangers to individual portfolios and institutions. In the words of Federal Reserve Chairman Alan Greenspan, they are also a potential source of "systemic disturbance." Perhaps nowhere are the destabilizing effects of financial and legal innovation felt more intensely than in OTC derivatives markets.

However, a *dynamic, functional* analysis of derivatives risks, given the pace of financial and legal innovation in derivatives markets, provides needed analytical stability. It is a robust aid to boards of directors, senior managers, trustees, corporate counsel, municipalities, legislators, regulators, and anyone else with a significant stake in derivatives markets—meaning, directly or indirectly, virtually all of us. Accordingly, this book adopts a functional approach to managing derivatives' risks.

The principal advantage of a functional approach is that it enables us to understand and keep abreast of the legal and business implications of rapid product innovation. A functional approach focuses on products' essential economic attributes and "characterizes products by the needs they satisfy."[12] A dynamic, functional approach also offers insight into the interplay among competing yet interdependent financial markets and intermediaries. OTC derivatives is a field in which technological, legal, regulatory, and product changes, as well as an institutionalized "product-migration and development cycle," quickly render obsolete any *static* product- or institution-based analysis.[13] Absent a functional analysis, one must memorize the never-ending flow of product names and myriad combinations and permutations of product features generated by derivatives dealers—a daunting prospect when every dealer is engaged daily in a fiercely competitive struggle to develop new products and differentiate existing products from the many close substitutes offered by other dealers.

A functional approach is viable, because the economic needs that products satisfy are essentially the same in all economies, regardless of time and place. The approach frees its user from dependence on the often intimidating proliferation of synonyms and acronyms describing functionally equivalent, sometimes identical products. As such, it enables senior management and its legal advisers to view the vast array of derivatives "like the goods on the shelf in a supermarket." A supermarket, of course, provides "better and faster service for...customers when they come to shop."[14] Likewise, a functional approach enables the customer—here, the derivatives user—quickly to locate the right aisle and section. It also enables the user to understand better the economic differences between competing types and brands of products and to analyze effectively a product's otherwise murky legal implications.

A functional approach provides the tools to answer such questions as:

What are the economic functions of derivatives?

What business and investment strategies do those functions serve?

What relevance do those functions and strategies have to the practical management of OTC derivatives risks, both financial and legal?

What are the implications of the migration of certain products from intermediaries to markets?

THEORETICAL BASIS FOR A FUNCTIONAL APPROACH

Many have explored the economic history of financial innovation and the origins of modern derivatives markets, but few have satisfactorily explained the driving forces behind financial innovation and the rise of modern derivatives markets. Preeminent among the latter is Robert C. Merton of Harvard University's Graduate School of Business Administration. In an article appearing in the Winter 1992 issue of the *Journal of Applied Corporate Finance,*[15] Merton examines the process of financial innovation, which he calls the " 'engine' driving the financial system toward its goal of improving the performance of what economists call the 'real economy.' "

Merton recognizes that financial innovation "does not, of course, proceed in a vacuum," but always takes place within a specific institutional and regulatory setting. However, because specific institutions and regulations are transient, an examination of any particular setting is generally unenlightening. Far superior in Merton's view is an analysis of the *basic functions* of the financial system. These functions remain "essentially the same in all economies—past and present, East and West." Merton analyzes financial innovation from a functional perspective "because the functions of the financial system are far more stable than the identity and structure of the institutions performing them," and also more stable than the "time path" of the products those institutions develop. Expressly adopting Merton's functional approach, Tufano argues that financial innovation is a "timeless" process and that the perpetual nature of financial innovation is a product of a stable, "immutable set of functions" financial systems perform in response to unchanging societal and institutional needs.

Nobel laureate Merton H. Miller, Professor of Finance Emeritus at the University of Chicago's Graduate School of Business, tacitly supports Merton's functional analysis. In Miller's article in the same issue of the *Journal of Applied Corporate Finance,* he asks, "Why the great burst of financial innovations over the last twenty years?" He responds that of all the potential causes, the most persuasive is that the modern derivatives boom is "merely a delayed return to the long-run growth path of financial improvement" that had lain dormant since the early 1930s.[16]

Miller reaches his conclusion partly through an examination of the "long prior history" of derivatives. He mentions, for example, the *puts* and *calls* traded on the Amsterdam Stock Exchange in the late seventeenth century, and he observes that exchange trading of futures has a history almost as long. Merton's article provides additional details. He mentions the existence of the Dojima rice market in Osaka, Japan, which began as a *forward* market in the seventeenth century and had evolved into "a fully organized futures market" by the eighteenth century. "Organized futures exchanges were created in Frankfurt in 1867 and in London in 1877. The Chicago Board of Trade was founded in 1848 and the New York Cotton Exchange was incorporated in 1872. Options on commodity futures were traded on the Chicago Board of Trade in the 1920s."

The rich history of derivatives exemplifies how the basic functions of capital markets remain the same, regardless of time and place.

Functions of Financial Systems

The primary economic function of a capitalist financial system is to enable households, individuals, and institutions to allocate their excess funds efficiently to those funds' most productive use, all in an uncertain environment. Investors—in economic jargon, "saver-lenders"—make excess funds available to organizations—"borrower-spenders"—that need more funds than those organizations can generate internally through retained earnings. Investment occurs when investors purchase debt and equity securities and other instruments issued by borrower-spenders. An investor's ability to earn a return above the "risk-free" rate, generally assumed to be that of U.S. Treasury obligations, depends on the investor's willingness to assume risk. "Economic life is a risky business."[17] "Eliminating all…risk often means eliminating all profit, a condition that most businesses cannot tolerate for long."[18]

According to Merton, six "core" mechanisms perform the basic resource allocation activities of the financial system "both spatially and across time, in an uncertain environment." In particular, the system: (1) facilitates payments for the exchange of goods and services, (2) pools funds to finance large-scale enterprises, (3) communicates price information essential to the coordination of decentralized decision making, (4) deals with asymmetries of information possessed by parties on opposite sides of transactions, (5) manages uncertainty and controls risk (i.e., "risk management"), and (6) transfers economic resources through time and across geographic regions and industries.[19]

Financial and Legal Risk

This book uses the term *financial risk* in the economic or statistical sense of uncertainty of outcome, meaning simply that more than one outcome of varying degrees of desirability is possible for any given decision.

The measurement of any given economic risk begins with two basic features: first, its *probability* of occurring (often designated either as a percentage from 0 to 100 or as a number between 0 and 1, with 0 meaning no possibility and 100% or 1 designating absolute certainty); second, its *magnitude*. A low-probability outcome of high magnitude may be considered equally risky to a high-probability outcome of low magnitude. Generally, for any two potential outcomes of different magnitudes to be considered equally risky, they must have different probabilities—that is, the potential outcome of greater magnitude must have a correspondingly lower probability.* A third important feature is the *direction* of the risk—that is, whether a given outcome is positive (e.g., a gain), negative (a loss), or neither.

In practice, a comparison of the riskiness of alternative decisions is rarely clear-cut. Most business decisions involve not a comparison of two potential outcomes but of a range of outcomes, each of varying probabilities. Seldom are probabilities and magnitudes of potential outcomes easily quantifiable, nor are they necessarily stable or constant over time. Many variables—such as the risk of a 200-basis-point (2% per annum) rise in applicable U.S. Treasury yields over a one-week period—are usually so remote or their probabilities so unquantifiable that any attempt to

---

*To use an extreme example, the "risk" associated with a 5% probability (.05) of winning $125,000 will almost always be considered greater than that of a 95% chance (.95) of winning $1100—although both may be good bets. Certainly, many rational investors would prefer to pay $1000 for a 5% (1 in 20) chance of winning $125,000 (on average they would expect to "earn" $5250 (or [$125,000 × .05] − $1000) on a $1000 investment!), rather than for a 95% chance of winning $1100 (on average they would earn $45 (or [$1100 × .95] − $1000) on a $1000 investment). Then again, someone who needs only the extra $45 and cannot afford to lose $1000 might choose otherwise. Likewise, because of the time value of money, if the $45 is to be earned immediately, that might be preferable to a $5250 payout earned only over an extended time frame.

value the true risk is guesswork. The realization that most probabilities and magnitudes are estimates based on extrapolations of historical data compounds the difficulty of quantifying risk: "Statistical figures referring to economic events are historical data. They tell us what happened in a nonrepeatable historical sense."[20]

Finally, many variables simply do not lend themselves to quantification. An important reason why legal risk is fundamentally different from financial risk is that legal risk is perhaps an archetypal case of unquantifiable risk. Laws rarely include precise quantitative measures. Rather, they include qualitative descriptors such as "reasonable," "material," "substantial," and "intentional." In addition, the potential consequences—or magnitude—of adverse legal outcomes are similarly unquantifiable. Will a contract be held entirely unenforceable or might offending provisions simply be stricken? Will a government agency allow a financial institution to continue operating in light of a given regulatory violation? Is the violation a civil or criminal matter? Law is replete with examples of what Laurence Tribe, Professor of Law at the Harvard Law School, refers to as "soft variables" that "resist ready quantification."[21] Hence, "lawyers rarely provide quantitative estimates of legal risk."[22]

The riskiness of any given outcome will vary over time and from economy to economy, organization to organization. The question of exactly how much risk is appropriate for a firm or portfolio at any given time will depend on its business and investment objectives and guidelines, its ability to absorb losses, and many other facts and circumstances. The nature of the risk is always an important consideration: Is it financial, legal, or something else, such as reputational?

Functions of Derivatives and Derivatives Dealers

Nondealer institutions use derivatives primarily to reduce or avoid unwanted business and investment risks. In theory, organizations and individuals are *risk-averse*. If faced with a decision that could result in a relatively large loss compared with its financial resources, a rational investor will act conservatively; in other words, the investor will assume significant risk or uncertainty only if the potential for gain is disproportionately large. "Because investors are generally risk-averse, they must be paid to carry uncertainty risk. Accordingly, the capital market[s] will establish a higher expected return for riskier capital assets through a positive risk premium."[23]* Conversely, a risk-averse investor is generally willing to pay a premium—that is, incur a certain, albeit small cost or loss—to avoid or protect against uncertain but large losses.†

In theory nonfinancial organizations seek to avoid or minimize exposures to financial uncertainties unrelated to their core business or investment activities. Financial uncertainties are, of course, inherent in all business and investment activities and are then necessary evils, but risks arising from exogenous or macroeconomic forces that a firm or investor cannot control often are not. Derivatives afford many firms and investors opportunities to manage their exposures to external risks, and they often do so in a way that is economically more efficient than other available alternatives. A frequent illustration is the firm that sources supplies or sells products overseas and is therefore exposed to significant currency risk.

Operational alternatives, such as establishing manufacturing facilities or sales centers offshore, are often effective means of reducing discrete currency exposures. By engaging in "operational hedging" a firm exposes its costs "to the same currency as revenues, reducing the exposure of profits to uncertain exchange rates."[24] Yet they can also become costly and cumbersome solutions if, for example, a firms's product markets are geographically dispersed and unstable. By relying on operational alternatives, a firm may diminish its strategic flexibility in responding to geographically shifting markets. In those instances, currency derivatives may be strategically preferable.

In general, perceptions of significant exposures to uncontrollable currency and other exogenous risks tend to depress overall economic

---

*In financial literature, financial instruments (whether assets or liabilities) are commonly "priced" or "quoted" from either of two economically equivalent perspectives. First, they can be priced according to their stated returns, or yields; second, they can be priced either at a discount to or premium over their face amount or par value. To avoid confusion, it is important to clarify which pricing convention is intended. The reason is that although the amount one would pay to purchase (or demand to sell) an asset bears an inverse relationship to the asset's risk, the return the asset must generate bears a positive relationship to the asset's risk. For example, other things being equal, a *highly risky* debt instrument might trade at a *discount* to its face or par value but pay a *high yield,* while a *low risk* instrument might command a *premium* but pay a *low yield.* See, e.g., Glaser, *Capital Asset Pricing Model, infra,* Chapter 12, note 11 (citing numerous authoritative sources of finance theory).

†Many recent derivatives slip-ups are directly attributable to management's abandonment (intentionally or through lack of effective oversight) of risk aversion in capital markets or assumption of excess risk without charging the necessary risk premium.

activity. The result is a loss of societal wealth through a reduction in the performance of what Merton refers to as the "real economy." Derivatives theoretically help financial intermediaries restore or enhance economic activity by providing nonfinancial organizations with efficient means of managing otherwise uncontrollable financial risks.

Importantly, derivatives do not—and are not designed to—eliminate risk entirely from the financial system. Rather, their economic function is to enhance the system's efficiency by "allow[ing] risks that formerly had been combined to be unbundled and transferred to those most willing to assume and manage each risk component."[25] The risk transfer function necessarily involves a high degree of complexity. As a result, it can be accomplished efficiently, including cost effectively, only through the active involvement of financial intermediaries—namely, derivatives dealers. The dealer's principal economic function is to facilitate, or intermediate, the transfer or reallocation of the risks borne by derivatives.

Originally, financial intermediaries acted as brokers who arranged, for a fee, transactions between counterparties with matching, or offsetting, financial exposures. Those counterparties would then enter into transactions directly between themselves, and the intermediary would not assume any risk of a principal. Almost immediately, however, most intermediaries developed the technological capacity, and the desire, to increase profits by acting as principals and, hence, true dealers. A dealer will, for a fee, enter into a transaction directly with an end user prior to arranging, and even if it cannot arrange, a precisely offsetting transaction. By acting as true dealers intermediaries inject liquidity into derivatives markets.

Modern derivatives dealers rely on sophisticated computer systems and quantitative techniques. Those technologies enable them to net out on a portfolio basis offsetting exposures created by individual transactions. The ability to identify and offset specific exposures regardless of how they are dispersed throughout a portfolio obviates the need to precisely offset the exposures created by individual transactions. Invariably, however, some residual exposure remains after all portfolio netting is performed, and the dealer must decide how to handle that exposure. It may choose to absorb the net exposure, depending on its market views and assuming it has the necessary capital base. Alternatively, the dealer can usually shed its residual exposure by entering into offsetting transactions, often by buying (i.e., taking a *long* position) or selling (a *short* position) relatively inexpensive financial futures.

Financial economists argue that derivatives and derivatives markets are best understood as facilities that enable organizations and investors to manage economic risks better. In the simplest terms, derivatives enable parties efficiently and with relatively minor transaction costs (compared with the costs of dealing directly in the underlying securities, assets, or

-
lated risk exposures—or uncertainties—over time. "Time and uncertainty are the central elements that influence financial economic behavior."[26]

By contributing to a more efficient and rational allocation of risk within the economy derivatives theoretically help increase overall economic activity. Considered in that light, derivatives and their markets benefit society. They encourage the risk taking essential to a more efficient and productive allocation of economic resources.

As discussed more fully in Chapter 4, any system of risk management, including one incorporating derivatives, can be analyzed in terms of its risk reduction functions and the risk management strategies those functions support.

Risk reduction functions

Theoretically, derivatives enhance economic efficiency by allowing the financial system to (1) unbundle complex packages of risks, (2) isolate the discrete risk components, then (3) transfer the individual risk components to those market participants most willing and able to manage or absorb them. Derivatives enable the financial system to perform the risk reallocation function with "vast savings in transaction costs, which for some institutions can be a tenth to a twentieth of the cost of using the underlying cash-market securities."[27] Stock index futures, for example, enable a firm or portfolio to acquire (or sell) in a single transaction a representative exposure to all of the securities comprising the index. Futures also enable dealers to offer equity index swaps that ordinarily have longer maturities and less frequent funding requirements than futures contracts. Certain credit derivatives (discussed below) enable lenders and investors to diversify in a single transaction exposures to multiple credits.

Once an end user has identified and quantified the components of its overall risk exposure (sometimes called its *risk profile* or *footprint*), it can determine which individual types of risks, and the amount of each risk type, it is willing and able to retain or assume and which risks and amounts it wishes instead to shed or reduce. Specifically, risk management reduces a firm or portfolio's risks by enabling it to (1) transfer, sell, or hedge the source of the unwanted risk, (2) *diversify* the unwanted risk, or (3) *insure* against any losses that might arise from the unwanted risk.

A DYNAMIC APPROACH—THE FINANCIAL INNOVATION SPIRAL

An understanding of the dynamic relationship between risk in the economy and what Merton calls the financial innovation spiral is essential to a practical and durable understanding of both derivatives and their risk management. The financial innovation spiral is the unending process whereby successful financial innovations stimulate demand for further innovation and lead to the creation of new products:

> The proliferation of new trading markets in standardized securities such as futures makes possible the creation of new custom-designed financial products that improve "market completeness." Next, volume in the new markets further expands as the producers themselves—typically, financial intermediaries—trade simply to hedge their own exposures. Such increased volume in turn reduces marginal transaction costs and thereby makes possible further implementation of new products and trading strategies—which in turn leads to still more volume...[and] additional markets, and so on it goes, spiraling toward the theoretically limiting case of zero marginal transaction costs and dynamically complete markets.[28]

As an example of the spiral effect, the Eurodollar futures market, enables financial intermediaries to offer end users customized interest rate swaps (examples of which are discussed in Chapters 2 and 3) in which floating-rate payments are linked to, e.g., LIBOR as an alternative to other indices, such as the U.S. Treasury rate.* Typically, intermediaries do not individually hedge each swap contract in their portfolio; rather, they hedge, through the Eurodollar futures market, the net or *residual* risk of

---

*Eurodollars are U.S. dollar deposits made with or claims against institutions at specified offices outside the United States and expressly denominated and payable in U.S. dollars. The London Interbank Offer Rate (LIBOR) is the fixed rate that central banks and large, creditworthy international banks and other institutions charge each other for sizable Eurodollar loans or deposits typically for periods of 1, 3, 6, and, less frequently, 12 months (although borrowing may range from periods of 1 day to 10 years). The Eurodollar futures market provides for organized trading of standardized three-month LIBOR deposits to be made at future dates. Eurodollar futures contracts are traded on the International Monetary Market (IMM) of the Chicago Mercantile Exchange and on the London International Financial Futures Exchange (LIFFE).

their entire portfolios after taking into account offsetting transactions. Generally, the availability of Eurodollar futures provides swap dealers with a readily accessible, low-cost hedging device.* Because dealers can now easily and cheaply hedge their residual portfolio risks, these products enable dealers to offer a wider array and higher volume of other, more customized products. Eurodollar futures have, as Merton says, made possible the evolution of organized swaps markets.

Moreover, swaps markets have evolved into competitive, transparent, liquid, and increasingly "commoditized" markets in which bid-offer spreads and other profit opportunities have declined so precipitously that most market makers look to other commercial activities and financial products as their primary sources of profits. Still, the demand for commoditized products motivates major dealers to maintain significant market presences. In addition, increasingly commoditized products can be used to synthesize or "manufacture" other, more complex and customized products that better serve the needs of end users. Merton states that "[m]arket trading of... 'pure vanilla' swaps expanded the opportunity for intermediaries to hedge, thereby allowing them to create customized swaps and related financial products more efficiently."[29] The general process whereby financial futures spur the growth of additional markets and further the cycle of product innovation and customization is the reason that Miller calls financial futures "industrial raw materials." Merton's list of raw materials also includes options, futures, and various other exchange-traded products.

Legal Innovation as Facilitating Financial Innovation

As Federal Reserve Governor Susan Phillips highlighted in a March 1998 address to the International Swaps and Derivatives Association (ISDA), the pace of financial innovation would not be sustainable without concurrent *legal innovation*. Tufano has examined the role of the private bar and

---

*Futures involve minimal credit risk, because the counterparty to each contract is a highly creditworthy exchange clearinghouse that marks to market and "settles up" contracts daily. Thus, futures markets are accessible to a wide range of participants, including retail customers. The results include lower bid-asked spreads, greater liquidity, more competitive pricing, and greater "market completeness." Futures have "substantially lower[ed] the costs of buying and selling the major foreign currencies." Miller, *The Last Twenty Years and the Next, infra,* Chapter 2, note 5: 465.

contract law in responding creatively to taxation, regulation, and other governmental market interventions as well as to macroeconomic shocks. He draws on a wealth of historical evidence in suggesting that a cycle of legal innovation rich in historical precedent supports today's explosion of financial innovation.* His historical research has centered, among other things, on the financial and legal innovations that ensued after unexpected judicial intervention in the restructuring of failed U.S. railroads and industrial corporations in the late nineteenth and early twentieth centuries.[30]

According to Tufano, the late 1800s witnessed exceptional financial distress, especially within the American railroad industry, "with as much as one-fifth of the nation's railroad mileage in the hands of court-appointed receivers."[31] Railroad firms suffered from "exceptionally high fixed costs…and bitter competition in many regions of the country." The distress, however, had a bright side; it triggered a number of resourceful responses by both public and private parties, the result of which was

> a period of rapid change in financial contracting. In particular, the American railroad industry pioneered the use of new kinds of securities and new means of corporate governance, including preferred stocks, income bonds, deferred coupon debt instruments, bond covenants, and voting trusts.

The accelerated pace of financial innovation was led mainly by investment bankers such as J. P. Morgan. However, it was triggered, even quickened by judicial intervention and the ensuing response of the private bar. The courts actively and unexpectedly intervened in an attempt to resolve the railroad industry's economic woes. They "changed the rules of the game" governing the rights and obligations of private parties and in the process "emasculated prior debt contracts." Private parties, in turn, responded with their own innovations. Those innovations "were that generation's financial engineering, and in many ways, they were no less sophisticated than our own": they consisted mainly of "new security contracts and governance structures." As discussed particularly in Chapters 16 and 17, the foundation of the structures included a system of corporate law fiduciary duties that courts only slowly began to enunciate.

In his analysis of the causes of the late nineteenth century's financial innovations, Tufano introduces an unconventional idea:

---

*Throughout this book, the term *innovation* is used to describe a private sector response either to government action or to exogenous stimuli. In contrast, economists use the term to describe both the stimulus and the response. See Mason et al., *Financial Engineering, supra,* note 2: 61.

The technological development that was probably more instrumental in explaining nineteenth century innovations was the *development of new legal techniques.* Just as financial engineers are indispensable to the production of modern financial innovations, the lawyers of the 1890s, such as Charles Stetson who served as J.P. Morgan's "attorney general," were essential to the production of the complicated corporate securities innovations a century ago. For example, during the late nineteenth century, the U.S. bar's skill at executing ever-more sophisticated and well-drafted security contracts improved dramatically. This *technical virtuosity* is exemplified by the Burlington Northern bonds issue of 1896. These bonds had a number of unique covenants, including the requirement that proceeds from asset sales be reinvested in the railroad. Apart from the specifics of the covenants, the innovation illustrates the degree to which securities lawyers had *perfected their art* by the turn of the century: subsequent generations of lawyers were unable to find a loophole through which to circumvent the original drafter's intent.[32]

Tufano's historical inquiry builds on Merton's functional product and institutional analysis to draw striking parallels between the financial engineering of earlier generations and that of our own. By so doing, it strongly suggests that today's legal engineers, primarily the modern derivatives bar, have applied and continue to apply similarly innovative legal techniques and technical virtuosity to facilitate the modern wave of financial innovation.

Noteworthy here are the successful, ongoing efforts of the derivatives industry to develop standardized documentation for a multitude of OTC derivatives. Several standard form agreements have achieved widespread market acceptance in the world's major derivatives trading centers. Although standardized documentation is now mostly taken for granted, dramatic documentation backlogs not long ago seriously threatened the future growth of OTC markets.

Moreover, industry groups have helped modernize and improve the laws and regulations governing many vital aspects of these transactions. One exemplary development is the recent adoption by federal agencies and most U.S. states of modifications to the Uniform Commercial Code provisions governing the perfection of security interests in investment securities. In addition, industry groups have pushed for modernization of bankruptcy and insolvency laws in all of the world's major derivatives trading centers. In Governor Phillips' words, those and many other important efforts help "ensure that any perceived reductions in risk rest on a sound legal foundation."

Whither Financial Equilibrium?

Merton and his Harvard colleagues discuss the constraints upon the financial system that preclude it from reaching its theoretical limit of zero marginal transaction costs and dynamically complete markets—in other words, financial equilibrium. The driving force behind the financial innovation spiral is the relentless competition between financial intermediaries and organized markets to be the provider of financial products. That competition initially bodes ill for intermediaries, especially because so many recent innovations—e.g., interest rate and currency swaps—that formerly rewarded them with handsome profits have long since lost most of their direct profit-generating potential. In 1995 *Financial Engineering* noted:

> Financial markets, as we know, tend to be efficient institutional alternatives to intermediaries when the products have standardized terms, can serve a number of customers, and are well enough 'understood' for transactors to be comfortable in assessing their prices. As we also know, intermediaries are better suited for low-volume products.

Many formerly innovative and low-volume derivatives have become standardized, well-understood products that readily trade in enormous volumes on organized markets with little assistance from intermediaries.

Nevertheless, Merton and his colleagues draw no ominous conclusions about the future of financial intermediaries. To the contrary, their qualified prognosis for financial intermediaries is bright, as a result of two important factors flowing from their focus on low-volume products best suited for intermediaries.

Critical to their analysis is the reason that a particular product is low-volume. Is it due to fundamental causes that are sustainable over the long term? Or is it simply because the product is new? The modern swaps market, for example, originated in isolated, low-volume transactions. However, almost immediately after the announcement in 1981 of the famous World Bank/IBM currency swap, volume in these products exploded.[33] Resulting publicity ensured a rapid growth in familiarity with, and understanding of, the relatively simple mechanics of both currency and interest rate swaps. The markets quickly assimilated swaps' pricing characteristics; eventually screen-based quotation services began broadly disseminating actual market prices. Finally, swaps' genuine mass appeal became obvious in the early 1980s during periods of high and volatile interest rates and enormously unstable exchange rates. Currency and interest rate swaps quickly migrated to organized OTC markets.

Financial Engineering explains that if a product exhibits the characteristics suitable for organized trading, it is *"expected* to migrate from intermediaries to markets. That is, once they are 'seasoned,' and perhaps after some information asymmetries are resolved, those products are structured to trade in a market." (Emphasis in original.)

Yet other types of transactions, should remain low-volume and largely within the domain of intermediaries. Those transactions either involve "fundamental information asymmetries" or are "highly customized."

> In sum, financial markets and intermediaries are surely *competing* institutions when viewed from the *static* perspective of a particular product activity. However, when viewed from the *dynamic* perspective of the evolving financial system, the two are just as surely *complementary* institutions, each reinforcing and improving the other in the performance of their functions.[34]

Information asymmetries

Classic examples of information asymmetries are complex asset-based financings for corporate borrowers whose future cash flows are questionable. Those transactions typically require considerable credit analysis. Further, the ability to circulate to prospective buyer-lenders information essential to a proper credit evaluation is often, for borrower-dictated confidentiality reasons, restricted. An additional example is the increasingly common case of high-technology start-up companies. Although these firms often enjoy rapid growth prospects, by definition they have no proven records of successful financial performance from which potential investors can gauge credit risk. Moreover, when these companies are involved in developing and marketing innovative technologies, outside investors may have great difficulty assessing the viability of the technologies, the firms, and the potential markets for the firms' products.

Customization

Plentiful examples can be found in trade and daily news reports and of client-specific demand for customized financial products and transaction structures. Satisfying this demand requires not only an understanding of the wide array of available derivative products and securities but equally, if not more importantly, familiarity with a client's goals, resources, and financial and strategic limitations. Intermediaries are ordinarily capable providing the customized products that organized markets can not efficiently offer. Thus, the need for customization argues strongly in favor of continuing pivotal roles in capital markets for financial intermediaries.

An article from the February 1996 issue of *Global Finance* provides an example of a trend among many financial intermediaries away from commoditized products and markets toward business lines as to which intermediaries enjoy a sustainable comparative advantage over organized markets.[35] "Derivatives marketers are sounding a very different note from two years ago. They aren't product pushers. *They're risk doctors.*" (Emphasis added.) Among other things, John Chrystal, head of Credit Suisse Financial Products' structured products team in New York, observes: "Before, the difficult thing was to understand the technology. Now, the difficult thing is to understand client needs." For present purposes, the article's significant theme is its argument in favor of financial engineering. "The 'let me understand your business and help you manage your risks' approach does not lead to large volumes. 'Creating a complex derivative used to be a mass production process,' explains a New York banker. 'We used to churn something out and sell it to 20 people; now it can be sold to only one.'"

Similarly, in what may prove to be an important development in the dealer community, Bankers Trust has reportedly begun decentralizing its risk management group to "client-focused" units. According to one consultant, "They no longer view risk management as a separate product but as an adjunct to helping clients achieve their objectives."[36]

But most significant of all may be a recent study that throws new theoretical and empirical light on the benefits of customized products. In one of the first reports taking advantage of heightened mandated derivatives disclosures, Géczy, Minton, and Schrand studied the use of foreign currency derivatives by the 1991 *Fortune 500* largest (based on sales) U.S. industrial corporations.[37] From footnote disclosures in publicly filed year-end 1991 financial statements, the authors gleaned data on the use of currency swaps, forwards, futures, and options. Their findings, reported in the September 1997 issue of the *Journal of Finance,* strongly suggest that the benefits of customization through OTC currency derivatives are greatest for firms with long-term foreign currency debt outstanding.

Such exposures normally require a predictable long-term stream of foreign currency cash flows to satisfy debt service requirements. Géczy, Minton, and Schrand found that large companies tend for several reasons to conclude that such exposures justify the higher costs of using customized OTC products. First, the decreased liquidity of customized products is less of a concern when a firm has a predictable exposure that it foresees little prospect of unwinding. Second, fees and expenses associated with initiating the transactions are generally nonrecurring. However, one noteworthy drawback of long-term swaps is that the user should

expect a matching long-term exposure to the credit risk of its dealer counterparty.

Test case: Credit Derivatives. These intriguing products display
many features favoring "migration" to organized market, yet simultaneously evince powerful constraints on their ability to migrate. Although
they can assume a variety of forms, common to all are payoff structures
tied to prespecified credit events concerning one or more "reference credits." Typical products are total return swaps, credit default swaps, credit
spread options, and credit-linked notes; common credit events are customary loan defaults such as bankruptcy, nonpayment, cross acceleration,
and credit downgrades. Credit derivatives are promising because they
derive from a ubiquitous underlying exposure—i.e., credit risk—and thus
have immense "commoditization" potential. As Governor Phillips notes,
the products are a way "to directly adjust credit exposures to specific firms
or to diversify industry or geographic concentrations. Their potential is
enormous." The products' rise appears to have been stimulated by concerns about massive credit concentrations in bank loan and derivatives
portfolios in the early 1990s.

Unfortunately, though, credit risk is a "particularly heterogeneous
underlying" notoriously difficult to standardize.*[38] Many lenders insist on
including their own "standard" credit provisions in documentation for
loans they originate or buy. Whether the provisions will be acceptable to
other lenders is not always clear. Further, questions remain as to the ability of institutional and individual investors that are not traditional lenders
to evaluate the underlying credit terms. In addition, Governor Phillips
notes that "[+] here really are no exchange-traded instruments that can be
used [by potential dealers] to effectively hedge [residual] credit risk.

Perhaps a more troubling hurdle is the absence of precise credit measurement tools, especially when borrowers are start-up firms or otherwise
have issued no publicly traded debt or equity that can be used as a benchmark. Some lenders have begun applying mathematical techniques to the
measurement and pricing of portfolio credit risk, yet this technology—so-
called credit value-at-risk—is in its infancy. (The measurement difficulty
is also present, though to a lesser degree, when confidentiality agreements
prohibit originating lenders from disseminating credit information.)

---

*ISDA has prepared a form of "Confirmation of OTC Credit Swap Transaction, Single Reference
    Entity, Non-Sovereign." Although drafted as a supplement to the 1992 ISDA Master
    Agreement, the form can also be used as a stand-alone agreement.

Furthermore, the business of lending continues to be highly relationship driven, with credit decisions made on a variety of subjective factors.

Overall, it is not surprising that in measuring credit risk many lenders "still rely largely on qualitative methods that predate the derivatives revolution."[39] Often, for example, they use credit scoring to batch credits into a few classes, with most performing credits ranking in the higher classes. The absence of meaningful credit differentiation can result in inefficient pricing that ultimately harms both originating lenders and credit protection providers. Logically, it should result in overcharging high quality credits and undercharging less creditworthy firms.

Far-Reaching Implications for Senior Management and Its Legal Advisers

The implications of the Harvard team's analysis are far-reaching. Especially important is their guidance as to the likely future path of financial innovation and their suggestions regarding the future direction of legal innovation. The thrust of the team's argument is that the focus of financial service organizations will continue moving in the direction of highly tailored, individualized, client-driven solutions, rather than mass-marketing of an unending supply of new products. The rise of financial and legal engineering as new disciplines represents a market effort to accommodate the need for customization.

Large profits on mass-marketed products are exceptionally difficult to maintain in capital markets because of the rapid speed at which innovations can be imitated by competitors. As Tufano observes:

> In the financial system,…new products receive virtually no patent protection. Reverse-engineering is a rapid process and manufacturing a 'knock-off' can be accomplished almost instantaneously in some cases. For this reason, it is not surprising that investment banking innovators can underwrite only (a median of) one deal before a competitor successfully underwrites a substitute product. In this super-charged competitive environment, competitors' innovations are quickly scrutinized by potential imitators, modified, and reoffered to clients.[40]

The inevitable result is increased product supply that tends quickly to drive down profit margins on even the most ingenious products.

The implications of the spiral effect are crucial for two additional reasons. First, the theory dispels concerns about the diminishing role of financial intermediaries in capital markets, and the deteriorating performance of many traditional markets, such as organized futures exchanges. Second, the theory suggests that government and industry efforts to arrest the momentum of financial innovation or materially alter the spiral effect are dangerous and should be undertaken only with great caution.*

In essence, the Harvard team states:

1. The financial innovation spiral cannot be stopped. It can only be controlled, and only then through informed, careful, coordinated oversight.
2. Formal changes in markets, institutions, and products should, rather than be alarming, be anticipated and managed, by both the public and the private sectors.

IMPLICATIONS FOR THE FUTURE

As mentioned earlier, the dynamism of derivatives markets and the financial innovation spiral has important and intriguing legal implications for all market participants, particularly senior management and its legal advisers at nondealer organizations. One critical implication builds on the realization that, if the reasoning of the Harvard team is correct—and the weight of authority in academic and government circles as well as among market professionals suggests that it is—derivatives markets will likely continue to grow rapidly and evolve. Tufano and others also argue that for many organizations derivatives are rapidly becoming an important if not essential element of competitive strategy. Derivatives can be used to help an organization solve its own vexing financial and regulatory problems; they can also be used creatively to help a firm solve the problems of oth-

---

*In Merton's words: "When treated atomistically, financial innovations in products and services can be implemented unilaterally and rather quickly by entrepreneurs. Innovations in financial infrastructure [including government regulation], by contrast, must be more coordinated and, therefore, take longer to implement. As we have seen in the case of recent U.S. thrift and banking legislation, major changes—which could conceivably include outright elimination of obsolete institutions and their surrounding regulatory structure—take place exceedingly slowly." Merton, *Financial Innovation, supra,* note 15:21. "[G]overnment actions can do much to either mitigate or aggravate their disruptive effects [i.e., those of the clash between new innovations and old infrastructure]. By analogy, hurricanes are inevitable, but government policy can either reduce their devastation by encouraging early warning systems or it can aggravate the damage by encouraging the building of housing in locations that are especially vulnerable." Mason et al., *Financial Engineering, supra,* note 2: 35–36.

ers, such as clients, customers, suppliers, and employees. The chance to use derivatives to solve others' problems presents intermediaries with competitive opportunities unavailable a few years ago.

Similarly, in late 1995, the Center for Study of Futures and Options Markets at Virginia Polytechnic Institute announced the results of its "study of studies," entitled *Derivatives: State of the Debate,*[41] sponsored by the Chicago Mercantile Exchange. *State of the Debate* surveyed over a dozen major private and global public sector derivatives studies, and it also reviewed and abstracted nearly 100 important derivatives articles. One of the study's most provocative findings is that

> improvements in risk management techniques that were first applied to derivatives are now spilling over into and improving the management of risks in other, more traditional businesses—banks taking deposits and making loans, securities firms purchasing and financing securities positions, or corporations managing their treasury functions. These improvements in risk management, in turn, enhance the safety and profitability of these institutions.

Numerous articles and studies since 1995 confirm that the spillover continues. More exciting, however, is that the expansion of risk management techniques beyond derivatives is undergoing a fundamental transformation. According to Gene Shanks, one of the developers of Bankers Trusts' well-known Risk Adjusted Return on Capital (RAROC) system, which many view as the earliest incarnation of value-at-risk (VAR): Enterprise risk management has come across as a good way to play defense. Its highest value is creating offensive gains for *competitive advantage.*[42]

Generally, *State of the Debate* found that the modern derivatives boom "has yielded substantial benefits to public and private institutions...and to the U.S. economy." In addition, "[n]ot a single study reviewed called for banning or severely restricting the use of derivatives." Since the publication of *State of the Debate,* nothing has occurred (with, as of the date of this writing, i.e., early Spring 1998, the potential exception of the escalating lawsuits and growing scope of losses from the Asian currency crisis) to change either of those findings.

On a different note, Tufano and Miller have issued warnings of concern to all senior management and its legal advisers responsible for legal risk management. An inevitable consequence of ongoing product generation is that many new financial products must fail. "The capital markets do not immediately arrive at optimal solutions, but they, like product markets, grope their way by experimenting and learning."[43] Consequently, "[t]he inherent nature of financial contracts virtually ensures that failure is more likely than not." [44] Failed experiments test risk management systems. They can also be painful, particularly when they produce headlines.

New SEC derivatives disclosure rules   Two recent studies point to one important benefit of recently adopted derivatives disclosure rules that has received little notice. The first is that of Géczy, Minton, and Schrand, mentioned earlier, who studied the use of currency derivatives by 372 of the *Fortune 500* nonfinancial firms in 1990; the second is a study by Peter Tufano, discussed in Chapter 10, who analyzed the risk management practices of the North American gold mining industry. Both studies were made possible by the availability of reliable data regarding the risk management practices at issue.

A substantial supply of new, reliable risk management data should be available soon, as the Securities and Exchange Commission's new derivatives disclosure requirements begin to take hold. [45] The new rules, adopted January 28, 1997, require new disclosures about the policies used to account for derivatives and about certain quantitative and qualitative information about market risk exposures. The rules became applicable at fiscal year-end 1997 for public companies with market equity capitalizations of more than $2.5 billion and for all banks and thrifts. They become applicable at fiscal year-end 1998 to all other public companies, except small business issuers.

Although, as discussed in Chapter 18, the new rules are highly controversial, one important point about them is not: namely, they will provide abundant empirical data for researchers to test extant theory both for and against corporate and investor derivatives use. If the few studies conducted to date are any indication, findings based on the new disclosures are likely to reinforce the notion that overall, derivatives play a legitimate and important role in the global financial system.

ENDNOTES: CHAPTER 1

1. Foreword by Robert C. Merton to Lillian Chew, *Managing Derivative Risks: The Use and Abuse of Leverage* (John Wiley & Sons, 1996) [the entire book is hereafter referred to as *Leverage*]: xiii. Merton, along with Myron S. Scholes of Stanford University, won the Nobel Memorial Prize for Economic Sciences in 1997 "for a new method to determine the value of derivatives....[They] developed this method in close collaboration with Fischer Black, who died in his mid-fifties in 1995." See announcement, The Royal Swedish Academy of Sciences, Information Department, Website: www.kva.se (October 14, 1997) [hereafter, *1997 Nobel Announcement*].

2. See Scott P. Mason, Robert C. Merton, André Perold, and Peter Tufano, *Cases in Financial Engineering: Applied Studies of Financial Innovation* (Prentice Hall, 1995) [hereafter, *Financial Engineering*]: 51.

3. Holbrook Working, "Futures Trading and Hedging," *American Economic Review* (June 1953) [hereafter, *Futures Trading and Hedging*]. A collection of Working's articles is reprinted in Anne E. Peck, ed., *Readings in Futures Markets, Book I: Selected Writings of Holbrook Working* (Chicago: Board of Trade of the City of Chicago, 1977) [hereafter, *Selected Writings of Holbrook Working*]. Except as otherwise noted, all citations to Working's writings are to their location in Peck, *Selected Writings of Holbrook Working, supra.*

4. Holbrook Working, "Economic Functions of Futures Markets" [hereafter, *Economic Functions of Futures Markets*], in Peck, *Selected Writings of Holbrook Working, supra,* note 3: 285.

5. Edward R. Tufte, *Visual Explanations: Images, Quantities, Evidence and Narrative* (Graphics Press, 1997) (emphasis in original) [hereafter, *Visual Explanations*]: 30.

6. "Bank of America Roundtable on Derivatives and Corporate Risk Management," *Journal of Applied Corporate Finance,* 8(3) (Fall 1995): 58–74.

7. Philip McBride Johnson, "Is Failing to Hedge a Legal Virus?" *Futures* (November 1993): 18; Gregory J. Millman, "The Risk Not Taken," *Barron's* (May 1, 1995): 46.

8. David Wessel, Darren McDermott, and Greg Ip, "Speculators Didn't Sink Indonesian Currency; Local Borrowing Did," *Wall Street Journal* (December 30, 1997): A1. See also Louis Lucas, "Turmoil Prompts Currency Rethink," *Financial Times* (October 31, 1997) ("it was not uncommon for companies to borrow in US dollars and remain unhedged because...it was superficially cheaper"): 20; John Lipsky and Karen Parker, "Currency Lesson Ignored," *Financial Times* (October 13, 1997) ("a long tradition of regional exchange-rate stability had encouraged domestic investors to assume significant currency risk"): 18.

9. Working, *Futures Trading and Hedging, supra,* note 3: 139.

10. James B. Conant, *On Understanding Science* (Yale University Press, 1947): 36.

11. Daniel P. Cunningham et al., "An Introduction to OTC Derivatives," *SWAPS and Other Derivatives in 1996,* Kenneth M. Raisler and Alison M. Gregory, Cochairs (Practicing Law Institute, 1996) [the article is hereafter referred to as *OTC Derivatives*; the book is hereafter referred to as *1996 PLI Derivatives*]: 275.

12. Mason et al., *Financial Engineering, supra,* note 2: xiv.

13. See *id.*: 21.

14. Merton H. Miller, "Financial Innovation: Achievements and Prospects," *Journal of Applied Corporate Finance,* 4 (Winter 1992) [hereafter, *Achievements and Prospects*]: 7.

15. Robert C. Merton, "Financial Innovation and Economic Performance," *Journal of Applied Corporate Finance,* 4 (Winter 1992) [hereafter, *Financial Innovation*]: 12–22.

16. Miller, *Achievements and Prospects, supra,* note 14: 4–11.

17. Paul A. Samuelson and William D. Nordhaus, *Economics,* 15th ed. (McGraw-Hill, 1995) [hereafter, *Economics*]: 181.

18. Franklin R. Edwards and Cindy W. Ma, *Futures and Options* (McGraw-Hill, 1992): 141.

19. The quotation and analysis in this paragraph are from Mason et al., *Financial Engineering, supra,* note 2: 1, 10–13; see also Merton, *Financial Innovation, supra,* note 15.

20. See Ludwig Edler von Mises, *Human Action* (1949).

21. See Laurence H. Tribe, "A Further Critique of Mathematical Proof," *Harvard Law Review,* 84 (1971): 1810.

22. Henry T. C. Hu, "Misunderstood Derivatives: The Causes of Informational Failure and the Promise of Regulatory Incrementalism," *Yale Law Journal,* 102 (April 1993) [hereafter, *Misunderstood Derivatives*]: 1457, 1491.

23. Note, "The Regulation of Risky Investments," *Harvard Law Review,* 83 (1970) [hereafter, *Risky Investments*]: 603, 620; see also William F. Samuelson and Stephen G. Marks, *Managerial Economics* (2nd ed.) (The Dryden Press, 1995) [hereafter, *Managerial Economics*]: 300–301.

24. Thomas J. O'Brien, "Operational Hedging, Strategic Flexibility, and Financial Hedging of Exchange Rate Risk" (unpublished manuscript; March 13, 1998 draft) [hereafter, *Financial Hedging of Exchange Rate Risk*]; *see also* Trevor S. Harris and Nathan D. Melumad, "An Argument Against Hedging by Matching the Currencies of Costs and Revenues," *Journal of Applied Corporate Finance* 9(5) (Fall 1996): 90–97.

25. See "Statement by Alan Greenspan, Chairman, Board of Governors of the Federal Reserve System, Before the Subcommittee on Telecommunications and Finance of the Committee on Energy and Commerce, U.S. House of Representatives, May 25, 1996," *Federal Reserve Bulletin* (July 1994) (emphasis added) [hereafter, *Statement Before Congress*]: 594.

26. Robert C. Merton, *Continuous-Time Finance* (Blackwell Publications, 1992, revised) [hereafter, *Continuous-Time Finance*]: xiii.

27. Foreword by Robert C. Merton to Chew, *Leverage, supra,* note 1: xiii.

28. This quotation and the following discussion of the Eurodollar futures market are from Merton, *Financial Innovation, supra,* note 15.

29. *Id.:* 18–19.

30. See Peter Tufano, "Business Failure, Judicial Intervention, and Financial Innovation: Restructuring U.S. Railroads in the Nineteenth Century," *Business History Review,* Spring 1997 [hereafter, *Judicial Intervention and Financial Innovation*]; see also Peter Tufano, "Securities Innovations: A

Historical and Functional Perspective," *Journal of Applied Corporate Finance,* 7(4) (Winter 1995) [hereafter, *Securities Innovations*]: 90–104; Mason et al., *Financial Engineering, supra,* note 2: 43–74.

31. All quotations in this paragraph are from Tufano, *Judicial Intervention and Financial Innovation, supra,* note 30.

32. Tufano, *Securities Innovations, supra,* note 30 (emphasis added) (citations omitted): 95; see also Mason et al., *Financial Engineering, supra,* note 2: 52.

33. See, e.g., Michael Wood, "Development of the Cross Currency Swap Market," *Cross Currency Swaps,* Carl R. Beidleman, ed. (Business One Irwin, 1992): 93–96.

34. Mason et al., *Financial Engineering, supra,* note 2: 22.

35. Joan Ogden and Robert McDermott, "Are You Ready to Buy a Ticket for Derivatives II?" *Global Finance* (February 1996) 24–40.

36. Liz Moyer, "Bankers Trust Dispersing Risk Management Group," *American Banker* (February 19, 1998): 7.

37. Christopher Géczy, Bernadette A. Minton, and Catherine Schrand, "Why Firms Use Currency Derivatives," *Journal of Finance,* 52(4) (September 1997) [hereafter, *Why Firms Use Currency Derivatives*]: 1323–1354.

38. Harry M. Kat, "Credit Derivatives: A New Addition to the Derivatives Toolbox," *Derivatives: Tax Regulation Finance,* 3(2) (November–December 1997): 90; see also Satyajit Das, "The Market for Credit Derivatives," *Financial Products,* 65 (May 8, 1997); Robert S. Neal, "Credit Derivatives: New Financial Instruments for Controlling Credit Risk," *Federal Reserve Bank of Kansas City Economic Review,* 81 (2nd Quarter 1996): 15–27.

39. Karen Spinner, "Managing Bank Loan Risk," *Derivatives Strategy,* 3(1) (January 1998) (also focusing on pricing concerns): 15. See also, in the same issue, Karen Spinner, "The Search for Credit-VAR": 18–19.

40. Tufano, *Securities Innovations, supra,* note 30: 101.

41. Donald L. Horwitz and Robert J. Mackay, *Derivatives: State of the Debate,* October 1995 [hereafter, *State of the Debate.*

42. "The World According to Gene Shanks," *Derivatives Strategy,* 3(1) (January 1998) (emphasis added): 32–37, 36.

43. *Id.*: 62.

44. Tufano, *Securities Innovations, supra,* note 30.

45. See Securities Act Release No. 7386, published in the Federal Register on February 10, 1997; see also the SEC's "Questions and Answers About the New 'Market Risk' Disclosure Rules" (available July 31, 1997). The required disclosures about accounting policies are specified in new Rule 4-08(n) of Regulation S-X and Item 310 of Regulation S-B. The required disclosures about market risk exposures are specified in new Item 305 of Regulation S-K and Item 9A of Form 20-F.

Developing an Analytical Framework

We must decide whether tetrahedrons belong in square or round holes.

Easterbrook, Circuit Judge
Chicago Mercantile Exchange v. SEC,
1989[1]

Because there exist three relevant categories...the court's definitional task involved not placing tetrahedrons in round or square holes, but in triangular holes as well.

Russo and Vinciguerra, New Product
Development, 1991
(Criticizing Chicago Mercantile
Exchange v. SEC)[2]

Domestic and international legislators, regulators, supervisory authorities, industry groups, news media, lawyers, accountants, and academics use the term *derivative products,* or simply *derivatives,* with widely varying meanings. The variations have important commercial and legal implications for individual firms, as well as for the effective functioning of the financial system. Definitional variations and uncertainties result, at opposite extremes, in stifling rigidity or unnerving instability in regulatory schemes. They also hamper private sector efforts to implement meaningful systems of internal controls, particularly as those controls attempt to comply with applicable law.

Serious definitional flaws inherent in existing law have led legal practitioners such as Russo and Vinciguerra to conclude that the "the present 'definitional' approach to market regulation" is by nature "innovation-inhibiting."[3] Definitional rigidity also contributes to what Miller scorns as "one size fits all" regulation. For example, the present U.S. regulatory scheme determines the respective jurisdictions of, the Securities and Exchange Commission (SEC) and the Commodity Futures Trading Commission (CFTC) over new financial products in the first instance on the basis of whether each product constitutes a "security," a "futures contract," or neither. Yet the innovation spiral is rendering such distinctions increasingly untenable, as many new exchange-traded and OTC derivatives combine features of both securities and futures. Furthermore, as Working wrote in 1953, even traditional products such as forwards cannot easily be distinguished from futures simply based on "superficial technical characteristics." Anticipating much of the current regulatory confusion, Working wrote that the problem with technical product definitions is that they have varied widely from time to time and from place to place. Consequently, definitions based on such characteristics show an historical trend toward *increasing complexity and obscurity* as later writers tried to remedy technical shortcomings found in earlier definitions.[4]

At the firm level, a definitional approach to the term *derivative* as the foundation for a system of risk management is similarly flawed. A functional approach is far superior.

The first part of this chapter constracts a conceptual model for visualizing the dynamics of financial innovation. The model shows that reliance on a definitional approach is potentially debilitating, because many derivatives definitions convey little useful information about a financial instrument's risk and return characteristics. The second part illustrates practical difficulties raised by current derivatives definitions used by regulators and other financial market participants.

SENIOR MANAGEMENT'S INFORMATIONAL NEEDS

Any system "is only effective if it serves the needs of some user"[5]—in our case senior management (e.g., trustees, boards of directors, and executive officers) and its legal advisers.

Decision making and oversight are the essence of management. The choice of either a functional or a definitional approach to the management of derivatives risks—both business and legal risks—can dramatically alter the quality of management decision making and oversight, because the two approaches often lead to practical differences in the content of information communicated to, by, and among senior management and its legal advisers. The quality of information, in turn, affects the choice and effectiveness of risk management and other business strategies. Specifically, it affects the diagnosis of decision problems, the design of potential solutions, and the ability to monitor and evaluate the performance of strategies once they are chosen. Adequate information about risks and opportunities is a cornerstone of sound decision making and oversight.

At the broadest level, management information falls into two categories, dictated by the purposes the information serves. The first is information needed for external reporting purposes; the second is that needed for internal use. External reporting primarily involves the dissemination of information to parties reporting entity—such as shareholders, creditors, tax authorities, and other regulators—regarding the institution's business, financial condition, results of operations, and other mattes. The nature of the reported information varies depending on the nature and legitimate needs of the intended recipient.

Likewise, different internal purposes require different types of information. The information needed to monitor a business's compliance with applicable law differs considerably from that needed to run the business profitably.

Valid, meaningful information regarding problems to be addressed and the range of potential solutions is critical to the process of financial innovation and to the disciplines of legal and financial engineering. To the extent that derivatives definitions fail to convey meaningful information about either the risk and return characteristics or the legalities of various products, those definitions are useless. To the extent that those definitions convey misleading information about likely legal and regulatory treatment or risk and return characteristics, they can be positively harmful. Unfortunately, existing derivatives definitions say little about products' risk and return features and legal and regulatory implications. Thus, they are often useless, even harmful.

In stark contrast, a functional approach begins with and is constructed from an analysis of risk and return characteristics. Moreover, it is sufficiently robust to help assess and accommodate existing and likely future legal and regulatory concerns. As such, a functional approach is far more informative to senior managers, legal advisers, regulators, shareholders, and other interested parties.

Innovating Around Prohibited Profitable Transactions

Merton Miller elevates the role of government in financial markets to the lofty status of an "initiating force in financial innovation."[6] But he likens the role of government to that of the "grain of sand in the oyster"—a "typically inadvertent" stimulus to the production of the "pearls" of financial innovation. By extension, he unmistakably implies that managers need and desire to know about potentially profitable transactions that existing law either prohibits or renders unduly expensive or burdensome.

Figure 2.1 helps us picture Miller's analysis. The figure depicts the "universe" of all possible activities. Circle L represents all lawful activi-

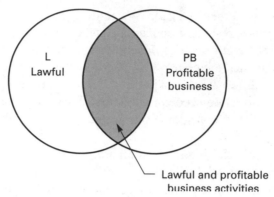

Figure 2.1   Universe of activities.

ties; any activity outside Circle L is unlawful. Circle PB represents all possible profitable business activities; any activity outside Circle PB is either not a business activity or, for any number of reasons including the imposition of burdensome taxes or regulatory requirements, not profitable. Miller's immediate concern is with those business activities located in the unshaded region of Circle PB—the profitable but unlawful business activities that financial innovation may be able to transform into *legal and profitable* activities that move over into the shaded region where Circles L and PB intersect. Consider the following examples.

Eurodollar markets: inadvertent pearls of Regulation Q

Beginning in 1933, the Federal Reserve's U.S. banking restriction known as Regulation Q placed a ceiling on the rate that commercial banks in the United States could pay for funds raised through the acceptance of consumer time deposits. Banks relied on those deposits as a primary source of inexpensive funding for the lending operations central to their business. Under Regulation Q, the payment of a rate above the ceiling rate constituted an illegal activity in the unshaded region of Circle PB.

So long as market rates were near or below the Regulation Q ceiling, this source of funding was economically viable. But, upward pressures on market interest rates in the late 1960s and early 1970s created more profitable consumer investment opportunities that weakened the ability of U.S. banks to attract needed time deposits. Heavy competition came from head offices and other non-U.S. offices of foreign banks, which were not subject to Regulation Q. Moreover, U.S. law enabled foreign banks to use their U.S. offices to open offshore deposit accounts for their customers located in the United States.*

An unforeseen consequence of Regulation Q was that much of the deposit-taking activity of U.S. money-center banks moved offshore. U.S. banks' foreign branches, particularly those in Western Europe, were free of Regulation Q's restrictions and therefore could offer more competitive free-market rates on their deposits than could their U.S. offices. The shifting of deposit-taking activity offshore was, from the depositor's standpoint, mechanically simple. Nevertheless, it imposed new operating costs on the U.S. bank. It also introduced "a series of legal complexities" and risks for both the U.S. bank and the depositor.[7]

The primary legal concern is that a Eurodollar deposit is not a contract governed by the laws of the United States. Rather, for legal purposes it becomes a contract made and to be performed at a place outside the United States, at the location of the foreign office at which the deposit is booked, regardless of the depositor's nationality or that of the obligor bank.

> The holder of a Eurodollar deposit, therefore, must accept the risks of the law at the place where his deposit is sited. Put differently, the holder of a Eurodollar deposit is not the owner of dollars; he is the owner of rights under an English contract if the deposit is made in London or under a German contract if it is made in Frankfurt. The significance of this fact is that the Eurodollar depositor must count on a *political* as well as an *economic risk.*[8]

The economic risk is the risk that, in an insolvency of the foreign bank, any award to be made to the depositor would be denominated not in dollars but in the bank's local currency. Thus a residual currency exchange risk exists. The political risk is that a foreign government might nullify or otherwise limit the bank's obligations as to the deposit.

---

*Henry Harfield uses a quaint illustration of the plight of U.S. banks under Regulation Q. He posits the case of a New Yorker who inherited $1 million at a time when U.S. banks were limited to paying a Regulation Q ceiling rate of $5\frac{1}{2}\%$. The New Yorker "learned that if he deposited his million dollars with the London branch of his friendly bank rather than at its main office in New York, he could enjoy a return of $7\frac{1}{2}\%$ on the million dollars. His friendly bank, however, had no branch in London so at this point our hero visited the New York branch of an English bank and thereafter opened a U.S. dollar account with its London head office." The friendly New York bank's failure to have a London branch cost it the million-dollar deposit, which went instead to the English bank's head office. The hypothetical illustrates the competitive pressures that forced U.S. banks to open foreign European branches to compete with their European counterparts for deposits, particularly those of U.S. customers. See Harfield, *The Eurodollar, infra,* note 7: 579–590.

Figure 2.1 explains the movement of deposit-taking activities off-shore to take advantage of a more favorable regulatory climate. Regulation Q made the payment of free-market interest rates in the United States an unlawful business activity in the unshaded region of Circle PB. Likewise, the payment of Regulation Q rates in the United States would fail to attract deposits and would, therefore, become an increasingly ineffective, unprofitable business activity outside Circle PB.

The opening of foreign branches from which U.S. banks could accept Eurodollar deposits enabled the banks to shift their deposit-taking activities from the unprofitable region outside Circle PB over into the shaded region, where Circles L and PB intersect—that is, the region of lawful, profitable business activities. In retrospect, the innovative use of Eurodollar time deposits enabled U.S. banks to overcome the anticompetitive effects of Regulation Q and compete effectively with foreign rivals to obtain deposits.*

OTC swaps: inadvertent pearls of foreign exchange controls

The modern OTC swaps market began in the late 1970s with OTC currency swaps. Those swaps, in turn, had their origins in two earlier transaction structures, both of which were unintended consequences of foreign exchange controls.

Parallel and back-to-back loans   The first involved "parallel" and "back-to-back" loan transactions entered into by private parties in the 1970s to avoid onerous exchange controls, particularly those imposed by the government of Great Britain beginning in 1957.

> The pound's weakness was fundamentally the result of Britain's weak economy that generated a lower rate of return on capital. As a result, British investors directed their investments abroad, mainly to the United States. This created a downward pressure on the pound [as British investors sold pounds and bought dollars]....Suffice to say that between 1973 and 1977 the pound sterling lost 30 percent of its value as measured against the dollar....[T]he [British] government took...steps to stop devaluation of the pound and instituted new internal controls.[9]

---

*Regulation Q was phased out under the Depository Institutions Deregulation and Monetary Control Act of 1980.

The British government designed the new controls to discourage British investors from making foreign investments. First, it imposed premiums on pound/dollar currency exchanges in which the dollars were earmarked for foreign investment. Further, the British government imposed additional costs on the repatriation of profits earned abroad. The combination of premiums plus additional costs often rendered both transactions prohibitively expensive.

Private parties initially devised a means of skirting onerous exchange controls through complex, offsetting borrowing arrangements called *parallel loans.* Several different structures were available. The simplest structure analytically was the four-party arrangement depicted in Figure 2.2. Three-party arrangements were also common. "The instruments for parallel...loans provide for two separate loan agreements, one for each currency, with an interest rate applicable to each....Three- or

1. Initial Loans

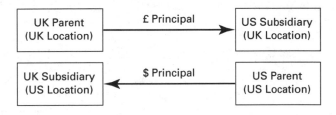

2. Periodic Interest Payments

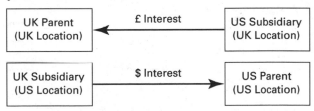

3. Repayment of Principal at Maturity (Interest Also)

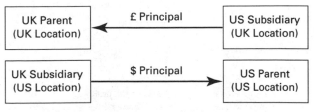

Figure 2.2   Parallel loans.

four-party loans provide for the direct lending of the funds to foreign subsidiaries of one or both of the parents."[10]

Parallel loans soon evolved into back-to-back loans. In a *back-to-back
loan,* the subsidiaries drop out of the structure and the cashflows move
directly between parent companies. However, the reason the loans are back
to back is that they typically involve the interposition of a financial intermediary between the two parent companies, as depicted in Figure 2.3.
Financial intermediaries were generally considered to be better able than
non-financial parent companies to evaluate the credit risk of each ultimate
counterparty to a transaction.

However, the early loan transactions, while effective, had serious
drawbacks. First, corresponding loans were documented in separate,
heavily negotiated agreements—a labor intensive, time-consuming, and
expensive process. Second, investment banks, brokerage houses, and
merchant banks typically commanded hefty fees for arranging the transactions. Next, accounting rules treated the loans as balance sheet items,
thereby inflating counterparties' balance sheets.* Finally, and most

1. Initial Loans of Principal

2. Periodic Payments of Interest

3. Repayment of Principal (and Interest) at Maturity

Figure 2.3   Back-to-back loans.

---

*On its books, each party would carry the full principal amount of the loan it made as an asset and
    that of the loan it received as a liability. Interest accruals would also be shown, both receiv-
    ables (as assets) and payables (as liabilities).

importantly, the offsetting loans exposed both counterparties to disproportionately large default risks: "Although such a risk exists with any
loan agreement, what [made] this situation more tenuous [was] that the
counterparty that did not default may still [have been] obligated to repay
its borrowing event after the cash flows had stopped coming in from the
other side."[11]

Currency and interest rate swaps   Private parties eventually turned to a
mechanism used since 1962 as part of the General Arrangement to Borrow
(GAB) entered into among 10 countries party to the Bretton Woods international monetary system. The "twin pillars" of the system were dollar and
gold prices; "[g]old was set at the prewar price of $35 per troy ounce."[12] By
the early 1960s, gold and dollar prices were under speculative pressure, and
as gold was bid up in world markets, the dollar declined. The GAB was an
effort to "defend the dollar" and the fixed exchange rate mechanism. GAB
countries agreed to preset lines of credit among their central banks and treasuries to fund the emergecy dollar purchases needed to prop up the dollar.
This intergovernmental "swap network" allowed GAB members temporarily to swap currencies during times of crisis, hoping to forestall currency crises. Early OTC currency swaps among private parties drew heavily on the experience of the GAB swap network.

  Financial and legal engineers used the GAB model to design a transaction structure that transformed offsetting and cumbrous loan transactions into a sequence of currency purchases and sales. The resulting documentation, which lacked the promissory notes of traditional loan
transactions, provided that on certain dates the parties would *exchange,* or
purchase and sell—not lend and borrow—specified amounts of currencies. "A currency swap is the purchase of a currency [at the outset of the
transaction] and the sale simultaneously of the same amount of that currency [upon maturity], but with different delivery dates for purchase and
sale." The initial exchange was thus viewed as a spot transaction in which
one party would sell a specified amount of one currency to the other party
against payment by that other party of a corresponding amount of another
currency. The parties would also agree to reverse the initial exchange on a
scheduled final maturity date—say, five years—at a preagreed exchange
rate, which was usually the same as that used for the initial spot transaction. Finally, "[o]ver the life of the transaction the two parties [would]
agree to exchange amounts calculated *as though they were interest* on
the...amounts exchanged initially."[13]

Early currency swap cashflows were identical to those of the loan transactions depicted in Figure 2.3 (although not all included the interposition of a financial intermediary). Both structures involved series of reciprocal payment obligations consisting of (1) initial exchanges of principal denominated in different currencies, (2) periodic payments of interest in the currency of the principal amount received, and (3) final scheduled reversals of the original principal exchanges.

As with the original loan transactions, there were early concerns about the default risks and the enforceability of swap payment termination rights, particularly with U.K. counterparties. There was also noticeable apprehension about the applicable accounting treatment. Nevertheless, the early concerns eventually dissipated, especially after the much-heralded World Bank/IBM currency swap. After that transaction was announced, the swaps market expanded with stunning speed. Markets quickly began to demonstrate remarkable indifference toward swaps' legal risks. Consider that professor Henry T. C. Hu of the University of Texas School of Law, who is a leading scholar of derivatives markets and financial regulation, finds that "[t]he apparent disregard of legal risks illustrated by [the early swaps market] is surprising."[14] That disregard was not limited to legal risks. For example, in 1984 a prominent swaps specialist wrote that "a certain lack of standardized accounting procedures in most countries [allows] consequently a considerable amount of leeway for reporting such transactions."[15]

Once the currency markets "seasoned" the swap technique, intermediaries easily and quite logically adapted it to the interest rate transactions that came into heavy demand in 1982, at a time of unsteady U.S. interest rates and economic recession. Interest rate swaps were first treated as simplified currency swaps—swaps with "[i]dentical currencies on the two sides." The use of a single currency obviates the need for exchanges of principal.

Figure 2.1 analysis   Figure 2.1 is helpful in visualizing the dynamics of the evolution of OTC swaps. By the early 1960s, market forces were increasing the price of gold and puting heavy downward pressures on the dollar. Nevertheless, currency exchange at free-market rates presumably remained a lawful protitable business activity located in the shaded region where Circles L and PB intersect. The GAB arrangement temporarily defended the dollar, keeping dollar exchanges in that shaded region.

Eventually the Bretton Woods mechanism broke apart, leaving exchange rates to float freely. The British government, shortly thereafter, unilaterally imposed exchange controls that threatened the ability of British investors to make foreign investments. The exchange controls forced affected investment transactions to move from the shaded region in Figure 2.1 to the unshaded (i.e., unlawful) region of Circle PB or to the region outside Circle PB (i.e., unprofitable). Yet soon the innovative, lawful use of parallel and back-to-back loan transactions, followed by currency swaps, enabled private parties to achieve the economic results of free market exchanges without incurring the penalties exacted by British exchange controls. In oter words, prohibitively expensive (or unlawful) transactions outside the shaded region were moved, through financial innovation, back into the shaded region of lawful, economic business activities.

The "essence of capitalist economics is that one obtains the best possible return on one's capital." When laws of governments rather than those of economics decree a limitation on the return capital can earn, capital will move to "a more productive environment, that is to say, one where [it can] produce subject to the laws of economics and not to the laws of the land."[16] In terms of Figure 2.1, the essence of capitalist economics is to shift activities out of the unlawful (unshaded) region of Circle PB or the unprofitable region outside of Circle PB into the profitable, lawful (shaded) region where Circles L and PB intersect.

Innovation Within the Region of Lawful, Profitable Business Activities

Critical to the analytical framework we are developing is that the placement of an activity within or outside the shaded region of Figure 2.1 is *logically in dependent of the riskiness* of that activity.

Safe business activities may yet fall outside the shaded region of Circle PB. For example, the British exchange controls that led to the development of currency swaps were not imposed to prevent British investors from making risky foreign investments. To the contrary, the imposition of those restrictions may even have induced many British investors to make riskier investments—that is, investments in a then fundamentally weak British economy.

Likewise, many activities, such as visiting friends, washing the car, and walking the dog, are under most circumstances entirely safe and lawful activities. However, given that those visits, washings, and walks tend not to be business activities, they would normally be in Circle L, but not Circle PB. Therefore, they would fall entirely outside Figure 2.1's shaded region.

Finally, many activities, such as drilling wildcat oil wells, playing professional football, and developing a new propulsion system for the launching of commercial satellites, may constitute highly risky activities. Nevertheless, they are often entirely lawful and profitable business activities that fall within the shaded region of Figure 2.1.

The urge to innovate around legal barriers to profitable transactions is a driving force behind financial innovation. Merton shows barriers are often unintended consequences of well-meaning but poorly conceived social policy. Miller faults taxes. Another driver is the desire to manage risk. Businesses actively seek innovative solutions to the problems posed by the economic and other risks of lawful, profitable transactions in the shaded region of Figure 2.1. Risk management tools are needed to protect the profitability of existing lawful business activities. Moreover, as Tufano explains, "[f]orward-looking managers" are finding they can use financial and legal engineering to "help create a competitive edge" and enhance profitability.[17]

The primary rationale cited by private industry for using derivatives is to manage the economic risks of their lawful business and investment activities, both to protect and strategically to improve the profitability of existing activities.[18] That rationale is consistent with the primary function of derivatives cited by economists and government officials such as Alan Greenspan, which is to enhance economic efficiency by enabling market participants to unbundle complex risk packages and transfer unwanted risks to parties better able to bear them.

Derivatives Crises and "Suspect" Transactions

Figure 2.4 identifies another subset of activities falling in Figure 2.1. Figure 2.4 adds a new Circle S, representing transactions publicly perceived to be "suspect," regardless of whether they are lawful or constitute profitable business activities. The addition of Circle S creates an analytical distinction helpful in thinking about the defects of a definitional approach to derivatives regulation or controls.

"Suspect" yet lawful, profitable transactions are those located in the intersection of the three circles. Activities outside Circle S—let us call them "nonsuspect" activities—do not on their face give rise to public concerns. Of interest are the lawful, profitable, nonsuspect transactions in the lower shaded sector of lawful business activities. Because of the

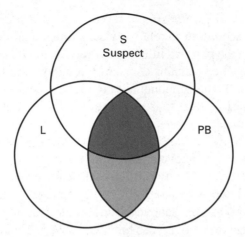

Figure 2.4 "Suspect" transactions.

many large and highly publicized losses of the last few years, many people feel that derivatives transactions automatically fall in the upper shaded region—that of lawful, profitable, yet suspect business activities. Managers, of course, realize this. For example, the *1995 Wharton/CIBC Wood Gundy Survey* reported in April 1996 that, of the surveyed firms that do not use derivatives, 39% "cite concerns about the perception of derivative use by the public, investors, and regulators as a significant reason."

Notwithstanding public perception, the placement of any lawful, profitable business activity at any specific location within or outside the shaded region of Figure 2.4 is *not logically dependent on the riskiness* of that activity. The implications of such an observation can be shown with a "plain vanilla" interest rate swap.

Interest rate swap

The most common OTC derivative is an interest rate swap in which two parties enter into a negotiated agreement to exchange periodically, at specified intervals, different types of interest rate payments—for example, floating-rate for fixed-rate payments. The amount of each payment is calculated on the basis of a hypothetical, or "notional," principal amount, which is never exchanged and is only used as a basis for calculating interest payments.

The term *plain vanilla* simply refers to an OTC derivative traded in a liquid market according to relatively standardized contracts and market conventions. "In the plain vanilla interest rate swap, the notional principal is nonamortizing [i.e., remains constant throughout the life of the swap], the payments are made semiannually, the reference rate for determining the floating [rate] payments is six-month LIBOR, and the swap is not callable or puttable."[19]

The price of a U.S. dollar denominated swap is usually quoted as a number of basis points above comparable maturity U.S. Treasury bonds, and the typical maturity is between 2 and 10 years. Dealer pricing takes the simple form of a two-way quote on a "swap spread," which is a specified number of basis points (bps) above the applicable Treasury rate. "For example, a dealer might quote five-year spreads as 22/26. That is, the dealer will use 22 bps to price the swap if [it] is paying the fixed rate and 26 bps if [it] is receiving [fixed]. In a $100 million deal, that spread amounts to $40,000 per annum."[20]

Application: CreditCo

A plain vanilla interest rate swap might be used, for example, by a publicly held finance company (CreditCo) that makes floating-rate consumer loans that it funds by issuing fixed-rate bonds. Assume CreditCo has no desire to speculate on interest rates. Rather, it is happy to earn income concentrating on what it does best: sourcing and financing loans. Aside from consumer defaults, CreditCo's primary business risk is that market rates will decline while the bonds are outstanding, reducing its revenues on its consumer loan assets and thereby decreasing the company's ability to service its fixed-rate bond debt.

A swap in which CreditCo were to receive fixed interest rate payments and pay floating would reduce the company's exposure to declining rates. Any resulting loan revenue shortfall could be covered by the fixed-rate payments received on the swap. CreditCo's costs in entering into the swap would be transaction costs, including the bid-offer spread payable to the swap dealer. The company would also forgo the upside of any favorable market rate movements.

CreditCo's swap would hedge the rate risk created by the company's mismatching floating-rate assets and fixed-rate liabilities. By transferring to a swap dealer the floating-rate risk with which CreditCo prefers not to contend, the swap enables CreditCo to concentrate its resources—including scarce management resources—on its core business of making loans.

Most observers would likely consider the swap (assuming reasonable pricing) a prudent transaction for CreditCo.

Perverse Incentives and Disincentives

The CreditCo swap illustrates several serious problems inherent in a definitional approach to derivatives regulation sandcontrols. The first is that merely characterizing the swap as a derivative could deter CreditCo from using it for prudent risk management. Studies show that many public companies that otherwise prefer to use derivatives to manage unwanted risks shun the products to avoid having to report them in public filings. Management's fear is that a valid hedging strategy might be criticized by shareholders and punished by financial markets, even if the strategy is perfectly designed and executed, and the company suffers no economic loss on the *combined* hedged activity and hedge. One reason is that a derivatives hedge such as that described is designed to perform in an equal and opposite manner to the hedged activity. (Fears are exacerbated by proposed accaunting rules that would in effect require separate reporting in income statements of swaysand their hedged instruments.

A hedge is often entered into to protect against an anticipated decline in the value of an asset (or portfolio of assets) or increase in the cost of a liability (or portfolio of liabilities). In a "perfect" hedge, all losses (gains) on the hedged activity will be offset by equal and opposite gains (losses) on the derivative. The goal of the hedge is "to *freeze* the value of the asset [or liability]. Any price rise or decline of the underlying asset [or liability] is offset by the derivative hedge. In fancier terms, a straight hedge is an attempt to *make the cash flows* between the asset [or liability] and the hedge instrument *symmetric* so that the *losses and gains cancel each other out*."[21] Figure 2.5 depicts the range of potential economic results of a perfect hedging strategy. In all cases, the economic result of the combined position of the derivative and the hedged underlying asset or liability is represented by the horizontal line.

CreditCo, for example, would, with a perfectly designed and executed hedging strategy and falling interest rates, realize a loss on its consumer loans. However, that loss would be offset by a gain on the swap. Obversely, if rates rise, the company will realize a gain on its consumer loans, offset by a loss on the swap. In either case, as the center horizontal line in Figure 2.5 indicates, the economic result is the same.

Nevertheless, CreditCo's management may still be concerned that the swap will be viewed in isolation from the hedged loans. If so, that

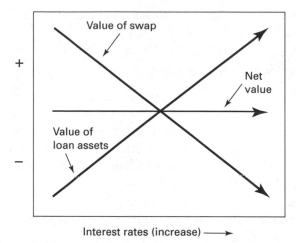

Figure 2.5   Perfect hedge.

could give an investor the perverse impression that the company, whether it gains or loses on the swap, is speculating on interest rates, when precisely the opposite is the case. The purpose of CreditCo's swap, as we assumed, was to lock in the spread it would earn on its floating-rate consumer loans regardless of the direction in which market rates moved. As one commentator notes:

> [I]t is common to lose money on the derivatives portion of the transaction even in a perfectly executed hedging strategy. This is a *normal* and *expected* *outcome in hedging,* and should be of no concern to the hedging firm or to the public. The only correct way to judge the performance of a particular hedge is to take both sides of the trade into account and to look at overall profit.[22]

Figure 2.4 Analysis—Serious Flaws Emerge

When the CreditCo swap is considered in light of Figure 2.4, several analytical flaws of a definitional approach to derivatives emerge. The swap portion of the transaction would be located within the intersection of all three circles and thus constitute a suspect transaction. Meanwhile, the hedged loans would be located in the shaded region where only Circles L and PB intersect; they would not be considered suspect. Immediately, four concerns arise.

1. Unnecessarily risky characterization of swap

The isolation of the swap from the consumer loan assets renders it difficult to appreciate the offsetting economic characteristics of the two. Hence, in isolation the swap may appear to be imprudently risky. If the market fails to discern the true nature of the hedging strategy from the review of the company's public filings, it may unnecessarily, from a pure risk perspective, penalize the price of CreditCo's stock because of the company's use of the swap.

2. Failures to appreciate the risk of floating-rate consumer loans

There are corresponding risks that, viewed in isolation, the "nonsuspect" consumer loan transactions will appear less risky than they truly are. A failure to appreciate the dangers of mismatching interest rates might lure CreditCo's management to cause the company to engage in inadequate lending and risk management practices. The failure to appreciate the interest rate risk of floating-rate consumer loans could reduce the company's incentive to manage those risks. Management might decide, if there is downward pressure on the company's stock that has been attributable to its derivatives use, to abandon the derivatives hedging strategy. In that event, CreditCo might be left entirely exposed to market interest rate movements and hence in a far riskier economic condition than it would be with swap in place. In the words of one corporate treasurer: "If we're not hedging, we're speculating."[23]

3. Lost strategic advantage; competitive disadvantage

Closely related to the immediately preceding risk is the danger that CreditCo will fail to take advantage of a strategic opportunity made available to it through interest rate swaps. Without the ability to manage interest rate risk using derivatives, the company may find itself forced to choose between one of two potentially inferior risk management strategies. The first is simply to assume the rate risk without attempting to manage it. That could be much riskier than using swaps.

The second alternative is for CreditCo to alter either its lending or its funding practices. It might, for example, cease issuing fixed-rate debt and attempt instead to borrow on a floating-rate basis. Or it might choose either to make only fixed-rate loans or to charge higher floating rates to compensate for the excess risk. In any event, the strategy of changing, lending, or funding practices is likely to either increase funding costs or reduce the quality or volume of consumer loans CreditCo can make.

The competitive risks facing the company may become acute once CreditCo's competitors, some of which might be privately owned and unconcerned with disclosure issues, successfully use derivative to manage their own rate risks. "Forward-looking managers need to keep abreast of their rivals' successful uses of promising breakthroughs like financial engineering."[24]

4. Potential needless waste of resources

If CreditCo determines for competitive or other business reasons to pursue the derivatives hedging strategy, reporting concerns may demand an inordinate dedication of management resources.

Basic Flaw: Definitional Approach Fails to Convey Essential Risk Information

One flaw inherent in any definitional approach to derivatives regulation or internal corporate controls is to the failure of definitions to account adequately for the riskiness—or lack thereof—of business and investment activities. Product definitions are essentially labels that may provide important cautionary risk signals; they can warn market participants and regulators alike that products fitting specific definitional criteria have, *at one time,* been identified as bearing undesirable economic traits and behavioral characteristics. In many circumstances, definitions used to categorize financial instruments can provide useful, stopgap measures in response to specific crises precipitated by particular products, the riskiness of which may not have been fully appreciated either by products' designers or by the products' users. Nevertheless, the adequacy of any definitionally based response tends to prove fleeting.

In Chapter 1 we explored the financial innovation spiral one result of which is a proliferation of new securities and trading markets as the economics of existing products become widely understood. Trading volumes increase, yet prices decline, as do the direct profits intermediaries earn on the products. Yet the technology of financial engineering and growing manu of standardized "raw materials" enable intermediaries to recapture profits lost to declining margins on standardized products—intermediaries are constantly customizing existing products to better satisfy current demand and designing new products in response to changing demand. By so doing they help fulfill specific needs of end users and improve "market completeness." With today's replication technologies, the range of potential new products is theoretically unlimited. A motivating force of innovation is the drive to profit by recreating the economics of problamatic products without falling into existing product definitions. Often innovation successfully leads to new products that lack the dangerous attributes of those they supersede. Yet Tufano reminds us that "the long history of innovation suggests a richer and more dynamic or evolutionary story of innovation, learning, and experimentation. A shock or an unfilled need typically leads to a series of innovations, *many of which prove to be unsuccessful.* Three sets of example—the evolution of income bonds, warrant contracts, and modern preferred stocks—demonstrate the point."[25]

The income bonds Tufano describes were used in the late nineteenth century by distressed firms. Their unusual feature was that the failure to pay specified interest would not result in a bond default if the bond issuer did not, over the relevant interest period, demonstrate sufficient accounting profits. But soon it became clear that accounting profits could easily be manipulated and moved to later periods to the detriment of bondholders, in effect forgiving affected interest payments. Income bonds, which "are a textbook case of how financial innovation is a process of learning and experimentation," are "virtually extinct." They are also a textbook case of how a contractual definition–i.e., profits–was easily circumvented.

Early equity warrants also exhibited serious design flaws when investors discovered to their chagrin that the warrants "did not protect their holders against cash dividends, stock dividends, or stock splits." Finally, the preferred stocks examined by Tufano provided their holders with a put in the event that the issuer paid dividends over a stated period in excess of a specified amount. Unfortunately for the holders, the first issuer of these securities "declared a dividend much larger than the one that would trigger the put feature, but made it payable seven months later, after the put feature had expired."

The Harvard team and others such as Merton Miller have demonstrated that financial innovations occurring at each phase in the cycle either introduce new complexities or reintroduce old complexities into financial markets through unfamiliar forms of instruments and transactions. That unfamiliarity of forms can often have two adverse side-effects.

First, the new forms may entail otherwise undesirable risks that, because of their unfamiliarity, elude definition-driven regulatory prohibitions or internal organizational controls. Economic forces provide strong incentives for market participants to develop products that possess high degrees of risk without displaying unsavory attributes that have been identified as obvious risk indicators. Furthermore, technological advances provide increasingly powerful means of developing new and risky instruments that satisfy the technical definitional requirements for less risky products.

Even well-regarded products intended for legitimate purposes may introduce new and unforeseen risks. As an example, Chapter 6 discusses recent criticisms of the foreign exchange options and currency swap options—swaptions—that have become an important tool of both public and private treasury departments worldwide. Generally, purchases of foreign exchange option products are considered to be, much like purchases of insurance policies, legitimate means of implementing prudent risk management strategies for public and private sector entities exposed to significant currency risk. Nevertheless, some argue that even such otherwise innocuous products as purchased foreign exchange options can be used by treasurers for disguised currency speculation.

Second, new forms of instruments and transactions may through hapless coincidence fall within prevailing definitions of prohibited transactions. Russo and Vinciguerra sharply criticize this result. They assert that the definitional approach embodied in current U.S. legislative solutions to derivatives problems, in the legitimate search to provide certainty and meaningful guidance and protections to financial market participants, threatens to "freeze" and "straitjacket" financial innovation. The results are "definitional impediments" that can have severe adverse consequences both for individual organizations and for the overall financial system. Russo and Vinciguerra conclude:

> Today, the fundamental question confronted in the development of an innovative financial product is not how the product could be developed to be efficient, to meet investors' needs, and to enhance U.S. competitiveness in the world financial market. Rather, the central issue has become whether or not a new product will ever be permitted to be offered or sold in the United States.

In their view, the fundamental problem is "the underlying premise of federal financial market regulation—that regulatory responsibility over new financial instruments should be allocated based upon whether an instrument falls within the definition of 'security' or 'futures contract.'"[26]

In essence, the rigidity of the definitional approach to market regulation and internal controls enables the risks of many products and transactions to go undetected for substantial time periods; conversely, it can inhibit the realization of the benefits of many relatively low-risk products that either fit into technical definitions of risky products or fall into traps caused by regulatory fragmentation resulting from fixed definitions. Thus, definitional labels, at least for many plain vanilla products, may be adequate indicators of risks that are generally well understood and manageable. However, for many other products—perhaps even for the plain vanillas—labels cannot long substitute adequately for vigorous risk analysis. They are, to the contrary, more likely over time to become increasingly irrelevant and potentially misleading risk indicators.

"Risk Oval"

A simple addition to Figure 2.4 helps explain the flaws of the definitional approach. Figure 2.6 adds to the realm of business activities a new oval representing business activities that are somehow unusually risky; activities outside the new oval are not unusually risky. Two consequences flow from the addition of the "risk oval." First, Figure 2.6 suggests that certain activities located in the intersection of all three circles—activities previously called "suspect" yet outside the risk oval and in the "NR" area—are not unusually risky. Second, Figure 2.6 suggests that certain activities located outside Circle S but in the intersection of Circles L and PB—"non-suspect" activities located inside the oval in area "UR"—are, nevertheless, unusually risky.

Finally, the current definitional approach fails to address the fact that laws, products, and product risks are dynamic. In terms of Figure 2.6, the

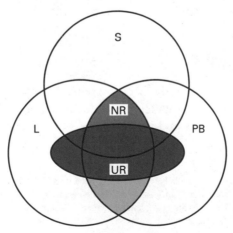

Figure 2.6   Risk oval.

size and contours of the risk oval as well as of each of the three circles are constantly shifting. The boundaries between the different shapes are often vague, and the relative locations of the three circles are subject to change. The dynamic character of derivatives risks casts further doubt on the definitional approach.

Senior management and its legal advisers, if they are to control an organization's true risk exposure, must develop an internal system of risk management that is independent of static statutory and regulatory definitions, one that focuses instead on the economic reality of products and product combinations. Any such system must facilitate comprehension of the essential functions and behavioral characteristics of the financial products that the organization is using or contemplating using, given the risk management strategy it is pursuing. Regardless of statutory, regulatory, and judicial definitions calling a product a "derivative," senior management must understand and employ a system of risk management that makes sense for its organization.

In making derivatives decisions, senior management and its legal advisers must remain cognizant of the distinction between statutory and regulatory definitions on the one hand and internal governance issues on the other. Many types of transactions may be considered entirely lawful and legitimate activities. Nevertheless, management certainly does not want its organization engaging in the full range of activities legally permissible. Conversely, many types of transactions that management may be eager to encourage—in light of the organization's economic objectives, risk appetite, and risk management strategy—might be unlawful. If so, management, together with its financial and legal engineers, may wish to attempt to innovate around the relevant prohibitions.

CURRENT DEFINITIONS

The Global Derivatives Study Group, sponsored by the Group of Thirty (G-30),* adopted the most widely accepted definition of the term *derivative* in its influential 1993 study of derivatives practices and principles. The

---

*The Group of Thirty is a supranational group formed by the Rockefeller Foundation in 1979 to bring senior financial leaders, academics, and regulators together to discuss and analyze important financial topics. The G-30 Study is available from the Group of Thirty, 1990 M Street NW, Washington, DC 20036, telephone number (202) 331-2472, facsimile number (202) 785-9423.

G-30's Paul Volcker, then former chairman of the Board of Governors of the Federal Reserve System (Federal Reserve), initiated the study, which was a voluntary private sector initiative to examine the global OTC derivatives industry. Among the study's participants were senior members and professionals of many of the industry's leading dealer institutions, a few large end users, and professionals from the related legal, accounting, and academic disciplines.

The Study Group's efforts led to a collection of reports and recommendations, commonly referred to as the G-30 Study, which is now rightly viewed as the benchmark against which all subsequent derivatives studies continue to be measured. It includes an Overview of Derivatives Activities (*G-30 Overview*), 20 risk management recommendations directed toward dealers and end users, and 4 recommendations for legislators, regulators, and supervisors. The breadth and scope of subject matter covered, as well as the divergent and often conflicting interests represented by the Study Group's participants, contributed to the industry's general acceptance of the study.

The G-30 Study remains the starting point for any serious effort to establish and implement sound derivatives risk management policies and procedures.

G-30 Definition

The *G-30 Overview* offers the following definition of derivative products:

> [A] derivatives transaction is a bilateral contract or payments exchange agreement whose value derives, as its name implies, from the value of an underlying asset or underlying reference rate or index....[D]erivatives also include standardized futures and options on futures that are actively traded on exchanges, and securities such as call warrants. The term "derivative" also is used by some observers to refer to a wide variety of debt instruments that have payoff characteristics reflecting embedded derivatives, or have option characteristics, or are created by "stripping" particular components of other instruments such as principal or interest payments.[27]

The *G-30 Overview* provides a table, reproduced in Figure 2.7, listing various derivatives contracts and derivatives securities. The G-30 Study focused primarily on the forms of derivatives contracts listed in boldface type. These contracts cover the entirety of what many market participants

---

Derivatives Contracts

Privately Negotiated (OTC) Forwards	**Privately Negotiated (OTC) Options**	Exchange Traded Futures	Exchange Traded Options
Forward Commodity Contracts	**Commodity Options**	Eurodollar (CME)	S&P Futures Options (MERC)
Forward Foreign Exchange Contracts	**Currency Options**	US Treasury Bond (CBT)	Bond Futures Options (LIFFE)
	Equity Options	9% British Gilt (LIFFE)	
Forward Rate Agreements (FRAs)	**FRA Options**	CAC –40 (MATIF)	Corn Futures Options (CBT)
	Caps, Floors, Collars	DM/$ (IMM)	
Currency Swaps	**Swap Options**	German Bund (DTB)	Yen/$ Futures Options (IMM)
Interest Rate Swaps	**Bond Options**	Gold (COMEX)	
Commodity Swaps			
Equity Swaps			

Derivatives Securities

Structured Securities and Deposits	Stripped Securities	Securities with Option Characteristics
Dual Currency Bonds	Treasury Strips	Callable Bonds
Commodity-Linked Bonds	IO's and PO's	Putable Bonds
Yield Curve Notes		Convertible Securities
Equity-Linked Bank Deposits		Warrants

Note: The Derivatives Contracts indicated in bold type are the primary subject of this G–30 Study.

Figure 2.7   Derivatives, contracts, and derivatives securities. (*Reprinted with permission from the Group of Thirty, Washington, DC.*)

and industry groups, the most prominent being ISDA, consider to be the OTC derivatives market.*

The scope of the formal G-30 definition is sufficiently broad to include instruments that many major derivatives dealers do not categorize as derivatives. The dealers' primary objection is that those instruments are

---

*The G-30 definition is premised on two concepts that should be kept in mind in interpreting market statistics and formulating risk management programs. First, the G-30 mentions the distinction between derivatives contracts and derivatives securities, but it does not explain *why* derivatives securities are excluded from the subject of the study. Second, the table accompanying the definition and reproduced in Figure 2.7 spans a far wider range of derivatives instruments than many market participants, most notably ISDA, consider appropriate. Again, the G-30 Overview does not explain Figure 2.7's wider product coverage.

different in kind from traditional derivative instruments. ISDA draws the clearest distinction between traditional and other derivatives. It distinguishes between, first, *"bilateral contracts* involving the exchange of cash flows and designed to shift risk between parties" and, second, *"securities* issued to *raise capital."* The rationale for excluding derivatives securities is that even though "some types of capital-raising instruments 'derive' their values or cash flows from the price of an underlying asset or index, such as mortgage-backed securities, they are securities designed to raise funds for their issuer. *Derivatives are privately negotiated bilateral contracts, not securities.* The *notional amount* used to calculate payments in a derivatives transaction is *not at risk."*[28]

In addition to analytical distinctions involving capital-raising versus risk-transferring activities, there are several practical reasons for excluding derivative securities from the coverage of the term *derivative product.* First, loose usage of the term *derivative* might pointlessly stigmatize traditional, plain vanilla swaps and other products whose risk and return features are relatively straightforward and easily managed. That could have serious repercussions on derivatives markets and, ultimately, the financial system; it would deprive the financial system of the benefits of many effective and efficient risk management tools.

Derivatives markets were tainted in the public press as a result of large losses incurred by holders of certain highly risky financial instruments. Among the most vilified products of 1994 were the mortgage-backed securities (MBS) derivatives that turned out to be disastrous investments for countless investors. The sudden upsurge in interest rates in early 1994[29] resulted in the "mortgage-backed mayhem" in the market for MBS derivatives. Certain MBS derivatives are highly risky, owing to their inherent leverage and dependence on mortgage loan prepayment rates. For example, *interest-only (IO) strips* are leveraged instruments, the price of which moves inversely to that of traditional bonds. Investors bought large amounts of IOs in mid-1992, only to watch the market bond prices continue to rise relentlessly until the Federal Reserve announced an interest rate hike in February 1994. To take the opposite extreme, *principal-only (PO) strips* are also leveraged instruments, but their prices move in sympathy with those of traditional bonds. Investors who had loaded up on POs prior to the February 1994 rate hikes were decimated by the market fallout that ensued.

A problem with MBS derivatives is that, "[a]lthough straightforward in concept—simply bundle together a bunch of home mortgages and sell the package as a security—[they] include some of the most complex financial instruments ever invented."[30] To date, no institution has generated a satisfactorily reliable model for predicting prepayment rates, rendering the pricing of the instruments more of an art than a science. *State of the Debate* includes an abstract of a Fall 1994 article from the *Journal of Applied Corporate Finance* that summarizes clearly the dangers of MBS derivatives. According to the abstract:

> The authors believe that recent losses on MBS derivatives do not stem from default (credit risk), but from "unexpected changes in interest rates, inaccurate models linking interest rates to changes in prepayment behavior, and, in some cases, ignorance of the risk profiles of the derivatives..."
>
> The findings conclude that managing an MBS portfolio "requires a model that can value and monitor the securities on a day-to-day basis. The relative value of the (MBS)...must be based on a relatively accurate and consistent model that links mortgagor prepayment behavior to changes in interest rates. Although such models exist and are constantly being refined, they are far from perfect." Moreover, "institutional investors may disagree not only about which model is correct, but also about the appropriate values for the various parameters in any given model.[31]

Given the unpredictability of prepayments and resulting riskiness of many MBS derivatives, protections for MBS holders are provided through transaction structures that stratify prepayment risk exposures. The outer strata, where IOs and POs reside, are highly risky.

The strata into which each structure is divided are called *tranches*. An examination of the risk characteristics of the various tranches reveals that many inner tranches are relatively safe. Their risk is, by virture of the structure, transferred to other tranches, which often absorb most of the prepayment risk of the entire structure. Those more risky tranches, mostly responsible for the MBS derivatives disasters, must remain highly risky if they are to fulfill their function of cushioning the inner tranches. The structures, then, purport to eliminate prepayment risk; instead, they redistribute it among various MBS holders.

Additional distinctions between MBS derivatives and traditional derivatives securities can be drawn. For example, mortgage-backed securities trade in different markets and otherwise display a number of economic features entirely distinct from traditional derivatives. However, a detailed discussion of MBS derivatives is beyond our present scope.

Another practical reason for avoiding loose usage of the term *derivative* is that such usage may cause a user incorrectly to associate the risk and return features of easily understood and managed products such as plain vanilla swaps with those of complex, exotic instruments. If so, the user may fail to appreciate the riskiness of the complex instrument and fail to implement appropreate controls. If so, the occurence of unexpectedly large losses may be only a matter of time.

Derivatives definitional concerns are heightened after each publicized loss, and they often lead to calls for additional legislation and stricter regulation. Concerns about the stigmatization of derivatives have caused many end users that might otherwise benefit from sound derivatives usage to avoid derivatives entirely. During most of 1994 the general public and media perception of derivatives was undeniably negative. Much unfavorable sentiment remains.*

Antiderivatives legislation in fact did pass in the spring of 1996 in Texas, restricting the ability of mutual funds to use even the simplest of derivatives. Recently enacted Ohio prohibitions are far more onerous. As reported in the August 1996 issue of *Derivatives Strategy,* Ohio adopted "the severest of any state's prohibitions on derivative investments by local government bodies….[The] mantra [of its proponent] is this: 'Public portfolios shouldn't hedge risk—they should be risk averse….If you have no risk, or low risk, you have no need for derivatives.'" The definition of derivatives adopted by the Ohio legislature is, according to the article, so broad that it even "comes down against reverse repurchase agreements…—even against 'purchasing an investment where there is not a reasonable expectation it will be held to maturity.'"†

---

*The following comments capture well the often negative public mood. A recent *Time* magazine article said "[d]erivatives are a kind of nuclear financial instrument. They are powerful and highly complicated…. [I]n derivatives, like nuclear mishaps, there are no small accidents." The same article proclams that because of derivatives, "many banks have a new sideline: gambling." Bernard Baumohl, "The Banks' Nuclear Secrets," *Time* (May 25, 1998). Similarly, shortly after the string of large losses that commenced in late 1993, Mary Schapiro, then Chairman of the CFTC, commented that "[b]ased on recent press reports, the current media definition [of derivatives] sometimes seems to be a derivatives transaction is any transaction in which a large amount of money is lost." *Futures* (March 1995): 16.

†However, there are also signs that the current perception of derivatives among politicians, investors, and potential end users has greatly improved. The same *Derivatives Strategy* article, for example, notes the "conventional wisdom" is that the political opprobrium around derivatives is lifting. A March 3, 1996 headline in the *Wall Street Journal* announced that "Derivatives Are a Tempting Option Again: Trading Is Up and Regulatory Fears Are Subsiding." That article reported that "participants at ISDA's 11th annual meeting…describe the mood as almost ebullient." In contrast, the same conference a year earlier was, according to one former ISDA board member, "'kind of like attending a wake.'" Finally, the *American Banker* recently reported on the willingness of even small banks to actively use derivatives, with some community banks even using structured notes and MBS derivatives. See, e.g., Aaron Elstein, "Afraid of Derivatives? Not These 3 Little Banks," *American Banker* (October 22, 1996): 1; James C. Allen, "Derivatives Gain Favor with Small Banks," *American Banker* (March 21, 1996): 22.

The understanding of risk embodied in the approach of the proponents of state antiderivatives legislation is fundamentally at odds with the views of many federal regulators. A useful example is provided by recent remarks of SEC Commissioner Wallman, which are directly contrary to those of the Ohio legislator quoted above:

> [T]he general public often tends to view those things that are not well understood and that have risk—such as derivatives—as inherently bad, instead of what they are—in this case, tools for managing risk.
>
> The danger here is readily apparent. Without a sufficient understanding of risk and return, investors may eschew risk that they ought to be willing to incur—at least for long-term retirement fund investments. In that case, these investors will not have sufficient funds for their later years. That portends poorly for them as well as for our economy going forward.[32]

Slippery Slopes

Statistics and arguments about derivatives are singularly susceptible to misinterpretation, exaggeration, and distortion. References to the market's "exponential growth" and "incomprehensible" size, for example, are legion and can induce queasiness, especially when combined with warnings about accelerating technological change and increasingly interconnected world financial markets. Derivatives numbers provide abundant fodder for "slippery slope" type arguments about derivatives dangers. Consequently, they can lead, particularly in times of crises, to urgent calls for regulatory action.

Frederick Schauer, Professor of Law at the University of Michigan, demonstrates that slippery slope and other forms of "Where do you draw the line?" arguments generally depend for their persuasive effect on a classic paradox: that the difficulty of making and defending a *precise* conceptual distinction may seem to suggest that no distinction is justified.[33] The difficulty is exacerbated when the distinction rests on concepts that are counterintuitive, as are many behavioral aspects of derivatives. Schauer wryly illustrates his point with the ancient Greek conundrum of the heap of salt from which grains are removed one at a time. He observes: "If the removal of one grain of salt from a heap still leaves a heap...and so too with the removal of the next grain, and the next, and the one after that, and so on, then it must follow that the removal of *all* the grains still leaves a heap. This is of course absurd, because we all know that heaps and empty spaces are different."[34]

Schauer's illustration demonstrates the power of the definitional paradox to blur distinctions "that do not rest on any point of natural or rigid demarcation." The absence of any "obvious stopping point along a continuum [does not render]...imprecise the point that is ultimately chosen."[35] His analysis is applicable to many related definitional matters, such as the distinction between speculation and hedging.

Generic definitions of derivatives inevitably lead to imprecision. Although generic descriptions are useful, they appear, in Schauer's terminology, incapable of identifying "toeholds" to prevent the slide down the slippery slope. However, both financial markets and the law are capable of handling practical and conceptual distinctions that do not lend themselves to analytically precise definitions. Lawyers and the law are comfortable with imprecise terms such as "reasonable," "material," "promptly," and "negligent." In *The Concept of Law,* H. L. A. Hart sums up the argument:

> The same predicament was expressed by some famous words of St. Augustine about the notion of time, 'What then is time? If no one asks me I know: if I wish to explain it to one that asks I know not.' It is in this way that even skilled lawyers have felt that, though they know the law, there is much about law and its relations to other things that they cannot explain and do not fully understand.[36]

There is no reason that lawyers and capital market participants cannot become, as Hart would say, "perfectly at home with the day-to-day use of the word in question."

The term *derivative* means different things to different people. Thus, the first goal in designing any system of risk management incorporating derivating should be to identify as precisely as practicable those transactions intended to be either avoided or authorized and encouraged. Second, one must continuosly monitor the effectiveness of the system ones inplemented and adjust it for changing circumstances. Feedback is crucial.

Where to Draw the Line? Practical Concerns; A Pragmatic Solution

Anyone responsible for developing a working definition of derivatives, whether for regulatory or internal control purposes, must determine "where to draw the line." Careful and informed judgment is especially important with derivatives, which often behave counterintuitively.*

As with the G-30 Study, the development of a working definition begins with a formal or generic definition that is then supplemented with a careful listing of the known categories of financial instruments intended to be included. To the extent practicable, known categories to be excluded should also be identified. Similarly, regulatory and statutory attempts to define derivatives begin with lists and categories, leaving to catchall phrases, such as "and all other similar items," the work of filling in the resulting definitional gaps.

The lack of a precise derivatives definition frequently makes it difficult for nonexperts to determine the extent to which there is both agreement and disagreement over the types of products covered by the term. Professor Hu writes: "Certain products are...indisputably derivatives."[37] According to Capital Market Risk Advisors, the "core" OTC products are those named in the inner oval of Figure 2.8. However, as to the "noncore" products listed outside Figure 2.8's inner oval, the views of regulators and various market participants (as well as their advisers), can and do differ significantly.

Often, published reports on the size of the OTC derivatives market simply use the phrase "OTC derivatives" without identifying precisely the scope of product coverage. Seldom do the reports indicate whether values and statistics cited are limited to core products or whether they include one or more noncore products. In this regard, two current reports are exceptions, with their insistence on clear terminology that greatly improves statistical comparability comparisons.

The first is the July 10, 1996 ISDA report on the size of the market for "[t]ransactions outstanding in interest rate swaps, currency swaps, and

---

*Counterintuitive behavior makes derivatives similar to many other aspects of modern finance.
    Bernstein, for example, in *Capital Ideas, infra,* Chapter 4, note 13, examines the implications of the theories of modern finance of such "giants" in economics as Fischer Black, Myron Scholes, Robert Merton, Franco Modigliani, and Merton Miller. He remarks that the theoretical origins of what has now become known as *contingent claims analysis* (CCA) lead to the strange conclusion that the entire capital structure of a corporation, its "outstanding debts and shares of stock...turns out to be a complex maze of options....[T]he stockholders do not own the company, they have a call option on its assets. They can exercise that option by paying off the company's debts." See *Capital Ideas, supra,* Chapter 4, note 13: 222. The importance of the CCA approach to the pricing of corporate liabilities and evaluating capital budgeting decisions is explored *infra,* particularly Chapters 11 and 15, which are derived largely from Merton, *Continuous-Time Finance, supra,* Chapter 1, note 26, and Mason et al., *Financial Engineering, supra,* Chapter 1, note 2: 353–375.

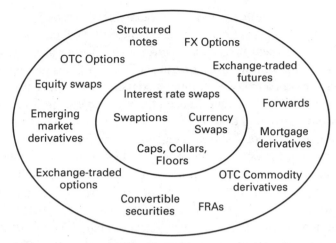

Figure 2.8   Derivatives universe (*Reprinted with permission from Capital Market Risk Advisors.*)

interest rate options at the close of 1995" (*1995 ISDA Report*). The second is the authoritative *Central Bank Survey of Foreign Exchange and Derivatives Market Activity 1995* (*1995 BIS Report*), released in April 1996 by the Bank for International Settlements (BIS), Basle, Switzerland. The *1995 BIS Report* "collected information on activity in a wider range of OTC instruments than previous surveys had."* A comparison of the 1995 ISDA and BIS surveys reveals that different OTC derivatives market estimates can be based on widely different product coverages. If product coverage or the range of institutions surveyed are not clearly stated, estimates are unlikely to be comparable.† For managers and practicing lawyers who are not provided with reliable information on which to base comparisons, the inconsistencies among reported estimates can be disconcerting.

---

*Included were the same core products identified by ISDA, along with products such as forward rate agreements (FRNs); interest rate warrants; "other interest rate derivative products" (meaning OTC derivatives with "leveraged payoffs and/or those whose notional principal amount varies as a function of interest rates,...[such as] swaps based on LIBOR squared as well as index amortizing rate swaps"); currency options and swaptions; currency forwards and foreign exchange swaps; options on interest-bearing underlying securities (such as futures on government securities); equity and stock index forwards, swaps, options, and warrants; and commodity forwards, swaps, and options.

†For example, ISDA surveyed 71 dealer institutions. In marked contrast, the BIS surveyed 2401 reporting entities, including end users.

Generic definitions are useful for rough overviews of derivatives concepts. Yet in practice it is imprudent to rely heavily on them for business or legal risk management purposes, regardless of whether terms are used to allow or prohibit various types of transactions. Policies and procedures, which may be broad in concept, must also identify with a degree of specificity appropriate to the circumstances the types or categories of products intended to be permitted or prohibited. Vagueness and ambiguity increase the difficulty of establishing meaningful policies and procedures. Managers who focus on them may engage intentionally or inadvertently in transactions that their boards did not intend to authorize, or as to which their firms have not instituted appropriate controls. Also, a lack of definitional precision can lead to legal uncertainty as to whether, among other things, an appropriate degree of managerial oversight has been exercised. Boards, senior managers, and their legal advisers will certainly be targets of criticism if large, unexpected losses result from transactions that were somehow inappropriate but nevertheless permitted by vague or ambiguous internal guidelines.

The creation of working policies and procedures must include a review of noncore products, regardless of whether they are called "derivatives," especially since the scope of any given set of "core products" may vary over time and from organization to organization, regulator to regulator, commentator to commentator. The starting point, therefore, is the identification of the functional characteristics of various products in a manner not driven by static definitions. Finally, because of fluid state of the derivative markets managers and lawyers must review and update policies and procedures frequently, reviewing relevant lost or categories of derivatives to be permitted or prohibited.

ENDNOTES: CHAPTER 2

1. 883 F.2d 537 (7th Cir. 1989): 539, *cert. denied sub nom. Investment Company Institute v. SEC,* 496 U.S. 936 (1990) [hereafter, *IPs case*].
2. Thomas A. Russo and Marlisa Vinciguerra, "Financial Innovation and Uncertain Regulation: Selected Issues Regarding New Product Development," *Texas Law Review,* 69, p. 1431 (May 1991; pagination used herein is from separate reprint, paginated 1–154) [hereafter, *New Product Development*]: 42.
3. See *Id.*: Part I.
4. Holbrook Working, *Futures Trading and Hedging, supra,* Chapter 1, note 3 (emphasis added; citations omitted): 142.

5. See Trevor Harris, "A Note on Accounting Principles and Their Development," unpublished manuscript, Fall 1995.

6. Merton H. Miller, "Financial Innovation: The Last Twenty Years and the Next," *Journal of Financial and Quantitative Analysis,* 21 (December 1986) [hereafter, *The Last Twenty Years and the Next*]: 461.

7. Henry Harfield, "International Money Management: The Eurodollar," *The Banking Law Journal,* 89(7) (July 1972) [hereafter, *The Eurodollar*]: 582.

8. *Id.* (emphasis added): 585.

9. Nasser Saber, *Interest Rate Swaps: Valuation, Trading, and Processing* (Irwin Professional Publishing, 1994) [hereafter, *Interest Rate Swaps*]: 12–19.

10. Carl R. Beidleman, "Characteristics of Cash Flows, Foreign Exchange Risk, and Forerunners of Currency Swaps," *Cross Currency Swaps,* Carl R. Beidleman, ed. (Business One Irwin, 1992): 13.

11. Keith C. Brown and Donald J. Smith, "Currency Swaps: Quotation Conventions, Market Structures, and Credit Risk," *Cross Currency Swaps,* Carl R. Beidleman, ed. (Business One Irwin, 1992): 63–90.

12. All quotations in this and the following paragraph are from Saber, *Interest Rate Swaps, supra,* note 8: 10–17. The 10 countries were the United States, Belgium, Canada, France, Great Britain, Germany, Italy, Japan, the Netherlands, and Sweden. Those countries later became the Group of Ten, with Switzerland participating as an associate member.

13. All quotations in this paragraph are from David Pritchard, "Swap Financing Techniques, or How to Make the Most of the World's Capital Markets," *Euromoney* (May 1984) (emphasis added).

14. Hu, *Misunderstood Derivatives, supra,* Chapter 1, note 22: 1487.

15. Boris Antl, *Parallel Loans, Swaps and Foreign Exchange Contracts* (1984): 7.

16. The quotations in this paragraph are from Harfield, *The Eurodollar, supra,* note 7: 583.

17. Peter Tufano, "How Financial Engineering Can Advance Corporate Strategy," *Harvard Business Review* (January–February, 1996) [hereafter, *Advancing Corporate Strategy*].

18. See, e.g., *1995 Survey of Derivatives Usage by U.S. Non-Financial Firms,* (Wharton/CIBC Wood Gundy, April 1996) [hereafter, *1995 Wharton/CIBC Wood Gundy Survey*]; *Strategic Derivatives: Successful Corporate Practices for Today's Global Marketplace* (The Economist Intelligence Unit, 1995) [hereafter, *Strategic Derivatives*].

19. John F. Marshall and Kevin J. Wynne, "Financial Engineering: Creative Engineering With Interest Rate Swaps," *Derivatives: Tax Regulation Finance* (May–June 1996): 233.

20. Saber, *Interest Rate Swaps, supra,* note 9: 129.

21. Greg Beier, "Understanding the Difference Between Hedging and Speculating," *Derivatives Risk and Responsibility,* Robert A. Klein and Jess

Lederman, eds. (Irwin Professional Publishing, 1996) (emphasis added): 25–41.

22. Stephen Figlewski, "How to Lose Money in Derivatives," *Journal of Derivatives* (Winter 1994) [hereafter, *How to Lose Money in Derivatives*]: 75–82.

23. Charles M. Seeger, "Protecting Profits As Currencies Fluctuate," *Export Today* (November–December 1994): 59.

24. Tufano, *Advancing Corporate Strategy, supra,* note 17.

25. This quotation and the discussion in the next two paragraphs are based on Mason et al., *Financial Engineering, supra,* Chapter 1, note 2 (emphasis added): 61–65.

26. All quotations in this paragraph are from Russo and Vinciguerra, *New Product Development, supra,* note 2.

27. G-30 Study: 28.

28. All quotations in this paragraph are from "ISDA Defines Derivatives," *Business Wire* (New York, August 9, 1994) (emphasis added) [hereafter, *ISDA Defines Derivatives*].

29. See e.g., Michael Carroll and Alyssa A. Lappen, "Mortgage-Backed Mayhem," *Institutional Investor* (July 1994) (cover story).

30. *Id.*

31. Horwitz and Mackay, *State of the Debate, supra,* Chapter 1, note 41: 77.

32. Steven M. H. Wallman, "Regulating in a World of Technological and Global Change," Remarks Before the Institute of International Bankers, Washington, DC (March 4, 1996).

33. See, generally, Frederick Schauer, "Slippery Slopes," *Harvard Law Review,* 99 (1985): 361.

34. *Id.:* 378.

35. *Id.*

36. Hart, *The Concept of Law, infra,* Chapter 6, note 14:13.

37. Hu, "Hedging Expectations: 'Derivative Reality' and the Law and Finance of the Corporate Objective," *Texas Law Review,* 73 (1995) [hereafter, *Hedging Expectations*]: 985, 996.

The Building Blocks of Functional Analysis

Twenty-five years ago it was comparatively easy to acquire a sound knowledge of the general investment field...(but now)...the different types of securities have multiplied in number to an almost unlimited extent....(T)he different types of (securities) which are daily sought for investment nowadays are often so different...that not only must each class be judged by itself, but a great many issues of the same general class have distinct traits which go far to affect directly their position and value as investments.   *John Moody, 1910[1]*

The array of derivatives contracts is not as complex as it first appears. Every derivatives transaction can be built up from two simple and fundamental types of building blocks: forwards and options.
                                          G-30 Overview, 1993

As with any other business activity, a primary concern of senior management and its legal advisers regarding the use of a derivative product is the potential effect on the organization's overall competitive strategy. According to Professor Michael Porter of Harvard University's Graduate School of Business Administration, "[A]t general management's core is strategy: defining a company's position, making *trade-offs,* and forging *fit* among activities." Further, "competitive advantage comes from the way [an organization's] activities *fit* and reinforce one another."[2] If the derivative enhances a portfolio or firm's other activities, it contributes to long-term organizational competitiveness. If it is incompatible with other activities, it drains resources, especially management resources, and can create other operating inefficiencies.

Fundamental to understanding whether a product will fit with other activities in an organization's overall competitive strategy is a functional analysis of:

1. The derivative
2. The assets or liabilities with which it is to be combined
3. The economic behavior of the resulting combination

A functional approach begins with an analysis of an individual product's and investment risk and return characteristics. Next, it analyzes the way the product combines, interacts, or fits with other assets, liabilities, and business activities.

ANALYZING ECONOMIC RISK AND RETURN CHARACTERISTICS

The first step in a functional analysis is to determine the individual product's economic risk and return characteristics. For most senior managers and legal advisers, an in-depth knowledge of derivatives' pricing is usually not essential—senior managers and lawyers do not have to be "math whizzes," "rocket scientists," or "number crunchers." Nevertheless, a basic understanding of the behavioral characteristics of any product under consideration is essential.

At the core of such understanding is the knowledge of the "basic building blocks" from which every derivative product is constructed—forwards and options. Every product, whether a "plain vanilla" transaction or a complex hybrid instrument, can be deconstructed, or "reverse-engineered," into its basic building blocks. Reverse engineering isolates and categorizes the individual risk components of every derivative, and it simplifies the understanding of the nature and magnitude of each component.

Forward-Based Contracts

The simplest building block is a forward contract, which "obligates one counterparty to buy, and the other to sell, a specific underlying [asset, rate, index, or commodity] at a specific price, amount, and date in the future." (We will refer to the underlying asset, rate, index, or commodity as a hypothetical instrument called a *fidget*—the financial instrument equivalent of a widget.)* "Forward markets exist for a multitude of underlying [fidgets],

---

*Before objecting that *fidget* seems a frivolous term, consider the problems inherent in the common alternatives, such as *cash, actual, spot, variable,* and *underlying.* As Holbrook Working wrote in 1953, each alternative is certainly well understood by those "who are intimately acquainted with…trading and its consequences"; yet its "usage is a bit frustrating and even misleading" to nontraders (who Working calls "inquiring novices").

Cash, a convenient term for traders, conveys little information to nontraders. Why? "Its application involved two shifts of meaning: (1) use of 'cash' to designate, not immediate *payment,* as is usual, but immediate *delivery*; and (2) extension of the altered meaning to cover all terms of delivery except those involved in futures contracts. These changes left the word with *no logical merit for the purpose except its brevity.*…Most seriously misleading is frequent resort to the use of '*actual.*'" Similarly, consider that commodities markets often employ the oxymoron "*spot-deferred* transactions."

Finally, experience teaches that when "inquiring novices" encounter a term such as the *variable* or *underlying,* they invariably wonder: The variable or underlying what? Sometimes they voice their question, and the problem is easily solved. More often they do not, and need less misunderstandings ensue. See generally Working, *Futures Trading and Hedging, supra,* Chapter 1, note 3 (emphasis modified): 314–343.

including the traditional agricultural or physical commodities, as well as currencies (referred to as foreign exchange forwards) and interest rates (referred to as forward rate agreements or 'FRAs')."[3] The reason a forward contract is the simplest derivative is that its value ordinarily changes in direct proportion to changes in the price of the underlying fidget. Consequently, calculation of the forward contract's expected value is relatively easy, and its price sensitivity to changes in the price of the underlying fidget can be plotted linearly.*

Any calculation of forward prices begins from the underlying fidget's current *spot price.* A spot price on any date is simply the market price for immediate delivery of the fidget on that date. Spot prices, which are determined by supply and demand, ordinarily fluctuate over the time period between the date the contract is entered into (the contract date) and the forward delivery date specified in the contract.

Gain or loss on a forward is determined primarily by the difference between the spot price on the delivery date and the purchase price set forth in the contract (the contract price). If on the delivery date spot prices *exceed* the contract price, the *buyer*—often referred to as the holder of the "long" position—of the underlying realizes a *gain* on the forward, and the seller, or "short," realizes a loss, each equal in an amount to the difference between the two prices. The reason is that the price of the fidget on the delivery date will be cheaper under the contract than it is on the open market.[†] Conversely, if the delivery date spot price is *less* than the contract price, the buyer realizes a loss and the seller a gain.

The payoff profiles of both long and short positions in a forward contract are depicted in Figure 3.1. In each case, the price of the underlying fidget is indicated by the horizontal axis, and the contract price is indicated by the point at which each diagonal line intersects the horizontal axis. The positions of the long and the short are exactly offsetting; thus a gain for the long is an equivalent loss for the short, and vice versa.

---

*Ease of calculation results in ease of price (or value) monitoring and, hence, risk management. This contrasts markedly with option-based products, the pricing and risk management of which, as we will see, are far more involved and subject to much theoretical and practical debate. Plotting reveals that an option's price sensitivity is *curved* and always changing, unlike that of a forward, which is linear and constant.

†The contract will be valuable to the long whether or not it chooses to take delivery. The reason is that the long can always sell the contract to a third party who wishes to take delivery. In a competitive market, that third party should be willing to pay up to the amount of the savings it would realize by purchasing the underlying fidget pursuant to the forward contract rather than on the spot market.

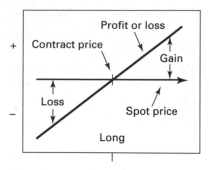

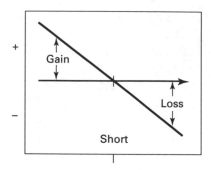

Figure 3–1a   Long forward position.   Figure 3–1b   Short forward position.

Forwards are OTC transactions. Therefore, their price, delivery, credit, and other terms are subject to negotiation. "At the time the [forward] contract is entered into, the delivery price is chosen so that the value of the forward contract to both parties is zero. This means that *it costs nothing to take either a long or a short position.*"[4] As Nasser Saber explains, forward contracts are agreements to enter into exchanges, and rational market participants "will only agree to an exchange of equal values." Therefore, the net present value* of the exchange to both sides at the time of contract formation "must be zero."[5]

The zero net present value feature of a forward-based transaction means that it commences as neither an asset nor a liability.[6] (For accounting purposes, as we discuss later, it has, then, no "historical cost" capable of being booked as a balance sheet item.) However, a contract that begins as neither an asset nor a liability can quickly become one or the other. The ability to enter into a forward-based contract with little, in the case of futures, or no money down is the primary source of the contract's *leverage*—that is, its potentially dramatic responsiveness to even small changes in the value of the underlying fidget.

Normally, a forward contract's value fluctuates over the contract's life as the following example demonstrates. "The easiest forward contract to value is one written on a security that provides the holder with no income. Nondividend paying stocks and discount bonds are examples of such securities."[7] Assume that today's spot price for a share of LMN com-

---

*Net present value means the face amount of the future payment, reduced by a discount factor
      appropriate to compensate the recipient for the opportunity cost of delayed the payment
      (and, with physical commodities, for storage, insurance, and delivery costs).

mon stock, which pays no dividend, is $10 and that the applicable "risk-free" interest rate is 5%.* The theoretical forward price of a round lot (100 shares) of LMN common stock for delivery one year from today is $1050, or the sum of today's $1000 spot price *plus* a $50 financing charge ($1000 × 5%). The financing charge is the cost of inducing the seller to wait one year before receiving payment for its LMN shares.

A seller must be paid to wait, because waiting to consummate the sale implies an opportunity cost to the seller. If the seller were instead to sell on today's spot market, it would receive its $1000 immediately. The seller could then invest that $1000 for one year, earning a risk-free return of $50.[†] If the risk-free rate were to rise to 6% prior to the contract date, the seller would demand an implied financing charge of $60. If the current spot price were also to decline to $9, the buyer would be willing to pay only $9 per share. The forward price would be $954, or $900 *plus* a $54 financing charge ($900 × 6%). Thus, the primary reason forward prices of financial instruments fluctuate is that spot prices, market interest rates, or both fluctuate.

Finally, all forward-based transactions create *two-way credit exposures,* because actual exchanges of value occur only at maturity. It is possible for either party to a forward to incur a loss or a gain, and therefore both are exposed to credit risk, or the risk of counterparty default.

For many end users, the two-way nature of credit risk is often the *central feature* distinguishing forwards from other types of credit transactions. Although most nonfinancial organizations purchase investment

---

*Often, the "risk-free" rate is the *repo rate.* "A *repo* or *repurchase agreement* is an agreement where the owner of securities agrees to sell them to a counterparty and buy them back at a slightly higher price later." Hull, *Derivatives, supra,* note 3: 50. The repo rate is considered risk-free, because a repo is economically equivalent to a loan in which the securities purchased with the loan proceeds fully collateralize the repayment obligation. "The difference between the price at which the securities are sold and the price at which they are repurchased is the interest earned by the counterparty. If structured carefully, a repo involves very little risk to either side. For example, if the borrowing [i.e., securities-buying] company does not keep to its side of the agreement [i.e., does not repurchase the securities or repay the loan], the lender simply keeps the securities." *Id.*

[†]Alternatively, if the seller does not own the LMN shares on the contract date, pricing theory assumes the seller will purchase the shares at today's spot price to "cover" its future delivery obligation. Otherwise, it runs the risk that spot prices will rise on or before it has a chance to cover. The seller is assumed to obtain funding for today's spot purchase price by borrowing at 5%.

Viewed differently, the discounted present value of the $1050 to be received in one year is $1050/(1.05) = $1000.

securities in their normal treasury operations and often borrow money, end users seldom act as outright lenders in arm's-length loan transactions. Therefore, the credit and legal analysis required for a proper assessment of the risks of forward-based derivatives may be unfamiliar to the end user and its legal advisers.

Credit risk creates exposures equal to a contract's replacement cost, or market value, which for forwards is the net present value of all future cashflows. Positive (negative) market value to one counterparty is negative (positive) to the other. A party whose contract has positive market value is "in the money" and has extended credit to the other party, which is "out of the money." Proper credit risk management begins with calculations of a portfolio's actual, or current credit exposure. Counterparties should also track future, or potential exposure based both on expectations of probable future market conditions and on worst-case scenarios.

Swaps: Combinations of Forwards

The basic building blocks of a swap are forward contracts. Chapter 2 contains examples of plain vanilla currency and interest rate swaps. Swaps constitute a series of simple forward contracts. An interest rate swap, for example, involves an exchange of interest payments on each designated future payment date. Each exchange can be analyzed and valued as a separate, individual forward contract. A currency swap is comparable, except that many involve initial spot exchanges of principal.

> As the name implies, a [plain vanilla] swap transaction obligates the two parties to the contract to exchange a series of cash flows at specified intervals known as payment or settlement dates....The cash flows from a swap can be decomposed into equivalent cash flows from a bundle of simpler forward contracts. For example, an interest rate swap can be decomposed in terms of cash flows into a portfolio of single payment forward contracts on interest rates. At each settlement date, the loss or gain in the currently maturing implicit forward contract is in effect realized."[8]

One reason swap markets have flourished is that the products' forward-based composition allows for relative ease of calculating swap prices. It also allows for simplicity of reconfiguring cashflows into any number of variations designed to meet an end user's cashflow needs. A wide variety of swaps is readily available. Among them are "amortizing" swaps, which have reducing notional amounts; "canapé" currency swaps, involving no initial or final exchanges of principal; "zero coupon" swaps, in which one side makes no payments until the final maturity date; and "forward swaps," which do not commence until a future date.

As discussed earlier, the objective in designing a forward-based contract (in this case, a swap) is to ensure that at the outset the net present value of all exchanges of the payments to be made by both sides will equal zero. The determination of the net present value of each side's obligations is simply a summation of the net present values of each of its payment obligations. Although the number of calculations (and iterations of the same calculations) necessary to determine and equalize the net present values of the two sides' payment obligations can be quite large, the calculation structure is straightforward.

Swaps contain two pricing uncertainties. First, usually one or both sides of the transaction will be making floating-rate payments, and therefore the floating-rate pay or can only estimate the face amount of any future payments to be made. Estimates depend on one's assessment of likely future interest rates (but *not* on the likely movement of underlying fidgets, such as commodity prices or equity values). Second, the discounting process requires assumptions about applicable interest rates to be used to discount future payments to present value, and those rates usually change during the life of the swap. Thus, the value of a swap will, over time, change as applicable rates change. Nevertheless, the calculation structure will remain constant. Therefore, for valuation purposes, the effect of each change in applicable rates can be determined simply by substituting the new rates into the original formula.

Futures: Highly Standardized Forwards Traded on Organized Exchanges

A futures contract, like a forward, is an agreement of one party to buy and the other to sell a specific underlying fidget at a specific price, amount, and date (or over a specified time period*) in the future. Futures are, essentially, forward contracts traded on organized futures exchanges. Their payoff profiles are identical to those of forwards described in Figure 3.1. Futures exchanges originally handled agricultural commodities, but "[t]he

---

*"One way in which a futures contract is different from a forward contract is that an exact delivery date is not usually specified. The contract is referred to by its delivery month, and the exchange specifies the period during the month when delivery must be made." Hull, *Derivatives, supra,* note 3: 4.

volume of the newer financial futures contracts involving interest rates, currencies, and equity indices now dwarfs the volume in traditional agricultural contracts."[9] Economically, futures contracts have four essential features.

First, to be eligible for exchange trading, a futures contract must conform to the applicable fully standardized features specified by the exchange. Standardization covers all aspects of a contract except price. Price is determined on major exchanges simply through an "open-outcry method" on futures trading pits that on many exchanges continues to survive despite technological advances that might otherwise appear to render the open-outcry method obsolete. Thus, the quantity and quality of the underlying fidget is specified by the exchange, as are the time, place, and method of payment or settlement.

Second, "standardization extends to the credit risk of futures. Credit risk is greatly reduced by marking the contract to market with daily (or more frequent) settling up of changes and value, and by requiring buyers and sellers alike to post margin as collateral for these settlement payments."[10] The margin requirement takes two forms and applies to each party to the transaction. First, both the buyer and the seller of the underlying fidget must post an initial margin at the outset of each contract, limiting to some extent the leveraging ability of futures market participants. Second, a party must post a "variation margin" each time the market moves against it by a specified amount, called a *tick.*

The frequent marking to market and posting of margin means that parties to futures contracts easily and constantly monitor changes in the value of an open position, settling losses and gains incrementally rather than all at once on contract maturity. On the delivery date for a financial futures contract, the market value of the contract will equal the spot price of the underlying fidget. The process by which prices move toward equality is known in futures markets as *convergence.* For contracting parties, the margining and collateralization process has two drawbacks in that it entails higher administrative costs and results in unpredictable cashflows when compared with forward-based products such as swaps.

Third, the immediate counterparty to every futures contract is a futures clearinghouse, essentially the middleman between contracting parties. Consequently, the credit risk to each counterparty to a futures contract is that of the clearinghouse. This feature further greatly reduces counterparty credit risk, because exchanges are funded by their members and enjoy the highest credit ratings. Generally, futures contracts are entered into and traded freely without concern about clearinghouse default, or counterparty credit risk.*

Finally, the minimization of credit risk in futures transactions means that, unlike participants in OTS forwards and swaps markets, can afford to remain anonymous. "The futures market…is an impersonal market in which there is no premium on knowing one's counterparty. The moral hazard of trading with strangers is solved by interposing an intermediary—the clearinghouse."[11] In addition, relatively small minimum contract sizes make futures contracts more readily available to retail investors than swaps and forwards, which are almost exclusively transactions between institutions (with perhaps equity swaps being the most notable exception).

Unbundling Forward-Based Transactions

Swaps and futures are relatively simple contracts to unbundle into their forward-based building blocks. However, the functional approach can also analyze the risks of more complicated structured transactions, as the following two examples demonstrate. Both structures manage currency exchange risks; the second also manages the spot price risks of oil and rice on behalf of an oil-producing nation that imports rice from Japan.

Creating a synthetic asset

Figure 3.2 diagrams a transaction designed in 1991 to enable an investor who had customarily held U.S. Treasuries to achieve its goal of improving its returns. The investor desired to invest instead in German "bunds" yielding 31 basis points more than comparable U.S. Treasuries. Bunds are German government bonds denominated and payable in deutshemarks (DM). As an alternative to purchasing a 10-year U.S. Treasury yielding 8.14%, the investor purchased an 8.45% 10-year bund and simultaneously entered into a matching currency swap. Under the swap, the investor agreed to exchange its DM cashflows over the life of the swap for U.S. dol-

---

*However, concerns about clearinghouse creditworthiness are not purely academic. An example is provided by "the collapse of the International Tin Council in 1986 and the fallout for the London Metals Exchange. To cope with large defaults, some exchanges explicitly insure contracts, raise assessments on members, or make special calls on them." See Hargreaves, *Swaps: Versatility at Controlled Risk.*

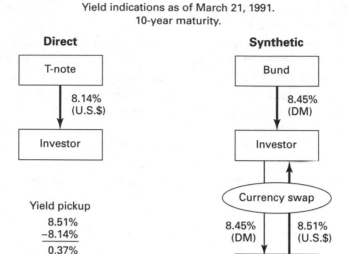

Yield indications as of March 21, 1991.
10-year maturity.

Measures of the dollar cash flow from a U.S. Treasury note compared with that from a German government bond (Bund) with its mark cash flow swapped into dollars. Against the yield pickup the investor would sacrifice a degree of liquidity, assume credit risk on the German government and the swap house, and be open to price risk if the maturities of cash flows of the Bund and swap fail to match exactly those of the Treasury note.

Figure 3.2   Synthetic asset for investors. (*Reproduced with permission from J.P. Morgan & Co. Incorporated.*)

lars. The net result (prior to transaction costs and without regard to tax effects) was an increased yield of 37 basis points.

The first step in a functional analysis of the transaction is to unbundle the risks the investor would have faced had it invested in the bunds directly without a swap. The obvious risk was that after buying the bund the dollar would strong then against the mark–i.e., U.S. $/DM exchange rate risk (assuming the investor desired to convert DM proceeds into U.S. dollars). A lesser risk was that of a German government default. Although the investor was comfortable with the default risk, it would not accept currency risk. To purchase the bund the investor needed to shed the unwanted currency risk. The swap enabled the investor to do precisely that.

However, the swap introduced two additional economic risks for the investor to consider, as well as one other risk about which it may have had concerns. The first was the risk of default of the dealer swap counterparty. The second risk stems from the possibility that the investor might over the 10-year life of the structure have desired to liquidate the investment early and sell the bund prior to the maturity of the swap. In that case, the investor might have been left with a swap for which it had no obvious use as a hedging instrument. Aside from possible adverse tax and accounting consequences, that result would have left the investor in precisely the same position it had set out to avoid—namely, exposed to U.S. $/DM currency exchange risk.

Had it liquidated the investment early, the investor would have had to either terminate the swap or assign it, perhaps the bund purchaser. The investor would have needed the legal right to assign the swap. Swap assignments are, however, usually contractually prohibited (see, e.g., section 7 of the ISDA Master Agreement) because they expose the other side ti the credit risk of a new conterparty. They are also more cumbersome than early terminations. Therefore, early termination would have been the more likely choice of all parties.* If the assignee desired a swap, it could easily enter into one on its own.

One other risk with which the investor may have been concerned, especially a public company or regulated entity, was that of holding an OTC derivative and engaging in a potentially "suspect" activity.

Synthetic barter

Figure 3.3 depicts a complex transaction in which a number of plain vanilla swaps were combined to achieve a remarkable result. The structure involved two plain vanilla commodity swaps, a plain vanilla currency swap, and a plain vanilla interest rate swap. The result was a synthetic barter arrangement that enabled an oil-producing nation to obtain a long-term supply of rice in exchange for a fixed long-term quantity of oil.

Prior to the transaction, the practice of the oil-producing nation was simply to sell oil on the spot market for U.S. dollars. It would then convert those dollars into Japanese yen and purchase rice in Japan on the spot market. The nation had exposure to three separate price risks: "the price of oil

---

*In evaluating the all-in cost of the structure, the investor needs to consider the potential of early
termination costs. Swap terminations require the payment of a termination value to the in-
the-money party. The termination value is usually the market value of the swap. However, a
dealer would also charge a bid-asked spread, because early termination is economically the
same as entering into a new swap with exactly offsetting terms.

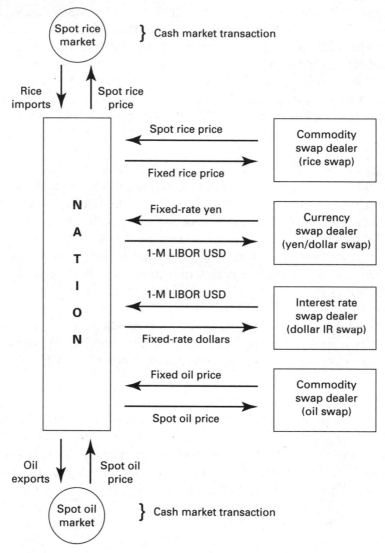

Figure 3.3   Synthetic barter. (*Reproduced with permission from Warren, Gorham & Lamont.*)

in dollars, the price of rice in yen, and the price of yen in dollars."[12] The transaction structure mitigated all three of those risks.

Although the structure is complicated and the complete details were unavailable,* the transaction exhibits the following cash and commodity flows. First, a commodity swap was entered into under which the oil producer locked in a long-term fixed dollar price for selling future specified oil production. Next, those dollars were indirectly converted into a fixed number of yen using a combination of (1) a fixed-for-floating U.S. dollar denominated interest rate swap followed by (2) a floating-rate dollar for fixed-rate yen currency swap. Finally, the fixed-rate yen (the amount of which was now also locked in) were converted, through a commodity swap, into the yen needed to buy a fixed quantity of rice on the spot market.

The primary risk introduced by the synthetic barter structure was the chain of counterparty risks arising from the possibility of involving up to four separate dealers in the transaction.[†]

Option-Based Contracts

"The other derivatives building block is the option contract."[13] All option-based products can be analyzed in terms of the two basic types of options: *puts* and *calls*. Because each put and call has two sides, a *long* and a *short*, "four basic option positions are possible": one can be long or short a put or a call. From those basic positions, together with long and short positions in forwards and underlying fidgets, a limitless number of other positions can be constructed[‡]

---

*A detailed analysis is scheduled to be published in Marshall and Wynne, "Synthesizing Countertrade Solutions with Swaps," *Global Finance Journal.*

†As with the preceding synthetic asset example, the oil-producing nation should consider, in evaluating the all-in cost of the structure, the possible costs of early termination. In the prior example, we noted that a bid-asked spread would be at issue in an early termination of the currency swap. Here, each swap would have its own bid-asked spread, so a total of four spread costs must be contemplated.

‡Discussions of options and option pricing can become extremely technical. Two classic authoritative texts, each of which explores the subject in great technical and theoretical detail, are Hull, *Derivatives, supra,* note 3, and Cox and Rubenstein, *Options Markets, (Prentice-Hall, 1985)* For the senior manager or lawyer seeking more general, less technical discussions that are nevertheless quite relevant in exploring issues of direct concern to derivatives risk management, see *G-30 Overview* and Chew, *Leverage, supra,* Chapter 1, note 1 (and introduction by Robert C. Merton).

Options are typically defined from the perspective of the option holder as a right, not an obligation.[14]

> In exchange for payment of a premium, an option contract gives the option holder the right *but not the obligation* to buy [i.e., a call] or sell [i.e., a put] the underlying (or settle the value for cash) at a price, called the strike price, during a period or on a specific date. Thus, the owner of the option can choose not to exercise the option and let it expire. The buyer benefits from favorable movements in the price of the underlying but is not exposed to corresponding losses.[15]

Thus defined, "'[t]he advantage of options over swaps and forwards is that options give the buyer the desired protection while allowing him to benefit from a favourable movement in the underlying price.'"[16]

However, in managing risk—both economic and legal—it is equally important to note the *disadvantage* of buying options. In particular, the buyer of an option, unlike a party entering into a swap or forward, must pay a premium to enter into the option contract. An option buyer is not exposed to losses in the price of the underlying fidget. Nevertheless, the buyer is still exposed to a smaller, albeit certain *cost* because of the premium that must be paid. Much like an insurance policy, this premium "substitutes a sure loss for the possibility of a larger loss."[17] If the call expires worthless, the payment of the premium constitutes an overall loss on the option; if at expiration the call is in the money, the payment of the premium reduces the holder's overall gain on the option. Likewise, the cost of the premium reduces any gain from favorable price movements. An accurate assessment of the economic performance of any option-based strategy or instrument requires that the premium be taken into account. Although that point may seem obvious, its significance can also easily be missed.*

---

*One article provocatively asserts: "In the absence of market imperfections, options strategies may simply be the best way for treasury to speculate with corporate funds while escaping the scrutiny of senior management, shareholders, and others." Ian H. Giddy and Gunter Dufey, "Uses and Abuses of Currency Options," *Journal of Applied Corporate Finance* (Fall 1995):49–57. For a convincing rebuttal, see Christopher S. Bourdain, "FX Option Myths that Aren't," *Derivatives Strategy,* 1(5) (April 1996). On a related note, Tufano mentions a director of a well-known U.S. consumer-products corporation [who] went out of his way to defend one of the company's financial transactions: 'We just bought *puts* to hedge our foreign currency risk, but we're not involved with derivatives.' My well-meaning acquaintance was attempting to distance himself and his organization from the 'd' word, despite the fact that options are in fact derivatives." *Using Derivatives: What Senior Managers Must Know, supra,* note 2: 35.

Expiration payoffs; Intrinsic Value

An examination of option payoff profiles at expiration is the beginning of an understanding of the economics of options. Payoff profiles can be determined solely from an option's *intrinsic value,* which at any time is simply "the maximum of zero and the value [the option] would have if exercised immediately."[18]* The intrinsic value of a call is the amount (if positive) by which the then market value of the fidget exceeds the call's strike price. Conversely, the intrinsic value of a put is the amount (if positive) by which the put's strike price exceeds the then market value of the fidget. An option's expiration payoff is simply its *intrinsic value* at expiration, as measured from the perspective of the *holder,* or the *long.* The issuer, or *writer,* of an option is referred to as the *short.*

   Figure 3.4 portrays the expiration payoff profiles to the option holder of both a call and a put. In each case, underlying spot fidget prices are indicated by the horizontal axis. Strike prices are indicated at each point marked "X." The point at which each diagonal line crosses above the horizontal axis is the option buyer's "breakeven point," meaning it has earned back its premium. Thus, if at the call's expiration the spot price *exceeds* the strike price, the holder will exercise the option. In contrast, if at the put's expiration the spotprice is *less than* the strike price, the holder will exercise the put. Yet that "the option has moved into-the-money does not necessar-

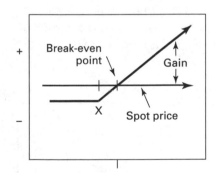

Figure 3.4*a*   Long call.

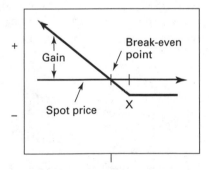

Figure 3.4*b*   Long put.

---

*Intrinsic value is never negative, because option pricing theory holds that a rational holders will not exercise an option if doing so would cause them to lose money—that is, if the strike price of a call (put) exceeds (is less then) the market price of the fidget. The holder could more cheaply buy (or profitably sell) the fidget on the open market.

ily imply that the transaction has been profitable, as the initial premium paid must be subtracted from the in-the-money amount to come up with a profit margin."[19]

For both economic and legal risk management purposes, it is imperative to understand the risk options pose to the option writer. In *Derivatives Risks and Speculative Capital,* Saber notes that options are typically (as in the *G-30 Overview*) defined from the holder's perspective. From the perspective of the option writer, an option is a contract that *obligates* the writer, in exchange for a premium, to sell (in the case of a call) or buy (a put) the underlying fidget (or settle the value for cash) at the strike price during the option period or on a specified date.

Figure 3.5 portrays the expiration payoff profiles to the option writer, or issuer, of both calls and puts. In each case, underlying fidget prices are again indicated by the horizontal axis and strike prices are indicated by the point "X." The point at which each diagonal line crosses the horizontal axis is the option issuer's "breakeven point." In other words, if at expiration fidget prices are between the breakeven point and the strike price, the holder will exercise its option and the writer must make a payment—yet the payment will not be a loss to the issuer but merely a return of all or part of the premium previously received.

Option valuation prior to expiration is considerably more complex than the valuation of forwards, for several reasons. After the contract date the value of a forward is determined by, and fluctuates primarily according to changes in, two variables: (1) the spot price of the underlying fidget and (2) the level of prevailing risk-free interest rates. The value of each of those variables can be obtained objectively from a newspaper, by tele-

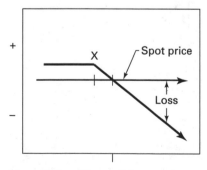

Figure 3.5*a*   Short call.

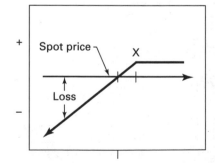

Figure 3.5*b*   Short put.

phone, or from a screen-based quotation system.[20] The same variables are involved in the determination of an option's price. Yet, option prices also depend on, and fluctuate with changes in, three additional factors: (3) the strike price, (4) the time to expiration, and (5) the anticipated volatility of underlying fidget prices. The strike price (which remains constant throughout the option's life) and time to expiration (which decreases over the option's life) are determined at the outset of the contract through negotiation.

TIME VALUE

The value of a forward contract can be calculated relatively easily and plotted linearly, because of its dependence on only the first two variables, spot prices and interest rates. Similarly, the *intrinsic value,* defined as the value of the option at expiration, can be plotted straightforwardly, as in Figures 3.4 and 3.5. However, the valuation of options prior to expiration is a more complicated matter, because in addition to intrinsic value options have *time value.* Although the mathematics of time value are extraordinarily complex, conceptually time value is simply the value that is attributable to *uncertainty* regarding the price of the underlying fidget over time prior to expiration.

An intuitive grasp of the time value of an option is easily within reach without mathematics. Consider the value of a call option prior to expiration under the following circumstances. Assume the intrinsic value is zero, because the price of the underlying fidget is below the strike price—no rational person would exercise a call option at a price below the strike price. Nevertheless, a call option with no intrinsic value prior to expiration obviously still has some value, because some time prior to expiration the fidget prices *might rise* above the strike price. Similarly, an in-the-money call option has both intrinsic and time value, because no matter what the intrinsic value at any given moment prior to expiration, fidget prices *might rise even higher* prior to expiration. An option holder can (except in extreme market circumstances) always capture the benefits of any temporary upticks in fidget prices.

The reason such benefits can be captured is that options come in two forms, either American style or European style. "*American options* can be exercised at any time up to the expiration date. *European options* can only be exercised on the expiration date itself."[21] The difference in exercise mechanics are not for present purposes terribly significant. Suffice to say that it seldom makes sense for an option holder to exercise an option prior to expiration, because that would destroy the option's remaining time value. It is generally preferable from the holder's perspective simply to sell the option on the open market. Thus, even though European options can be exercised only on expiration, their values behave similarly to those of American options: the holder of a European option is always (absent contractual restrictions) free to sell the option at any time, regardless of whether the option is currently exercisable.

Time value of an option is, then, a function of three factors. First, it depends on the time remaining to expiration—the longer the time remaining, the greater an out of the money option's chance of moving into the money, and the greater an in-the-money option's chance of moving further into the money. Second, time value depends on the proximity of underlying fidget prices to the option's strike price. If, for example, the fidget's price just before expiration equals the strike price, any small change in the fidget price will render the option either in the money or out of the money at expiration. Similarly, if the fidget's price just prior to expiration is far out of the money, only a massive movement in underlying fidget prices will cause the option to expire in the money.

Third, time value depends on the volatility (more accurately, the anticipated or implied volatility) of underlying fidget prices. Again, the greater the volatility of—meaning the degree of fluctuations in—fidget prices, the more likely that the option will move into the money or further into the money at some time prior to expiration. Thus, in valuing an option prior to its expiration, "[t]he sole item that requires judgment is…volatility."[22] Of the three factors that determine time value, there is no doubt about the first two—the strike price and the time remaining to maturity. The only doubt relates to volatility.

An entire industry has grown out of attempts to estimate volatility accurately, because that is really the only one of the five option valuation factors over which there can be significant disagreement. For those who rely on mathematical modeling to guide their option grades, differences of opinion about option values—the differences that generate active option trading—are driven mainly by different methods of calculating volatility. Normally, one might expect the value of an option to be based on one's view of the future value of the underlying fidget. But that is not the case: "Intuitively, this implied volatility can be thought of as the combined but current judgment of the market about the *future uncertainty* of a given for-

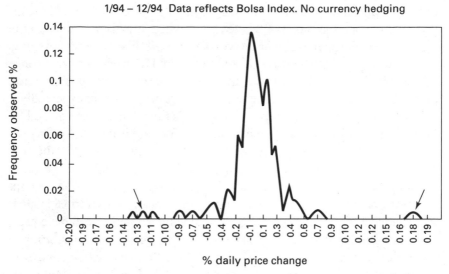

Figure 3.6   Mexican Equity Market Volatility: January to December 1994. (*Reprinted with permission from* Derivatives Risk Management, *Warren Gorham & Lamont, Boston, Mass.*)

ward price—the higher the implied volatility the more uncertain they are about the forward price."[23]

Figure 3.6 illustrates the risks involved in attempting to predict volatility. From January through November 1994, the price of equity securities in the Mexican equity market tended to fluctuate within a band of plus or minus two percentage points. However, in December 1994 the Mexican peso was devalued, leading to three separate individual daily market moves (indicated by the arrows) of greater than 10% (i.e., plus or minus 0.10).

> Based on historical analysis through November, a move of this magnitude would be regarded as virtually impossible. A more thorough analysis into the background of the sources of risk [i.e., of volatility] would have revealed that the peso exchange rate was pegged to the U.S. dollar. From this one should expect the exchange rate to typically change very little from day to day but [that] periodically [it] could change by very large amounts.[24]

As the Mexican equity market example suggests, efforts to estimate volatility can be perilous. An "incorrect" choice of the historical time horizon on which future volatility is to be estimated can result in unexpectedly large option price changes.

Although the time value of an option can be grasped intuitively without much difficulty, the mathematical computation of time value is complex and beyond the scope of this text. Likewise, it is usually beyond the scope of a senior manager's or lawyer's responsibility. Nevertheless, it is important in risk management for managers and lawyers to have a sense of the complexity that may make any derivative (or any other transaction that displays "optionality") behave counterintuitively and unexpectedly.

A sense of the complexity of an option's time value can be gained by observing that whereas the market value of a forward is plotted linearly (as is the intrinsic value of an option, with the one difference that the line changes its mathematical sign at point X in Figures 3.5 and 3.6), the value of an option, as indicated in Figure 3.7, displays curvature. The straight line at the base of the shaded region represents the option's intrinsic value. The shaded region indicates the additional value an option will have prior to expiration, because of its *time value.* As Figure 3.7 indicates, prior to expiration, the price of an option will be greater than the option's intrinsic value; in other words, the time value of an option is positive. A comparison of the lengths of lines b, c, and d in Figure 3.7 illustrates that the time value of an option varies depending on the price of the underlying fidget. When the fidget price is b', the time value will be the length of line b; when the fidget price is X, the time value will be the length of line c.

The significance of a linear plot is that the rate of change in value, and hence the *value sensitivity,* is constant: for every one dollar change in value of the fidget underlying a forward contract, the corresponding unit value of the forward contract will change by the same amount. Thus, the *rate* of change of the value of a forward is *independent* of underlying fidget prices.

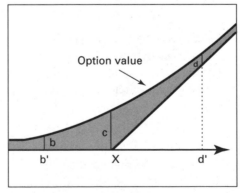

Figure 3.7   Long call option time value.
(*Reprinted with permission from the Chicago Mercantile. Exchange*)

In contrast, the rate of change in the value of an option is *dependent* on underlying fidget prices. Because an option's time value plot is curved, its value sensitivity depends on underlying fidget prices. Graphically, the value of a call option is indicated by the curved line in Figure 3.7. In other words, the rate of change is not constant; rather, it changes *instantaneously* upon any change in the price of the underlying fidget.* Suffice to say that the value of a deeply out of the money option will change very slowly—its rate of change approaches zero. By contrast, the value of a deeply in the money option will change at almost exactly the same rate as the rate of change in underlying fidget prices—its rate of change approaches 1.0 (or 100%). Finally, the rate of change in the of value of an option that is at the money (the underlying fidget price equals the strike price) is 0.5 (or 50%).

Thus, an option's value does not change at a constant rate. Rather, the rate of change depends on several factors, the first of which is whether the option is out of the money, at the money, or in the money. If an option is deeply out of the money and close to expiration, it will usually have some slight value. As indicated in the region in Figure 3.7 far to the left of point X, the value of the option will move to the left along the horizontal axis as fidget prices decline. The farther left it moves, the more the option value curve will converge toward the base of the shaded region, which is the line indicating that the option has a zero value. If the option is far enough out of the money, even a large movement in fidget prices is unlikely to cause the option to move into the money on the expiration date. Therefore, on a percentage basis, the change in the price of a deeply out of the money option near expiration will be close to 0% of the change in underlying fidget prices.

The reverse is also true. If an option is close to expiration and deeply in the money, its value should move in direct proportion to fidget prices. That value may not converge toward equality immediately, because prior to expiration there is always uncertainty that fidget prices will decline. But generally, in terms of Figure 3.7, the option's price will converge toward the diagonal line as fidget prices increase beyond point X. Finally, an

---

*The computation of an instantaneous rate of change of any quantity is calculated using a mathematically defined function, also called a *derivative*. The mathematics of the calculation of any rate of change (and of changes in the rate of change) involve differential calculus. For a useful introduction, see Salin N. Neftci, *Mathematics of Financial Derivatives* (Academic Press, 1996).

option that is exactly at the money just prior to expiration is in a highly uncertain position. A slight change in fidget prices may or may not result in the option being in or out of the money. Mathematically, the rate of value change at point X is 50%.

Caution: For risk management purposes, the resolution of both the theoretical and practical aspects of option pricing arguably remains the most challenging academic and practical problem of modern finance. The well-known Black-Scholes option pricing model has been called both "'the most important discovery ever made in financial economics,' [and] 'the most successful theory not only in finance but in all economics.'"[25] Yet, given that in practice many important assumptions on which the model depends are seldom if ever satisfied, the model is unsuitable for many practical applications.

Academics and practitioners alike are, therefore, constantly search-ing for alternatives to the model as well as other ways to improve on its predictive capabilities.* In sum, as we discuss in a moment:

> The non-linear price profile of options is the *first warning sign* to users that they are venturing into unfamiliar territory....[T]he curvature of options is dynamic....The landscape becomes more alien with two risks that are unique to options, *time decay* and *volatility.* Both increase or decrease the uncertainty of asset flows inherent in all options and both affect the value of an option in such a way that the *underlying asset's price need not change for the price of the option to change....*Anything with an *embedded option* also takes on the *risks of options.*[26]

FUNDAMENTAL OPTION RISKS

The sensitivity—or exposure—of an option's value to changes in fidget prices creates absolute value risk. This risk is usually expressed as a prob-ability ranging from 0 to 1. The probability value is referred to by the Greek letter *delta*; options are said to have *delta risk.* As just demon-strated, *delta values* vary depending on where in relation to point X on the horizontal axis underlying fidget prices are located. Variation in delta is also measured and given its own Greek letter, *gamma.* Thus, options are

---

*See, e.g., George Yu, "Learning Curve: American Options Valuation," *Derivatives Week* (October 21, 1996): 5–6. Yu discusses three of the latest developments in the pricing and hedging of American options: the *analytical valuation method,* the *analytic method of lines,* and the *approximation by bounds method.*

also said to have *gamma risk*. The greater the non-linearity (i.e., [curvature]) the greater the [gamma] risk."[27] The relationship between delta and gamma is analogous to that between speed–the change in distance over time and acceleration–the change in speed over time.

Regardless of whether there is any change in the value of the underlying fidget prices during the life of the option, the time value of the option will eventually decay to zero. Graphically, that means that, as expiration approaches, all other things being equal, an option's price will converge toward the option's intrinsic value. Figure 3.8 depicts that result. The process by which an option's price decreases simply as a result of the passage of time is referred to as *time decay* and given its own Greek letter, *theta*. Thus, options also have *theta risk*.

Finally, arguably the most distinctive option risk is an option's volatility, or *vega risk*. "The more variable are the spot price movements of an asset, the more volatile the asset is said to be." In other words, the more uncertainty there is regarding an asset's future price, the higher its volatility. The volatility of an option is defined as "the risk of an option position changing in value as a result of the underlying asset's volatility." Volatility is critical to option pricing because it is the only one of the five primary option pricing variables (i.e., strike price, interest rate, expiration date, price of underlying, and volatility) not determined either through negotiation or by reference to some other market or rate. Volatility is determined purely by judgment, which is often based on complex mathematical models. "Viewed in this way, it is clear that the market for an

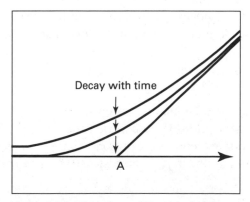

Figure 3.8 Time decay. (*Reprinted with permission from the Chicago Mercantile Exchange.*)

option on any underlying asset is in fact the market's price for the volatility on that underlying asset, quite separate from the price of the underlying asset itself. That's why some traders quote the price of an option in terms of volatility rather than the premium one has to pay."[28]

Volatility's critical role in option pricing is the primary reason that option pricing models are so important:

> Since implied volatility is the number that justifies an option price, an option buyer or seller can use that number to evaluate whether his or her option is cheap or expensive, by comparing it with the implied volatility of other options in the market. But since the number derived is dependent on the pricing model being used, different models can yield different results....[T]he discrepancies in volatility numbers can give rise to results which are significantly different.[29]

Combined Effect

The combined effect of the "Greek letter" risks leads to a highly dynamic risk profile for individual options. Generally, the only way to perfectly eliminate option risks is by entering into an equal and opposite option contract. However, that result is seldom satisfactory because it involves the payment of an option premium, which is a guaranteed though perhaps relatively small loss. The difficulty of managing option risks is compounded by the tendency of various risks to move simultaneously yet in opposite directions. For example, as time passes, *theta* risk causes the time value of an option to decay at an accelerating rate, pushing the option value curve ever closer to the option's intrinsic value. Yet a sudden and simultaneous increase in volatility can force the option value curve in the opposite direction.

The foregoing analysis of the Greek letter risks used a call option and focused on the position of the long, or the option holder.

Caps, floors, and collars: options on interest rates

"Much as forwards can be bundled to create swaps, options can be bundled to create other option-based contracts called caps, floors, and collars."[30] Caps, floors, and collars are option-based products used to manage the risk of changes in underlying interest rates.* Each comprises a series

---

*Each of the three products constitutes a series of simple European, as opposed to American, interest rate options.

of options. Unbundled, each option entitles the holder to receive a portion (which may be zero) of the interest accrued (or assumed to have accrued) over an interest period on a notional amount and at a specified rate. The amount of that portion is calculated as the difference between a specified strike rate and a floating reference rate. Payments are usually made at the end of the interest period (i.e., the option's expiration date), although the reference rate used to compute the amount, if any, of each payment is the rate in effect at the start of the interest period.

A cap is a series of call options, each of which entitles the holder to receive the amount, if any, by which interest accrued on a notronal amount at the reference rate exceeds interest accrued at the strike rate. In contrast, a floor is a series of put options, each of which entitles the holder to receive the amount, if any, by which interest assumed to have accrued at the strike rate exceeded interest accrued at the reference rate. A collar is simply a combination of a cap and a floor. The "buyer" of a collar is considered to be a counterparty that has simultaneously purchased (the long position) a cap and sold (the short) a floor.

Caps, floors, and collars are usually written in relation to specific loan transactions. A buyer of a cap is usually an end user that has borrowed money at a floating rate and wishes to lock in a maximum rate it will pay on the borrowing. In contrast, a floating rate borrower that believes interest rates are unlikely to decline may agree to sell a floor. If so, it forfeits in exchange for an immediate premium at least a portion of any subsequent decline in floating rates. Finally, a floating rate borrower that wishes to cap its floating interest rate exposure without paying a premium may offset the cost of the cap premium by selling a floor. In that case, the borrower has set both an upper and a lower limit on, and thus to some extent fixed, its interest rate exposure.

Unbundling complex structures involving options

A functional approach is helpful in analyzing the risks of transactions involving embedded options as well as outright options.

Embedded option   Perhaps the most common embedded option is that found in floating-rate home mortgages. Most residential floating-rate mortgage loans provide that interest rates will be reset periodically to reflect changes in some specified underlying rate. However, they also contain limits on the size of any one-period rate change and on the maximum interest rate over the life of the loan. Both the short-term and the long-term limits are considered to be options, although they are exercised automatically without need of any action on the part of the option holder—here, the borrower.

In other words, the maximum rate limit over the life of the loan represents the economic equivalent of an unbounded floating-rate loan combined with an interest rate cap. Although the cap is valuable, the purchaser of the option—here, the borrower—should not assume that the cap is free of cost. Option pricing involves the payment of a premium. A premium does not have to be stated explicitly; in the case of capped home mortgages it is instead reflected as an increase, though perhaps slight, in the applicable interest rate and effectively amortized (or paid-in installments) over the life of the loan.

Similarly, the contractual limit on short-term rate movements is economically a collar, with a notional amount that ratchets up or down on each reset date. The collar suggests two valuation questions that the homeowner may wish to consider. First, what is the cost to the buyer of the cap portion of the collar? In many cases, the premium payable by the borrower for the cap is offset by the premium for the floor that the buyer is entitled to receive. Second, is the collar properly valued? This question is complex, given that low introductory mortgage loan rates usually make it highly likely that the applicable rate will increase on each reset date, at least in the early years of the mortgage. If so, that means the floor at issuance (i.e., the date of the borrowing) is deeply out of the money to the lender, while the cap portion of the collar is in the money to the borrower. What, then, is the real cost of the in the money option to the borrower? Probably a higher mortgage interest rate.

Short straddle: transaction structure   Figure 3.9 diagrams the payoff profile and time decay of a complex and fascinating transaction consummated in the mid-1980s. The transaction involved a single issuer's simultaneous sale of an equal number of three-year American put and call options on the same underlying asset, at the same strike price. The underlying asset was "one quarter of the...value of one trading unit" as of a specified date on the Nikkei 225 Index, which is a weighted-average measure of the aggregate price performance of 225 well-known stocks trading on the Tokyo Stock Exchange. The structure contemplated a dollar-denominated purchase price and dollar-denominated cash settlement value. Assume for convenience that the issuer was hedging its exposure through a strategy that involved the purchase of certain equities that were included in the index, along with certain offsetting Nikkei 225 Index options. The issuer's only obligation was to deliver yen, which would then be converted according to a preset spot exchange rate mechanism built into the documentation. Nevertheless, the options were "general contractual obligations of the [i]ssuer and...not secured by any options or futures purchased by the [i]ssuer or any form of collateral or security."

For simplicity, assume that the value of one quarter of a trading unit several weeks prior to the transaction's closing date was approximately ¥ 5000, or $150 at then spot foreign exchange rates. To facilitate the closing, that value, though it was several weeks old, was set in the offering documentation as the strike price for both the puts and the calls. The parties' intention was to adjust the put and call premiums on the closing date to reflect any changes in the value of the Nikkei 225 Index between the date at which the strike price was set and the actual closing date. Assume that by the closing date, the value of the Nikkei had fallen slightly—it had moved just to the left of point X—so that one quarter trading unit was worth approximately ¥4985. In contrast, assume that on the issuance date, the value of the Japanese yen had risen against the value of the dollar. Thus, the put premium at issuance was $6.50, and the call premium $9.25, with the aggregate premium received by the issuer net of transaction fees and costs exceeding $15 million.

This transaction structure, commonly called a *short straddle,* is used by an issuer when, in the words of the Chicago Mercantile Exchange (CME), "you [the issuer] expect [that the] market is stagnating. Because you are short options, you reap profits as they decay—as long as market remains near X."

The CME also includes the following caution to the option writer: "**Loss characteristics:** Loss potential open-ended in either direction.

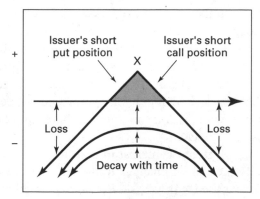

Figure 3.9   Short straddle.

Position, therefore, must be closely monitored and readjusted to neutrality if market begins to drift away from [X]." (Bold emphasis in original.) In contrast, the issuer's potential profit on the transaction, indicated by the shaded region in Figure 3.9, is limited to the net premium received, less any transaction costs incurred thereafter.

Short straddle: functional analysis   The first step in a functional analysis is to unbundle the risks of the transaction. Four major risks are readily apparent: (1) the risk of changes in the value of the Nikkei 225 Index, (2) currency exchange rate risk, (3) political risk, and (4) credit risk of the issuer and any provider of credit support. For convenience, we will focus only on risks (1) and (2).

Both the long and the short positions in both options were exposed to currency exchange rate risk. All other things being equal, and since we assumed that the issuer was actively hedging its exposure in Nikkei equity securities or actual trading units on the index, any change in exchange rates would not have directly affected the issuer's obligations. Rather, a strengthening of the dollar would likely have reduced the dollar-denominated profit to an option holder, because the same number of yen would have purchased fewer dollars; likewise, a weakening of the dollar would have increased the dollar-denominated profit.

This currency risk would have been quite difficult to hedge, other than through purchases of foreign exchange options. Yet any such options would have also commanded a hefty premium. Moreover, the contingency on which the foreign exchange option would be based would not match the underlying contingency driving the value of the puts and calls. In other words, there is no necessary connection between currency exchange rate changes and changes in the value of the Nikkei 225 Index. Thus, no matter what happens with the value of the Nikkei, the currency options will have an independent value and risk structure. An equity put may expire in the money, whereas the currency option may expire out of the money. In that case, the put would be exercised but not the currency option. Conversely, the put may expire out of the money while the currency option may expire in the money. In that case, the put would not be exercised but the currency option would. Currency options here might not have provided a well-designed hedge.

In any event, of greatest interest to both the issuer and the option holders was likely the risk of changes in the value of the Nikkei Index. Both parties were exposed to price risk. But, as explained by the CME, the issuer was especially exposed to adverse price movements, because its risk was "open-ended in either direction"—that is, whether the value of the index increased or decreased. The management of price risk requires *dynamic hedging*. It is essential that the issuer monitor the delta, gamma, theta, and vega risks discussed earlier. It is useful to examine briefly the likely consequences of each risk from the issuer's perspective in light of a large market drop, such as occurred repeatedly in the late 1980s. Such an event would cause the value of the Nikkei to plummet, moving rapidly to the left along the horizontal axis of Figure 3.9.

First, *delta* (or absolute value) risk increases dramatically as the index's value moves left, and the amount by which the put grows more deeply out of the money to the issuer increases rapidly. Graphically, the put price curve would begin to approach the straight, intrinsic value line, but at an ever lower point along that line. *Gamma* risk, or the acceleration of *delta* or absolute price risk, is likely to decline rapidly as price risk approaches the solid line. That, however, cannot be adequate to counteract the effects of the *delta* risk. The effects of *theta* risk, or time decay, would depend entirely on when the market move occurs, whether near expiration or substantially prior to it.

Finally, a dramatic increase in volatility, or *vega* risk, might cause the call option to acquire a value to the holder even though it was quite far out of the money. But the greater risk to the issuer was likely with respect to the puts. Increasing volatility would have caused the entire option value curve to shift downward, increasing the degree to which the options were out of the money to the issuer.

EFFECTS OF OPTION CHARACTERISTICS ON PLAIN VANILLA TRANSACTIONS

Options are truly risky to the holder of the "short" position.* The ability of a derivatives dealer to offer optionlike features to counterparties usually implies that the dealer is offsetting the option risk by assuming somewhere else in its portfolio a corresponding long position. To cover the costs of that offset, the dealer must change its option buyer a premium.

---

*When options are used to speculate, they can also be risky to the holder of the "long." The reason
    is that the holder of the long position stands to lose the entire value of its premium paid if the
    option expires out of the money.

This is so even with plain vanilla products, which with minor modifications can be "enhanced" through optionlike features such as puts, or early termination rights. At least three risk management issues arise under such circumstances.

First, management must confirm that the persons responsible for designing the transaction have identified clearly the manner in which the premium is being charged. Sometimes a premium is explicit, in the form of an upfront fee. Other times, it is implicit, resulting, perhaps, in a slightly less favorable rate payable by the holder of the option. The most risky manner in which a premium is paid, as many recent derivatives fiascoes have demonstrated, is through the issuance of an offsetting option. For example, we saw in the case of a collar that a cap premium can be offset by the simultaneous sale of a floor. Although the floor may seem to be a relatively painless way of obtaining the desired cap, a floor is an option that implies option risks. Thus, the provider of the floor must consider the optionlike exposure in calculating the all-in costs of the transaction.

Second, it is equally important, after the manner in which the premium is being charged has been determined, to calculate whether the price being paid for the premium is fair.

Third, under certain circumstances, embedded option features may create legal risks, particularly when investment or transaction guidelines to which a firm or portfolio is subject specify that the organization is not to engage in "derivatives" or options transactions. The embedding of option features within other products, and the uncertainty of derivatives definitions, can create a real risk that particular products may exceed those guidelines. In that case, exposure to legal liability may arise, especially if losses are incurred and transactions are reverse-engineered to reveal their optionality only after the fact.

PUT-CALL PARITY

Options and foewards are not as different from each other as they might otherwise seem. For example, assuming equal strike prices, the diagonal segments of the intrinsic value plot of a short put (Figure 3.5) can be attached to the diagonal of a long call (Figure 3.4) for a position equivalent to a long forward (Figure 3.1). Conversely, a long put (Figure 3.4) plus a short call (Figure 3.5) is equivalent to a short forward (Figure 3.1).

This fundamental relationship also works in reverse, because "option payoff profiles can be duplicated by a dynamically adjusted combination of forwards and risk-free securities."[31] However, "dynamic-hedging" is a demanding mathematical task that summons into play the Greek letter risks just discussed. It also implies greater risks than managing forward, or linear exposures. It necessarily demands sophisticated computer facilities and skilled mathematicians. Nevertheless, the important point for present purposes is that the use of forwards (and risk-free assets) to create options, and vice versa, is possible because of a basic mathematical relationship formally called "put-call parity."

ENDNOTES: CHAPTER 3

1. Quoted in Mason et al., *Financial Engineering, supra,* Chapter 1, note 2: 43 (citation omitted).
2. Quotations in this paragraph are from Michael E. Porter, "What Is Strategy?" *Harvard Business Review* (November–December 1996) (emphasis modified) [hereafter, *What Is Strategy?*]: 61–78; see, generally, "Using Derivatives: What Senior Managers Must Know," *Harvard Business Review* (January–February 1995) [hereafter, *Using Derivatives: What Senior Managers Must Know*]: 33–41.
3. The quotations in this paragraph are from the *G-30 Overview:* 30–31; see also Charles W. Smithson, "A Building Block Approach to Financial Engineering: An Introduction to Forwards, Futures, Swaps and Options," in *SWAPS and Other Derivatives in 1997,* Kenneth M. Raisher and Alison M. Gregory, Co-chairs (Practising Law Institute, 1997): 9–22; John C. Hull, *Options, Futures, and Other Derivatives,* 3rd ed. (Prentice Hall, 1997) [hereafter, *Derivatives*]: 1–3.
4. Hull, *Derivatives, supra,* note 3: 2.
5. Saber, *Interest Rate Swaps, supra,* Chapter 2, note 9: 57.
6. See, e.g., Don M. Chance, *An Introduction to Derivatives,* 3rd ed. (The Dryden Press, 1995) [hereafter, *Introduction to Derivatives*]: 509.
7. Hull, *Derivatives, supra,* note 3: 51.
8. *G-30 Overview:* 31.
9. *Id.:* 32.
10. *Id.*
11. Miller, *The Last Twenty Years and the Next, supra,* Chapter 1, note 13: 465.
12. John F. Marshall, and Kevin Wynne, "Currency Swaps, Commodity Swaps, and Equity Swaps," *Derivatives: Tax Regulation Finance,* 2(1) (September–October 1996): 43–48.
13. *G-30 Overview:* 32.
14. Hull, *Derivatives, supra,* note 3: 8

15. *G-30 Overview*: 32.

16. Bob Reynolds, *Understanding Derivatives: What You Really Need to Know About the Wild Card of Corporate Finance* (Pitman Publishing, 1995) [hereafter, *Understanding Derivatives*]: 91.

17. Mason et al., *Financial Engineering, supra,* Chapter 1, note 2: 9.

18. See Hull, *Derivatives, supra,* note 3: 142.

19. Susan Ross Marki, *Derivative Financial Products* (HarperCollins Publishers, 1991): 34.

20. Hu, *Misunderstood Derivatives, supra,* Chapter 1, note 22: 1475.

21. Hull, *Derivatives, supra,* note 3: 5.

22. Hu, *Misunderstood Derivatives, supra,* Chapter 1, note 14: 1475; see also Hull, *Derivatives, supra,* note 3 (adding as to stock options the factor of "dividends expected during the life of the option"): 151.

23. Chew, *Leverage, supra,* Chapter 1, note 1 (emphasis in original): 158; see, generally, Hull, *Derivatives, supra,* note 3: chapter 7; Hu, *Misunderstood Derivatives, supra,* Chapter 1, note 22: 1475.

24. Dr. Saied Simozar, "Measuring Derivatives Risk," in *Derivatives Risk Management Service,* ed. G. Timothy Haight (Warren, Gorham & Lamont, 1996) [this service is hereafter referred to as *Derivatives Risk Management Service*]: ¶ 5B.04.

25. See Hu, *Misunderstood Derivatives, supra,* Chapter 1, note 22: 1475.

26. Chew, *Leverage, supra,* Chapter 1, note 1 (emphasis added): 139.

27. *G-30 Overview*: 44.

28. All quotations in this paragraph are from Chew, *Leverage, supra,* Chapter 1, note 1: 158.

29. *Id.*: 158–159.

30. *G-30 Overview*: 33; see, generally, Hull, *Derivatives, supra,* note 3: Chapters 16 and 17; Peter A. Abken, "Interest-Rate Caps, Collars, and Floors," *Economic Review* (November–December 1989) [hereafter, *Caps, Collars, and Floors*]: 2–24.

31. See Smithson et al., *Managing Financial Risk, infra,* Chapter 11, note 28: 37-44, 41.

CHAPTER 4

Strategic "Fit" and the Building Blocks of Risk Management

The economic function of these [derivatives] contracts is to allow risks that formerly had been combined to be unbundled and transferred to those most willing to assume and manage each risk component. The importance of this function has increased, as competitive pressures have intensified in many economic sectors and as interest rates, exchange rates, and other asset prices have tended to be quite volatile.

Alan Greenspan, Chairman, Federal Reserve Bank
Statement Before Congress, May 25, 1994[1]

Without a clear set of risk-management goals, using derivatives can be dangerous.

Froot, Scharfstein, and Stein
Harvard Business Review,
November–December 1994[2]

The functional analysis of derivatives in Chapters 2 and 3 focused mainly on the economic characteristics of individual products. However, as Alan Greenspan warns, for the risk management function of derivatives "to be effective and the efficiency to be realized, end users must retain ultimate responsibility for transactions they choose to make. In a wholesale market, sophisticated and unsophisticated end users alike must ensure that they fully understand the risks attendant to any transaction they enter."[3] This chapter examines how derivatives, because of their essential "risk management function,"[4] form an integral part of an organization's overall business and investment strategy.

Absent the implementation of a clear set of risk management principles, any derivatives user runs an unavoidable risk of incurring unforeseen and unacceptable derivatives losses. Even without such losses, derivatives activities can easily lead to management inefficiencies, because they require a high degree of senior management attention. That attention is required even if the products are used for nonspeculative risk management purposes. If derivatives activities divert management resources away from their most productive use, those activities will detract from, rather than enhance, a firm or portfolio's competitive strategy.

STRATEGIC "FIT"

Ultimate economic and legal responsibility for understanding derivatives risks, as every major derivatives study to date has concluded, resides solely with senior management, and mainly with the trustees, directors, or comparable supervisory personnel. "Contrary to what senior managers may assume, a company's risk-management strategy cannot be delegated to the corporate treasurer—let alone to a hotshot financial engineer. Ultimately, a company's risk-management strategy needs to be integrated with [the firm's] overall corporate strategy."[5]

An organization should engage in a business activity only if the activity is compatible with the organization's other activities. Choices must be made among potentially incompatible business activities. "Trade-offs occur when activities are incompatible. Simply put, a trade-off means that more of one thing necessitates less of another....[A business] cannot do both [activities] without bearing major inefficiencies." Inefficiencies detract from long-term sustainable strategic positioning. To avoid ineffi-ciencies, a core responsibility of senior management is to define the orga-nization's overall strategy "—and to say no. Strategy renders choices about what not to do as important as choices about what to do. Indeed, set-ting limits is another function of leadership."[6]

CONSTRUCTING A RISK MANAGEMENT STRATEGY

Derivatives activities are susceptible to two basic lines of criticism. The first attacks management's goals in the use of derivatives. For example, critics might allege that a corporation is using derivatives imprudently to generate extra earnings—as a so-called independent profit center. That use is incompatible with the overall business strategy of a nonfinancial insti-tution and directly inimical to risk management.

The second line of criticism focuses on the implementation of risk management strategies. When large losses occur, critics often blame sup-posedly inadequate senior management supervision. Lax supervision, it is commonly charged, permitted derivatives activities that increased rather than reduced risk. Alternatively, critics may argue that incentives for risk management were poorly designed, thus "incentivizing" or encouraging rogue traders to engage in derivatives activities incompatible with sound risk management.

An effective risk management strategy requires both a clear definition of the strategy's *goals* and a clear specification of the measures to be
executed to *implement* the strategy.

TRANSFORMING BUSINESS
ACTIVITIES TO REDUCE RISK

Reproduced as Figure 4.1 is a modified version of Figure 2.6, which illustrates schematically, at the broadest levels, the goals of risk management.
(Relevant regions within Figure 4.1 have been numbered for simplicity.)
Figure 4.1 provides a useful starting point for an analysis of risk management strategies, of which the use of derivatives is merely one alternative.
It demonstrates how laws and public perceptions can at times strongly
influence business strategies—whether or not they employ derivatives—
in unintended and undesirable ways.

Recall that profitable business activities (located in Circle PB) outside the "risk oval" of Figure 4.1 are not especially risky for the relevant
organization, whereas those within it are. Moreover, business activities
within Circle S are considered imprudent and publicly suspect, regardless
of whether they are lawful (CircleL) or profitable.

As we noted earlier, the determination of whether a preferable business activity suspect (S), lawful (L), or both depends largely on the activity's definition. Yet definitions do not necessarily provide any information
about the activity's riskiness. Consider the following examples.

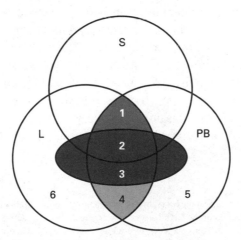

Figure 4.1   Goals of risk management.

Arbitrage Savings by Moving from Region 4 to Region 1

Lawful business activities in region 1 of Figure 4.1 are not highly risky,* even though they may be "suspect." Many plain vanilla swap transactions that either reduce risk or result in significant transaction cost savings without appreciably increasing risk fall within this region, simply because they are labeled derivatives. Likewise, most other "core" OTC derivatives listed in Figure 2.8 would fall in region 1.

A common example of a plain vanilla currency swap used to obtain cost savings without appreciably increasing risk is provided by the *G-30 Overview.* Many sovereignties (Finland is the G-30's prime example) and multinational companies exhibit disparate borrowing costs from country to country, currency to currency. In many cases, borrowers can significantly reduce borrowing costs by issuing debt in markets and currencies in which their costs of funds are comparatively cheapest, then swapping the borrowed funds into other desired currencies. The swap effectively converts the currency of the borrowing from the inexpensive currency into the desired currency, yet at an overall lower cost.

For example, assume a hypothetical company, TechCo, wishes to fund new operations in Italy at a time when TechCo's cheapest source of funds is pound sterling denominated debt issued in the U.K. capital markets. Temporary relative cost disparities might arise if, for example, U.S. and Italian capital markets are somewhat saturated with TechCo paper at the time when TechCo has issued comparatively little debt in the United Kingdom. In that case, U.K. demand for TechCo paper might be higher, enabling TechCo to command a relatively lower sterling interest rate. TechCo could issue paper in the United Kingdom and use a currency swap to convert sterling proceeds into Italian lira. The *G-30 Overview* notes that through such transactions "in the early days of the swap market, funding could be obtained at savings of as much as 50 basis points (0.50%) given the significant arbitrage opportunities that then were available. Today [July 1993] arbitrage savings are more likely to be in the range of 10 to 25 basis points (0.10% to 0.25%)."[7] Hu noted more recently that even though

---

*The assumption, for discussion purposes, that activities are or are not highly risky sets aside temporarily the question of the circumstances under which *identical* activities used by the same institution but for different purposes, or used improperly or mistakenly, can be transformed into highly risky activities.

many arbitrage savings opportunities have diminished over the years, "there is reason to believe that some gains are available for the clever and fleet-footed."[8]

Arbitrage and the "Law of One Price"

Arbitrage opportunities in efficient markets—that is, markets where prices completely account for all relevant information—are fleeting.* True arbitrage occurs when a market participant notices that an identical asset is simultaneously selling at different prices in two different markets. Once the alert arbitrageur identifies the pricing disparity, it can immediately locks in a theoretically risk-free return by simultaneously selling the asset in the market where it is selling at the higher price and buying it (to cover the simultaneous sale) in the market where it is selling at the lower price. Arbitrage opportunities are fleeting because the mere act of executing the arbitrage trades tends to eliminate the price disparity. According to the laws of supply and demand, the purchase increases demand, driving up the price of the asset in the lower-priced market the simultaneous sale decreases demand and drives down the price of the asset in the more expensive market. "The rule that states that prices must be driven into line in this manner is called the Law of One Price."[9]

The Law of One Price is in effect in the TechCo example, and it should, all other things being equal, drive away the pricing disparity—that is, the difference in rates at which TechCo can borrow in U.K. and Italian capital markets. Indeed, TechCo's issuance of debt in the United Kingdom at a different rate—or price—from that in the Italian market will itself tend to drive prices between the two markets into alignment.

Although TechCo is willing to fund its Italian operations in sterling, presumably it does not wish to assume the risk of sterling/lira exchange rate fluctuations over the life of the new sterling-denominated debt. Without the swap, TechCo would experience a curency mismatch upon each scheduled debt service payment, because its source of funds for repayment is in lira. Hence, each payment would expose TechCo to currency exchange rate risk in converting the lira back to sterling. A currency swap would enable TechCo to lock in currency exchange rates over the life of the swap, which could be customized to be identical to the maturity of the U.K. debt. Having

---

*They also entail transaction costs, taxes, trading delays, and other "market imperfections." Consequently, it is not unusual to see minor "violations" of the Law of One Price persist indefinitely. See, e.g., Tucker, *Financial Futures, infra,* note 10: 11.

eliminated *the spot market* exchange rate risk, TechCo can comfortably move to take advantage of the arbitrage opportunity.

Summary

Arbitrage savings transactions would lie in region 1 of Figure 4.1, because they involve low risk currency swaps used prudently to minimize exchange rate risk. Nevertheless, the use of the swaps might give rise to shareholder and regulatory scrutiny and criticism of TechCo, even if the transactions (1) were economically beneficial to all concerned, (2) involved no appreciable increase in economic risk, and (3) because of their simplicity, required little senior management oversight.

Modern Futures Markets: Transforming a Region 3 into a Region 1 Activity

Modern agricultural and industrial commodities futures markets provide another example of transactions inappropriately labeled as suspect. The modern U.S. origins of those markets are traceable to the Chicago Board of Trade (CBOT), which was established in 1848 by a group of 82 private merchants. Initially, the role of the exchange was merely to provide a centralized trading location where buyers and sellers could gather to purchase and sell commodities. At the outset, all exchange transactions were for immediate delivery.

By the mid-1800s Chicago had emerged as the distribution center of the U.S. farming economy, because of its strategic location at the base of the Great Lakes and proximate to the Midwest farmlands. As the early grain trade expanded, problems of supply and demand, transportation, and storage led to chaotic market conditions. Harvest season was especially tough on farmers, who brought their crop to market at a time when supply vastly exceeded demand for current delivery. Warehouse and storage facilities in the city began to prove inadequate to accommodate the vast quantities of agricultural products flowing through the city during harvest season. Farmers were ill equipped to manage the resulting costs and price risks.

Because of their need to lower costs and risks, farmers began informally contracting with merchants to sell their product for future delivery. Yet those early forward contracts proved troublesome, because they exposed both sides to counterparty default risk. Thus, in 1865 the CBOT began formalizing grain trading using standardized *futures contracts*.

Futures contracts required that both parties post performance bonds as margin. They also called for product to be delivered at some time in the future, say September or December, and at specified delivery points, if delivery was desired. Futures could be entered into or traded at any time during the year. Thus, they allowed farmers to sell product prior to harvest, while their crop was still in the fields or perhaps not even yet planted. Alternatively, farmers could store their product in local grain elevators for future delivery under a futures contract.

The economic impact of futures trading was that by preventing over-supplies of grain from being delivered simultaneously, it helped stabilize prices and contributed to rational price formation. To understand how the mechanism works economically, note that in the spring a farmer might be considering selling product during the fall harvest. She or he could then determine from the exchange the currently quoted price for futures contracts calling for fall delivery. A low price quote would signal to the farmer that the harvest season was not the most economic delivery period. Thus the farmer would have the information available well in advance to determine that traveling to the market to sell during the Fall was likely to result in unfavorable prices. The farmer might, then, decide to store her or his harvest in a local elevator for later sale at stronger prices.

The result was that farmers could sell their products over an exchange on one day for delivery on a future, presumably less congested date. "The process helped to smooth the distribution of commodities by alleviating the burden on Chicago's storage facilities at storage time."[10] During the late 1800s the CBOT eventually began offering trading in a variety of grain futures and other agricultural futures contracts having standardized grade, quantity, and delivery terms.

Over time, the number and variety of contracts offered by the CBOT expanded rapidly, and in 1874 the second oldest futures exchange was established, the Chicago Mercantile Exchange (CME). The economic function that these exchanges served primarily for the benefit of farmers was efficient price formation and risk allocation.

Futures markets transformed many aspects of farming and agriculture from risky activities in region 3 to less risky region 1 activities. Nevertheless, futures transactions, when used by farmers, and merchants, grain elevators, and processors for legitimate risk management purposes have long been subjected to suspicion, scrutiny, and criticism: Indeed, Working explains that not until the late 1940s did the idea that futures markets were predominantly hedging markets begin to take hold. Prior to then they were viewed as predominantly speculative. Still, as noted earlier, futures trading has long been subject to periodic legislative attacks.[11]

Modern Futures Markets: Creating a
New Region 2 Activity

Early in the development of the CBOT and CME, speculators entered into futures markets, discovering they could use futures contracts as a means of trying to profit on commodity price movements. They could achieve the same "action" as on the underlying asset for a fraction of the capital that outright dealing in the underlying asset itself demanded, because they did not have to take actual positions in or possessin of the underlying asset.

Part of the reason futures and other derivatives attract speculators is that they rarely involve actual physical delivery of the underlying commodity and are virtually always settled by cash payments. Rather than take delivery, the buyer (or long) or seller (short) of the underlying commodity can at any time effectively extinguish the futures contract. One does so simply by entering into an offsetting transaction with the exchange clearinghouse. The result, after payment has been made or received, is a net zero exposure. Miller noted in 1986 that the additional "abstraction" introduced into futures markets by the right of cash settlement created "enormous new potential applications for financial futures, a potential that has only just begun to be tapped."

Notwithstanding losses suffered by many speculators in futures markets, the presence of futures markets allows those markets to flourish and is an important reason for the markets' depth and efficiency. Without speculators, futures markets would be inefficient. Working explains that some speculators (whom he, perhaps unfortunately, calls "scalpers") offer a service much like market makers in other markets. Namely, in the hope of turning a quick but small profit on a trade, they offer to buy from "urgent" sellers and sell to "urgent" buyers at slight discounts or markups, which the sellers and buyers are willing to accept as a tradeoff for not having to shop around for a better deal.[12] When futures markets lack the liquidity provided by speculators they are unable to fulfill their essential hedging function and often fail. Speculators are necessary for futures markets to perform their essential risk management function.

In the approving words of the U.S. Supreme Court:

> The advent of *speculation in futures markets produced well-recognized benefits* for producers [i.e., farmers] and processors of agricultural commodities. A farmer who takes a "short" position in the futures market is protected against a price decline; a processor who takes a "long" position is protected against a price increase. Such *"hedging"* is *facilitated by the availability of speculators* willing to assume the market risk that the hedg-

ing farmer or processor wants to avoid. The speculators' participation in the market substantially enlarges the number of buyers and sellers of executory contracts and therefore makes it easier for farmers and processors to make firm commitments for futuree delivery at a fixed price. The *liquidity* of a futures contract, *upon which hedging depends,* is *directly related to the amount of speculation* that takes place.

Persons who actually produce or use the commodities that are covered by futures contracts are not the only beneficiaries of futures trading....In a broad sense, futures trading has a direct financial impact on three classes of persons. Those who actually are interested in selling or buying the commodity are described as "hedgers"; their primary financial interest is in the profit to be earned from the production or processing of the commodity. Those who seek financial gain by taking positions in the futures market generally are called "speculators" or "investors"; *without their participation, futures markets "simply would not exist."* Finally, there are the futures commision merchants, the floor brokers, and the persons who manage the market; they also are essential participants, and they have an interest in maximizing the activity on the exchange."[13]

Proposed Currency Risk Management: Transforming a Region 1 Activity into a High-Risk Region 3 Activity

Consider a hypothetical multinational baby products firm, Alpha Products. Alpha produces and sells a line of "medium-end" baby products, consisting largely of lotions, diapers, and other nonfood products. Alpha's line of products has over the past decade sold very well in the Americas, although mainly outside the United States. Alpha is headquartered, and has all its research and production facilities, in the United States. It imports most raw materials used for its lotions from Latin America. Most of its other products have high paper content, and Alpha imports most of its paper from Canada. The company's stock is publicly traded in the United States.

Alpha has staffed its treasury department with a talented corps of financial engineers who have proved to be adept at identifying and pricing intricate currency exchange derivatives, especially those involving Latin American currencies. Treasury's ability to manage Alpha's exchange rate risk over the past decade has enabled the company to prosper and enjoy steady and solid earnings growth in a highly competitive industry. Alpha's treasury people have developed and monitored an accurate risk profile of the company. They attempt to isolate the major components of Alpha's currency risks, in terms of both particular currencies and currency pairs.

Currently, the company's international operations expose it to exchange rate risk arising primarily in four currencies. Alpha's marketing department has historically been accurate at forecasting both foreign sales and corresponding raw materials needs. Treasury has worked closely with marketing and successfully used marketing's projections as the basis for Alpha's currency risk management program.

Even when derivatives fell out of public favor in 1994, senior management was satisfied with Alpha's hedging program; all losses to date fell within acceptable ranges. Management realized and publicly disclosed that derivatives losses were to be expected even in a "perfectly executed hedging strategy" and that those losses should be of no concern either to management or to public shareholders. Management, following treasury's advice, has always judged the performance of any hedge by looking at the overall performance of the entire transaction—both the derivative and the underlying purchase or sale. On that basis, the program has exceeded expectations. Indeed, it is an important reason that Alpha's overall profits have been consistently high and its growth sustainable. Alpha's well-designed hedging program has neutralized most of the company's massive currency exposure, enabling management, unlike the management of many close competitors, to concern itself with other, more pressing issues, such as research and development, improvements in the production process, labor relations, and marketing.

Senior management and the company's shareholders remained comfortable with Alpha's treasury operations throughout the wave of adverse derivatives publicity in 1993 and 1994. The company had aggressively disclosed the nature and extent of its activities, forestalling significant shareholder concerns about Alpha's derivatives program. However, toward the end of 1994, treasury reported several large derivatives gains that, while welcome, troubled certain senior managers. It was difficult to discern any obvious direct tie to the company's hedging program. Nevertheless, the gains were not repeated and were eventually, for all practical purposes, forgotten.

Recently, however, shareholders have begun to express concerns about several unusual losses on Alpha's currency derivatives, which similarly appear to have served no direct hedging purpose. On the basis of Alpha's financial statements, many shareholders have indicated concerns that the losses may be unrelated to the company's manufacturing, marketing, and distribution activities. In response, Alpha's board has retained an independent derivatives consulting firm to analyze and monitor the company's derivatives activities.

The problems

Adding to senior management's concerns are recent treasury reports containing unsettling news about increasing unpredictability of future currency movements. One of treasury's researchers, it seems, has predicted future increased volatility in key exchange rates as a result of indications of political and economic instability in several regions that constitute key Alpha markets. Treasury is seeking a mandate to expand the maturities, volumes, and types of its derivatives. So far, only short-term, forward-based products have been specifically authorized by senior management. However, internal corporate guidelines are in many respects vague—they do not specifically preclude trading in synthetic currency options or the embedding of option features into forward-based transactions. Marketing, unusually silent, has not decided what to make of treasury's findings.

To management's surprise, the consultant's preliminary findings suggest that reported derivatives-related losses may have been too low. Evidence is emerging that certain members of the treasury department had been incurring, without properly reporting, significant currency losses through purchases of currency options. The transactions, called *long strangles,* are depicted in Figure 4.2.

A long currency strangle position, which consists of simultaneous purchases of puts and calls on the same underlying currency at different strike prices, is designed to enable the option buyer to benefit from any major market move in either direction in relevant exchange rates. Unfortunately, the premiums paid for strangles are totally wiped out over time if rates remain stagnant, which is exactly what has been happening.

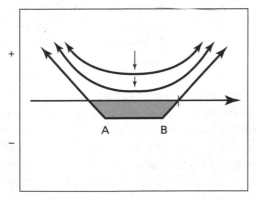

Figure 4.2   Long strangle.

The traders had been taking views—speculating—on the U.S. dollar/Mexican peso exchange rate. They thought the rate was about to explode out of its recent trading range, although none of the traders had any clear view on which direction the currencies would move. Unfortunately, exchange rates have remained relatively stable over the past 18 months, and losses have begun to mount. It appears that rather than abandon their speculative activity, the traders attempted to make up for prior losses by steadily increasing the size of their option positions.

It is beginning to appear from the consultant's report that poor management controls allowed large losses deep within the treasury department to remain mostly undetected. Treasurers, in the hope of avoiding having to report the losses, gambled by taking increasingly larger positions. The treasurers have been indefinitely suspended with reduced pay, pending senior management's analysis of the consultant's final report and recommendations.

Alternatives under consideration

Senior management generally agrees with the researcher's predictions about future exchange rate volatility. Nevertheless, it and its legal advisers are reluctant to suggest any increase in derivatives activities, given the near certain shareholder backlash that already will result upon disclosure of the newly discovered losses. Faced with this derivatives embarrassment, management (in addition to determining senior management accountability issues) is looking for some means of effectively managing the anticipated level of currency volatility without using derivatives.

One solution management is seriously considering is abandoning the company's derivatives operations and relocating manufacturing facilities outside the United States to areas where key markets are located. That might cause short-term operating disruptions and result in lost jobs in the United States. It would also expose the company to a range of new political and tax issues. Yet, on balance, several members of management believe this to be the best way of handling large exchange rate exposures. Without a large derivatives operation, the only way to manage that risk is to coordinate the currencies of production costs more closely with those of corresponding revenues. Thus, labor and fixed costs, which represent the majority of Alpha's costs of production, would after relocation be denominated in the same currency as sales. One drawback, however, is that the relocation strategy does not address the currency risks relating to importing raw materials.

Overlooked alternatives

The inordinate time and attention senior management and its advisers have devoted to derivatives' legal and economic risks has distracted them from considering a full range of potential alternatives. For example, management has failed to consider seriously the alternative of developing new markets not subject to the projected economic instabilities. If the research report is correct, the underlying economic uncertainty is likely to affect not only exchange rates but also product demand in the affected regions. If so, there may simply be "nothing a risk-management program can do to improve the underlying bad economics."[14] Certainly, building new offshore facilities is a risky strategy. Perhaps a more auspicious plan of action would be to invest in developing new products or to explore new markets in other regions and countries.

Second, management appears to be too ready to scrap all derivatives activities, thus significantly increasing Alpha's exposure to currency risks. The derivatives mandate sought by treasury, even though it implied a new level of sophistication and risk, might be well suited to the company's needs, assuming the program is managed properly.

In sum, abandoning the derivatives operation would likely transform Alpha's current activities into potentially volatile region 3 activities.

SEC Disclosure Rules: Transforming a Low-Risk Region 1 Activity into a High-Risk Region 3 Activity

Shareholders have an important and legitimate interest in knowing the risk profile of the companies in which they invest. That interest is only enhanced when one considers the importance of information about financial and other business risks to a shareholder attempting to achieve a well-diversified investment portfolio. Nevertheless, the shareholder's interest in disclosure must be weighed against the potential costs and competitive disadvantages to a corporation of overly burdensome disclosure requirements.

There are circumstances under which derivatives disclosure rules applicable to public companies might have an adverse impact on a company's business, independent of the inherent riskiness of the derivatives themselves, as shown in the Alpha Products example. First, the use of derivatives, if it dramatically increases a company's disclosure burden, could impose significant reporting and compliance burdens on public companies. An argument can also be made that increased disclosure subjects a company to greater litigation exposure, although safe harbors for forward-looking statements have been built into the new rules. Finally, disclosure relating to proprietary information about commodity price expectations could jeopardize one of the company's well-deserved competitive advantages.

Professor Don Chance of Virginia Tech offers an interesting illustration of the potential disadvantages of any rigorous SEC derivatives disclosure requirements. He discusses the case of a hypothetical publicly held airline that purchased a large supply of jet fuel in anticipation of heavy traffic in the following year.

Chance assumes that the company in the current year "puts on a hedge by purchasing oil futures." Therefore, at the end of the current year the company must provide details about its oil-hedging program in its public filings. "This forces it to reveal to its competitors that it is hedging oil. The competitor now knows that if oil prices decrease, the hedging airline will not benefit." A competitor that either is not hedging or does not have shares publicly traded in the United States will not be required to disclose that it is not hedging:

> Clearly the firm that is hedging is taking less risk than the firm that isn't. Yet the SEC is forcing the hedging firm to report and justify, at considerable cost, its activities as if those activities place the shareholders and creditors at greater risk. One might argue that such information should be useful to shareholders and creditors; it might conceivably result in a higher bond rating or increased stock price. On the other hand, it might tell outsiders that this firm is using derivatives and that can often be just enough of a negative implication to hurt it.[15]

One important guideline for using derivatives as part of any risk management program is: "Companies should pay close attention to the hedging strategies of their competitors."[16] Surely, the hedging airline above could find itself in an adverse competitive position, if its competitors are not similarly required to report their hedging strategies or lack thereof. The use or nonuse of derivatives for risk management purposes often constitutes important competitive information.

If the airline were sufficiently concerned about the financial cost effects of derivatives disclosure, it might decide to forgo its hedging program. In the highly competitive airline industry, even minor fuel price fluctuations can have a tremendous impact on a company's profitability. Thus, a less risky region 1 activity could easily be transformed into a potentially risky region 3 activity.

Eurodollar Markets: Transforming
an Unprofitable Region 5 Activity into
a Profitable Region 4 Activity

Chapter 2 discussed how Regulation Q's ceilings on interest rates payable on U.S. time deposits spawned the creation of Eurodollar markets. The payment of a rate above the ceiling rate would, absent Regulation Q, have constituted a low-risk activity. However, the payment of legal rates eventually rendered deposit taking in the United States unprofitable for many money-center and other banks that had to start paying more competitive rates to attract deposits. Therefore, the ceiling rendered deposit-taking activities for many banks an unprofitable activity located in region 6 of Figure 4.1. Upward pressure on interest rates forced U.S. banks to move much of their deposit-taking activity offshore, particularly to their foreign branches in Western Europe. Deposits taken at those locations were free of Regulation Q's restrictions. Therefore, the foreign branches could offer more competitive and legal free-market rates. Deposit taking was thereby transformed into a region 4 activity.

Equity Swaps: Diversification Through
Region 1 Transactions

Many wealthy Americans have for decades held "founder's stock" or other "low-basis stock" in U.S. companies. Much of the stock has experienced extraordinary appreciation over the applicable holding periods. Although many holders have no need to raise cash, they are often concerned about their lack of diversification. Others would also like to take defensive measures to lock in the benefits of stock currently trading at historic highs. If not for heavy adverse tax consequences, the holders' preferred approach would be to sell a large portion of their stock and use the proceeds to construct a well-diversified equity portfolio.

Because of the tremendous appreciation in the price of the stock over the applicable holding periods (much of which appreciation is attributable to inflation), current sales may result in massive capital gains taxes. In many cases, the tax costs would exceed more than one-third the value of the low-basis stock. Rather than sell the stock outright, many holders prefer to enter into equity swaps, whereby they agree for a stated period of time to exchange the return on their single stock for the return on a larger index or basket, less a financing charge usually in the form of a spread that is deducted from the return on the larger index or basket. A typical equity

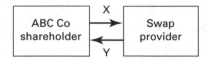

X: Total return of ABC Co, including
dividends plus net price change.

Y: Total return on Index, less spread,
with total return including dividends
plus net price change.

Figure 4.3   Stock swap.

swap is depicted in Figure 4.3. Alternatively, other techniques involving
equity derivatives are available for diversifying out of low-basis stock.
Included are "shorting against the box" and borrowing against a hedged
position. Although a comparison of the alternatives is beyond our present
scope,[17] the result of each is that otherwise lawful but unduly burdensome
stock sales, which can be thought of as region 6 transactions, can be converted into region 1 transactions.

Figure 4.1 Summary

Figure 4.1 demonstrates the adverse transactional consequences of the
current approach to derivatives regulation and of ongoing public criticism
of derivatives use. The adverse effects that have generated some of the
loudest industry complaints are that, by failing to focus on transactions'
inherent riskiness, many transactions are included in the "suspect" area,
region 1, even though they are demonstrably less risky than nonderivatives alternatives. Conversely, many transactions fall into the "nonsuspect" area, region 3, even though they may be demonstrably riskier than
derivatives solutions located in region 1.

In both cases, dependence on product definitions as a short cut far
avoiding a searching analysis of risks and controls can distort the allocation of management resources away from their most productive use.
Management and legal advisers are often forced to exert inordinate effort
monitoring and carefully disclosing and explaining safe, plain vanilla
derivatives transactions. Alternatively, mischaracterizations or fears of
public criticism may induce management to forgo the benefits derivatives
offer in reducing risk. Management may instead implement more costly
and cumbersome nonderivatives solutions or simply choose to leave oth-

erwise manageable risks unmanaged. The experience of many derivative professionals beginning in 1994 is consistent with that recounted by Jeffrey Larsen, a managing director and head of international capital markets at Chase Manhattan Bank. He explains that after the derivatives crisis began, "We had people coming in to take derivatives off their books, even though it increased their risk."[18] And that applied not only to exotic deals but also to the low-margin, plain vanilla products.

Concerns about derivatives that are not tailored to the products' riskiness, or lack thereof, can have the economically perverse effect of encouraging highly risky nonderivatives solutions, while simultaneously discouraging comparatively nonrisky derivatives solutions.

Against the foregoing risks must be weighed the legitimate interests of shareholders, particularly in attempting to realize the diversification benefits of modern portfolio theory, in obtaining all relevant risk information. Otherwise, labeling a company an "oil company" or an "industrial company" may—especially if the oil company uses derivatives to hedge most of its oil exposure and the industrial company uses them to speculate in financial markets—be misleading. Moreover, shareholders have the right to judge for themselves whether management has made the necessary infrastructure investments appropriate for any given level of derivatives risk management. Shareholders also need information with which to judge the merits of management's risk management strategy.

Current Disclosure Controversy

Concerns about such potential perverse incentives drive much of the criticism of the new SEC derivatives disclosure rules and newly published Financial Accounting Standards Board (FASB) standards on derivatives disclosure. For example, in April 1997, after holding hearings, a U.S. Senate Subcommittee issued a report highly critical of the SEC's rules and the proposed FASB initiative (since modified). Doubtless, the most serious concerns raised in the report are that the new rules: (1) reveal sensitive information to competitors; (2) single out derivatives "as if they were especially risky"; (3) discourages prudent use of derivatives; (4) mask actual risks of transactions by isolating derivatives from the risks they are being used to manage; and (5) lead to reporting that will not be comparable between companies.[19] Generally, these same concerns, along with concerns about costs and disclosure burdens, have been raised by many reporting companies that are or will be affected by the new rules.

An important distinction to bear in mind (and that may not be obvious to nonaccountants) in evaluating the current controversy is the fundamentally distinct purposes behind securities law disclosures and accounting rules. The two sets of requirements are designed to serve different investor needs. Perhaps the most essential distinction is the difference between forward-looking and "historical" information: the SEC rules are forward-looking, designed to give the reader an idea of a company's current and future derivatives exposures; FASB's accounting rules are intended to tell the financial statement user how derivatives have been used and how they have performed to date.

The SEC's rules include detailed quantitative disclosures about market risks of derivatives and other market sensitive instruments (essentially, what we referred to in Chapter 2 and Figure 2.8 as "core" and noncore derivatives). The disclosures can take the form of either (1) a tabular presentation of anticipated cashflow needs, (2) a detailed portfolio sensitivity analysis, or (3) a description of approximated "value at risk." In contrast, the FASB rules address "how past transactions should be portrayed to investors in the body of the financial statements."[20] Should, for example, gains and losses on hedging instruments be marked-to-market and reported in the income statement or as changes to shareholders equity prior to the unwinding or termination of the hedged transaction? When should changes in the value of derivatives be recorded on the balance sheet?[21]

STRATEGIC PREREQUISITE— DEVELOPING A RISK PROFILE

As a first step in strategic planning, an end user must develop an overall risk profile. A risk profile identifies, and attempts to quantify where feasible, the economic and financial variables to which the end user is exposed and which are likely to affect competitive strategies and economic performance.

Having initially identified the variables, the end user then identifies those which are capable of derivatives solutions. The five broadest categories of risks that lend themselves to derivatives solutions are fluctuations in (1) interest rates, (2) exchange rates, (3) equity prices, (4) commodity prices, and (5) credit exposures. The number of subcategories used and the degree of specificity within each category will depend greatly on

- Technology risk
- Basis risk
- Political risk
- Suitability risk
- Personnel risk
- Optional risk
- Concentration risk
- Contract risk
- Systems risk
- Limit risk
- Rollover risk
- Hedging risk
- Interpolation risk
- Extrapolation risk

- Credit risk
- Market risk
- Interest rate risk
- Prepayment risk
- Reinvestment risk
- Volatility risk
- Netting risk
- Currency risk
- Commodity risk
- Equity risk
- Call risk
- Yield curve risk
- Curve construction risk
- Raw data risk

- Regulatory risk
- Tax risk
- Accounting risk
- Legal risk
- Daylight risk
- Capital risk
- Liquidity risk
- Bankruptcy risk
- Collateral risk
- Modelling risk
- Cross-market risk
- Systemic risk
- Time lag risk
- Knowledge risk

Partial listing

Figure 4.4   Galaxy of risks. (© *1996, Capital Market Risk Advisors, Inc.*)

the needs and resources of each end user and the complexity of its operations. For purposes of properly evaluating potential derivatives solutions, a risk profile should also include any additional risks introduced by derivatives. For illustration purposes, Figure 4.4 provides a "partial listing" of the types of risks that an organization may wish to consider in constructing its risk profile.

Once an accurate risk profile has been drawn, senior management is in a better position to make informed decisions regarding the activities from which the organization will attempt directly to earn its profits in terms of the types of risk, and the amount of each type, the organization is willing and able to assume. An accurate risk profile will also enable management to identify unavoidable but unwanted risks. From among those unwanted risks that can be managed with derivatives, senior management can choose those that the organization will so manage.

The foregoing decisions depend on several factors, three of which predominate. The first is the expected contribution of each activity to the organization's competitive strategy. An activity's contribution will depend on its economic return and the degree to which the activity strategically fits, and does not interfere, with the organization's other business and investment activities. The second factor is each activity's legality. Finally, the cost of each activity must be considered, including, for public companies and regulated entities, the costs of regulatory compliance.

STRATEGIC GOALS—THE THREE
DIMENSIONS OF RISK MANAGEMENT

An effective risk management strategy involves more than an identification of product risks; it also requires that choices be made in implementation among functionally defined *strategic goals* of risk reduction. Functional analysis provides a methodology enabling senior management and its legal advisers to choose the appropriate "dimension," or combination of dimensions, of risk management to be adopted for their organization. Although the overarching goal of any risk management strategy is risk reduction, a risk reduction strategy requires additional refinement in terms of second-order goals.

Merton describes three second-order goals, which he calls the "three dimensions of risk management."[22] The first dimension involves the reduction of risk by transferring, selling, or *shedding* its source: "In general, adjusting a portfolio by moving from risky assets to a riskless asset to reduce risk is called *hedging*." Diversification, the second dimension, "consists of simultaneously pooling and subdividing risks. While it does not eliminate risk in the aggregate, it redistributes it to reduce the risk faced by each individual." The third and final dimension is purchasing insurance against large losses: "Insurance permits the owner of an asset to retain the economic benefits of ownership while eliminating the uncertainty of possible losses. Of course, this retention of the 'upside' while deleting the 'downside' of an asset ownership is not free. The fee or premium substitutes a sure loss for the possibility of a larger loss."*

The choice of which, if any, of the three strategic goals of risk reduction to be adopted can have legal as well as economic consequences.

Hedging

Many practitioners and commentators alike use the term *hedging* indiscriminately to mean any form of risk management, whether pure hedging, diversification, or insurance. However, for a clear understanding of the

---

*"The combined set of futures and options contracts and the markets, formal and informal, in which they are transferred has thus been likened to a gigantic insurance company—and rightly so. Efficient risk sharing is what much of the futures and options revolution has been all about. And that is why the term "risk management" has come increasingly to be applied to the whole panoply of instruments and institutions that have followed in the wake of the introduction of foreign exchange futures…in 1972." Miller, *Achievements and Prospects, supra,* Chapter 1, note 14: 7.

legal and economic implications of derivatives, it is beneficial to use the term in its strict sense, as an activity distinct from diversifying and insuring.

A hedge is a transaction usually entered into to protect against either an anticipated decline in the value of an asset (or portfolio of assets) or the anticipated increase in the cost of a liability (or portfolio of liabilities). In a "perfectly" executed derivatives hedge, all losses (gains) on the hedged activity will be offset by equal and opposite gains (losses) on the derivative. The goal of the hedge is to *freeze* the value of the asset or liability. Any price rise or decline of the underlying asset or liability is offset by the derivatives hedge. The purpose of a hedge is to make the cashflows of the derivative and the hedged instrument symmetrical, so that losses and gains will cancel each other out both as an accounting matter and in terms of the timing of actual cashflows. Figure 2.5 depicts the economic results of a perfectly executed hedging strategy.

Our earlier TechCo arbitrage savings transaction contained a hedge in the form of a currency swap. TechCo was seeking to raise Italian lira financing by issuing debt in pounds sterling and then swapping the proceeds into lira. The swap would have consisted of three components: (1) an initial exchange of principal, with TechCo paying pounds sterling and receiving lira, (2) subsequent exchanges of interest, with TechCo paying lira and receiving pounds sterling (which it would use to fund its U.K. interest obligations), and (3) a reversal of the original principal exchanges. Assuming for convenience that the interest payments were at a fixed rate, TechCo's lira-based financing costs—compared with the pound—would have been fixed from the outset of the transaction. Fluctuations in exchange rates between the pound and the lira during the life of the swap would have had no direct affect on the lira-denominated costs of the financing.

Diversification

Modern "portfolio theory" holds that investors and firms face two kinds of risk, often called "systematic" and "unsystematic" risk. By properly diversifying one's investments and exposures, it is possible to reduce exposure to price changes of any particular asset or liability—that is, unsystematic risk. "'Unsystematic' risk stems from the fact that many of the perils associated with a specific company are unique to the company and perhaps its immediate competitors. 'Systematic' risk arises from economy-wide perils that affect all businesses."[23] Systematic risk, in other words, is simply all risks that cannot be diversified away.

"Even a little diversification goes a long way to reduce volatility" of a portfolio.[24] According to modern portfolio theory, a portfolio of 15 randomly picked stocks eliminates about 95% of all unsystemic risk. A randomly picked portfolio is assumed to result in a portfolio of investments in organizations across a broad range of industries. To the extent that the portfolio consists of investments in companies that are in the same industry, much of the benefits of diversification will be lost.For a diversification stratedy to be effective, it must be the right kind of diversification.

In our earlier discussion of an undiversified portfolio of "founder's stock," the holder was initially assumed to be completely exposed to unsystematic risk. Any movement in the price of the founder's stock would have had a corresponding and proportionate effect on the value of the holder's portfolio. In contrast, diversification theory is based on the premise that factors causing changes in the price of one asset or liability will not necessarily affect the price of other assets or liabilities, or may not affect them to the same extent or in the same manner. The technical term used is *covariance*. Investments with strong covariance will move in lockstep with each other; investments with little covariance will move relatively independently; investments with strongly negative covariance will move in opposite directions.

Insurance

As understood in our analysis, "the reference to 'insurance' here is to a class of contracts that serve an explicit *function*."[25] As noted earlier, that function is, for a price, to protect a purchaser of the contract from adverse price movements while preserving for the purchaser the benefits of favorable price movements. In other words, insurance in a functional analysis generally refers to holding options. "In general, the owner of any asset can eliminate the downside risk of loss and retain the upside benefit of ownership by the purchase of a put option. Furthermore, the purchase of a call option is economically equivalent to owning the asset and insuring its value against loss by purchasing a put option."

Functional analysis provides a methodology enabling senior managers and their legal advisers to choose the appropriate dimension, or combination of dimensions, of risk management to be adopted by their organization. Put differently, it enables managers and advisers to identify and choose those strategic goals that an organization is capable of achieving through derivatives solutions.

SELECTING AMONG STRATEGIES

Functional analysis enables senior management and its legal advisers to choose among strategies available to implement the organization's risk management goals and evaluate the vast array of products and product combinations, any of which may increase or decrease an organization's overall exposure to risk—both economic and legal. It does so by providing information about the costs, benefits, legalities, and likely effectiveness of different alternative strategies. In many instances, functionally equivalent products can be used to implement different strategies. Conversely, functionally distinct products can be used to implement the same strategies.

Generally, knowledge about the functional characteristics—that is, the economic risks and returns—of specific products and product combinations provides the basis not only for comparing derivatives strategies but also for comparing derivatives with alternative strategies not involving derivatives. As an illustration, consider a hypothetical Japanese automobile manufacturer, with its manufacturing facilities in Japan, during the seemingly unstoppable rise of the U.S. dollar in the first half of the 1980s.*

To date, the dollar's climb against the Japanese yen has greatly aided the company's competitive strategy by enabling the company constantly to lower its U.S. car prices (the bulk of its sales) and thereby capture U.S. market share. The ever-strengthening value of the dollar is driving down the company's yen-denominated labor costs compared with those of U.S.-based manufacturers. However, senior management has grown concerned that the dollar's rise is not sustainable and may soon begin to reverse. Management is therefore seeking to reduce the company's massive currency risk. Senior management makes the following comparison of available derivative products and product combinations with other available business alternatives prior to making any business decision. In effect, it conducts a functional analysis.

---

*For discussion purposes, this illustration makes the assumption that the major determinant of the company's production cost advantage over its U.S. rivals is its lower costs of labor. The assumption is somewhat artificial, because Japanese car makers during that time period imported a host of raw materials from the United States. Therefore, the rise of materials' costs would have constituted a countervailing force offsetting to some extent labor cost advantages attributable to the weakening yen.

Derivatives Solution

Under consideration is entering into either a series of dollar/yen currency swaps or purchasing comparable currency *swaptions* (i.e., options to enter into, in this case, currency swaps). However, in management's view, the all-in costs of those transactions are still somewhat unfavorable, because of the novelty of the transactions. Moreover, swaps and swaption markets, still in their infancy, are insufficiently deep; no one is offering products that are adequately long-term to provide the company with the protection it seeks for a meaningful time period. Also, the Japanese company is having significant difficulty projecting U.S.-based car sales, owing to uncertainties about the future of the U.S. economy. Finally, though the company's treasurer is well versed in foreign exchange trading and anxious to enter into the swaps market, senior management is not yet comfortable with the new products, and it is concerned that none of its Japanese competitors appear to be using them.

Nonderivatives Alternative

A nonderivatives approach to hedge the company's long-term currency exposure is to build a manufacturing facility in the United States, creating a *natural hedge*. By shifting manufacturing operations to the United States, the company will match the currency of its labor costs with the currency of its U.S. revenues. However, the costs to the company are many. First, the company incurs the large initial cost of building a U.S. plant. Next, it has created a threat to Japanese employee morale by raising the prospective loss of, or at least the reduced increase in, jobs available to Japanese workers. Finally, the company is in effect forfeiting the possibility of any future strengthening of the U.S. dollar, arguably putting itself at a competitive disadvantage compared with other *Japanese* automobile exporters that have operations located in Japan.*

Alternative Means Summary

The preceding illustration demonstrates a set of circumstances under which a company may choose to use a natural rather than a derivatives hedge. Had the decision been made several years later, as currency deriv-

---

*The U.S. dollar appreciated by about 50% during the first half of the 1980s, only to retreat back to its original starting point by 1988. See Froot et al., *Risk Management Framework, supra,* note 2: 91.

atives grew to become both less expensive and well-understood plain vanilla transactions, the risks of which were quite easily manageable, the company's evaluation would have been different, whether or not the ultimate result was the same.

STRATEGIC IMPERATIVE: FIT AND SUSTAINABILITY OF COMPETITIVE ADVANTAGE

By assisting firm and portfolios in the management of inescapable but unwanted risks, derivatives hold the promise of providing many users with what Porter calls a "strategic fit." "Strategic fit among many activities is fundamental not only to competitive advantage but also to the sustainability of that advantage....Positions built on systems of [interlocked] activities are far more sustainable than those built on individual activities."[26]

For most businesses, strategic fit necessitates management of exposures to interest rates, exchange rates, and other volatile asset prices. During the seemingly unending string of massive derivatives losses in early 1994, Alan Greenspan defended derivatives activities in his House of Representatives testimony* by explaining that derivatives were being actively used by many financial and nonfinancial entities, including federally sponsored agencies and state and local governments, which "have concluded that active management of their interest rate, exchange rate, and other financial market risks is essential. They recognize that *such risks, if left unmanaged, can jeopardize their ability to perform their primary economic functions successfully.*"[27] In terms of Porter's analysis, Greenspan's statements suggest that active risk management using derivatives is in many cases necessary to sustain the effective performance of a business's primary mission. Unquestionably, risk management is an essential activity for virtually every business in today's economy. To achieve competitive viability, a business must integrate risk management into its entire system of business and ivestment activities. Derivatives are an effective means of doing precisely that.

---

*Greenspan also noted: "[I]t would be wrong to draw sweeping conclusions from these events [i.e., derivatives losses]. Changes in interest rates and other market variables necessarily affect the fortunes of individual economic units. Many entities undoubtedly decreased their vulnerability through use of derivatives, and many others that elected not to use derivatives undoubtedly suffered losses."

Waves of adverse derivatives headlines in recent years have obscured the surge in the use of derivatives by nonfinancial organizations to advance corporate strategies. These organizations use derivatives to isolate and manage various financial risks, freeing them to concentrate their resources, including managerial talents, on activities in which those organizations enjoy competitive advantages.

COMPETITIVE STRATEGY: USING DERIVATIVES TO SOLVE OTHER PARTIES' PROBLEMS

In a *Harvard Business Review* article, Tufano offers several intriguing examples of the creative use of financial engineering by successful businesses to help build "long-term relationships with customers, suppliers, employees, and shareholders."[28] He highlights five corporations that faced well-defined strategic objectives in their core businesses, which involved the production and marketing of gas, electricity, chemicals, cement, and oil. In each case, traditional means of achieving the stated objectives seemed unsatisfactory, because they imposed costs or risks considered unacceptable by the parties with which the businesses sought to enter into long-term relationships. The leaders of those business needed "to act quickly to ensure that short-term obstacles [would] not disrupt their long-term strategies." Yet in so doing, the companies would either have to absorb or manage those risks themselves or pay others to do so. To determine the optimal means of managing those risks, the companies turned to "the concepts, tools, and markets of financial engineers." Those businesses used innovative solutions to further their strategic objectives by assisting their customers, employees, and counterparties in shedding unwanted risks.

The following is an abstract of one of the five case studies—Enron Capital & Trade Resources (Enron)—described by Tufano and examined in greater detail in *Financial Engineering*; also included is a synopsis of a second transaction, the Viacom/Blockbuster deal, described in greater detail in the January 1996 issue of *Institutional Investor.*

Enron

In commodity markets, the only way to compete successfully long term is to be a least-cost producer or to differentiate one's product. Methane gas, the heart of Enron's business, is a simple commodity tough to differentiate; by the late 1980s, methane producers were suffering from tremendous price volatility and supply shortages, thus making least-cost production competition perilous. In this volatile market, Enron's management identified customer concerns about "reliable delivery and predictable prices" as competitive factors. Enron used financial engineering to *redefine* its business by transforming the company into a "gas bank"—or, more accurately, a gas derivatives dealer. Enron invested heavily in sophisticated risk management systems and highly trained personnel, and the company began successfully offering customers "a variety of derivative products, including natural gas swaps, caps, floors, collars, swaptions[,] forwards, and other structured risk-management products."

Viacom

Viacom used an equity-derivatives play to acquire Blockbuster Entertainment. Viacom's initial $69-a-share cash/stock offer was unsuccessful. An offeror's share price often declines once its offer is announced, whereas the target's share price usually increases. Thus, an acquiror's use of its own equity ordinarily depresses that equity's price, diminishing the attractiveness of the offer. Viacom eventually enhanced its offer to include $20 worth of "Viacom warrants, debentures, and equity derivatives called contingent value rights [CVRs]." According to *Institutional Investor,* the CVRs were designed so that their value would move inversely to movements in the market price of Viacom's stock. Thus, Blockbuster's shareholders obtained significant price protection, while Viacom capped its purchase price. Viacom's bid prevailed.

Strategic Use Summary

Through financial and legal engineering, derivatives are quickly, though with little public fanfare, becoming integrated into the basic business and investment strategies of many major corporations and other businesses. Firms and portfolios are using derivatives directly to solve their own complex and vexing business problems. Many businesses are also using them indirectly to solve the business problems of *other parties* as part of those businesses' long-term strategies. The economic problems to which derivatives solutions are being applied are no longer narrowly defined financial issues, such as "shaving a few basis points off financing costs or shedding transaction exposures arising from sales abroad"; rather, they are far broader issues of corporate competitive strategy. As Tufano asserts, "the failure to appreciate their [derivatives'] true competitive value can be shortsighted and ultimately hazardous."*

ENDNOTES: CHAPTER 4

1. See Greenspan, *Statement Before Congress, supra,* Chapter 1, note 25: 594.
2. Kenneth A. Froot, David S. Scharfstein, and Jeremy C. Stein, "A Framework for Risk Management," *Harvard Business Review* (November–December 1994) [hereafter, *Risk Management Framework*]: 91–102.
3. Greenspan, *Statement Before Congress, supra,* Chapter 1, note 25: 600.
4. See Merton, *Financial Innovation, supra,* Chapter 1, note 15: 17; Mason et al., *Financial Engineering, supra,* Chapter 1, note 2: 8.
5. Froot et al., *Risk Management Framework, supra,* note 2: 92.
6. All quotations in this paragraph are from Porter, *What Is Strategy? supra* Chapter 3, note 2.
7. See *G-30 Overview*: 35–38.
8. Hu, *Hedging Expectations, supra,* Chapter 2, note 37: 1025.
9. Chance, *Introduction to Derivatives, supra,* Chapter 3, note 6:11 (emphasis omitted); see also Dwight R. Lee and James A. Verbrugge, "The Efficient Market Theory Thrives on Criticism," *Journal of Applied Corporate Finance,* 9(1) (Spring 1996): 35–40.
10. See, generally, Alan L. Tucker, Ph.D., *Financial Futures, Options, and Swaps* (West Publishing Company, 1991) [hereafter, *Financial Futures*]: 4–5. Similar historical information can be obtained directly from the CBOT's Internet site (http://www.cbot.com).
11. See, generally, Working, "New Concepts Concerning Futures Markets and Prices" [hereafter, *New Concepts Concerning Futures Markets*], in Peck, *Selected Writings of Holbrook Working, supra,* Chapter 1, note 3; Working, *Economic Functions of Futures markets, supra,* Chapter 1, note 4: 293.
12. See Holbrook Working, "Price Effects of Scalping and Day Trading," in Peck, *Selected Writings of Holbrook Working, supra,* Chapter 1, note 3: 181–194.

---

*See Tufano, *Advancing Corporate Strategy, supra,* Chapter 2, note 17: 137. Several other informative books, studies, surveys, and articles focus on creative, strategic applications of derivatives and the techniques of financial engineering, rather than on the use of the products to speculate in capital markets. *Financial Engineering* provides dozens of case studies documenting the use of financial engineering techniques by many well-known organizations and public sector entities. The Economist Intelligence Unit has published a study entitled *Strategic Derivatives: Successful Corporate Practices for Today's Global Marketplace* (sponsored by Bankers Trust and Coopers & Lybrand, L.L.P.). *Institutional Investor* and other magazines such as *Global Finance* have been spotlighting early each year the prior year's most successful derivatives deals.

13. *Merrill Lynch, Pierce, Fenner & Smith v. Curran,* 456 U.S. 353, 358–360, 72 L.Ed. 2d 182, 188–190, 102 S.Ct. 1825 (1982) (footnotes omitted; emphasis added) [hereafter, *Curran*].

14. See Froot et al., *Risk Management Framework, supra,* note 2: 98.

15. Don M. Chance, "Derivatives Disclosure," *Derivatives Research Unincorporated,* 2(6) (formerly available on the Internet, http://www.vt.edu:10021/business/finance/dmc/DRU/-contents.html) April 22, 1996 [hereafter, *Disclosure*]. Paragraph reprinted with permission.

16. See Froot et al., *Risk Management Framework, supra,* note 2: 101.

17. For a general description of equity derivatives, see Mary L. Harmon and Daniel P. Breen, "The Changing World of Equity Derivatives," in *Tax Strategies for Corporate Acquisitions, Dispositions, Spin-offs, Joint Ventures, Financings, Reorganizations and Restructurings* (Practising Law Institute, 1996) [hereafter, *Equity Derivatives*].

18. Robert Clow, "Beyond the Scarlet Ledger," *Institutional Investor* (February 1998): 53.

19. See, generally, "Proposals by the Securities and Exchange Commission and the Financial Accounting Standards Board for the Accounting Treatment of Financial Derivatives," *Report of the Subcommittee on Securities* (April 21, 1997).

20. See Michael H. Sutton, "Dangerous Ideas: A Sequel," [Personal] Remarks by Michael H. Sutton, Chief Accountant, Office of the Chief Accountant, U.S. Securities and Exchange Commission, to the 1997 Annual Meeting of the American Accounting Association (August 18, 1997).

21. See, generally, Thomas J. O'Brien, "Accounting Versus Economic Exposure to Currency Risk," *Journal of Financial Statement Analysis* (Summer 1997): 21–29; Mark J. P. Anson, "Accounting for Derivatives Part II: New Rules from FASB," *Derivatives Quarterly,* 4(2) (Winter 1997); George J. Benston, "Accounting for Derivatives: Back to Basics," *Journal of Applied Corporate Finance,* 10(3) (Fall 1997): 46–58.

22. All quotations in this paragraph and the next are from Mason et al., *Financial Engineering, supra,* Chapter 1, note 2 (emphasis in original): 8; *see also* Merton, *Financial Innovation, supra,* Chapter 1, note 15: 17.

23. Hu, *Hedging Expectations, supra,* Chapter 2, note 37: 1016.

24. Peter L. Bernstein, *Capital Ideas: The Improbable Origins of Modern Wall Street* (The Free Press, 1992) [herein, *Capital Ideas*]: 54.

25. Both quotations in this paragraph are from Mason et al., *Financial Engineering, supra,* Chapter 1, note 2: 9.

26. Porter, *What Is Strategy? supra,* Chapter 3, note 2: 73.

27. All quotations in this paragraph are from Greenspan, *Statement Before Congress, supra,* Chapter 1, note 25: 594–595.

28. Tufano, *Advancing Corporate Strategy, supra,* Chapter 2, note 17: 136.

CHAPTER 5

Legal Risk:
A Functional Analysis

Imbalances between derivative-product innovation and the evolution of
the infrastructure to support it are inevitable.

Robert C. Merton
Harvard University, 1996[1]

Contract risk is an area in which the law tends to lag behind the
innovations in derivatives and the complexity of financial markets.

Maarten Nederlof
Capital Market Risk Advisors, Inc.,
October 1995

The functional characteristics of individual products and product combinations result in legal risks that are different in kind from their economic
risks. Economic risks can, in theory, be quantified and objectively measured, although the choice and applicability of any given qualitative
methodology is often the subject of lively debate. In contrast, legal risks
"do not readily lend themselves to measurement."[2] They are qualitative
rather than quantitative. Nevertheless, legal risks are no less real than their
quantitative counterparts.

Any well-designed risk management system must adequately
address legal risks. In addition, the system's legal risk controls must "fit"
into the organization's overall competitive strategy. This chapter continues the functional analysis of derivatives risks by providing a framework
for analyzing the main categories, or "building blocks," of derivatives
legal risks.

"LEGAL RISK"—TRADITIONAL
DEFINITION

The *G-30 Overview* summarizes the prevailing definition of legal risk
used in OTC derivatives markets as follows:

> Legal risk is the risk of loss because a contract cannot be enforced. This
> includes risks arising from insufficient documentation, insufficient capac-
> ity or authority of a counterparty (*ultra vires*), uncertain legality, and unen-
> forceability in bankruptcy or insolvency.
>
> Although financial institutions have encountered these legal risks in
> their traditional lending and trading purposes, the risks come in new forms
> with derivatives.[3]

127

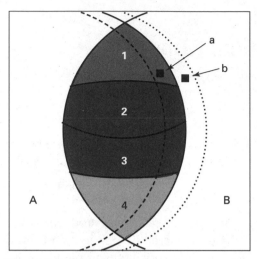

Figure 5.1   Uncertain legality.

The foregoing definition of legal unenforceability risk can be depicted using the portion of Figure 4.1 reproduced above as Figure 5.1. Uncertainty as to the location of the border of Circle A creates uncertainty as to the enforceability of transactions that lie near the border. A transaction located at point a, for example, would be considered enforceable, whereas a similar transaction located at point b would be considered unenforceable.

The *G-30 Report* observes: "In the early days of derivatives, lawyers confronted a host of issues (e.g., corporate, constitutional, tax, regulatory) that were beyond the scope of existing laws and regulations."[4] Many of the early enforceability concerns have been resolved, providing greater legal certainty as to many transactions. Nevertheless, "there remain issues related to the enforceability of over-the-counter (OTC) derivatives transactions that need to be clarified to provide the requisite legal framework for these growing activities."

The *G-30 Enforceability Working Paper* identified several main enforceability risks that present the most serious counterparty concerns at different transaction stages. A major theme underlying these concerns is that a counterparty, or its trustee or receiver in bankruptcy or insolvency, might assert various legal deficiencies either as legitimate justifications or as pretexts for disaffirming or rejecting transactions constituting large losses. Led by fears about the "systemic risks" posed by potential dealer insolvencies, many regulators and industry groups have focused in detail on the hazards to dealers posed by enforceability risks.

To date, however, there has been little discussion of the potential impact of these enforceability concerns on end users. The reason is likely that although the great bulk of derivatives activity is concentrated at a handful of dealer institutions, few if any derivatives end users have large enough portfolios to warrant serious systemic concerns to the financial system. For example, whereas Chemical Bank (before its merger with Chase Manhattan Corp.) had a $3.2 trillion derivatives portfolio at the end of 1994, the largest portfolio among industrial companies was that of Ford Motor Co.—$66.4 billon, or approximately one-fiftieth the size of Chemical's portfolio.[5] Notwithstanding the lack of specific focus on the impact of enforceability issues on end users, all market participants should consider these issues carefully for several reasons.

First, as discussed earlier, derivatives provide an efficient and cost-effective tool for managing many financial risks to which end users may choose to limit their exposure. The growing awareness of senior management, investors, and regulators of the potential benefits of derivatives, when used properly, is rapidly transforming derivatives usage for many organizations from a competitive advantage into a competitive necessity. The advantages of derivatives in "lowering hedging costs...facilitating risk transfer, [and] providing opportunities to enhance returns...[mean that] those who neglect the new technology run the risk of losing out to those who exploit it."[6]

Consequently, many current and potential end users have a competitive need for ongoing and effective access to OTC derivatives markets. A dealer that asserts legal technicalities as a basis for avoiding large losses would imperil the dealer's reputation and jeopardize its ability to maintain a profitable derivatives business. Similarly, an end user's attempt to renege on large losses could undermine its reputation, thus greatly restricting its access, or increasing the cost of its continuing access, to OTC derivatives markets.

Second, many of the most troubling enforceability concerns arise upon a counterparty's bankruptcy or insolvency. In the 1980s, during the early stages of the OTC markets, derivatives dealers tended to enjoy superior credit ratings to most of their end user counterparties. Those writings enabled end users comfortably to ignore seemingly minimal dealer bankruptcy or insolvency default risk. Since the late 1980s, many large dealers have suffered materially adverse credit events, as well as rating downgrades. It is no longer uncommon for an end user to carry an equal or higher credit rating than its dealer counterparty. There is now little reason to assume that a potential counterparty bankruptcy or insolvency is any less of a concern to users than to dealers. Accordingly, well-advised derivatives users incorporate general counterparty risk limits into their internal controls. This has rapidly become a standard, widely recommended practice for all market participants.

Third, the documentation process resolves many enforceability concerns. An end user must provide in its agreements representations and warranties as to its contractual and regulatory status and other significant matters. Material inaccuracies in those representations and warranties may constitute events of default entitling a dealer to exercise contractual early termination rights and "close out" all transactions with the defaulting counterparty, as well as to apply any collateral held by the dealer toward net amounts owed to it. In extreme (though today far less common) cases, dealers have the contractual right upon default simply to "walk away" from a contractual arrangement under which the dealer is a net obligor. A full understanding of the nature of enforceability risks resolves many problematic representation and warranty issues.

MAIN ENFORCEABILITY CONCERNS

Contract Formation: Statute of Frauds

The effective functioning of high-speed OTC derivatives markets depends on the ability of market participants quickly and confidently to enter into binding transactions. Fast execution is needed because of the acute sensitivity of many product prices even to minor market moves. As one swaps specialist commented in a 1984 *Harvard Business Review* article, describing market practices: "An interest rate swap is normally executed on the telephone and may begin to accrue immediately. The two parties sign a legal contract that governs the exchange of cash flows at a later date."[7] In that respect, market practices have not changed much since 1984. OTC derivatives markets, especially for plain vanilla transactions, continue to be dominated by telephonic transaction execution (although many efforts are under way to develop real-time, screen-based markets).

Telephonic transaction execution gives rise to two risks. First, any agreement executed telephonically is necessarily incomplete. The most that is expected to be achieved by telephone is agreement on a transaction's principal economic terms, "together with any requirements for credit support (e.g., collateral, letter of credit or guarantee)."[8] Second, even as to those terms, there can be substantial uncertainty as to whether the parties have in fact clearly reached agreement. There is an ever-present danger of miscommunication and resulting lack of a true "meeting of the minds."*

Typically, formal legal documentation manages the risks of incomplete agreements and imprecise identification of principal terms. However, the speed and volume of OTC derivatives transactions can give rise to serious delays in the preparation, negotiation, and execution of final legal documentation. During the period between reaching telephonic agreement and finalizing documentation, some uncertainty as to the parties' intentions and the content of their agreement is inevitable. In the event of an intervening market movement, there is always a risk that the party adversely affected may dispute a transaction's terms in an effort to disavow it socalled buyer's or sellers remorse.

The uncertainty persisting in documentation delays can be significant, particularly in times of market turmoil. Although documentation practices have improved dramatically in recent years, significant "backlogs" have persisted throughout the growth of modern OTC derivatives markets. Even simple transaction confirmations, which are intended to be transmitted promptly after a telephonic agreement has been concluded, are often negotiated over for lengthy time periods and so cannot completely eliminate the uncertainty of documentation delays. Moreover, confirmations are limited to the major economic terms of a transaction; they relegate to other agreements the remainder of the terms of the relevant counterparties' contractual relationship.

> Although most parties intend the initial exchanges of terms letters or telexes and confirmations to constitute binding agreements, these initial agreements typically do not contain all the noneconomic provisions that most parties require for arrangements that may last as long as 10 to 15 years. For example, the confirmation letter or telex often does not include provisions covering representations and warranties, covenants, events of default, liquidated damages, assignment, judgment currency, consent to jurisdiction and closing documents.[9]

---

*Screen-based transaction execution may greatly reduce ambiguities as to the precise principal economic terms of any agreement. However, screen-based technologies introduce their own problems, such as the need for instantaneous delivery of messages and the possibility of inaccurate routing.

Thus, the issue arises as to whether, under the applicable governing law, "an oral agreement made prior to a signed writing represent[s] a binding contract."[10]

Under the law of many jurisdictions, such as England, France, Germany, and the Canadian provinces of British Columbia and Quebec, no particular form of agreement is necessary to constitute a binding agreement. Therefore, oral agreements governed by the laws of those jurisdictions are generally binding. However, in other important jurisdictions there are dangerous gaps in the law governing oral transactions. The "statute of frauds" contained in the contract law of many jurisdictions resolves uncertainties inherent in significant oral agreements—generally those either not performable within one year or involving monetary amounts exceeding a minimum threshold*—by requiring that the agreements be evidenced by a note or memorandum in writing signed by the party to be charged (or its authorized agent).

New York's solution: end user caution

Major gaps in New York law have been filled, although the solution continues to warrant counterparties' careful consideration. On September 18, 1994, New York amended its statute of frauds[11] to provide greater certainty of enforceability for telephonically and electronically concluded "qualified financial contracts." The qualified financial contract definition covers most core OTC derivatives and, in effect, states that contracts will not be void for lack of a writing, if (1) there is "sufficient evidence" that a contract was made (including electronic communications by means of telephone recordings or computer output) *or* (2) the parties have agreed to be bound by the qualified financial contract from the time they reach agreement on it, whether by telephone, exchange of electronic messages (including telexes, telefacsimiles, and other electronic messages), or otherwise. Under the amendment, the terms of a confirmation *actually or constructively* received within *five business days* (or such longer time as

---

*$500 is the applicable threshold under the Uniform Commercial Code applicable to sales of goods. And foreign exchange contracts, in which currencies are treated as goods, are subject to the Uniform Commercial Code. See *Intershoe Inc. v. Bankers Trust,* 77 N.Y.2d 517, 521 (1991). "The *Intershoe* decision suggests that other derivatives products that could be deemed to involve the 'sale' of a 'good,' such as currency and cross-currency swaps, also may be subject to the statute of frauds requirement in Article 2 of the UCC." See Cunningham et al., *OTC Derivatives, supra,* Chapter 1, note 11· 286–287.

the parties may have agreed in writing) of a trade are binding if the counterparty does not object within *three business days of such receipt.**

English or New York law governs the vast majority of OTC derivatives contracts. Therefore, most OTC derivatives contracts entered into telephonically are immediately enforceable. Market participants must recognize that the *failure promptly to discover and object to an error* in a confirmation governed by New York law will, absent a provable agreement to the contrary, cause them to be bound by that error.

Many counterparties seldom respond within three business days to confirmations received from their dealers, who almost always prepare the initial confirmations. In addition, "[i]t is not unheard of for a market participant to discover after the fact [sometimes long after the fact] that the signed confirmation of a swap does not correctly reflect its understanding of what the parties agreed."[12] That may expose the end user to unexpected legal liability, or possibly leave it with unenforceable gains, if the terms of a confirmation contained in the version sent by the dealer are incorrect. Counterparties are under no legal obligation to renegotiate "incorrect" terms. Many dealers strongly resist later requests to renegotiate terms on which they have relied in hedging their own exposures.

Capacity

Transactions involving corporations and financial institutions seldom give rise to capacity issues. However, for many other end users, capacity issues have emerged as chief dealer concerns. Capacity issues predated the large derivatives losses that commenced in 1993 and accelerated in frequency in 1994. In the preceding decade, almost half of all OTC derivatives "default losses" were due to a single judicial decision. It was the 1991 U.K. House of Lords decision in the case commonly known as *Hammersmith and Fulham,* "which held that English local authorities did not have the capacity to enter swap and other derivatives transactions."[13] In July 1993 the *G-30 Enforceability Working Paper* noted:

> As a result of the *Hammersmith and Fulham* decision, dealers have become cautious about entering into swaps and other derivatives with governmental entities in jurisdictions where these entities' capacity to enter into the transactions in question is not clearly set forth in statute....
>
> Dealers were also asked the extent of their concern with respect to vari-

---

*Unless the parties otherwise agree, however, the burden of proving receipt is on the sender.

ous counterparties. The entities causing "serious concern" are municipalities (41%), followed by sovereigns (10%), and pension funds (9%). The three entities most commonly causing "some concern" are unit trusts, pension funds, and insurance companies.

Since the *G-30 Report* was released, concerns regarding the capacity of many market participants to engage in OTC derivatives transactions have intensified. Numerous pension funds, municipalities, other public sector entities, charitable institutions, mutual funds, and other noncorporate users have suffered massive derivatives losses. In many cases, losing parties have attempted to disavow the losses by claiming that they lacked the requisite capacity to enter into the transactions. Dealers are, therefore, often understandably reluctant to engage in OTC derivatives with many noncorporate, nonfinancial institution end users without receiving satisfactory legal assurances that those end users have the capacity to engage in the subject transactions. Often, such assurances take the form of legal opinions confirming that specific transactions are expressly within the end user's capacity and have been duly authorized. Related opinion issues can become more complex as transaction types become increasingly customized and specialized to fit a particular firm or portfolio's needs.

Capacity issues are determined by reference to the organic documents and law governing the organization of the relevant party:

> The power of an entity to enter into a transaction generally flows from its charter and by-laws or, in some cases, the special organic law under which it was created. Where sovereigns and public-sector entities are concerned, a local or national constitution may also be relevant, or a charter or statute, in the case of a public corporation, and, where trusts are involved, the deed of trust will be the source of power.[14]

When an end user's capacity to engage in OTC derivatives is not immediately obvious, based on a review of the foregoing sources, noncorporate, nonfinancial institution counterparties often confront serious impediments to engaging in those transactions.

Early Termination: Bankruptcy and Insolvency

Early termination due to either bankruptcy or insolvency formerly created another area of significant legal concern. Most of that concern has been greatly minimized since the passage, beginning in 1990, of corrective legislation in the United States and many other countries where major financial centers are located. Nevertheless, the lessons of functional analysis and the effects of the "financial innovation spiral" suggest that issues still exist and additional issues are likely to arise. The *G-30 Enforceability Working Paper* notes:

> In dealing with a counterparty organized in the United States, participants in the derivatives market once faced an element of uncertainty in assessing the bankruptcy and insolvency risks involved. The risks could vary depending upon the type of counterparty—bank, savings institution, or corporation—with which one was dealing, since each was subject to a separate set of laws and regulations.
>
> The most significant area of concern was that, in a proceeding under the U.S. Bankruptcy Code, termination rights under master swap agreements were subject to an automatic stay.[15]

The automatic stay formerly raised serious concerns over the ability of a nondefaulting counterparty to enforce early termination rights, closeout netting provisions, rights against collateral, and related contractual rights that arise upon bankruptcy or insolvency.

In the late 1980s, fears heightened that prior to receiving relief from the automatic stay—which often involves lengthy proceedings—a nondefaulting party would be exposed to substantial market risk. More important, however, was the risk that bankruptcy and insolvency rules might permit a trustee or receiver to "cherry pick" a portfolio—in other words, it might reject all of an insolvent counterparty's out-of-the-money contracts while simultaneously accepting, or continuing in force, all of its in-the-money contracts. Cherry picking could cause severe losses, because nondefaulting parties would have to continue making full payments on losing trades while receiving only a claim in bankruptcy for offsetting gains.

Amendments to bankruptcy and insolvency laws have mitigated such concerns on the enforceability of important contractual rights. Nevertheless, for several reasons every counterparty's senior management and its counsel should familiarize himself or herself with applicable bankruptcy and insolvency issues.

First, the intricate definition-driven treatment of swaps and other OTC derivatives under most bankruptcy and insolvency regimes is significantly different from that of many other types of commercial contracts. Given their complexity, bankruptcy and insolvency rules often engender confusion. Therefore, notwithstanding the analytical density, the amendments do provide an essential degree of certainty as to a number of products and institutions.

Second, although many jurisdictions have adopted express legislation resolving these issues, others have not. An end user should be aware of the effects of applicable bankruptcy and insolvency regimes on the enforceability of its documentation on counterparties organized in Spain, Portugal, Italy, and other non-U.S. jurisdictions as to which bankruptcy and insolvency concerns persist. Industry trades groups, primarily ISDA, have obtained legal opinions that provide significant comfort as to the bankruptcy and insolvency laws of many important countries. Nevertheless, all counterparties should study those opinions and consider, if warranted, establishing credit limits for firms organized in countries under which applicable bankruptcy and insolvency laws do not fully and clearly recognize early termination rights, closeout netting, or rights against collateral. They should also avoid, or lower exposure limits for, particular products as to which legal assurances cannot be obtained.

Third, bankruptcy and insolvency concerns are particularly important with regard to the highly rated derivative products subsidiaries through which many major financial institutions conduct their OTC derivatives businesses. These "bankruptcy remote" structures can be controversial. An understanding of bankruptcy and insolvency rules can help an end user evaluate the merits of alternative structures and dealer counterparties.

Fourth, although there are few recognized difficulties regarding the applicability of U.S. bankruptcy and insolvency rules to currently offered products and existing institutions, uncertainties persist. ISDA and the Public Securities Association (PSA) (PSA has changed its name to The Bond Market Association) in April 1996 jointly released a position paper (1996 Position Paper), directing attention to various inconsistencies in U.S. insolvency regimes that warrant legislative correction. The 1996 Position Paper notes:

> Because the applicable provisions of the Bankruptcy Code were incorporated piecemeal, in an entity by entity and product by product fashion, they at times seem to distinguish arbitrarily between similarly situated creditors and similar types of transactions. The policy rationale supporting broad termination and setoff rights, which is to ensure the efficient functioning of the marketplace, particularly in times of market stress, applies equally to similarly situated creditors and products.[16]

One important question the 1996 Position Paper raises is the extent to which inconsistencies among legislation will "taint" cross-product netting contemplated under master agreements. *Cross-product netting* refers to the process of combining and offsetting gains and losses between particular counterparties over a range of different instruments, so long as the instruments are all governed by the same master agreement. The 1996 Position Paper poses the following unsettling question:

> [A]ssume that a counterparty enters into a forward foreign exchange transaction, which is clearly a "swap agreement" under the Bankruptcy Code, and a cash-settled equity option, which is a "securities contract" under an ISDA Master Agreement. The ISDA Master Agreement provides that all transactions thereunder constitute a "single agreement." The question becomes whether it is a single swap agreement or a singly, potentially unprotected swap/securities agreement contract.

Similarly, different statutory treatments of "securities contracts" and "swaps" may lead to unintended and unexpected results as to transactions between certain types of OTC derivatives counterparties:

> Upon commencement of a bankruptcy proceeding, Counterparty may terminate the swap pursuant to Section 560 of the Bankruptcy Code, but will be unable to liquidate the securities contract if it is not a stockbroker, financial institution, or securities clearing agency. If, however, Counterparty is a bank (and thus a "financial institution"), it would be able to terminate both contracts.

Fifth, as Merton explains, "[t]he standard mode of analysis for financial regulatory policy is still the institutional approach."[17] That applies equally to bankruptcy and insolvency rules. Although recent amendments to applicable legislation have at least temporarily minimized the number and importance of most issues, functional analysis suggests that over time the lines between various institutions, products, markets, and services are "likely to become less distinct."

Institutional and product definitions, supplemented by products lists, largely form the basis for current legislation. Although the definitions and lists are extensive, arguably exhaustive for present purposes, one of the goals of financial engineering is to create innovative and new institutions and products. The power of financial engineering and the drive of Merton's "financial innovation spiral" dictate that markets, products, and market participants will constantly change, leading to constant uncertainty.

Sixth, there is significant uncertainty regarding the likely treatment of multibranch netting provisions under applicable bankruptcy and insolvency laws of many jurisdictions. The *G-30 Enforceability Working Paper* notes:

Banks use multibranch master agreements to "book" individual derivatives transactions through any branch designated in the agreement. The use of such master agreements involves a netting issue that has not received sufficient attention from participants and regulators: whether upon the insolvency of a counterparty, parties to a multibranch master agreement can terminate that agreement and net across branches to achieve one net amount owed by or to a counterparty.[18]

The difficulty with multibranch netting agreements is that they affect the assets of branches and agencies that local administrators may have a distinct interest in preserving for the benefit of local depositors. *Ringfencing* occurs when a local administrator disallows netting across branches (including head offices). The problem arises if the derivatives transactions booked at a local branch show a net profit due to that branch. In that case, "the local administrator might consider [that profit] as a net asset for paying off local depositors....If this happens, the local branch's counterparty might be required to pay the profit to the local branch."[19] Yet if the multibranch netting agreement is enforced in a different jurisdiction, the counterparty adversely affected by the local administrator's actions is unlikely to receive credit for any lost netting benefits. The ringfencing problem is, in some respects, analogous to cherry picking, although it occurs at the level of cherry picking among branches, rather than among contracts.

New York State enacted legislation in July 1993 designed, among other things, to recognize the enforceability of contractual multibranch netting rights against New York branches and agencies of non-U.S. banking institutions. That legislation was the "first step toward the global recognition of the legal enforceability of multibranch netting agreements."[20] ISDA has obtained a number of legal opinions, particularly from G-10 countries (which now include Belgium, Canada, England, France, Germany, Italy, Japan, Luxembourg, the Netherlands, Sweden, Switzerland, and the United States). "Altogether, ISDA has obtained 31 netting opinions, 28 of which conclude that bilateral and multibranch close-out netting would be enforceable under a[n]...ISDA Master Agreement governed by New York or English law, with the exception of Italy, Spain, and Portugal."[21]

Legality/Enforceability of OTC Derivatives

The final enforceability risk discussed in the *G-30 Enforceability Working Paper* consists of a number of related concerns, such as gaming, wagering, and gambling prohibitions, as well as an increasingly important force majeure issue raised by the prospect of a potential European Monetary Union.

Gaming, etc.

The *Working Paper* noted in 1993 that "Brazil, Canada, Japan, and Singapore each indicates that issues exist whether swaps or other derivatives transactions could be deemed gambling contracts, and thus illegal or unenforceable." Similar concerns exist under the laws of Australia. In the United States, specifically in New York, three types of statutes "bear on the legality issue with respect to gambling....There once was a risk that a court might use one of these three statutes to invalidate a swap agreement; however, the exemptions from the Commodity Exchange Act provided to swap agreements and hybrid instruments [both of which are discussed below] substantially reduce this concern."[22]

Also, in the United States, "there was once the risk that all swap transactions with U.S. counterparties would be deemed off-exchange traded commodity futures contracts, which would have made them unenforceable." As discussed in Chapter 7, concerns in this regard persist, although they have been greatly minimized. Although most of the foregoing concerns relating to the enforceability of transactions with U.S. counterparties have been resolved, the resolution still raises matters that need to be addressed by transacting parties. Moreover, the process of resolving those concerns has not been without costs. The resulting legal uncertainties in the United States caused potentially important market segments and financial activities to relocate elsewhere, particularly to London and other major financial centers. The extent to which that process could easily repeat itself and may now be recurring, particularly in light of current litigation and regulatory initiatives, warrants further examination of the process.

1989 Swap Policy Statement:
swaps exemption

Prior to 1987, there was little serious concern among swaps market participants that the Commodity Exchange Act (CEA) or the attendant jurisdiction of the Commodity Futures Trading Commission (CFTC) might apply to swap contracts or options involving interest rates. However, the CFTC published in 1987 an Advance Notice of Proposed Rulemaking (Advance Notice) announcing its intention to assert jurisdiction "over virtually all hybrid instruments, with only limited exclusions or exemptions for hybrid instruments having '*de minimis*' or 'incidental' futures or commodity option features."[23]* Significantly, the Advance Notice also stated that the CFTC was considering jurisdiction over a wide range of swaps transactions.

> At the same time, the CFTC initiated certain investigations and enforcement proceedings against institutions that were beginning to engage in commodity price swap transactions. These actions had the effect of halting any development of a commodity price swap market in the U.S. and [they] forced U.S. institutions and others to shift the principal focus of this market to London and other financial centers.[24]

To alleviate market concerns caused by the Advance Notice and concurrent enforcement and related actions, in July 1989 the CFTC issued a policy statement (1989 Swap Policy Statement) creating a nonexclusive "safe harbor" exempting most interest rate and currency swaps from the exchange-trading requirements of the CEA.[25] However, the 1989 Swap Policy Statement could not, alone, offer sufficient comfort for swaps and related markets. Thus, on January 14, 1993, at the direction of Congress, the CFTC adopted regulations exempting swap agreements (as defined in Section 101 of the U.S. Bankruptcy Code) (Swaps Exemption) under the authority granted to it by the Futures Trading Practices Act of 1992 (FTPA).[26] The Swaps Exemption clarified and expanded the scope of the 1989 Swap Policy Statement's nonexclusive "safe harbor." In January 1993, the CFTC also issued a Hybrid Exemption under the authority granted by the FTPA, pursuant to which the CFTC exempted specified categories of hybrid instruments from most provisions of the CEA.[27]

To be eligible for the Swaps Exemption, a transaction must constitute a *"swap agreement...entered into solely between eligible swap participants."* (Emphasis added.) A "swap agreement" includes most currency and interest rate products, including options to enter into any of the foregoing, together with master agreements. An "eligible swap participant" includes most institutional investors, and it also covers individuals with "total assets exceeding at least $10,000,000."

---

*Hybrid instruments are financial instruments that, although styled as securities (usually, debt securities) or depository instruments, contain payment features that are "economically equivalent" to those of commodity futures or commodity options. As such, the parties may consider the instruments to be securities subject to state and federal securities laws or depository instruments subject to federal banking laws. Nevertheless, the CFTC may assert exclusive jurisdiction over the instruments if it finds that the value of the instruments is somehow based on futureslike or commodity optionlike components. See Chapter 7.

In addition, the Swaps Exemption seeks to ensure that exempted transactions do not function like futures contracts. Futures are highly standardized products that are traded on exchanges and that involve minimal credit risk. Therefore, for the exemption to apply, (1) the product must not be part of a "fungible class of agreements that are standardized as to their material economic terms," (2) the creditworthiness of the counterparty (or any guarantor or other obligor) must be a "material consideration" in determining whether to enter into the transaction, and (3) the product cannot be "entered into and traded on or through a multilateral transaction execution facility."

The Swaps Exemption contains a corresponding preemption of state gaming laws. It also preempts state "bucket shop" laws "adopted to protect the public against unscrupulous practices that involved taking orders for the purchase or sale of commodities or securities without actually effecting the transactions on an exchange or arranging for delivery. The orders were actually, or for all practical purposes, thrown in the 'bucket.'"[28]

The requirements for the applicability of the Swaps Exemption can generally be set forth in checklist form. However, difficulties will likely arise over time as new generations of products fit less and less clearly within the definitions of the precise parameters of the exemption. The financial innovation spiral suggests further difficulties, because the "migration" of successful products to organized trading markets does not necessarilymeans a migration to regulated exchanges.

Trade option exemption

In addition, the CFTC has adopted a "trade option" exemption (Trade Option Exemption) to protects off-exchange trading of commodity options under limited circumstances relating to the nature of the offeree. Specifically, the exemption is limited to a "producer, processor or commercial user," or a "merchant" who handles the underlying commodity and who enters into the transaction "solely for purposes related to its business as such." Although it may be easy to determine who is a producer, processor, or merchant, determining "commercial user" status is often difficult.

> The CFTC has provided little guidance concerning the business activities that qualify as "commercial uses" of a commodity for purposes of the trade option exemption, other than to indicate that "persons engaged in the occasional sale of commodities or their byproducts, who may be unsophisticated in the use of options," may not take advantage of the exemption. The pur-

pose of the requirement, the CFTC has indicated, is to ensure that offerees are experienced commercial enterprises.[29]

European Monetary Union (EMU)

The third stage of EMU, scheduled to commence January 1, 1999, raises a number of potential legal, accounting, tax, and financial issues. The third stage commences the planned introduction of a single currency–the "euro"– that will become the official currency of the 11 participating member countries, and will potentially affect payment flows involving any members former national currency. However, the number of countries that will eventually join the currency union is unclear. Some commentators believe the consequences of the euro could be dramatic not only for EMU participants but also for counterparties located in the United States. "Nearly 100 percent of all swap contracts between U.S. counterparties, irrespective of the currency in which the deal is made, are governed by New York law. Perhaps half of *all* derivatives contracts are governed by New York law....Consequently, New York law will have to be prepared to deal with the issues arising."[30]

Private industry groups have worked on both legislative and contractual solutions to what some consider to be a potential problem of frustration of contract that may result upon true unification. The problem purportedly arises, in effect, because the individual currencies involved will simply disappear, and be replaced by the euro." That may cause legal difficulties to the extent that derivatives contracts refer to payments in the disappearing currencies. The currencies themselves will be unavailable in a few years, and so will the availability of pricing from which payments can be determined. Some lawyers believe that if legislative solutions are not satisfactorily achieved, "there's serious potential for widespread disputes and litigation."[31] Therefore, an ISDA documentation task force has prepared an EMU provision that can be included in both existing and new master agreements involving the affected currencies:

> "By incorporating this new clause under your master agreements, you can mitigate the risk that the proposed single currency might lead to frustration of contracts," says ISDA chairwoman Gay Evans. Dealers will nonetheless have to get their counterparties to agree to the new language.

Although serious doubt exists as to the validity of the claim that the introduction of the euro may frustrate contracts calling for payments denominated in currencies that will disappear upon monetary union, New York has passed protective legislation dealing with the introduction of the euro. The legislation provides, in relevant part:

> If a subject or medium of payment of a contract, security or instrument is a currency that has been substituted or replaced by the euro, the euro will be a commercially reasonable substitute and substantial equivalent that may be either: (i) used in determining the value of such currency; or (ii) tendered, in each case at the conversion rate specified in, and otherwise calculated in accordance with, the regulations adopted by the council of the European Union.[32]

The reason for doubt as to the seriousness of the frustration issue is that in several cases courts have held that by selecting a foreign currency as a means of payment, the parties to a contract have intended to mean the currency of the country at the time the obligation becomes due. "This is the only logical solution. The idea that it would not be governed by the law of the currency...is absurd."[33]

"LEGAL RISK"—A FUNCTIONAL PERSPECTIVE

A functional analysis reveals that although the traditional definition of legal risk may be appropriate for certain purposes, without more, it provides an inadequate foundation on which to build a system of OTC derivatives legal risk management. Events of the past few years have demonstrated that the legal risks confronting an end user involve more than the risk that, because of legal deficiencies, an in the money contract might be deemed unenforceable. They also include at least the following five general categories of risks:

1. *Legal and compliance.* Legal and regulatory sanctions might be imposed on end users, particularly those in regulated industries, for failure to conform to statutorily mandated risk management practices.

2. *Fiduciary duties.* Directors of corporations generally have state law fiduciary duties to conform to "the standard dictates of corporate process: decisionmaking that is informed, careful documentation of the informed nature of the decisionmaking, and sound internal controls."[34] Normally, those duties are owed to a corporation's shareholders. However, important Delaware case law provides that when a corporation is insolvent or even "in the vicinity of insolvency,"[35] the directors' duties extend to a corporation's creditors. Similarly, other fiduciaries, such as trustees and many investment managers, owe fiduciary duties to investors and trust

beneficiaries. Generally, the use—conceivably even the nonuse—of derivatives can create risks of violations of fiduciary duties. In addition, the recent Delaware court's *Caremark* decision, discussed in Chapters 16 and 17, has thrown a new spotlight of directors' and officers' oversight responsibilities.

3. *Documentation/transaction structure.*   The documentation covering a product, as opposed to the product itself, may not perform in accordance with the parties' expectations. Although standard forms pervade the OTC derivatives industry and have facilitated enormously the documentation process, the documentation, even as it applies to plain vanilla products, is sophisticated. In the words of a leading industry spokesman (written in 1986 with direct regard to the early "swaps code," but equally applicable to the full range of current OTC derivatives documentation), the documentation is generally not for "novices," but is instead

> expected to make the lives of professional traders and their counsel simpler by permitting them all to speak the same language while, at the same time, preserving the flexibility needed to accommodate the varied and evolving needs of the growing number of participants in the swap market.[36]

Moreover, structural concerns relating, among other things, to collateralization and the use of other forms of credit support, also need to be considered. In the United States and in non-U.S. jurisdictions in which major financial centers are located, efforts are under way to establish clearer and more commercially reasonable structural protections for collateralized transactions. These include amendments to applicable law and attempts to establish workable and efficient collateral depositories. Nevertheless, real issues remain and are likely to persist.

4. *Reporting.*   Despite its overlap with the legal/compliance and documentation categories, the reporting category warrants its own discussion. Basically, public companies in the United States have a duty to disclose material information to their shareholders. The benefits of such disclosure must, however, be weighed against the financial costs and other burdens of such disclosure on the corporations. As mentioned there is an ongoing debate about the nature and extent of applicable SEC and FASB reporting requirements, one that is highly unlikely to lend itself to anything more than temporary stopgap solutions. Moreover, corporations and other end users have contractual reporting requirements to creditors and other third parties, and public sector entities have reporting obligations to their respective constituencies.

5. *Regret.* A counterparty that is otherwise fully capable of performing its contractual obligations might "choose" not to do so. This is a risk that has assumed enormous proportions in OTC derivatives markets, particularly with regard to "sales practices" and related "codes of conduct" applicable to such markets. Usually, this is a risk that applies in the first instance to dealers. The circumstances under which a solvent dealer that wishes to remain in business might attempt to renege on a contract by claiming that an end user somehow took advantage of the dealer's inferior knowledge or sophistication are at worst still remote. Nevertheless, the impact of this issue on dealer and end user relationships, negotiations, and documentation practices warrants discussion.

ENDNOTES: CHAPTER 5

1. Chew, *Leverage, supra,* Chapter 1, note 1: xiv.
2. See "Executive Summary," *GARP: Generally Accepted Risk Principles* (Coopers & Lybrand, 1996) [hereafter, *GARP*]: 11; see also Saber, *Interest Rate Swaps, supra,* Chapter 2, note 9 ("Transaction risks are difficult to quantify but must nevertheless be taken into consideration"): 69.
3. All quotations in this paragraph are from the *G-30 Overview*: 51–52.
4. The quotations in this paragraph are from the "Working Paper of the Enforceability Subcommittee" contained in *Appendix I: Working Papers to the G-30 Report* [hereafter, *G-30 Enforceability Working Paper*]: 43.
5. See "Chase Manhattan Top Holder of Derivatives," *Investor's Business Daily* (May 13, 1996): A29.
6. See, generally, Anthony G. Cornyn, CFA, "Financial Derivatives: Regulatory Quagmire or Opportunity for Reengineering," in *Derivatives Risk and Responsibility,* Robert A. Klein and Jess Lederman, eds. (Irwin Professional Publishing, 1996) [this anthology is hereafter referred to as *Derivatives Risk and Responsibility*]: 597.
7. Tanya S. Arnold, "How to Do Interest Rate Swaps," *Harvard Business Review* (September–October 1984): 96.
8. See, generally, Cunningham et al., *OTC Derivatives, supra,* Chapter 1, note 11: 286–290.
9. Cunningham et al., *OTC Derivatives, supra,* Chapter 1, note 11: 288.
10. *G-30 Enforceability Working Paper, supra,* note 4: 45.

11. Section 5-701 of the General Obligations Law and § 1-206 of the Uniform Commercial Code.

12. Anthony C. Gooch and Linda B. Klein, "A Review of International and U.S. Case Law Affecting Swaps and Related Derivative Products," in *Advanced Strategies in Financial Risk Management,* Robert J. Schwartz and Clifford W. Smith, Jr., eds. (New York Institute of Finance, 1993) [this article is hereafter referred to as *1992 Review of Case Law*]: 398.

13. This and the immediately succeeding quotation are from the *G-30 Enforceability Working Paper, supra,* note 4: 43, 46–47. The citation for the *Hammersmith and Fulham* is 2 W.L.R. 372 (H.L. 1991).

14. See, generally, Gooch and Klein, *1992 Review of Case Law, supra,* note 12: 403–412; *G-30 Enforceability Working Paper, supra,* note 4: 46–47.

15. *G-30 Enforceability Working Paper, supra,* note 4: 47; see, generally, Seth Grosshandler, Sandra M. Rocks, and Lech Kalembka, "Securities, Forward and Commodity Contracts, and Repurchase and Swap Agreements Under the U.S. Insolvency Laws," in the course materials for the conference entitled *Documentation for OTC Derivatives* (Institute for International Research, October 1996); Cunningham et al., *OTC Derivatives, supra,* Chapter 1, note 11: Part VI.

16. This and the following quotation are from *Financial Transactions in Insolvency: Reducing Legal Risk Through Legislative Reform,* a position paper prepared jointly by the International Swaps and Derivatives Association, Inc. and the Public Securities Association (April 2, 1996).

17. Quotations in this paragraph are from Mason et al., *Financial Engineering, supra,* Chapter 1, note 2: 33–38.

18. *G-30 Enforceability Working Paper, supra,* note 4: 48.

19. See, generally, Barry W. Taylor, "Customizing ISDA Masters & Opining on ISDA Masters," in *1996 PLI Derivatives, supra,* Chapter 1, note 11: 133–136.

20. See Cunningham et al., *OTC Derivatives, supra,* Chapter 1, note 11: 305.

21. Daniel P. Cunningham and Thomas J. Werlen, "Memorandum for ISDA Members," dated September 12, 1997, regarding "ISDA Netting Opinions," in *SWAPS and Other Derivatives in 1997,* Kenneth M. Raisler and Alison M. Gregory, Co-Chairs (Practising Law Institute 1997): 149, 151.

22. All quotations in this and the following paragraph are from *G-30 Enforceability Working Paper, supra,* note 4: 48–54.

23. See Advance Notice of Proposed Rulemaking, 52 Fed. Reg. 47022 (December 11, 1987); see, generally, Cunningham et al., *OTC Derivatives, supra,* Chapter 1, note 3: 315–320. For a general description of the regulatory treatment of hybrid instruments, see Greene et al., *U.S. Regulation, infra,* Chapter 8, note 2: §§ 13.04[4], 13.05[5][a]; see also Thomas A. Russo, "Regulation of Equity Derivatives," in *SWAPS and*

Other Derivatives in 1994, William P. Rogers, Jr., Chairman (Practising Law Institute, 1994) [hereafter, *Regulation of Equity Derivatives*]: 595-660.

24. See, generally, Cunningham et al., *OTC Derivatives, supra,* Chapter 1, note 11: 315–316.

25. *Policy Statement Concerning Swap Transactions,* 54 Fed. Reg. 30, 694 (July 21, 1989).

26. 17 C.F.R. § 35.2 (1993), effective April 30, 1993.

27. CFTC Regulations Part 34, 58 Fed. Reg. 5580 (January 22, 1993).

28. Anthony C. Gooch and Linda B. Klein, *Documentation for Derivatives* (Euromoney Publications, 1993) (citations omitted) [hereafter, *Documentation for Derivatives*]: 14–15; see also Gooch & Klein, *Credit Support Supplement* (Euromoney Book, 1995) [hereafter, *Credit Support Supplement*].

29. Greene et al., *U.S. Regulation, infra,* Chapter 8, note 2 (citations omitted): § 13.05[5][d][i]; see 17 C.F.R. § 32.4; 50 Fed. Reg. 10786 (March 18, 1985); see also *Industry Association Brief, infra,* Chapter 8, note 29: 12–13.

30. Simon Boughey, "The EMU Threat," *Derivatives Strategy,* 1(10) (October 1996) [hereafter, *The EMU Threat*]: 26–30; see also Michael Peltz, "Bracing for EMU," *Institutional Investor* (June 1996) [hereafter, *Bracing for EMU*]: 113–119.

31. Quotations in this paragraph are from Peltz, *Bracing for EMU, supra,* note 30.

32 N.Y. Gen. Oblig Law §§ 5-1604 (McKinney Supp. 1977). The New York added a new title 16 to the New York General Obligations Law. Similar legislative initiatives are underway in Illinois and California.

33. Michael Gruson, Luncheon Address, "The Euro and the New York Lawyer," summarized in the *Newsletter of the American Foreign Law Association, Inc.* (Winter 1998). For a more far reaching discussion of legal issues raised by the introduction of the euro, see generally Michael Gruson, "The Introduction of the Euro and Its Implications for Obligations Denominated in Currencies Replaced by the Euro," *Fordham International Law Journal,* 21(1) (November 1997): 65–107.

34. Hu, *Hedging Expectations, supra,* Chapter 2, note 37: 1015.

35. *Credit Lyonnais Bank Nederland, N.V. v. Pathé Communications Corp.,* 17 Del. J. Corp. L. 1099, 1155 (Del. Ch. 1991); see, generally, Hu, *Hedging Expectations, supra,* Chapter 2, note 37: 1014–1031.

36. Daniel P. Cunningham, "Swaps: Codes, Problems and Regulation," *International Financial Law Review* (August 1986): 26–35.

CHAPTER 6

Legal Engineering: Innovations in Legal Risk Management

The general attitude of the Study towards regulation is plain....Where the official priority should be placed, in the view of the Study, is in clarifying legal uncertainties, and resolving legal inconsistencies between countries that may impede risk-reduction procedures.

Paul Volcker
Foreword, G-30 Study, *1993*

Legal rules defining the ways in which valid contracts...are made....provide individuals with facilities for realizing their wishes, by conferring legal powers upon them to create, by certain specified procedures and subject to certain conditions, structures of rights and duties within the coercive framework of the law.

H. L. A. Hart
The Concept of Law, *1961[1]*

The legal responsibilities of senior management and its counsel encompass a wide variety of activities, all of which flow from a limited number of distinct commercial relationships. However, the particular rights, duties, and obligations of derivatives market participants are subject to constant change, largely because of the "financial innovation spiral." The spiral effect and other social changes lead to constant evolution of organizations, markets, products, legislative regimes, and regulatory structures.

Although the range of possible commercial relationships and activities is theoretically unlimited, the present discussion is limited to those relationships that, in the experience of senior managers and practicing lawyers, commonly rise to the level of practical, day-to-day significance in the management of derivatives' legal risks. Figure 6.1 depicts such relationships from a corporate end user's perspective (it can easily be modified for other types of relationships and entities). The activities, or responsibilities, of legal risk management are indicated by circles and ovals, whereas the parties that are the immediate subject of those activities are indicated by rectangles.

Figure 6.1, which depicts the domain of the legal engineer, illustrates several important points. First, the *G-30 Report* and all other significant public and private derivatives risk management studies to date have emphasized that sound derivatives risk management begins with a market partici-

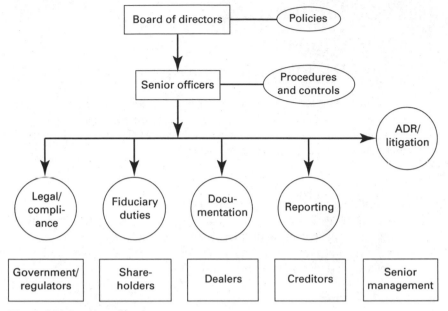

Figure 6.1   Legal engineering.

pant's senior management. The board of directors (or analogous governing body, in the case of noncorporate organizations) must determine an organization's risk management policies, while its senior officers must adopt specific procedures and controls designed to implement those policies. The effectiveness of any set of policies, procedures, and controls will determine in large part the organization's exposure to both the economic and the legal risks of derivatives. Legal exposure (the circle on the far right) depends principally on how well the policies, procedures, and controls address the activities indicated by the other four circles in Figure 6.1.

Much of the remaining chapters of this book will focus on various aspects of relationships depicted in Figure 6.1 to illuminate the major activities and parties involved in legal engineering and risk management. It will do so by, among other things, examining the main categories of legal and regulatory risks that affect today's transactions and that are certain to affect future transactions. It will also offer specific solutions, where appropriate, to today's legal risks and suggestions as to methods for achieving and maintaining state-of-the-art systems for analyzing and controlling both current and future legal and regulatory risks.

FOUNDATIONS OF A LEGAL RISK
MANAGEMENT SYSTEM—
FUNCTIONAL ANALYSIS

Functional analysis suggests that the manner in which both the rights and the obligations constituting the legal relationships among various parties (e.g., those indicated in Figure 6.1) will constantly evolve. Innovations in financial products and technologies, as well as changes in political and social realities, will affect over time the availability and choice of products that different organizations use and the manner in which those products are used. The expected "migration" of successful products from institutions to organized markets also suggests changes-over time in the nature of the institutions selling particular products. Furthermore, the heated competition among organized exchanges and OTC markets for business in financial products will likely lead to further blurring of lines between products. It could also foster the consolidation and convergence of previously distinct types of markets. If a risk management system is to remain viable in today's fluid financial environment, that system must similarly evolve and innovate.

Legal innovation will be necessary at both a public, or systemic level and in the private sector. Innovation at a public level refers to changes in the applicable external legal and regulatory environment governing markets, products, and market participants, and to some extent their interactions. Innovation at a private level consists of changes in the legal structure chosen by private market participants and evidenced in organic documents as well as in contractual relationships with managers, employees, investors, and outside interested third parties. Another analytically distinct level might be called "quasi-public." It consists primarily of the self-regulatory organizations that are assuming growing prominence in many financial markets and legal regimes because of their superior flexibility and responsiveness, when compared with government bodies, in reacting constractively to changing market forces rather than in a way that detracts from legitimate business interests.

The three levels of innovation must be coordinated: the internal structure and contractual relationships chosen by an organization or self-regulatory body are subject to external legal and regulatory constraints; the external legal and regulatory environment is in principle designed to permit and encourage socially optimal organizational structures and contractual relationships.

Recall that Figure 5.1 suggests that, because of legal and regulatory uncertainty, products and activities in Circle become riskier as a legal matter as they approach the border of Circle L. This is particularly so if the border is evolving or if there otherwise is material uncertainty as to its location. Figure 6.2 expands on Figure 5.1. It suggests that in many respects product and activity risks lie along a modified continuum.* Thus, the closer a product approaches the center line separating regions 2 and 3, the riskier that product becomes.

Each of the three arrows in Figure 6.2 points in the direction of increasing risk. The closer an activity moves toward the center line between regions 2 and 3, all other things being equal, the riskier that activity becomes as an *economic* matter. Similarly, the closer an activity approaches that portion of the border of Circle L that lies within Circle PB, the riskier that activity becomes as a *legal* matter. An activity located at point "a" would, therefore, have high economic and legal risk; an activity located at point "b" would have low economic and legal risk; and an activity located at point "c" would have high economic but low legal risk.

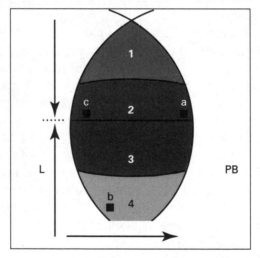

Figure 6.2   Risk.

---

*The greater the degree of "market completeness," the greater the range of available risky products and activities. Customization of products helps "complete" or "span" markets by enabling private parties to manufacture, or synthesize, products with risk and return profiles that might not otherwise be available on standard markets. For a discussion of the economics of market "spanning," see Judge Easterbrook's comments in the *IPs case, supra,* Chapter 2, note 1:544.

The benefit of the "private law" established by an organization's organic documents and contracts is that it permits the organization to determine for itself the products that it chooses to use and the resulting riskiness of its activities. One organization may, for example, choose to avoid as much risk, both economic and legal, as practicable by engaging in an activity located at point "a", while another organization with the opposite risk appetite and tolerance might choose activities located at "b".

The principal benefit of successful legal innovation, whether at the private, public, or quasi-public law level, is that it enables market participants to reduce the riskiness of existing activities and, at times, to engage in new activities, the risk of which can now be better controlled. Legal innovation occurs in regulatory regimes, internal governance structures, product documentation, and counterparty contractual relationships.

Both "private" and "quasi-public" law are presumptively more responsive and flexible than legislatively mandated systems and controls. These traits are vital in a highly competitive global economy where individual firms and entire markets must continue to respond rapidly to competitive challenges while simultaneously maintaining state-of-the-art risk management systems and techniques. Miller, in his 1986 article *The Last Twenty Years and the Next*,[2] provides a cogent example of the disadvantages of "public" regulation of financial markets:

> All new futures contracts must have CFTC approval before trading can begin. Delays in granting approval often run to a year or more: and even when the end is almost in sight and the traders are virtually lined up waiting for the starting bell, contracts have been sent back for further low-order but, at that point costly revisions. All this [means]...new contracts whose potential had previously been studied in depth by the exchanges whose members will bear the risks if the contract fails (as, indeed, most of them do). And the amounts involved are too large for frivolity.

Thomas Russo of Lehman Brothers, who has now in many ways become an industry spokesperson, draws a sharp contrast when he describes the benefits of industry self-regulation as follows:

> An industry-driven effort contains the flexibility that purely governmental initiatives simply cannot. Under an industry-led initiative, there would be no need to navigate a law through the Congressional committee system or publish proposed rules in the Federal Register, that often languish while the agency awaits comment and languish further until it adopts final rules. The government is slow while derivatives are dynamic. Derivatives, therefore, are most appropriately regulated in a way that assures that change can be addressed and resolved expeditiously.[3]

THE HISTORICAL ANTECEDENTS OF
LEGAL INNOVATION

Financial economists, especially those from the "Chicago School," often consider law and regulation to be at best necessary social evils. Miller, throughout *The Last Twenty Years and the Next*,[4] expresses the strong form of the foregoing proposition. For many years he has credited regulation and taxes with being "two longstanding spurs to innovation." He has repeatedly asserted that financial innovation is not the result of government design, but rather is the inadvertent outcome of misguided regulatory interventions that motivate private capital to seek innovative ways of skirting arbitrary regulatory barriers and avoiding unnecessary taxes. In Miller's words, "the role of government in producing the *pearls of financial innovation* over the past twenty years has been essentially that of the *grain of sand in the oyster.*"[5]

Yet Miller's analysis, at least with regard to the law, is incomplete in one critical respect. He focuses only on the grain of sand (i.e., ill-advised regulations and taxes). He does not explicitly address either the role of contract law, which gives individuals the power to act as "private legislators," or the role of private practitioners in creating the pearls of financial innovations.

Tufano has examined the role of the private bar and contract law in responding creatively to government action. Tufano's research has centered, among other things, on the pearls of financial and legal innovation that often followed unexpected judicial intervention in the restructuring of failed U.S. railroads and corporations in the late nineteenth and early twentieth centuries.[6] His work makes great progress in demonstrating that bursts of both financial and legal innovation are historically recurring, cyclical phenomena dating back centuries. In that regard, he shares Miller's view that the middle years of the twentieth century, during which little financial innovation occurred, were arguably the most aberrant period in U.S. financial history. Miller succinctly explains the reasons for the dearth of major financial innovations during the period of world economic stagnation that began in the early 1930s and continued well into the 1950s: "In that depressed and war-scarred period, and even more so during the war and slow recovery years that followed, there were better outlets for innovative talents. We were just too poor and too distracted with other, more pressing concerns."[7]

Tufano's research raises the likelihood that a cycle of legal innovation rich in historical precedent facilitated greatly today's explosion of financial innovation. His historical analysis includes, for example, a list of 23 different types of securities—among them, zero-coupon bonds, no-par and low-par stock, convertible bonds, exchangeable and extendible bonds, currency option bonds, and warrants—all of which were developed between 1830 and 1930, and most of which are either in use today or have close contemporary cousins. He also describes briefly the appendix to the first edition of Benjamin Graham and David Dodd's 1934 investment classic, *Security Analysis,* a book that focused on stocks and bonds.

As Tufano notes in *Financing Engineering,* Graham and Dodd were stymied by the difficulties introduced into their analysis by the already tremendous variety of complex hybrid securities. Many of the hybrid's examined by Graham and Dodd exhibit economic characteristics nearly identical to today's most sophisticated securities, including complex financial instruments containing embedded options. The hybrids included "pay-in-kind bonds, step-up bonds, putable bonds, bonds with stock dividends, zero coupon bonds, inflation indexed bonds, a variety of exotic convertible and exchangeable bonds, 23 different types of warrants, voting bonds, [and] nonvoting shares." Graham and Dodd's "Partial List of Securities Which Deviate from the Normal Patterns" spanned 17 pages and covered 258 different securities.

The capital markets, trade journals, and daily newspapers provide abundant potential subjects for case studies of the precedent for today's financial innovations. Numerous examples are found in an article by John D. Finnerty of Fordham University and McFarland Dewey & Co. that appeared in the Winter 1992 issue of the *Journal of Applied Corporate Finance.* Finnerty's "An Overview of Corporate Securities Innovations," contains an analysis of the "revolutionary changes in the array of financial instruments available [in 1992] to corporate treasurers and investors." In words that echo those penned 58 years earlier by Graham and Dodd, Finnerty states that "many of the new securities defy categorization." He also provides, in the style of Graham, Dodd, and Tufano, four tables listing "some 60 new securities I have been able to identify."

An example of a current innovation receiving attention is the U.S. Treasury Department's inflation-indexed bond program commenced in January 1997. Generally touted as a new instrument—as *Investor's Business Daily* reported on October 3, 1996—the first inflation-indexed bond "on free soil" was issued to combat the rampant inflation of the Revolutionary War. According to the report, the war bonds were issued by the rebel state of Massachusetts in response to the calls by barefoot troops for "just pay." Soldiers had been complaining, because inflation was eating up seven-eighths of the value of their military pay between the time they received it and the time it arrived back home to the soldiers' families. To address the problem, the Massachusetts legislature in 1780 enacted a law to pay the troops with 6% interest-bearing notes indexed to inflation. But no preexisting inflation index was available, so the Bay State simply "slapped one together" and printed it on the face of the bonds:

> Both Principal and Interest to be paid in the then current Money of said State, in a greater or less Sum, according as Five Bushels of Corn, Sixty-eight Pounds and four-seventh Parts of a Pound of Beef, Ten Pounds of Sheeps Wool, and Sixteen Pounds of Sole Leather shall then cost.[8]

Bringing the innovation process full circle, even prior to their issuance the new bonds spurred the creation of an entirely new class of derivatives for hedging against or speculating on inflation rates.[9]

THE IMPORTANCE OF LEGAL INNOVATION

According to Tufano's research, the accelerated pace of financial innovation in the late nineteenth century is best explained as a response to financial crises suffered by corporations and railroads. As discussed in Chapter 1, commenting on the likely explanation for the spate of innovations during that period, Tufano introduces an unconventional idea among economists: that is, that "the technological development that was probably more instrumental in explaining nineteenth century innovations was the development of new legal techniques."[10] Furthermore, he suggests that nineteenth century lawyers were indispensable to the securities innovation then occurring. Tufano's historical inquiry, which builds on Merton's functional product and institutional analysis, strongly suggests that the modern OTC derivatives bar has applied and continues to apply similarly innovative legal techniques and technical virtuosity.

Yet in the opinion of many active derivatives market participants, the hypothesis is valid. If so, that is important for several reasons. First, it implies that any understanding of the dynamic process of financial and legal innovation can be greatly improved by a study of the historical path of innovation. Second, historical research is important for a reason explained by Congressman Newt Gingrich in his highly controversial Kennesaw State College and Reinhardt College lectures:

> Every major figure read history for a practical reason. History can be the
> most practical of disciplines, because it is teaching you about what you
> want to do. Studying how others have done things gives you a *wider menu
> of solutions* than people who don't read history....*It's cheaper to imitate
> than to invent.*[11]

Politics aside, his explanation of the importance of history holds.

The third and most important reason for studying the contribution of lawyers and contract law to financial innovation is that history provides an appreciation of how the private bar, at its best, is capable of generating constructive solutions to exasperating commercial issues. At times, constructive legislative or regulatory measures are needed, and the legal solutions often originate with private industry groups. The four recommendations for legislators, regulators, and supervisors contained in the *G-30 Report* are a useful example. Alternatively, other issues are, perhaps, only inefficiently, at times counterproductively, resolved by regulatory or legislative action. A glimpse into the difficulty with government action was recently provided by Securities and Exchange Commission (SEC) Chairman Arthur Levitt: "You can't address fast-changing instruments with ironclad regulations."[12] To the extent the private bar is capable of providing constructive solutions that can be implemented without legislative or regulatory action, those solutions will be preferable. Private measures are more easily modified and customized to fit changing circumstances and are, therefore, more flexible than the regulatory and legislative alternatives.

The essence of the private bar's contribution is the generation of new types of private contractual arrangements and new corporate governance structures. Those contributions can provide protections that are more precisely tailored to specific circumstances and thus in context superior to existing law or new legislation and regulation. Tufano pays particular attention to the design of the new contracts in the late nineteenth century that established voting trusts. Voting trust arrangements enabled investors to better monitor the actions of management of reorganized railroads and to trace those railroads' financial performance; they also alleviated some of the harsher effects of information asymmetries in securities markets. Those asymmetries were caused by the failure of outside investors to have as much information available to them as their "agents" who run the organizations in which they have invested.

A modern development comparable in its innovative impact to the voting trust structure is the proliferation of the special purpose vehicles that provide the bulwark for, in the words of one market participant, the "[s]tructured securitized credit [which provides] a new technology for lending....At a time when the traditional lending system is clearly in trouble [i.e., 1988], this new technology is offering us a framework for a fundamentally different and better financial system."[13]

A detailed theoretical analysis of the flexibility and creative potential of the private contractual approach to resolving nettlesome financial and legal problems is also found in H. L. A. Hart's classic work, *The Concept of Law.*[14] The following is an exploration of immediately pertinent highlights of that analysis.

"THE ELEMENTS OF LAW," AND "PRIVATE LEGISLATORS"

In a section entitled "The Elements of Law," *The Concept of Law* elaborates on three defects inherent in every legal system derived from "primary rules of obligation." Primary rules include "restrictions on the free use of violence, theft, and deception to which human beings are tempted but which they must, in general, repress, if they are to coexist in close proximity to each other." The three defects are, first, the *uncertainty* caused by doubts that may arise about the sources and scope of given rules and the procedures for settling this doubt; second, "the *static* character of the rules" (emphasis in original); and, third, the *inefficiency* of any system of enforcing these rules. "The remedies for each of these three main defects in this simplest form of social structure consists in supplementing the *primary* rules of obligation with *secondary* rules, which are rules of a different kind." (Emphasis in original.)*

Secondary rules "specify the ways in which the primary rules may be conclusively ascertained, introduced, eliminated, varied, and the fact of their violation conclusively determined." Hart discusses secondary rules essential to remedy the three principal defects. He calls these the "rules of recognition, change, and adjudication." "The simplest form of such a rule is that which empowers an individual or body of persons to introduce new primary rules for the conduct of the life of the group, or of some class within it, and to eliminate old rules." Some of these secondary rules, those which Hart refers to as "private power-conferring rules,"

---

*Interestingly, as the italicized words indicate, Hart's legal analysis borrows much of its terminology from the fields of statistics and modern finance.

enable individuals to vary their respective legal rights and obligations through the power to enter into private contracts. Contract law enables individuals through the exercise of "limited legislative powers" to attempt to redress the defects of the uncertainty, static character, and inefficient nature of public law and regulation.[15] The "possession of these legal powers makes of the private citizen, who, if there were no such rules, would be a mere duty-bearer, a *private legislator.*" Moreover, "[t]he power thus conferred on individuals to mould their legal relations with others by contracts, wills, marriages, etc., is *one of the great contributions of law to social life.*"[16]

In light of Hart's theoretical analysis, a comparison of the results of Tufano's historical research with those of Finnerty's study of modern financial innovation suggests a further unconventional hypothesis. That is, that a study of earlier legal innovations and the reasons for those innovations' failure or continuing success, in one form or another, provides practical guidance to modern financial and legal innovators, as well as to those who would regulate innovative activities. Both legal theory and the history of innovation argue strongly in favor of government moderation and circumspection prior to the exercise of regulatory or legislative power in response to derivatives fiascos.

EXAMPLES OF MODERN LEGAL TECHNICAL VIRTUOSITY IN OTC DERIVATIVES

Contemporaneous legal innovations facilitated, if not catalyzed, many financial innovations of prior generations. A modern paradigm of legal innovation is the development of the standard industry form "master agreements" that now pervade both OTC derivatives and other financial markets. In its proper historical perspective, the master agreement innovation constitutes a remarkably successful private industry response to serious legal uncertainties that initially threatened to stunt the growth of modern OTC derivatives markets.

Of particular concern with early OTC transactions was the risk that courts would not give effect to contractual netting arrangements. Early transactions were structured as offsetting or matching loan transactions, called parallel or back-to-back loans. Hence, the documentation provided for a series of opposite but equal one-way funds flows, under which either party could stop its payments if its counterparty defaulted in the performance of its payment obligations. Many lawyers were concerned that a court might be unwilling to enable one "borrower" to terminate its payment obligations simply because another borrower had defaulted on its obligations. The concern, especially among U.K. lawyers, was that termination rights might be found "incompatible with the concept of debt" and that, therefore, U.K. courts might not enforce them. Hence, parties feared that a nondefaulting party might be required to continue making payments even after its counterparty had defaulted.

The use of master agreements served to alleviate these concerns, because they expressly conditioned each party's payment obligations on the other party's performance of its respective payment obligations. Over time, the master agreement approach became "seasoned" and accepted in capital markets. Regulators and lawyers also grew increasingly comfortable with the use of master agreements. Eventually, the legal enforceability concerns faded, at least outside of bankruptcy and insolvency. For example, in Section 3.3 of its June 1, 1987 "Memorandum for the Bank of England and the Board of Governors of the Federal Reserve System," a British law firm opined that "a *future* payment obligation under a Swap Agreement does not constitute a debt....Rather the obligations of the parties are in the nature of obligations to exchange certain amounts at certain times and we do not consider that, in relation to any of those amounts, a debt comes into existence until the stated time for payment of such amount." (Emphasis in original.)

Indeed, master agreements have been so successful that their use is now effectively mandated by international banking regulators pursuant to the risk-based capital guidelines (Capital Guidelines), agreed to in July 1988 (and subsequently amended) by bank supervisory authorities from 12 countries meeting in Basle, Switzerland. The Capital Guidelines, as implemented in the United States, were amended on December 7, 1994 to reduce applicable capital charges for those banks that are using legally enforceable bilateral netting contracts. In effect, international and domestic regulators as well as private industry groups have provided ringing testimony to the modern bar's creativity and technical skills. Now, banks that engage in derivatives transactions without enforceable bilateral netting arrangements implemented through master agreements will almost certainly be subject to higher capital charges than are banks that have entered into enforceable netting agreements. Banking regulators in particular have forcefully emphasized that bilateral netting arrangements embodied in private contracts contribute to the overall safety and soundness of the banking system. For example, Chairman Greenspan, in a 1992 letter to Senator Donald Riegle, estimated that on a bilateral basis netting results in an average reduction in counterparty credit exposure of between 40% to 60%.[17]

As discussed earlier, master agreements enabled private market participants to overcome dangerous documentation backlogs in the early years of the OTC derivatives market. Those backlogs had given rise to substantial legal uncertainty regarding the enforceability of many early swaps contracts, especially in light of statute of frauds concerns that suggested oral swap agreements were of questionable validity. The uncertainty inhibited the willingness of particular counterparties to continue entering into contracts with each other. Hence, many practitioners believe the use of master agreements explains much of the size of the current OTC derivatives markets.

OTC derivatives markets, as alternatives to regulated exchanges, needed a solid legal foundation on which to mount Merton's "engine of financial innovation" that drives financial markets, including those for derivatives. For exchange-traded products, termination rights and offset problems are solved by the interposition of highly creditworthy clearinghouses as the immediate counterparty to every transaction. In addition, parties transacting on exchanges are subject to rigorous "margin requirements" forcing them to post collateral for their outstanding obligations. Thus, the exchanges effectively act as guarantors of each transaction and eliminate for all practical purposes concerns about counterparty credit risk. In OTC transactions, clearinghouses for routine payments are never used. Therefore, the ability and willingness of a counterparty to perform its payment obligations is a crucial concern.

Master agreements, supplemented by enormously successful industry efforts to obtain corresponding statutory protections for contractual netting arrangements in almost all of the world's major financial centers, have effectively resolved the netting issue for the vast majority of derivatives contracts. Master agreements' netting provisions can in that regard be viewed as analogous to the exchange clearing mechanism. Indeed, J. P. Morgan's Mark Brickell, a leading spokesperson for derivatives dealers, once noted in 1994 that, in a sense, clearinghouses do in fact exist for swaps, "embedded in the bilateral and multilateral netting arrangements of the financial institutions themselves."[18] Bilateral (and multibranch) netting arrangements are set forth in master agreements.

MASTER AGREEMENTS AND RELATED STANDARDIZED DOCUMENTATION

In *The Last Twenty Years and the Next* Miller enumerated a set of requirements that must be met before he will consider any financial improvement to constitute a "significant and successful financial innovation."[19] In sum, to qualify an improvement must first in some important sense be surprising and unanticipated. Additionally, it must have some fundamentally unusual quality about it that enables the innovation to endure and its application to be further extended long after the original stimulus for its creation—which he typically attributes to regulatory intervention or the imposition of new taxes—has either been abandoned or ceased to be relevant. Miller's award for "the most significant and successful financial innovation" of the last few decades went to *financial futures,* the "industrial raw materials" of the derivatives dealer.

According to similar standards, the application of master agreements to swap markets constitutes a significant and successful legal innovation. Those agreements now form the solid legal foundation for essential private contractual rights throughout OTC derivatives markets. The development and application of standardized master agreements to OTC swap transactions has certainly constituted a truly major and lasting improvement, the application of which has been extended to a vast array of additional products. By now, "[s]everal organizations around the world have developed standard documentation for global derivatives transactions which helps deal with and reduce enforceability risks. These organizations include the British Bankers Association (BBA), the Australian Financial Markets Association (AFMA), a group of German banks, the Association Franáaise (AFB), [the International Swaps and Derivatives Association, Inc. (formerly, the International Swap Dealers Association, Inc.)] ISDA, and others."[20]* In fact, the potential breadth and applicability of the standard form master agreement prepared by ISDA is sweeping.

Indeed, the breadth and applicability of the ISDA Master Agreement is at least theoretically unlimited. Consequently, one legal expert recently asked a group of derivatives lawyers, who in their practices might be called upon from time to time to render or accept legal opinions on ISDA

---

*These and other organizations also engage in legal engineering at the public law level by proposing and advocating the passage of legislation and regulations designed to give greater legal certainty to private law contractual rights relating to OTC derivatives.

Master Agreements and, therefore, be responsible for ensuring the legal validity of any covered contracts:

> Did you know you can sell soap and greeting cards under the ISDA Master? Or restricted stock subject to the securities laws? Or fungible futures contracts in violation of the commodities laws? Or property to an affiliated mutual fund in violation of Section 80a-17 of the Investment Company Act? And so on.[21]

The foregoing remark was not then and is not now intended as a criticism of the ISDA form, but rather as a testimony to its extraordinary versatility and its nearly automatic acceptance among derivatives practitioners and other transactional lawyers.

Equally important is that many other standard ISDA documents are intended to apply to cross-border transactions. As we discuss shortly, the OTC derivatives market is truly global and thus transactions and transacting parties are potentially subject to the vagaries of a wide range of legal regimes. Therefore, to achieve international acceptance, ISDA needed to and did elicit the active support of a large number of lawyers from law firms and financial institutions throughout most of the world's major financial centers—a remarkable achievement in and of itself. In fact, the effort was so successful that two leading derivatives practitioners observed with no apparent exaggeration in a 1992 article: "Not only were the [early] 1987 ISDA forms a much-needed solution to the documentation problem, but they have also contributed to the standardization of the currency swap market itself."[22] Furthermore, the successful documentation effort set the stage for further successful international cooperation among market participants on crucial industry matters, not the least of which was the achievement of a high degree of international uniformity on critical rules applicable upon a counterparty bankruptcy and insolvency.

Cautionary Note on Master Agreements

Standard industry form master agreements constitute the end product of extraordinarily sophisticated and wide-ranging international efforts at "private legislation." That alone suggests that the agreements, despite their widespread acceptance, are the result of much negotiation and compromise. Moreover, the expansive potential breadth of product coverage, especially in the ISDA forms, and the necessity that the integrity of the forms withstand judicial scrutiny in jurisdictions throughout the world means that the forms and their supporting materials are based on intricate and sophisticated legal reasoning. Users must not expect all material implications of the document's structures and detailed provisions, even when accompanied by user guidelines, to be self-evident.

OTHER ONGOING EFFORTS

Industry groups, exchanges, and other interested parties are continuing the attempts to improve the legal certainty and efficiency of derivatives markets. An important focus of attention are counterparty credit risk issues. Credit issues are, as Merton emphasized many years ago, key constraints on the effective functioning of derivatives and capital markets. Aside from developing new credit derivatives, many contributors—e.g., Bankers Trust, the Chicago Mercantile Exchange—are attempting, for example, to establish services for improving the efficiency of collateralization arrangements. These developments are augmented by recent fundamental improvements in the Uniform Commercial Code and attempts to achieve greater international harmony concerning collateral security issues. For example, both Euroclear and Cedel Bank believe they have developed systems to address collateral security risks. One other area of considerable importance to fiduciaries, as discussed in Chapters 16 and 17, involves ongoing efforts to conform the law of fiduciary duties to the realities of modern financial markets.

ENDNOTES: CHAPTER 6

1. H. L. A. Hart, *The Concept of Law* (Oxford University Press, 1961) (emphasis omitted) [hereafter, *The Concept of Law*]: 27.
2. Merton H. Miller, *The Last Twenty Years and the Next, supra,* Chapter 2, note 6: 468.
3. Nigel Page, "Russo Drives Moves to Self-Regulation," *International Financial Law Review* (January 1996) [hereafter, *Move to Self-Regulation*]: 20.
4. Miller, *The Last Twenty Years and the Next, supra,* Chapter 2, note 6: 459–471.
5. *Id.:* 461 (emphasis added).
6. Peter Tufano, *Judicial Intervention and Financial Innovation, supra,* Chapter 1, note 30; see also Peter Tufano, "Securities Innovations: A

Historical and Functional Perspective," *Journal of Applied Corporate Finance,* 7(4) (Winter 1995) [hereafter, *Securities Innovations*]: 90–104.

7. Miller, *The Last Twenty Years and the Next, supra,* Chapter 2, note 5: 470–471.

8. Roger Lowenstein, "Inflation Bonds: Revere, Rubin & Leather," *Investor's Business Daily* (October 3, 1996): C1.

9. See, e.g., Sam Pang, "Learning Curve: Inflation Derivatives," *Derivatives Week* (December 15, 1997): 6–7; Robert H. Scarborough, "Tax Issues and Strategies: Inflation-Indexed Bonds May Lead to New Derivatives," *Derivatives Tax Regulation Finance,* 2(2) (Warren, Gorham & Lamont, November–December 1996): 83–87.

10. Mason et al., *supra,* Chapter 1, note 2: 52.

11. "Gingrich's Lessons of American Civilization," *Investor's Business Daily,* September 18, 1996: A2 (emphasis added).

12. Arthur Levitt, "Defusing Derivatives: The SEC's Flexible Approach," *Risk/Latin American Derivatives* (April 1996): 42–43.

13. Lowell L. Bryan, "Structured Securitized Credit: A Superior Technology for Lending," *Journal of Applied Corporate Finance,* 1(3) (Fall 1988).

14. Hart, *The Concept of Law, supra,* note 1.

15. See, generally, *id.:* 89–96.

16. See *id.:* 26–41 (emphasis added).

17. Letter from Alan Greenspan, Chairman, Board of Governors of the Federal Reserve System (Federal Reserve), to Senator Donald Riegle, Jr., September 11, 1992.

18. Mark C. Brickell, "Clearinghouse Arrangements for Privately Negotiated Derivatives," *World of Banking,* 13 (1994).

19. Miller, *The Last Twenty Years and the Next, supra,* Chapter 2, note 6: 459–471.

20. *G-30 Enforceability Working Paper, supra,* Chapter 5, note 4: 43.

21. Barry W. Taylor, "Customizing ISDA Masters and Opinion on ISDA Masters," *SWAPS and Other Derivatives in 1996* (Practising Law Institute, October 1996): 145.

22. Daniel P. Cunningham and Michael Wood, "Standardized Swap Definitions and Documentation," *Cross-Currency Swaps,* Carl R. Beidleman, ed. (Business One Irwin, 1992): 117.

CHAPTER 7

Market Regulation:
A Functional Analysis

[T]hose of use in the U.S. should recognize that the technology that
makes our capital markets so accessible to others also represents a two
way street....It is just as easy for U.S. capital providers to move to direct
off-shore investments.

Steven Wallman, SEC Commissioner
Regulating in a World of Technological
and Global Change, 1996[1]

This regulatory approach worked well for a long time, but over the last 20
years or so it has been quite thoroughly overtaken by events.

Sheila Bair, Acting Chairman
Commodity Futures Trading
Commission, October 1993[2]

Financial innovation has produced many new products that include
"swaps, hybrid instruments and sophisticated new varieties of forward
contracts, many of which combine...features of traditional debt or equity
instruments with those of futures contracts."[3] Many debt and equity
instruments traditionally fall within the ambit of federal and state securities laws (collectively, Securities Laws), whereas commodity futures and
commodity options are generally governed by the Commodity Exchange
Act (CEA).

Many innovative derivatives cast in the form of traditionally unregulated products such as interest rate swaps include features that alter the
products' "economic reality," thereby potentially subjecting the products
to regulation under the Securities Laws, the CEA, or both. Other innovative products, especially so-called hybrid instruments, combine in one
instrument different economic characteristics traditionally subject to disparate regulatory regimes. Thus, derivatives transactions that contracting
parties may consider either to be unregulated or regulated by a specific
regulator may instead be subject not only to regulation but also to inconsistent regulation.

REGULATORY UNCERTAINTY

In the United States, securities and commodities regulation is premised on
imprecise and ambiguous product definitions. In practice, the results of
the application of a definitional scheme to a financial product often

depends on who is making the determination—the SEC, the CFTC, or a court—rather than on any clearly articulated or agreed-upon mode of analysis. The definition or classification issue is particularly nettlesome in its application to OTC derivatives, because of its broad jurisdictional implications in the ongoing "turf battle"[4] between the CFTC and the SEC. The lack of international supervisory coordination over OTC derivatives markets exacerbates the adverse effects of interagency disputes between the CFTC and the SEC. This problem is being rapidly addressed on many fronts by international banking, securities, and futures regulators, but nevertheless defies easy resolution.*

The lack of a clear regulatory framework, particularly for new products, complicates any regulatory analysis. *Foreseeable* legal uncertainty often causes market participants either to alter the terms of transactions or otherwise to avoid altogether transactions governed by U.S. law that would otherwise make economic sense for all concerned, including the U.S. economy. "In this environment, the potential for losses of creativity as well as jobs and business has become a reality."[5] In addition, recent litigation and enforcement actions by both the SEC and the CFTC indicate that certain OTC derivatives transactions display characteristics, the undesired regulatory implications of which were likely *unforeseen* either by the products' designers or by the parties to the relevant transactions.

Figure 4.1 is reproduced in modified form as Figure 7.1 to depict the effects of legal uncertainty. Recall that the "risk oval" illustrates why singling out derivatives—that is, region 1 and 2 activities—for new regulation or legislation does not efficiently address the problems that "risk" raises. Economically, activities in region 3 can be as risky as those in region 2, while products in region 1 can be as safe as those in region 4.

Moreover, as Figure 7.1*a* indicates, even if there were a consensus regarding derivatives' economic risks, unavoidable definitional uncer-

---

*For example, (1) as of early 1998, 66 futures exchanges and clearinghouses had signed a "Declaration on Cooperation and Supervision of International Futures Markets and Clearing Organizations"; (2) in May 1995, securities regulators from 16 countries signed the so-called Windsor Declaration, calling for closer cooperation and better information flow; (3) on March 15, 1994, the SEC and CFTC, together with UK regulators, issued a "joint statement" on "OTC Derivatives Oversight" designed primarily to improve international oversight of derivatives trading through enhanced information sharing; and (4) under the auspices of the BIS, international banking supervisors have been working since the 1980s on improved capital adequacy guidelines and other matters relating to derivatives. For a bibliography of international cooperative efforts in recent years, see, e.g., David Shirreff, "The Agony of the Global Supervisor," *Euromoney* (July 1996): 48–52.

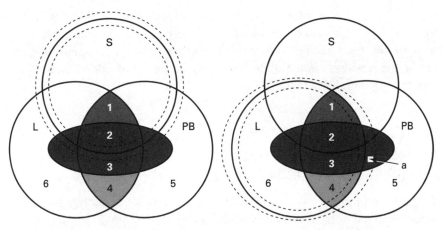

Figure 7.1a   Derivative uncertainty.   Figure 7.1b   Legal uncertainty.

tainty makes it difficult to determine which products truly are derivatives—thus, the location of the border of Circle S is and will continue to be unclear. Partly for this reason, Alan Greenspan, among others, urges that efforts to control risk "should not be confined to derivatives activities but should encompass all risk activities."[6] Derivatives, however defined, constitute only one means of creating (or reducing) financial exposures. And the mathematical relationship of "put-call parity" teaches that virtually any financial risk that can be created with derivatives can just as easily be created without them: "Without realizing that all derivatives can be synthetically replicated with the underlying cash markets, some skeptics have even commented that trading in the underlying cash markets is less risky than trading in the derivatives market."[7]

Figure 7.1(b) illustrates that financial and legal engineering necessitate an understanding of the applicable legal and regulatory structure—the location of the border of Circle L. A transaction that is intended to result in, for example, a region 3 activity but that results in a transaction located at point a will have been entirely unsuccessful. Uncertainty in the current regulatory framework applicable to derivatives can be visualized as uncertainty as to the boundaries of Circle L.

Traditional securities and commodities law regulatory structures—which do not use the term *derivatives* but instead focus on definitions of the key terms security, *commodity, futures contract,* and *commodity option*—provide limited assistance in determining whether many OTC derivatives fall within Circle L. With respect to these products, the location of Circle L's border is, because of definitional uncertainty, often unclear. Thus, Greenspan again appropriately emphasizes that risk controls should be based not "on *legal definitions* of the instruments used to create the positions in the underlying risk factors" but on the underlying risk factors themselves.

ESSENTIAL REGULATORY INFORMATION—DEFINITIONAL CATEGORIES AND ECONOMIC REALITY

To ensure compliance with applicable law and avoid regulatory surprises, senior management and its legal advisers must have two different types of meaningful product information. To begin, they must be able to determine whether a product on its face fits within any of the obvious definitional categories upon which complex regulatory schemes are initially based. These schemes rely on definitional categories to determine in the first instance whether a product appears to constitute a security, futures contract, or commodity option.

A product that appears to fit neatly within any of the standard definitional categories is likely to be subject to regulation under either the securities or the commodities laws. If it fits neatly into the standard definitional categories of both regulatory schemes, it is therefore potentially subject to inconsistent regulation. In that case, complex statutory, regulatory, and common law rules must be followed to determine, as best as possible, which of the two schemes will prevail.

Next, managers and legal advisers must also obtain adequate information about a product's economic characteristics. A product that nominally fits within a standard definitional category might not, as an economic matter, constitute the type of product intended to be regulated. In that case, the product could, despite features that facially suggest otherwise, remain unregulated. In contrast, a product that lacks any of the features that would cause it neatly to fall within any of the standard regulatory categories might nevertheless exhibit economic characteristics that replicate those of products that fall neatly within the standard definitions. In that case, securities or commodities regulators, or both, might decide that in "economic reality" the product meets the statutory definitions and therefore warrants regulation.

Once senior management and legal advisers have obtained needed information about a product's relevant regulatory characteristics, they can then analyze (or revisit) the product's economic features to consider the products' likely profitability. As discussed earlier, not all lawful business activities are profitable and not all profitable business activities are lawful. In many instances, products that are potentially profitable—either standing alone or because of their ability to enable users to manage unwanted risks of other profitable business activities—may be subject either to regulatory prohibitions or to regulatory burdens that would render the use of those products unprofitable. Conversely, often products that would not otherwise be economically viable become valuable by virtue of their legal characteristics.

Whenever a product is potentially either prohibited or subject to costly regulatory burdens, information about its profitability is essential. Profitability information will motivate management's decision whether to avoid the product altogether or instead seek to apply the techniques of legal and financial engineering to innovate around the regulatory barriers and burdens.

THE "BUILDING BLOCKS" OF REGULATORY ANALYSIS

A functional analysis of OTC derivatives regulation is intuitive and conforms to the way business managers actually make decisions. In practice, a senior manager (or perhaps a trader or financial officer) first identifies an economic need to be satisfied or function to be performed. The manager then considers the existing products that might satisfy that need or perform that function efficiently over the relevant time period, in light of the organization's needs. The manager's analysis, which should factor in the organization's resource and other constraints, typically results in a range of available products (including derivatives) and strategies.

Although a functional analysis cannot resolve the inconsistencies and uncertainties inherent in U.S. or other applicable law, it provides an early warning system for detecting potential regulatory problems. Moreover, functional analysis, with its emphasis on the creative benefits of financial and legal innovation provides business managers and lawyers with the instruments they need to navigate turbulent legal waters once early warning signals have been received.

As discussed earlier, a functional product analysis provides information about a product's economic characteristics. A functional analysis involves first "unbundling" the product—or "reverse engineering" it—

into its "basic building blocks." The "building block" approach to product analysis isolates and categorizes individual risk components that may or may not be likely to attract the attention of securities or commodities regulators by (1) illuminating forward- and option-based product components and (2) separating a derivative from its underlying "fidget."

Both aspects of the analysis are critical, because a failure to appreciate either aspect may unexpectedly result in a product becoming subject to regulatory regimes, as discussed in more detail in Chapter 8. Typically, forward-based products that do not involve underlying securities or traditional "commodities" within the meaning of the CEA are not subject to securities or commodities regulation. If, however, the fidget is an agricultural product listed within the CEA's "commodity" definition, then the derivative may be subject to the CEA's exchange-trading requirement (absent an applicable exemption) and antifraud provisions and to CFTC jurisdiction. If the fidget is, for example, an interest rate or currency exchange rate, it might be considered by the CFTC to constitute a "commodity" that (depending on the nature of the transaction and the counterparties) is exempt from the CEA's exchange-trading requirement but still subject to its antifraud provisions.

If the fidget is any other financial instrument, the analysis is often more complex. When a product is derived from individual securities or narrow baskets of securities (in each case, ones that are not exempt from the registration requirements of the federal securities laws), then the derivative will potentially be subject to the securities laws and to SEC jurisdiction. If the underlying instrument is an exempt security under the federal securities laws or if it otherwise constitutes a broad-based securities index or basket of securities (i.e., if it meets what is known as the "substantial segment criterion"), the derivative may instead be subject to the CEA and to CFTC jurisdiction.

UTILITY OF A FUNCTIONAL ANALYSIS OF DERIVATIVES REGULATION

Uncertainty in recent years as to the proper regulatory treatment of various OTC derivatives has generated controversy regarding many simple products and efficient markets that, because of high volume and low margins, depend on legal certainty to function effectively—especially plain vanilla products such as interest rate and currency swaps and options on foreign exchange.

Economic Reality and Functional Analysis

By breaking down a transaction into its fundamental building blocks of forwards and options, and by isolating the derivative instrument from the underlying fidget, a functional approach focuses the analysis precisely on the transaction's economic characteristics. As such, the approach provides a useful if not essential guide, given the enormous definitional gaps, in determining the potential applicability of federal and state securities laws and the CEA to any OTC derivatives transaction. Functional analysis does not, however, end the inquiry or eliminate all legal uncertainty. Existing regulatory structures only loosely conform to functional guidelines. Nevertheless, a functional analysis provides an essential analytical starting point.

Equally important is that, particularly in the initial product design stages, once the necessary regulatory analysis has been completed, a functional approach can guide efforts to avoid undesirable legal uncertainties that may jeopardize otherwise economically beneficial transactions. Economic factors motivate managerial decision making and constitute the first-order managerial priorities. Legal and regulatory regimes, at their finest, may facilitate the achievement of economic objectives, but they can just as easily impede or thwart the realization of those objectives. When they present obstacles, financial and legal engineers may devise, using the tools of functional analysis, methods of minimizing regulatory constraints or avoiding regulatory barriers altogether.

Timelessness and Stability of Functional Approach

The parameters of any particular regulatory regime, whether in or outside the United States, are often unpredictable, based primarily on local historical, political, and cultural circumstances. Nevertheless, functional analysis—in particular, its emphasis on the effects of the financial innovation spiral—provides senior management and its legal advisers with analytical tools that can help in understanding most applicable regulatory structures.

The main benefit of a functional analysis is that it provides guiding principles free of the instability of institutional approaches to regulation and to the unpredictable and arbitrary nature of definition-based product approaches. Moreover, it does so in a manner that enhances an understanding of transitory institutions and product definitions.

An appreciation of the transitory nature of institutions and products is essential to regulatory compliance in OTC derivatives markets. As Merton explains, "[T]he most efficient institutional arrangements for fulfilling [economic] functions will generally change over time and differ across countries. Even when the names of institutions are the same, the functions they perform often differ dramatically. For example, banks in the U.S. today are very different from what they were in 1925 or 1955, and they are also quite different from the institutions called banks in Germany or the U.K. today."[8]

Likewise, Russo and Vinciguerra argue that in modern financial markets definition-based regulatory distinctions are archaic and unworkable. Their central concern is with the "definitional impediments to financial innovation"[9] wrought by a regulatory structure that allocates jurisdiction over new financial products between the CFTC and SEC on the basis of inherently "imprecise legislative definitions" of futures and securities. They demonstrate that "[t]he distinctions between futures and securities...have become ambiguous in light of the development of products, such as exchange-traded options, index participations (IPs), and stock index futures, that combine characteristics of both."* Additional examples are provided by Professor John Coffee of Columbia University Law School, who describes regulatory turf wars involving the Federal Reserve (which, according to Coffee, seemingly always wins) and other regulators. In contrast, a functional approach to products and institutions is, as Merton emphasizes, principled and predictable.

A functional analysis suggests, however, that legal uncertainty will gradually mount because of the dynamics of the financial innovation spiral, the global nature of derivatives markets, accelerating financial industry "interrelatedness," and the efforts of financial and legal engineers to innovate around legal and regulatory barriers. Over time, formerly useful statutory distinctions on which most of the U.S. financial regulatory structure is predicated have been demonstrating a glaring need for modernization.

---

*Russo and Vinciguerra criticize a "functional" approach, unrelated to the one that the G-30 advocated and that is adopted in this book: "Theories that seek to justify or allocate regulatory jurisdiction [between the CFTC and SEC] typically rely upon *functional* grounds." (Emphasis added.) The functional grounds they criticize are so-called functional attempts to distinguish between "securities" and "futures." That approach tends toward obscure, unhelpful terms such as *futurity*. Compare, for example, the *G-30 Overview:* 28–34, with Russo and Vinciguerra, *New Product Development, supra,* Chapter 2, note 2: 11–16.

END-USER CONCERNS

The potential applicability of the Securities Laws or the CEA to an OTC derivatives transaction is often considered to be a dealer rather than an end-user concern. The reason is that most OTC derivatives controversies have been the result of one counterparty's attempt to disavow responsibility for large, unforeseen losses. So far, primarily end users have sought to disavow such losses. In practice, it is unlikely that a dealer that wishes to remain in the market would—because of reputational, legal liability, and regulatory concerns—seek to avoid contractual obligations on products it had structured and sold.

Still, there are many reasons that end users and their counsel need to be aware of potential legal and regulatory issues.

Availability of Legal Rights and Remedies

The most important reason for understanding the potential applicability of federal and state securities laws and the CEA to any OTC derivatives transaction is to gain an understanding of the range of potential remedies and liabilities for violations of those laws. It is equally important to appreciate the wide range of transactions to which *neither* regulatory regime is likely to apply. When neither applies, an aggrieved party's remedies are generally limited to those available under state common law for breach of contract and fraud claims.

Similarly, much attention has been paid to federal regulatory guidance addressed to different types of financial institutions directing them, in effect, to know and assess the ability of their counterparties to understand the risks of OTC derivatives. Alternatively, various regulators such as the National Association of Securities Dealers (NASD) and self-regulatory organizations (SROs) such as the New York Stock Exchange and the American Stock Exchange have adopted "suitability" rules applicable to derivatives and related instruments. However, suitability requirements are generally enforced directly by SROs against members through fines, censure, suspension, expulsion, and other sanctions; they do not generally entitle the customer to a right of action for damages against the SRO member.

Generally, then, it is inadvisable for an end user to rely on institutional regulatory guidance for protection. The objective of the guidance is to protect the safety and soundness of regulated institutions, not their customers. According to Merton, this guidance "takes as given the type of institutions that provide particular financial services and then analyzes what can be done to help these institutions perform those services more effectively. Framed in terms of *the* thrifts, *the* banks, or *the* insurance companies, policy issues are posed in terms of what can be done to make these institutions safe and sound."[10]

A further explanation is provided by Ernest Patrikis, First Vice President, and Diane Virzera, an attorney, both of the New York Fed:

> The ultimate rationale for this guidance is to ensure that banks engage in derivatives activities safely and soundly by protecting themselves from attendant credit, legal, and reputational risks. Although the guidelines address issues of appropriateness, they do so in the context of risk management at the bank and *do not establish suitability standards for the protection of unsophisticated customers. They are prudential supervision examiner guidelines, not customer protection rules.*[11]

Participation in the Development of Self-Regulatory Apparatus and Codes of Conduct

To the extent that the regulatory emphasis moves in favor of industry self-regulation, end users have an interest in participating in that effort. To date, for understandable reasons, end-user involvement has been modest. For example, Patrikis spoke before the End-Users of Derivatives Association (EUDA) at its April 1996 annual meeting in Washington, DC. In explaining the absence of EUDA from the effort by a number of industry groups to create, under the auspices of the New York Fed, a "code of conduct" for OTC derivatives market participants—subsequently embodied in the "Principles and Practices for Wholesale Financial Market Transactions" (Principles and Practices)—he explained: "When we started down this path there was no EUDA. That is why EUDA was not invited as a sponsoring trade association."[12] Similarly, few end users were involved in the preparation of the *G-30 Study,* and those who were involved were large users of derivatives not necessarily representative of the broader end user community.

According to Patrikis and Virzera, the Principles and Practices are intended to "articulate the basic assumptions in the OTC derivatives markets—participants transact business at an arm's-length basis."[13] While that statement alone is hardly controversial, note that the Principles and Practices by their express terms do not apply to a counterparty relationship unless expressly adopted by those counterparties. They are expressly intended to be "sets of 'best practices' that OTC derivatives market participants voluntarily may choose to follow." However, the voluntary nature of the Principles and Practices has been rendered problematic, as Patrikis and Virzera indicate:

> Nevertheless, the "best practices" *may prove to be useful to courts as standards* to evaluate the nature of relationships between OTC derivatives counterparties and define their respective responsibilities under the common law.

Compliance Costs

The costs of complying with regulatory requirements must be borne by market participants, both dealers and end users alike. The most obvious result of unnecessary or overly burdensome compliance requirements is that the costs will to the extent possible be passed on by dealers to end users, most likely in the form of increased product prices. Alternatively, economic theory dictates that dealer inability to pass compliance costs on to end users will eventually result either in more limited product offerings or in decreased dealer competition. In addition, end users are subject to their own direct legal and compliance costs.

Market Incompleteness

Financial Economists repeatedly emphasize that one unintended beneficial result of arbitrary regulation and regulatory competition between financial institutions and markets is their contribution to financial innovation. However, Coffee has concluded, on the basis of an evaluation of "the history of the SEC and the CFTC turf battles throughout the 1980s,"[14] that the competition between these two agencies when their jurisdiction has overlapped has had a demonstrably negative effect on U.S. financial markets. The reason? "[E]ach agency is likely to possess some blocking power or veto authority over transactions that market participants regulated by the other wish to engage in. The result can be a *dead-weight social loss,* as presumptively efficient and value maximizing transactions are barred by both agencies. Indeed, the SEC/CFTC jurisdictional wars provide a paradigm of this process at work."

According to Coffee, one cost of legal uncertainty is that dealer unwillingness to offer complex OTC products, owing to regulatory concerns, may result in more limited product offerings. "Hence, if these hybrid instruments are chilled by the specter of dual [SEC/CFTC] jurisdiction, there is presumably some efficiency loss, and the capital market no longer 'spans' all combinations of risk and return. The bottom line then is that regulatory competition restricts the products that the market can offer."

However, Coffee eventually offers support for the financial economists when he states that although the "chilling effect" may stifle domestic innovation, it certainly has not done so on a global basis:

> To be sure, the new products did not disappear. The Toronto Stock Exchange began trading an index participation product [which the CFTC successfully blocked in the United States], apparently with some success. Foreign futures exchanges have begun to trade futures on individual stocks [which the SEC has effectively vetoed in the United States]....Just since 1986, the share of the world's futures trading conducted on American exchanges fell from eighty percent to under fifty.

U.S. markets may be rendered less complete and less competitive by regulatory concerns. However, end users that are aware of the full range of products offered internationally may be able to obtain desired risk management products, and perhaps at better pricing, in foreign markets.

Effect on Documentation

Regulatory issues tend to insinuate themselves into OTC derivatives documentation, particularly representations and warranties. A counterparty's failure to appreciate the legal ramifications of contract terms may later affect the availability to it of contractual rights and remedies.

Public Companies

The expectations of shareholders of public companies regarding those companies' business activities may be based to a significant extent on regulatory product classifications, the descriptions of which may be based upon Securities Laws and CEA product definitions.

Dealer Insolvency

A healthy dealer is highly unlikely to disavow its OTC derivatives losses. However, in the event of a dealer insolvency, its trustee or receiver might attack the enforceability of OTC transactions that arguably constitute, for example, illegal off-exchange futures contracts. Greenspan, partly for this reason, asserts that it is important that "end users of derivatives…implement sound risk management practices," including "the consistent application of counterparty credit limits to the dealer."[15]

End User as Issuer of Securities

As we discuss below, the SEC has initiated enforcement actions based on its view that certain swaps are securities because they are functionally equivalent to cash-settled put options written by end users on underlying Treasury securities. A logical extension of this reasoning is that an end user may be deemed to have sold a security in a manner that technically violates, for example, restrictive covenants in public debt instruments, or in a manner that violates or otherwise risks liability under the Securities Laws. Coffee notes, with reference to Bankers Trust's 1994 settlement with the SEC, that "if swaps can be deemed securities (as appears likely under the SEC's theory), then both parties to a swap have standing to sue under Rule 10b-5."[16] Conceivably, knowing or reckless end user misrepresentations—for example, regarding sophistication and ability to assess transaction risks independently, or legal authority to enter into particular products—might be deemed to violate of antifraud provisions of the Securities Laws.

ENDNOTES: CHAPTER 7

1. Steven M. H. Wallman, "Regulating in a World of Technological and Global Change," Remarks Before the Institute of International Bankers, Washington, D.C. (March 4, 1996) (www.sec.gov/news/speeches/spch087.Txt); see also Craig Torres and Michael Siconolfi, "Leverage: Wall Street's Two-Edged Sword," *Wall Street Journal* (August 21, 1992) ("The private derivatives markets, for the most part, are beyond the expertise, surveillance and laws of regulators"): C1.
2. Sheila Bair, "United States Regulation of Derivative Instruments: Reflections from a Crucial Crossroads," in *Derivative Instruments,* Edward J. Swan, ed. (Kluwer Academic Publishers Group, 1994) [hereafter, this paper is referred to as *Crossroads* and this anthology is referred to as *Derivative Instruments*]: 14–15.
3. See Joseph Dial, "Overseeing Exchanges: How the CFTC Does It," *Risk/Emerging Markets Investor* (April 1996) [hereafter, *How the CFTC Does It*]: 48.
4. See Russo and Vinciguerra, *New Product Development, supra,* Chapter 2, note 2: 5, 14; see also John C. Coffee, Jr., "Competition Versus

Consolidation: The Significance of Organizational Structure in Financial and Securities Regulation," *The Business Lawyer* 50(2) (February 1995) [hereafter, *Organizational Structure*]: 447–484. Merton H. Miller and Christopher L. Culp, "Rein in the CFTC," *Wall Street Journal* (August 17, 1995) [hereafter, *Rein in the CFTC*].

5. Russo and Vinciguerra, *New Product Development, supra,* Chapter 2, note 2: 11.

6. This and the quotation in the next paragraph are from Greenspan, *Statement Before Congress,* Chapter 1, note 25 (emphasis added): 599.

7. K. Ravindran, *Customized Derivatives: A Step-By-Step Guide to Using Exotic Options, Swaps, and Other Customized Derivatives* (McGraw Hill, 1998): 3.

8. Merton, *Financial Innovation, supra,* Chapter 1, note 15: 20.

9. This and the remaining quotations in this paragraph are from Russo and Vinciguerra, *New Product Development, supra,* Chapter 2, note 2: 2–5.

10. Both quotations in this paragraph are from Merton, *Financial Innovation, supra,* Chapter 1, note 15: 20.

11. Ernest T. Patrikis and Diane L. Virzera, "Over-the-Counter Derivatives Sales Practices: Disclosure, Suitability, Appropriateness, and 'Best Practices'" (unpublished manuscript; may be available through the New York Fed) (May 30, 1996) (emphasis added) [hereafter, *Sales Practices*]: 11.

12. See Ernest T. Patrikis, "Dealer/End-User Relationships—What They Are and What They Should Be," *Remarks Before the End-Users of Derivatives Association Second Annual Conference and Member Meeting,* April 9–10, 1996 (available on the Internet at: www.ny.frb.org/pihome/news/speeches/ep9660409.html) [hereafter, *Dealer/End-User Relationships*].

13. All quotations in this paragraph are from Patrikis and Virzera, *Sales Practices, supra,* note 11 (emphasis added): 15.

14. The quotations in this section are from Coffee, *Organizational Structure, supra,* note 4 (emphasis added): 465–466, 470.

15. See Greenspan, *Statement Before Congress,* Chapter 1, note 25: 595.

16. See John C. Coffee, Jr., "Bankers Trust Settlement: Whither the Swaps Market?" *New York Law Journal* (January 26, 1995) [hereafter, *Whither the Swaps Market?*]; see also *In the Matter of BT Securities Corporation,* Admin. Proc. File No. 3-8579, Securities Act Release No. 35136, 1994 SEC LEXIS 4041 (December 22, 1994).

CHAPTER 8

Market Regulation: Overview

[T]he nature of derivatives activities clearly demonstrates that [the current regulatory system] has not kept pace with the dramatic and rapid changes that are occurring in domestic and global financial markets. Banking, securities, futures, and insurance are no longer separate and distinct industries that can be well regulated by the existing patchwork quilt of Federal and State agencies.

Charles A. Bowsher, Comptroller
General of the United States
Testimony Before the U.S. Senate, May
19, 1994[1]

There has never been a greater need for us to work together. We regulate one of the most innovative industries on the face of the earth, whose main commodity—capital—has little regard for national borders. If anything, the pace of change has become even more pronounced in recent years, bringing a host of challenges for all of us.

Arthur Levitt, SEC Chairman
Remarks Before International
Association of Securities Commissions
(IOSCO), September 18, 1996

Historically, statutes, regulations, and decisions governing derivatives and their markets have been woven into the fabric of existing law on an ad hoc basis, usually in response to legal disputes or economic crises. In this regard, U.S. law is an evolving "patchwork quilt" of statutes, regulations, and judicial and agency decisions. It has been called "fragmented" and "inefficient,"[2] lacking any overriding, coherent logical structure. Far-reaching consequences often flow from strained judicial and regulatory interpretations of key statutory terms, most of which were adopted in an era before the advent of modern derivatives and related financial markets and technologies.

Nevertheless, it would be a mistake to overstate the practical effects of U.S. regulatory fragmentation on most existing OTC derivatives and their markets. As in any other area of the law, the confusion generated by hard derivatives cases (usually those involving exotic products, egregious conduct, and anachronistic regulations) belies the considerable degree of judicial and regulatory consistency and predictability as to the vast majority of existing OTC products. Virtually all famous cases, including an important one decided by the Supreme Court in 1997, have involved serious allegations of misconduct, mismanagement, or both. Unsurprisingly, they have led to inconsistent and contradictory judicial decisions and agency rulings. As Coffee reminds us: "To some, this only proves the old adage: hard cases make bad law."[3]

OVERVIEW OF CURRENT U.S. DERIVATIVES REGULATION— CLASSIFICATIONS AND CONSEQUENCES

"Financial market oversight in the United States is both compartmentalized and overlapping."[4] The law is driven by a regulatory classification scheme that reflects to a greater or lesser degree an ongoing "battle of philosophies"[5] and competing "financial regulatory policies"[6] regarding the proper goals of regulation and the best methods of achieving those goals. The consequences of any given regulatory classification can be dramatic.

Generally, any OTC derivative can be classified in three different ways. If it is (1) neither a "security," a "commodity future," nor a "commodity option," it will fall outside the Securities Laws and the CEA and mainly be a matter of state common law; (2) a "security" (a term that includes certain security options), it is potentially subject to the Securities Laws; and (3) a "commodity future" (also called a "futures contract" or just a "future") or "commodity option," it is potentially subject to the CEA.[7] Complexities arise in particular with "futures" on "securities."

Common Law

Generally, a derivative that is neither a security, a futures contract, nor an option on a security or a futures contract (in which case, it generally cannot be a hybrid instrument either) can be entered into on an OTC basis free of the registration requirements of the Securities Laws, the exchange-trading requirements of the CEA, and the antifraud and antimanipulation prohibitions of both the Securities Laws and the CEA. "[I]t is 'home free all'; the contract is exempt from any regulatory regime. The legal concerns are largely those under the common law: agreement on terms and the capacity to act."[8]

Most OTC derivatives, particularly plain vanilla products, fall outside the domain of federal and state regulatory schemes.* As federal district court Judge John Feikens noted in his opinion dismissing the complaints—other than the common law fraud counts—of Procter & Gamble Company (P&G) against Bankers Trust Company and BT Securities Corp. (collectively, BT): "At present, most derivatives transactions fall in 'the common-law no-man's land beyond regulation—...interest-rate and equity swaps, swaps with embedded options ("swaptions"),' and other equally creative financial instruments."[9]

Securities Laws

A product that falls within the definition of a "security" is potentially subject to the Securities Laws and the jurisdiction of the SEC. In addition, any OTC derivative that has as its underlying fidget a "security" or a formula tied somehow to the value of a security is potentially itself a security. The SEC has unequivocally stated that the inclusion of optionlike features linked to underlying securities may lead it to treat a transaction documented as a swap as itself constituting a security. However, the SEC has to date relied on this reasoning only in limited circumstances involving allegations of egregious dealer conduct.[†]

The theoretical potential of the SEC's position is still troubling, particularly as to swaps and swap-related products: "It has long been the position of the dealer community that privately negotiated over-the-counter ('OTC') derivatives are neither securities nor futures contracts subject to the federal regulatory jurisdiction of the Securities and Exchange Commission or the Commodity Futures Trading Commission, respectively."[10] Swaps have traditionally been thought of as risk managemen

---

*Residual uncertainty remains as to whether many plain vanilla products exempt from the CEA's exchange-trading requirement are futures contracts subject to the CEA's antifraud and antimanipulation provisions. See note 15, *infra,* and accompanying text. For example, on January 19, 1996, Mary L. Schapiro, then chairman of the CFTC, wrote to two Congressmen that the CFTC had "not taken a position on whether swap agreements are futures contracts." CFTC exemptive actions, including the Swaps Exemption, make no specific finding as to whether swaps are futures. Implicit in the CFTC's controversial May 7, 1998 "Concept Release" announcing its intended reexamination of its approach to OTC dervatives markets is, as the Treasury has criticized, the notion that swaps are futures.

†For example, in a series of releases relating to the dispute between BT Securities Corporation and Gibson Greetings, Inc. (Gibson), the SEC has taken the position that the inclusion in swaps of option-based functional characteristics derived from the price or yield of an underlying security may cause those swaps to become securities under the federal securities laws.

instruments consisting of series of forward exchanges of cashflows, not as investments constituting part of the capital formation process. Moreover, market participants and legal advisers have long believed that the bilateral nature of swaps also distinguishes them from securities. Although financial economists and the press may at times refer loosely to swaps as "securities,"[11] prior to recent SEC enforcement actions (discussed below), few seriously considered them to be securities for regulatory purposes.*

Furthermore, under the "economic reality" test (discussed below) that the Supreme Court uses in determining whether an instrument is a security, a transaction nominally structured as a swap but that constitutes for all practical purposes a unilateral extension of credit lacks any significant forward-based component. If the transaction functions in reality more like a unilateral extension of credit, an extension of the SEC's reasoning would suggest that the product might, depending on other factors (such as the existence or lack thereof of a broad plan of distribution), be considered a security.

"Whether a financing transaction is a security is a weighty issue for the participants. If the 1933 Act covers the arrangement, two consequences result. One, the arrangement must be registered with the Securities and Exchange Commission, unless an exemption applies. Two, with or without a registration exemption, the antifraud provisions of the 1933 Act and the...1934 Act...will apply."[12] Additional complications may also arise. For example, if a swap transaction is deemed to be a security, both parties will "have standing to sue under Rule 10b-5, private placement procedures must be followed more carefully, dealers may have to register as broker-dealers with the SEC, and the SEC's net capital rules may apply to some bank subsidiaries."[13]

In addition, nonbank "financial intermediaries that deal in the securities that fall within the definitions under the [Securities Laws] face close substantive regulation by the Securities and Exchange Commission."[14] In contrast, those that deal in "derivatives that do *not* fall within the definition of security...are not subject to similar regulation." "Securities and com-

---

*Market participants and legal experts have long believed that two features of swaps clearly distinguish them from securities. First, although swaps may be thought of as extensions of credit, they are not notes and any credit extension is bilateral—either party, depending on market forces, may at any time be either in or out of the money on its swap transaction. Next, as discussed in Chapter 2, explicitly designing early swaps as sequences of currency purchases and sales, rather than loans or extensions of credit, was meant to alleviate concerns about default risks and the enforceability of early termination rights of swap agreements.

modities laws, together with requirements issued by the Federal Reserve Board and the Office of the Comptroller of the Currency [governing commercial banks], broadly affect derivatives markets by imposing upon derivatives traders, mandatory rules and guidelines." Among them are registration requirements, capital adequacy standards, and reporting requirements, as well as guidelines regarding effective policies and procedures relating to client selection and suitability requirements, marketing and sales practices, and product pricing and valuation procedures.

Commodity Exchange Act

The CEA regulates "commodity futures" and "commodity options" trading. It provides, among other things, that commodity futures and options transactions, with certain exceptions, (1) must take place on a contract market and (2) are subject to the CEA's antifraud and antimanipulation provisions.[15] Transactions that fall within a statutory exclusion (such as the Treasury Amendment) are not covered by the CEA *at all* and thus are subject neither to the exchange-trading (or contract market) requirements nor to CEA antifraud and antimanipulation provisions. Transactions that fall within a regulatory exemption (such as the Swaps Exemption, the Hybrid Exemption, and the Trade Option Exemption) are exempt from the exchange-trading requirements only—they are *not* exempt from the CEA's antifraud and antimanipulation provisions. A commodity futures or option transaction that is neither excluded nor exempt and that is not entered into on a contract market is illegal and unenforceable.

The CFTC also regulates "futures commission merchants" (FCMs), "floor brokers," "commodity trading advisers," and "commodity pool operators."

Theoretically, an OTC derivative that contains forward-based components is potentially subject to the CEA and to the exclusive jurisdiction of the CFTC.* The reason is that the CEA does not define key statutory

---

*Often option- and forward-based product components are understood to result in the potential applicability of either the Securities Laws or the CEA (or, for depository instruments, federal banking laws). Yet, a functional analysis often reveals that a product is rather a "hybrid" that displays characteristics potentially subjecting it to the CFTC's exclusive jurisdiction. The instrument may, in particular, be a security or depository instrument that nevertheless has limited futures-like or commodity option-like characteristics. Thus, the value of the instrument will to some extent be tied to the value of a commodity futures or option.

terms on which CFTC jurisdiction is predicated with regard to financial futures. Thus, the CFTC has primary responsibility for interpreting the statute and, in effect, providing a definition. While CFTC decisions are subject to judicial review, CFTC cases are usually litigated in the Seventh Circuit, where the CFTC is, in Coffee's words, "the home team."*

The CFTC's Hybrid Exemption determines for all practical purposes the applicable regulatory regime. It include a "predominance test" for CEA exemptions that specifically requires a comparison of value of the "commodity-dependent" and "commodity-independent" components of the instrument.[16†] The predominance test requires that the instrument be "decomposed" into its component commodity option or futures components. In the case of commodity options: "In the most straightforward case, a commodity-dependent payout that is option-like is viewed as a long or short put or call. A futures-like payout is decomposed into a combination of options positions." Thus, a futures-like payout formula must be broken down into a combination of puts and calls on the same fidget having the same strike price. As shown in Chapter 3, the payoff profile of such a combination replicates the payoff profile of a forward, or futures, contract.

> The premiums for the options are then summed or netted, as appropriate, to arrive at the commodity-dependent value of the commodity-dependent components of the instrument. Instruments in which the sum of the commodity-dependent values of the commodity-dependent components is less than the present value of the commodity-independent component and meeting certain other criteria are exempted.[17]

---

*Merton Miller and his colleague Christopher Culp, echoing the words of Holbrook Working from decades earlier, emphatically state what they perceive to be the danger of leaving to the CFTC the primary task of resolving definitional uncertainty as to financial futures:

> Because *futures contracts have no specific economic attributes of their own* other than exchange trading *to distinguish them from ordinary forward contracts or swaps* (a forward contract is any contract for the future purchase of a commodity at a fixed price, and a "swap" is merely a package of forwards), the quest for any objective definition of "off-exchange futures" among contracts not already exchange-traded is *doomed from the start.* An overzealous regulator fishing for "illegal off-exchange futures" thus confronts a virtually unlimited supply of possibilities.

See Miller and Culp, *Rein in the CFTC, supra,* Chapter 7, note 4 (emphasis added).
†The predominance test is applied only once—upon issuance of the instrument. Changes in the value or price of the underlying fidget can easily move, and changes in the value of the option-like features can fluctuate dramatically depending on changes in volatility, over the life of the instrument. Without the one-time test, ongoing certainty regarding the applicability of the exemption would be difficult and perhaps impossible to obtain or provide.

The overriding CEA difficulty for parties to OTC derivatives is the danger that an existing product will be deemed to be a futures or commodity option as to which no exemption or exclusion is available. If so, the product will be illegal and unenforceable. With new products that have not yet been sold, two problems arise.

First, to be traded on an exchange a product must receive the prior approval of the CFTC as part of the CFTC's "contract designation" process, which includes in essence a review of the product's intrinsic merits. Under CEA § 5(7), the CFTC must conclude that the contract has an "economic purpose" and that trading in the instrument "will not be contrary to the public interest." The generality of the "economic purpose" standard and the "public interest" test necessarily convey wide agency discretion and raise difficult problems of proof for the proponents of new products. Consequently, the contract designation process is at best time-consuming—it can take years.

Second, even if a product survives the merit review, there still might not be any exchange that wishes to offer it for trading.*

DEFINITIONAL UNCERTAINTY AND INTERAGENCY JURISDICTIONAL DISPUTES

Just as the meaning of the term *derivative* as discussed in Chapter 2 is elusive, so also are the meanings of the key terms *security, commodity, commodity futures,* and *commodity options.* The definitions of the terms *security* and *futures* have, according to Russo and Vinciguerra, generated more literature and, probably, litigation than any other issue arising under the Securities Laws or the CEA.

In evaluating whether it will consider a derivative to be a security,

---

*For example, the result of the *IPs case* was not that Index Participations would be traded on a designated futures exchange or contract market. Rather, because the SEC regulates exchanges, which wanted to trade the products but could not do so (owing to CFTC exclusivity over the products), and because of the lack of desire of any CFTC-regulated exchange to trade the products, "these products 'are not trading today in any U.S. financial market *in any form.*'" See Russo and Vinciguerra, *New Product Development, supra,* Chapter 2, note 2 (citation omitted): 9. However, successful offshore markets for the products have developed.

the SEC has in actuality based its reasoning on a functional analysis (although the agency has not used that term in this context) that looks beyond product labels to examine the "economic reality" of transactions. Similarly, the CFTC's product analysis attempts to look into the economic substance of transactions. Therefore, a functional product analysis can alert market participants to product characteristics that may facilitate SEC or CFTC efforts to assert jurisdiction over various OTC derivatives and market participants.

Traditionally, in determining questions of economic reality or substance, courts look to judicial precedent as well as customary usage and the reasonable expectations of the parties. However, given the youth of OTC derivatives markets and the paucity of OTC derivatives cases that proceed past the initial pleadings stage, little direct judicial precedent is currently available. Further, judicial attempts to determine customary usage and parties' expectations are similarly uncertain.

Prior to the passage of the Commodity Futures Trading Commission Act of 1974 (CFTC Act)[18] the definition of commodity, set forth in CEA § 1(a)(3), included simply "a couple dozen edible items 'and all other goods and articles' (except onions for some reason)."[19] The CFTC Act comprehensively overhauled and expanded the CEA and created the CFTC. It also expanded the definition of the key term commodity to include "all services, rights, and interests in which contracts for future delivery are presently or in the future dealt in." As a result, the meaning of commodity, while clear as to specifically enumerated agricultural products, is vague as to all others, especially financial instruments.[20] By so expanding the definition of commodity, the CFTC Act effectively granted the CFTC potentially exclusive jurisdiction over all financial futures—as well as over options on certain financial products.

The breadth of the potential jurisdictional grant has resulted in interagency disputes between the CFTC and the SEC. The literal language of § 1(a)(3), as the SEC realized, effectively enabled the CFTC to designate a contract market for trading futures on single securities. Such a market would then compete directly with securities exchanges and OTC markets. Moreover, the contract market designation process applies under the CEA to futures and options involving underlying commodities. Therefore, the mere fact of designation of a market for the trading of futures or options on securities would necessarily (but circularly) imply that securities are commodities. Therefore, options on single securities would have been commodity options and thus subject to the CFTC's exclusive jurisdiction.

Attempts to resolve the interagency dispute have resulted in a series of compromises and exceptions to the CFTC's exclusive jurisdiction. The most important has been the so-called Shad/Johnson Accord, agreed to by the SEC and the CFTC, and named after their then respective chairmen, in 1981. Doubts about the validity of the Accord were resolved when Congress codified it in 1983 via amendments to the CEA. Under the Accord, "the SEC retained jurisdiction over (i) options on securities and securities indices, (ii) options on foreign currencies traded on a U.S. national securities exchange, and (iii) the offer and sale of securities issued by commodity pools."[21] The CFTC, on the other hand, retained exclusive jurisdiction over (1) commodity options; (2) futures contracts and options on futures contracts on all commodities, including any individual securities exempt from the Securities Laws, certain permitted broad-based securities indices (the so-called *substantial segment criterion,* purportedly intended to make sure the CFTC does not allow trading of futures on small enough indices that are the equivalent of futures on individual securities), and foreign currencies; and (3) options on foreign currencies not traded on a U.S. national securities exchange.

Unfortunately, complications persist. For example, transactions that fall within the exclusive jurisdiction of the CFTC but that have not received contract market designation are illegal. Moreover, the CFTC has stated that "[i]n determining whether a transaction constitutes a futures or option contract," it will not simply accept the parties' characterization of a transaction as dispositive. It will instead consider the transaction's economic reality: "the Commission assesses the transaction as a whole with a critical eye toward its underlying purpose."[22]

The lack of definitional guidance in the CEA partly explains the frustration of Merton, Culp, Russo, Vinciguerra, Coffee, and many others with the theoretically extraordinary scope of CFTC jurisdiction. The CFTC's aggressiveness in stepping in to provide "guidance," whether in interpretive releases or in enforcement actions, explains much of the remaining frustration. The controversy has resurfaced with the Federal Reserve's Greenspan, Treasury Secretary Rubin, and the SEC's Levitt jointly condemning the May 1998 CFTC Concept Release.

Thus, the comprehensive and expansive reach of the CEA, "together with the proliferation of derivatives financial instruments, has given rise to regulatory problems, including, in particular, recurring *uncertainty* about whether the CEA applies to derivative and hybrid instruments that were not contemplated" in 1974, when the CFTC Act was passed.[23]* The financial spiral effect is constantly producing and promises to continue to produce OTC derivatives that create the possibility for further CEA and CFTC difficulties.

ONGOING DEFINITIONAL AND JURISDICTIONAL STRUGGLE—*DUNN v. CFTC*[24]

A topical example of continuing definitional difficulties and jurisdictional struggles involves an issue of statutory construction argued before the Supreme Court on November 13, 1996 and decided February 25, 1997. The *Dunn* case addressed interpretative differences among several federal circuit courts and between the U.S. Treasury Department and the CFTC.

In *Dunn,* the Court had to decide whether, under the so-called 1974 Treasury Amendment[†] to the CEA, foreign currency options (FX options) constitute "transactions *in* foreign currency" or "transactions *involving*

---

*One area of particular confusion is equity derivatives. For example, the CFTC asserted jurisdiction in its enforcement action against MG Refining & Marketing Inc. and MG Futures Inc. (both are subsidiaries of Metallgesellschaft, AG). The action, which had nothing to do with equity derivatives, resulted in a July 1995 settlement based on a three-part test for determining when certain off-exchange contracts contained "all the essential elements" of futures contracts. The test refers to a contract that (1) calls for "future delivery at a price or formula set at the contract's inception, (2) can be satisfied either by physical delivery or an offsetting transaction, and (3) is used either to speculate or hedge rather than take delivery."

As Miller and Culp point out, many financial transactions, perhaps all derivatives, not traditionally considered futures contain all three elements. They all involve a reference price or formula set up front. "Because the terms of many derivatives allow some form of cash settlement, they may also meet the second part of the test. And if derivatives are *not* used either to speculate or hedge, what are they used for?" After pointing out the apparent "signalling" by the CFTC of its intention to begin narrowing significant CEA exemptions, Miller and Culp note: "Swaps on equities and certain swaps on securities, for example, are not covered by the swaps exemption and hence are not protected from the CFTC's new three-point acid test."

However, representatives of the CFTC, in subsequent statements, have stated that the commission was not trying to signal a tightening of the exemptions in the MG action— another case of hard facts potentially making bad law. See Miller and Culp, *Rein in the CFTC, supra,* Chapter 7, note 4; see, generally, Russo, *Regulation of Equity Derivatives, supra,* Chapter 5, note 23.

†The Treasury Amendment provides:

> Nothing in this chapter [the CEA] shall be deemed to govern or in any way be applicable to transactions in foreign currency, security warrants, security rights, resales of installment loan contracts, repurchase options, government securities, or mortgages and mortgage purchase commitments, unless such transactions involve the sale thereof for future delivery conducted on a board of trade. See 7 U.S.C. § 2(ii); CEA § 2(a)(1)(A)(ii)

foreign currency." The Treasury Amendment excludes transactions "in" foreign currency (other than those that take place "on a board of trade") from the CEA's coverage and from CFTC jurisdiction. Transactions "involving" foreign currency, if not so excluded, are potentially subject to the CEA's exchange-trading requirement and antifraud provisions and to CFTC jurisdiction.

The technical issue had potentially far-reaching consequences, directly affecting the U.S. OTC markets in FX options. The OTC market in FX options is an extremely efficient global market that operates on thin margins but has *daily average* trading of $40 billion, half of which takes place in the United States.[25] Thin-margin, high-volume markets depend on legal certainty for their viability. Commercial and investment banks and other regulated and unregulated financial institutions, many of which are members of important capital market industry associations ("Industry Associations")—e.g., the Foreign Exchange Committee, the Futures Industry Association, and the Public Securities Association—have for many years been engaging in the transactions with highly sophisticated counterparties in the United States and around the world on an OTC basis on the understanding that FX options are not subject to the CEA.

In its *amici curiae* brief opposing the CFTC's position in *Dunn,* the Industry Associations expressly acknowledged that, if the Treasury Amendment were not to exclude OTC FX option transactions from the CEA, both the Swaps Exemption and the Trade Option Exemption would likely still render most FX options enforceable as exempt OTC transactions. Even so, the brief stated that the exemptions are "significantly more limited in scope than the Treasury Amendment....By their very nature, moreover, regulatory exemptions are subject to the CFTC's jurisdiction and regulatory discretion. Indeed, the CFTC could decide to restrict the scope of these two exemptions even further or eliminate the exemptions altogether." In other words, in markets as important, sensitive, and mobile as these, the highest degree of legal certainty is warranted and essential.

The CFTC took the seemingly hyper-technical position that none of the Treasury Amendment's language or legislative history indicates any congressional intent to exclude FX options markets from the CEA.[26] According to the *CFTC Brief,* when Congress intended in other contexts that the CEA cover options, it specifically used the key terminology "involving" rather than "in":

For example, Congress distinguished between transactions "in" and transactions "involving" commodities in other sections of the CEA. The CEA's exclusive jurisdiction provision, 7 U.S.C. 2(i), and its general options provision, 7 U.S.C. 6c, both describe commodity options as transactions "involving"—rather than transactions "in"—the commodity. See, e.g., *Brown v. Gardner,* 115 S.Ct. 552, 556 (1994).

Assuming for argument's sake the dubious proposition that Congress had in other contexts carefully used the word "involving" when describing options contracts, the proper question before the Court was whether Congress' use of thc "in" phraseology in the Treasury Amendment was intended to be read restrictively to exclude FX options. That result is highly improbable. In 1974, when the CFTC Act was passed, Congress was almost certainly unaware that FX options would come into existence—the only foreign currency transactions then traded were "off-exchange...foreign currency futures."

Stripped to its essence, the one unambiguously valid—though logically weak —point raised by the CFTC's argument is that in upholding the CFTC's position in the lower court decision, the Second Circuit considered itself bound by its prior decision in *CFTC v. American Board of Trade, Inc.,* 803 F.2d 1242 (1986). However, the *American Board of Trade* decision involved CFTC efforts to protect certain defrauded individuals. In support of the CFTC's position, the Second Circuit based its decision in *American Board of Trade* on legislative history regarding the source of the request for inclusion of the Treasury Amendment. The source was a letter from the Treasury Department in which Treasury asserted that the protections of the CEA were not necessary for the protection of sophisticated financial institutions, because they were already subject to regulation. The Treasury letter led the Conference Committee to conclude that:

> A great deal of the trading in foreign currency in the United States is carried out through an informal network of banks and tellers. The Committee believes that this market is more properly supervised by the bank regulatory agencies and that, therefore, regulation under this legislation is unnecessary.   803 F.2d at 1249.

Nevertheless, as the *Industry Association Brief* asserted, nothing in the express language of the Treasury Amendment (or the quoted legislative history) necessarily limits the amendment's scope to transactions involving sophisticated institutions. Indeed, the Supreme Court's "plain meaning" doctrine of statutory intcrpretation, which the Court relied on heavily in deciding *Dunn* against the CFTC, strongly suggested the opposite.*

Moreover, the Fourth Circuit's decision in *Salomon Forex, Inc. v. Tauber,* 8 F.3d 966 (1993), *cert. denied,* 114 S.Ct. 1540 (1994), the only other comparable case, flatly rejected the argument that the Treasury Amendment's exclusion applies only to transactions which result in actual delivery of currency. *Salomon Forex* held: "Once we conclude that the clause is to be read to broadly include futures, it is a short step to conclude that the Treasury Amendment applies to *all* transactions in which foreign currencies are the subject matter."[27]

In addition, the CFTC acknowledged that an FX option is, under the Treasury Amendment, excluded from the CEA once it is exercised, because then there actually is a transaction "in" foreign currency—that is, the delivery of the relevant foreign currencies. The logic of that argument leads to strange conclusions.

First, it predicates CFTC jurisdiction over FX options not on the nature of the instrument itself or of the parties to the transaction. Instead, jurisdiction is based solely on subsequent market movements. The decision whether to exercise any option is for all practical purposes driven by market forces. Rationally, an option holder always exercises (or sells) an in the money option, including an FX option, which at expiration has value. Furthermore, no rational option holder would ever exercise an out of the money FX option, because it has either no or negative intrinsic value—its exercise would therefore *increase* the option holder's loss beyond the simple loss of its option premium.

Second, the kind of fraud that would have concerned Congress—had it directly considered the issue—would certainly have been the writing of an in the money option on which the writer attempts to renege. But that could happen only upon favorable market movements. Why would anyone care about an unenforceable out of the money option—which has no intrinsic value and would never be exercised? Under the CFTC's logic, an in-the-money option, which raises real fraud possibilities, is precisely the

---

*This doctrine dictates that the correct starting point for statutory interpretation is the "plain meaning" of a statute itself, unless there is some indication that the plain meaning was not intended. In other words, the Court has established an interpretive presumption against unnatural or illogical meanings. For a further discussion of the "plain meaning" doctrine, see *Consumer Prod. Safety Comm'n v. GTE Sylvania, Inc.,* 447 US 102, 108 (1980); *Gordan v. United States Van Lines, Inc.,* 130 F. 3d 282 (7th Cir 1997): 286.

kind of option excluded from the CEA via the Treasury Amendment. Certainly, that result is difficult to support, especially under the Supreme Court's "plain meaning" doctrine.

Nevertheless, *Dunn* was in some sense a "hard case." It involved (1) bad facts (a Ponzi scheme by "unscrupulous promotors" who defrauded individual investors); (2) unforeseen, and perhaps unforeseeable, market events (the development and growth of OTC options markets through the application of revolutionary option valuation theory and technology only *after* the passage of the Treasury Amendment); (3) outdated statutory language; (4) ambiguous legislative history; and (5) a clash of regulatory mandates (the Federal Reserve, which regulates banks and needs highly liquid and effective OTC markets to promote safety and soundness and implement national currency policy, *versus* the CFTC, whose basic mandate includes protecting individual investors against fraud). Virtually any judicial outcome would have, in some sense, constituted "bad law." As noted, the Court held in favor of Dunn and against the CFTC. The "bad" part of that result is the ultimate failure to punish (aside from obvious costs and expenses) unsavory conduct.

In early 1997, corrective legislation modifying the Treasury Amendment in relevant part was reintroduced in both the U.S. House of Representatives and the U.S. Senate. To date, no action has been taken on either bill. The CFTC and Treasury Department are also currently struggling to settle any future disputes out of court.

GOVERNMENT RESTRAINT AND INCREMENTALISM

To date, government responses to derivatives disputes and crises have tended to be modest and incremental. Regulators, market participants, and commentators generally agree for three primary reasons that continued legislative, judicial, and regulatory restraint is essential to the effectiveness of derivatives markets.

Global Markets; No Principal Physical Location

Unlike exchanges, OTC derivatives markets lack any fixed, identifiable physical location. They are, as Miller observes, "classic 'upstairs' market[s]"[28] that operate telephonically, electronically, and by computer.

These markets are "highly evolved, sophisticated, and very active. Trading is conducted twenty-four hours a day, from 6:00 a.m. Sydney, Australia time on Monday until 5:00 p.m. New York time on Friday, with [foreign currency] exchange rate [and other] quotations available on computer screens and similar electronic devices. OTC transactions are not conducted on organized exchanges. Instead, most trading is conducted over the telephone directly with dealers or through brokers. These markets are extremely sensitive to political and financial developments around the world and around the clock."[29] The *1995 BIS Report* remarked that the first feature "worth noting" about expansive OTC derivatives markets is their "global nature."[30]

Lacking a definite physical location, the markets are, in effect, highly "mobile." If confronted with adverse regulatory or judicial treatment, they can, as the following examples illustrate, quickly and easily "relocate" to more hospitable legal climates.*

Brent oil market

"A case in point is the Brent oil market"; after the District Court for the Southern District of New York held that certain Brent 15-day oil contracts constituted futures contracts subject to the provisions of the CEA, certain major U.S. oil companies moved their trading activities offshore "and never fully returned," even after the CFTC issued a statutory interpretation clarifying that the contracts fell within the CEA's "cash forward exclusion."[31]

---

*According to the Industry Association's *amici curiae* brief in *Dunn,* a Supreme Court decision that FX options were subject to the CEA would have jeopardized the competitiveness of U.S. OTC FX option markets and market participants. Subjecting OTC FX options to the CEA, according to the brief,

> creates significant legal uncertainty over the enforceability of a substantial volume of foreign exchange option contracts, could impose great regulatory and transactional costs on the OTC foreign currency markets, and *could possibly drive those OTC markets out of the United States.* [CEA coverage] may also put market participants in this country, including certain members of the Industry Association, at a disadvantage in global competition.

The *Industry Association Brief, supra,* note 29 (emphasis added): 6–13. Of further relevance here is that the CFTC expressly concede in its *Dunn* brief the legitimacy of concerns that "excessive domestic regulation may drive [the OTC FX option] market to overseas financial centers that provide a more hospitable regulatory environment."

CFTC advance notice

Another case in point, as discussed in Chapter 5, is the manner in which swaps markets reacted in 1987 to the CFTC's publication of its Advance Notice—in which, among other things, the CFTC intimated that it might assert jurisdiction over a wide range of swaps and related transactions. The combined effect of the Advance Notice and other actions taken by the CFTC around that time was to drive important market segments offshore, principally to London and other financial centers. Generally, the regulatory approach taken in the Advance Notice and subsequent CFTC actions, rulings, and interpretations—an approach often based on complex and unpredictable tests used to determine whether an instrument bears an "economic equivalence" to futures and commodity options—has been to discourage many major financial institutions from participating meaningfully in U.S. markets for certain derivatives and hybrid instruments.

Regulatory arbitrage

The search for a favorable regulatory environment is variously referred to by lawyers and economists as "regulatory arbitrage" or its closely related counterpart, "rent seeking." Governments and regulators that knowingly participate in the process through "regulatory competition" are often said to be participating in a regulatory "race to the bottom."[32]

Regulatory arbitrage is difficult if not impossible to prevent by any single nation or individual regulator. CFTC Commissioner Dial recently noted: "As financial institutions with worldwide operations seek the best returns, the global financial marketplace becomes more tightly integrated every day, with capital moving from country to country and time zone to time zone at the tap of a computer key."[33] Similarly, SEC Commissioner Wallman warns that "the walls...built by geographic boundaries and time zones which once dictated and furthered nationalistic views toward commerce are now generally nonexistent....[T]hose of use in the U.S. should recognize that the technology that makes our capital markets so accessible to others also represents a two way street....[I]t is just as easy for U.S. capital providers to move to direct off-shore investments."[34]

Host governments attempting to attract business activity, or regulators attempting to expand their jurisdictional reach, can easily undermine legitimate attempts to halt the arbitrage effect. They can lower the relevant regulatory burdens on prospective participants who would then be attracted to their markets or jurisdictions. Or, in the case of competing regulators, they can attempt to create legal uncertainties that will in effect act as what Coffee calls a "regulatory tax" on firms regulated by others.

Consider, for example, the supervisory complexities raised by the following hypothetical transaction: "If the Italian branch of a British securities firm uses a remote terminal to trade a German bund [instrument] for a customer in Paris, where did the transaction take place, which supervisor has oversight of the trader's conduct, and which supervisor monitors the integrity of the deal?"[35] Similarly, one commentator, quoting from the 1993 report by the Bank of England entitled *Derivatives: Report of an Internal Working Group,* noted that "the ability of unregulated foreign dealers to act as counterparties in the United States places a 'hole [in] the...heart of the derivatives market.' However, it is the fact that derivatives markets function internationally, largely beyond the reach of regulators, which is a hole in the heart of the regulatory structure."[36]

Simply put, the globalization of OTC derivatives markets and fundamental product demand weaken attempts at meaningful regulation of OTC derivatives markets solely on a nationalistic basis or by any single regulator. Impositions of unilateral regulatory hurdles without corresponding changes in economic demand "are more likely to force innovators underground or overseas, where they will deliver the needs demanded by their clients cloaked in forms acceptable to regulators."[37] Likewise, Russo and Vinciguerra assert that "firms that can afford to do so take their innovative products to overseas markets. [Alternatively,] [f]irms that cannot afford to export innovation *simply refuse to offer new products.*"[38]

Need for Comprehensive Solutions

The second reason for incrementalism has been perhaps best stated by Federal Reserve Chairman Greenspan:

> As the Board has stated repeatedly, there is a pressing need to modernize the U.S. financial system and regulatory structure. However, the Board believes that *legislation directed at derivatives* is *no substitute for broader reform* and, absent broader reform, could actually *increase risks* in the U.S. financial system by creating a regulatory regime that is itself ineffective and that diminishes the effectiveness of market discipline."[39]

Remedial legislation will be efficacious only if it is comprehensive and addresses the need to revamp and modernize the *entire* U.S. regulatory system—without singling out derivatives.

Market Discipline; Development of Self-Regulatory Apparatus

Any major legislative or regulatory changes risk adversely affecting successful industry efforts toward self-regulation and the development of industry-standard "best practices." OTC derivatives markets are primarily wholesale markets that depend on counterparty creditworthiness and sound business practices. Wide-ranging and ongoing efforts of the G-30, the Futures Industry Association, the Derivatives Policy Group,[40]* stock and futures exchanges, the legal and accounting professions, and others have been designed to improve risk management practices in a manner that is both more effective and responsive to technological and other innovations than government action can realistically aspire to be.

Private sector responses to the challenges posed by derivatives are largely responsible for the concerted opposition of most federal regulators to any new remedial derivatives legislation. As Greenspan stated in his May 1994 congressional testimony:

> the Board believes that remedial legislation relating to derivatives is neither necessary nor desirable at this time....Market forces, reinforced by broad acceptance of the risk management principles appear to be effectively constraining risk-taking by nonbank dealers and encouraging implementation of sound risk management practices. Counterparties to derivatives contracts are generally quite sensitive to credit exposures and often transact only with dealers they judge to be of the highest credit rating."[41]

Similarly, others argue that additional regulation "would be expensive and counterproductive. Whether a derivative instrument is appropriate for a particular end user ultimately depends upon an entity's management and internal controls, not upon regulatory policy."[42]

---

*This group (DPG) was formed at the suggestion of SEC Chairman Arthur Levitt in August 1994. Shortly thereafter, Mary L. Schapiro, then Chairman of the CFTC, joined Chairman Levitt as the principal official public sector contacts for the DPG. The six institutional members of the DPG are Merrill Lynch, CS First Boston, Goldman Sachs, Morgan Stanley, Salomon Brothers, and Lehman Brothers. The report is entitled "Framework for Voluntary Oversight" (*DPG Framework*).

DRAWBACK OF INCREMENTALISM—
LEGAL UNCERTAINTY

Although its benefits are readily apparent, incrementalism also demonstrates serious drawbacks. Limited responses may temporarily resolve discrete crises, yet, as previously discussed in the United States they have generally failed to achieve fundamental resolution of two overriding issues. First, there is considerable uncertainty regarding the extent to which new and existing products are or may be subject to securities or commodities regulation; second, once a product is clearly subject to securities or commodities regulation, there is often significant uncertainty as to which of the two regulatory regimes will control.

ENDNOTES: CHAPTER 8

1. Cited in Saul S. Cohen, "The Challenge of Derivatives," 63 Fordham L. Rev. 1993 (1995) [hereafter, *Challenge of Derivatives*]: 2028.
2. See Edward F. Greene, et al., *U.S. Regulation of International Securities and Derivatives Markets,* 3rd ed., II (Aspen Law and Business, 1996) [hereafter, *U.S. Regulation*]: § 13.04[1].
3. John C. Coffee, Jr., *Whither the Swaps Market?, supra,* Chapter 7, note 16. Justice Harlan first popularized the adage in the United States by in his dissenting opinion in *U.S. v. Clark,* 96 US 37, 49, 24 L.Ed. 696 (1878), citing Lord Campbell in *East India Co. v. Paul,* 7 Moo. 85, 111, 13 Eng. Rep. 811, 821 (P.C. 1849) ("it is the duty of all courts of justice to take care, for the general good of the community, that hard cases do not make bad law").
4. Joanne T. Medero, "Swaps and Other Derivatives: Regulatory and Legislative Developments," *Review of Banking and Financial Services,* 10(11) (Standard & Poor's, November 9, 1994) [hereafter, *Regulatory Developments*]: 117; see, generally, Greene et al., *U.S. Regulation, supra,* note 2: Chapter 13.
5. See, e.g., Louis Loss and Joel Seligman, *Fundamentals of Securities Regulation, Third Edition* (Little, Brown and Company, 1995) [hereafter, *Fundamentals of Securities Regulation*]: 22–33.
6. See Merton, *Financial Innovation, supra,* Chapter 1, note 15: 20.
7. The CEA does not use or define futures contract or commodity futures. Instead, it refers to "contracts of sale…for future delivery." But "future delivery" is also not defined, other than to specifically exclude forward contracts—or sales of cash commodities for "deferred shipment or

delivery." See CEA § 1a(11); see, generally, Miller and Culp, *Rein in the CFTC, supra,* Chapter 7, note 4; Greene et al., *U.S. Regulation, supra,* note 2: § 13.05[2][a].

8. Cohen, *Challenge of Derivatives, supra,* note 1: 1998.

9. *Procter & Gamble Company v. Bankers Trust Company,* 925 F.Supp. 1270 (S.D. Ohio, May 9, 1996) [hereafter, *Procter & Gamble*]; see also *Bankers Trust International PLC v. PT Dharmala Sakti Sejahtera,* 1994 Folio Nos. 2168 & 1396 (High Ct. of Justice, Queens Bench Div., Dec. 1, 1995) (LEXIS, Enggen Library, Cases file) [hereafter, *Dharmala*].

10. Warren N. Davis and James M. Cain, "The P&G/Bankers Trust Settlement and Opinion: Views and Implications," *Futures and Derivatives Law Report,* 16(4) (June 1996) [hereafter, *Views and Implications*]: 3.

11. See, e.g., Hull, *Derivatives, supra,* Chapter 3, note 4: 1; Tucker, *Financial Futures, supra,* Chapter 4, note 10: 1.

12. Christopher Olander and Cynthia Spell, "Interest Rate Swaps: Status Under Federal Tax and Securities Laws," *Maryland Law Review,* 45 (1986): 21, 53–54.

13. See, generally, Coffee, *Whither the Swaps Market?, supra,* Chapter 7, note 16; Coffee, *Organizational Structure, supra,* Chapter 7, note 4.

14. All quotations in this paragraph are from Thomas C. Singher, "Regulating Derivatives: Does Transnational Regulatory Cooperation Offer a Viable Alternative to Congressional Action?" *Fordham International Law Journal,* 18 (1995) (emphasis added): 1419–1422, 1405.

15. See 7 U.S.C. §§ 2, 6(a) and (c), 6c(b); *Curran, supra,* Chapter 4, note 13. As noted earlier, the CFTC on May 7, 1998 issued a Concept Release [hereafter, *CFTC Concept Release*] as part of its comprehensive regulatory reform effort concerning both exchange and off-exchange markets. Part of this effort is a review of regulation of OTC derivatives markets.

16. 58 Fed. Reg. 5580 (January 22, 1993); see also 55 Fed. Reg. 13582 (April 11, 1990); see, generally, Russo, *Regulation of Equity Derivatives, supra,* Chapter 5, note 23: 613–614, 617–624. The quotations in this paragraph are from Russo, *Regulation of Equity Derivatives:* 622–623.

17. Russo, *Regulation of Equity Derivatives, supra,* Chapter 5, note 23: 622–623.

18. Pub. L. No. 93-463, 88 Stat. 1389. The overhauled and expanded Commodity Exchange Act is codified, as amended, at 7 U.S.C. § 1 *et seq.*

19. See Loss and Seligman, *Fundamentals of Securities Regulation, supra,* note 5: 233.

20. See Greene et al., *U.S. Regulation, supra,* note 2 ("The precise meaning of the phrase 'dealt in' is not entirely clear."): § 13.05[1].

21. The Accord is codified at Futures Trading Act of 1982, Pub. L. No. 97-444,

tit. 1, 96 Stat. 2294 (1983). The quotation is from Greene et al., *U.S. Regulation, supra,* note 2 (citation omitted): § 13.04[3].

22. Statutory Interpretation Concerning Certain Hybrid Instruments, 54 Fed. Reg. 1128 (January 11, 1989), CFTC Regulations Part 34: 1139; see also Greene et al., *U.S. Regulation, supra,* note 2: § 13.05[2][b].

23. Greene et al., *U.S. Regulation, supra,* note 2 (emphasis added): 13–26.

24. See *Dunn v. Commodity Futures Trading Commission,* 1997 U.S. Lexis 1451, 117 S.Ct. 913,137 L.Ed. 2d 93 (February 25, 1995) [hereafter, *Dunn*]; see, generally, "Brief of the Foreign Exchange Committee, The New York Clearing House Association, The Futures Industry Association, The Managed Futures Association, and The Public Securities Association as *Amici Curiae* in Support of the Petitioners," filed with the U.S. Supreme Court on July 12, 1996 in *Dunn, supra,* note 24 [hereafter *Industry Association Brief*]; see also John M. Quitmeyer, "Supreme Court to Decide If Off-Exchange Currency Options Are Regulated," *Derivatives: Tax Regulation Finance* (January–February 1997) [hereafter, *Supreme Court to Decide*]: 138–142.

25. See *1995 BIS Report*; *Central Bank Survey of Derivatives Markets Activity Results of the Survey of the United States* (Federal Reserve Bank of New York, December 18, 1995): Annex II, Table 5—U.S.; see, generally, *Industry Association Brief, supra,* note 24: 9–10.

26. The quotations in this and the following paragraph are from "Brief for the Commodity Futures Trading Commission," filed August 30, 1996 with the U.S. Supreme Court in *Dunn, supra,* note 12 (available at 1996 WL 501987, SCT-BRIEF) [hereafter, *CFTC Brief*].

27. 8 F.3d at 976 (emphasis in original).

28. See Miller, *The Last Twenty Years and the Next, supra,* Chapter 2, note 6: 465.

29. Sce *Industry Association Brief, supra,* note 24: 8. The quotation is from Miller, *The Last Twenty Years and the Next, supra,* Chapter 2, note 6: 465.

30. See *1995 BIS Report:* 24.

31. See Russo, *Regulation of Equity Derivatives, supra,* Chapter 5, note 23: citing *Transnor (Bermuda) Limited v. BP North America Petroleum,* 738 F.Supp. 1472 (S.D.N.Y. 1990): 1489, and the CFTC's "Statutory Interpretation Concerning Forward Transactions," 55 Fed. Reg. 39188, 39192 (September 25, 1990)): 612, n. 11.

32. See Merton, *Financial Innovation, supra,* Chapter 1, note 15; Coffee, *Organizational Structure, supra,* Chapter 7, note 4: 447–484.

33. Dial, *How the CFTC Does It, supra,* Chapter 7, note 3: 49.

34. Steven M. H. Wallman, "Regulating in a World of Technological and Global Change," Remarks Before the Institute of International Bankers, Washington, DC (March 4, 1996) [hereafter, *Regulating in a World of*

Technological and Global Change]; see also Swan, *Derivative Instruments, supra,* note 2 ("the nature of the derivative instrument markets is that they are international, and consequently extremely difficult to regulate with purely national regulatory systems"): x; Similarly, Craig Torres, and Michael Siconolfi, "Leverage: Wall Street's Two-Edged Sword," *Wall Street Journal* (August 21, 1992) ("the private derivatives markets, for the most part, are beyond the expertise, surveillance and laws of regulators"): C1.

35. David Shirreff, "The Agony of the Global Supervisor," *Euromoney* (July 1996) [hereafter, *Agony of the Global Supervisor*]: 51.

36. Cohen, *Challenge of Derivatives, supra,* note 1 (citation omitted): 2028.

37. See Mason et al., *Financial Engineering, supra,* Chapter 1, note 2: 66; see, generally, Hu, *Misunderstood Derivatives, supra,* Chapter 1, note 22.

38. See Russo and Vinciguerra, *New Product Development, supra,* Chapter 2, note 2 (emphasis added): 10.

39. Greenspan, *Statement Before Congress,* Chapter 1, note 25 (emphasis added): 603.

40. The *DPG Framework*'s introduction states:

> The DPG was organized to respond to the interest that has been expressed by Congress, agencies and others with respect to public policy issues raised by the OTC derivatives activities of unregulated affiliates of SEC-registered broker-dealers and CFTC-registered futures commission merchants. These issues include the understandable interest in more meaningful information regarding the risk profile of professional intermediaries and the quality of their internal controls as well as a clearer articulation of the nature of their relationships with nonprofessional counterparties and related transaction responsibilities. The DPG's objective was to formulate a *voluntary oversight* framework intended to address these public policy issues.

41. Greenspan, *Statement Before Congress,* Chapter 1, note 25: 603.

42. See, e.g., Cohen, *Challenge of Derivatives, supra,* note 1: 1996.

CHAPTER 9

Market Regulation:
Case Law Road Map

Judge Feikens'....surprise opinion...may prove to be a landmark because it is the first time that an American court has ruled on a number of critical legal issues affecting the multi-trillion dollar derivatives markets....People will be spinning this one for a long time.

Warren Davis
Counsel to EUDA, American Banker,
May 21, 1996

These correct and long-anticipated rulings do not change the legal or regulatory landscape for swaps in the United States....End users, therefore, should not take false comfort that Judge Feikens' decision will provide an effective remedy for any swap that ends up being unprofitable.

Daniel P. Cunningham
Counsel to ISDA, American Banker,
June 20, 1996

The Law, like the traveler, must be ready for the morrow. It must have a principle of growth.

Justice Benjamin Cardozo[1]

Until Judge Feikens issued his May 9, 1996 opinion* in *Procter & Gamble,* little directly relevant judicial guidance regarding the potential regulatory or judicial treatment of OTC derivatives was available in the United States. His opinion constituted the first published decision by a U.S. court addressing the broad range of legal issues applicable to swaps and swap-related

---

*As of this writing, the potential for new judicial guidance both in the U.S. and elsewhere presents itself as a consequence of the recent Asian currency crisis. Reportedly, J.P. Morgan & Company is already involved in litigation in the United States and South Korea over derivatives deals that expose the bank to hundreds of millions of dollars of potential losses. See, e.g., Timothy L. O'Brien, "J.P. Moran In Korea Battle On Derivatives," *New York Times* (February 27, 1998): D1.

products.* The judge held that certain complex interest rate swaps, documented on a standard form ISDA Master Agreement, together with a customized ISDA Schedule and separate written confirmations, were not "securities" under the 1933 or 1934 Act or Ohio's securities laws. He also found that the Swaps Exemption excluded the transactions in question from the CEA's exchange-trading requirement and that the transactions were otherwise not actionable by P&G under the CEA. His opinion also draws seemingly straightforward common law conclusions that have, nevertheless, been subject to remarkably divergent interpretations.

Technically, *Procter & Gamble* has limited precedential authority. Indeed, as discussed below, Judge Feikens was careful to note that his rulings were narrow and not intended to cover any OTC derivatives other than the swaps at issue in the case. In addition, his opinion in any event constitutes merely a series of unappealed trial court rulings—there is no certainty that the rulings would have been upheld on appeal or that they will be followed by other courts, whether in the same or in other jurisdictions.†

Nonetheless, as the first relevant decision in this area, it received both national and international press coverage. Consequently, it will receive considerable legal scrutiny, both by market participants and by later courts and lawmakers called on to handle OTC derivatives legal issues. Perhaps even more important is that Judge Feikens' careful and thorough analysis of the relevent legal issues suggests an unmistakable effort to establish a comprehensive framework for analyzing the regulatory and common law

---

*Market participants may find instructive a recent case addressing the nature of counterparty relationships in OTC foreign exchange transactions governed by New York law, *Campania Sud-Americana de Vapores, S.A. v. IBJ Schroder,* 785 F.Supp. 411 (S.D.N.Y. 1992). CSAV sued its FX dealer for alleged overcharges in a series of currency transactions from 1984 to 1990. The opinion involved 175 transactions (out of 1087) between the parties during that period. The court held no fiduciary relationship existed, despite a relationship between the parties for over 40 years. It concluded: "CSAV's allegations that it reposed trust and confidence in Schroder and relied upon Schroder to give CSAV the best rates are merely an *effort to avoid the repercussions of its lack of diligence* in monitoring the rates at which conversions were made for over six years." 785 F.Supp. at 422 (emphasis added). The court emphasized the absence of a duty to disclose information "to one who reasonably should be aware of it." *Id.* For an excellent discussion of the case, see John P. Emert, Vice President and Counsel of Citibank, N.A., "New York Case Finds Arm's-Length Dealing with OTC Foreign Exchange Transactions Does Not Create a Fiduciary Relationship," *Derivatives* (Warren, Gorham & Lamont, July–August 1996): 277.

†The reason neither party appealed appears unrelated to the content of the opinion. According to press reports, the opinion was filed just before the parties reached an out-of-court settlement. Apparently, neither party had seen the opinion before the settlement was reached. See, e.g., Davis and Cain, *Views and Implications, infra,* note 13.

treatment of swaps. To that extent, the opinion should provide welcome analytical support to later courts and lawmakers, as well as legal advisers, whether or not they agree with the Judge's ultimate conclusions. Until further meaningful judicial guidance is provided, the *Procter & Gamble* decision provides the best available "road map" for analyzing many of the legal issues of greatest importance to the U.S. OTC derivatives industry.

DESCRIPTION OF THE P&G SWAPS

Procter & Gamble involved two "highly specialized" swap transactions.[2] One—called the "5s/30s swap"—involved floating-rate payments calculated for the first six months based on a rate lower than privaling commercial paper (CP) rates. That amount would, after six months, be increased by a complex "spread." A simple mathematical transformation converting bond prices to yields would have shown that the spread formula was highly sensitive to any change in the existing mathematical relationship between yields on five-year Treasury notes and prices of 30-year Treasury bonds. Because basic corporate finance teaches that prices and yields on long-term fixed-rate instruments respond far more dramatically than those of short-term instruments to changes in prevaling interest rates, P&G's representatives were, or should have been, well aware of the enormous volatility inherent in a 5s/30s spread. The other derivative—the "DM swap"—involved payments "based on [the] value of the German deutschemark."

The "5s/30s Swap"

The 5s/30s was a five-year fixed- for floating-rate swap with a notional amount of $200 million. Under this swap, Bankers Trust (BT) agreed to pay P&G a 5.30% fixed rate for five years. In exchange, P&G agreed to pay a floating rate for the same period. For the first six months, the floating rate was to be the prevailing CP rate *minus* 0.75%—that is, 75 basis points (bps)— amended in January 1994 to *minus* 88 bps. After the first six months, P&G's payment obligations would be reset to include the spread described above.

If the spread formula produced a negative number—which could have happened if interest rates declined, thereby reducing P&G's payment obligations—it would instead be deemed to be zero. Thus, the spread could only *increase* P&G's costs, not lower them. The spread formula resulted in massive leverage that, according to Judge Feikens, "meant that even a small movement up or down in prevailing interest rates results in an incrementally larger change in P&G's position in the swap."

An instant result of the 5s/30s swap was that P&G reduced its floating-rate funding costs for the first six months beneath its target of the CP rate *minus* 40 bps—P&G's initial rate was CP *minus* 88 bps. But to achieve the reduction, P&G assumed risks equivalent to those of the writer of a highly leveraged put option in which "each basis point move was magnified up to 31 times."[3] P&G had to assume such extraordinary leverage because in efficient capital markets "there is *no free lunch*. P&G could not achieve its funding target by executing a plain vanilla interest rate swap. To achieve such off-market rates, it had to assume some risks. It did so by *selling* a *put option* on 30-year US Treasuries whose *payoff profile was repackaged into the spread formula*. The premium it earned for selling this option was 75 basis points per year for five years."

The "DM Swap"

The DM deal was also a highly leveraged swap (apparently also a five-year maturity) with an option-like payoff profile. Floating-rate payments were calculated according to a complex formula with a "leverage factor...shown in the formula as ten." For the first year, BT would pay a floating rate plus 233 bps, while P&G would pay the same floating rate plus only 133 bps. Thus, P&G received a 1%, or 100 bps, premium for the first year. Given that there is no "free lunch," P&G had to assume some risk to obtain that primium. That risk took the form of an additional spread payable by P&G "if the four-year DM swap rate ever traded below 4.05% or above 6.01% at any time [over the first year of the swap]....If the DM swap rate stayed within the band of interest rates, the spread was zero." Thus, P&G effectively *wrote* two options: a call option payable if DM rates rose above 6.01%, and a put option payable if rates dipped below 4.05%.

OTC DERIVATIVES—COMMON LAW BASICS

Judge Feikens' decision also contains important common law rulings. In this regard, it complements the English commercial court in the December 1995 *Dharmala* decision.[4]*

---

*Dharmala is also an important OTC derivatives decision. Like *Procter & Gamble,* It involved swaps documented on standard ISDA forms that expressly provide for (unless otherwise specified) New York or English governing law. Most transactions involving ISDA documentation are governed by New York or English law. The *Procter & Gamble* swaps were expressly governed by New York law; *Dharmala* involved an English governing law provision.

Fiduciary Relationships and
Related Claims

Procter & Gamble

The first of two significant common law aspects of *Procter & Gamble* is Judge Feikens' dismissal of P&G's claims that (1) under New York law a fiduciary relationship existed between the parties and, therefore, (2) BT owed P&G fiduciary duties with respect to their swap transactions. P&G had alleged that BT's failure to satisfy those fiduciary duties effectively voided transactions in which P&G had suffered losses approximating $200 million. Second, Judge Feikens dismissed P&G's claims of negligent misrepresentation and negligence that were based on P&G's assertions that a "special relationship" existed between the parties.

The fiduciary relationship, fiduciary duty, and special relationship issues are important matters great to dealers. In the majority of OTC derivatives transactions, especially those involving complex products, dealers have superior knowledge of the products' risks and return features. Uncertainty as to the nature of the parties' relationship could jeopardize a large number of OTC transactions, because derivatives are generally zero-sum transactions in which there is a "winner" and a "loser." Counterparties might opportunistically try to use common law caims to void losing transactions.

P&G's relationship and duties claims rested on its assertion that it "agreed to the swap transactions because of a long relationship it had with BT and the trust that it had in BT, plus the assurance that BT would take on the responsibility of monitoring the transactions and that BT would look out for [P&G's] interests....P&G points to its trust in BT in that it divulged confidential corporate information to BT. By entering into complex swaps transactions with BT, which represented itself as experts in such transactions, P&G relied on that expertise and BT statements that it would tailor the swaps to fit P&G's needs."[5]

Nevertheless, Judge Feikens held that those factors, even if true, were insufficient grounds for establishing a fiduciary or special relationships or "negligent misrepresentations" under New York law. He found that the parties' relationship was at "arm's length" and that

> New York law is clear that a fiduciary relationship exists from the assumption of control and responsibility and is founded upon trust reposed by one party in the integrity and fidelity of another. No fiduciary relationship exists...[where] the two parties were acting and contracting at arm's length.

Furthermore, he found that P&G and BT were in a "business relationship" and that New York courts reject "the proposition that a fiduciary
relationship can arise between parties to a business relationship." He
found a business relationship even though "BT had superior knowledge in
the swaps transactions." The dealer community welcomed the finding in
Procter & Gamble that no fiduciary or special relationship existed, particularly when combined with the *Dharmala* decision.

Dharmala

Dharmala involved an English Commercial Court proceeding brought by
Bankers Trust Company and Bankers Trust International against an
Indonesian investment holding company, PT Dharmala Sakti Sejahtera.
The swaps transactions at issue were documented under ISDA documentation, and the parties had expressly chosen English jurisdiction and governing law. Bankers Trust won a judgment of US$69 million, constituting
the full amount it had claimed, together with interest thereon and costs.
"On the facts of the case, the judge was only prepared to allow a very limited duty of care owed by Bankers Trust to Dharmala and *rejected the contention that the bank had assumed an advisory role.*"[6]

Other Common Law Duties

The second significant common law aspect of *Procter & Gamble* and
Dharmala is that the cases do not eliminate *all* duties owed by a dealer to
its counterparty (or, for that matter, by an end user to its dealer). To begin,
end users are always free to agree with dealers to a heightened duty of care
than otherwise would exist under applicable law. In light of these decisions, prudence dictates that if a counterparty wishes to impose a heightened duty of care on its dealer, it should expressly so provide in its written agreement.

New York law

As characterized by one attorney who advised P&G in the suit against BT,
Judge Feikens merely dismissed P&G's "peripheral" Securities Laws and
CEA claims but was prepared to allow "the core of P&G's case—its common law fraud count"—to proceed.[7] As noted earlier, Judge Feikens
issued his ruling "only hours before the parties agreed to a settlement in
which P&G will pay $35 million of the amount BT claims it owes."[8]

Therefore, a detailed judicial application of the relevant common law of fraud to the facts of that case is lacking.

Nevertheless, in allowing the fraud count to proceed, Judge Feikens made several observations regarding applicable New York contract law. Legal advisers to dealers and end users have drawn markedly different conclusions from those observations.P&G's counsel states:

> In fact, in this ruling Judge Feikens enhanced considerably the strength of P&G's case by finding that a legal requirement exists that the dealer disclose material information even if there is no fiduciary duty. In short, the center of P&G's legal position held…and (to the extent that there was any doubt) P&G's position in challenging the transactions was vindicated.[9]

An adviser to end users (and counsel to EUDA), is even less reserved: "Well, the only court ever to have spoken to this matter has now firmly stated that dealers must disclose material information of which they have superior knowledge to their counterparties. However you want to spin it, this make good common sense and represents a *victory for the end-user community.*"[10]

English law

One British lawyer commenting on the *Dharmala* decision notes:

> It is of course always possible that a wider duty of care [than in *Dharmala*] may be allowed by the English courts in, for example, a case involving a highly sophisticated transaction and a relatively unsophisticated counterparty. In those circumstances, the courts may be more likely to accept evidence that a bank [or other dealer] had assumed a responsibility to advise the counterparty on issues such as risk and suitability. However, cogent and convincing evidence of the nature of the relationship, of the counterparty's reliance on the advice given, and of the fact that the advice caused the loss, will be required.

In *Dharmala,* no such wider duty of care was found. That case involved relatively straightforward transactions and a highly sophisticated swap counterparty. Moreover, it lacked any "cogent and convincing" evidence that an advisory relationship existed.

End user caution

In contrast to the end user comments on *Procter & Gamble* noted above, ISDA's counsel prudently warns: "End users…should not take *false comfort* that Judge Feikens' decision will provide an effective remedy for any swap that ends up being unprofitable.…It only applies to a *very limited category* of transactions and situations where the dealer '*knows*' that the end user 'is *acting on the basis of mistaken knowledge.*'"[11] There are several reasons an end user would be well advised, as ISDA's counsel suggests, to note carefully the precise language and context of Judge Feikens' ruling.

First, certain of the Judge's statements, taken out of context, might be read to suggest that "the duty to disclose…may arise [simply] when one party to a contract has superior knowledge which is not available to both parties." However, Judge Feikens emphasized that one party must be aware of the other's *mistaken* knowledge. In relevant part, he states: "New York case law establishes an implied contractual duty to disclose in business negotiations. Such a duty may arise where (1) a party has superior knowledge of certain information; (2) that information is not readily available to the other party; and (3) *the first party knows that the second party is acting on the basis of mistaken knowledge.*"[12]

Dealers, with their often formidable technological and legal infrastructure and market knowledge, typically have superior market knowledge to that of end users. Whether this superiority rises to the level of being legally significant absent awareness (or even constructive awareness) that a counterparty is operating on a misunderstanding of the relevant product is an entirely different question, and one not before Judge Feikens.

As EUDA's counsel points out, in an April 2, 1996 hearing involving the disclosure issue, Judge Feikens emphasized that one of P&G's

> allegations…is that what they were never able to obtain was a full understanding of how the [spread] formula worked…what the elements were that went into that pricing formula. They allege…that Bankers Trust would not give them the elements of this proprietary formula that they had to price the swap. Isn't there a duty—a contractual duty, where one party possesses this information and it's vital in the understanding and interpretation and execution of the contract, to disclose?"[13]

One day later, Judge Feikens further elaborated that "what Procter & Gamble is saying…is, 'Look, you didn't tell us about all this intricacy. You didn't disclose that this pricing formula would be that subjective, that you had the ability to make those determinations [as to the formula's inputs] under this swap transaction without advising us about that.'" Plainly, the Judge found there were triable issues as to whether P&G was operating under a mistake of fact and BT knew (or should have known) of that mistake. The issues raised involved more than mere superior knowledge.

Second, Judge Feikens repeatedly emphasized that the standard of proof required under New York law for a violation of the duty to disclose is difficult to meet. In allowing P&G's claims to proceed, he stated: "No matter how plaintiff proceeds to prove its case under New York law the burden of proving fraud requires clear and convincing evidence, and not mere preponderance....This evidentiary standard demands a 'high order of proof'...and forbids the awarding of relief 'whenever the evidence is loose, equivocal or contradictory.'"

Finally, as ISDA's counsel states, "swaps overwhelmingly involve sophisticated entities as dealers and end users in transactions that entail bilateral extensions of credit."[14] That is clearly the prevailing view among banking regulators. Greenspan's 1994 congressional testimony is particularly telling in this regard:

> [T]he burden of being informed in the marketplace, especially a wholesale marketplace, must not fall only on the dealer....For the transfer of risk [function of derivatives] to be effective and the efficiency to be realized, *end users must retain ultimate responsibility for transactions they choose to make.* In a wholesale market, sophisticated and unsophisticated end users alike must ensure that they fully understand the risks attendant to any transaction they enter....Thus, the Board does not see the need for legislative or regulatory protection for end users.[15]

Similarly, Patrikis offers the following advice: "[A] participant should satisfy itself that it has the capability, internally or through independent professional advice, to understand or make independent decisions about its transactions....Some would say that an end-user stands no chance against a 'dealer.' What I think this boils down to is the tendency of some to be unable to acknowledge that they do not comprehend the transaction being pitched to them by a marketing staff."[16]

Securities regulators, on the other hand, such as the SEC, the NASD, and various state authorities, are more sympathetic to end user concerns. However, the ability of securities regulators to aid end users, absent a judicially cognizable finding that an OTC derivative constitutes a security under the Securities Laws, is limited. Judge Feikens cited unambiguous Supreme Court precedent for the proposition that "[t]he 'courts are the final authorities on the issues of statutory construction and are not obliged to stand aside and rubber-stamp their affirmance of administrative decisions that they deem inconsistent with a statutory mandate or that frustrate the congressional policy underlying a statute.'"[17]

In addition, allegations of violations of "know your customer" or "suitability" rules are unlikely to help an aggrieved end user: "A broker-dealer's violation of the NYSE's 'know your customer' rule or the NASD's suitability rule generally will not entitle the customer to bring a civil claim against that broker-dealer."[18]

In sum, barring any presently unforeseeable legislative changes, it is prudent for all market participants and their counsel to treat OTC derivatives markets as *wholesale—not retail*—markets in which participants will be presumed to act with sophistication and on an arm's-length basis. Banking regulators and economists view these markets and their institutional participants as serving an essential economic function. Participants in wholesale markets are seldom viewed as warranting the special protections afforded, for example, under the Securities Laws to individual retail investors.

Absent demonstrable fraud, other outrageous dealer conduct, or the violation of a written advisory or fiduciary agreement, end users should as a precautionary measure assume that they will be unlikely, in the event of large losses, to find that federal courts are receptive to claims based on assertions of advisory, fiduciary, or other special relationships.

APPLICATION OF SECURITIES LAWS TO OTC DERIVATIVES—"ECONOMIC REALITY"?

The applicability of the Securities Laws in *Procter & Gamble* depended on the resolution of the "threshold issue" of whether either of the highly specialized swaps at issue constituted a "security" within the meaning of the 1933 or 1934 Act.[19] Judge Feikens' analysis is instructive. Equally useful is a comparison of how his analysis of the legal consequences of the swaps' option-based economic features diverges from the SEC's analysis.

The 1933 and 1934 Acts contain definitions of the term security that are "virtually identical" for present purposes. The definitions begin with extensive lists of covered products and conclude with broad catchall language covering any "instrument commonly known as a 'security.'" Judge Feikens expressly considered whether the swaps in question were one of the myriad financial transactions that fall within any of the recognized definitional categories asserted by P&G: "(1) investment contracts; (2) notes; (3) evidence of indebtedness; (4) options on securities; and (5) instruments commonly known as securities."

In any event: "Economic reality is the guide for determining whether these swaps transactions that do not squarely fit within the statutory definition are, nevertheless, securities....In order to determine whether these swaps are securities, commodities, or neither, I must examine each aspect of these transactions and subject them to the guidelines set forth in Supreme Court cases." He found that the swaps fit into none of the foregoing categories and therefore held that they were not securities under either the 1933 or 1934 Act.

Investment Contracts; Investments Commonly Known as Securities

In deciding whether the swaps were securities under either of these categories, Judge Feikens applied the Supreme Court's guidelines set forth primarily in *SEC v. Howey*[20] and elaborated upon in *United Housing Foundation, Inc. v. Forman.*[21] Quoting *Forman,* he stated that "the test whether an instrument is an investment contract is whether it entails 'an investment in a common venture premised on a reasonable expectation of profits to be derived from the entrepreneurial or managerial efforts of others.'"[22] He found that several essential elements of the *Howey* test were lacking in the present case.

First, he found that there was no "common enterprise," because "P&G did not pool its money with that of any other company or person in a single business venture." Second, BT was not managing P&G's funds, and P&G's assertion that the swaps were part of BT's derivatives business was irrelevant. Finally, he noted that "the value of the swaps depended on market forces, not BT's entrepreneurial efforts. The swaps are not investment contracts."

Judge Feikens also explained that "[t]he Supreme Court uses the *Howey* test for both 'investment contracts' and the more general category of an 'instrument' commonly known as a 'security.'" In examining instruments that arguably fall under "non-specific categories of securities, those instruments must nevertheless comport with the *Howey* test. Again, there was no common venture, and the value of the swaps depended on market forces, not BT's entrepreneurial or managerial efforts. On this point also, "[t]hese swaps do not qualify as securities."

Notes or "Family Resemblance" to Notes

Applying the Supreme Court's *Reves* test, Judge Feikens considered four factors in determining whether the swaps were notes or bore any "family resemblance" to notes.[23] "Those four factors are: (1) the motivations of the buyer and seller in entering into the transaction (investment for profit or to raise capital versus commercial); (2) a sufficiently broad plan of distribution of the instrument (common trading for speculation or investment); (3) the reasonable expectations of the investing public; and (4) whether some factor, such as the existence of another regulatory scheme, significantly reduces the risk of the instrument, thereby rendering application of the securities laws unnecessary."

Acknowledging that there is no "neat and tidy" way to apply the first factor—i.e., the parties' motivations—he still concluded that it provided insufficient grounds for suggesting the swaps were securities. Although the parties' motives were complex, he found that overall the "motives are tipped more toward a commercial rather than investment purpose."

As to the second factor, Judge Feikens easily concluded that the swaps were highly customized products and that they "could not be sold or traded to another counterparty without the agreement of BT. They were not part of any kind of general offering" or plan of distribution.

His application of the third factor, the expectations of the investing public, led him to conclude that the swaps again were not securities. "They were not traded on a national exchange, 'the paradigm of a security.'" Furthermore, while recognizing that "some media refer to derivatives generally as securities and that some commentators assume that all derivatives are securities....[O]ther commentators understand that many swap transactions are customized, bilateral contracts not subject to regulation....However, what is relevant is the perception of those who enter into swap agreements, not the public in general." He found that P&G did not perceive the swaps as securities, because P&G "knew full well" that its swaps were not registered as securities. He noted critically that "P&G's 'perception' that these swap agreements were securities did not arise until after it had filed its original Complaint" and the SEC and CFTC issued their rulings in Gibson.*

Judge Feikens found that the final factor was less conclusive, because the only alternative regulatory scheme available consisted of guidelines intended to protect the banking industry. "[T]heir focus is on the protection of banks and their shareholders from default or other credit risks. They do not provide any direct protection to counterparties with whom banks enter into derivatives transactions." Nevertheless, even

---

*"If P&G itself had really though it was dealing with securities, it is fair to assume that P&G would have included securities counts in its original complaint."

though he found that the swaps might meet this prong of the *Reves* test, he decided that, without more, it was insufficient for the swaps to be deemed securities under the Securities Laws. In his words: "Balancing all the *Reves* factors, I conclude that the 5s/30s and DM swaps are not notes for purposes of the Securities Acts."

Evidence of Indebtedness

Judge Feikens determined that the test of whether an instrument is a security under this category "is essentially the same as whether an instrument is a note."[24] On that basis, he concluded that the swaps were not securities under this factor. In his conclusion he relied on the absence of a missing "essential element of debt instruments—the payment or repayment of principal. Swap agreements do not involve the payment of principal; the notional amount never changes hands."*

Options on Securities[25]

Optionality is the most controversial aspect of Judge Feikens' Securities Laws analysis. Significantly, neither party disputed his functional analysis of the optionality of the 5s/30s and DM swaps. Indeed, BT acknowledged that "both swaps contained terms that functioned as options." The pivotal issue was whether this optionality was sufficient to cause the swaps to fall within the statutory definition of an option on a security.[26]

The 5s/30s swap

The 5s/30s swap presented a more challenging effort at statutory construction. Economically, the spread formula contained "at least two put options,"[27] the value of which was derived from the value of underlying Treasury securities. To determine whether these embedded options caused the entire transaction to fall within the statutory definition of a security, the Judge considered the nature of their "underlying instrumentality." He concluded that they did not.

---

*Although this aspect of his reasoning is correct as to interest rate and many other types of swaps, it is not necessarily applicable to many currency swaps in which principal amounts actually do change hands. But, a court could find, as discussed in Chapter 2, that even with currency swaps involving principal exchanges, the exchange obligation is not "indebtedness" but rather a sequence of forward purchases and sales of currencies. Otherwise, virtually any monetary obligation begins to look like indebtedness and, thus, a security.

Judge Feikens acknowledged that the formula's payoff profile was that of a put option on a Treasury note—in other words, a put option on an individual security. However, for three reasons, he considered that payoff profile alone an insufficient reason to treat the host swap as a security. The reasoning on two points is strained. On the third—his reading of the applicable legislative history—his reasoning is more persuasive, although his reason for even inguiring into the legislative history is not. As Justice Scalin notes in his concurring opinion in *Dunn,* there's no reason to inquire into the legislative history if the statute's "plain meaning" is clear.

First, he found it significant that the spread formula did not give either party the "right to take possession of a security." But this ignores the economic reality that most options on securities are cash-settled and that, therefore, the economic impact of cash settlement is usually insignificant.

Second, Judge Feikens found that "[n]either party could choose whether or not to exercise an option; the stream of interest payments under the swap was mandatory." Based on economic theory, this is at best a strained interpretation of the term *option.* Economic theory, particularly theories used to price option securities, assume that option holders are rational actors who will not make the irrational decision *not* to exercise in the money options. Put differently, Judge Feikens reasons that the legal status of an instrument with option-like payoffs depends on whether the holder *has the right to act irrationally.**

Third, the Judge noted that the "parenthetical phrase '(including any interest therein or based on the value thereof)'…could lead to a reading of the statute to mean that an option based on the *value of a security* [rather than on the security itself] is a security." That reasoning hardly seems problematic: undoubtedly, few would argue that one ought to be able to defeat the accepted security status of an option on an individual security simply by eliminating the economically insignificant right to demand physical delivery. Yet he thought the controlling statutory language "jumble[d]." To determine the correct reading of the jumble d language, Judge Feikens examined the legislative history of the relevant 1982 amendments to the 1933 and 1934 Acts that added that language.

He finds that the legislative history "makes it clear" that Congress

---

*Supportive of Judge Feikens' reasoning on the first two points is that "commentators do not agree on whether an agreement that replicates the economic effect of an option on a security may itself be a security in the absence of an exercise election and a right to take delivery of the security." See Becker and Fisher, *Federal Securities Laws After P&G, supra,* note 19 (citations omitted): 1034, n. 5.

did not intend to treat an option on the *value* of an individual security—as opposed to on the security itself—as a separate security:

> The U.S. House of Representatives Report ("House Report") on the 1982 amendments that added this parenthetical phrase provides that the definition of "security" includes an option on "(i) any security, (ii) any certificate of deposit, (iii) any group or index of securities (including any interest therein or based on the value thereof), and (iv) when traded on a national securities exchange, foreign currency."…Thus, even though the statute jumbles these definitions together, it is clear from the House Report that the parenthetical phrase "(…based on the value thereof)" was intended only to modify the immediately preceding clause—"group or index of securities"—and not the words "any option" or "any security."

Judge Feikens' reading of the quoted legislative history is, as a matter of grammatical construction, unassailable. So is his reading of the statute *as he quoted it* in his discussion of "options on securities." Unfortunately, he *misquoted* it there, despite quoting it accurately earlier.

His misquotation is material. The Supreme Court, elaborating upon its "plain meaning" doctrine, has held that "the starting point for interpreting a statute is the language of the statute itself."[28] A court is to examine legislative history only if the language *of the statute itself* is somehow unclear. Judge Feikens effectively reversed the process—he started with the legislative history, *then* read into the statute a grammatical error that did not exist.

Here is Judge Feikens' misquotation of the relevant statutory language: "any put, call, straddle, option or privilege on any security, group or index of securities (including any interest therein or based on the value thereof)." So quoted, the language lacks proper sentence structure and so becomes ambiguous—it lacks proper "enumeration" "parallel construction"[29] of a series.

One way to see his error is to rewrite the quoted language as follows: "security, group of securities or index of securities (including any interest…based on the value thereof)." So written, each item in the series is plainly modified by the parenthetical. The Judge's error also readily emerges when we correctly quote the statute (modifications needed to correct the misquotation are indicated in brackets): "any put, call, straddle, option[,] or privilege on any security, [certificate of deposit, or] group or index of securities (including any interest therein or based on the value thereof)." Quoted correctly, the parenthetical modifies the entire series, "any security, certificate of deposit, or group or index of securities." Hence, an option on the value of a security should itself be a security *according to the plain language* of the statute.

However, even if the plain meaning suggests that such an option is itself a security, that does not end the inquiry here. The definitional sections of both the 1933 Act and the 1934 Act begin with the words "unless the context otherwise requires...." Judge Feikens could have held that the context did otherwise require that these swaps not be considered securities. After all, the "Supreme Court has held...that Congress did not 'intend' the Securities Acts 'to provide a broad federal remedy for all fraud.'"[30]

The DM swap

The discussion of the DM swap is noncontroversial. The statutory language would not classify the DM swap as a security even if it were an option, because the underlying was not itself a security. According to Judge Feikens, "the underlying instrumentality of the DM swap was not a security, because the value of the DM swap was based on a foreign currency, which is not a security as defined in the 1933 and 1934 Acts."

SEC's Disagreement with *Procter & Gamble*

The SEC has formally announced that it disagrees with Judge Feikens' analysis of swaps that function as options on the value of securities. Unfortunately, the SEC has not presented its own analysis of the statutory language or legislative history of the 1933 or 1934 Act. So, the basis for its disagreement with Judge Feikens is unclear.

In its 1994 settlement with BT Securities Corporation relating to Gibson, the SEC ruled that a transaction documented as a swap and called a "Treasury-Linked Swap" was, nevertheless, "within the class of options that are securities, within the meaning of the federal securities laws."[31] Based on the swap's functional characteristics, the SEC ruled that the Treasury-Linked Swap was "in actuality a *cash-settled put option* that was written by Gibson and based initially on the 'spread' between the price of the 7.625% 30-year U.S. Treasury security maturing on November 15, 2022 and the arithmetic average of the bid and offered yields of the most recently auctioned obligations of a two-year Treasury note."

In *Procter & Gamble*, Judge Feikens expressly considered, but rejected, the SEC's above reasoning in *BT Securities* and its reasoning in the related *Vazquez* order.[32] He noted that the swaps there at issue "have some similarities to the 5s/30s swap." Nevertheless, he held:

> In both Orders the SEC acknowledged that its findings were solely for the purpose of effectuating the respondents' Offers of Settlement and that its

findings are not binding on any other person or entity named as a defendant or respondent in any other proceeding. They are not binding in this [*Procter & Gamble*] case, in part because of the differences between the transactions; nor do they have collateral estoppel effect....Even though both the Gibson Greetings, Inc. swap and the P&G 5s/30s swap derived their values from securities (Treasury notes), they were not options.

After the *Procter & Gamble* decision, the SEC reiterated its view that the Treasury-Linked Swap was a security. In a June 11, 1996 order relating to *BT Securities,* the SEC agreed that there were some similarities and some differences between the Treasury-Linked Swap and the 5s/30s swap. Nevertheless, it stated that "the Commission disagrees with the Court's [Judge Feikens'] analysis and reiterates its position that the Treasury-Linked Swap is a security within the meaning of the federal securities laws because it was in actuality a cash-settled put option on the spread between the price and yield of two different Treasury securities."[33]

The legal issues, then, are whether the right to demand physical delivery of a security and whether the distinction between a *security* and *its value* are legally significant under the Securities Laws. Fortunately, the dispute is unlikely to affect the great majority of "core" OTC derivatives transactions, especially those of the plain vanilla variety. Although many such products often contain option features, such as early termination provisions (i.e., puts) and caps or maximum rates (i.e., calls), unless those features are somehow explicitly tied to the value of individual securities there is unlikely to be any reason for those option-like features alone to render the products securities.

Unresolved federal securities law issues

Several federal Securities Laws issues that remain unresolved after *Procter & Gamble, Missner, BT Securities,* and *Vazquez* warrant comment.

First, Judge Feikens carefully confined the scope of his holdings: "I do not determine that all leveraged derivatives transactions are not securities, or that all swaps are not securities. Some of these derivative instruments, because of their structure may be securities. I confine my ruling to the 5s/30s and the DM swaps between P&G and BT."[34] Whether other courts will follow his rulings and analyses is unclear.

Second, the SEC's position in *Missner, BT Securities,* and *Vazquez* appears to be that the entire Treasury-Linked Swap was an option, whereas Judge Feikens expressly considered only embedded option features. Thus, a further complication to any comparison between *Procter & Gamble* and the SEC's orders concerns the extent to which "an instrument that contains an option in addition to other non-security elements [might] be a security."[35]

Third, Judge Feikens' three stated justifications for his conclusions regarding whether options on the value of securities are in themselves securities are strained and arguably incorrect. Whether his ultimate conclusion is incorrect is another question, because alternative reasoning likely would have led him to the same result. One promising alternative path that has been suggested is that he might instead have analyzed the underlying instrumentality as, not a single Treasury security, but as an underlying group or index of Treasury securities.[36]

Finally, this end user caution deserves consideration (ignoring, for the moment, the controversial assertion of a "jurisdictional gap"):

> Judge Feikens' ruling [suggests]…an option on a security which is packaged as a swap would seem to be outside the jurisdiction of the SEC so long as the embedded option is cash settled by the party "out of the money" and there is a mandatory nominal payment from the party "in the money." It is not difficult to envision dealers creating instruments that are the economic equivalent of options on individual securities, but which fall within the jurisdictional gap suggested by Judge Feikens' opinion.[37]

It is unlikely that the reasoning of *Procter & Gamble* could support a holding that a swap that is economically equivalent to an option on an individual security would not be a security under federal Securities Laws. Among other things, the quotation suggests that the parties' to the envisioned transaction would, unlike P&G and BT, *expect* the instrument to be a security. Moreover, the quoted language suggests that the option feature is not embedded within an instrument that contains other material nonsecurity elements. The economic reality of the entire instrument would clearly be that of an option. Finally, given the SEC's aggressive posture on this area, it is doubtful that any dealer would consciously try to take advantage of such a "jurisdictional gap."

APPLICATION OF CEA TO OTC DERIVATIVES

Recent CFTC enforcement actions over widely publicized derivatives losses add to an understanding of the applicability of the CEA to, and of the potential for the CFTC to assert jurisdiction over many OTC derivatives. The *Dunn* case and accompanying briefs and lower court opinions

also provides substantial valuable information The Supreme Court's opinion, along with ongoing legislative proposals should now be required
reading. However, Judge Feikens' opinion provides guidance in understanding the relevance of the CEA to swaps and swap-related OTC derivatives.[38]

Swaps exemption

"BT asserts that the swaps are not futures contracts; P&G claims that they
are." The swaps were entered into on an OTC basis, not on a contract market. Therefore, if the swaps were futures and not eligible for an exemption
or exclusion, they would have been illegal and unenforceable. Judge
Feikens did not have to decide this issue of whether the swaps were
futures, because he first found that both the 5s/30s and the DM swap transactions met all the eligibility criteria for the Swaps Exemption.

As described in Chapter 5, to qualify for the Swaps Exemption a
transaction must first constitute a swap agreement (within the meaning of
Section 101 of the U.S. Bankruptcy Code) and be entered into between eligible swap participants. Judge Feikens easily found (without analysis) that
both swaps fit the literal language of the swap agreement definition and
that both BT and P&G met the literal definition of eligible swap participant. By implication, he perceived no reason to look beyond the literal language of either definition. He also easily found that the swaps met the
three remaining criteria:

> [T]hese swaps are customized and not fungible as they could not be sold to
> another counterparty without permission....[C]reditworthiness is a consid-
> eration of the parties....[T]he swaps are private agreements not traded on
> any exchange.

Thus, the swaps were exempt from the exchange-trading requirement.
But that did not end the inquiry, because even transactions that satisfy
the Swaps Exemption arguably, and in the CFTC's view, remain subject
to the antifraud provisions of Sections 4b and 4o of the CEA and Section
32.9 of the CFTC Rules, C.F.R. § 32.9.

Section 4b

Section 4b, in relevant part, makes it unlawful for anyone, in connection
with a commodity futures transaction entered into on behalf of any other
person, to engage in certain fraudulent conduct. "BT asserts that Count
XII, alleging a violation of Section 4b, should be dismissed because BT

did not act 'for or on behalf of' P&G. Rather, BT 'acted solely as a principal, dealing with—not for—P&G on an arm's length basis.'"

Judge Feikens acknowledged P&G's contention that BT's advertisements and representations constituted "promises that BT would use its experience, sophistication and expertise on behalf of its clients to advise them in the complex financial area of leveraged derivatives." Yet he found that the parties' relationship was one in which each acted as principal—that is, on its own behalf—in a bilateral contractual relationship. Therefore, he held that "BT was not acting for or on behalf of P&G." Moreover, based on an analysis of case law, he held that P&G had no private right of action under Section 4b.

Section 4o

Section 4o is an antifraud provision applicable to "commodity trading advisors." Judge Feikens had to decide "whether BT was P&G's commodity trading advisor."

As defined in relevant part in CEA § 1a(5)(A), a commodity trading adviser is someone who, for profit, (a) advises others regarding trading in (I) a futures contract to be entered into on or subject to the rules of a contract market, (II) an authorized commodity option, or (III) any "leverage transaction" or (b) regularly issues or promulgates reports regarding any of the activities specified in clause (a).

Clause (I) did not apply, because the swaps were exempt from the exchange-trading requirement. Clause (II) was perhaps a more difficult though still not very troublesome matter. Judge Feikens simply said that "Section (II) may not be applicable," because of the Swaps Exemption. Clause (III) did not apply, "because the 5s/30s and DM swaps do not fit within the CFTC's regulations for leverage contracts referred to in 7 U.S.C. § 23(a)," which must be for 10 years or longer.

To remove all doubt about whether BT was P&G's commodity trading adviser, Judge Feikens also examined closely the nature of the parties' discussions leading up to the transactions. He noted that BT representatives "gave P&G a sales pitch regarding the potential benefits of their product." Also, they discussed BT's market views. Yet although he found that "BT Securities representatives came close to giving advice, P&G representatives used their own independent knowledge of market conditions in forming their own expectation as to what the market would do in the 5s/30s and DM swaps." Because that expectation "was clearly P&G's sole decision," the Judge found that BT had not acted as P&G's commodity trading adviser and he dismissed the Section 4o claims.

Judge Feikens compared the facts of *Procter & Gamble* to those at issue in *BT Securities,* in which the CFTC indicated that BT Securities had an advisory relationship with Gibson. However, the facts there were distinguishable. "Apparently, Gibson did not understand the ramifications of the transaction, and BT Securities was aware of that lack of sophistication." In addition, he noted that although the CFTC's order in *BT Securities* "indicated that the CFTC viewed BT Securities as a commodity trading advisor as to Gibson, the CFTC's Order is not binding here." The distinction then was that Gibson implicitly lacked sophistication and BT Securities knew it, whereas "P&G's representatives used their own independent knowledge of market conditions in forming their own expectations as to what the market would do."

Violation of 17 C.F.R. § 32.9

Judge Feikens dismissed the claim of violation simply on the basis that § 32.9 does not provide for a private right of action.

Unresolved CEA issues

Two important CEA issues that remain unresolved in light of *Procter & Gamble* and *BT Securities* warrant comment.

First, not surprisingly, a counterparty's level of sophistication and the degree to which a dealer engages in sales pitches or makes statements that might constitute "advice" are fact-intensive issues.

Second, formerly the question of whether the CFTC considers swaps to constitute futures was uncertain. Judge Feikens began his CEA analysis by noting that as of January 19, 1996, as evidenced by a "Letter from Mary L. Schapiro, Chair of U.S. Commodity Futures Trading Commission to Congressmen Roberts and Bliley," the CFTC "had not taken a position on whether swap agreements [even those meeting the eligibility requirements of the Swaps Exemption] are futures contracts." The May 1998 *CFTC Concept Release* removes any ambiguity as to the CFTC's view. As John Hawke, Jr., Treasury Under Secretary for Domestic Finance, recently asserted, the *CFTC Concept Release* "is premised, inescapably, on the CFTC's apparent canclusion that many swaps are subject to their jurisdiction as futures contracts and can be appropriately regulated as such."

The question remains relevant because the antifraud provisions of the CEA apply to exempt transactions. More importantly, if a swap transaction failed to satisfy the requirements for the Swaps Exemption or any other exemption or exclusion, because, again, it would likely violate the CEA's exchange-trading requirement and thus be unenforceable. Although the probability of such failures is not great today—in the vast majority of cases the checklist nature of the exemption requirements makes compliance easy to determine, and given that the exemptions are nonexclusive—the cost of legal uncertainty may still be high.

Moreover, an exemption is always less preferable to an exclusion; an exclusion is not subject to agency jurisdiction or regulatory discretion. The *CFTC Concept Release* explicitly raises precisely this point, because the CFTC is expressly contemplating "comprehensive regulatory reform" with "no preconceived goal in mind." The OTC derivatives industry, along with the Federal Reserve, Treasury, and SEC, is understandably alarmed over the possibility that the CFTC could decide to restrict (or expand) the scope of the Swaps Exemption and the Trade Option Exemption or to eliminate either or both exemptions altogether.[39]

ENDNOTES: CHAPTER 9

1. Quoted in Dennis Lloyd, *The Idea of Law: A Repressive Evil or Social Necessity?* (Penguin Books; first published, 1964; 6th reprint with revisions, 1987): 326 [hereinafter, *The Idea of Law*].
2. Except as otherwise noted, all quotations from this discussion of the P&G swaps are from the *Procter & Gamble* opinion.
3. This and the immediately following quotation are from Chew, *Leverage, supra,* Chapter 1, note 1 (emphasis modified): 35. For a thorough and informative discussion of the economic effects of the "5s/30s swap," including the remarkable leverage factor incorporated into the swap via the complex floating rate spread formula, see *id.:* 33–37.
4. *Bankers Trust International PLC v. PT Dharmala Sakti Sejahtera,* 1994 Folio Nos. 2168 & 1396 (High Ct. of Justice, Queens Bench Div., Dec. 1, 1995) (LEXIS, Enggen Library, Cases file) [hereafter, *Dharmala*].
5. All quotations in this and the next paragraph are from 925 F.Supp. at 1289 (citations omitted).
6. This and the quotation from the next paragraph are from Andrew Clark, "UK Court Limits Duty of Care in Derivatives Transactions," *International Financial Law Review* (February 1996): 10–13.
7. Denis Forster, "The State of the Law After Procter & Gamble v. Bankers Trust," *Derivatives Strategy* (June 1996) [hereafter, *State of the Law*]: 55.

8. "P&G v. BT: The Debate Continues," *Derivatives Strategy* (June 1996) [hereafter, *The Debate Continues*]: 12.

9. See Forster, *State of the Law, supra,* note 7.

10. See Warren Davis, "Spinning the P&G–Bankers Trust Settlement," *American Banker* (May 21, 1996) (emphasis added) [hereafter, *Spinning the P&G Settlement*]: 36.

11. Daniel P. Cunningham, "What Did the BT–P&G Judge Really Say?" *American Banker* (June 20, 1996) (emphasis added) [hereafter, *What Did Judge Feikens Really Say?*]: 22.

12. This quotation and that in the following paragraph are from 925 F.Supp. at 1290–1291 (citations omitted) (emphasis added).

13. The quotations in this paragraph are from Warren N. Davis and James M. Cain, "The P&G/Bankers Trust Settlement and Opinion: Views and Implications," *Futures and Derivatives Law Report,* 16(4) (June 1996) [hereafter, *Views and Implications*]: 4–5.

14. Cunningham, *What Did Judge Feikens Really Say?, supra,* note 11.

15. Greenspan, *Statement Before Congress,* Chapter 1, note 25 (emphasis added): 600.

16. Patrikis, *Dealer/End-User Relationships, supra,* Chapter 7, note 12.

17. 925 F.Supp. at 1281 (quoting *SEC v. Sloan,* 436 US 103, 118, 98 S.Ct. 1702, 1711–1712, 56 L.Ed.2d 148 (1978)). *Cf.* NASD Manual (CCH)— Conduct Rule 2310, "Recommendation as to Customers (Suitability)," and related Interpretive Materials, particularly IM-2310-2(e), "Fair Dealing with Customers with Regard to Derivative Products or New Financial Products."

18. Patrikis and Virzera, *Sales Practices, supra,* Chapter 7, note 11: 6.

19. The quotations in this and the following paragraph are from 925 F.Supp. at 1277 (citations omitted). For an analysis of the relevant Ohio securities laws issues addressed in *Procter & Gamble,* see 925 F.Supp. at 1283–1284. For a general analysis of the federal securities law issues addressed in *Procter & Gamble* and related SEC orders, see, generally, Brandon Becker and Joshua Fisher, "OTC Derivatives and the Federal Securities Laws After Procter & Gamble v. Bankers Trust," in *SWAPS and Other Derivatives in 1996,* Kenneth M. Raisler and Alison M. Gregory, Co-Chairs (Practising Law Institute, 1996) [hereafter, *Federal Securities Laws After P&G*]: 1029–1046.

20. 328 US 293, 66 S.Ct. 1100, 90 L.Ed. 1244 (1946).

21. 421 US 837, 95 S.Ct. 2051, 44 L.Ed.2d 621 (1975).

22. The quotations and analysis of the "investment contract" issue are from 925 F.Supp. at 1277–1278 (citations omitted); the quotations and analysis of the "instruments commonly known as securities" issue are from 925 F.Supp. at 1282–1283 (citations omitted).

23. *Reves v. Ernst & Young,* 494 US 56, 110 S.Ct. 945, 108 L.Ed.2d 47 (1989). All quotations relating to the "notes" test are from 925 F.Supp. at 1278–1280 (citations omitted).

24. All quotations relating to this "evidence of indebtedness" test are from 925 F.Supp. at 1280 (citations omitted).

25. Except as otherwise noted, all quotations relating to this "options on securities" test are from 925 F.Supp. at 1280–1282 (citations omitted) (emphasis added).

26. The key language quoted by Judge Feikens—or rather misquoted because the judge omitted the bracketed words and failed to indicate the omission with ellipses—was added to both the 1933 and 1934 Acts in a 1982 amendment. See Act of October 13, 1982, Secs. 1 and 2, Pub. Law 97-303, 96 Stat. 1409. The need as late as 1982 to add language relating to options provides support for Greenspan's insistence on the need to modernize the current statutory framework governing derivatives, and perhaps securities as well.

27. See Davis and Cain, *Views and Implications, supra,* note 13: 5.

28. See *Consumer Prod. Safety Comm'n v. GTE Sylvania, Inc.,* 447 US 102, 108 (1980).

29. See William Strunk, Jr. and E. B. White, *The Elements of Style,* 3rd ed., (MacMillan, 1979): 26–28. In their section on parallel construction, Strunk and White show repeatedly that grammatical errors can be demonstrated and "corrected by rearranging the sentence." Certainly they would agree that grammatical errors can also be created by rearranging otherwise correct sentences.

30. *Marine Bank v. Weaver,* 455 U.S. 551, 556, 102 S.Ct. 1220, 1223, 71 L.Ed.2d 409 (1982).

31. The quotations in this paragraph are from *In re BT Securities Corporation,* Securities Act Release No. 33-7124, Exchange Act Release No. 35136, 58 SEC Doc. (CCH) 1145 (December 22, 1994) (emphasis added) [hereafter, *BT Securities*]; see also *In re Mitchell A. Vazquez,* Securities Act Release No. 7269, Exchange Act Release No. 36906, Release No. AAER-766 (February 29, 1996) [hereafter, *Vazquez*]; see, generally, Becker and Fisher, *Federal Securities Laws After P&G, supra,* note 19: 1034–1035.

32. The quotations in this paragraph are from 925 F.Supp. at 1281–1282.

33. *In re Gary S. Missner,* SEC Rel. No. 33-7304, 34-37301, AAER No. 791 (June 11, 1996) [hereafter, *Missner*]: note 4. In the June 1996 issue of *Derivatives Strategy,* unnamed sources at the SEC are quoted as follows concerning the *Procter & Gamble* decision:

> "This is not a major court, it's not in New York or any other financial cen-ter, or a Federal appellate court," says one senior official. "It's just a district court decision. We've established our position in many of these matters,

based on the Gibson Greetings–Bankers Trust consent decree in which certain swaps are treated as securities. We expect to go forward with this position in future cases." An SEC spokesman adds that the commission is standing by its position that "certain types of transactions can still be classified as securities."

The Debate Continues, supra, note 8: 12–13.

34. 925 F.Supp. at 1283.

35. See Becker and Fisher, *Federal Securities Laws After P&G, supra,* note 19: 1042.

36. See *Id.,* note 19: 1041, note 15.

37. Davis and Cain, *Views and Implications, supra,* note 13: 3.

38. All quotations from the *Procter & Gamble* opinion contained in this discussion of the applicability of the CEA are (unless otherwise noted) from 925 F.Supp. at 1284–1288.

39. For other examples of comparable CFTC rethinking of existing regulations, see CFTC Proposed Rules, *Section 4(c) Contract Market Transactions; Swap Agreements,* 59 Fed. Reg. 54,139, 54,150 (1994); see also *Industry Association Brief, supra,* Chapter 8, note 9: 12–13.

CHAPTER 10

Role of Senior Management: A Functional Overview of Governance

Unfortunately, the insights of the financial engineers do not give managers any guidance on how to deploy the new weapons [i.e., derivatives] most effectively.

Froot, Scharfstein, and Stein
Harvard Business Review,
November–December 1994

While theorists continue to advance new rationales for corporate risk management, empiricists seeking to test if practice is consistent with these theories have been stymied by a lack of meaningful data.

Peter Tufano
Journal of Finance, September 1996

Dramatic theoretical advances and the development and proliferation of powerful computers and telecommunications facilities have greatly accelerated the pace of financial innovation and transformed global capital markets. In so doing, they irreversibly altered the economic environment in which actual and potential users of derivatives operate. Most organizations now have unprecedented capabilities for ridding themselves of unwanted financial and operating risks and modifying or reshaping those risks that they willingly choose to take. Nevertheless, "it is safe to say that there is no single, well-accepted set of principles that underlies their hedging programs....Without a clear set of risk-management goals, using derivatives can be dangerous."[1]

Derivatives' dangers have both a legal and a financial dimension, neither of which can be adequately understood or managed in isolation. Nor can either dimension be satisfactorily controlled in isolation from an organization's overall risk management system, which in turn must "fit" within overall competitive strategy. The failure to integrate derivatives usage and risk management properly within overall strategy can easily result in unacceptable trade-offs. The most damaging trade-offs are likely to manifest as newly created derivatives risks or inordinate commitments of senior management and legal resources.

Senior management is responsible for choosing among alternative risk management strategies and for overseeing the implementation and continuing effectiveness of those choices. A functional approach provides senior management and its legal advisers with superior analytical tools for managing the legal and financial risks of derivatives. By so doing, it enhances a user's ability to use derivatives to manage other risks, whether its own and those of its customers, suppliers, employees, and other business "partners." A functional approach provides a key to understanding how derivatives can be used to achieve risk management goals without incurring trade-offs that detract from long-term strategy.

ROLE OF SENIOR MANAGEMENT— OVERVIEW

Decisions regarding the risks an organization will manage and those it will choose, implicitly or explicitly, to take are among the most important an organization can make. Day-to-day responsibility for implementing the strategies may be delegated to corporate officers (or analogous personnel in noncorporate organizations). However, both legally and as a matter of prudence, responsibility for determining, reviewing, and continuously monitoring and updating the goals of risk management and the strategies to be employed to achieve those goals—whether or not involving derivatives—resides at the highest levels of management.

For Derivatives users, active senior management involvement in managing derivatives' risks is widely recommended as a business matter and in ondated as a legal matter. Domestic and international banking supervisors and securities and commodities regulators; the G-30, ISDA, EUDA, the London-based Futures and Options Association (FOA), and the Risk Standards Working Group (Risk Standards Group; which consists of individuals from the institutional investment community); and many other respected commentators, private industry groups, and market participants have repeatedly stressed that the first, most important "line of defense"[2] against OTC derivatives risks is an organization's trustees, board of directors, or comparable supervisory body. For that line of defense to be effective, senior management and its legal advisers must understand the financial and legal dimensions of risk management in general and OTC derivatives risk management in particular. They must also understand whether a risk management system enhances or undermines overall organizational effectiveness.

The precise nature of senior management's business responsibilities and legal obligations varies among organizations and jurisdictions. Nevertheless, important general observations can be made.

Fiduciary Duties

Regardless of its particular legal form, every organization is ultimately managed by its directors, trustees, or regents, or by other individuals or entities who exercise comparable supervisory and oversight responsibilities. Those persons or entities are generally charged with fiduciary duties that dictate the degree of skill, care, and loyalty—alternatively called trust and confidence—the law requires of them. As discussed more fully in Chapters 16 and 17, different standards of skill, care, and loyalty apply to different fiduciaries, depending on specific facts and circumstances.

The range of different types of fiduciaries is expansive. It includes directors of corporations,[3] both public and private; general partners of general and limited partnerships; directors and trustees of management and investment companies "organized as corporations, unincorporated associations, or business trusts [that] normally have a board of directors or trustees with considerable investment freedom"[4]; and other types of trustees and trusteeships with diverse operations and operating structures, including corporate trustees, bank trust departments, law firms, and individuals or panels of individuals operating with or without significant investment expertise and the support of full-time staff.

Officers and Executives

Directors, trustees, and other fiduciaries at the highest management levels typically delegate to other executives responsibility for day-to-day management. For example, corporate officers are the agents of the board through whom the board acts. Their responsibilities are generally determined by statute, corporate organizational documents (including the certificate of incorporation, by-laws, and directors' resolutions) and employment agreements. Similarly, trustees may delegate responsibility for the daily management of funds and portfolios under their supervision to internal administrators or executives as well as to outside money managers, investment advisers, and other professionals. The responsibilities of these delegatees are similarly set forth in organizational documents, employment agreements, and investment management contracts.

Under the securities laws, officers of publicly held companies owe fiduciary duties to investors. As the SEC constantly reiterates: "The Commission has long viewed the issue of corporate governance and the fiduciary obligations of corporate officers and directors to their investors as one of paramount importance to the integrity and soundness of our capital markets."[5]

"BEST" VERSUS ACTUAL DERIVATIVES RISK MANAGEMENT PRACTICES

"Best" Practices

Under current industry "best practices" for both dealers and end users, directors and other comparable fiduciaries at the highest levels of management should formulate, monitor, and periodically update their organizations' derivatives policies. In turn, corporate officers and others to whom executive or day-to-day managerial responsibilities are delegated should design procedures and guidelines to implement board (or comparable) level policies. Managers at all levels are responsible for enforcing procedures and guidelines. For example, the first recommendation of the *G-30 Report* provides:

> *The Role of Senior Management.* Dealers and end-users should use derivatives in a manner consistent with the overall risk management and capital policies approved by their boards of directors. These policies should be reviewed as business and market circumstances change. Policies governing derivatives use should be clearly defined, including the purposes for which these transactions are to be undertaken. Senior management should approve procedures and controls to implement these policies, and management at all levels should enforce them (emphasis modified).

Similarly, the FOA published its *Guidelines for End-Users of Derivatives* (*End User Guidelines*), in December 1995.[6] The FOA's first two end user guidelines are:

> Principle 1. The **board of directors (or its equivalent)** should establish and approve **an effective policy for the use of derivatives** which is consistent with the strategy, commercial objectives and risk appetite of the underlying business of the organization, and should approve the instruments to be used and how they are to be used.
>
> Principle 2. **Senior management** should establish **clear written procedure for implementing the derivatives policy** set by the board covering such matters as dealing authority, reporting lines, risk limits, counterparty and documentation approvals and valuation procedures and should regularly review their operation and effectiveness (emphasis in original).*

---

*The derivatives guidelines of the Office of the Comptroller of the Currency (OCC), provide "guidance on risk management practices to national banks and federal branches and agencies engaging in financial derivatives activities." The first guideline addresses "Senior Management and Board Oversight." See *Risk Management of Financial Derivatives,* Banking Circular 277 (BC-277), dated October 27, 1993.

Actual Practices

The extent to which actual practices conform to industry guidelines varies considerably across firm's and industries. While some evidence suggests dealer practices tend to conform well to the guidelines, there is ample evidence that end user practices, while improving, in many instances fall short of recommended best practices. For example, the *1995 Wharton/CIBC Wood Gundy Survey* reports that only

> 76% of the firms using derivatives have a documented policy with respect to use of derivatives, and 49% of the firms regularly report on derivatives to their boards....16% of the firms neither have a documented policy nor report regularly to their boards.

Shortfalls in actual practices are potentially most hazardous when they occur at the board or other comparable supervisory level.

The foregoing survey results, while suggesting lagging problems, represent significant progress compared with the findings of an earlier survey conducted by the G-30. Appendix III to the *G-30 Report* includes, among other things, the early 1993 responses of end users to the question: "What depth of understanding of derivative products and associated risks is possessed by your board of directors?" Only 53% of the respondents answered that their boards had a "sufficient understanding relative to the use of derivatives at [their] organization[s]." Another 18% said their boards had a "good understanding of the concepts and the risks of derivatives," and 29% said their boards had "little understanding of derivatives."

The uncomfortably low level of board understanding reflected in the G-30 survey is perplexing, given that 42% of the respondents considered their use of derivatives to be *"imperative,"* another 42% considered such use to be *"very important,"* and 19% considered such use to be *"important."* (No respondent considered derivatives either unimportant or of little risk management value.) Similarly, a follow-up bulletin as to frequently asked questions about BC-277 states: "The OCC has general concerns that not all derivatives users both understand the associated risks and have adequate risk measurement, monitoring and control systems and policies in place. The OCC has particular concerns about the extent of *senior management* and *board of director knowledge and oversight* of derivative activities, for *both dealers and end-users."*[7]

Interpreting Survey Results

Upon first inspection, current surveys suggest material ongoing weaknesses in senior management understanding of derivatives. Yet the survey results should be interpreted judiciously. Outsiders can

> know remarkably little about corporate risk management practices.... Corporations disclose only minimal details of their risk management programs, and, as a result, most empirical analyses have to rely on surveys and *relatively coarse data* that at best discriminate between firms that do and do not use specific types of derivative instruments.[8]

Until more extensive and verifiable data is made available to researchers and analysts, there is no way to confirm the accuracy and reliability of the results of even detailed and carefully designed industry surveys.* One notable exception is an industry that Tufano describes as "almost tailor-made for academic investigation: the North American gold mining industry."

That industry consists of over 50 firms, 48 of which Tufano studied. Public companies constitute over 90% of the industry (based on gold production) and they are all closely followed by analysts. Almost all are undiversified, single-industry firms that provide detailed and meaningful disclosure about both their risk exposures and their diverse risk management practices. Their opportunities for risk management are numerous: the firms have a "rich menu" of risk management vehicles from which to choose. Among them are forwards, futures, swaps, and bullion loans. Because the firms deal with gold, a "globally-traded, volatile commodity," outsiders can readily observe and assess exposures to gold price risks. "Detailed disclosure of gold mining firms' use of the full range of risk management instruments permits analysts to measure the firms' gold price exposure."

Anecdotal evidence suggests that analysts and shareholders monitor gold price exposures and care about the extent to which risk management practices conform to stated policies. For example, two firms Tufano studied are Homestake Mining Company and Barrick Gold Corporation. Homestake has flatly stated that it does not hedge its gold production, whereas Barrick hedges a substantial amount. Hu notes that in 1994, when Homestake temporarily "departed from its general no-hedging policy with

---

*As discussed in Chapters 1 and 5, recent SEC derivatives disclosure requirements will surely result in more useful data being made available. Most of the new requirements become effective for banks, thrifts, and certain large registrants after June 15, 1997. For other registrants, the rules do not become effective until one year later.

respect to...one specific high-cost, extremely short-lived mine, some shareholders are reported to have immediately called Homestake's Chief Financial Officer to complain. When Barrick announced in 1996 that it was cutting back the amount of production it would hedge, the action attracted wide attention."[9]

According to Tufano, even though academic theory "might predict that no firms manage gold price risk....To the contrary, the gold industry has *embraced* risk management: over 85 percent of the firms in this industry used at least some sort of gold price risk management in 1990–1993 [the period studied]." And their risk management practices vary widely from firm to firm. Roughly one-sixth of the firms hedge more than 40% of their exposures and one-sixth hedge none of their exposures.

The results of the *1995 Wharton/CIBC Wood Gundy Survey,* the *G-30 Report,* and other surveys may also merely be symptomatic of an important reality of business life—namely, that the function of boards of directors and other supervisory bodies in practice does not conform to traditional theory. In a modern economy, "with the rise of a professional managerial class, the idea that the board of directors *actually manages* the company is being replaced with the idea that the board's primary function is to *monitor* management."[10] Certainly, directors retain ultimate *legal* responsibility for corporate management. However, in reality, senior executives, whether or not board members, often exercise more actual managerial authority than corporate law so far formally contemplates.

In practice, the power and influence of executive officers (and other comparable officials in noncorporate organizations) tend to far exceed, on a day-to-day basis and at the highest strategy and policymaking levels, the degree of power and influence assumed by legal theory. Although there is reason to believe that tendency is to be changing, it still persists.

COMPARING PRACTICE
WITH THEORY

In a 1995 article in the *Harvard Business Review,* five leaders of major corporations presented their views of the realities of corporate governance.[11] Among the questions addressed were: "What role should a board dominated by outside directors play in formulating and reviewing the company's strategy?...How does a board ensure that its members have the expertise to judge management's performance?" The article begins by noting: "Most directors and managers seem to agree that the objective is to make the board a more effective watchdog without undermining management's ability to run the business." Nevertheless, the opinions of the senior managers expressed in the article reveal that, in reality, the effectiveness of boards in fulfilling their "watchdog" function is questionable.

Several opinions reveal that the extent to which boards actually act as outside watchdogs is limited. For example, one chairman states flatly that "at the end of the day, most independent directors get neutralized in one fashion or another." "It is hard for outside directors not to be taken by surprise at some point, because they are dependent on the information that management prepares for them." Another executive writes: "The notion that nonexecutive directors who meet only once a month should determine the company's strategic direction is, quite frankly, unrealistic." If that reality is indeed changing, the SEC and powerful institutional investors are leading the effort.

Shareholder Activism: Increasing Officer and Director Accountability

An important trend affecting public companies beginning in the 1990s is the growing activism of institutional investors and other significant shareholders in matters of corporate governance. Market dynamics have in recent years resulted in far greater institutional securities ownership. Changing ownership patterns have forced large investors to become more active in asserting their rights as security holders to affect change in corporate management.

In an increasingly competitive environment, pension funds, money managers, and other large investors are driven to improve investment performance. However, attempts to achieve superior performance through active trading strategies, even when effective, are usually not enough. Capital markets are highly competitive and difficult to beat merely through portfolio management strategies.

One of the two "pillars of modern finance" is that markets are "efficient" in that "[i]nformation that is freely accessible is incorporated in prices with sufficient speed and accuracy that one cannot profit by trading on it."[12] Relying on empirical evidence, the current movement toward modernizing the law of trusts explicitly endorses the "efficient market hypothesis":

> Economic evidence shows...the major capital markets of this country are highly efficient, in the sense that available information is rapidly digested

and reflected in the market prices of securities. As a result, fiduciaries and other investors are confronted with potent evidence that the application of expertise, investigation, and diligence in efforts to "beat the market" in these publicly traded securities ordinarily promises little or no payoff, or even a negative payoff after taking account of research and transaction costs....[S]killed professionals have rarely been able to identify underpriced securities (that is, to outguess the market...) with any regularity.[13]

In addition to being increasingly competitive, markets now are flush with capital. One major indicator is the massive inflow of funds in recent years into stock and bond markets, both directly and, more commonly, indirectly through institutional investment managers. In September 1996 *The Wall Street Journal* noted that "fund managers are grappling with fierce competition and a torrent of new money to manage."[14] Similarly, *Investor's Business Daily* reported that "[s]trong inflows into stocks in January [1997] and a steadily rising market have pushed trading levels to new highs....On the New York Stock Exchange, the past five weeks [ending February 14, 1997] have seen nine of the top 16 volume days in history. The Nasdaq's hit three of its top 10 volume days in that time."[15] The success of the Dow Jones in early 1998 in surprising the 9,000 barrier suggests strongly that the flow of funds has not dramatically changed direction. An important caveat is that recessionary fears in East Asian appear to be having an effect an asset allocations. Many investors have begun shifting capital invested in equities over to bonds and cash markets.

The combination of market efficiency and massive inflows of funds into the hands of institutional investors often forces institutions to take larger positions in individual companies.[16] Consequently, many trades by institutions, which now constitute "about 80% of all trading activity in the stock market,"[17] are large enough to move markets. In addition, the mere volume of funds invested with institutions automatically increases the difficulty of finding suitable investment opportunities.

To counteract the effects of huge transaction costs in the form of unfavorable prices, institutional investors and many other major shareholders have aggressively sought alternative means of improving the performance of portfolio companies. Often, the best means of improving performance is to get more actively involved in the internal governance of portfolio companies. "'The public funds have so much money that they find it's harder to find new companies to invest in than to try to turn around poorly performing ones.'...The funds have therefore begun to single out underperformers, demanding more say in their governance, and, increasingly, proposing changes in board composition and strategy."[18]

Among institutional investors, the California Public Employees' Retirement System, or "Calpers," has taken a high-profile role in efforts to turn around companies it considers to be underperforming. According to the February 11, 1997 *Wall Street Journal*:

> Businesses target by Calpers, the nations's biggest public-employee pension fund, often come under widespread institutional-investor pressure to overhaul their top management and corporate-governance practices. In recent years, the giant fund has played an influential role in the departure of leaders from General Motors Corp., Eastman Kodak Co., International Business Machines Corp. and others.[19]

In March 1998, Calpers made headlines simply by "backing away from a sweeping staff proposal that would pressure many big businesses to embrace strong corporate-governance practices."[20]

At times, shareholders have resorted to litigation to influence management performance.[21] Yet other developments, the most important being changes commencing in late 1992 to the SEC's proxy rules,[22] have liberalized rules governing shareholders communications thereby giving shareholders greater ability to freely express their views on matters of corporate governance. Shareholders now have greater power to embarrass or oust existing management for perceived business failures or inadequate performance. "Virtually all major public corporations now acknowledge that they have no choice but to make their managements more accountable to their shareholders and that, in general, strengthening the hand of outside directors is the logical way to do so."[23]

Generally, shareholder activism leads to greater directorial responsibility for, and involvement in, corporate governance and increased outside director independence from incumbent management. In the words of John G. Smale, then nonexecutive chairman of General Motors Corporation, regarding the highly publicized, "industry-leading" internal governance policies instituted in 1994 by GM:

> Their [the policies'] existence formally recognizes that the board of directors is *separate from the management* of the company—and that the board has separate specific obligations to the owners of the business. The board's basic responsibility is to see that the company is managed in a way that serves the owners' interest in successfully perpetuating the business. It has to act as an independent monitor of management, *asking the tough questions* that management might not ask itself.[24]

SEC Enforcement Actions

Likewise, the SEC has aggressively pursued increased accountability for officers and directors and the independence of directors from senior executives.[25] In issuing its formal report in *Cooper Companies,* the SEC said it was doing so "to emphasize that corporate directors have a significant responsibility and play a critical role in safeguarding the integrity of the company's public statements and the interests of investors when evidence of fraudulent conduct by corporate management comes to their attention."[26] Evidence that calls into question the accuracy of outstanding public reports makes it "incumbent on the Board to ensure the candor and completeness of the company's public statements." The SEC's views expressed in the *Cooper Companies* report explain the SEC's aggressive stance in *Gibson Greetings.*[27]

GIBSON GREETINGS

The SEC found[28] that Gibson and two of its senior officers violated the securities laws by reporting materially inaccurate information about the size of the company's unrealized derivatives losses. The SEC also found violations resulting from Gibson's failure to maintain accurate internal books and records and its lack of adequate internal controls.

The overall findings may initially seem surprising because the SEC acknowledged that Gibson's misstatements were "caused" by its dealer's misrepresentations. The SEC noted, for example, that dealer "representatives misled Gibson....As a result, Gibson remained unaware of the actual extent of its losses." Nevertheless, the SEC asserted that those misrepresentations and issues of causation were relevant in its enforcement action against the dealer, but that *Gibson Greetings* was a separate case involving only the securities law obligations of Gibson and its senior officers: "Those obligations are not excused by the [dealer's] fraud."

A closer look at the "hard facts" of the case enables an outsider to appreciate the SEC's actions. Gibson originally entered into two plain vanilla interest rate swaps designed to convert $30 million out of a total of $50 million principal amount of outstanding fixed-rate debt into floating rate obligations. However, Gibson voluntarily terminated those swaps early and at a gain. After that, the company soon began to enter into a series of new or amended OTC derivatives transactions: some of which produced gains, most of which produced losses. Although Gibson cashed out of certain gains (thereby recognizing income), the SEC stated that "at no time did Gibson pay cash to terminate a derivative with an unrealized loss. Instead, rather than incur a realized loss by terminating a derivatives position, Gibson consistently attempted to trade out of losses by agreeing to new or amended derivatives." But "each time Gibson shifted unrealized losses into new or restructured derivatives positions, the overall mark-to-market value of its derivatives portfolio worsened."

Along the way, the aggregate notional amounts of the outstanding transactions grew to $167.5 million, an amount totally out of proportion to the principal amount of Gibson's outstanding debt. In addition, the new and amended transactions grew increasingly complex and involved higher leverage. The SEC easily found that at some point Gibson's derivatives no longer bore any relation to Gibson's underlying debt obligations; it found that what originally began as a hedging program eventually transformed into pure speculation. According to the SEC: "The derivative transactions entered into by Gibson resulted in losses primarily because interest rate movements were not correctly anticipated."

The SEC also found that the unrelated nature of the transactions rendered them ineligible for hedge accounting treatment and its corresponding deferral of recognition of gains and losses. Therefore, applicable law required the company to mark-to-market the value of its portfolio, thus taking both gains and losses into income on a more frequent basis. Nevertheless, the company continued to apply hedge or deferral accounting and deferred recognition of its growing losses.

Moreover, the SEC found that although the company's board had approved a resolution authorizing derivatives relating to the outstanding debt, "[n]o specific procedures were put in place to implement that resolution, such as procedures to place limits on the amounts, types or nature of derivatives transactions, or to assess the risks of derivatives transactions. Gibson also lacked adequate controls designed to ensure that its derivatives positions were accounted for in accordance with Generally Accepted Accounting Principles."

Finally, as the losses grew, and the company was apparently aware of the losses (even if not the full magnitude), Gibson failed to discuss in the MD&A portion of its annual and quarterly filings the potential materially adverse effect the losses might have on it.

IMPLICATIONS FOR OTC DERIVATIVES
DECISION MAKING AND OVERSIGHT

Currently, little authoritative guidance is available (except, perhaps, in the case of regulated entities such as banks and insurance companies) to senior management concerning its risk management responsibilities over derivatives. While *Cooper Companies* and *Gibson Greetings* provide some assistance, any lessons drawn must be tempered by the recognition that those cases involved egregious conduct. Until definitive guidance about senior management's responsibilities concerning derivatives activities becomes available, senior management and its legal advisers must rely on general precepts of corporate, trust, and other applicable law. One important point that should not be overlooked is that the absence of specific derivatives guidance is likely due to the growing appreciation that derivatives risks are not necessarily different in kind from the risks of any other business or investment activity.

An important initial observation is that all fiduciaries are subject to inherently conflicting legal duties. There is significant tension between the law's desire to discourage imprudent risk taking and the reality that every business and investment activity must assume some risk to earn a profit. That tension dictates that fiduciaries generally engage exclusively in neither risk taking nor risk avoidance, but rather in risk management.

Likewise, prudence dictates that fiduciaries assume the law will hold them to a high standard of independent judgment in analyzing and monitoring the effectiveness and implementation of derivatives policies. Day-to-day managerial responsibilities usually must as a practical matter be delegated to officers, administrators, outside money managers, and others. For example, a manager of a large pension fund who invests fund assets through outside money management firms that make day-to-day investment decisions remains responsible for the activities of those money managers. Thus, the fund manager should adopt, and actively monitor compliance with, formal policies and guidelines governing the range, amounts, and types of investments that outside managers will be permitted to make. Nevertheless, ultimate responsibility for derivatives use resides at the highest levels of management.

That responsibility includes a duty to exercise skill and care in selecting and supervising delegatees (such as chief executive officers and fund managers) and in monitoring their business and investment performance. Senior management remains ultimately responsible regardless of the particular organizational form or the structure of a rela-

tionship that may devolve significant responsibilities to outside agents
or advisers.

> The board must know the business well enough to be able to participate in
> forming the company's vision and direction. It must be able to arrive at an
> independent judgment of the soundness of the company's strategies for the
> future and to exercise the oversight necessary to fulfill its responsibilities to
> the owners.[29]

Fiduciary duties to owners and, at times, others (such as creditors when a
company is in the vicinity of insolvency) are a function of both business
reality and legal requirements.

A firm's supervisory body does not necessarily need to ensure that
all or even most of its members possess "on-the-job derivatives experience" or other derivatives expertise. Rather, as discussed in later chapters,
the appropriate level of senior management experience and training is a
matter for supervisory level consideration in light of all relevant facts and
circumstances. Included among those are the nature and volume of a
firm's derivatives activities and the existence of an independent risk management function that reports directly to the board (or comparable body).
It may also be more efficient to set up a committee structure whereby
immediate responsibility for derivatives matters can be assigned to a sub-
group that reports periodically to the full board (or comparable body).

OVERSIGHT SKILLS OR OPERATIONAL
EXPERTISE? THE BENEFITS OF
FUNCTIONAL ANALYSIS

Among the greatest challenges confronting senior management is the need
to understand the effects of alternative risk management strategies. In considering the use of derivatives, management must ask: "Will (or does) our
derivatives usage (1) reduce our risk, (2) increase it, or (3) simply result in
costs, implicit or explicit, without providing any overall risk reduction
benefit?" To answer those questions, management must further ask: "(4)
What do we mean by 'risk' and (5) how do we measure or quantify it if it
is capable of quantification? And (6) if derivatives will (or do) cost us
money without reducing our risk, do they offer a potential competitive
advantage by enabling us to help reduce the risks facing our customers,
suppliers, employees, or other business 'partners'?"

Answering those questions requires two skills: first, the ability to
understand derivatives' risk management functions; second, the ability to

measure and understand the magnitude and direction of the expected risk reduction benefits, the "confidence level" of that expectation, and the costs, implicit and explicit, of achieving those benefits. A functional approach to derivatives provides the first skill; familiarity with certain principles of modern finance and related quantitative techniques helps provide the second.

Derivatives present daunting mathematical, or quantitative, challenges. "Even the more sophisticated corporate trading rooms master only a few types of transactions and instruments."[30] Derivatives give rise to natural concerns over whether individuals who lack advanced training in mathematics can properly understand and supervise the use of the products. The functional, "building block" approach to derivatives addresses this concern directly. It provides insight into many behavioral characteristics of products that might otherwise easily be missed because they are complex, obscure, or counterintuitive. In so doing, the functional approach reveals its virtues.

Recommending the functional approach is its analytical simplicity. Managers and lawyers who lack mathematics backgrounds can without inordinate difficulty learn the principal behavioral characteristics of the individual building blocks of forwards and options. A functional approach enables even the most complex products to be broken down into their individual building blocks, or risk components. After that, the task of understanding the interactions of product combinations is far simpler. Much of the remaining analysis is a matter of measuring probabilities and magnitudes of the individual risk components. And risk measurement is a task that usually can and must be delegated. On the other hand, the final, most important analytical step is interpreting the meaning of the measurements—a task that cannot be delegated.

Nevertheless, summary statistics and estimates, as well as explanatory reports, prepared by internal staff or outside consultants can usually facilitate the interpretation of risk measurements without loss of meaningful information. Therefore, they can greatly simplify senior management's duties in fulfilling its supervisory function, provided senior management already possesses an "ability to deal comfortably with fundamental notions of number and chance."[31] Certainly, most successful business managers and business lawyers have that ability. "Mathematics is not primarily a matter of plugging numbers into formulas and performing rote computations. It is a way of thinking and questioning that may be unfamiliar to many of us, but is available to almost all of us."[32]

For supervisory purposes, the law requires an ability to appreciate product risks and applications. However, it seldom requires "operational expertise":

> They [senior managers] do not need to become number crunchers, but their legal obligations to make informed decisions will require them to understand how the derivatives transaction process works and how certain characteristics of derivatives relate to the company's objectives, structure, and culture.[33]

Senior managers have no legal obligation to be able to perform complex calculations or design and execute derivatives-based (or other) risk management strategies. Their responsibility is to exercise informed and independent judgment in evaluating the risks, costs, effectiveness, and "fit" of relevant business activities, whether or not involving derivatives.

In reaching informed and independent judgments, senior management may rely on employees, staff, and outside consultants and advisers[34] for explanations of even the most sophisticated products and strategies. Moreover, systems can be designed to capture and report relevant information to management on a routine basis and not merely in response to crises. Here, it is useful to consider the advice of Robert McKnew, an executive vice president of Bank of America: "And when I say 'reported,' I mean expressed in such a way that somebody in senior management can look at your decisions and evaluate them against an explicit, unambiguous standard. I am talking about *meaningful internal* or management accounting systems, *not just adhering to external reporting conventions.*"[35]

Similarly, Don Chance cautions managers that their inability to grasp technical explanations of mathematically complex processes or products may have nothing to do with their lack of quantitative skills: "Many mathematicians and economists have consistently demonstrated to me that they cannot communicate what they are doing in simple terms. If it can't be explained to a nontechnical person, either they [i.e., the mathematicians and economists] don't understand the problem or it isn't very important."[36] As both a legal and a business matter, however, responsibility for the miscommunication or lack of understanding is irrelevant. Senior managers have an obligation not to approve policies or authorize transactions they do not adequately and independently understand.

ENDNOTES: CHAPTER 10

1. Froot et al., *Risk Management Framework, supra,* Chapter 4, note 2: 91.
2. See Maarten Nederlof, "Risk-Management Programs," in printed materials relating to *Risk Management* conference (Association for Investment Management and Research, October 1995) [hereafter, *Risk-Management Programs*]: 15.

3. Directors are fiduciaries whose powers, duties, and obligations are governed by applicable state corporate law. See, generally, *Pepper v. Litton,* 308 US 295, 306, 60 S.Ct. 238, 84 L.Ed. 281 (1939).

4. See Loss and Seligman, *Fundamentals of Securities Regulation, supra,* Chapter 8, note 5: 36–37.

5. *Cooper Companies, Inc.,* Release No. 34-35082, '94–'95 CCH Dec. ¶ 85,472 (citation omitted) [hereafter, *Cooper Companies*]. *Cf. Solash v. Texas Corp.,* [1987–1988 Transfer Binder] Fed. Sec. L. Rep. (CCH) ¶ 93,608 (Del. Ch. Jan. 19, 1988) ["it is possible to say broadly that the duty of loyalty is transgressed when a *corporate fiduciary,* whether *director, officer* or controlling shareholder, uses his or her corporate office…to promote, advance or effectuate a transaction between the corporation and such person…and that transaction is not substantively fair to the corporation" (emphasis added)]: 97,727; Edward P. Welch and Andrew J. Turezyn, *Folk on the Delaware General Corporation Law: Fundamentals* (Little, Brown and Company, 1996) ("Apart from this single statutory requirement [of minute taking], *the powers and duties of officers are fixed by the by-laws or by board resolution,* and generally such provisions are valid, unless inconsistent with some clear policy of the statute or common law or with an overriding provision of the certificate of incorporation" (emphasis added)): ¶ 142.6.

6. As the FOA's Foreword explains, the guidelines are intended mainly for end users: "While numerous studies and reports have been published on aspects of risk management associated with derivatives, the majority of these reports (and the practical recommendations contained in them) have been primarily directed at brokers or dealers rather than end-users."

7. *Answers to Frequently Asked BC-277 Questions* (emphasis added): 8.

8. Except as otherwise noted, this and the quotations in the following three paragraphs are from Peter Tufano, "Who Manages Risk? An Empirical Examination of Risk Management Practices in the Gold Mining Industry," *The Journal of Finance,* 51(4) (September 1996) (emphasis added) [hereafter, *Who Manages Risk?*]: 1097–1137; see also Géczy, Minton and Schrond, *Why Firms Use Currency Derivatives, supra,* Chapter 1, note 37; Rene M. Stulz, "Rethinking Risk Management," *Journal of Applied Corporate Finance,* 9(3) (Fall 1996) (discussing, among other things, Tufano's survey and article) [hereafter, *Rethinking Risk Management*]: 8–24.

9. See Henry T. C. Hu, "Behind the Corporate Hedge: Information and the Limits of 'Shareholder Wealth Maximization,'" *Journal of Applied Corporate Finance,* 9(3) (Fall 1996) [hereafter, *Behind the Corporate Hedge*]: 49.

10. James Hamilton, James Motley, and Andrew Turner, "Responsibilities of Corporate Officers and Directors Under Federal Securities Laws," *Federal*

Securities Law Reports (*Extra Edition*), No. 1701 (February 15, 1996) [hereafter, *Securities Law Responsibilities*]: ¶ 104.

11. The quotations in this and the following paragraph are from "Redraw the Line Between the Board and the CEO," *Harvard Business Review* (March–April 1995) [hereafter, *Redraw the Line*]: 153–165; see, generally, *Pension Fund Excellence, infra,* Chapter 16, note 33.

12. Stulz, *Rethinking Risk Management, supra,* note 8: 11.

13. *Restatement of the Law Third, Trusts, Prudent Investor Rule,* as Adopted and Promulgated by the American Law Institute, Washington, DC, May 18, 1990 (American Law Institute Publishers, 1992) [hereafter, *Rest. 3rd, Trusts* (*Prudent Investor Rule*)]; see also Lee and Verbrugge, *The Efficient Market Theory Thrives on Criticism, infra,* Chapter 11, note 11.

14. Robert McGough and Charles Gasparino, "Fund Managers: No More Mr. Nice Guy," *The Wall Street Journal* (September 9, 1996): C1.

15. Walter Hamilton, "Volume Is Rising Along with Stock Prices," *Investor's Business Daily* (February 14, 1997): A19.

16. If anything, the trend toward increasing institutional ownership of individual securities is likely to continue. According to Merton, this trend is part of the financial innovation spiral:

> Retail customers ("households") will continue to move away from direct, individual financial market participation such as trading individual stocks or bonds where they have the greatest and growing *comparative disadvantage.* Better diversification, lower trading costs, and less informational disadvantage will continue to move their trading and investing activities toward aggregate bundles of securities such as mutual funds, basket-type and index securities, and custom-designed products issued by intermediaries. This secular shift…will cause liquidity to deepen in the basket/index securities while individual stocks become relatively less liquid.

Mason et al., *Financial Engineering, supra,* Chapter 1, note 2 (emphasis added): 32.

17. Bernstein, *Capital Ideas, supra,* Chapter 4, note 24: 4.

18. Thomas A. Stewart, "The King Is Dead," *Fortune* (January 11, 1993): 36; see, generally, Thomas W. Briggs, "Shareholder Activism and Insurgency Under the New Proxy Rules," *The Business Lawyer,* 50(1) (November 1994): 99.

19. Joann S. Lublin, "Calpers Targets Apple, Reebok, Others in Its Latest List of Worst Performers," *The Wall Street Journal* (February 11, 1997).

20. Joann S. Lublin, "Calpers Softens Its Proposed Standards For Corporate Governance in the U.S." *Wall Street Journal* (March 13, 1998): A2; see also Bruce Orwall and Joann S. Lublin, "Investors Take Aim at Disney Board Again," *Wall Street Journal* (February 20, 1998): C1; Joann S. Lublin, "Calpers Considers Seeking Board Seats," *Wall Street Journal* (December 26, 1997): A3.

21. Recently, the Delaware Court of Chancery addressed in dictum the oversight element of corporate directors' fiduciary duty of care. *In re Caremark International Inc. Derivative Litigation,* No. 13670 (Del.Ch. Sept. 25, 1996), involved a shareholders' derivative action against members of Caremark International Inc.'s board. The plaintiffs claimed the board breached its fiduciary duty of care concerning alleged violations by Caremark employees of federal and state regulations applicable to health care providers. While the immediate impact of the case, discussed in later chapters, is arguably unclear, consider the following newspaper account: "The ruling...lays the groundwork for expanding directors' obligations and good faith duty of care, shifting their role from passive observer to active guardian of corporate integrity." Dominic Bencivenga, "Words of Warning: Ruling Makes Directors Accountable for Compliance," *New York Law Journal* (February 12, 1997) (emphasis added): 5.

22. See "Regulation of Communications Among Shareholders," Exchange Act Release No. 31326, 1992 Fed. Sec. L. Rep. (CCH) ¶ 85,051 (October 16, 1992).

23. *Redraw the Line, supra,* note 11: 153.

24. *Id.* (emphasis added): 154–155.

25. "A directorship is increasingly being recognized more as a responsibility than as an honor or courtesy, and the non-monetary rewards of the post are not nearly so compelling as they once were....This has prompted the SEC to conclude that the interests of shareholders are best served by a board of directors able to exercise *independent judgment, ask probing questions* of management, and bring to the company a broader perspective than that entertained by management." Hamilton et al., *Securities Law Responsibilities, supra,* note 10: ¶ 104.

26. This and the following quotation are from *Cooper Companies, supra,* note 5.

27. *In re Gibson Greetings, Inc., et al.,* Exchange Act Release No. 36357, Release No. AAER-730 (October 11, 1995) [hereafter, *Gibson Greetings* or *Gibson*]. All quotations in the following discussion of the case are taken therefrom.

28. The findings were consented to by Gibson and the two named senior officers (collectively, Respondents) as part of an Offer of Settlement that the SEC accepted. The Respondents consented to the SEC's Order Instituting Proceedings and to the entry of the SEC's findings, but they did so without admitting or denying any of those findings.

29. *Redraw the Line, supra,* note 11: 155.

30. "Using Derivatives: What Senior Managers Must Know," *Harvard Business Review* (January–February 1995) (remarks of David Yeres of Rogers & Wells) [hereafter, *What Senior Managers Must Know*]: 37.

31. John Allen Paulos, *Innumeracy* (Vintage Books, a division of Random House, 1990) [hereafter, *Innumeracy*]: 3.

32. John Allen Paulos, *A Mathematician Reads the Newspaper* (BasicBooks, a division of HarperCollins Publishers, 1995) [hereafter, *A Mathematician Reads the Newspaper*]: 3.

33. *What Senior Managers Must Know, supra,* note 30.

34. For organizations that lack suitable sophisticated internal systems, or that are concerned about the speed with which any state-of-the-art risk management system can quickly become outdated, "[i]ndependent valuation service can give you the sophisticated advice you need." See Miriam Bensman, "Risk Managers for Rent," *Derivatives Strategy,* 1(1) (November 1995): 16.

35. "Bank of America Roundtable on Derivatives and Corporate Risk Management," *Journal of Applied Corporate Finance,* 8(3) (Fall 1995) [hereafter, *1995 BofA Roundtable*]: 72.

36. Don M. Chance, "A Nontechnical Introduction to Brownian Motion," *DRU,* Vol. 1, No. 40 (January 29–February 5, 1996) to appiar in (unforthcoming book to be published by Frank J. Fabozzi Associates).

Essential Managerial Information: Overview of Modern Finance

The two pillars of modern finance theory are the concepts of efficient markets and diversification....The lesson of market efficiency for corporate risk managers is that the attempt to earn higher returns in most financial markets generally means bearing large (and unfamiliar) risks....[D]iversification should also discourage some companies from hedging financial exposures incurred through their normal business operations. To explain why, however, requires a brief digression on the corporate cost of capital.

René M. Stulz
Journal of Applied Corporate Finance,
Fall 1996

Unlike individual risk management, corporate risk management doesn't hurt, but it also [except in limited circumstances] doesn't help. Corporate finance specialists will recognize this as a variant of the Modigliani and Miller theorem, which was developed in the 1950s and became the foundation of "modern finance."

Froot, Scharfstein, and Stein
Harvard Business Review,
November–December 1994

Directors, trustees, fund managers, executive officers, and other fiduciaries can fulfill their fiduciary duties regarding derivatives more effectively through greater familiarity with the principles of modern finance. These principles affect, directly or indirectly, all risk management strategies that employ derivatives. In addition, many criticisms of and attacks on derivatives strategies are rooted in the principles of modern finance. An organization that uses derivatives inconsistently with these principles may be using the products incorrectly or for purposes other than risk management. Either way, the organization may be increasing rather than reducing risk. It may even be transforming the very nature of its business.

SUPERVISORY-LEVEL UNDERSTANDING

Modern finance informs both sides of the ongoing derivatives debate. But what does "modern finance" mean?* Equally important, how can we synthesize its principles to convey practical information useful in constructing and supervising a system of encompassingly business and legal risk management? The American Law Institute (ALI) offers a useful starting point for answering both questions.

Stable Supervisory Definition

The ALI recognizes that there are "endless variations in reasonable strategies for...the prudent management of risk, with a variety of legitimate theories of investment to support and incorporate into those strategies."[1] A practical definition of modern finance is one that, like the functional building-block approach to individual derivative products, offers a simplified, stable approach to evaluating the business and legal implications of the endless risk management strategies and theories. It is one that enables fiduciaries and their legal advisers quickly to grasp the basic attributes of a financial risk management program, whether or not it employs derivatives. Knowledge of those attributes enables one to judge, initially, the merits and importance of financial risk management as a business and investment objective. It then provides the functional tools for comparing the costs and benefits of alternative techniques for implementing appropriate risk management systems, strategies, and controls.

Costs and benefits

For present purposes, we define the costs of risk management broadly to include (1) the purchase price and other direct financial costs of alternative risk management instruments and activities, (2) any new risks intro-

---

*Merton, whose concern is financial theory, uses an extraordinarily broad definition that encompasses a massive, changeable corpus of theory and practice: "It is generally agreed that financial management of firms and households, intermediation, capital market and microinvestment theory, and much of the economics of uncertainty fall withing the sphere of modern finance. As is evident from its influence on other branches of economics including public finance, industrial organization, and monetary theory, the boundaries of this sphere, like other specialties, are both permeable and flexible. The theoretical and empirical literatures covering this large and imperfectly defined discipline are truly vast." See Merton, *Continuous-Time Finance, supra,* Chapter 1, note 26: 3.

duced by those instruments and activities, including new legal and financial risks, (3) direct transaction costs, such as bid-offer spreads for purchasing and selling financial assets and the legal, accounting, and other professional fees incurred in establishing and maintaining a risk management program, and (4) indirect costs. The indirect costs include "the opportunity costs of senior management education and attention and the costs of appropriate internal controls"[2]; they also include the opportunity costs of lost strategic flexibility resulting from any long-term contractual commitments.

Commenting on the loss of strategic flexibility, Walter Dolde notes a common deficiency of textbook arguments in favor of natural (i.e., operational) hedges that avoid using derivatives. In his opinion, those arguments typically ignore "the effects of fluctuations in international activity. Downsizing in a particular currency—labor force, production and distribution facilities, and debt service—is a rather blunt instrument to use in response to a recession or seasonal downturn. These actions do not occur costlessly, nor do their reversals when growth resumes. Using FX derivatives—the scalpel, if you will, instead of the cleaver—reduces unwanted side effects from such adjustments."[3]*

The benefits of using derivatives over other risk management techniques include direct items, such as (1) the reduction of risk at a fraction of the costs of transacting directly in underlying assets, instruments, and indexes (our financial insrument widgets, or "fidgets"). They also include (2) indirect benefits such as preserving strategic flexibility by avoiding cumbersome operating solutions (e.g., reducing currency exposure through local foreign currency borrowing or by building or buying overseas production facilities) that would deprive a firm of strategic operating options, such as the ability to (a) enter or exit an industry, (b) abandon or delay projects, (c) temporarily shut down facilities, or (d) vary rates of production in response to changing market conditions. Derivatives' indi-

---

*Operational, on-balance-sheet risk management strategies are often the solution of choice for those who have difficulty finding appropriate liquid markets for satisfactory long-term financial hedges. "But such on-balance-sheet methods can be costly and, as firms such as Caterpillar have discovered, inflexible." Moreover, if those strategies involve financings, such as gold loans (which combine dollar financings with forward gold sales), they increase debt and thus leverage. Derivatives strategies, used properly, maximize the benefits of risk management while minimizing transaction costs. See Smithson et al., *Managing Financial Risk, infra,* note 28: 31, citing "Caterpillar's Triple Whammy," *Fortune* (October 27, 1986). But see Logue, *Hostile Market for FX, infra,* note 12; Anthony and Smith, *Managing Risk Without Resorting to Derivatives, infra,* note 13.

rect benefits also include (3) the preservation of manufacturing and other economies of scale that depend on production through a single plant or nearby facilities. "As an officer of one Fortune 500 MNC [multinational corporation] observed, 'we cannot sacrifice the scale economies available in manufacturing in order to create natural FX hedges.' Consequently, that firm's FX risk management actively uses financial instruments."

Common themes of modern finance

For trustees, investment companies, and other money managers responsible for supervising portfolio investments, modern finance is best understood as referring to the handful of common themes loosely referred to as "modern portfolio theory" and the "efficient market hypothesis." These themes provide portfolio managers with the analytic tools they need to (1) maximize expected returns for any given level of risk and (2) minimize the risks they must assume to generate targeted expected returns.

Officers, directors, and other fiduciaries of operating entities also need familiarity with modern portfolio theory and efficient market theory. They will also benefit from familiarity with the so-called Modigliani-Miller propositions, "contingent claims analysis," and other related concepts generally falling under the rubric of "corporate finance." Corporate finance encompasses two types of activities. The first are the "capital budgeting" decisions that allocate capital expenditures among projects and investments. The second are the "financing" decisions that determine how to raise funds to pay for capital expenditures. Capital budgeting affects the left, assets side of a firm's balance sheet; financing decisions affect the right, liabilities side.

Fundamentals

The foregoing themes of modern finance are, as the ALI notes, independent of any particular risk management, financing, or investment technique. Thus they offer "an instructive conceptual framework for understanding and attempting to cope with" the fundamentals of modern finance that are "not derived from or legally defined by the principles of any particular theory."[4] The fundamentals of particular importance to a functional understanding of derivatives legal risk management are the way modern finance:

    1. Reevaluates basic notions of *risk and return* and, in the process, (a) redefines risk in the statistical sense of *uncertainty* of outcomes, whether good or bad, as opposed to the commonly understood sense of the possibility of bad outcomes, (b) explicitly *balances* risk against expected return, (c) is concerned with the effect of individual investments and business activities on the overall risk and return of entire *portfolios* and *firms* rather than on that of the individual investments and business activities considered in isolation, and (d) shows how *borrowing* (i.e., leverage) and *lending* can be used efficiently to alter risk and return features of portfolios and firms

2. Identifies the limited conditions under which corporate financing and risk management decisions can *enhance firm value:* namely, by reducing (a) the probability of bankruptcy and the associated direct and indirect costs of financial distress that can be incurred in and prior to bankruptcy, including the costs of (i) underinvesting, (ii) harming key business relationships, and (iii) suffering bankruptcy court interference with business operations, (b) transaction costs, and (c) taxes

3. Provides techniques for valuing financial claims whose payoff profiles are contingent on the values of one or more underlying assets, instruments, or indexes

4. Combines powerful mathematics, particularly statistical techniques, with classical economic theory, enabling many business and investment decisions previously thought incapable of objective analysis to be studied with the tools of scientific research

The remainder of this chapter covers two topics. The first is primarily a historical description of the four separate lines of inquiry from which the foregoing fundamentals are derived. The second pertains to the essential role, and limitations, of mathematics in financial risk management.

ORIGINS OF MODERN FINANCE

Historical perspective is essential to an understanding of how to use derivatives to manage other risks and how to manage the business and legal risk the products introduce. Without it, one can easily misjudge the extent to which the legal infrastructure of modern derivatives markets fails to accommodate the revolutionary pace of change in the theory and practice of finance. Merton, for example, warns of the "interdependence between product and infrastructure innovations and of the inevitable conflicts that arise between the two."[5] He likens financial innovation and infrastructure mismatches to "the creation of a high-speed passenger train" operating on "the tracks of the current rail system[, which] are inadequate to handle such high speeds."

Four distinct lines of inquiry have led to the modern theory of finance: efforts to (1) minimize portfolio risk while maximizing expected portfolio returns, (2) determine the efficiency of capital markets and, hence, whether stock, commodity, and other prices are predictable, (3) determine optimal firm capital structures, and (4) determine the prices of securities whose payoffs are contingent on underlying asset prices.[6] The ideas resulting from each line of inquiry continue, separately and in combination, to influence profoundly the effectiveness and validity of all financial risk management strategies, whether or not they employ derivatives.

Portfolio Risk and Return

Modern finance traces its immediate origins to the publication in 1952 of an arcane article in the *Journal of Finance* entitled "Portfolio Selection." The article was authored by future Nobel laureate Harry Markowitz, who was then an unknown graduate student at the University of Chicago. Markowitz proved mathematically how diversification could (1) reduce portfolio risk with minimal loss of expected return and (2) maximize expected return for any specified level of risk.

Before "Portfolio Selection," investors commonly diversified their investments; the law of trust investments, for example, has long contained an express diversification requirement. Yet the defining characteristic of early diversification practices and legal requirements is that their sole objective was (and where applicable still is) to avoid loss—that is, to minimize the risk of having all one's capital wiped out by a loss on a single investment. Early diversification practices lacked any formal analysis of risk-return trade-offs. Markowitz's proof illuminated portfolio dynamics and the mathematical trade-offs between risk and return.

In its original form, Markowitz's portfolio theory was, as a computational matter, extraordinarily unwieldy. Still, it provided a theoretical foundation for many later empirical studies and theoretical developments. Eventually, financial economists constructed full-fledged theories of investment risk and return on Markowitz's theoretical foundation. John Lintner and Nobel laureates James Tobin and William Sharpe made key insights and simplifying assumptions—eventually subsumed within the capital asset pricing model—that enriched Markowitz's theory and rendered it useful for practical investment and risk management applications.

Yet many of the assumptions introduce other difficulties, the implications of which are hotly debated.

Note on terminology: Much of modern finance has, since the publication of "Portfolio Selection," extensively relied on securities market terminology. Yet, as discussed later, the principles of modern finance are applicable to the entire spectrum of business and investment activities, including corporate finance and capital budgeting. The reason for the current terminology is happenstance: modern financial theory is largely the unintended by-product of academic attempts to determine the extent to which stock prices are predictable. Academics have long been drawn to stock and commodity markets by the markets' unusual wealth of statistical data.* In the words of M. F. M. Osborne, an eminent astrophysicist at the U.S. Naval Research Laboratory and student of stock markets:

> The stock market is a gigantic decision-making phenomenon. It deserves scientific attention from those who would like to understand how decision making occurs, naturally, and in the large. As an economic phenomenon, we believe the market can reproduce in a few weeks a scaled version of supply-demand relations that would take many years to complete in a different setting.[7]

Efficient Markets; Predictability of Prices

Nearly two decades prior to "Portfolio Selection," Holbrook Working, a statistician from Stanford University, published the results of his study on the predictability of prices in U.S. commodity markets. Working found

---

*Around 1900, Louis Bachelier, a French mathematician whose interest in markets was evidently entirely academic, "laid the groundwork on which later mathematicians constructed a full-fledged theory of probability." He also provided theoretical support for later attempts systematically to value financial instruments "such as options and futures, which had active markets even in 1900. And he did all this in an effort to explain why prices in capital markets are impossible to predict!" Bernstein, *Capital Ideas, supra,* Chapter 4, note 24: 18.

Bachelier's work was essential to efforts beginning in the 1950s to develop a coherent theory of investment risk and return. "Bachelier was so far ahead of his time....[that] one of the leading finance scholars of the 1960s...once delivered this accolade: 'So outstanding is his work that we can say that the study of speculative prices has its moment of glory at its moment of conception.'" *Id.*; see also Merton, *Continuous-Time Finance, supra,* Chapter 1, note 26 (praising Bachelier's "magnificent dissertation on the theory of speculation" and noting the "direct and indisputable" lineage from Bachelier to modern finance): xiv; Brealey and Myers, *Principles of Corporate Finance, infra,* note 10 (Bachelier's mathematical study of random processes was so advanced it "anticipated by 5 years Einstein's famous work on the random Brownian motion of colliding gas molecules"): 326.

that although price levels may be somewhat predictable, price *changes,* the practitioner's primary concern, are mostly random. "Working's discoveries were revolutionary."[8] Nevertheless, after the publication of Working's paper, "almost complete silence reigned until 1953."

In 1953, Maurice Kendall, a renowned professor of statistics at the London School of Economics, published a paper in the British *Journal of the Royal Statistical Society.* The paper outlined Kendall's conclusions drawn from his analysis of weekly data on diverse groups of stocks traded on the British stock market from 1928 to 1938. The paper also covered monthly average prices of wheat on the Chicago commodity markets from 1883 to 1934 and of cotton on the New York Mercantile Exchange from 1816 to 1951. Kendall's findings, which reportedly "horrified" and "created an uproar" among his fellow statisticians at the Royal Statistical Society, confirmed Working's. "[Kendall] found no structure of any sort in this wide variety and long history of price patterns." Each series of prices appeared to be "a 'wandering' one, almost as if once a week the Demon of Chance drew a random number from a symmetrical population of fixed dispersion, and added it to the current price to determine next week's price....*The best estimate of the change in price between now and next week is there is no change."* This "wandering" of prices is now popularly known as a *random walk.*

Working's and Kendall's conclusions continue to inspire prodigious studies of the predictability of market prices. Those efforts have culminated in the now dominant theory known as the *efficient market hypothesis.* Among its most notable contributors are Eugene Fama, Harry Roberts, Michael Jensen, and Nobel laureate Paul Samuelson. Samuelson was apparently the first to combine extensive knowledge of statistical techniques with a rich background in classical economics. In his view, "[t]he nonpredictability of future prices from past and present prices is the sign, not of failure of economic law, but the triumph of economic law after competition has done its best." In efficient markets, the theory goes, intense competition generates fair prices.

Enter, economics

Samuelson tied vast statistical data on the unpredictability of prices to the basic economic forces of supply and demand. He acknowledges that actual market prices may not equal hypothetical "true" or "intrinsic" values (which Samuelson calls "shadow prices" and Hu calls "blissful prices"). Yet he asserts that market prices, which are the product of vigorous competition, at any given moment represent the market's then current best estimate of true values: "no other estimate of intrinsic value is likely to be more accurate than what buyers and sellers agree on in the market-place." The underlying force that drives price changes, that motivates market competition, is *information* about supply and demand. Because the timing and content of information is unpredictable, price changes are unpredictable too. Samuelson's conclusion, evident in the title of his groundbreaking 1965 paper, is that financial markets provide "Proof That Properly Anticipated Prices Fluctuate Randomly."

Forms of efficient market theory

As now understood, an efficient market is one in which available information affecting supply and demand is rapidly impounded into current market prices. "A (perfectly) efficient market is one in which every security's price equals its investment value at all times."[9] Three forms of efficiency have been postulated: (1) a "weak" form holding that current prices reflect all available information about past prices (thus, one cannot predict future prices from past prices); (2) a "semistrong" form under which prices reflect all publicly available information; and (3) a "strong" form holding that prices reflect or at least instantly adjust to all available information, including "monopolistic" information (defined to include not only "inside" information but also superior investment skills and market insight of outstanding investors). Academics and market professionals have long debated the relative merits and drawbacks of the three forms.

Status of efficient market theory

In an important 1970 paper recapitulating test results in capital markets of the three forms of the efficient market hypothesis, Fama concludes: "[T]here is no important evidence against the hypothesis in the weak and semi-strong form tests…and only limited evidence against the hypothesis in the strong form tests (i.e., monopolistic access to information about prices does not seem to be a prevalent phenomenon in the investment community)."[10] In its 1990 report, the ALI, in the tradition of Working, Kendall, Fama, and others, proffers this advice to fiduciaries and other investors:

> Economic evidence shows that, from a typical investment perspective, the major capital markets of this country are highly efficient, in the sense that available information is rapidly digested and reflected in the market prices

of securities. As a result, fiduciaries and other investors are confronted with potent evidence that the application of expertise, investigation, and diligence in efforts to "beat the market"...ordinarily promises little or no payoff, or even a negative payoff after taking account of research and transaction costs. Empirical research...reveals that in such markets skilled professionals have rarely been able to identify under-priced securities (that is, to outguess the market with respect to future return) with any regularity.[11]

Clearly, "[t]he efficient market theory applied to financial markets has been an unquestionable success....But like all successful theories, the efficient market theory has come under attack. An academic cottage industry has grown up around attempts to discover efficient market 'anomalies'—that is, observations that are inconsistent with the operation of efficient markets."[12] Nevertheless, the theory has flourished, if only for one obvious reason: in highly competitive markets, once an anomaly that provides opportunities for abnormal returns is discovered, "the behavior (or lack of behavior) that gives rise to it will tend to be eliminated by competition among investors for higher returns....The implication here is rather striking. The more empirical flaws that are discovered in the efficient market theory [as evidenced by fleeting opportunities for above-average returns], the more robust the theory becomes."

Efficient Market Hypothesis and Derivatives Disclosure

The evolution of the SEC's derivatives disclosure requirements and the related Financial Accounting Standards Board derivatives accounting rules present an ongoing test of the efficient market hypothesis.* Unquestionably, many public companies use derivatives to manage the results contained in their financial reports. Consider, for example, the results of the *1995 Wharton/CIBC Wood Gundy Survey.* That survey asked firms that use derivatives for managing risk to rank the relative importance of four risk management objectives: managing (1) cashflows, (2) balance sheet accounts, (3) firm market value, and (4) accounting earnings.

Not surprisingly, 49% of the respondents claimed their "most impor-

---

*SEC derivatives disclosure and FASB derivatives accounting issues are discussed further in Chapter 18.

tant" risk management objective is to stabilize cashflows (discussed in Chapter 12). Less expectedly:

> Managing the *fluctuations in accounting earnings is a close second with 42%* of firms indicating that this is the "most important" objective of their hedging strategy. While in many cases the impact of hedging on reported earnings and cash flows may be similar, the popularity of this objective may suggest that some firms focus hedging strategy more on stabilizing the reported numbers presented to investors than stabilizing the actual economic internal cash flows (emphasis added).

Two important questions are immediately raised by such survey evidence. First, does the use of derivatives to stabilize reported earnings vitiate the usefulness of the information reported to investors? Second, does such use result in uneconomic trade-offs for reporting firms?

The answers to those questions depend on the extent to which investors, both individual and institutional, are able to analyze reported numbers and answer the following additional questions: Has a reporting firm's use of derivatives altered its securities' overall risk-return features in a way that affects the securities' contribution to the investor's portfolio?* Is a reporting derivatives user entering into otherwise uneconomical derivatives transactions simply to manage its reported financial results? Equally important, is a firm that might otherwise benefit economically from derivatives avoiding them out of concern over potentially misleading accounting and disclosure requirements?[†] Shortly after the large deriv-

---

*Hu poses the example of an investor who holds oil company stock, not necessarily because of bullish views on oil prices but because of the portfolio effects of an oil investment: "[A]n investor may have purchased the shares...because of the presumed way in which a change in the oil price would affect the prices of other assets in his portfolio. That is, from the point of view of optimizing his portfolio, he was seeking shares that would provide such an exposure to the price of oil. If a corporation takes hedging actions and the investor had assumed the corporation would not hedge or if the corporation takes hedging actions unanticipated by the investor, the corporation has undermined the ability of the investor to optimize his portfolio." Hu, *Behind the Corporate Hedge, supra,* note 2: 48–49.

†Hu offers an intriguing, but all too common, scenario: "[A]ssume that hedge accounting treatment is not available for a particular hedging transaction. Rejecting the hedging transaction because of concerns over the quarter-to-quarter impact on reported earnings could be justified only if the share price impact of such fluctuations were destructive enough to outweigh whatever benefits to the actual or blissful [i.e., intrinsic] share price would otherwise flow from entering the hedging transaction. This is an empirical issue. The traditional conception may reinforce a possible tendency on the part of some managements to exaggerate the importance of [reported] earnings." Hu, *Hedging Expectations, supra,* Chapter 2, note 37: 1022.

atives losses of 1994 many fund managers and reporting companies, seeking to dispel investors' concerns and keep or attract funds, heavily advertised that they do *not* use derivatives. That trend persists.[13]

Additional important questions include: Is the inordinate time and attention often devoted to derivatives reporting and accounting detracting from senior management performance? Is it detracting from investor performance and portfolio results? Are heightened disclosure concerns creating economic distortions? Do they, for example, mislead investors into treating derivatives risks as disproportionately greater than core business risks of reporting firms? If investors lack the analytic capabilities needed to analyze and compare the effects of derivatives on similar firms in comparable industries, are other sources of reliable comparative information economically available? For example, do published *beta values*—statistical measures that rely on historical prices to determine a security's sensitivity to changes in overall market conditions—satisfactorily account for derivatives use or nonuse, given that the staggering growth rate of derivatives markets limits the usefulness of historical data?

The opacity of derivatives accounting and reporting may preclude investors and analysts from obtaining meaningful information about securities' true risks. Efficiency arguments suggest that *if* that is so and *if* markets can be made aware that reported information is deficient, *then* markets will punish the stock prices of reporting firms whose disclosures are deficient. Firms that provide less meaningful disclosure are by definition riskier than those whose reporting is more useful; investors are more likely to shun—thus reducing the demand for and price of—securities of firms that provide less reliable information, regardless of conformity to specific disclosure mandates. The lesson of efficiency is that *if* derivatives indeed serve essential risk management functions, those stock prices of firms that use derivatives effectively should benefit significantly from full and meaningful *voluntary* disclosures. Indeed, market efficiency suggests that a critical concern of any regulatory body is the protection of voluntary disclosures of meaningful derivatives and other information.

Efficiency arguments suggest that (absent countervailing forces) market forces encourage firms to provide voluntary information, regardless of regulatory and accounting requirements. Once investors, directly or in reliance on securities analysts, gain comfort in markets' ability accurately to price derivatives' true economic (as opposed to accounting) effects, derivatives should play a more useful role in capital markets. Markets must first, however, be capable of, among other things, distinguishing between efficient *uses* and inefficient *failures to use* derivatives. Once that distinction can be made and is made, economic forces should cause appropriate price adjustments in reporting firms' securities:* "as derivatives accounting and disclosure improve and securities analysts better understand derivatives... devoting real economic resources for cosmetic accounting earnings purposes will become increasingly questionable."[14] Likewise, avoiding derivatives for cosmetic reporting purposes may also become suspect.

MM Theory and the Search for Optimal Capital Structure

Shortly after the publication of "Portfolio Selection," two other academics began collaborating on a problem described as the "mirror image" of that with which Markowitz had wrestled. Markowitz had wondered whether he could devise a strategy for *purchasing* assets that maximizes expected portfolio returns while minimizing risk. Franco Modigliani and Merton Miller "turned that question around by asking how a corporation should select securities to *sell* to arrive at an optimal balance between debt and equity—the claims of creditors versus the claims of stockholders."[15] The near heretical results of their research, now popularly known as Modigliani-Miller theory (typically called MM, or M and M), transformed the theory and practice of corporate finance. Modigliani and Miller won Nobel prizes for their efforts.

---

*Anecdotal evidence suggests that investors care strongly about firms' risk management policies and their adherence in practice to those policies—at least when the policies and practices are comprehensible. Tufano's study of the North American gold mining industry included two firms with contrasting risk management approaches: Homestake Mining Company generally does not hedge, and Barrick Gold Corporation hedges a lot. "When Homestake, in 1994, departed [slightly] from its general no-hedging philosophy..., some shareholders are reported to have immediately called Homestake's Chief Financial Officer to complain. When Barrick announced in 1996 that it was cutting back the amount of production it would hedge, the action attracted wide attention." See Hu, *Behind the Corporate Hedge, supra,* note 2: 49; see also Hu, *Hedging Expectations, supra,* Chapter 2, note 37 (citing the few "studies done on the impact of 'earnings management' on shareholder wealth"): 1020, note. 168.

Proposition I

MM theory rests on two propositions. Proposition I holds that in "perfect," "frictionless" capital markets,* assuming a firm's investment and capital expenditure policies (hence, the left side of its balance sheets) are predetermined, the value of the firm is "independent of its capital structure (that is, its debt/equity ratio)."[16] Market value is a function of a firm's real resources, and those resources ultimately are the cashflows produced by the firm's real assets. Securities represent claims on that market value, which is derived from expected cashflows. Thus, market value is based on the total of a firm's expected cashflows; it is irrelevant how the firm divides its cashflows among the holders of different classes of debt and equity securities, because the division cannot increase aggregate cashflows.

Miller explains that, in a perfect market, capital structure simply determines how "to partition the earnings (and their attendant risks) among the many separate [securities holders]." He suggests that investors consider a firm with only one issue of bonds and one class of equity securities outstanding. To determine the value of the firm's equity, the investors would begin by first "capitalizing its operating earnings *before* interest and taxes. The value of the shares would then be found by subtracting out the value of the bonds."

Arbitrage proof

Modigliani and Miller support Proposition I with an "arbitrage proof." They posit two firms of identical cashflows and equivalent riskiness—this is their so-called risk class assumption, which Miller labels a useful but nonessential "expository device" (discussed further below). One firm has a capital structure consisting entirely of equity securities; the other is levered, with both debt and equity securities outstanding. "Lastly, suppose that the levered firm's value is less than that of the unlevered firm."[17] If so, an arbitrage opportunity—that is, a chance for a risk-free profit—would arise.

---

*A perfect, frictionless market is one with (1) no taxes, transaction costs, costs of bankruptcy, or costs of financial distress. And it is an ideal market in which, among other things, (2) individuals can borrow and lend on the same terms as the firms in which they invest (so borrowing and short selling are unrestricted), (3) all investors have the same costless access to reliable information about firms' future prospects and earnings power, and (4) trading takes place continuously.

To see the arbitrage, notice that a holder of shares of the all-equity firm could simultaneously sell them and buy a proportionate percentage—a "cross section"—of the levered firm's debt and equity securities.* The purchase price for the cross section would be less than the proceeds received by the arbitrageur ("equilibrators," as Miller calls them) in the sale of the all-equity firm's shares. Yet the proportionate holding of the debt and equity securities of the levered firm would continue to entitle the investor "to exactly the same cash flow. Such an arbitrage possibility would raise the price of the levered firm's equity and lower that of the unlevered firm until the two firms had the same value [i.e., reached equilibrium]....Conversely, if the levered firm were relatively overvalued, then by combining the unlevered firm's equity with borrowing—that is, by creating 'homemade leverage'—the investor could duplicate the return on the levered firm's equity at lower cost."

The initial impact of MM theory is attributable to Proposition I's counterintuitive "paradox of indifference"[18] (also called an "invariance" or "irrelevance" proposition)—its proof that in a perfect market, changes in capital structure should not affect a firm's market value (or, as some say, that capital structure "does not matter"). According to Proposition I: by either (1) using "homemade leverage" to lever an all-equity firm or (2) buying cross sections of debt and equity of a levered firm to "undo the leverage," investors in perfect markets can "wash out" any firm's debt-equity ratio or capital structure. For Miller, given the impregnable logic of Proposition I, the all-important question for empiricists was:

> Could investors, acting on their own, really replicate and, where required, wash out corporate capital structures? Even if they could not do so completely and immediately as in the formal proof, could they act completely enough and quickly enough to make the invariance proposition useful as a description of the central tendency in the real world capital market?

---

*A similar arbitrage could be performed by an outside investor who did not already own the shares of the all-equity firm. The investor could simultaneously make a short sale of shares in the all-equity firm and purchase a proportionate percentage of the levered firm's securities. To effect the short sale, the investor would temporarily borrow shares and sell them, incurring interest charges over the life of the securities loan. Those charges would reduce the profitability of the overall transaction. The investor's strategy would be to wait for the market prices of the two firms' securities to reach their true economic equilibrium—the price of the all-equity firm's shares should fall and the prices of the securities of the levered firm should rise. Thereafter, the investor would purchase the all-equity firm's shares at their fallen price and use those shares to "repay" its securities loan.

Beyond Arbitrage Proof: Efficient Market Hypothesis

Miller notes that in 1958 M and M used the "then-novel" arbitrage proof "essentially as a metaphor—an expository device for highlighting hidden implications of the 'law of one price' in perfect capital markets." The arbitrage is no longer needed to explain MM; it has been displaced by the efficient market hypothesis. However, the dynamics of market efficiency are in many ways similar to those of the arbitrage proof and warrant examination.

As mentioned earlier, the efficient market hypothesis holds that a security's current price is the market's best estimate of that security's value, and in well-developed capital markets discrepancies between market price and true value are rare. In the language of classical economics, Sharpe and colleagues explain why such discrepancies are uncommon:

> Major disparities between price and investment value will be noted by alert analysts who will seek to take advantage of their discoveries. Securities priced below value...will be purchased, creating pressure for price increases due to the increased demand to buy. Securities priced above value...will be sold, creating pressure for price decreases due to the increased supply to sell. As investors seek to take advantage of opportunities created by temporary inefficiencies, they will cause the inefficiencies to be reduced, denying the less alert and the less informed a chance to obtain large abnormal profits.[19]

Proposition II

According to Miller, Proposition II "showed that when Proposition I held, the cost of equity capital was a linear increasing function of the debt-equity ratio. Any gains from using more of what might seem to be cheaper debt capital would thus be offset by the correspondingly higher cost of the now riskier equity capital. Our propositions implied that the *weighted average* of these costs of capital to a firm would remain the same no matter what combination of financing sources the firm actually chose."*

---

*Thus, a change in leverage forces a realignment of the market values of the firm's debt and equity. For example, (1) an increase in debt and hence leverage must cause a proportionate increase in the expected return on both debt and equity (which become riskier); and (2) a decrease in leverage must proportionately reduce the expected return on both debt and equity (which become less risky, although costlier equity now accounts for a greater proportion of the firm's value than before). If either result were not to obtain, an arbitrage opportunity would arise. If, for instance, increased leverage did not reduce market equity values to compensate for the additional risk borne by equity holders, the equity, all other things being equal, would be overpriced. Alert traders would short the equity, earning risk-free profits while forcing, through their sales, the realignment predicted in (1) above. See, e.g., Brealey and Myers, *Principles of Corporate Finance, supra,* note 10: 216.

Proposition I implies that an increase in leverage will not increase the value of equity shares, even though the expected proportion of cash-flows to be paid to equity holders increases (the capital structure now includes more debt with lower cashflow requirements). The problem for the firm is that, as equity cashflows increase, so do those flows' risks. Thus, the greater the firm's leverage, the riskier its equity securities: because of the increased risk, "the change in the expected earnings stream [dedicated to the equity] is exactly offset by a change in the rate at which the earnings are capitalized."[20]

Proposition II demonstrates that "[t]he expected rate of return on the common stock of a levered firm increases in proportion to the debt-equity ratio (D/E), expressed in market values; the expected rate of increase depends on the spread between...the expected rate of return on a portfolio of all of the firm's [debt and equity] securities...[and] the expected return on the debt." As the firm's leverage increases, the risk and return characteristics of its debt begin to more closely resemble those of an all equity firm—the debt holders are exposed to greater cashflow variability; eventually, as debt holders become entitled to virtually all the firm's cashflows, they will require equity-like returns. Proposition II, therefore, implies that as leverage increases, the expected return to equity must increase, but at an ever decreasing rate—as the firm approaches an all-debt capital structure, there is little or no cashflow left over to allocate to equity holders.

MM summary

MM theory has been controversial, sometimes bitterly so. The reason, as Miller observed in 1988, is the skepticism caused by

> almost daily reports in the financial press, then [1958] as now, of spectacular increases in the values of firms after changes in capital structure. But the view that capital structure is literally irrelevant or that "nothing matters" in corporate finance, though still sometimes attributed to us... is far from what we ever actually said about the real world applications of our theoretical propositions. Looking back now, perhaps we should have put more emphasis on the other, upbeat side of the "nothing matters" coin: showing what *doesn't* matter can also show, by implication, what *does*.

As discussed in later chapters, the application of the upbeat, constructive side of MM theory to risk management, and the theory's implications for derivatives users, has received abundant scholarly attention in recent years.

Option Pricing; Contingent Claims Analysis; Dynamic Replication

Attempts began at least as far back as the early 1900s to determine a formal theory for pricing put and call options. Those efforts have led to a variety of robust option pricing formulas as well as a new branch of finance called contingent claims analysis, or CCA. A revolutionary advance occurred with the publication in 1973 of Fischer Black and Myron Scholes's famous paper on option pricing.[21] The paper helped trigger the "explosion of theoretical, applied, and empirical research on option pricing"[22] that undergirds much of modern derivatives markets.

CCA applies a variety of techniques to financial decision problems, ranging "from the pricing of complex financial securities to the evaluation of corporate capital budgeting and strategic decisions. [It also] has an important place in the theory of financial intermediation." CCA, which is independent of any specific option pricing formula, resulted from combining dynamic portfolio theory (i.e., one that contemplates continuous portfolio adjustments) with key qualitative insights underlying the Black-Scholes formula. CCA is now "one of the most powerful tools of financial analysis in modern finance."

Corporate liabilities as options

The qualitative insight of Black and Scholes, "which may prove to be of greater practical significance than their famous quantitative formula," is that "*corporate liabilities, in general, can be viewed as combinations of simple option contracts.* This insight provides a unified framework in which to view the structure of corporate liabilities and implies that option pricing models can be used to price [all] corporate securities" and their derivatives.[23] In combination with CCA, option pricing theory enables intermediaries and other market participants to price both explicit option contracts and embedded options (such as an issuer's right to call a bond). Also implicit in the option pricing framework is the notion that option risk management techniques can be extended beyond simple option contracts; they can now be applied to entire portfolios that exhibit option-like features, whether or not those portfolios contain explicit options.

In addition, the methodology can be further extended to synthesize and price virtually any derivative, including nonexistent or hypothetical products. According to Merton: "[C]ontingent-claims analysis (CCA) can be used to determine the production process and cost for an intermediary to create virtually any financial product that has the properties of a derivative security.... [I]t is in principle no more difficult to create derivative securities with specialized payoff patterns than it is to create ones with standard patterns (e.g., call options). CCA thus provides the means for intermediaries to create custom financial products in an 'assembly-line' fashion."[24] Put differently, CCA provides "the 'blueprints' or production technologies for financial intermediaries to manufacture derivative[s]."

Modern origins of dynamic replication

In their 1973 paper, Black and Scholes show "it is possible to construct a portfolio involving positions in the stock and the risk-free asset where the return to the portfolio over a short time interval exactly replicates the return to the option."[25] They also demonstrate "precisely how the composition of the portfolio must continually change in response to movement in the stock price and the passage of time, such that the replication of the return to the option is maintained." In other words, once a replicating portfolio has been created, perfect replication (and, therefore, perfect hedging) can be maintained only through theoretically continuous adjustments in the stock and risk-free asset positions. As discussed in Chapter 3, the mere passage of time will reduce an option's value even if all other inputs to that value (such as the price and volatility of the underlying stock) are held constant.* The process of constantly adjusting replicating portfolios to maintain a hedge is referred to as *dynamic* or *delta hedging*. Chapter 12 contains a functional explanation of dynamic hedging.

Dynamic portfolio hedging

The ability to view liabilities (including risky debt, whether senior or subordinated, as well as guarantees, convertible debt instruments, and all types of equity interests) as simple options explains the logic of dynamic replication that underlies portfolio hedging strategies. We noted earlier that much of the extraordinary growth of derivatives markets is directly attributable to dealers' capacity to hedge their derivatives exposures on a

---

*Recall that option values change in proportion to the square root of time. So the passage of half an option's life should reduce the option's value by one-quarter (i.e.,

$$\tfrac{1}{2} \times \tfrac{1}{2} = \tfrac{1}{4}, \text{ so } \sqrt{\tfrac{1}{4}} = \tfrac{1}{2}).$$

portfolio basis.* "Hence, by the application of CCA, risk management of the intermediary's complex portfolio [could] be reduced to the manage-[26]

Nevertheless, dynamic portfolio hedging is no longer confined to derivatives dealers; it is integral to the risk management strategies of many significant derivatives users, including government entities, private pension funds, and corporate treasury departments.

Dynamic replication enables all market participants, not only dealers, to unbundle complex, dissimilar instruments then isolate and aggregate their similar risk components. Offsetting exposures can be netted across dissimilar instruments and residual portfolio risks can be hedged inexpensively, usually in relatively cheap cash and futures markets. Dynamic replication offers a simple, elegant solution to what might otherwise constitute insurmountable portfolio risk management obstacles. And so it has rightly been called "a cornerstone of modern financial risk management."[27]

Importance of Modern Finance to Derivatives Users

Modern portfolio theory, the efficient market hypothesis, MM theory, CCA, and their progeny have many important implications for derivatives users. Among them are the following.

First, the theories explain many of the unavoidable trade-offs that investors and businesses must make between risk and return. In mature financial markets, it is difficult to increase portfolio returns or firm values without also increasing risks or altering the nature of a firm's business. A solid grasp of risk-return trade-offs is essential in properly analyzing any derivatives decision problem.

---

*Replication strategies enabled dealers to quickly create the hedging positions needed to manage the risks they assumed in selling option products. The demand for option products accelerated as markets became familiar with options' new and innovative uses. "[T]he flow of applications grew from a trickle to a flood. Options were incorporated into the entirely new and complex debt instruments that blossomed during the 1980s. They are responsible for the mushrooming of the market for government-guaranteed home mortgages. Their hedging features made possible the development of...interest rate swaps..., the explosion in daily trading in the foreign exchange markets, the ability of banks to shield themselves from the vagaries of the money markets...and the willingness of major investment banking firms to provide many millions of dollars of instant liquidity to their institutional customers." Bernstein, *Capital Ideas, supra,* Chapter 4, note 18: 230.

Second, modern finance explains why "attempts to outpredict markets as efficient as the financial markets are unlikely to succeed."[28] For derivatives users, the lessons of efficiency are that: (1) in open and competitive capital markets it is extraordinarily difficult to use any trading strategy, whether or not including derivatives, consistently to beat the market; (2) the difficulty of beating the market is compounded by the infrastructure costs of controlling new risks introduced by derivatives themselves; and (3) because efforts to outguess the market cannot be relied on to eliminate risks, "the remaining alternative is to manage the risks."

Third, to use derivatives properly to manage financial risks, fiduciaries and their legal advisers must understand each theory, "not because it is *universally* true but because it leads you to ask the right questions."[29]* And "financing decisions seem overwhelmingly complex if you don't...ask the right questions." For trustees, the right questions include whether and how derivatives might help maximize portfolio returns while minimizing risks; officers and directors should ask whether and how derivatives might contribute to maximizing firm value.

Fourth, a point that is likely to grow in legal significance is that in efficient capital markets, "investors will not pay others for what they can do equally well themselves. As we shall see, many of the controversies in corporate financing center on how well individuals can replicate corporate financial decisions." The propriety of "entity level" use of derivatives to manage financial risks is an important economic issue, the legal implications of which for derivatives users have only recently begun to receive attention.

Many critics argue that the virtues of entity level risk management are either overrated or misunderstood; they assert that investors can more efficiently manage many financial risks on their own and so will not com-

---

*A constant theme running throughout modern finance is that, because of unavoidable simplifying assumptions, no theory is perfect. A theory's usefulness depends on the ability of its assumptions to isolate specific matters under investigation. One important difficulty, however, is that the isolation must ordinarily be conducted in a dynamic environment involving numerous interacting random variables, many of which resist quantification—attempts to study all variables and interactions at once are seldom successful. Hence, according to Nobel laureate Milton Friedman, "the relevant question to ask about the 'assumptions' of a theory is not whether they are descriptively 'realistic,' for they never are, but whether they are sufficiently good approximations for the purpose in hand." Milton Friedman, *Essays in the Theory of Positive Economics* (University of Chicago Press, 1953): 15, quoted in Sharpe et al., *Investments, 5th ed., supra,* note 9: 262.

pensate firms (either by paying higher prices for the firms' securities or by accepting lower debt or equity returns) to manage those risks for them. Entity level risk management may waste firm resources, reducing firm value.* The criticisms are, to a limited degree, powerful. Senior managers of derivatives users, and their legal advisers, need to understand the criticisms. In a proper context, the criticisms reveal their limitations, meaning the conditions under which they cease to be valid. An understanding of those conditions is important in the defense of entity level use of derivatives. The defense, rooted in finance and economics, has an unmistakable legal dimension.

MODERN FINANCE AS A SCIENCE— THE ROLE OF MATHEMATICS

A subject of growing concern to derivatives users (and to those who invest in firms and portfolios that use derivatives) is modern finance's reliance upon mathematics. Indeed, to many observers, *"modern finance* connotes the employment of mathematics in finance."[30] For present purposes, much of the power of modern finance lies in its ability to prove mathematically how derivatives, used properly, can reduce rather than increase overall business and investment risk.[†] What emerges from the proof is insight into the effective use of derivatives.

Precision and Objectivity of Scientific Analysis

An easily overlooked aspect of Markowitz's portfolio theory is "its methodology...its introduction of mathematics into finance....Prior to 'Portfolio Selection,' it was generally thought that investment decisions

---

*Consider, e.g., the following: "Adolf A. Berle, Jr., and Gardiner C. Means argue in their classic book *The Modern Corporation and Private Property,* that the modern corporate form of organization was developed precisely to enable entrepreneurs to disperse risk among many small investors. If that is true, it's hard to see why corporations themselves also need to reduce risks investors can manage on their own." Froot et al., *Framework for Risk Management, supra,* Chapter 4, note 2: 93.

†Modern finance has also proved mathematically how other financial strategies, that are in isolation or in the abstract, are risky or speculative can be used to reduce risk. Examples include investing in junk bonds, selling securities short, buying securities on margin, or borrowing money to optimize a capital structure and thereby increasing leverage.

were too subjective to lend themselves to scientific analysis....Employing mathematics meant that finance could now be studied by the tools of scientific research."[31]* By virtue of its mathematics, portfolio theory introduced new precision and objectivity into investment practice and theory. According to Merton:

> It was not always thus. Finance was first treated as a separate field of study early in this century, and for the next 40 years it was almost entirely a descriptive discipline with a focus on institutional and legal matters. As recently as a generation ago, finance theory was little more than a collection of anecdotes, rules of thumb, and manipulations of accounting data. The most sophisticated tool of analysis was discounted value and the central intellectual controversy centered on whether to use present value or internal rate of return to rank corporate investments.[32]

After "Portfolio Selection," mathematical rigor quickly progressed throughout the field of finance, including corporate finance. Many rapid advances in risk management and capital budgeting techniques and in the general study of financial decision making under conditions of uncertainty are directly attributable to mathematical precision and objectivity. Here, it pays to consider the profound impact of Markowitz's methodology in light of the words of James Conant concerning science in general:

> [A] theory is only overthrown by a better theory, never merely by contradictory facts. Attempts are first made to reconcile the contradictory facts to the existing conceptual scheme by some modification of the concept. Only the combination of a new concept with facts contradictory to the old ideas finally brings about a scientific revolution. And when once this has taken place, then in a few short years discovery follows upon discovery and the branch of science in question progresses by leaps and bounds.[33]†

Undoubtedly, Conant's view of scientific progress aptly describes the modern revolution in the theory and practice of finance and the sudden burgeoning of modern derivatives markets.

---

*Consider this 1971 comment made by the head of the top-performing mutual fund for the first half of that year: "I just don't see how you can measure risk in a meaningful way or make a formula for buying a stock. There are just too many variables. Look, this is an art, not a science." Chris Welles, "The Beta Revolution," *Institutional Investor* (September 1971) (quoting Arthur Reynolds, who ran the Channing Venture Fund): 24.

†Compare Chapter 16's discussion of the well-established principle of American jurisprudence that changes in legal doctrine should ordinarily be cautious and incremental. In making that argument, Bayless Manning relies directly on parallels from the development of knowledge in the fields of science.

Fiduciaries and their legal advisers can, through mathematics, gain a superior understanding of the decision-making and oversight aspects of derivatives. Quantitative methods, particularly statistical techniques, underlie most systems of derivatives business risk management. They are also responsible for providing theoretical pricing of most products, especially those with explicit or embedded optionality.* Quantitative methods provide strategies and procedures for organizing, evaluating, and interpreting information that bears on managers' and lawyers' derivatives responsibilities. Because of the increasing amount of data efficiently accessible through high-speed and rapid data communications, there is an ever-growing dependency on statistical methods as a means of making sense of that data. Without these methods, the data would appear as disorganized, unstructured phenomena. Mathematics provides a way to abstract useful *information* from the *data*.

Quantitative methods generally help managers "impose order on and interpret reality" in a manner that "gives practical meaning to it in terms the human mind can grasp and that might otherwise escape our attention."[34] These methods can arbitrarily be classified as deterministic or stochastic:

> Deterministic methods assume the relationships among the relevant factors of a decision problem are fixed or invariant and can therefore be solved with mathematical procedures. Tell me A, and I can tell you B with certainty. Stochastic methods on the other hand assume the relationships among the relevant factors are stochastic, i.e. variable or uncertain, and therefore require statistical procedures. Tell me A, and I can tell you the probability of B, but B may or may not happen.

Probability analysis attempts to quantify a critical aspect of the uncertainty involved in decision making. Yet new uncertainties are introduced by the nature of the order that quantitative methods impose. When the imposed order is inconsistent with reality, or if it obscures other important aspects of reality, new risks arise. To control the resulting business and legal risks, it is not enough for fiduciaries and legal advisers to understand the benefits of mathematics. They also need a supervisory understanding of the limitations inherent in quantitative methods.

---

*Market prices are, of course, determined in the first instance by supply and demand. Quantitative methods and their models influence supply and demand by providing means of determining when market prices are high, low, or fair.

Limitations of Quantitative Methods

The introduction of mathematics into finance can create difficulties, especially for those who supervise others who are more adept at applying the quantitative tools of modern finance. Mathematics solves and simplifies many data problems, yet, as noted above, it introduces new risks. Those of paramount supervisory concern (aside from computational errors) are risks introduced by (1) attempts to quantify the unquantifiable, (2) cognitive biases, (3) oversimplifications of complex matters, and (4) exposures to discontinuity.

Quantifying the unquantifiable

As mentioned earlier, legal risks are paradigmatic, unquantifiable risks. Lawyers seldom render probabilistic opinions on legal issues, and when they do the opinions are usually phrased in language such as "more likely than not." Part of the reason for that approach is that the resolution of legal issues often turns on matters of subjective, unpredictable discretion and judgment, as influenced by cultural and political forces. The law, as written, interpreted, and applied under a wide range of circumstances by diverse legislatures, courts, government agencies, lawyers, and private parties, can vary considerably.

Similarly, economics and other social sciences are inexact sciences; they depend largely on subjective judgments and preferences. Economic decisions often display patterns that lend themselves to probabilistic reasoning and thus quantitative analysis. Yet the ability to assign probabilities to many aspects of economic decision making should not lead managers to ignore the many social aspects of economics that resist quantification. With regard to derivatives, the temptation to overemphasize the quantitative aspects of decision making is exacerbated by the enormous data and the powerful analytical capabilities at the disposal of decision makers. Merton warns that

> powerful analytics are a temptation to excessive focus on mathematical rigor with the unhappy consequence of leaving the accompanying substantive economics inaccessible to all but a few. Attention to formal technique without equal attention to the underlying economics assumptions leads to misplaced concreteness by confusing rigor in the mathematical sense with rigor in the economic sense.[35]

The degree of rigor that can be applied in the "economic sense" is limited. Managers and lawyers need to resist drawing unwarranted inferences and taking false comfort in masses of statistics.

The message here is plain: one should not "limit [one's] deliberations only to those variables that do lend themselves to quantification, excluding all serious consideration of the unquantifiable."[36] Fiduciaries and their legal advisers must be careful to avoid mistaking quantitative precision for legal, economic, and other types of certainty. Still, anecdotal evidence suggests that many executives and their advisers continue to overstate the degree to which risks can be quantified. For example, a representative of a premier accounting firm recently asserted in front of a large audience of derivatives users that the "golden rule of risk management" is that one should "avoid risks that can't be priced or quantified."

Cognitive biases: the expert and availability effects

Hu describes three types of objectively verifiable cognitive biases that affect perceptions and judgments of derivatives' risks. Two are closely related. The first, which he labels the "availability effect," refers to the tendency of people to "estimate the probability of an event by the ease with which related associations come to mind."[37] This bias is responsible for the tendency of a "damaging event, if timed appropriately and widely publicized, [to] induce...people to behave as if the likelihood of such events had increased." One well-known mathematician describes this tendency as a "tendency to personalize—to be misled by [one's] own experiences, or by the media's focus on individuals and drama."[38]

The second bias is the "expert effect," or the tendency of "people...to overemphasize the importance of field they understand best." The concern is that this bias may lead derivatives professionals to "fail to integrate legal risks into their calculations." As noted earlier, "hard statistical data tends to 'dwarf the soft variables' in the minds of decisionmakers." Experts trained in derivatives' analytics can easily overlook other factors, especially the classical economics that explain much of capital market activities. Saber offers an explanation for why many derivatives professionals are particularly susceptible to cognitive biases against variables that cannot be readily (if at all) quantified:

> [T]he discipline of finance in its new metamorphosis [after the publication of "Portfolio Selection"] required scholars with knowledge of mathematics. One obvious place to look for such experts was in the physics departments of universities. Mathematics is considered to be the language of nature, and the job of the physicist is to apply mathematics to solve the problems of nature....Unfortunately, the cross-discipline migration of physicists into finance...had a cultural component....The physicists who flocked to finance did not have a firm schooling in the principles of economics as developed by

the classical thinkers. One is at a loss to find a reference to Ricardo, Smith, Marx, Franklin or even contemporary Keynes in their writings.[39]

Cognitive biases: the threshold effect

"Individuals tend to ignore low probability catastrophic events.... Psychologists theorize that individuals do not worry unless the probability of the event is perceived to be above some critical threshold."[40] This bias has enormous implications for the management of derivatives risks, both economic and legal. Analytic models used to measure and manage derivatives risks can easily underestimate or "ignore low probability states"—outliers, as statisticians call them—that would otherwise skew valuations. "A bad model is one which...attempts to consider too many marginally relevant states of the world or, given a set of accounted-for variables with no 'surprises,' produces a poor valuation."

Many derivatives risk management models assume "normal distributions" for some or all relevant random variables. The normal distribution is the common statistical name for the symmetrical, bell-shaped probability distribution depicted in the solid curve of Figure 11.1. As discussed in Chapter 12, "the assumption of normality is used because normal distributions have statistical properties that make problem solving very easy."[41]

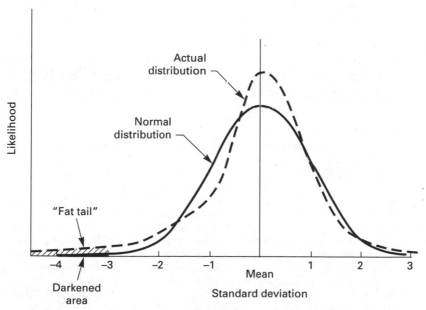

Figure 11.1   Normal versus "fat tail" distribution.

Yet, for present purposes, working with the distribution mathematically is unnecessary.

Misleading "tail" probabilities: a hypothetical

What is important is an understanding that from the relevant area under the curve of the normal distribution one can easily estimate using standardized tables with the probability of any specified event occurring. An example is the probability of a firm entering financial distress. "When one is especially concerned about 'tail' probabilities—the probabilities of the worst and the best outcomes—the assumption about the statistical distribution of the gains and losses is important. Research...suggests that default probabilities across different classes of debt are generally larger than implied by the normal distributions[, that]...default probabilities have 'fatter tails' than those implied by a normal distribution."[42]*

Assume the horizontal axis of Figure 11.1 represents the annual income distribution of HealthyCo, a publicly held consumer appliance company with outstanding floating-rate debt. Although sales have long been steady, many consumers finance their purchases, rendering HealthyCo's earnings sensitive to market interest rates. The company is reviewing its risk management strategy over the next 18 months, the remaining life of the outstanding debt. Assume management has determined that HealthyCo has the financial ability to withstand a decrease in earnings of up to three standard deviations (denoted "3σ") over that period; however, any greater decrease would likely force the company to default on its loan.

Moreover, short of actual default, the company might begin experiencing difficulties with customers, employees, managers, suppliers, and distributors if default becomes more likely.[†] HealthyCo has several essen-

---

*"The normal distribution has great practical utility because it can be used as a reasonably good approximation to the behavior of many segments of reality (the normal distribution models no practical situation perfectly). Many variables, however, are *not well modeled by the normal distribution* even though well meaning people continue to misapply it to them. It is important to be able to judge when the normal is and is not a good model of the segment of reality under study." Pardew, *Managerial Statistics, supra*, note 34.

†"Employees demand higher wages if the probability of layoff is greater. Managers demand higher salaries (or perhaps even an equity stake in the company) if the risks of failure, insolvency, and financial embarrassment are great. Suppliers set more unfavorable terms in long-term contracts with companies whose prospects are more uncertain. And customers, concerned about a company's ability to service their products in the future or fulfill warranty obligations, with be reluctant to buy its products." Smith and Stulz, *The Determinants of Firms' Hedging Policies, infra,* Chapter 13, note 17: 399, n. 17.

tial business relationships with groups that "are frequently unable to diversify risks specific to their claims on the corporation. Because they are risk-averse, these individuals require extra compensation to bear the nondiversifiable risk of the claims." Customers depend upon the continuing viability of the company for assurances of their ability to obtain postsale servicing and maintenance of their purchases, especially to the extent covered by product warranties. "Special guarantees may have to be given to customers who doubt whether the firm will be around to service its products."[43] Employees and managers look to HealthyCo for long-term, stable employment and opportunities for advancement. "The odds of defections by key employees are higher [for a highly levered firm] than if the firm had started out with less debt." Suppliers often extend trade credit by shipping parts and appliances prior to receipt of payment (and payments might not be made until retail sales occur), and distributors need assurances during their wait as to the company's viability. In short, once the potential for default becomes material, it can threaten vital business relationships.[44]

HealthyCo's treasury department has just recommended that HealthyCo purchase an out-of-the-money interest rate cap to ensure its ability to service its public debt if floating rates should, unexpectedly, suddenly dramatically increase. Management, concerned about adverse derivatives publicity and the necessity of disclosing in its public filings that it is purchasing derivatives, is considering whether to authorize the proposed interest rate derivative. An additional concern is that the pricing for the swap seems out of line with management's expectations, although treasury assures management that the price is entirely appropriate.

For analytical guidance, HealthyCo's management may decide to look to the normal distribution for a sense of its likelihood of default, based on the company's historical income volatility. If management does so, it will find that the probability of financial distress (as measured by an income decline of three standard deviations or more over the relevant period) is less than 0.5%. In other words, the chances that the company will default on its loan are less than 1 in 200. In Figure 11.1, the very thin, darkened area under the normal distribution to the left of -3σ (i.e., minus three standard deviations) depicts those odds. Such a low probability might easily lead management to simply *ignore* for all practical purposes the possibility of financial distress inherent in the floating-rate loan agreement. So management decides to forgo the cap, not wanting to get involved in derivatives.

Notice, however, that if earnings are actually more variable than implied by the normal distribution, the actual probability of distress could be many times that of an estimate generated by a review of the normally distributed probabilities. Instead of 0.5%, Figure 11.1 suggests that the actual probability is greater than 5%. The diagonally marked area under the normal distribution to the left of -3σ depicts the actual percentage in Figure 11.1. Its area is far larger than that of the comparable thin, dark area under the normal curve. Management appears to have significantly understated the riskiness of HealthyCo's income, perhaps by a factor in excess of 10. Thus, it has potentially materially underemphasized the importance of risk management to the firm's viability.

Recent history teaches that low-probability, one-time events are relatively common over long time periods. Although one cannot predict with any degree of accuracy what the specific one-time events will be, fiduciaries should assume that some unlikely events will occur. "The paradoxical conclusion is that it would be very unlikely for unlikely events not to occur."[45] "Recent [relevant] examples are the devaluation of the Mexican peso, the 1987 stock market crashes, and commodity volatility during the Gulf War."[46]

Oversimplification

All derivatives pricing models and risk management systems are necessarily dependent on "parameters, data, assumptions, and methodology."[47] For example, Capital Market Risk Advisors (CMRA) analyzed "value at risk," or VAR, calculations. VARs provide a means of measuring the amount of capital an organization has at risk (in the traditional sense of risk of loss) over a specified time horizon.* They are statistical estimates based on historical data of how much money an organization should *expect* occasionally to lose over a given time frame. For example, "a daily VAR would tell an institution that it could expect, in 95 cases out of 100, to lose no more than $x\%$ of its value."[48] VAR techniques are highly attractive, because they greatly simplify data. However, the

> simplicity is seductive. Used to the extreme, in a single statistic a firm can measure its exposure to markets worldwide....VAR can be dangerous, however. A review of dozens of dealers' and end-users' VARs revealed radically different approaches to the calculation....[T]he magnitude of the discrepancy among these methods is shocking, with VAR results varying by more than 14 times for the same portfolio.

Equally shocking is that all the alternative methods employed to reach those dramatically different results were based on *plausible* assumptions.

---

*VAR methodologies are one of three alternative quantitative disclosure formats mandated by SEC in its new derivatives disclosure rules. See Chapter 18.

Indeed, often "senior management and directors or trustees are shocked to learn that their firm's risk reports can change dramatically under alternate assumptions. This fact is even more surprising when the 'alternate' assumptions are those they consider to be likely or reasonable."

Stulz argues that VAR methodologies are seldom useful for end users, because of the data on which those methodologies rely. VAR results are totally dependent on current market or historical data for predictions. The methodologies are most effective in measuring risk over small time periods. Yet nondealer organizations are usually far more concerned with the amount of capital they have at risk over extended time periods. Unfortunately, reliable data to feed into the VAR models to obtain predictions for use over long periods does not exist:

> If we attempt to move from a daily to, say, a one-year VAR at the...99th percentile [which is a more meaningful measure for most end users], it becomes very difficult to calculate such a model, much less subject it to empirical testing. Since an annual VaR at the 99th percentile means that the loss can be expected to take place in only one year in every 100, one presumably requires numerous 100-year periods to establish the validity of such a model.[49]

Similarly, an IBM treasury official recently commented that "VAR alternatives still need improving. 'It is a useful measure when you are looking at a one-basis-point shift, but the world doesn't move in single basis points.'"[50]

Discontinuity

Stochastic systems and the quantitative methods used to understand (to impose order on) them are necessarily dependent on historical inputs. The methods themselves cannot detect whether the occurrence of an unusual event is a reasonable though unusual result or, instead, evidence of a basic underlying shift in key relationships or parameters. This problem is particularly acute as to attempts to monitor the value of securities and investment portfolios. Consider that many calculations are required to perform modern portfolio analysis. Then consider that the analysis assumes that covariances, or relationships among securities, as well as the risk and return features of individual securities, are stable. But in reality covariances are not stable. "Market prices, investor expectations, and the riskiness of assets do not stand still. They are dynamic, not static....The consequence is that the necessary conditions for an accurate calculation of risk may not prevail."[51]

Nederlof of CMRA provides a recent example of the kind of "paradigm shift" that quantitative models cannot recognize. In recent years a thriving mortgage brokerage industry has emerged. This industry has affected structured vehicles that issue securities (whether or not categorized as derivatives) backed by consumer mortgages. The payoff characteristics of the securities depend on the rate at which consumers refinance and prepay their mortgages. Before mortgage brokers, models used to price different tranches of structured securities relied upon projections based on historical prepayment frequencies. Those frequencies, in turn, bore relatively predictable relationships to significant declines in mortgage interest rates. Mortgage brokers, however, changed that frequency, suddenly rendering the historical data useless. The brokers caused a dramatic upsurge, based on past data, in prepayment activity even upon what had previously been considered to be minor rate decreases. Time lags between rate declines and subsequent refinancings shortened from months to weeks. Unfortunately for many security holders, few pricing models for the securities had factored in, or were even capable of factoring in, that "paradigm shift."

It is worth noting here Alan Greenspan's testimony before Congress in May 1994 about the importance, and limitations, of quantitative methods, capital requirements, and internal controls. He asserted that, despite all quantitative measures, occasionally "adverse market circumstances" will arise in which "market forces threaten to build momentum and break loose of economic fundamentals." It is unrealistic, he argued, to attempt in advance to develop risk management systems that will infallibly respond to every such crisis. He preferred instead to insist that Congress avoid saddling banking and other financial institutions with burdensome derivatives regulatory requirements. No economical way exists, he argued, to ensure that institutions are "capable of withstanding every conceivable set of adverse circumstances." Therefore, he emphasized that only one meaningful solution exists to the infrequent but unavoidable market crises: namely, sound policy action taken at the time by individual firms and, if necessary, by regulators.

ENDNOTES: CHAPTER 11

1. See, generally, "Reporter's Comments," *Rest. 3rd, Trusts* (*Prudent Investor Rule*), *supra,* Chapter 10, note 13: 18–19, 28, 75–79.
2. See Henry T. C. Hu, "Behind the Corporate Hedge: Information and the Limits of Shareholder Wealth Maximization," *Journal of Applied Corporate Finance,* 9(3) (Fall 1996) [hereafter, *Behind the Corporate Hedge*]: 40, n. 2.

3. This and the following quotation are from Walter Dolde, "The Trajectory of Corporate Financial Risk Management," *Journal of Applied Corporate Finance,* 6 (Fall 1993) (emphasis omitted) [hereafter, *Trajectory of Corporate Financial Risk Management*]: 36; see also Merton, *Continuous-Time Finance, supra,* Chapter 1, note 26: 423–427.

4. See "Reporter's Comments," *Rest. 3rd, Trusts (Prudent Investor Rule), supra,* Chapter 10, note 13: 19. Note that the quoted language in the text refers primarily to modern portfolio theory and the investment decisions that must be made by trustees and other money managers. Nevertheless, the comments are equally applicable to directors, officers, and other executives of operating enterprises.

5. For the quotations in this paragraph, see Mason et al., *Financial Engineering, supra,* Chapter 1, note 2: 35; see also Merton, *Financial Innovation, supra,* Chapter 1, note 15.

6. See generally Bernstein, *Capital Ideas, supra,* Chapter 4, note 24: 91–145, 203–230; Jonathan B. Baskin and Paul J. Miranti, Jr., *A History of Corporate Finance* (Cambridge University Press, 1997); Mason et al., *Financial Engineering, supra,* Chapter 1, note 2: 353–375; Merton, *Continuous-Time Finance, supra,* Chapter 1, note 26: 3–15, Part IV.

7. M. F. M. Osborne, "Periodic Structure in the Brownian Movement of Stock Prices," *Operations Research,* 10 (May–June 1962): 145–173, quoted in Bernstein, *Capital Ideas, supra,* Chapter 4, note 24: 106.

8. All quotations in this and the following three paragraphs are from Bernstein, *Capital Ideas, supra,* Chapter 4, note 24 (emphasis added): 95–96, 117–119. The full citations for the articles referred to in the text are Holbrook Working, "A Random Difference Series for Use in the Analysis of Time Series," *Journal of the American Statistical Association,* 29 (March 1934): 11–24; Maurice G. Kendall, "The Analysis of Economic Time-Series, Part I. Prices," *Journal of the Royal Statistical Society,* 96 (1953): 11–25; Paul A. Samuelson, "Proof That Properly Anticipated Prices Fluctuate Randomly," *Industrial Management Review,* 6 (Spring 1965): 41–50.

9. William F. Sharpe, et al., *Investments,* 5th ed. (Prentice Hall, 1995) [hereafter, *Investments (5th)*]: 105.

10. See Eugene F. Fama, "Efficient Capital Markets: A Review of Theory and Empirical Work," *Journal of Finance,* 25 (May 1970) [defining efficiency as the condition in which (a) the difference between (i) actual market prices and (ii) the price that would prevail if all participants had perfect information (b) is zero]: 383–417; see, generally, Richard A. Brealey and Stewart C. Myers, *Principles of Corporate Finance,* 5th ed. (McGraw-Hill, 1996) (emphasis in original) [hereafter, *Principles of Corporate Finance*]: Chapter 13; Bernstein, *Capital Ideas, supra,* Chapter 4, note 24: 126–145.

11. "General Note on Comments *e* through *k*," *Rest. 3rd, Trusts (Prudent Investor Rule), supra,* Chapter 10, note 13 (emphasis added): 75; see Dwight R. Lee and James A. Verbrugge, "The Efficient Market Theory Thrives on Criticism," *Journal of Applied Corporate Finance,* 9(1) (Spring 1996) ("Certainly there is no evidence of a trading rule that has generated above-average returns for a sustained period") [hereafter, *Efficient Market Theory Thrives on Criticism*]: 35–40, 37; see also Ray Ball, "The Theory of Stock Market Efficiency: Accomplishments and Limitations," *Journal of Applied Corporate Finance* (Spring 1995): 4–17; Eugene F. Fama, "Efficient Capital Markets: II," *Journal of Finance,* 46 (December 1991): 1575–1617; Michael C. Jensen, "Some Anomalous Evidence Regarding Market Efficiency," *Journal of Financial Economics,* 6 (June–September 1978): 95–101; Harry V. Roberts, "Stock Market 'Patterns' and Financial Analysis: Methodological Suggestions," *Journal of Finance,* 14(1) (March 1959) (Roberts was the first to identify the three forms of efficiency): 1–10.

12. Lee and Verbrugge, *Efficient Market Theory Thrives on Criticism, supra,* note 11: 35. But see Dennis E. Logue, "When Theory Fails: Globalization as a Response to the (Hostile) Market for Foreign Exchange," *Journal of Applied Corporate Finance,* 8(3) (Fall 1995) (noting, among other things, as to the theory of "purchasing power parity"—which holds that exchange rates between two currencies will respond quickly to reflect home country inflation differentials—that "the reality has not lived up to expectations.... [especially] in the short to intermediate term") [hereafter, *Hostile Market for FX*]: 39–48.

13. See, e.g., Jamie R. Anthony, Jr. and Brian L. Smith, "How to Manage Risk Without Resorting to Derivatives," *American Banker* (November 14, 1996) (arguing, curiously, that risk management programs such as AAA guaranteed, or collateralized, asset-backed securitizations and loan-loss-reserve programs are "simpler, safer, and extremely flexible alternative[s]" to derivatives; also asserting boldly that such programs enable financial institutions to "meet almost any risk issue") [hereafter, *Managing Risk Without Resorting to Derivatives*].

14. Hu, *Behind the Corporate Hedge, supra,* note 2: 44.

15. Bernstein, *Capital Ideas, supra,* Chapter 4, note 24 (emphasis in original): 166; see, generally, Brealey and Myers, *Principles of Corporate Finance, supra,* note 10 ("it should be no surprise that we can use the capital asset pricing model to derive MM's proposition I"): 447–473.

16. Except as otherwise noted, the quotations in this and the following four paragraphs are from Merton H. Miller, "The Modigliani-Miller Propositions After Thirty Years," *Journal of Economic Perspectives,* 2(4) (Fall 1988) (emphasis in original) [hereafter, *MM Theory After Thirty Years*]: 99–120; see also, companion articles in the same issue of the *Journal of Economic*

Perspectives, by Joseph E. Stiglitz, "Why Financial Structure Matters" [hereafter, *Why Financial Structure Matters*]: 121–126; Stephen A. Ross, "Comment on the Modigliani-Miller Propositions" [hereafter, *Comment on MM Theory*]: 127–133; Sudipto Bhattacharya, "Corporate Finance and the Legacy of Miller and Modigliani": 135–147; Franco Modigliani, "MM— Past, Present, Future": 149–158. The original MM theory is contained in Miller and Modigliani, "The Cost of Capital, Corporation Finance, and the Theory of Investment," *American Economic Review,* 48(3) (June 1958): 655–669.

17. This and the quotations in the following paragraph are from Ross, *Comment on MM Theory, supra,* note 16: 128. For a detailed description of arbitrage mechanics, see Philip H. Dybvig and Stephen A. Ross, "Arbitrage," in *New Palgrave, A Dictionary of Economics,* J. Eatwell, P. Milgate, and P. Newman, eds. (The MacMillan Press, Ltd., 1987): 100–106; Hal Varian, "The Arbitrage Principle in Financial Economics," *Journal of Economic Perspectives,* 1(2) (Fall 1987): 55–72.

18. The quotations in this and the following paragraphs are from Miller, *MM Theory After Thirty Years, supra,* note 16: 100–102.

19. Sharpe et al., *Investments (5th), supra,* note 9: 106.

20. This and the following quotation are from Brealey and Myers, *Principles of Corporate Finance, supra,* note 10: 454–455.

21. See Fischer Black and Myron Scholes, "The Pricing of Options and Corporate Liabilities," *Journal of Political Economy,* 81 (May–June 1973): 637–654; see, generally, John C. Cox and Mark Rubenstein, *Options Markets* (Prentice Hall, 1985); Mason et al., *Financial Engineering, supra,* Chapter 1, note 2: 353–375; Merton, *Continuous-Time Finance, supra,* Chapter 1, note 26: xv, 9, 11, 413–427; Chew, *Leverage, supra,* Chapter 1, note 1: 96–101.

22. This and the quotations in the following paragraph are from Merton, *Continuous-Time Finance, supra,* Chapter 1, note 26: 9, xv.

23. See Mason et al., *Financial Engineering, supra,* Chapter 1, note 2 (emphasis in original): 353.

24. This and the following quotation are from Merton, *Continuous-Time Finance, supra,* Chapter 1, note 26: 451, 429.

25. This and the following quotation are from Mason et al., *Financial Engineering, supra,* Chapter 1, note 2: 363.

26. Merton, *Continuous-Time Finance, supra,* Chapter 1, note 26: 453; see also *Id.* ("The focus of CCA is on the hedging and pricing of an individual security or financial product. However…CCA, together with general dynamic portfolio theory, can be used to measure and control the total risk of an intermediary's entire portfolio"): 430.

27. See Chew, *Leverage, supra,* Chapter 1, note 1 (also observing: "Not only is delta a great simplifying mechanism; it also facilitates aggregation across all instruments (be they derivatives or cash) because delta expresses them in units of their underlying. Market participants can thus manage their price risks on a residual exposure basis, since all the derivative and cash positions can be netted off each other, to arrive at a final number."): 99.

28. The quotations in this paragraph are from Charles W. Smithson and Clifford W. Smith, Jr., with D. Sykes Wilford, *Managing Financial Risk: A Guide to Derivative Products, Financial Engineering, and Value Maximization* (Irwin Professional Publishing, 1995) [hereafter, *Managing Financial Risk*]: 31; see also Stulz, *Rethinking Risk Management, supra,* Chapter 10, note 8: 11–12.

29. The quotations in this and the following paragraph are from Brealey and Myers, *Principles of Corporate Finance, supra,* note 10: 323, 344.

30. Nasser Saber, *Derivatives Risks and Speculative Capital,* forthcoming, manuscript draft dated February 4, 1997 (emphasis in original) [hereafter, *Derivatives Risks*].

31. Saber, *The Course of Modern Finance,* in *Derivatives Risks, supra,* note 30; see also Bernstein, *Capital Ideas, supra,* Chapter 4, note 24 ("The innovations triggered by the revolution in finance and investing....have added a measure of science to the art of corporate finance"): 6–7.

32. Merton, *Continuous-Time Finance, supra,* Chapter 1, note 26: xiii.

33. James B. Conant, *On Understanding Science* (Yale University Press, 1947): 36–37; see also Lee and Verbrugge, *Efficient Market Theory Thrives on Criticism, supra,* note 11 ("In Kuhn's view of scientific progress, a theory is typically discarded only when a better theory is available"): 35, citing Thomas S. Kuhn, *The Structure of Scientific Revolutions* (University of Chicago Press, 1962).

34. The quotations in this paragraph are from Donald L. Pardew, "Managerial Statistics," Columbia University Graduate School of Business, unpublished paper on file with author (Fall 1995) [hereafter, *Managerial Statistics*].

35. Merton, *Continuous-Time Finance, supra,* Chapter 1, note 26: xv.

36. Peter L. Bernstein, "Have We Replaced Old-World Superstitions with a Dangerous Reliance on Numbers?" *Harvard Business Review* (March–April 1996) [hereafter, *Superstitions?*]: 51.

37. Except as otherwise noted, the quotations in this section are from Hu, *Misunderstood Derivatives, supra,* Chapter 1, note 22 (citations omitted): 1490–1491.

38. John Allen Paulos, *Innumeracy: Mathematical Illiteracy and Its Consequences* (Vintage Books, a division of Random House, 1990) [hereafter, *Innumeracy*]: 6.

39. Saber, *The Course of Modern Finance,* in *Derivatives Risks, supra,* note 30. Reprinted with permission.

40. The quotations in this paragraph are from Hu, *Misunderstood Derivatives, supra,* Chapter 1, note 22: 1488–1490. The statement regarding good and bad analytic models is quoted by Hu from Paul Scura et al., "Financial Innovation and New Corporate Securities," in *Corporate and Municipal Securities,* III, Robert L. Kuhn, ed. (1990).

41. See, generally, Chew, *Leverage, supra,* Chapter 1, note 1: 161–162; Watson, Billingsley, Croft, and Huntsberger, *Statistics for Management and Economics,* 5th ed. (Allyn and Bacon, 1993) [hereafter, *Management Statistics*]: § 6.3.

42. This quotation is from, and a more detailed discussion of a similar risk management problem to that discussed in the text is available in, Stulz, *Rethinking Risk Management, supra,* Chapter 10, note 8: 8–24.

43. This and the following quotation are from Stewart Myers, "The Search for Optimal Capital Structure," in Donald H. Chew, Jr., ed., *The New Corporate Finance: Where Theory Meets Practice* (McGraw-Hill, 1993) [the article is hereafter referred to as *The Search for Optimal Capital Structure*; the book is hereafter referred to as *The New Corporate Finance*]: 148.

44. See, generally, *Id.:* 142–150; Bradford Cornell and Alan C. Shapiro, "Financing Corporate Growth," in Chew, ed., *The New Corporate Finance, supra,* note 44: 195–211; Clifford W. Smith and René M. Stulz, "The Determinants of Firms' Hedging Policies," *Journal of Financial and Quantitative Analysis,* 20 (1985) (developing the theory of how risk management, by reducing the cost of financial distress, can increase a firm's expected value): 391–405; Alan C. Shapiro and Sheridan Titman, "An Integrated Approach to Corporate Risk Management," in Joel Stern and Donald H. Chew, Jr., eds., *The Revolution in Corporate Finance* (Basil Blackwell Ltd., Oxford, England, and Basil Blackwell, Inc., Cambridge, Mass., 1986) (extending the cost of financial distress argument to focus on relationships with buyers and suppliers). For an empirical analysis of the validity of the theories referred to in the foregoing materials, see Tufano, *Who Manages Risk?, supra,* Chapter 10, note 8: 1106–1112; Géczy, Minton, and Schrand, *Why Firms Use Currency Derivatives, supra,* Chapter 1, note 37.

45. Paulos, *Innumeracy, supra,* note 38: 37.

46. Except as otherwise noted, this and all quotations in the following paragraph are from Tanya Styblo Beder, "VAR: Seductive But Dangerous," *Financial Analysts Journal* (September–October 1995) (emphasis added) [hereafter, *Seductive But Dangerous*]: 12–24.

47. Except as otherwise noted, all quotations in this paragraph are from Beder, *supra*; see also Stulz, *Rethinking Risk Management, supra,* Chapter 10, note 8. The Stulz quotations in this section are from *Rethinking Risk Management.*

48. Stulz, *Rethinking Risk Management, supra,* Chapter 10, note 8: 21.

49. *Id.*

50. "Giant Reawakening," *Risk,* 10(3) (March 1997): 41.

51. Bernstein, *Capital Ideas, supra,* Chapter 4, note 24: 60.

CHAPTER 12

Fundamentals of Modern Finance: Risk and Return; Modern Portfolio Theory

Under New York's "prudent man rule" which the new law replaces, the propriety of each investment was determined separately....[Y]ou might have been prohibited from buying some of the market's newer products, such as options and so-called derivatives, because they were considered inherently imprudent.

"New Prudent Investor Rule Will
Impact Most New York Trusts"
The New York Community Trusts,
March 1996

Under conventional modern portfolio theory, for instance, there are two kinds of risk faced by corporations and by investors. "Unsystematic" risk....[and] "Systematic" risk....Investors can substantially eliminate their exposure to unsystematic risk simply by buying a large enough number of stocks. It is only systematic risk that investors are concerned about.

Henry T. C. Hu, University of Texas
School of Law
Hedging Expectations, *1995*

Fiduciaries may be held responsible for violating legal duties, if their portfolios or organizations increase risk through the incorrect or improper use of derivatives and losses materialize. Even without losses, fiduciaries may be criticized for flawed derivatives strategies or improper oversight. Thus, derivatives users and their counsel would be well advised to anticipate and be prepared to respond to arguments against derivatives use. Likewise, those who choose not to use derivatives may need to defend their own strategies. Either way, effective responses require familiarity with the fundamentals of modern finance introduced in Chapter 11. We discuss those fundamentals in greater detail in this chapter and in Chapter 13.

EVOLVING DEFINITION OF RISK

Traditional Definition: Risk of Loss

Traditionally, investors, businesses, capital markets, and the law viewed risk in the ordinary, intuitive sense of downside exposure. Few financial institutions, large corporations, or institutional investors continue to analyze risk that way. In contrast, many areas of the law, and a surprisingly large number of firms and individual investors, still rely on the traditional view.

Questions about the meaning of risk and the nature of risk-return trade-offs remain vital today, especially when the subject turns to derivatives. As SEC Commissioner Wallman recently explained to an audience of international bankers:

> How to describe risk and return presents a fascinating issue. Everyone here knows that high risk investments demand higher expected returns, and that searching for higher returns entails incurring additional risk. Sounds relatively simple, doesn't it? But how much risk for how much extra return? And what does risk really mean? And how best would you measure it? And, once measured, how best would you describe it, especially to individuals not expert in finance? When one considers the results of various studies,…you have to wonder whether all [investors] have a solid grasp on the fundamentals."[1]*

Commissioner Wallman concluded that the need for a better understanding of risk and return is especially important to derivatives users: "[t]he danger here is readily apparent. Without a sufficient understanding of risk and return, investors may eschew risk that they ought to be willing to incur….Similarly, an overreaction to complex and novel instruments such as derivatives caused by a lack of understanding of risk could lead to a stifling of innovation in these areas and the loss of their accompanying benefits."

---

*According to the commissioner, a Towers, Perrin study "found that 39% of employees polled did not know how their 401(k) or savings plan dollars were being invested, and that 50% of employees polled said that a guaranteed return on their investment was the most important factor in making retirement fund investment decisions." No mention was made of the rate of return employees required or whether that rate was one that, for example, would be calculated after adjusting for inflation (and taxes, as applicable). See also "Recent Developments in Retirement Planning: Workers Need More Retirement Planning Information," *Tax Management Financial Planning Journal* (May 16, 1995): 113–114.

Modern Finance Definition:
Uncertainty Risk

Modern finance defines risk as uncertainty risk, or the chance that actual returns* on investments or portfolios will differ from expected, or mean, returns. The expression *mean return* is used in the statistical sense of the average return expected on an investment or activity repeated a large number of times; it does not necessarily correspond to the actual return one might expect on a one-time investment.

The new definition of risk addresses the dispersion, or distribution, of above- and below-average returns around a mean value. Thus, it measures both downside exposure and upside potential. Further, modern measures of risk indicate both the probability that actual returns will vary from expected returns and the magnitude of the expected variations. The greater either the probability or the magnitude of expected variations, the higher the risk.

Risk, Expected Return, and
Normal Distributions

In practice, investors assume for convenience that most returns are symmetrically distributed about their mean. In other words, they assume that favorable and unfavorable returns are equally likely, that variability—or risk—is "directionless."[2] The assumption that risk is directionless enables investors to utilize the common statistical term *variance,* and its square root, *standard deviation,* as standard measures of risk.[†] These terms are "computationally easier to work with than the alternative [one-sided measures]. Proofs and applications of various risk-return investment principles typically are simpler to derive using standard deviation as the measure of risk."[3] (However, as discussed later, simplification introduces its own risks.)

Finally, investors also assume asset and portfolio returns display—or through routine mathematical transformations can be converted into pat-

---

*The "return" or "rate of return" on an investment generally comprises (1) changes in market price (i.e., appreciation, which can be either positive or negative) and repayments of invested capital and (2) other cash receipts or earnings (most importantly, interest and dividends). Return is expressed as a proportion of the overall outlay of funds, or capital, invested over time. See, generally, *MIT Dictionary, infra,* note 13; "Comment *g*" to Reporter's Notes, *Rest. 3rd, Trusts (Prudent Investor Rule), supra,* Chapter 10, note 13: 26.

[†]In basic risk notation, standard deviation is denoted by the lowercase Greek letter sigma, σ. Variance, which is the square of standard deviation, is thus denoted σ^2.

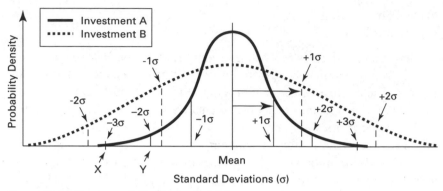

Figure 12.1   Two normal distributions with same mean.

terns that display—the familiar bell-shaped probability distribution called the *normal distribution,* examples of which are shown in Figure 12.1. The normal distribution "underlies modern portfolio theory."[4] It is extraordinarily easy to work with compared to all available mathematical alternatives. It also enhances comparability of analyses by enabling investors to use variance and standard deviation as common measures of risk. Although the mathematics of calculating probabilities associated with the normal distribution are complex, that is seldom problematic: "[A]ny random variable whose values follow a normal distribution occurs with probabilities that can be developed....[by] sidestep[ping] the formula and mathematics associated with it and instead find[ing] the probabilities...using a table."[5] The assumption of normality is usually appropriate, because most returns, at least over the long term, are either roughly normally distributed or easily transformed into such a distribution.

Equally important, the normal distribution greatly simplifies an analysis of *portfolio* diversification (discussed below) in two ways. First, statistical theory holds that combined returns of assets whose individual returns are normally distributed also display a normal distribution. Second, the dispersion of normally distributed returns are completely defined (explained below) by their mean and standard deviation. Consequently, the normality assumption enables an investor to learn *all* relevant information about the risk and return characteristics of an asset or a portfolio simply from its standard deviation (risk) and mean (expected return). Thus, an entire portfolio can be regarded as a single investment, and the contribution to it of any one investment can easily be evaluated by determining that investment's relation to the entire portfolio. If that were *not* the case, the investment's contribution could be evaluated only by determining its separate relation to every other investment in the portfolio.

A normal distribution's standard deviation defines the dispersion of returns in two senses. First, it indicates the likelihood that actual returns will vary from the expected average; second, it indicates the magnitude of the likely variations. A normal distribution simplifies greatly, because about (1) 68% of all its outcomes lie in a range of plus or minus one standard deviation of the mean (e.g., in Figure 12.1 the limits of the range are indicated for each bell-curve by the respective vertical lines marked -1σ and $+1\sigma$); (2) 95% lie within two standard deviations (-2σ and $+2\sigma$); and (3) 99% lie within three standard deviations (-3σ and $+3\sigma$).* If, for example, a portfolio's expected return is normally distributed with a mean of 9.0% and a standard deviation of 1.0%, then an investor can be 99% confident of receiving an annual return between 6.0% (i.e., $9\% - 3\sigma = 6.0\%$) and 12.0% (i.e., $9\% + 3\sigma = 12.0\%$).†

Figure 12.1 depicts two investments with the same mean, or expected, return. Yet investment B has a standard deviation almost twice that of investment A. Expected returns on A, because of its smaller standard deviation, are clustered around the mean (making the solid curve taller and narrower); those of investment B are more widely dispersed. Investment B is riskier than A, because it has a greater chance of generating returns significantly above or below the common mean. For example, consider point X, located at the -2σ point of investment B. Investment B's dotted curve is much higher at X (indicating a greater probability of X occurring) than A's, which for all practical purposes is flat at X. Statistically, based on inspection of the curves' comparative heights, one would expect occasionally to realize a negative return (a loss) of magnitude X or greater on investment B, but rarely if ever a loss as large as X on investment A (although a loss of Y or greater on investment B would be expected occasionally to occur).

Figure 12.2 depicts two normally distributed risky investments with different means and different risk profiles. Investment A has an expected return of 12%, investment B, 20%. Because A's distribution is more tightly

---

*More precise probabilities can be rendered easily for normally distributed random variables. "One can take any normally distributed random variable, convert it to a standard normal...statistic, and use a table to determine the probability that an observed value of the random variable will be less than or equal to the value of interest." See, generally, Chance, *Introduction to Derivatives, supra,* Chapter 3, note 6: 119–123.

†Put differently, in 99 out of 100 cases the investor would expect to receive (or be confident of receiving) a return somewhere between 6.0% and 9.0%.

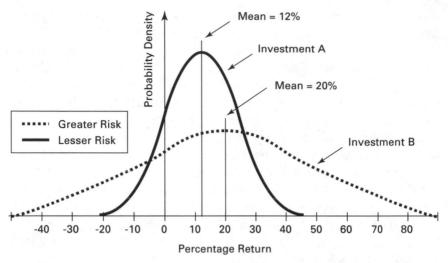

Figure 12.2   Comparison of two risky securities with different means.

clustered about its mean, A is less risky than B, whose distribution is more widely dispersed. One would, for instance, consider it reasonable for B to experience a negative return (a loss) of 25%, but the probability of A losing that large an amount is negligible. Investors with different desires for return and tolerances for risk might reasonably disagree on whether A or B is the superior investment. An aggressive investor would likely prefer B; a conservative investor would likely choose A.

Caution: Despite the assumptions of normality that investors and business managers make for computational ease, the normal distribution does *not* model accurately the expected returns on many securities, projects, and investments. Fiduciaries and other investors are well served by at least an intuitive sense of when the normal distribution is and is *not* a useful model. If nothing else, recommendations and analyses stated in probabilistic terms logically assume some form of underlying probability distribution—questioning those assumptions is entirely appropriate. Two examples help illustrate this point.

First, out-of-the-money options are one of the most common examples of the practical limitations of the normal distribution. As discussed in earlier chapters, option pricing is generally driven by the models used to measure the volatility of underlying fidget prices. Those models assume underlying fidget prices are normally distributed. Yet out-of-the-money options usually have much higher implied volatilities (meaning volatilities determined solely on the basis of inferences from current market prices) than those predicted by option pricing models. The reason? Empirical evidence suggests that, "because option buyers and sellers realize that the possibility of more frequent extraordinary moves in the underlying asset is higher than that suggested by the normal distribution, out-of-the-money options are far more valuable (maybe two to three times) than the theoretical prices dictated by the pricing model[s]."[6]

Second, the pricing of common stocks displays an asymmetrical, right-skewed distribution (one that appears to lean left, because it has a short left "tail" stopping at zero and a long, theoretically unlimited right tail). The reason for the skewing effect is that, although stockholders can realize potentially unlimited gains, their potential losses are legally limited to the amount of their investments. Many asymmetrical distributions, such as those of common stock returns, can often be converted into normal distributions (or into distributions that approximate the normal) through mechanically straightforward mathematical transformations. As Sharpe and colleagues explain:

> If we add 1.0 to a security's return and then compute the natural logarithm of this value, the resulting transformed return distribution may appear to be normally distributed. Consequently, researchers are often concerned with whether security returns are "lognormally" distributed rather than normally distributed. Although the empirical evidence is open to debate, most observers consider lognormality to adequately characterize common stock returns.[7]

RISK-RETURN TRADE-OFFS

Modern finance recognizes that "decision making under uncertainty is two-dimensional. Any investment option has two fundamental characteristics: expected return and the uncertainty risk associated with that return....Current economic theory indicates that...a trade-off between the risk and return of a security characterizes the capital markets."[8] In contrast, as discussed in Chapters 16 and 17 much of existing corporate, securities, and trust investment law pays little explicit attention to risk-return trade-offs.

Example of Risk-Return Trade-off

Consider the investments depicted in Figure 12.3. Assume that for $100 an investor can purchase either common stock A or corporate bond B. Assume also the investor is certain that at the end of one year each investment will have either of two possible values, each of which is equally likely (so each

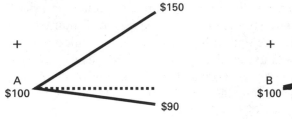

Figure 12.3a   Common stock.   Figure 12.3b   Corporate bond.

value has a .5, or 50%, probability). At the year's end, security A will be worth either $150 or $90, while B will be worth either $110 or $108. Therefore, the expected return on A is $20 [(.5 × $50) + (.5 × −$10) = $20]; the expected return on B is $9 [(.5 × $10) + (.5 × $8) = $9].

A traditional investor or legal regime focusing only on risk of loss would deem security A *inferior* to B. Why? Even though A's expected return is more than double B's, A has a 50% chance of loss. Under traditional legal rules, "the merits of investing in each security are evaluated in terms of some ceiling probability of a capital loss."[9] If the ceiling loss probability were, say, 10%, then security A, with a 50% chance of loss, would be legally impermissible. If the ceiling were stated as a dollar amount, say, $5, then A's $10 potential loss would again exceed the stated ceiling. A traditional legal regime might even characterize A as *speculative* and B as *risk free* (B cannot lose money, ignoring for discussion purposes the effects of inflation and taxes). Thus, traditional law could easily ignore the extra $11 of expected return on security A, because of the law's exclusive focus on risk of loss.

Under modern finance, security A would almost always be deemed superior to B, because of A's greater expected, or average, return. Yet if the investor is considering making a one-time, one-year investment (and is doing so without regard to the investment's contribution to a portfolio), the law of averages will have no opportunity to apply. As a one-time investment, security A cannot return $20—we know it can only gain $50 or lose $10. Moreover, because the returns of A are more variable, security A might be considered too risky for many conservative investors.* If, for example,

---

*Measures of variability that ignore the larger magnitude of positive returns are said to discriminate against investments with upside volatility. See, generally, Sharpe et al., *Investments (5th)*, *supra,* Chapter 11, note 9: 178–179.

the investor could not afford a $10 loss and had no need for a return greater than $8, then modern finance would agree that B is superior.

Diversification; Borrowing and Lending

Markowitz's original portfolio theory rests on two propositions. The first is derived from a mathematical proof of the validity of diversification's risk reduction benefits. The mathematics are laborious, but the gist is easily stated: Although the expected return of a portfolio equals the weighted average expected return of its component securities, overall portfolio risk is *proportionately less* than the weighted average risk of those securities. According to the ALI, portfolio risk is less, because individual investments rarely respond in precisely the same manner and extent to any given event. The differing responses of risky investments within a portfolio tend, in varying ways and degrees, to cancel each other out. In a properly constructed portfolio, they do so *without loss of overall expected return.*

Markowitz's second proposition is also easily summarized: For any given level of portfolio risk, a single portfolio (or substitute portfolios with identical risk and return features) can be constructed that offers the maximum expected return; likewise, a single portfolio can be constructed to minimize the risk that must be assumed to generate a desired expected return. Markowitz labels "efficient" a portfolio that has either the highest expected return for a given risk or the lowest risk for a given expected return.[10] As depicted in Figure 12.4, the "efficient frontier" for any group of securities is the set of all efficient portfolios that can be constructed from that group.

In Figure 12.4, all portfolios between points B and D lie along the frontier and are efficient. Any portfolio that plots directly below a point on the frontier is inefficient, because the point above it on the frontier (and each point in between) will yield a greater expected return for the *same* risk. Thus, portfolio 2 is inefficient; portfolio 1 yields a greater expected return for the same risk. Portfolios that plot along the curve between points A and B are inefficient. For every such portfolio—say, portfolio A—a point lies on the frontier directly above it—point C—that yields a greater expected return for the same risk. Finally, portfolio E is inefficient, because portfolio D offers a higher expected return for less risk.*

---

*Portfolio E also suggests that at some point it does not pay to assume added risk, because the extra risk eventually begins to decrease rather than increase overall expected returns. "There is some evidence that very high risks are not worth the incremental return produced, and that extremely high risks actually reduce return on the average." Chris Welles, "The Beta Revolution," *Institutional Investor* (September 1971): 55.

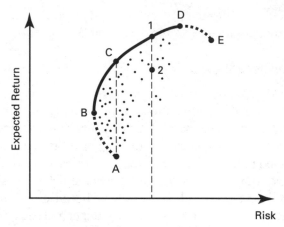

Figure 12.4   Efficient frontier.

An investor should always attempt to construct an efficient portfolio, one that lies along the efficient frontier. "Once on the frontier, the objective should be to move elsewhere on the frontier" if the investor desires a higher expected return or lower level of risk.[11] Any movement to a portfolio plotting below the frontier would either unnecessarily sacrifice some expected return or assume some risk that is otherwise avoidable.

Covariance and Portfolio Risk

Although Markowitz's achievements would win him a Nobel Prize today, his portfolio theory went unnoticed for many years. The problem then (and now) is that the theory is mechanically unwieldy; it depends on statistical procedures that, although somewhat straightforward, require numerous estimates and calculations, even for portfolios containing modest numbers of securities.*

To apply the theory, investors must first "make reliable estimates of [the risk of] each individual security. They also have to estimate the expected return for each individual security. But that is the easy part."[12] They then have to determine "how each of the many securities under con-

---

*Portfolio selection problems can be solved by those able to "employ a variant of linear programming known as *quadratic programming.*" Nevertheless, as discussed *infra,* one still has to "estimate the expected return and standard deviation" for each security under consideration for inclusion in the portfolio. See Brealey and Myers, *Principles of Corporate Finance, supra,* Chapter 11, note 10: 174–178.

sideration will vary in relation to every one of the others." That determination is calculated using a common statistical measure called *covariance,* or *correlation coefficient.*

In statistical terms, covariance is a measure of the direction and strength of a linear relationship between two random variables.[13] It is expressed as a number between -1 and $+1$. In portfolio theory, the relevant random variables are the expected returns on two paired securities. Covariance tells how one would expect those returns to vary in relation to each other. "At either extreme $[-1$ or $+1]$ we have perfect correlation. When we have perfect correlation, the fluctuations in one asset's return are perfectly predictable in terms of the fluctuations in the other asset's return."[14]

A covariance of $+1$ means returns are perfectly positively correlated; a change in the return of one security predicts a perfectly proportionate change in the return of the other. A covariance of -1 means that the returns are perfectly negatively correlated; a change in the return of one security equals a proportionate but opposite change in the return of the other. A covariance of zero means that expected returns are independent; knowledge of the return of one security conveys no information about the return of the other. For returns whose covariances are neither -1 or $+1$, nor zero, suffice to say that "a 'big' positive covariance indicates that the variables move together, a 'big' negative covariance indicates that they move inversely, and a 'small' covariance indicates that they are uncorrelated with one another."[15]

Constructing a Portfolio

The measure of covariance between two securities determines whether diversifying between those securities (i.e., investing a portion of portfolio wealth in both securities) makes sense. At one extreme, diversification cannot reduce the risk of securities with a covariance of $+1$; any event affecting the relevant market and causing a change in one security's return will cause a proportionate, corresponding change in the other. "When two securities' returns are perfectly positively correlated, the risk of a combination...is just a weighted average of the risks [of] the component securities, using market values as weights....[D]iversification does not provide risk reduction, only risk averaging."[16] Risk averaging protects only against those risks that are unique to the particular stock. Examples might include, say, for a pharmaceuticals company, FDA approval of an important new drug or an adverse result of a major lawsuit.

At the other extreme, diversification can theoretically eliminate entirely the risk of two securities with a covariance of -1. "When two securities' returns are perfectly negatively correlated, it is possible to combine them in a manner that will eliminate all risk. This principle motivates all hedging strategies."* Finally, as Sharpe states, theoretically "[d]iversification provides substantial risk reduction if the components of a portfolio are uncorrelated. In fact, if enough are included, the overall risk of the portfolio will be almost (but not quite) zero!"

Yet Sharpe acknowledges that zero risk is an undesirable, often unfeasible, objective of most investors. The strict logic of perfect hedging implies not only zero risk but also zero expected return. At a minimum, investors can do better than that by simply investing in risk-free U.S. Treasury securities.† Moreover, "common stocks move together, not independently. Thus most of the stocks that the investor can actually buy are tied together in a web of positive covariances which set the limit to the benefits of diversification."[17]

Most investors seek returns exceeding the risk-free rate. Diversification theory shows how to obtain those returns most efficiently. Efficiency here has a precise meaning. When a portfolio lies along the efficient frontier, the only way to increase expected returns is by increasing assumed risk. An efficient investment is one that either (1) assumes the least additional risk to earn the desired additional increment of expected return or (2) sacrifices the least expected return to achieve a desired reduction of risk. As discussed below, a properly diversified portfolio does not eliminate all risk; it eliminates only as much "diversifiable" risk as practicable. The capital asset pricing model (CAPM) shows how diversification, combined with risk-free borrowing and lending, theoretically enables the investor to construct not a riskless portfolio but one lying on the upward-sloping "capital market line" of Figure 12 5.

In Figure 12.5, the expected return on a risk-free investment is designated by the point on the vertical axis labeled Rf. The upward-sloping capital market line illustrates the additional highest return an investor can expect to generate for any given level of assumed risk. Points under the

---

*Negative correlation "almost never occurs" and perfect negative correlation never occurs between real common stocks. See Brealey and Myers, *Principles of Corporate Finance, supra,* Chapter 11, note 10: 159.

†From 1926 to 1995, Treasury bills provided a 0.6% average annual *real* return after adjusting for inflation. Average nominal T-bill returns were 3.7%. See *Stocks, Bonds, Bills, and Inflation, 1995 Yearbook* (Ibbotson Associates, Chicago, 1995).

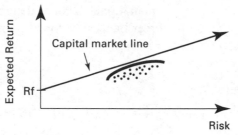

Figure 12.5   Diversification.

capital market line represent inefficient portfolios: for any portfolio plotting below the capital market line, greater expected return is obtainable for the same level of risk. As discussed below, that can be accomplished by combining risk-free borrowing or lending with an optimal efficient portfolio of risky investments.

MODERN PORTFOLIO THEORY; SEPARATION THEOREM; CAPM

In its original form, portfolio theory is at best extraordinarily cumbersome to apply, even today.* Since Markowitz's original theoretical formulation, a number of assumptions and models have been developed that greatly simplify the analysis. Of particular relevance here are the "separation theorem" developed by James Tobin and CAPM, which is attributed to William Sharpe, John Lintner, and James Treynor.[18] These works have direct relevance to trustees' and other portfolio managers' use, and thus the legal risks, of derivatives. Tobin developed a simplifying strategy, once a theoretical optimal portfolio had been identified, for helping investors construct portfolios lying along the efficient frontier, although he did not

---

*For a sense of the mathematical chore involved, consider that a portfolio of 10 securities requires 45 covariance calculations and a portfolio of 50 securities requires 1225. "[B]y the time the universe of stocks to be analyzed reaches 2,000—not an unrealistic number for large bank trust departments or major investment advisory organizations"—the number of covariance calculations reaches 1,999,000. Consider also that after figuring out the covariances of all the securities to be considered for inclusion in the portfolio, "[e]ven today…the investor has only begun to fight." The investor must then calculate the risk and return characteristics for each possible portfolio, using previously determined covariances (as noted earlier, it is only here that quadratic programming enters the process). From those calculations, *then* the investor identifies the efficient frontier. See Bernstein, *Capital Ideas, supra,* Chapter 4, note 24: 64, 57.

reduce the initial enormous computational tasks of determining the optimal portfolio. Sharpe, on the other hand, developed a theoretical model that greatly simplifies the math.

Separation Theorem

Tobin assumes all investors have unlimited ability to invest in risk-free assets (e.g., Treasury securities) and borrow (to leverage or margin their assets, including securities portfolios) at a risk-free interest rate. He uses this simplifying assumption* to reach a powerful conclusion—namely, that the composition of risky assets in the efficient portfolio is the same for *every* investor. In Tobin's words: "[T]he proportionate composition of the noncash [i.e., risky] assets is independent of their aggregate share in the investment balance."[19] The immediate implication of Tobin's analysis is dramatic: namely, the massive number of calculations required to identify and choose at any time from the portfolios along the efficient frontier need be made only once for all investors—it need *not* be made separately for each investor. Once the single optimal portfolio is identified, it becomes the preferred efficient portfolio for all investors. Thus, "[t]he optimal combination of risky assets for an investor can be determined without any knowledge of the investor's preferences toward risk and return."[20]

Using Tobin's system, an investor with risk and expected return preferences other than those of the optimal portfolio can achieve them in one of two ways. First, to achieve lower risk than that of the optimal portfolio, an investor invests a portion of her or his wealth in the optimal portfolio and the remainder in risk-free assets (i.e., those having a return known with certainty). Alternatively, to achieve a higher expected return than that of the optimal portfolio, an investor combines her or his original wealth with funds borrowed at the risk-free rate and uses all borrowed funds to make a levered investment in the single optimal portfolio. The benefits of both strategies are illustrated in Figure 12.6.

In Figure 12.6, the line tangent to the efficient frontier again begins on the vertical axis at the risk-free rate (Rf) and extends through, and beyond, the point on the efficient frontier representing the optimal portfolio. (Hence,

---

*Note that "assumptions need to be simplistic in order to provide the degree of abstraction that allows for some success in building [a] model. The *reasonableness* of the assumptions (or lack thereof) is of little concern. Instead, the test of a model is its ability to help one understand and predict the process being modeled." Sharpe et al., *Investments (5th), supra,* Chapter 11, note 9 (emphasis in original): 262.

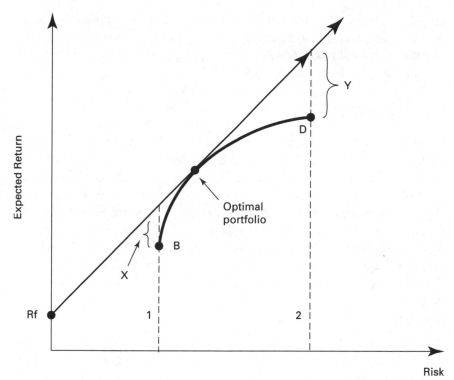

Figure 12.6   Separation theorem.

the optimal portfolio is often called the *tangency portfolio*.) A conservative investor whose risk tolerance is that indicated by line 1 and who would otherwise invest all her or his wealth in portfolio B can thus achieve a higher expected return for the same risk. The investor places a portion (calculated straightforwardly) of his or her wealth in the tangency portfolio and the remainder in risk-free assets. The investor thus generates the added increment of expected return indicated by line segment X. There is no reason for an investor with a line 1 risk tolerance ever to hold portfolio B. In contrast, an investor with the risk appetite indicated by line 2, who would otherwise invest in portfolio D, can earn additional return for the same risk. This investor can borrow money and invest all original wealth plus borrowed funds in the tangency portfolio. This investor thereby generates the additional increment of expected return indicated by line segment Y.

Separation theorem provides the rationale underlying the ALI's observations that "[b]orrowing [i.e., leverage] may play an inverse role to that of lending and is permissible for trustees, provided the tactic is employed selectively and cautiously."[21] In addition, as discussed below, to the extent that leverage increases risk, trustees should takes steps to ensure that the additional risk is adequately compensated. According to the ALI, "compensated risk is not inherently bad."

Capital Asset Pricing Model

Sharpe pursued Markowitz's observation that "[t]he returns on most stocks are correlated. If the Standard & Poor Index rose substantially, we would expect United States Steel (Common) to rise. If the Standard & Poor Index rose substantially, we would also expect Sweets Company of America (Common) to rise. For this reason, it is more than likely that United States Steel will do well when Sweets Company does well."[22] Sharpe believed the correlation among stocks is due to a single underlying factor. That factor, he eventually concluded, is the market as a whole. And the overall market turns out to be, for Sharpe, Tobin's tangency portfolio.

Assumptions; market portfolio

A discussion of Sharpe's model, CAPM (also jointly attributed to Lintner and Treynor), helps illuminate many of the issues that drive the current debate over corporate or "entity level" use of derivatives. It is not necessary to agree with the model to understand its impact on derivatives strategies, especially for trustees and other money managers. The ability to follow the debate regardless of whether one agrees with CAPM is helpful, because the model, as discussed below, has at times been heavily criticized.

CAPM makes many assumptions that, as Sharpe readily acknowledges, are unrealistic. In particular, it relies upon perfectly efficient, frictionless markets. It assumes, among other things, that (1) all investors have unrestricted access to borrow and ability to lend funds at the risk-free rate, (2) transaction costs and taxes are irrelevant, (3) information is freely and instantly available to all investors, and (4) all investors agree on the future prospects of all securities. Finally, it concludes that (5) "in equilibrium the proportions of the tangency portfolio will correspond to the proportions of what is known as the *market portfolio,* defined as follows:

> The market portfolio is a portfolio consisting of all securities where the proportion invested in each security corresponds to its relative market value. The relative market value of a security is simply equal to the aggregate market value of the security divided by the sum of the aggregate market values of all securities.[23]

Sharpe and other theoreticians developed the notion central to CAPM that a substantial proportion of every security's covariance, or risk, is attributable to the riskiness of the overall market, or the market portfolio so defined. Note, however, that the model's central concept of a measurable market portfolio, or even a discernable overall market, is controversial.*

Partitioning Risks

In modern portfolio theory, a security's total risk "consists of two parts: (1) *market* (or systematic) risk; and (2) *unique* (or unsystematic) risk."[24] In theory, unique risk can be avoided by proper diversification; market risk, however, cannot. The reason? "Unique risk stems from the fact that many of the perils that surround an individual company are peculiar to that company and perhaps its immediate competitors. But there is also some risk that you can't avoid, regardless of how much you diversify....Market risk stems from the fact that there are other economywide perils which threaten all businesses. That is why stocks have a tendency to move together. And that is why investors are exposed to 'market uncertainties,' no matter how many stocks they hold."[25]

Pricing Implications

The distinction between market and unique risk is fundamental to CAPM. The model holds that diversification cannot eliminate market risk; it results only in *averaging* the market risks of the securities comprising a portfolio. In contrast, diversification can sharply *reduce* unique risk. The

---

*Sharpe acknowledges that "the market portfolio is *surprisingly ill defined....*In reality, actually identifying the *true* market portfolio (or even a close approximation) is beyond the capability of any individual or organization....These days we should think globally....[W]e should also include common stocks, preferred stocks, and corporate bonds....the value of proprietorships and partnerships. How about government debt[,]...real estate, cash holdings, monetary metals (primarily gold), and art. But we have not finished yet. We should also consider consumer durable[s]....[and] the largest asset of all, the training and education...called *human capital.*" Sharpe et al., *Investments (5th), supra,* Chapter 11, note 9 (emphasis modified): 266–267.

Saber suggests a more fundamental problem. He states that the market portfolio is not ill defined, it is *undefinable.* See Nasser Saber, Letter to the Editor, *Barron's* (January 8, 1996) ("Those who think that the S&P 500 index is the market, or roughly approximates it, should think again. The market CAPM is the market for everything, not just equities. It includes commodities, real estate, oil and gas, ventures in Silicon Valley, IPOs, etc....[T]he foundation of CAPM is a non-definable value....Any conclusion drawn from it...can be correct only accidentally").

differing effects of diversification on market and unique risk under CAPM lead to the model's cardinal conclusion regarding pricing: namely, efficient markets will compensate investors for bearing systematic risk, but *not* for bearing unique risks.

The reasoning behind the pricing conclusion begins with CAPM's assumption that investors are rational and risk-averse. By definition they will, other things being equal, pay more for less risky investments than for riskier ones. Given two investments opportunities of differing risk and equal expected return, an investor will pay more for the less risky of the two. Likewise, investors will, other things being equal, demand greater expected return to hold riskier investments than less risky ones. Given a choice between two investments of different risk, an investor will hold the riskier one only in the expectation of receiving a higher return.

Further, in "equilibrium," efficient markets will not compensate for the bearing of diversifiable and hence unnecessary risks. Well-diversified investors compete to sell temporarily "overpriced" securities, meaning those that bear diversifiable risk (i.e., unique and, from the perspective of the well-diversified investor, unnecessary risk). The competition drives down the securities' prices, quickly eliminating the overpricing and restoring pricing equilibrium. The same but opposite dynamic holds for securities temporarily "underpriced." Thus, in efficient markets diversification eliminates unique risks. In contrast, diversification cannot reduce systematic (market) risk. The "web" of positive covariances among stocks precludes investors from successfully ridding themselves of systematic risks if they are to continue holding stocks.

In considering the merits of the pricing argument, it is helpful to have a sense of how easily an investor can realize the benefits of diversification. Most academics and practitioners believe that a majority of the benefits can be achieved with a surprisingly small number of well-diversified investments. "Roughly speaking, a portfolio that has 30 or more randomly selected securities in it will have a relatively small amount of unique risk. This means that its total risk will be only slightly greater than the amount of market risk that is present."[26]

Although the precise number of investments needed to achieve most of the benefits of diversification is a matter of debate, the benefits can easily be visualized. Figure 12.7 illustrates how quickly diversification begins to minimize the unique, nonmarket risks (using standard deviation as the measure of risk) of a portfolio, based on the number of investments in that

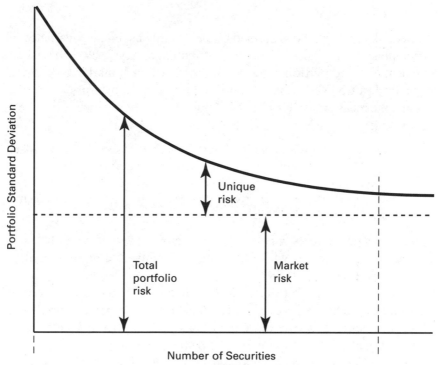

Figure 12.7   Diversification and risk.

portfolio.* As Figure 12.7 makes plain, even with limited diversification, portfolio risk—labeled "total portfolio risk" in the diagram—is mainly a function of the average market risk of the securities comprising the portfolio. The more securities in the portfolio, the more closely portfolio risk will asymptotically approach the average market risk of those securities; eventually, virtually all uncompensated, unique risk will be eliminated, leaving the portfolio bearing only compensated, systematic risk.†

---

*As to the number of investments needed to achieve most of diversification's benefits: "Some analysts are happy with 15 [investments] while others require at least 60. The general rule of thumb is 30. Finally, since systematic risk does not disappear with diversification, it must be dealt with and managed." Marshall and Bansal, *A Complete Guide to Financial Innovation, supra,* note 14: 120.

†"*All* the risk of a fully diversified portfolio is market risk." Brealey and Myers, *Principles of Corporate Finance, supra,* Chapter 11, note 10 (emphasis in original): 173.

Portfolio Effects; Beta

Market risk of a portfolio is defined as the weighted average covariance of its component securities.[27] The risk contribution of any stock to the risk of a well-diversified portfolio is essentially that stock's market risk. Beta, introduced in Chapter 11, is one commonly accepted measure of market risk and the measure used in CAPM. Applied to individual securities, beta can be understood in terms of the following:

> If you want to know the contribution of an individual security to the risk of a well-diversified portfolio, it is no good thinking about how risky that security is in *isolation*—you need to measure its *market* risk, and that boils down to measuring how sensitive it [the security] is to market movements. This sensitivity is called *beta* (β).

Applied to a portfolio, beta is "simply a weighted average of the betas of its component securities, where the proportions invested in the securities are the respective weights."[28]

CAPM's market portfolio is defined to have a beta of 1.0. By definition, stocks and portfolios "with betas greater than 1.0 tend to amplify the overall movements of the market. Stocks [and portfolios] with betas between 0 and 1.0 tend to move in the same direction as the market, but not as far."[29] Thus, a portfolio with a beta of, say, 0.5 will tend to move in the same direction as the overall market, but only half as far; one with a beta of 1.5 will also tend to move in the same direction as the overall market, but its reaction will be 50% greater than the market's. "This brings us to one of the principal themes of [modern portfolio theory]: The risk of a well-diversified portfolio depends on the market risk of the securities included in the portfolio."

For example, a portfolio of 100 randomly selected high-beta stocks with an average beta of, say, 1.5 (consistent with our earlier example) would by any estimate be well diversified. Including such a large number of stocks in the portfolio removes virtually all unique risks. As suggested by Figure 12.8, this portfolio's returns will move "almost in lockstep with the market. However, this portfolio's standard deviation would be...1.5 times that of the market. A well-diversified portfolio with a beta of 1.5 will amplify every market move[, positive or negative,] 50 percent and end up with 150 percent of the market's risk." Likewise, a portfolio of 100 randomly selected low-beta stocks with an average beta of 0.5 would be well diversified. This portfolio's standard deviation would be only half that of the market portfolio. The effects of diversification on both 100 security portfolios described above are depicted in Figure 12.8 (using betas as measures of risk).

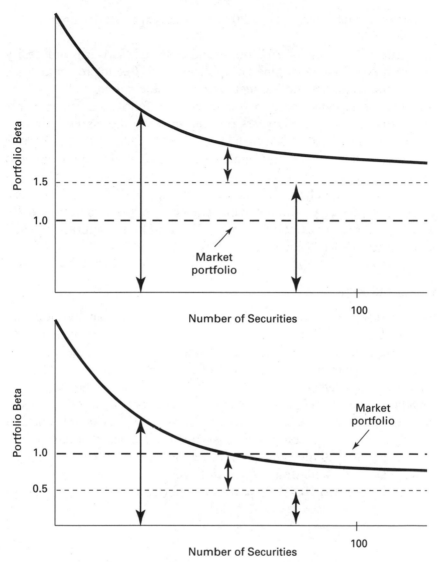

Figure 12.8   Above- and below-average portfolio betas.

Calculating Risk Premium

The message of CAPM is "both startling and simple. In a competitive market, the expected risk premium varies in direct proportion to beta....The expected risk premium on an investment with a beta of .5 is, therefore, *half* the expected risk premium on the market; and the expected risk premium on an investment with a beta of 2.0 is *twice* the expected risk premium on the market."[30]

The calculation of risk premium is straightforward and easily demonstrated. First, determine the applicable risk-free interest rate—say, 6.0% per annum. Second, estimate the applicable *market risk premium,* meaning the expected return on the market portfolio *minus* the risk-free rate. "Over a period of 69 years [ending in 1994] the market risk premium...has averaged 8.4 percent a year." Finally, multiply the market risk premium by the relevant portfolio's beta. Applying this methodology to our earlier examples (and assuming annual returns) reveals that (1) the 0.5 beta portfolio would have a market risk premium of 8.4% × 0.5 = 4.2%, and (2) the 1.5 beta portfolio would have a market risk premium of 8.4% × 1.5 = 12.6%. Thus, the first portfolio would have a total expected annual return of 10.2%; the second, 18.6%.

Beta and Risk Premium

The message of CAPM and modern portfolio theory is that investors will choose riskier portfolios, and thus assume additional beta (moving upward to the right along the capital market line), only in the expectation of receiving a commensurate increment of additional return. The additional expected return demanded in excess of the risk-free rate is the *market risk premium* applicable to the particular level of risk, or beta, that the investor chooses to assume. The broad stock market is defined as having a beta of 1.0. Treasury bills, in contrast, are risk-free investments that have a beta of zero. Figure 12.9 illustrates the risk-return trade-off implied by CAPM as it applies to (1) a portfolio of risk-free securities, (2) the market portfolio, and (3) the two 100-stock portfolios referred to in Figure 12.8. (For

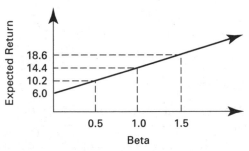

Figure 12.9   Beta and risk premium.

simplicity, we assume that the annual risk-free rate is 6.0% and that the annual 8.4% market risk premium is applicable.)

Figure 12.9 plots the capital market line beginning at the risk-free rate of 6.0 and moving upward to the right through the 1.0 beta value of the market. At that point, the expected market return is 6.0 + 8.4% = 14.4%. Similarly, the first 100-stock portfolio had a beta of 0.5. As we found earlier, its expected portfolio return is therefore equal to 6.0% + 4.2% = 10.2%. The second stock portfolio had a beta of 1.5, and we found that its expected portfolio return is equal to 6.0% + 12.6% = 18.6%.

ENDNOTES: CHAPTER 12

1. This and the following quotation are from Wallman, *Regulating in a World of Technological and Global Change, supra,* Chapter 2, note 32 (emphasis added): 8–9.
2. See Sharpe et al., *Investments (5th), supra,* Chapter 11, note 9 ("The chances of a positive outcome a certain distance away from the center of the distribution are just as great as the chances of a negative outcome an equal distance in the opposite direction"): 178; see, generally, William F. Sharpe, *Investments,* (3rd ed.) (Prentice Hall, 1985) [hereafter, *Investments (3rd)*]: 122–130.
3. Sharpe et al., *Investments (5th), supra,* Chapter 11, note 9: 178.
4. Tucker, *Financial Futures, supra,* Chapter 4, note 10: 36; see also Brealey and Myers, *Principles of Corporate Finance, supra,* Chapter 11, note 10 ("standard deviation and variance are the correct measures of risk if the returns are normally distributed"): 149–151; Pardew, *Managerial Statistics, supra,* Chapter 11, note 20; Watson et al., *Management Statistics, supra,* Chapter 11, note 28: § 6.3.
5. See Watson et al., *Management Statistics, supra,* Chapter 11, note 41: 245.
6. Chew, *Leverage, supra,* Chapter 1, note 1: 162.
7. Sharpe et al., *Investments (5th), supra,* Chapter 11, note 9: 178–179.
8. *Id.* (footnote omitted): 619.
9. *Risky Investments, supra,* Chapter 1, note 23: 603.
10. See, generally, Sharpe et al., *Investments (5th), supra,* Chapter 11, note 9: 194; Brealey and Myers, *Principles of Corporate Finance, supra,* Chapter 11, note 10: 173–194.
11. Jeffrey S. Glaser, "The Capital Asset Pricing Model: Risk Valuation, Judicial Interpretation, and Market Bias," *The Business Lawyer,* 50 (February 1995) [hereafter, *Capital Asset Pricing Model*]: 690.
12. Bernstein, *Capital Ideas, supra,* Chapter 4, note 24: 57.

13. See, generally, Watson et al., *Management Statistics, supra,* Chapter 11, note 41: 624–632; see also *The MIT Dictionary of Modern Economics,* 4th ed., David W. Pearce, ed. (The MIT Press, 1992) [hereafter, *MIT Dictionary*].

14. John F. Marshall and Vipul K. Bansal, *Financial Engineering: A Complete Guide to Financial Innovation* (New York Institute of Finance, 1992) [hereafter, *A Complete Guide to Financial Innovation*]: 109–110.

15. Watson et al., *Management Statistics, supra, Chapter 11* note 41: 627.

16. This and the quotations in the following two paragraphs are from Sharpe, *Investments (3rd), supra,* note 2 (emphasis omitted): 131–134.

17. See Brealey and Myers, *Principles of Corporate Finance, supra,* Chapter 11, note 10: 160–161.

18. See, generally, Glaser, *Capital Asset Pricing Model, supra,* note 11: 687, n. 1. For the original articles on separation theorem, portfolio theory, and CAPM, see James Tobin, "Liquidity Preference as Behavior Toward Risk," *Review of Economic Studies,* 67 (February 1958): 65–86; William F. Sharpe, "A Simplified Model for Portfolio Analysis," *Management Science,* 9 (January 1963): 277–293; William F. Sharpe, "Capital Asset Prices: A Theory of Market Equilibrium Under Conditions of Risk," *Journal of Finance,* 19(3) (September 1964): 425–442; John Lintner, "Security Prices, Risk, and Maximal Gains from Diversification," *Journal of Finance,* 20 (1965): 587; John Lintner, "The Valuation of Risk Assets and the Selection of Risky Investments in Stock Portfolios and Capital Budgets," *Review of Economic Statistics,* 47 (February 1965): 13–37. Treynor's article is unpublished. For a detailed discussions of security valuation techniques, modern portfolio theory, diversification, CAPM, and related topics, see Sharpe et al., *Investments (5th), supra,* Chapter 11, note 9.

19. James Tobin, "Liquidity Preference as Behavior Toward Risk," *Review of Economic Studies,* 67 (February 1958) (also quoted in Bernstein, *Capital Ideas, supra,* Chapter 4, note 24): 65–86.

20. Sharpe et al., *Investments (5th), supra,* Chapter 11, note 9: 263.

21. The quotations in this paragraph are from *Rest. 3rd, Trusts (Prudent Investor Rule), supra,* Chapter 10, note 13: 28–29, 19–20.

22. Quoted in Bernstein, *Capital Ideas, supra,* Chapter 4, note 24 (citation omitted): 77.

23. Sharpe et al., *Investments (5th), supra,* Chapter 11, note 9 (emphasis modified): 263.

24. See, generally, Sharpe et al., *Investments (5th), supra,* Chapter 11, note 9 (emphasis modified): 212–217; Brealey and Myers, *Principles of Corporate Finance, supra,* Chapter 11, note 10: 153–156; "General Comment *e,*" *Rest. 3rd, Trusts (Prudent Investor Rule), supra,* Chapter 10, note 13 ("non-market risk, or somewhat less precisely 'specific' or 'unique'

risk…can be reduced through proper diversification"): 19; Glaser, *Capital Asset Pricing Model, supra,* note 11: 693.

25. Brealey and Myers, *Principles of Corporate Finance, supra,* Chapter 11, note 10: 156.
26. Sharpe et al., *Investments (5th), supra,* Chapter 11, note 9: 215; see also Brealey and Myers, *Principles of Corporate Finance, supra,* Chapter 11, note 10 ("once you have a portfolio of 20 or more stocks, diversification has done the bulk of its work. For a reasonably well-diversified portfolio, only market risk matters"): 156.
27. Brealey and Myers, *Principles of Corporate Finance, supra,* Chapter 11, note 10 (emphasis modified): 160. The quotation following is from *Id.:* 160.
28. Sharpe et al., *Investments (5th), supra,* Chapter 11, note 9: 271.
29. The quotations in this and the following paragraphs are from Brealey and Myers, *Principles of Corporate Finance, supra,* Chapter 11, note 10 (emphasis omitted): 160–165.
30. This and the quotation in the following paragraph are from *Id.:* 180, Chapter 7.

CHAPTER 13

Fundamentals of Modern Finance: MM Theory

The firm pays its debts not just because the law says it must, but because the value of the stock to its shareholders is greater to them if the firm pays the debts than if it doesn't. Otherwise the shareholders can default on the payment, invoke limited liability and turn the keys over to the bondholders.

Merton H. Miller
"The Modigliani-Miller Propositions
After Thirty Years," Journal of
Economic Perspectives, *Fall 1988*

[T]he prevailing legal view of corporate risk management fails to acknowledge some of the important insights achieved by modern corporate finance theory—particularly, with respect to the valuation of shares.

Henry T. C. Hu, University of Texas
School of Law
Journal of Applied Corporate Finance,
Fall 1996

This chapter continues the discussion of the fundamentals of modern finance, paying particular attention to issues of importance to corporate risk management. It builds on the discussion of economic fundamentals begun in Chapter 12. The ideas discussed here and in Chapters 12, 14, and 15 are a cornerstone of derivatives financial and legal risk management, particularly for corporations and other operating business entities (versus investment vehicles).*

MM THEORY: FROM "PERFECT MARKET" ASSUMPTION TO REAL-WORLD APPLICATIONS

Modigliani and Miller (MM) theory is in an important sense the complement of modern portfolio theory—specifically, the capital asset pricing model (CAPM). Both MM and CAPM offer methodologies for determin-

---

*To conform to accepted usage in academic finance literature, *corporate finance* refers to the theory and practice of finance as applied to many different types of operating business entities. It covers not only corporations, but also the multiplicity of alternative organizational forms available under state, federal, and foreign law (e.g., limited liability companies, limited partnerships, and unincorporated associations).

ing optimal mixes of debt and equity securities under conditions of uncertainty: CAPM approaches the subject from the perspective of the investor, or securities holder; MM approaches it from that of the firm, or securities issuer. Portfolio theory helps investors construct optimal investment portfolios, given subjective risk-return preferences; it helps determine precise combinations of risky and risk-free investments to hold to maximize expected returns while minimizing overall portfolio risk. MM provides a theoretical basis on which a firm can choose the particular mix of securities to issue to maximize firm value. The most important factor in that choice is the proportion of debt the firm desires in its capital structure. That in turn depends on the nature of the firm's assets, its expected tax liability, management's (and investors') appetite for risk, and management's desire to maintain reserve borrowing capacity.

MM's power lies in its paradoxical proof that in ideal markets one cannot increase firm value merely by altering capital structure—this is MM's so-called value-invariance proposition.[1] Its basic insight is that assets, booked on the left side of the balance sheet, are the source of firm value. At any moment, a firm's capital structure—the right side of its balance sheet—is nothing more than the coincident aggregate of claims to the value on the left. In a perfect market, changes in capital structure merely reallocate claims to firm value without affecting the underlying assets. Put differently, those changes simply modify claimants' relative rights *inter se,* or among themselves, to a (momentarily) fixed value; a change in capital structure has no effect on firm value and therefore "*doesn't* matter."

MM theory broke sharply with conventional thinking by distinguishing "the real value of a firm [from] its financial packaging." With that distinction as foundation, Modigliani and Miller began constructing a theoretical edifice to explain how in real markets capital structure *does* affect firm value and therefore *does* matter. Others have extended the MM analysis to show how financial risk management and derivatives in particular can be used to increase firm value. Yet despite significant scholarship in the literature of corporate finance on the benefits of derivatives, the corresponding legal implications have received little attention from legal scholars.*

Miller, Modigliani, and others show that MM's "real-world applications" readily emerge from its internal logic. Those applications offer

---

*Professor Hu's articles—including *Behind the Corporate Hedge, supra,* Chapter 11, note 2, and other works cited herein—are the primary exception.

guidance to managers and investors not only in determining and identifying appropriate capital structures but also in assessing financial risk management strategies, whether or not they employ derivatives. As Miller and others have asserted, many firms can increase their market value by altering capital structure and changing risk management strategies—both of which flow from MM's "'new' intuition"*—if they do so in the right way and for the right reasons. Here, revisiting the context in which Miller and Modigliani first made their once radical argument is instructive.

According to Modigliani, the dominant view in 1958 was that "some debt in the capital structure had to reduce the cost of capital even in the absence of taxes simply because the interest rate was lower than the earnings-price ratio on equity."[2] He and Miller believed that view to be mistaken. Yet before they could show why, they first, in Miller's words, "had to convince people (including ourselves!) that there could be *any* conditions, even in a 'frictionless' world, where a firm would be indifferent between issuing securities as different in legal status, investor risk and apparent cost as debt and equity."[3] They chose to introduce their subject in its simplest and most vigorous form by assuming away all capital market imperfections. In that assumption lies the key to the prudent use of derivatives to manage financial risk.

By isolating real-market imperfections and carefully reintroducing them into an MM framework, one can surmise how firm market value will respond to each of those imperfections. In that sense, the imperfections point the way to a qualitative, supervisory-level understanding of how financial policy, particularly the use of derivatives, can enhance firm value. The prospect of enhancing firm value by reducing the adverse impact of market imperfections is important economically and legally, because it comports with both MM and CAPM. Both of those theories hold that investors will not compensate firms for unnecessary risk management. When conducted by a firm, financial risk management is redundant and even wasteful from an investor's perspective, if the investor can

---

*As discussed *infra*, this intuition is "new" only compared with prevailing thinking in 1958, which "took it as self-evident that there was a unique, value-maximizing debt ratio" for all firms. Today, the error of that view and the strength of MM's value-invariance proposition are supported by overwhelming empirical evidence. Firms both within the same industry and across different industries display a vast array of capital structures despite comparable degrees of risk and profitability. The evidence is so compelling that Modigliani senses that the original MM insight, once so extraordinary, now "seems almost trivial." See Modigliani, *MM—Past, Present, Future, infra*, note 2: 150.

efficiently manage the relevant risks on its own. Yet many market imperfections, several of which we examine below, affect not risks but *costs*. Some of the costs, such as excess corporate taxes, are by-products of systematic distortions in the financial system. Others are *deadweight costs* of inefficiencies inherent in markets' legal and financial infrastructure.

COMPANY COST OF CAPITAL

With its perfect market assumption stated, the MM argument begins with the premise that firm market value equals the market value of a firm's assets. More specifically, it equals the discounted present value of the firm's expected, or future, operating earnings, net of interest and taxes.* So defined, assets include any property or characteristic of the firm that investors expect to contribute to future net cashflows. Assets include real assets already in place, whether tangible or intangible,† as well as valuable strategic alternatives, including growth opportunities and operating options.

Assets create *current* market value by generating expected *future* cashflows. MM posits that, in valuing a firm, the market views the firm as a "black box" producing operating cashflows. It assigns a risk-adjusted value to those flows, ignoring transient capital structures and such "details" as "technology, production, and sales."[4] MM theory assumes that investors "price the whole firm by capitalizing its operating earnings *before* interest and taxes," factoring in the amount, timing, and uncertainty of expected cashflows. The theory isolates the valuation of cashflows from that of investor claims to those flows. MM gives primacy to asset values, which cannot be enhanced merely by reshuffling claims to the assets.

MM hypothesizes that in valuing a firm, investors first construct a *market value* balance sheet (as opposed to book value, which, mainly

---

*Corporate finance uses several other terms for the same concept. Often, the terms *operating income, operating cashflows,* and even the unadorned *cashflows* are used interchangeably to mean cashflows, income, or earnings, in each case from normal operations and before adjusting for interest and taxes. Normal operations include all continuing activities other than "extraordinary" items, such as sales of real estate or other major capital assets outside the ordinary course of business.

†Intangibles cover contract rights and intellectual property, including patents, trademarks, and copyrights. The expression also covers any other right or characteristic that adds to an assessment of a firm's expected cashflows. Examples include (1) experienced management teams with reputations for integrity and sound judgment, (2) a reputation for making high-quality products backed by strong warranties, and (3) a highly motivated, well-trained work force. (Items 1 and 3 are sometimes included in human capital.)

because it relies on historical asset costs, can be and usually is quite different), such as that below. The left, asset side of the balance sheet contains a single entry for the market value of the firm's expected cashflows (ECFV). Those flows are the end product of investment and capital budgeting decisions (often called, simply, "investments"), defined broadly to cover any choice of how funds are to be spent.[5] The right, liability side consists of all entries for the market values of claims against those cashflows. Claims result from decisions about how to raise money. The market derives the aggregate value of claims, or liabilities, from the value of expected cashflows. Therefore, the market value of liabilities is logically dependent on that of expected cashflows.

**Market Value
Balance Sheet**

ECFV (A) 100	Debt value (D) 30
	Equity value (E) 70
Asset value (V) 100	Firm value (V) 100

Initially, MM depended on its novel arbitrage proof that in ideal financial markets investors are indifferent to capital structure. The arbitrage proof has been superseded by many alternative proofs, including CAPM.[6] In a CAPM world, markets determine firm values from risk-adjusted expected cashflows. Risk adjustments are based on the firm's betas, which are historical estimates of the sensitivity of firm cashflows to overall market movements. Thus, the "market, in setting the values of companies, effectively assigns minimum required rates of return on capital that vary directly with the companies' level of risk,"[7] meaning overall asset risks.*

---

*Financial analysts commonly use beta as a measure of sensitivity of equity to overall stock market movements. Equity betas can be derived directly from the beta of a firm's assets, if the firm has no outstanding risky debt (and little operating leverage). If a capital structure contains risky debt, equity betas depend on both asset betas and the debt-equity ratio, or leverage. Of course, all corporate debt is risky, by definition. Nevertheless, financial economists, beginning with MM, often make the "troublesome tactical simplification" that, with little debt outstanding, a firm's debt is "of no risk whatever." See, e.g., Miller, *MM Theory After Thirty Years, supra,* Chapter 11, note 16: 106.

As shown in Chapter 12, the overall expected rate of return on a portfolio is a weighted average of the expected returns on the component securities.[8] The portfolio perspective applies to issuers as well as investors. If an investor held a portfolio consisting solely of all the outstanding securities of a single firm (which has no other liabilities), the expected returns on the portfolio would equal the issuer's expected return on assets—which is just a thinly disguised restatement of the accounting principle that the value on the left side of the market balance sheet equals that on the right. To the issuer the expected portfolio return is a cost, called its *company cost of capital*. A company calculates its cost of capital prior to partitioning cashflows and their attendant risks among holders of various classes of debt and equity securities. Because capital costs are independent of capital structure, changes in capital structure (i.e., in leverage, meaning the debt-equity ratio) affect expected returns on individual securities but *not* on the overall portfolio of the issuer's securities.

According to MM's Proposition II, the cost of both debt and equity capital, based on a given return on a firm's assets, is a linear function of the debt-equity ratio.[9] To see this relationship, consider again market value balance sheet. The market value of the firm's debt and equity securities, on the right, equals that of the firm's assets, on the left: $D + E = V = A$. Proposition II states that when Proposition I holds (i.e., when firm value is independent of capital structure), debt and equity returns are a linear function of total asset returns. In other words, knowing a firm's leverage ratio and asset returns enables debt returns to be calculated directly from equity returns, and vice versa. The general relationship is expressed as

$$r_A = \frac{D}{V} r_D + \frac{E}{V} r_E$$

where:
r_A = return on assets
r_D = return on debt
r_E = return on equity

(Equation 13.1)

We now insert numbers into Equation 13.1 to show how to find (1) a firm's market value from that of its securities; and (2) given an expected rate of return on debt (equity) securities, the expected return on equity (debt) securities. If the above firm's return on equity were 20% and return on debt 10%, that would imply a total asset return of 17%:

$$r_A = \frac{D}{V} r_D + \frac{E}{V} r_E$$

$$= \frac{30}{100} (.10) + \frac{70}{100} (.20)$$

$$= .03 + .14 + .17, \text{ so:}$$

$$r_A = .17, \text{ or } \underline{17\%}$$

Knowing total asset returns enables us to see how equity and debt returns ought to respond to the substitution of new debt (equity) for existing equity (debt).

Assume, for example, that the firm engaged in a highly leveraged transaction (HLT) in which it borrowed 50 new units of debt to repurchase 50 units of its outstanding equity. Immediately after the HLT, all outstanding debt, including that issued previously, would be riskier. The reason is that the amount of equity, or the "equity cushion," beneath the debt would have declined from 70 to 20 units. Market returns on the now riskier debt would rise (and prices fall).* Let us assume that debt returns were to rise to 15%. We know that changing the capital structure would not alter the riskiness or amount of overall cashflows available to service investor claims.[10] If investors on average received a 17% return before the HLT, and the transaction did not affect the firm's assets, investors on average would expect to receive 17% afterward. According to Miller, one could determine equity returns after the HLT directly by "subtracting out" of the 17% return on assets the new 15% debt returns. We do so momentarily.

Meanwhile, note that the transaction would cause leverage (the debt-equity ratio) to balloon from 0.43 (30/70) to 4.00 (80/20). Financial markets would, as a result, demand higher returns on both new and preexisting debt and equity. Required debt returns would increase, because of the smaller equity cushion. The equity would likewise have become riskier. In

---

*The rates of return at issue here are market rates. So if holders of preexisting debt that has become far riskier because of the HLT have no right to demand increased interest payments (or other compensation) from the company, the price of the debt securities they hold would decline to reflect a loss in the value of *those securities* resulting from the added risk. A famous example of this phenomenon was RJR Nabisco's 1988 management leveraged buyout, in which the announcement of the proposed HLT caused the company's $2.4 billion of outstanding debt to drop by $298 million. RJR is discussed in Brealey and Myers, *Principles of Corporate Finance, supra,* Chapter 11, note 10: 493.

a bankruptcy, equity is junior to debt, which enjoys legal "priority" in its right to receive distributions of value—in theory, equity claims are paid only after debt claims have been fully satisfied. Stockholders, then, by giving lenders a prior claim on assets, assume greater risk than lenders. The proposed HLT must increase equity returns to induce investors to buy and hold the riskier equity securities.

To calculate post-HLT equity returns, given a 4% (11% to 15%) increase in debt returns, we apply Equation 13.1:

$$r_A = \frac{D}{V} r_D + \frac{E}{V} r_E$$

$$.17 = \frac{80}{100} (.15) + \frac{20}{100} r_E$$

$$.05 = .20\, r_E$$

$$.25 = r_E, \text{ so:}$$

$$r_E = \underline{25\%}$$

The post-HLT market return on equity should be 25%. Consider what would happen if, instead of issuing new debt to buy back old equity, the firm used 30 units of new equity to prepay all its outstanding debt. The firm would have no financial leverage, so its equity and assets would be equally risky. Thus, overall equity returns would simply equal asset returns—namely, 17%. All asset returns and associated risks would be partitioned to the equity.*

The logic of MM thus illuminates (1) the interplay between changes in risk and expected return, on the one hand, and changes in securities' market values, on the other, and (2) the way market values of a firm's debt and equity securities are anticipated to respond to specified changes in an issuer's capital structure.† Since the publication of the original MM paper,

---

*An analogous line of reasoning to that in the text, and a corresponding equation to Equation 13.1, shows that (1) the beta of a firm's assets can be determined from a weighted average of the betas of the firm's debt and equity and (2) an increase (decrease) in leverage will increase (decrease) the betas of both debt and equity. The general equation is: $\beta_{assets} = (D/V)$ $\beta_{debt} + (E/V)\, \beta_{equity}$. See, generally, Sharpe et al., *Investments (5th), supra,* Chapter 11, note 9: 524–538.

†Complex illustrations can be constructed to show how MM applies not only to the broad mix of debt and equity but also to distinct classes of debt securities, equity securities, and hybrids. MM applies, for example, to the interplay of changes in the market value of secured debt to that of unsecured and subordinated debt and that of preferred stock. See, e.g., Brealey and Myers, *Principles of Corporate Finance, supra,* Chapter 11, note 10: 465.

academics have also examined the relationship between capital structure and financial risk management, including that involving derivatives.[11]

Their efforts include important works on the use of derivatives to reduce financial risk. Stulz, for example, has shown how derivatives can be "a direct substitute for equity capital. That is, the more the firm hedges its financial exposures, the less equity it requires to support its business."[12] If a hedging firm requires less equity, that suggests its derivatives make the firm's debt less risky. With these new insights, we can begin to analyze MM's real-world applications for derivatives users, and we do so shortly. But first, it helps to review in a derivatives context MM's first lesson: that one "can make a lot more money by smart investment decisions than by smart financing decisions."[13]

WHY NOT TRADE DERIVATIVES FOR PROFIT? AN MM RESPONSE

MM emphasizes that value is created on the left, not right, side of the balance sheet. If management is trying to maximize firm value, its dominant goal should be to make value-enhancing investments, those that strengthen the left side of the balance sheet. Derivatives are value-enhancing investments only if they are profitable activities on a stand-alone, risk-adjusted basis.[14] Moreover, to attract investors, expected derivatives' profits must exceed investors' opportunity costs, or the returns that investors forgo by not investing their capital elsewhere. Thus, to increase firm market value, derivatives must offer an expectation of sufficient profits to compensate investors for all their associated risks and costs.

The difficulty with derivatives is that they are (ignoring for the moment bid-offer spreads and other transaction costs) priced as zero-sum transactions. In other words, at inception they are exchanges of equivalent value: in theory, neither party has an expectation of risk-adjusted gain from the transaction unless it somehow has a comparative advantage in predicting underlying market movements. Another way of looking at this is that derivatives, when sold and priced in competitive markets, are zero net present value (NPV) transactions.* Even if a par-

---

*Because derivatives are entered into at a zero NPV, they have no historical "cost" that would permit them to be accounted for as on-balance sheet items. Applicable accounting rules require that the applicable cost be determined as the sum that a dealer would charge or offer to enter into the contract on its start date. Thus, most derivatives, certainly most nonoption products, are booked off-balance sheet. See Chapter 18. See also Elizabeth MacDonald, "FASB Moving Ahead on Rule on Derivatives," *Wall Street Journal* (July 7, 1997): A2.

ticular transaction is more likely than not to result in, say, a gain, the amount of that gain must be discounted by the corresponding degree of risk. In other words, the amount of the more frequent gains must be sufficient to offset the less frequent but larger losses. (One example is from the issuance of deeply out-of-the-money options. Although the options should generate premium income more frequently than they produce losses, the size of any loss could easily overwhelm any single premium, the amount of which is fixed.) On a risk-adjusted basis, the transaction should still have a zero NPV. Individual transactions "sometimes lose money and sometimes make money, but on average they break even."[15]

Furthermore, especially for derivatives users, the transactions have added transaction and other *deadweight* costs—that is, costs in excess of the additional interest or return payable as implied by MM's risk-return trade-off. Deadweight costs include bid-offer spreads, professional fees, and systems costs. They may also include nonquantifiable strategic fit costs, especially if a potential exposure diverts senior management's focus away from the firm's core business. If anything, derivatives are likely, on a stand-alone basis after factoring in all relevant costs, to decrease overall cashflows and lower firm market value.

Lacking special information or other comparative advantages, market participants should not expect to sustain profitable derivatives trading over the long term. Moreover, in derivatives markets, obtaining any comparative advantage is usually arduous. Most derivatives markets are highly competitive and efficient, making it difficult for any participant consistently to beat the market. Still, as Stulz observes, "the world remains full of corporate executives who are convinced of their own ability to predict future interest rates, exchange rates, and commodity prices."[16] One reason is that, over the short term, it is rarely easy to distinguish skill from luck. Even in efficient markets, the laws of probability dictate that any market participant can experience a gain on any given transaction. Sustainable, long-term profitability, however, is rarely achieved through mere good luck. It requires some market advantage that few nonfinancial firms have. Thus, for most nonfinancial firms, once all risks and direct and indirect costs are considered, "setting up the corporate treasury to trade derivatives is a value-destroying proposition."

USING DERIVATIVES TO REDUCE COSTS OF MARKET IMPERFECTIONS

Financial economists recognize one paramount objective* of value-maximizing firms that use derivatives as "part of overall corporate financial policy."[17] That objective is to minimize potential adverse effects on firm market value of variable cashflows and after-tax earnings. Variability can adversely affect firm value by its "potential to impose 'real' costs on the corporation."[18] Academic finance literature identifies several such costs. Here, we analyze[†] them according to the following taxonomy: (1) higher expected annual tax payments, (2) higher expected costs of financial distress, including bankruptcy, (3) higher compensation and more exacting contractual demands of noninvestor stakeholders, and (4) underinvestment caused by funding shortfalls relative to investment opportunities. Derivatives and other forms of financial risk management can enhance firm value by reducing each of these costs. Before analyzing how they do so, we first review the general effects on firm value of variable cashflows.

Cashflow Variability and Firm Market Value

Firm value is a positive function of expected net cashflows: as those flows increase (decrease), firm value increases (decreases). If cashflow expectations are sensitive to movements in interest rates, exchange rates, commodity prices, or other financial risks, firm market value should be similarly sensitive. We know that, other things being equal, greater variability ordinarily implies higher risk, and risky investments are less valuable than safe ones. It seems, then, that cashflow variability and firm market value

---

*Alternatives to the "standard variance–minimization models" referred to *infra* are discussed in
    Chapter 16. Particularly popular is the use of hedging or risk management to (1) capitalize
    on comparative advantages in particular markets about which firms may have specialized
    information or expertise and (2) transform the nature of a business.
†Consistent with the functional approach taken throughout this book, the ensuing analysis prefers
    illustrations and simple equations to mathematical proofs. Readers interested in the proofs
    should refer to the materials cited in the text, particularly Smith and Stulz, *Determinants of
    Firms' Hedging Policies, supra,* note 17; Froot et al., *Risk Management: Coordinating
    Corporate Investment and Financing Policies, supra,* note 18; and Myers, *Determinants of
    Corporate Borrowing, infra,* Chapter 14, note 10.

ought to be inversely related: that an increase in cashflow variability should decrease firm value. That inverse relationship further suggests the "tantalizing conclusion...that the value of the firm will necessarily rise if exposure [to cashflow variability] is managed. But however appealing, this conclusion does not directly follow."[19]

Modern portfolio theory holds that efficient markets do not reward firms for risk management services that investors can efficiently perform themselves. Cashflow variability is a nonsystematic risk that most investors can diversify away on their own.[20] Likewise, MM theory, with its subsequent extensions, holds that firms cannot decrease their company cost of capital or increase market value merely by reducing nonsystematic risks such as cashflow variability.[21] If a firm wishes to increase its market value through derivatives risk management, modern finance instructs that it must do so for reasons other than mere cashflow stabilization.

Example

Assume that a U.S. public company sources all inputs and manufactures and sells all final product within the United States.[22] The firm has no *direct* currency exposure, because all its costs and revenues are dollar-denominated. The company (USAuto) makes luxury automobiles and faces tough competition at home market from a German exporter, Auto AG. Auto AG has a sizable direct currency exposure: most of its costs are denominated in deutschemarks (DM), while its revenues, most of which are generated in the United States, are mainly in dollars.

The two companies' cars are close substitutes for each other, and aggregate demand for both products has long been constant within relevant price bands. Still, the number of cars sold by each firm, along with each firm's dollar cashflows, is greatly affected by the pricing and output decisions of the other firm: the firms are highly competitive with each other. Pricing and output decisions depend primarily on the dollar-deutschmark exchange rate, which determines relative cost differentials. When the dollar weakens, it reduces the DM value of Auto AG's repatriated U.S. revenues. Auto AG must usually raise prices, reduce its U.S. exports, or both; those actions forfeit sales to USAuto. When the dollar strengthens, repatriated DM revenues increase. Auto AG then often lowers its prices and increases sales, putting competitive price pressure on USAuto. Although USAuto has no direct dollar-deutschmark exposure, it has significant *indirect* exposure, which it is now considering managing more aggressively.

USAuto is contemplating using derivatives to reduce its currency exposure and stabilize its cashflows. USAuto's analysis of its exposure reveals that the firm effectively holds a short dollar position against the DM: its cashflows are inversely related to the dollar's value against the DM; as the dollar strengthens (weakens), USAuto's cashflows decrease (increase). USAuto's currency risk is analogous to that of a forward transaction in which it pays dollars and receives deutschmarks. With that insight, senior management is considering several alternative strategies to establish offsetting long dollar positions (i.e., USAuto receives dollars, pays deutschemarks). Many different types of FX derivatives would work, including swaps, futures, forwards, and individual or combinations of options.

USAuto's goal is to enhance its share price and firm market value by using derivatives to stabilize cashflows. Yet modern finance teaches that the stock market is unlikely to reward USAuto's proposed hedging strategy if it is undertaken merely for such stabilization.[23] An investor that wishes to reduce the currency exposure of USAuto stock can easily purchase any of the multitude of other stocks that benefit from a rising dollar. One obvious strategy is to buy shares of Auto AG. Another possibility is to purchase shares of U.S. firms that import heavily from Germany, or shares of foreign firms whose products are sold in the United States and whose home currencies, compared with the dollar, are closely correlated with the DM. Many investors may also want USAuto's existing exposure. They may use it, for example, to reduce the risk of holding Auto AG shares. If hedging and cashflow stabilization are to enhance USAuto's market value, the strategy must produce something more than mere cashflow stabilization.

COSTS OF MARKET IMPERFECTIONS[24]

Academics advance several theories (often called variance-minimizing models) to explain how reducing cashflow and earnings variability can increase firm value. The theories begin with a recognition that MM's perfect-market assumption sidesteps significant costs that market imperfections, or frictions, impose on variable cashflows.* They show how finan-

---

*In particular, the original MM theory assumes, among other things, that (1) taxes are insignificant, (2) bankruptcy is speedy and costless, (3) contracts are perfectly and costlessly enforceable, and (4) all investors and firm managers have equal, unlimited access to information about a firm both to monitor its compliance with its contracts and to assess its financial condition, risks, and prospects.

cial policy, by reducing cashflow variability, can reduce those costs. The theories do not discard MM. To the contrary, they build on its basic insight that a perfect market would be indifferent to changes in capital structure. With MM as foundation, the theories explore market responses to the reintroduction of various frictions. In so doing, they identify for financial managers the types of imperfections that may afford their firm an opportunity to increase firm value through financial risk management and the use of derivatives. By implication, they also cast doubt on the economics—and, as we revisit in later chapters, the legal validity—of risk management strategies designed to reduce cashflow variability regardless of its effects on firm value.

Before we examine the theories, it helps to illustrate the effects of risk management on cashflow variability. The dotted curve of Figure 13.1 depicts the distribution of a firm's expected annual cashflows without risk management. In contrast, the solid curve represents the same distribution after cashflows have been partially stabilized through risk management. The reduction in variability attributable to risk management explains the greater height and narrower dispersion of the solid curve.

In later chapters, we frequently refer back to Figure 13.1 to show how firms can use derivatives to reduce cashflow variability and the resulting costs of market imperfections inapplicable to MM's perfect market.

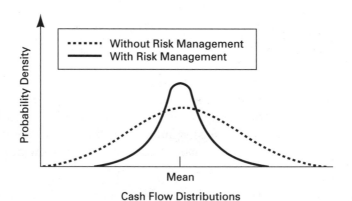

Figure 13.1   Managing cashflow variability.

ENDNOTES: CHAPTER 13

1. Except as otherwise noted, the quotations in this and the following two paragraphs are from Miller, *MM Theory After Thirty Years, supra,* Chapter 11, note 16: 100–103; see, generally, Brealey and Myers, *Principles of Corporate Finance, supra,* Chapter 11, note 10: 447–473; Myers, *The Search for Optimal Capital Structure, supra,* Chapter 11, note 43. The value-invariance proposition, as discussed in Chapter 12, is Proposition I.

2. Franco Modigliani, "MM—Past, Present, Future," *Journal of Economic Perspectives,* 2(4) (Fall 1988) [hereafter, *MM—Past, Present, Future*]: 150.

3. See, generally, *Miller,* MM Theory After Thirty Years, supra, Chapter 11, note 16 (emphasis in original): 100.

4. The quotations in this paragraph are from Miller, *MM Theory After Thirty Years, supra,* Chapter 11, note 16 (emphasis in original): 100–103.

5. See Brealey and Myers, *Principles of Corporate Finance, supra,* Chapter 11, note 10: 321; Henry T. C. Hu, "Risk, Time, and Fiduciary Principles in Corporate Investments," *UCLA Law Review,* 38 (1990) ("Broadly construed, the term 'investment' comprehends any use of current resources to achieve a future return"): 277, 279.

6. See Brealey and Myers, *Principles of Corporate Finance, supra,* Chapter 11, note 10 (noting that in 1958, when Miller and Modigliani developed MM theory, "the capital asset pricing models…and their later extensions that now dominate empirical research in finance had yet to come on the scene"; and after noting that "Proposition I can be proved umpteen different ways," deriving it from CAPM): 103, 465, n. 23, 466; Modigliani, *MM — Past, Present, Future, supra,* note 2 (commenting that "by now, countless alternative proofs of the theorem have been provided"): 150.

7. Stulz, *Rethinking Risk Management, supra,* Chapter 10, note 8: 12.

8. See, e.g., Brealey and Myers, *Principles of Corporate Finance, supra,* Chapter 11, note 10: 217, 454–466.

9. See, e.g., *Id.:* 214–217.

10. See, generally, *Id.:* 213–214; Myers, *The Search for Optimal Capital Structure, supra,* Chapter 11, note 43 ("Increased leverage diverts a larger fraction of the firm's operating income to lenders, and a smaller fraction to stockholders. However, the total going to all investors in the firm must be exactly the same. Lenders and stockholders *considered jointly* receive no more and no less than before"): 145.

11. See, generally, Stulz, *Rethinking Risk Management, supra,* Chapter 10, note 8; Stiglitz, *Why Financial Structure Matters, supra,* Chapter 11, note 16: 122. Note that most of the scholarly work to date has been theoretical, because of the dearth of reliable data. That may change with the SEC's new derivatives disclosure rules, discussed in Chapter 18.

12. See Stulz, *Rethinking Risk Management, supra,* Chapter 10, note 8: 16–17.
13. This and the quotations in the following paragraph are from Myers, *The Search for Optimal Capital Structure, supra,* Chapter 11, note 43: 142–143; see also Brealey and Myers, *Principles of Corporate Finance, supra,* Chapter 11, note 10: 239–270.
14. See, generally, Stulz, *Rethinking Risk Management, supra,* Chapter 10, note 8: 23.
15. See Froot et al., *Risk Management Framework, supra,* Chapter 4, note 2: 93; Brealey and Myers, *Principles of Corporate Finance, supra,* Chapter 11, note 10 (noting that even in costless and completely efficient markets derivatives trading is at best a zero net present value activity): 707.
16. This and the following quotation are from Stulz, *Rethinking Risk Management, supra,* Chapter 10, note 8: 11–12.
17. See, generally, Clifford W. Smith and René M. Stulz, "The Determinants of Firms' Hedging Policies," *Journal of Financial and Quantitative Analysis,* 20 (1985) (noting, among other things: "We treat hedging by corporations simply as one part of the firm's financing decision") [hereafter, *Determinants of Firms' Hedging Policies*]: 391–405.
18. This and the following quotation are from Stulz, *Rethinking Risk Management, supra,* Chapter 10, note 8: 12; see, generally, Brealey and Myers, *Principles of Corporate Finance, supra,* Chapter 11, note 10: 474–510; Smithson et al., *Managing Financial Risk, supra,* Chapter 11, note 28: Chapters 4 and 19; Froot et al., *Risk Management Framework, supra,* Chapter 4, note 2; Kenneth A. Froot, David S. Scharfstein, and Jeremy C. Stein, "Risk Management: Coordinating Corporate Investment and Financing Policies," *Journal of Finance,* 48(5) (December 1993) [hereafter, *Risk Management: Coordinating Corporate Investment and Financing Policies*]: 1629–1658; Deana R. Nance, Clifford W. Smith, Jr., and Charles W. Smithson, "On the Determinants of Corporate Hedging," *Journal of Finance,* 48(1) (March 1993) [hereafter, *Determinants of Corporate Hedging*]; Smith and Stulz, *Determinants of Firms' Hedging Policies, supra,* note 17.
19. Smithson et al., *Managing Financial Risk, supra,* Chapter 11, note 28: 101.
20. See, e.g., Stulz, *Rethinking Risk Management, supra,* Chapter 10, note 8 (noting that "most of a company's interest rate, currency, and commodity price exposures will not increase t he risk of a well-diversified portfolio. Thus, most corporate financial exposures represent 'nonsystematic' or 'diversifiable' risks"): 12; Henry T. C. Hu, "New Financial Products, the Modern Process of Financial Innovation, and the Puzzle of Shareholder Welfare," *Texas Law Review,* 69(6) (May 1991) (noting that a corporation hedging nonsystematic risk is "hurting its shareholders that happen to be diversified:...[such] a shareholder...would generally consider such

corporate behavior to be wasteful") [hereafter, *The Puzzle of Shareholder Welfare*]: 1273–1317, 1308.

21. See, generally, Hu, *Behind the Corporate Hedge, supra,* Chapter 10, note 9 ("In the Modigliani-Miller world, corporate-level hedging cannot increase the firm's value because individual shareholders can engage in hedging on their own if they so desire"): 44; Ross, *Comment on MM Theory, supra,* Chapter 11, note 16 ("even if the random characteristics of a firm's cashflows differ dramatically from those of other firms in the economy, nevertheless the idiosyncratic components of the cashflow will be valueless"): 128–131; see also Christopher L. Culp, Dean Furbush, and Barbara T. Kavanaugh, "Structured Debt and Corporate Risk Management," *Journal of Applied Corporate Finance,* 7(3) (Fall 1994) ("reductions in the variability of earnings or cashflow achieved by hedging firm-specific price risks do not add value *in and of themselves*" (emphasis in original)): 73; see also Nance et al., *Determinants of Corporate Hedging, supra,* note 18 ("portfolio theory implies that given well-diversified investors, corporate hedging does not benefit shareholders by reducing the firm's cost of capital"): 268.

22. See, generally, John Pringle, "A Look at Indirect Foreign Currency Exposure," *Journal of Applied Corporate Finance,* 8(3) (Fall 1995) (analyzing detailed examples of indirect currency exposures): 75–81; John J. Pringle and Robert A. Connolly, "The Nature and Causes of Foreign Currency Exposure," *Journal of Applied Corporate Finance,* 6(3) (Fall 1993) ("*Indirect* exposure occurs when the firm has a supplier, customer, or competitor that is exposed" (emphasis in original)) [hereafter, *Foreign Currency Exposure*]: 61–72; see also Trevor S. Harris, Nahum D. Melumad, and Toshi Shibano, "An Argument Against Hedging by Matching the Currencies of Costs and Revenues," *Journal of Applied Corporate Finance,* 9(3) (Fall 1996) (critically examining the practice, in imperfectly competitive markets, of "matching currency footprints," i.e., altering sourcing and selling patterns to match the currencies of costs and revenues) [hereafter, *An Argument Against Matching Currencies*]: 90–97; Dennis E. Logue, "When Theory Fails: Globalization as a Response to the (Hostile) Market for Foreign Exchange," *Journal of Applied Corporate Finance,* 8(3) (Fall 1995) (advocating such matching): 39–48.

23. See, e.g., Smith and Stulz, *Determinants of Firms' Hedging Policies, supra,* note 17 (MM theory implies that in perfect markets "if a firm chooses to change its hedging policy, investors who hold claims issued by the firm can change their holdings of risky assets to offset any change in the firm's hedging policy, leaving the distribution of their future wealth unaffected"): 392.

24. See, generally, Brealey and Myers, *Principles of Corporate Finance, supra,* Chapter 11, note 10: Chapter 18.

Using Derivatives to Reduce the Costs of Market Imperfections

One of the biggest costs in business is variability.

Norbert Ore, Sonoco Products Co.
Wall Street Journal, *August 18, 1997*

No sane lawyer attempts to write a contract requiring management to "abstain from suboptimal [investment] decisions."

Stewart C. Myers, M.I.T.
Determinants of Corporate Borrowing,
1977

A number of theories are available to explain how derivatives, by reducing cashflow and earnings variability, can increase firm value. All these variance-minimizing models build on the recognition that the perfect-market assumption of Miller-Modigliani (MM) theory fails to address the real costs that market imperfections impose on variable cashflows. Often firms can, by reducing cashflow variability, reduce the costs of market imperfections.

USING DERIVATIVES TO REDUCE TAXES[1]

One way risk management can add value is by reducing excess tax liabilities attributable to volatile pretax earnings. The logic of the argument is plain: because of the structure of a tax system (other things being equal), volatility of pretax incomes can lead to higher expected taxes. As shown in Figure 14.1, the structural feature that causes higher expected taxes is the *convexity* of a firm's effective tax schedule. In other words, as a firm's pretax income rises, its marginal tax rate also rises.* In Figure 14.1, the

---

*A famous mathematical expression called Jensen's Inequality reveals that the same logic also applies to the opposite situation. In other words, the expected value of a random variable with a *concave* function "is smaller than the value of the function evaluated at the expected value of the random variable." In terms of our example, if effective tax schedules were concave and not convex, that would mean that as pretax income rises, the marginal tax rate would *decline*. See Smith and Stulz, *Determinants of Firms' Hedging Policies, supra,* Chapter 13, note 17: 400–401; see also Merton, *Continuous-Time Finance, supra,* Chapter 1, note 26: 21, 326.

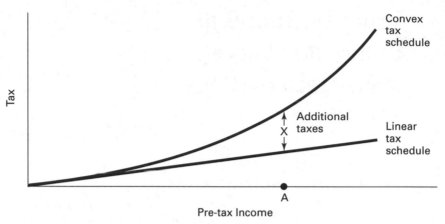

Figure 14.1   Convexity in the tax function.

additional tax paid because of convexity corresponds to the region between the convex and linear tax schedules. The distance, X, represents the additional tax attributable to convexity for a pretax income of A.

In the United States (and many other countries), convexity is caused by two factors. The first is the progressivity of the corporate tax code. "Statutory progressivity" can increase significantly the marginal effective tax rates (particularly for small, growing firms) as taxable incomes increase. In practice, however, the range of statutory progressivity is modest. The pretax incomes of many large, profitable U.S. firms quickly reach the constant, maximum marginal rate and would, without more, effectively be taxed at that rate. In that case, convexity would be little more than a minor detail for most large, profitable firms. In practice, however, a second factor slows the climb to the maximum rate, reintroducing convexity in the process. Namely, under the U.S. tax code, various "tax preference items (for example, tax loss carry forwards, foreign tax credits, and investment tax credits...make the effective tax schedule convex."[2] When that happens, the firm again faces higher expected taxes with volatile pretax cashflows.

Interest rate, foreign exchange rate, and commodity price volatility contribute to the cashflow variability of many firms. Firms whose cashflows vary widely as a result of such exposures may be able to use derivatives to stabilize their earnings and lower their expected taxes. Generally, the benefits of risk management are more pronounced (1) the greater the convexity of a firm's effective tax schedule and (2) the more volatile the

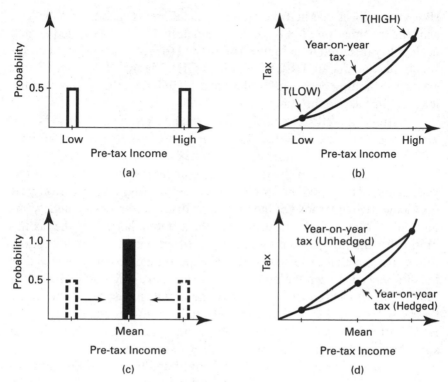

Figure 14.2   Reducing taxes with risk management.

firm's pretax earnings. To see how risk management achieves these benefits, consider the highly stylized example depicted in Figure 14.2.[3]

Assume HLCo's annual pretax income is subject, among other
things, to significant interest rate and FX exposures, all of which are fully
hedgeable.* As shown in Figure 14.2(a), the firm expects pretax income,
unhedged, to have either of two values—high or low—each of which is
equally likely. As shown in Figure 14.2(b), both values plot in the convex
region of HLCo's effective tax schedule. Over a large number of years,

---

*As mentioned in Chapter 1, the academic literature of finance often uses the term *hedging* generi-
cally to refer to all three forms of risk management: the reduction of risk by (1) shedding its
source by converting to a riskless asset, (2) diversifying away its nonsystematic aspects, or
(3) insuring against loss. See, e.g., Smith and Stulz, *Determinants of Firms' Hedging
Policies, supra,* Chapter 13, note 15 ("we define hedging as the acquisition of financial
assets that reduce the variance of the firm's payoffs"): 399. For simplicity, we occasionally
use the term *hedging* in its generic sense.

HLCo can expect that half the time its annual pretax income will be low, and half the time it will be high. Consequently, HLCo's expected annual tax liability (referred to in Figure 14.2(b) and (d) as "year-on-year tax") is simply the average of T(LOW) and T(HIGH). Figure 14.2(b) shows that average as plotting between T(LOW) and T(HIGH), at the midpoint of the diagonal line above the curve.

Assume that HLCo's management is considering whether to hedge. Treasury has prepared the data shown in Figures 14.2(c) and (d). Figure 14.2(c) shows that when fully hedged, pretax income can have only a single value equal to mean. Figure 14.2(d) compares expected, or year-on-year, taxes for a hedged pretax income of mean, designated "year-on-year tax (hedged)," with those of the unhedged distribution, designated "year-on-year tax (unhedged)." Inspection of the different heights of the tax liabilities for the hedged and unhedged distributions shows that hedging offers HLCo a chance to save taxes. If expected tax savings, depicted as the difference between the two heights, exceed hedging costs, HLCo can increase its after-tax income. Equally important, investors could not on their own have achieved the same tax reduction. Because hedging by HLCo offers investors a benefit they cannot achieve on their own, it should increase the firm's value.

Figure 14.3 is derived from the hedged and unhedged distributions of Figure 13.1. It shows the benefits of risk management to a firm with an expected cashflow distribution that is more realistic than HLCo's. Recall that in Figure 13.1 the wider, flatter dotted curve depicted an unhedged distribution and the narrower, steeper solid curve depicted a partially

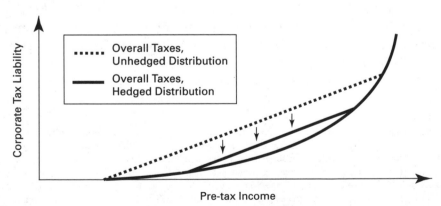

Figure 14.3   Reducing taxes on normally distributed cashflows.

hedged distribution. Hedging in Figure 13.1 narrowed the width of the cashflow distribution. It did not, however, compress the distribution into a single point, as with HLCo in Figure 14.2(c). Figure 14.3 shows that although partial hedging lowers expected taxes, it still leaves a firm's expected tax liability above the convex tax schedule.

REDUCING DEADWEIGHT COSTS OF FINANCIAL DISTRESS; TRADE-OFF THEORY

Another way that derivatives can increase firm value is by reducing the *current* costs of potential future financial distress. These costs depend on (1) the probability of distress and (2) the present value of the costs of distress, should it occur.[4] The most obvious distress costs are the direct and indirect costs of bankruptcy. Direct bankruptcy costs include court fees and legal, accounting, financial advisory, and other professional fees. Indirect costs include the opportunity costs of lost operating and investment flexibility while under bankruptcy court supervision; they also include the inefficiencies and difficulties arising because of senior management's distraction from its normal management and long-term strategic planning responsibilities.

Finance theory posits that the mere possibility of financial distress imposes deadweight costs on a firm. Many of these costs, such as lost strategic opportunities, are incapable of precise measurement. Direct inference from trading prices of publicly held stock is unreliable, because many factors besides distress costs determine stock prices. Still, despite measurement problems, the costs of distress are real and grow as a firm's risk of bankruptcy increases. If bankruptcy risks are at all due to hedgeable exposures, a firm may be able to use derivatives to reduce those risks. If so, derivatives may, depending on their costs, materially increase firm value, even when bankruptcy is not imminent.

Academic literature defines the costs of financial distress in a way that may at first seem peculiar. The peculiarity is that, although many important distress costs are obscure or counterintuitive, MM and CAPM teach that other costs that appear important may not affect firm value. Moreover, the phrase "financial distress" connotes a firm that is on the brink of bankruptcy, if not already insolvent. Yet distress costs can impact any levered firm, even when its financial condition is healthy. Because distress costs are peculiar, it is helpful to identify and examine them carefully before we look into how derivatives can reduce them.

Leverage and Interest Tax Shields

Originally, MM assumed away all tax-related market imperfections. Unfortunately, that assumption cast doubt on the theory's usefulness, because with it, the theory seemed to ignore a major corporate finance issue. Given the assumption, MM could not explain why, despite huge potential tax savings from corporate borrowing—up to 50 cents on the dollar in the late 1950s—many profitable firms borrowed little. As Miller freely acknowledges, the corporate tax system is one respect in which everyone agreed that, notwithstanding MM, capital structure and debt policy really do matter.[5]

In the United States, the tax savings from corporate debt result from the Internal Revenue Code's system of "double taxation" of most corporate net income. Income already taxed at the corporate level is again taxed when paid out to stockholders, usually as dividends. So dividends are effectively taxed twice. But interest payments on corporate debt are taxed only once, as income to the lender (often, a bondholder). Interest payments escape corporate-level taxation; they are deductible from the corporation's gross income in determining the corporation's net income and tax liability.

By 1963, the potential tax savings from deductible interest payments compelled Modigliani and Miller to publish a "tax correction" (MMC) of their original paper.[6] The sheer size of potential *interest tax shields* eventually persuaded them that firm market value could not be totally independent of leverage. They concluded that, on the basis of their model, many profitable firms should be able to realize greater after-tax income with more debt in their capital structures. According to Miller, "under conditions which can by no means be dismissed out of hand as implausible, [MMC] showed that the...optimal capital structure might be all debt!"[7]

MMC provoked more controversy than the original theory. It suggested that unlevered, highly rated firms were leaving "too much of their stockholders' money on the table in the form of unnecessary corporate income tax payments." Initial attacks focused on the increased riskiness of levered shares. Those attacks failed, because both the original Proposition II and the MMC version accounted explicitly for the risks of leverage.

MMC also "dutifully acknowledged" the more difficult argument that increased leverage heightened other "well-known" costs of debt. Among them are the renegotiation costs of bankruptcy, especially when numerous claimants are involved, and other "second-order" transaction costs, such as those of monitoring and enforcing loan agreement covenants. Yet that argument also seemed to fall short. The costs it identified seemed unable satisfactorily to account for the highly conservative capital structures prevalent throughout U.S. industry. Despite enormous potential tax savings, debt ratios in the late 1950s were not much higher than they had been, say, in low-tax and zero-tax periods of the early 1900s. MMC seemed to carry the unflattering suggestion that, given unexamined assumptions about the perils of debt, many unlevered, highly rated firms were wasting potentially huge tax savings that could benefit shareholders.

Offsetting Costs of Debt

MMC posed what Miller calls an "unhappy dilemma": either firms did not appreciate the extent to which they were overpaying taxes or the MMC model had missed "something major." Since 1963, academics have devoted prodigious energies to solving that dilemma. Their efforts have been fruitful, yielding deeper insight into many formerly baffling costs of leverage. The theory of corporate finance now offers a more satisfying explanation of why few firms choose target debt ratios as high as those predicted by the tax-adjusted Proposition II. Specifically, the theory now views leverage decisions as complex *trade-offs* between the tax benefits of debt and the offsetting costs—some obvious, some not—of financial distress.

A major theoretical breakthrough came in 1973 with the publication of Black and Scholes' famous option pricing paper. As noted earlier, the paper contained the "qualitative insight" that, in general, corporate liabilities can be viewed as combinations of simple options. Quickly, that insight helped academic researchers clarify many previously little understood sources of distress costs. We revisit the details and application of that insight in Chapter 15. For present purposes, a brief overview of the effects of those costs, along with a mention of important alternative explanations for the formerly elusive costs of leverage, is useful.

Alternative Explanations for Low Leverage

In addition to trade-off theory, other arguments partially explain the "gross underleveraging" criticized by MMC. One is the availability of tax shields other than interest deductions. Among them are loss carryforwards, accelerated depreciation, and foreign and investment tax credits. Moreover, firms view interest and other shields as valuable only if they anticipate future profits to shield; deductions are useless to unprofitable firms. Tax losses can often be carried forward up to 15 years, but their effect surely cannot be that powerful: the present value of a tax deduction erodes quickly the longer its use is delayed. A tax dollar saved today is considerably more valuable than the present value of a tax dollar saved 15, 5, or even 3 years from now.

Financial economists have also studied the effects of leverage on the interaction between personal and corporate taxes. When both levels of taxation are considered jointly, much of the advantage of corporate leverage vanishes. Individual shareholders, through capital gains treatment or deferred recognition of gain, can often greatly reduce their effective tax rates on equity income. Interest income, however, is usually taxed in the year it is received and at ordinary income rates, which tend to be higher than capital gains rates. Prior to the Tax Reform Act of 1986, many tax advantages of corporate debt were clearly offset by favorable tax treatment of equity income. Since 1986, however, the potential benefits of leverage for healthy, profitable firms have undeniably increased.[8] Still, their exact extent is unclear.*

Illustration of Trade-off Theory.[9]

A central goal of any financial manager is to find a capital structure that maximizes firm value. From the preceding discussion, we can conceptualize a levered firm's market value in terms of a simple equation:

$$V_L = V_U + PV(tax\ shield) - PV(COFD) \quad \text{(Equation 14.1)}$$

where V_L is the total value of the firm when levered
V_U is the total value of the firm, unlevered, or capitalized only with equity
$PV(tax\ shield)$ is the present value of the interest tax shield
$PV(COFD)$ is the present value of offsetting costs of financial distress

Equation 14.1 can be rearranged to show that leverage increases firm value only if the value of the interest tax shield exceeds the costs of financial distress. First, Equation 14.1 implies that

$$V_L - V_U = PV(tax\ shield) - PV(COFD)$$

---

*Several more explanations are available. For references to some, and for a more elaborate discussion of trade-off theory, see Myers, *Determinants of Corporate Borrowing, infra,* note 10.

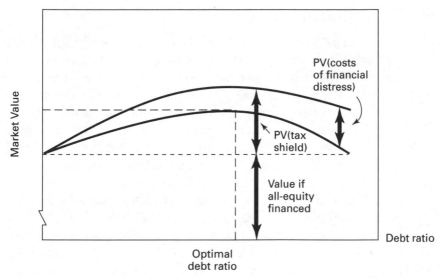

Figure 14.4   Tradeoff theory. (*Source: Richard A. Brealey and Stewart C. Myers, Principles of Corporate Finance. Copyright© 1996; reproduced with permission of The McGraw-Hill Companies.*)

According to the equation, a firm is more valuable levered ($V_L > V_U$) only if the present value of the interest tax shield is greater than that of distress costs [$PV(tax\ shield) > PV(COFD)$]. Conversely, the firm is more valuable unlevered ($V_L > V_U$) only if the present value of distress costs exceeds the present value of the interest tax shield [$PV(tax\ shield) < PV(COFD)$].

Figure 14.4 illustrates that for most firms moderate debt increases firm value above what it would be with all-equity financing. Too much debt, however, can be costly. As an all-equity firm begins to borrow, its interest tax shield should easily exceed its distress costs. As leverage increases, however, distress costs grow in relative significance, because the odds of bankruptcy increase. Stated differently, "the incremental tax advantage of borrowing declines as more debt is issued and interest tax shields become less certain."[10] Eventually, borrowing reaches an optimal point where the disadvantages of additional distress costs exactly balance, or offset, the tax advantage of additional borrowing. Beyond that point, the incremental increase in distress costs associated with any additional debt will exceed the corresponding incremental tax benefit. In Figure 14.4, that point is the "optimal debt ratio" lying along the horizontal axis. Once that optimal ratio is reached, any increase in leverage reduces firm value.

REDUCING "STAKEHOLDER" COSTS[11]*

Diversification enables most investors to manage the nonsystematic risks of their portfolios. Given such an efficient risk management tool, investors do not demand, nor can they expect to earn, extra compensation for bearing a security's nonsystematic risks. The costs of effectively eliminating nonsystematic risks are, to well-diversified investors in efficient markets, negligible. In contrast, many other interested parties are exposed to specific risks with little or no ability to manage those exposures. These parties, called *stakeholders,* include managers, directors, employees, suppliers, and customers.[†] Most stakeholders are vital to a firm's success and assume nonsystematic risks as an incident to their business relationships with the firm.

Because they are presumably risk-averse, stakeholders demand extra compensation to induce them to bear the firm-specific risks of their business relationships. That compensation is costly and borne by the firm, decreasing its market value. Alternatively, the firm may decide to use derivatives to manage the underlying firm-specific exposures and reduce the corresponding costs. If the savings realized from decreased stakeholder compensation exceed overall derivatives costs, the use of the products will increase net cashflows and firm market value.

Stakeholder Exposures; Firm Costs

Managers and employees

Few managers or employees can realistically manage the specific risks inherent in employment by a risky firm. The reasons are clear. A logical solution might be to "hedge" or "diversify" those risks by simultaneously holding multiple positions with unaffiliated firms. Few senior executives could successfully manage the resulting workload and potential conflicts of interests. For other employees, that solution is also unlikely to succeed. Few workers would hold multiple jobs for any reason other than to augment their income or acquire new skills.

Generally, a manager or employee seriously concerned about a firm's financial future either leaves the firm or demands greater compensation

---

*See also the HealthyCo discussion in Chapter 11 (Figure 11.1).
†Investors with most of their wealth tied up in closely held firms are in similar positions to the stakeholders discussed here. Communities and states in which firms are located also have important interests and therefore are often important stakeholders.

(including equity incentives) for the risks of staying. Risky firms bear the costs of either losing managers and other employees or having to offer higher compensation to retain them. The alternative is likely to be either hiring less qualified personnel or settling for less satisfactory work product and lower levels of motivation and commitment from qualified personnel.

Suppliers

Suppliers have better opportunities to minimize firm-specific risks. Many do so by maintaining expansive customer bases. However, for many firms that is but a partial solution. Firms frequently rely upon key relationships with significant customers or clients, and often products and services are customized to meet their particular needs. If so, those products and services may not be easily repackaged and resold to other buyers upon the loss of a major customer or client. In many cases, a significant customer's or client's failure can strike a hard financial blow to a supplier. The impact of a firm's demise can be onerous, especially if it occurs while the firm owes large receivables to a supplier.

To limit their potential exposures, suppliers tighten credit terms extended to risky firms by limiting the amounts those firms can purchase on credit and by shortening the periods during which firms earn discounts for prompt payment. Both actions connote real credit costs, because they deprive a firm of valuable free credit. The shorter the discount period or smaller the credit line, the greater the loss. If a firm is highly risky, suppliers may even refuse to ship prior to actual receipt of payment or of satisfactory assurances (e.g., letters of credit or guarantees) of payment. Such assurances are costly.[12]

Customers and clients

Customers of risky firms maintain access to alternative suppliers, because the loss of a major supplier can cause both temporary disruption and real "switching" costs. Consider the case of a customer invested heavily in the technology of a firm that subsequently fails. After the failure, the customer may have to convert to a new technology. The costs of converting would probably include out-of-pocket expenses for new hardware and software. More damaging is the potential that a major change in technology will drain revenues and weaken competitive positioning by interrupting or otherwise hampering business. If a failed supplier's technology is important to a firm's operations, the costs of substituting and integrating a new system into existing operations may be quite high.

Customers and clients anticipate those costs and factor them into decisions on whether to do business with a risky firm and, if so, the terms on which they will do business. For a risky firm to induce customers to enter into long-term relationships, it may have to offer significant price concessions or other benefits, such as free servicing and product upgrades. If a firm's product would be "mission critical" or otherwise strategically important to a client or customer, even substantial concessions may be inadequate.

Derivatives Risk Management Solutions

Derivatives help reduce stakeholder costs by enhancing a firm's ability to manage unwanted risks. Attendant to many firms' primary lines of business are undesired financial exposures. Derivatives can add value by enabling firms to shed or reduce unwanted exposures, thus tailoring the set of exposures they retain to those that they are best able, on the basis of principles of comparative advantage, to manage. Few nonfinancial firms enjoy any comparative advantage in bearing FX or interest rate risks. Similarly, with the exception of major commodity merchants, few nonfinancial firms enjoy any comparative advantage in managing commodity price risks.

Many firms whose stakeholders believe in their products and services but worry about discrete financial exposures might use derivatives to reduce stakeholder costs. Consider a U.S. customer that is excited about a technology firm's new suite of products and contemplating entering into a large purchase contract. The customer may fear the firm's FX exposures—for example, its vulnerability to any significant short-term weakening of the U.S. dollar against the Japanese yen. The customer may consider such a dollar decline, which would have a materially adverse impact on the technology firm, unlikely but possible. If so, the firm might consider using derivatives to manage its FX risks over the life of the customer's contract. It might, for example, shed some of the risks through FX options entitling it to purchase yen at a preset dollar price. If exchange rate volatility is high, option prices may seem steep; given the options' strategic value in getting the new customer contract, those prices may be cheap.

Implications of Modern Finance

The inability of stakeholders to manage their firm-specific risks can cause conflicts of interests between stakeholders and investors. As noted earlier, diversified investors consider the management of specific risks wasteful, whereas stakeholders strongly prefer to have those risks managed. "The bankruptcy of an airline company, for example, might be a disaster for its employees and managers who lose their jobs but a matter of indifference to its investors who own shares in other airline companies that obtain the bankruptcy company's routes."[13] The conflict arises because "shareholders as a class want managers to take more risk than they might otherwise be willing to [take]." As between stakeholders and stockholders, stockholders are the "superior risk bearers."

The resolution of the conflict lies in the recognition that the conflict is more apparent than real. Stakeholders demand extra compensation for bearing firm-specific risks, and the costs of that compensation increase the firm's costs and reduce its revenues and profits: adverse supply contracts and trade credit terms increase the costs of sales; customer discounts and other incentives lower revenues; higher salaries and wages increase costs of doing business. All these factors combine to strip out operating cashflows and lower firm market value. A decline in firm market value reduces stockholder wealth.

Many firms enjoy economies of scale and other comparative advantages that enable them to manage specific risks efficiently on behalf of stakeholders. Many advantages result from the institutional nature of derivatives markets. Economies of scale further enable many firms to obtain better pricing for risk management products than that available to individuals and small firms. Economies of scale also enable large firms to surmount more efficiently the investment barriers to establishing and maintaining adequate internal risk management controls and infrastructures. Through corporate risk management, firms can furnish stakeholders with valuable risk management services and in the process lower their own costs of transacting with stakeholders. "Thus, as long as the reduction in compensation of managers and employees and other suppliers plus the increased revenues from customers exceed the costs of hedging, hedging increases the value of the firm."[14] Because it is not redundant, such risk management can benefit investors without violating the precepts of MM or modern portfolio theory.

REDUCING COSTS OF SUBOPTIMAL INVESTMENTS

Cashflow variability can undermine the investment strategies of rational, value-maximizing firms in two basic ways: by increasing funding costs and by decreasing investment returns. To avoid the increased costs, many firms cut back investment spending. Yet such a move often leads to systematic underinvestment as compared with a firm's investment opportunities. Alternatively, firms may try to increase their returns by stabilizing investment spending. Yet few firms' investment opportunities long remain constant; most fluctuate, and with varying predictability. Because of fluctuating investment opportunities, stable spending sometimes leads to underinvestment and other times to overinvestment.

A combination of varying cashflows and fluctuating investment opportunities can throw a firm's supply of investment funds out of alignment with its investment demand. The resulting misalignment can induce a firm systematically to underinvest or overinvest compared with its valuable opportunities. Each practice is suboptimal and may diminish a firm's market value. Derivatives are efficient tools for managing cashflow variability caused by, among other things, interest rate, exchange rate, and commodity price fluctuations. If a firm's cashflows vary as a result of those external factors, derivatives may enable the firm to better align its supply of and demand for investment funds. Derivatives may significantly reduce the harmful effects of the firm's cashflow variability on its investment practices. To see why, revisiting basic MM insights is useful.

MM Overview: Derivatives as "Enabling" Value-Enhancing Investing.[15]

MM teaches that firm value is created on the left side of the balance sheet through value-enhancing investments, or those with a positive net present value (NPV). Further, according to MM's value-invariance proposition, financial policy, or decisions about how to fund investments, would be irrelevant in a perfect market; the source of funds would not affect the operating cashflows that determine a firm's market value. Whether a firm funds investments with new debt or fresh equity or reinvestment of retained earnings would be a matter of indifference to investors.

In real markets, however, access to external funds is often highly imperfect. Two types of market imperfections are most troublesome. The first are *information asymmetries,* or disparities in the relevant firm-specific information available to firm management and that available to outside investors. The second are imperfections inherent in the *contracting process.* If not for market imperfections, the supply of external funds available to a firm would be perfectly elastic; it could instantly expand or contract in response to the firm's changing funding needs. In real markets, supplies of external funds can be quite inelastic.

Market imperfections impose direct and indirect deadweight costs on firms seeking external funding. Rather than incur those costs, firms prefer to fund investments from internally generated cashflows, meaning retained earnings. Unfortunately, internal funding can be vulnerable to such "external factors" as fluctuating exchange rates, interest rates, and commodity prices. External factors can disrupt supplies of internal cash or lower supplies to an amount insufficient to fund a firm's preferred, or optimal, investment strategy. Either way, the firm has a shortage of internal funding for its positive NPV investments.

According to Froot, Scharfstein, and Stein, "simple accounting" dictates that, when confronting a shortage of internal cash, a firm has two choices: cut investment spending or raise funds externally. Given the direct and indirect costs of external funding—costs that in real markets can be reduced but never eliminated—most firms choose to cut investment spending. Many make such cuts even though doing so may result in *underinvestment* that compromises long-term strategy. Or, to guard against funding shortfalls that lead to underinvestment, firms may engage in the opposite practice, *overinvestment,* which has its own pitfalls.

Costs of underinvestment

Underinvestment means that a firm is rejecting valuable investment opportunities and scaling back investment spending. Doing so reduces the demand for investment funds and the concomitant risk that a firm will, at least in the short run, encounter a funding shortfall. Yet lowering investment spending does nothing to redress the underlying imbalance of funding supply and demand. More ominously, it may encourage a firm to forgo valuable investments regularly. If so, the firm's expected long-term cashflows and, most likely, its market value will decrease. The problem is particularly acute for firms whose cashflow variability and hence investment spending is uncorrelated with the frequency or magnitude of valuable investment opportunities.

Underinvestment refers, at a minimum, to a firm's failure to maintain adequate funding for future discretionary outlays essential to maintaining short-term competitive positioning. Most firms try to keep pace with ever-improving industry standards in operational effectiveness, which "means performing similar activities *better* than rivals perform them."[16] That requires regular spending not only for maintenance of plant, property, and equipment but also to match rivals' improvements in technology, training, advertising, and research and development. All this makes sense, because "in a competitive industry the firm should have to work hard simply to keep up."[17]

Underinvestment also refers, more fundamentally, to the failure to fund future discretionary investments needed to further long-term strategic positioning. Long-term success depends upon a firm's willingness to invest in the numerous functions essential to preserving and furthering strategic advantages. Most firms' success depends on an ability to outperform their rivals in the host of activities that together constitute organizational advantages or strategic fit. Over the long term, firms outperform competitors only when they establish strategic advantages that they can continue to preserve and deepen. Doing so requires constant, ongoing investment.

Costs of overinvestment

Overinvestment refers to the retention of funds for which a firm has no immediate need or profitable use. Retaining excess funds may preserve a firm's ability to exploit unpredictable business opportunities in a timely manner as they arise. Yet although this strategy preserves flexibility, it can also undermine efficiency and profitability. Often, the best use of excess funds is to return them to investors through debt repayments, dividends, or stock repurchases. Otherwise, firms must put the funds to use somehow, rather than leave them idle. Often, firms temporarily invest in cash equivalents, such as U.S. Treasury securities.

Cash equivalents pay returns below most firms' costs of capital. They are low-yield, highly marketable securities that are issued by government agencies or highly rated corporations and that pay yields at or slightly above risk-free rates. Investing in cash equivalents may be prudent, especially if a firm needs cash on hand to pay invoiced or anticipated expenses and extra funds to cover unforeseen items. Alternatively, the firm may simply be temporarily undecided about how best to use the funds. Yet as a policy matter, such purchases reduce a firm's overall profitability. Firms are in business to take risks, not avoid them. Risk-free returns will satisfy few investors. Any stockholder, for example, content to invest in U.S. Treasury bills can surely do so more efficiently on its own or through investment vehicles structured specifically for that purpose. Investors buy stocks to earn returns above risk-free rates.

Rather than invest excess funds in cash equivalents, some firms may be tempted to invest them in ways that foster organizational inefficiencies. A firm may, for example, make value-destroying acquisitions or create unnecessary executive perks. Besides providing low returns, holding significant excess funds may enable managers to "indulge an easy or glamorous corporate lifestyle."[18] Alternatively, it may encourage a firm to undertake unsound corporate acquisitions. Generally, excess funds can lead to organizational inefficiencies and otherwise harm competitive strategy. Therefore, overinvestment is a potentially serious drawback of excess cash.[19] However excess funds are used, their retention can diminish firm value.

As noted earlier, Porter explains that an essential aspect of senior management's function is "defining and communicating the company's unique position, making trade-offs, and forging fit among activities." Senior management's choice of what not to do, and by extension what *not* to invest in, is as important as choices about what to do or to invest in. Corporate leaders must set limits, including limits on investments.

Derivatives as "competitive weapons"

Both underinvestment and overinvestment are either caused, or exacerbated, by cashflow variability. In real markets, a key to maximizing firm value and avoiding the hazards of suboptimal investing is matching a firm's internal cashflows with its need for investment funding. Internal cash, drawn from retained earnings, is cheaper and has a lower implied cost of capital than external funds. Consequently, internal cash is a superior source of investment capital. Froot, Scharfstein, and Stein emphasize that internal cash can be a "competitive weapon" enabling firms to achieve their preferred investment states.[20] Derivatives, and risk management generally, reduce the variability of cashflows and enhance a firm's ability to match internal flows with investment needs. By helping ensure that a firm has adequate internal cash to fund its preferred investment strategy, derivatives also facilitate value-enhancing investments. They, too, are competitive weapons.

Example: cashflow variability and investment targets

Assume that a closely held U.S. exporter maintains a steady sales volume. Yet it is in a declining industry and has been forced consistently to lower prices, putting pressure on profit margins. To restore its former profitability, the firm is considering a strategically advantageous new line of business. The new business will require lots of funding over the next three to five years to pay for—among other things—product development, recruiting, marketing, and labor. Management is formulating an investment strategy for the new business. The firm prides itself on funding new investments from retained earnings. It uses bank credit sparingly and has no desire to go public.

A threshhold issue for management is the size of the new investment program, or the targeted level of investment spending. Although it has identified a preferred size program, management is uncertain whether retained earnings will be sufficient to fund it. Management realizes that too large a program may require outside funding, especially given treasury's warning that too great a dependence on retained earnings is risky. Management's preference, then, is to limit the size of the program, at least in its early phases, to one the firm can safely fund entirely from retained earnings. Management has so informed treasury. It has also asked for treasury's recommendations on an optimal program and whether to manage any related financial exposures.

Treasury projects that the firm will have, on average, just the right amount of retained earnings over the next five years to fund the maximum-size program. Yet cashflows and retained earnings, particularly during the first year, which should be the riskiest, will depend on several volatile exchange rates. Treasury is confident that the rates will remain within acceptable ranges, at least during the early years of the program. Still, historical volatility suggests that rates will fluctuate, with potentially dramatic spikes, throughout the five years. Because any fluctuation will directly affect operating cashflows and retained earnings, treasury is conservative. It recommends that the firm undertake only 65% of the maximum program. It further suggests that the firm purchase a few deeply out-of-the-money currency swaptions (options on currency swaps). Swaptions are OTC transactions that could be customized to be exercisable, for example, at any time over the first year of the program. They could, if exercised, give rise to currency swaps at favorable rates and with terms coextensive with the remaining life of the program. Alternatively, the firm may wish to purchase FX options. If these steps are supported by a strong derivatives strategy, treasury estimates that the firm can safely increase the program 75% to 80% of its maximum size. The following helps explain treasury's reasoning.

Using Derivatives to Lower Funding Costs

Earlier we noted that variable cashflows can undermine otherwise sound investment strategies by increasing funding costs and decreasing investment returns. Shortly we will examine how firms can use derivatives to reduce funding costs. First, however, it is important to review two major sources of external funding costs. The sources are two market imperfections, or frictions, that would not arise in MM's perfect market.

"Pecking order" theory of funding preferences; costly external funds

In an MM market firms could, for many reasons, instantly adjust their supplies of external funds to offset temporary imbalances between supplies of internal funds and investment demand. For example, the value of an investment would be verifiable by outsiders independently of information supplied by management. With complete information, markets could set appropriate risk-adjusted prices for securities and contracting parties could easily agree on all nonprice terms. Moreover, a firm's compliance with its contractual obligations would be objectively observable and could be costlessly monitored by outsiders. The prospect of a breach would matter little, because contracts would be perfectly and costlessly enforceable.[21]

MM's assumptions permit the conclusion that in a perfect market firms would be indifferent among alternative financing sources for positive NPV investments. A firm could expect fluctuating cashflows to cause temporary imbalances between supplies of internally generated funds and investment demand. No matter. Those imbalances need not affect the firm's investment strategy. If an investment were valuable, the firm could instantly adjust its external funding to offset any internal cash shortfall. Moreover, it could do so without incurring deadweight funding costs. Interest rates and returns on external funds would have to reflect the riskiness of repayment obligations, but they would involve no transaction fees or other costs.

In real markets things are different. Persistent funding imbalances driven largely by varying cashflows create a constant need to adjust supplies of external funds. However, market frictions make adjustments costly. Information asymmetries and limitations inherent in the contracting process (both discussed more fully below) impose deadweight costs on any change in external funds. The costs differ according to the funding source. To reduce deadweight costs, most firms refrain from frequent adjustments. Moreover, given the cost differentials among funding sources, when firms do adjust supplies of external funds they do so according to a distinct *pecking order* of funding preferences.

Specifically, to finance new investments, firms draw first on the cheapest source, retained earnings, second on debt, and, finally, on the most expensive source, external equity. As a firm draws from more expensive sources, funding costs grow. Rather than incur the comparatively higher costs of external equity, many firms with unused debt capacity will borrow from banks and other lenders or issue debt securities. Others, however, take the more radical step of cutting investment spending. One study found that firms cut capital expenditures by 35 cents for every dollar reduction in internal cashflow.[22] Many cuts in investment spending surely are warranted and improve organizational efficiency. Others, however, may imply a trade-off between the firm's current financial condition and its long-term competitive positioning.

Agency costs, generally

A clear understanding of how derivatives help ensure adequate cash for making value-enhancing investments requires knowledge of the causes of funding imbalances. That, in turn, requires consideration of the nature of the modern corporation.[23] A chief benefit of the modern corporate form is that it separates ownership and management functions.[24] Ideally, the separation promotes economic efficiency for the good of all concerned. It enables stockholders, who are a firm's owners and furnish equity capital, to delegate management responsibilities to experts with presumptively superior management skills. Theoretically, the result is better firm management. Stockholders further benefit because, freed of management responsibilities, they can concentrate their limited time and resources on diversification strategies involving many firms.

A chief drawback of the public corporation is that by entrusting firm management to third parties, stockholders assume a fundamental risk of any agency relationship: namely, that the agent, in discharging its duties, will prefer its own or some other party's interests to those of its principal. Potential conflicts of interests are a basic source of agency costs. Investors anticipate the conflicts and factor them into their valuations. Potential conflicts lower the price that investors are willing to pay for a security. For public companies, management's potential conflicts are numerous. Management may, for instance, favor the interests of some stockholders over those of others, or over the interests of creditors[25]; or it may prefer its own interests to those of outside investors and the firm.[26]

Information asymmetries; market signaling

A principal source of agency costs is asymmetrical information. Management has far better access than outsiders to key economic facts affecting a firm's cashflows and investment opportunities. It also controls the public reporting of firm-specific information. Normally, management's information advantage presents few problems. Public stockholders, for example, have little need or desire for active involvement in the management of individual firms. The detailed information essential to such involvement is of limited utility to an effective diversification strategy, interwined as it is with general risk and return parameters.

Moreover, stockholders usually have a number of other means of protecting their interests. Besides legal rights, they have many other common-sense protections. For example, "[t]here is…pervasive monitoring of performance in public corporations. Inside directors monitor officers; top- and lower-level managers monitor each other; independent directors monitor insiders. Managers who make good decisions thrive; those who do not also do not advance or are replaced."[27] Finally, management is ordinarily subjected to the scrutiny of outside lenders, securities analysts, institutional investors, regulators, large public shareholders, attorneys, and public accountants. Thus, one should expect diversified investors to be fully cognizant of and normally content with management's firm-specific information advantage.[28]

Nevertheless, outside investors have limited ability to assess the value of investments made by a firm independently of management's information and recommendations. "Because of the specialization of function in public corporations, shareholders, absent extraordinary circumstances, will follow management's recommendation when deciding how to vote."[29] Therefore, shareholders are vulnerable to any conflicts of interests that managers may have with all or some investors. Compounding information problems is the fact that management often has legitimate competitive reasons to withhold important information from investors about a firm's investment plans and opportunities.[30] Detailed information about valuable investments might be useful to the firm's investors and securities analysts. Yet the same information may be even more valuable to the firm's competitors, and its disclosure may thus be detrimental to the firm and its stockholders.

Investors are naturally skeptical of statements made by managers that might be construed as self-serving. Investors realize that, besides possessing superior information, management has several reasons to exaggerate a firm's prospects. For example, management of a firm nearing insolvency might be seeking fresh equity in an honest but unrealistic belief that an ambitious and risky investment will save the firm for the benefit of all investors. If so, management's optimism may tempt it to downplay the odds of financial distress and the risks of the new investment. Or management may simply delay disclosure of the true extent of a firm's financial difficulties, trying to buy time to give business a chance to rebound. Even under normal circumstances, management has incentives to embellish the firm's financial condition and the value of new investment opportunities. Managers often derive private benefits from their positions—such as power, prestige, and compensation—that they are reluctant to jeopardize.[31]

Finally, many announcements of corporate actions send important *signals* to the market about a firm's financial condition and prospects. Included are announcements of new securities issuances, changes in capital structure, and changes in dividend policies. Aware of management's information advantages, markets scrutinize public announcements to see if they are accompanied by consistent corporate behavior. Optimistic statements alone have little impact on a firm's market value, since managers routinely try to sound enthusiastic about their firms' prospects.[32] To do otherwise may drive away investors, customers, and suppliers and harm other valuable business relationships. To gauge management's true beliefs, markets care more about what management does than what it says. Optimistic statements supported by consistent behavior are credible; announcements at odds with a firm's behavior are not.

High costs of external equity

Available evidence suggests that markets are skeptical of most attempts to raise equity capital. Investors worry in particular that a public company may issue new equity not to finance new investments but simply because management thinks the firm's stock is overvalued. Absent a clear explanation to the contrary, investors assume that the shares of most firms issuing new equity are overvalued. They act on that assumption, typically reasoning as follows.

A firm may need new capital, but given the adverse signaling effects of new issuances, public equity can be an expensive funding source. Investors assume that if cheaper funds were available, an issuer would use them first.[33] Firms with significant and obvious unused borrowing capacity, for example, are unlikely to be credible issuers of new equity. Further, management acting in the interests of existing stockholders will logically sell new equity only if it believes that the market has fairly priced or overpriced the firm's stock. If management considered the firm's equity to be underpriced, any new issuance would be illogical. New investors could buy at a discount, diluting the ownership interests of existing stockholders, who would thus lose real economic value to new investors.

Even if management believes that the market has fairly priced its firm's stock, it could have trouble convincing risk-averse investors of the sincerity of its belief. Merely announcing that belief is seldom enough to convince skeptical investors. Markets usually demand proof in the form of extensive disclosures, often including the disclosure of information that management might consider to be competitively sensitive. By issuing new equity, especially if the issuance involves sensitive information, a firm appears to be sending a clear signal to the market that the stock is over-valued.[34] Rational, risk-averse investors assume the worst—namely, that the new equity is overpriced. They assume that management is more pessimistic than the market about the firm and its prospects. Importantly, that assumption reduces the value of the entire firm, not only the new equity. It therefore adversely affects the price of other equity already outstanding. Indeed, new issues tend to depress the price of outstanding stock by an estimated 3%, which on average amounts to about one-third the value of the proceeds from the new issue.[35] "The result: most companies perceive equity to be a costly source of financing and tend to avoid it."

Some firms and industries are credible issuers of new equity. The most obvious, as Myers points out in an important 1977 article,[36] are those, such as advertising agencies and high-technology or pharmaceutical firms, whose assets depend on future discretionary spending. Such assets, or "growth opportunities," are distinct from "assets in place," which Myers defines simply as assets whose value does not require future discretionary spending.* Growth opportunities are analogous to call options with exercise prices equal to the amount of the applicable discretionary payments. The failure to make those payments, such as expenditures for advertising or research and development, will cause the investment opportunities to "expire" worthless. Assets in place—a frequent example of which are utilities, hotels, and other real properties—may lose some of their value and cosmetic appeal if not maintained. Yet a borrower's failure to make additional discretionary expenditures is less likely to render the asset worthless. Thus, upon foreclosure after a default a lender should find it easier to restore or sell a hotel that has not been maintained well than to complete a research project for a new drug or the devel-

---

*The distinction between growth opportunities and assets in place is more a matter of degree than of kind. Virtually all assets require some future spending, if only for ordinary maintenance. Growth opportunities are not necessarily the same as intangibles, because many intangibles, such as patents and trademarks, are readily marketable.

opment of a new computer technology. The same reasoning explains why other credible borrowers include airlines, banks, and companies in heavy, capital-intensive industries such as steel and petroleum.

As the foregoing suggests, growth opportunities support less borrowing than assets in place. The reason is that the value of growth opportunities is usually either firm-specific (in this case, meaning valuable only to that particular firm) or, marketable only in imperfect, illiquid markets. If the assets are firm-specific or difficult to sell, they will have little collateral value and therefore support little borrowing. Doubtless, few secured lenders actually intend to use their collateral themselves. For example, banks normally face strong regulatory as well as economic pressures to dispose of foreclosed properties quickly. Similarly, many assets that are valuable to their current owners would require deep discounts to sell to third parties. Generally, the more firm-specific an asset's features, the greater the required discount. There may be, for example, an active market for used airplanes, automobiles, or real estate, but few companies could readily profit from, say, purchasing a patent to manufacture a new surgical instrument guided by an innovative computer technology.

Further, employees, customers, suppliers, and other stakeholders of a borrower whose assets are growth options are less likely to remain committed to the firm once it begins experiencing financial straits. They realize at least intuitively that the firm will have little value other than as a going concern and that its continuation as a growing concern may require continued external financing. Most suppliers would be quicker to abandon a growth firm, or stop extending its trade credit, upon signs of serious economic trouble that might trigger a debt default and the firm's failure.

With limited exceptions, most firms have difficulty selling new equity without simultaneously depressing the prices of their outstanding shares. Even firms that can act as credible issuers must explain why anticipated revenues will be inadequate to fund future growth. Investors must always judge for themselves the credibility of any assurances given. For firms with unused borrowing capacity, the obvious question is: Why not use cheaper private placements or loans to finance new investments? Private lenders, unlike public stockholders, can agree to maintain the confidentiality of sensitive information that they must receive to evaluate difficult credit decisions. Moreover, a firm may realize net tax benefits by borrowing.

Management foresees that, given potential conflicts of interests, convincing investors of the value of an equity offering and the fairness of a security's price will be difficult. Usually, investors are willing to pay much less than what management honestly believes to be a fair price for a firm's equity securities. In an effort to obtain the best price it can, management may be tempted to bargain with prospective investors. But that can be dangerous. If successful, the bargaining may bring in more cash over the short term. Yet investors that pay too high a price for securities are likely to be disappointed with eventual returns. If so, and if those investors somehow feel cheated, management may have sacrificed for a short-term benefit its reputation for honesty and integrity. Meaningful long-term access to capital markets demands a good reputation.

High costs of external debt; contracting costs

Rather than issue undervalued equity, firms with unused debt capacity often borrow to finance investments. Yet debt can be costly in both obvious and unexpected ways. First, new loans reduce a firm's reserve borrowing capacity—its ability to borrow in the future to finance other valuable investments. Second, perceived tax advantages of debt are of limited value to firms unable, or uncertain of their ability, to use interest deductions. Third, borrowing also increases leverage and the risk of a capital structure. As discussed earlier, firms with risky capital structures incur additional costs of doing business with suppliers, customers, employees, and others. Finally, the greatest deadweight costs of borrowing often are the nonmonetary costs of contractual restrictions imposed on borrowers' investment and operating activities. Contractual restrictions grow increasingly onerous with increases in a firm's level of outstanding debt.

To maximize the likelihood of repayment, lenders commonly seek direct and indirect contractual assurances that borrowers will use loan proceeds only to make valuable investments. One difficulty, the cost of which is borne by borrowers and, ultimately, their stockholders, is that a borrower's management's primary allegiance is to the firm's stockholders, not its lenders. For reasons discussed in Chapter 15, the investment objectives of stockholders and lenders can diverge, sometimes widely. Other things being equal, the divergence expands with greater debt in the capital structure. At times management may have an incentive to reject valuable NPV investments that would benefit lenders but be contrary to stockholders' interests. At other times management may even have an incentive to accept negative NPV investments that are contrary to the interests of the firm and its lenders but valuable to stockholders. Each situation presents opportunities for investment decisions that are suboptimal from lenders' and the firm's perspectives. In imperfect markets, the risks and corresponding agency costs of suboptimal investment decisions increase, as does the proportion of debt in the capital structure.

Lenders anticipate suboptimal investment decisions. To protect themselves, they take two important precautions. First, they adjust their loan pricing—that is, increase their interest rates and fees—partially to compensate for agency risks. Second, lenders try to minimize those risks by imposing contractual restraints—affirmative and negative covenants—on borrowers' investment and operating activities. Both monetary and contractual precautions, as the following discussion shows, are highly imperfect. Furthermore, both result in borrowing costs that would not arise in MM's perfect market.

Intrinsic flaws of the contracting process   Contracting parties have difficulty structuring, negotiating, monitoring, and enforcing loan documentation. The reasons are many. Obviously, the preparation and negotiation of loan documentation can result in significant professional fees and other out-of-pocket costs and expenses. However, more fundamental problems exist, because the contracting process associated with lending, like that of financial innovation, is imperfect. It involves, as Tufano says, much "learning by experimentation."[37]

It is impossible for the language or "four corners" of a document to define fully all legal rights and obligations of contracting parties. The parties cannot envision every conceivable circumstance that might arise during the term of a contract. Instead, they try to identify a limited set of contingencies or categories of contingencies to address from the potentially unlimited number of things that might go wrong. No one can anticipate and address in advance every circumstance that might distort the plain meaning of written words. Writings are subject to unavoidable gaps, errors, and ambiguities. Even if the parties could perfectly define all their respective rights and obligations, some uncertainty would remain as to how a future court might interpret what they wrote. Further, the law (even the meaning of written words) may change in subtle, but meaningful and unanticipated ways after a contract is signed and delivered. And a contract's governing law may render the enforcement of any provision, no matter how carefully drafted, dubious; the law does not afford contracting parties unlimited freedom as to the terms to which they can agree.

Further, there is always a risk of a "design defect," meaning that the structure or form of a contract may be poorly conceived. Or the contract may not reflect *both* parties' subjective intentions—there may not have been a real "meeting of the minds." If the parties interpret identical words differently, or if either party fails to understand the other's intent, the risks of a future dispute obviously increase. The chance of a misunderstanding and, so, a future dispute can be expected to grow in proportion to the unfamiliarity of each party with the other's business. For example, the rationales of many contractual constraints may seem obvious and unobjectionable to lenders. But borrowers unfamiliar with the business of lending may find "boilerplate" terms that lenders consider innocuous to be unfair, or they may wrongly but understandably interpret the terms as conveying unflattering connotations. A common example is the manager of a financially strong firm who finds it distasteful to spend endless hours negotiating points that can arise only in proverbial "disaster scenarios." Why not worry about reality?

Likewise, a lender is seldom as expert as its borrower at the borrower's business. Thus, a lender may not recognize that standard contractual protections it considers essential may, to *this* borrower, be utterly ineffective. Or standard terms that lenders have had no problem negotiating in prior transactions may be overly burdensome to a new borrower in an industry unfamiliar to the lender. How does a lender inexpert at a borrower's business identify and draft meaningful rules for the borrower to follow in deciding whether to accept or reject specific investment opportunities? Any rule must be stringent enough to assure the lender that its loan will not be endangered but flexible enough not to stifle the borrower's necessarily risky business.

One suggestion is to cast the decision rule in generalities. Yet, as Myers poignantly observes, "[n]o sane lawyer attempts to write a contract requiring management to 'abstain from suboptimal decisions.' "[38] Nor would a contract requiring a borrower to "engage in all optimal decisions" make sense. Either standard would be so vague as to be meaningless and legally unenforceable. In enforcing contracts, courts try to discern the parties' "objective manifestations of intent." That means that any decision rule must somehow be objectively verifiable. But how would a manager, or judge, decide what "suboptimal" or "optimal" means, or what investments qualify? Optimal to whom and under what circumstances? Optimal to the borrower may be suboptimal to the lender, or vice versa. How would a lender or a court judge an investment's potential value? Will the lender not require the expertise and cooperation of the borrower and its management? If so, how does a borrower avoid having its true, honest valuation appear deceptive? Or how does a lender avoid being misled by a deceptive borrower's unfair valuation, if the borrower is the only party capable of truly valuing an opportunity? If a decision rule requires further expenditures, what happens if adequate funds are not available? Stockholders, with limited liability, cannot be forced to contribute more capital.

Contracting parties unfamiliar with each other's business can easily have trouble identifying and agreeing upon legitimate and sensible contractual provisions. Even when they (and their advisers) are familiar with each other's businesses, problems remain. Each party, like a diversified stockholder, has limited resources available to dedicate to any given transaction.

Contractual decision rules restrict investment, operating, and financing freedom. Risky debt can saddle a firm with restrictions upon even safe positive NPV investments that would benefit all parties. Those investments may require creditor approval. Debt covenants "may not only be costly to monitor but may foreclose, if only by the time delay in renegotiating the original terms, the implementation of valuable initiatives that might have been seized by a firm less constrained."[39] Finally, the mandatory nature of debt service obligations, unlike dividend payments, which are discretionary, may precipitate bankruptcy for distressed firms. A publicly held firm might damage its reputation if it fails to live up to dividend expectations, and the failure to pay dividends on preferred shares may trigger other rights—such as conversion features or enhanced voting rights—favoring preferred stockholders. Still, missed dividend payments usually give stockholders no right to force bankruptcy.

Making the best of it: imperfect documentation   Necessity forces borrowers and lenders to rely on imperfect documents and an imperfect documentation process. Typically, the parties use customary contracts, modified as appropriate for each transaction. The gist of all loan contracts is the same: preserve for the borrower the maximum investment flexibility consistent with granting lenders meaningful protections against suboptimal investing. The important protections are those designed to ensure the integrity of a borrower's capital structure. Unfortunately, appropriate protections are almost always difficult to structure and negotiate.

Much of the relevant information necessary to create meaningful protections is under a borrower's control. "Managers often possess information that they cannot or will not disclose to investors, and investors often disagree among themselves as well as with managers regarding future prospects. As a result, defining and monitoring contractual relationships between managers and various classes of [investors] is extremely complex and imperfect."[40] Commercially, it would be pointless to try to craft perfect loan documents, assuming that were even feasible.

Hence, customary negative covenants include prohibitions on mergers and asset sales, the making of large investments, and the making of dividend and other payments to stockholders and affiliates. They also prohibit additional borrowings above agreed-upon amounts and may require borrowers to comply with accounting-based financial tests. Such tests might require a borrower to maintain at least a specified minimum net worth and minimum amount of working capital. Negative covenants may also expressly require the borrower to maintain sufficient current assets to make regularly scheduled payments of principal and interest. Affirmative covenants include reporting obligations that enable lenders to confirm that a borrower is complying with financial tests and thus monitor the integrity of the borrower's capital structure. Lenders further demand rights to inspect the borrower's books and records to ensure the accuracy of financial reports.

When default occurs, the most important right is the right of lenders to accelerate the due date of any outstanding loans. Acceleration permits lenders, in emergencies, to prevent failing borrowers from depleting their remaining assets in futile attempts to restore profitability. Lenders also demand rights to terminate future lending commitments and may insist on the right to collect overdue amounts by selling collateral.

Critical, however, is that negotiated covenants and rights upon default combine to form the most economically efficient solution to the problem of distorted investment incentives. Although managers and stockholders often object to covenants and the operating restrictions they impose, both groups, and lenders, obviously prefer them to the alternative: if not for contractual restraints, lenders would have little choice but to increase dramatically the prices they charge or, perhaps, simply refuse to lend to many borrowers. Thus, "we must conclude that managers and shareholders have found that it pays to accept them. They freely choose to accept constraints today which rule out behavior which seems rational tomorrow."[41]

Monitoring and enforcement   Once contracting parties agree upon a decision rule and appropriate documentation, other problems quickly arise. Written documents do not work automatically. Ensuring that their terms are fulfilled requires the time and effort of contracting parties and others. First, compliance must be monitored to ensure that each party is fulfilling the terms of its agreement. Monitoring presents significant problems for a lender. Although a borrower's investment opportunities and financial performance may be "costlessly observable to company insiders...[they] are observable to external creditors only at some cost."[42] Lenders often incur substantial monitoring costs.

Monitoring costs might include independent auditors' fees and the opportunity costs of time spent reviewing a borrower's financial reports. To reduce these costs, lenders rely on information furnished by the borrower's management. But again, management's loyalties are divided, so the costs can never be eliminated totally. To bear monitoring costs, lenders demand compensation in the form of up-front fees or higher interest rates, both of which reduce a borrower's market value. The alternative is harsher, but easier to monitor, restrictions. By limiting investment discretion, harsher terms might reduce market value even further.

Finally, many parties to an agreement, especially lenders, assume substantial "regret risk": namely, the risk that, because of changing market conditions or other circumstances, a borrower my regret its decision to borrow and try avoid its repayment obligations. Lenders insist on contractual provisions designed to ensure the enforcement of a borrower's obligations. Yet any contractual provision is of questionable utility once a borrower incurs significant financial difficulties. Again, stockholders cannot be assessed additional amounts because of limited liability. Thus, the costs of lending incur compensation for loans that, although not specifically identifiable in advance, are statistically unlikely to be repaid fully.

Pecking order theory, revisited

As the foregoing suggests, monetary and nonmonetary contractual protections for lenders are imperfect and costly. The costs are ultimately borne by stockholders. All solutions require structuring, negotiation, monitoring, and enforcement. More important is that the process of specifying contractual limitations and decision rules for determining when to allow, or require, borrowers to make investments is inherently flawed. A decision rule, if too restrictive, may prevent a firm from making investments that are in the interests of all parties. If the rule is not restrictive enough, or too loosely drafted, management may be able to evade the restrictions when they are needed most.

Given agency costs, many firms, absent a clear tax incentive, prefer not to borrow at all. However, they usually prefer borrowing to raising new equity capital. Still, in most cases firms prefer to finance new investments by reinvesting prior profits or retained earnings. By so doing, they avoid the agency costs caused by asymmetrical information between managers and investors. They also avoid the additional transaction costs of investment contracts, whether in the form of loan agreements or securities-offering documents. Those costs include the obvious investment banking, legal, accounting, and other related fees and expenses. More important, perhaps, are the costs of distorted investment incentives.

How derivatives, by reducing cashflow variability, lower funding costs

To see how cashflow variability can systematically increase a firm's funding costs, recall the HLCo example discussed earlier in this chapter. There, we examined the adverse effects of variable cashflows on HLCo's expected taxes, given a convex tax schedule. Over the long run, variability increases expected taxes. Similarly, the global convexity of a firm's funding *cost* function generally increases funding costs when a firm's supply of external funds varies.

Convexity in the cost function of external funding causes external funding costs to increase when cashflows and therefore investment levels vary. Figure 14.5 (derived from Figure 14.3), illustrates why. It applies the convexity analysis of the costs of external funding to a firm with normally distributed cashflows and pretax income.

In Figure 14.5, hedging narrows the width of the underlying normally distributed cashflows and pretax income. Yet, again, it does not compress the distribution to a single point (as with the HLCo example). Figure 14.5 shows that partial hedging lowers average annual expected funding costs, but not all the way down to the convex cost curve. Nor does hedging affect the shape of the curve by, say, flattening it out. Yet by narrowing the range of expected variations in external funds supplies, hedging counteracts the adverse effects of convexity in a firm's cost function.

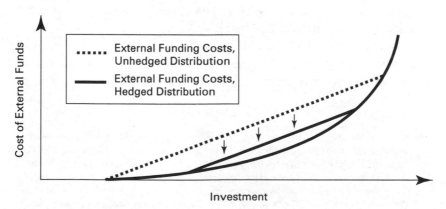

Figure 14.5   Reducing funding costs with risk management.

Market frictions make it costly to obtain and constantly adjust a firm's use of external funds in response to varying supplies of internal cash. Firms use either of two approaches for avoiding those costs. The first is to cut investment spending, which as noted earlier can lead to systematic underinvestment and its accompanying adverse effects. The second is to maintain excess supplies of cash, either by raising more external funds than the firm immediately needs or by maintaining large supplies of highly liquid investments. Either approach can lead to overinvestment and its associated drawbacks.

Using Derivatives to Increase Investment Returns

Previously, we saw that cashflow variability undermines the investment strategies of rational, value-maximizing firms in two ways. We have looked at the first way, which is systematically to increase a firm's funding costs. In particular, we examined the increased costs that result solely from the global convexity of a firm's investment funding cost function. An analogous but mathematically opposite phenomenon reduces expected returns on varying levels of investment spending.

Specifically, most investment return functions are not convex but *concave,* or dome-shaped. That means, other things being equal, investment is subject to the economic "law" of diminishing returns: that is, as total investment rises, marginal or extra return on each new unit of funds invested generally declines.* Figure 14.6 returns to the HLCo example to illustrate how variable cashflows can adversely affect expected investment returns, given a concave return function. (Figure 14.6 assumes that HLCo's annual investment spending is derived directly from the firm's pretax income.) Over the long run, variable cashflows, which induce variable levels of investment spending, ultimately reduce expected investment returns.

Assume that HLCo's annual investment spending is subject to the same fully hedgeable interest rate and FX exposures as its pretax income. Recall that, as shown in Figure 14.6(a), if cashflows are unhedged, the

---

*More formally, the law of diminishing returns holds that, all else being equal, less and less extra output is obtained from each additional unit of input. In the case of investing, funding is the input and investment return is the output. For example, one would expect each additional dollar invested to generate some extra increment of return. Yet the amount of that extra increment of return generated by each new investment dollar will decrease as the number of dollars invested increases. For a general discussion of the law of diminishing returns, see Samuelson and Nordhaus, *Economics, supra,* Chapter 1, note 17: 93–97.

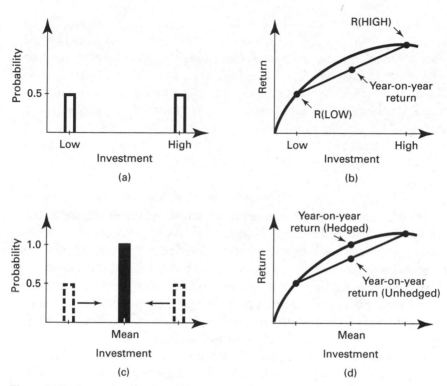

Figure 14.6   Increasing investment returns with risk management.

firm can expect pretax income and thus investment spending in any year
to assume either of two amounts—high or low—each of which is equally
likely. Figure 14.6(b) locates both amounts along HLCo's concave investment return function. Over a number of years, HLCo can expect that half
the time its annual investment will be low and the other half of the time it
will be high. Therefore, HLCo's expected annual return on investment
[labeled "year-on-year return" in Figure 14.6(b)] is simply the average of
R(LOW) and R(HIGH). Figure 14.6(b) shows that the average of those
returns plots between R(LOW) and R(HIGH), at the midpoint of the diagonal line below the curve.

In contrast, Figure 14.6(c) shows that if cashflows are fully hedged,
annual investment assumes a constant amount equal to mean. Figure 14.6(d)
makes several points. To begin, if the firm's pretax income is unhedged, its
expected, or year-on-year, investment will vary but be expected to *average*
mean. An average mean return derived from variable investment spending

is indicated by the point labeled "year-on-year return (unhedged)." If pre-tax income were, instead, fully hedged, annual investment would be constant at mean, as indicated by the point along the curve labeled "year-on-year return (hedged)." Figure 14–6(d) shows that hedging offers HLCo a chance to increase expected returns. A constant investment of mean (plotting along the curve) yields a higher expected return than a varying rate of investment averaging mean (plotting on the line below the curve). If the expected increase in return exceeds anticipated hedging costs, HLCo can increase its expected investment returns and presumably enhance firm market value by hedging.

The HLCo example is, again, for many reasons, unrealistic. As to the supply of investment funds, it assumes an unrealistic pretax income distribution and variations that are fully hedgeable. As to the demand for investment funds, the example assumes that HLCo's demand is constant from year to year. Yet in real markets opportunities to make value-enhancing investments fluctuate, causing corresponding fluctuations in demand for investment funds. Still, the important point is that the example illustrates the essential logic of any risk management policy designed to facilitate value-enhancing investing. Specifically, it shows the importance of maintaining a steady, constant level of investment spending compared with investment opportunities. Investment results are optimized when the level of investment spending is driven by investment opportunities, not by the level of internal funds available. Although investment opportunities and funds supplies are often strongly correlated, they can easily be largely independent.

Note on "Natural Hedges"; Closely Correlated Supply and Demand[43]

Firms attempting to articulate sound investment programs must first judge the extent to which supplies of internal funds are correlated with investment demand. For many firms, increases (decreases) in internal supplies are largely offset by increases (decreases) in investment demand. To the extent that such offsetting occurs, the firm's exposures are "naturally hedged." A frequently cited example is that of an oil company whose demand for investment funds fluctuates in sympathy with changing oil prices. An oil company's investment demand is often highly correlated with price levels, which in turn directly affect the company's internally generated supply of funds. When prices are high, the firm has an incentive to spend more to explore for and develop new wells. Thus, demand for investment funds is high. Likewise, high oil prices imply that the company's existing wells are yielding high cashflows. Those cashflows can be applied toward financing valuable investment opportunities. In contrast, when prices are low, the firm should have lower cashflows and thus less ability to finance similarly less valuable exploration and development activities.

When the internal supply of and demand for investment funds is naturally hedged, there is less that derivatives and other forms of financial risk management can do to manage the risks of being in that particular business. If, for example, the underlying economics of a business or industry are bad, financial risk management can offer little help. Thus, when oil prices are low, "[i]t's simply less profitable to be in the oil business....[T]here is nothing a risk-management program can do to improve the underlying bad economics of low oil prices."[44] Similarly, if prices are high, there may be no need for risk management.

In contrast, consider a manufacturer in a basic industry that sources most of its materials and production abroad even though it sells all its production in its domestic market. Assume that product demand is uncorrelated with exchange rates. Still, FX fluctuations will affect profit margins and may cause price pressures. The manufacturer, whose exposures are unlikely to be naturally hedged, might benefit from financial risk management using derivatives. Similarly, Froot, Scharfstein, and Stein mention "R&D-intensive firms" whose valuable investment opportunities consist largely of "growth options." They note that those growth options are "likely to represent valuable investments whose appeal is *not correlated* with easily hedgeable risks, such as interest rates. Thus, the logic [of their argument] would imply more hedging for R&D firms."[45]

The important point is that the goal of risk management is to ensure that a firm's internal supply of funds is properly aligned with its investment demand for those funds. Risk management cannot "insulate [firms] completely from risks of all kinds," but it can improve that supply-demand alignment.[46] Once the "first step" of aligning supply and demand has been taken, the "real challenge of risk management is to apply it to developing strategies that deal with the variety of risks faced by different companies."

ENDNOTES: CHAPTER 14

1. See generally, Nance et al., *Determinants of Corporate Hedging, supra,* Chapter 13, note 18: 268–269; Smith and Stulz, *Determinants of Firms' Hedging Policies, supra,* Chapter 13, note 17; Smithson et al., *Managing Financial Risk, supra,* Chapter 11, note 28: 102–105.

2. This and the following quotation are from Nance et al., *Determinants of Corporate Hedging, supra,* Chapter 13, note 18 (citations omitted): 268; see also Stulz, *Rethinking Risk Management, supra,* Chapter 10, note 8: 14.

3. The example, along with Figures 14.1 and 14.2, are from Smithson et al., *Managing Financial Risk, supra,* Chapter 11, note 13: 102–105. The illustrations are reproduced with permission.

4. See, generally, Stulz, *Rethinking Risk Management, supra,* Chapter 10, note 8: 13; Brealey and Myers, *Principles of Corporate Finance, supra,* Chapter 11, note 10: 485; Nance et al., *Determinants of Corporate Hedging, supra,* Chapter 13, note 18: 269.

5. See Miller, *MM Theory After Thirty Years, supra,* Chapter 11, note 16: 110–118.

6. See, generally, Modigliani, *MM—Past, Present, Future, supra,* Chapter 13, note 2: 151–155; Miller, *MM Theory After Thirty Years, supra,* Chapter 11, note 16: 112.

7. This and the quotations in the following two paragraphs are from Miller, *MM Theory After Thirty Years, supra,* Chapter 11, note 16 (emphasis added): 111–118.

8. Brealey and Myers, *Principles of Corporate Finance, supra,* Chapter 11, note 10: 484; see also Miller, *MM Theory After Thirty Years, supra,* Chapter 11, note 16 (asserting that "the incentive to leverage out the corporate tax may now actually be as high or higher than it was back in 1963"): 112. But see Modigliani, *MM—Past, Present, Future, supra,* Chapter 13, note 2 (finding the advantages of leverage, at least in 1988, to be "rather small"): 155.

9. See, generally, Brealey and Myers, *Principles of Corporate Finance, supra,* Chapter 11, note 10: 484–485; Froot et al., *Risk Management: Coordinating Corporate Investment and Financing Policies, supra,* Chapter 13, note 18 (noting, among other things, that the deadweight costs of external financing contribute to the convexity of its cost function); Robert C. Higgins, *Analysis for Financial Management,* 4th ed., (Richard D. Irwin, 1995) [hereafter, *Analysis for Financial Management*]: 220–230.

10. Stewart C. Myers, "Determinants of Corporate Borrowing," *Journal of Financial Economics,* 5 (1977) [hereafter, *Determinants of Corporate Borrowing*]: 147–175.

11. See, generally, Stulz, *Rethinking Risk Management, supra,* Chapter 10, note 8: 13–14; Smith and Stulz, *Determinants of Firms' Hedging Policies, supra,* Chapter 13, note 17: 399–403; see also Tufano, *Who Manages Risk?, supra,* Chapter 10, note 8; Géczy, Minton, and Schrand, *Why Firms Use Currency Derivatives, supra,* Chapter 1, note 37.

12. See, e.g., Stulz, *Rethinking Risk Management, supra,* Chapter 10, note 8: 14.

13. This and the remaining quotations in this paragraph are from Daniel R. Fischel, "The Business Judgment Rule and the *Trans Union* Case,"

Business Lawyer, 40 (August 1985) [hereafter, *The Trans Union Case*]: 1447–1455, 1442; see also Pringle and Connolly, *Foreign Currency Exposure, supra,* Chapter 13, note 22 (discussing stakeholder risks when a firm with significant FX exposure does nothing to manage it: from a stockholder's perspective, that is a reasonable result, "[b]ut for those other corporate stakeholders whose claims are not so diversified, including managers themselves, that may not be an acceptable answer"): 72.

14. Smith and Stulz, *Determinants of Firms' Hedging Policies, supra,* Chapter 13, note 17: 399.

15. See, generally, Froot et al., *Risk Management Framework, supra,* Chapter 4, note 2; Brealey and Myers, *Principles of Corporate Finance, supra,* Chapter 11, note 10: 498–503; Froot et al., *Risk Management: Coordinating Corporate Investment and Financing Policies, supra,* Chapter 13, note 18; see also Myers, *Determinants of Corporate Borrowing, supra,* note 10.

16. Porter, *What Is Strategy?, supra,* Chapter 3, note 2: 62.

17. Myers, *Determinants of Corporate Borrowing, supra,* note 10: 156; see also Porter, *What Is Strategy?, supra,* Chapter 3, note 2 (discussing, among other things, the inability generally to maintain competitive advantages through improvements in "operational effectiveness").

18. Brealey and Myers, *Principles of Corporate Finance, supra,* Chapter 11, note 10: 505.

19. See Brealey and Myers, *Principles of Corporate Finance, supra,* Chapter 11, note 10 (discussing the "dark side of financial slack" and, among other things, the leveraged recapitalization of Sealed Air Corporation, as an austerity measure undertaken at a time of excess cash to prepare the firm for a competitive future): 501–503; see also Michael C. Jensen, "Agency Costs of Free Cash Flow, Corporate Finance and Takeovers," *American Economic Review,* 26 (May 1986) [hereafter, *Agency Costs of Free Cash Flow*]: 323.

20. This and the following quotation are from Froot et al., *Risk Management Framework, supra,* Chapter 4, note 2 (concluding that "the role of risk management is to ensure that companies have the cash available to make value-enhancing investments."): 94.

21. See, generally, Myers, *Determinants of Corporate Borrowing, supra,* note 10 (noting that the value of most corporate investments is not objectively observable by outsiders but must instead be estimated by management): 157–159; Donald R. Lessard, "Global Competition and Corporate Finance in the 1990s," *Journal of Applied Corporate Finance,* 1 (1990) (discussing an "idealized world characterized by complete information, perfect enforceability of all contracts, and neutral taxation") [hereafter, *Global Competition and Corporate Finance*]: 59–72.

22. See Froot et al., *Risk Management Framework, supra,* Chapter 4, note 2 (citation omitted): 94.

23. See, generally, Adolph A. Berle, Jr. and Gardiner C. Means, *The Modern Corporation and Private Property* (1934) (the seminal work analyzing the nature and workings of the modern corporation).

24. See, generally, Hamilton, Motley, and Turner, "Responsibilities of Corporate Officers and Directors Under Federal Securities Laws," *CCH Federal Securities Law Reports, Extra Issue,* 1754 (February 21, 1997) (discussing the importance of the separation of ownership and control in the modern corporation and its relevance to directors' responsibilities, as well as the rise of a "professional managerial class") [hereafter, *Responsibilities of Officers and Directors Under Federal Securities Laws*]: § 104. For leading economic analyses, see Eugene A. Fama, "Agency Problems and the Theory of the Firm," *Journal of Political Economy,* 88 (1980): 288; Eugene A. Fama, and Michael C. Jensen, "Separation of Ownership and Control," *Journal of Law and Economics,* 26 (1983): 301.

25. See, e.g., Myers, *Determinants of Corporate Borrowing, supra,* note 10 (an important article analyzing the results of conflicts of interest between managers pursuing the interests of stockholders over the interests of creditors); Lawrence E. Mitchell, "The Puzzling Paradox of Preferred Stock (and Why We Should Care About It)," *Business Lawyer,* 51 (February 1996) (comparing management's duties to preferred stockholders to those owed to other investors) [hereafter, *Paradox of Preferred Stock*]: 443–477.

26. See, generally, David J. Denis, Diane K. Denis, and Atulya Sarin, "Agency Problems, Equity Ownership, and Corporate Diversification," *Journal of Finance,* 52(1) (March 1997) (finding support for the argument that managers' personal or private benefits are responsible for firms maintaining diversification strategies that reduce firm value) [hereafter, *Agency Problems, Equity Ownership, and Corporate Diversification*]: 135–160.

27. Fischel, *The Trans Union Case, supra,* note 13: 1442–1443.

28. See Sharpe et al., *Investments (5th), supra,* Chapter 11, note 9: 619.

29. Fischel, *The Trans Union Case, supra,* note 13: 1450.

30. See Lessard, *Global Competition and Corporate Finance, supra,* note 21: 61.

31. *Cf.* Denis et al., *Agency Problems, Equity Ownership, and Corporate Diversification, supra,* note 26 (examining managers' private benefits from corporate diversification; concluding that "[r]ecent evidence suggests that, on average, the costs of diversification to shareholders and firms outweigh the benefits"): 135–136.

32. Brealey and Myers, *Principles of Corporate Finance, supra,* Chapter 11, note 10: 395; see also Stewart C. Myers and Nicholas S. Majluf, "Corporate Financing When Firms Have Information That Investors Do Not Have," *Journal of Financial Economics,* 13 (June 1984); 187–222.

33. See Stephen A. Ross, "The Determination of Financial Structure: The Incentive Signalling Approach," *Bell Journal of Economics,* 8(1) (Spring

1977): 23–40; see also Sharpe et al., *Investments, 5th ed., supra,* Chapter 11, note 9: 619.

34. Froot et al., *Risk Management Framework, supra,* Chapter 4, note 2: 94; Brealey and Myers, *Principles of Corporate Finance, supra,* Chapter 11, note 10 ("investors are not stupid. They can predict that managers are more likely to issue stock when they think it is overvalued and that optimistic managers may cancel or defer issues"): 394–395.

35. The number given and the following quotation in the text are from Froot et al., *Risk Management Framework, supra,* Chapter 4, note 2 (among other things, examining a typical issuer's reasoning process; noting, for example, that "less than 2% of all corporate financing comes from the external equity market") (citations omitted): 94; Lessard, *Global Competition and Corporate Finance, supra,* note 21 (noting that investors who are "unable to tell if the firm really faces profitable investment opportunities…are likely to reduce their estimate of a company's value, especially in anticipation of a new equity issue"): 66; see also Brealey and Myers, *Principles of Corporate Finance, supra,* Chapter 11, note 10: 393–395; Sharpe et al., *Investments, 5th ed., supra,* Chapter 11, note 9: 619.

36. Myers, *Determinants of Corporate Borrowing, supra,* note 10; see also Brealey and Myers, *Principles of Corporate Finance, supra,* Chapter 11, note 10 (citing other materials; distinguishing the types of firms that make credible borrowers from those that make credible issuers of common stock): 474, 500; Froot et al., *Risk Management: Coordinating Corporate Investment and Financing Policies, supra,* Chapter 13, note 18 (noting the difficulty "R&D-intensive firms" have in raising any external financing, because of asymmetric information problems and the nature of their assets): 1652–1653.

37. See, generally, Mason et al., *Financial Engineering, supra,* Chapter 1, note 2 (discussing the process of learning and experimentation as it plays out in financial markets): 61–65.

38. See, generally, Myers, *Determinants of Corporate Borrowing, supra,* note 10 (discussing many of the contracting issues addressed in the text): 157.

39. Miller, *MM Theory After Thirty Years, supra,* Chapter 11, note 16: 113.

40. Lessard, *Global Competition and Corporate Finance, supra,* note 21.

41. Myers, *Determinants of Corporate Borrowing, supra,* note 10 (emphasis omitted): 161–162.

42. See Froot et al., *Risk Management: Coordinating Corporate Investment and Financing Policies, supra,* Chapter 13, note 18: 1636; Myers, *Determinants of Corporate Borrowing, supra,* note 10: 158.

43. See, generally, Froot et al., *Risk Management Framework, supra,* Chapter 4, note 2 (showing, among other things, how factors that affect cashflows may be positively correlated to factors that affect the profitability of

investments, thus creating "natural hedges"); Froot et al., *Risk Management: Coordinating Corporate Investment and Financing Policies, supra,* Chapter 13, note 18 (presenting a mathematical model for optimal hedging under conditions of changing investment and financing opportunities).

44. Froot et al., *Risk Management Framework, supra,* Chapter 4, note 2: 96–98.

45. Froot et al., *Risk Management: Coordinating Corporate Investment and Financing Policies, supra,* Chapter 13, note 18: 1652–1653.

46. This and the following quotation are from Froot et al., *Risk Management Framework, supra,* Chapter 4, note 2: 96–97; see also Froot et al., *Risk Management: Coordinating Corporate Investment and Financing Policies, supra,* Chapter 13, note 18 (noting also that it is optimal to hedge fully when there is no correlation between investment opportunities and the availability of internal funds): 1630–1631, 1640.

CHAPTER 15

Surprising Applications of Contingent Claims Analysis and Option Pricing Theory

> This note presents an overview of CCA and its application to a variety of corporate financial decision problems. The focus is on providing a functional understanding of the technique.
>
> *Mason, Merton, Perold, and Tufano*
> *"Contingent Claims Analysis," in*
> Financial Engineering, *1995*

> Bonus or stock option provisions of compensation plans can make the manager's expected utility a convex function of the value of the firm. If [so]... the manager will behave like a risk-seeker.
>
> *Smith and Stulz*
> Determinants of Firms' Hedging
> Policies, *1985*

Contingent claims analysis, or CCA, is a technique originally developed to explain the pricing of securities whose payoffs are contingent on the prices of other securities.[1] The technique benefited from the major conceptual breakthrough in 1973 embodied in the Black-Scholes option pricing model. That model rests on the qualitative insight that one can view corporate capital structures, along with their component debt and equity liabilities, as combinations of simple options. The literature of corporate finance has since expanded CCA's applications far beyond the pricing of traditional securities. CCA now helps explain the pricing behavior of many types of contingent rights, opportunities, and obligations that display "optionality" but that might not ordinarily be thought of as options.

The applicability of CCA to many areas of corporate decision making remains in its infancy. Still, CCA has a number of important implications for derivatives users, many of which have received little attention in legal literature. Our present concern is with the use of CCA to explain two key aspects of derivatives risk management. First, CCA and option pricing theory illuminate the dynamics of the conflicts of interests underlying the costs of financial distress introduced in Chapter 14's discussion of "trade-off theory." With the dynamics exposed, many legitimate and competitively advantageous benefits emerge by using derivatives to manage financial risks.

Second, CCA and option pricing theory have important implications for firms that compensate managers with incentive equity or option-like bonuses. In particular, they show that the *form*—common stock or options to purchase common stock—of managerial equity can dramatically affect a manager's incentives in directing the firm to manage its financial risks. As such, the choice of the form of managerial equity incentive should be a fundamental board policy issue considered integral to any system of derivatives risk management. A failure to recognize the link between management incentives and derivatives strategies can be harmful.

OPTION THEORY AND THE COSTS OF FINANCIAL DISTRESS

Lenders obviously care greatly about a corporate borrower's potential for bankruptcy.* An important reason is that the corporate form legally insulates stockholders from personal liability for corporate obligations. Ordinarily stockholders have no obligation to pay the debts of a defaulting corporation whose stock they hold. With limited liability, the amount

---

*The terms *bankruptcy* and *insolvency* are used in this chapter without reference to any state, federal, or foreign bankruptcy or insolvency regime. Likewise, this chapter uses terms such as *claim, interest,* and *creditor* for expository purposes only, without technical legal meaning. Our immediate concern is the theory and practice, not the legalities, of corporate finance. The relevant corporate finance literature seldom addresses legal niceties. We pay close attention to conflicts between legal and economic conceptions in Chapter 16.

For an engaging example of corporate finance's tendency to downplay legal issues, see Miller, *MM Theory After Thirty Years, supra,* Chapter 11, note 16: 103–109. Miller notes how, despite MM's attempts to abstract from the "purely cash-flow consequences" of corporate shares, "once again, the special [legal] properties of the corporate form intrude." These intrusive properties? Voting rights, majority and supermajority voting provisions, and stockholder limited liability! For a response from the legal profession, see Hu, *The Puzzle of Shareholder Welfare, supra,* Chapter 13, note 20: n. 66 and accompanying text. Hu notes that "in contrast to what finance texts teach, common stock is different from a properly constructed package of put and call options." Specifically, common stock carries legal properties, such as voting rights and a right to require managers to maximize the stock's economic value, not inherent in puts and calls. See also Bernard Black, "Shareholder Passivity Reexamined," *Michigan Law Review,* 89 (1990): 563.

a stockholder has at risk is limited to its investment in the corporation. Absent guarantees or other third-party credit supports, the value to which lenders have recourse upon a corporate borrower's default is, then, limited to that of the corporation's assets. Lenders care that the value of those assets, particularly in bankruptcy, may be insufficient to satisfy a borrower's obligations. Further, limited liability, given the vagaries of any bankruptcy proceeding, may jeopardize the true economic value of any lender's recovery.

Doubt about a lender's ability to recover its full value in bankruptcy is not the only problem that is raised by the corporate form and that derivatives can help solve. Lenders are also quite concerned about two other types of direct and indirect bankruptcy costs. First, the bankruptcy process itself imposes direct transaction costs upon all parties to a proceeding. Moreover, the bankruptcy process imposes significant business constraints upon bankrupt debtors while they remain subject to the supervision of bankruptcy courts. Constraints upon a firm's operating and investment flexibility can deprive it of the benefits of its management's skill and expertise. Firms hire managers because of their "special resources that increase the value of the firm. Managers cannot use their expertise unless they have some discretion in the choice of their actions."[2] That discretion may be precisely what is needed either to save a business and enable a debtor to reorganize successfully or, in a liquidation, to maximize recoveries.

Second, lenders worry just as much, perhaps more, about how limited liability can, prior to bankruptcy, distort the investment incentives of management, which is assumed to act strictly in the interests of stockholders. Limited liability may warp management's investment and operating incentives as a firm approaches financial distress. Stiglitz and Merton have separately shown that firms with substantial debt outstanding may undertake negative net present value (NPV) projects that benefit stockholders at the expense of the firm and its lenders. Myers has shown that firms with significant noncallable debt may forgo positive NPV investments that would benefit the firm and its lenders but reduce the market value of common equity.[3] Simply put, firms with significant debt in their capital structures may be tempted to accept investments with negative NPVs and reject those with positive NPVs. By distorting management's incentives, limited liability exacerbates potential conflicts of interests between lenders and stockholders. Option pricing theory and CCA help show why.

Corporate Liabilities as Options: Basic Concepts[4]

Recall from Chapter 12 that CCA views the capital structure as a combination of simple options; the value of debt and equity claims are contingent on the value of the underlying assets that are the source of firm value. Assume that a simple firm has only two liabilities: a zero-coupon bond with a market value, D, and a face amount, B, and one share of no-dividend common stock with a market value, E. Assume further that the firm will not raise any additional financing. Simple accounting tells us that total market value of all assets, A, must equal that of total liabilities, $D + E$. We also know that total asset value, A, equals firm value, V. Simplifying, $D + E = V$. From that equation, we can show that the common stock is analogous to a call option on the firm's assets. The option's exercise price is B, the face amount of the debt, and the option expires on the maturity date of the bond. The option is exercised by paying all outstanding bond obligations. If not exercised upon bond maturity, the option, meaning the common stock, becomes worthless.

If at bond maturity the firm's market value exceeds the face amount of the bond obligation, or $V > B$, the stock will be economically equivalent to an in-the-money call option. Management, acting in the stockholder's interest, can retire the bond (exercise the option) by paying its face amount (the exercise price), B. Once the bond is retired, the stockholder will hold the only claim to the firm's assets, so $E = V$. In contrast, if at maturity the firm's value is less than the bond obligation, or $V < B$, the firm will have insufficient assets to repay the bond (i.e., the value of the underlying assets will be less than the exercise price). The firm must default on the bond, allowing the "option" to retire the bond to expire unexercised. The equity, which is a right to residual asset values after the bond has been paid, will be economically equivalent to a call option on the firm's assets that expires out of the money. There is no residual asset value: the assets are not even worth enough to pay the bond. The bondholder, to mitigate its loss, will assume all rights to the firm's assets. In theory, the stockholder will surrender the firm to the bondholder and walk away without further liability.

Illustration: Ace Limited and Ace Unlimited

A stockholder's right to walk away without liability—the right that creates optionality—is valuable.[5] To see why, consider the payoff profiles in Figure 15.1 for investors in Ace Limited and Ace Unlimited. The two

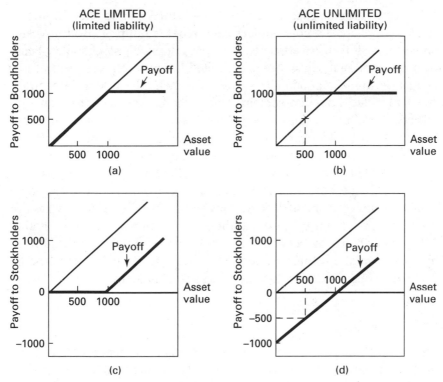

Figure 15.1   Ace Limited and Ace Unlimited. (*Source: Richard A. Brealey and Stewart C. Myers,* Principles of Corporate Finance. *Copyright© 1996; reproduced with permission of The McGraw-Hill Companies.*)

firms are identical, except that Limited's stockholders enjoy limited liability, while Unlimited's do not. Each firm's only debt is $1000 of zero-coupon bonds. The heavy "payoff" lines depict bondholder [Figure 15.1(a) and (b)] and stockholder [Figure 15.1(c) and (d)] recoveries. Those recoveries are a function of the value of the two firms' assets, V, at their respective bond maturities.

Notice from both Limited's and Unlimited's respective payoff profiles that bondholder and stockholder recoveries do noy depend upon limited liability when asset values equal or exceed $1000. In that case, bondholders receive $1000, stockholders own their firms outright, and each firm's residual value after the bonds have been paid is its total asset value minus $1000: i.e., $V = A - \$1000$. Notice also that, if assets are worth less than $1000, bondholder and stockholder recoveries of Limited are the reverse of those of Unlimited.

Let us assume that the assets are worthless. If so, Ace Limited's stockholders and its bondholders each receive nothing. Both investor groups lose all their investments. However, Limited's stockholders benefit in an important sense, because limited liability relieves them of any obligation to make bondholders whole for their $1000 loss. In contrast, Ace Unlimited's bondholders are made whole over the entire range of potential firm asset values—they always recover $1000, from either the firm or its stockholders, or a combination of both. If Unlimited's assets are worthless, its stockholders lose whatever they have invested in the firm and they have to pay another $1000 to bondholders.

Stockholders of both Ace Limited and Ace Unlimited lose the entire amount of any investment they may have made. Yet each company has lost not only the amount of its stockholders' investments but also another $1000 contributed by bondholders. Thus, another $1000 loss is suffered by each firm and it must be borne by someone. That loss is borne by Limited's bondholders but by Unlimited's stockholders.

CCA, option analysis

The shape of the payoff profile of Limited's stockholders is identical to a *long call* position, with a $1000 strike price, on the firm's assets [ignoring premiums, compare Figure 15.1c with Figure 3.5a]. Limited's bondholders hold the opposite position. It is identical to a combined *risk-free asset* worth $1000 plus a *short put* position, with a $1000 strike price [compare Figure 15.1a with Figure 3.6b].* The payoff profile of Unlimited's stockholders is identical to that of a *long* position in the firm's assets [compare Figure 15.1d with Figure 3.1a]. The payoff profile of Limited's bondholders is a horizontal line, indicating a risk-free asset worth $1000.

Ace Limited's bondholders have, from their perspective, sold an

---

*The payoff profile of common equity, which is a *long call*, has the same shape as a long position in the underlying asset combined with a long put on that underlying asset. The payoff profile of risky debt, which is a *risk-free asset* combined with a *short put*, has the same shape as a *covered short call* position—one in which the call seller (here, the bondholders) holds the underlying security (here, the right to Ace Limited's assets). By similar reasoning, the guarantor of a loan has a short put position: it pays an increasing amount to the guaranteed party (the lender) as the value of the firm falls further below the face amount of the debt; it pays nothing if firm value exceeds the amount of the debt.

uncovered put (or a covered call)* against the firm's assets. If at maturity the assets are worth less than \$1000, the firm will be unable to pay the bonds and must default. Stockholders have the right simply to walk away, "putting" the firm back to the bondholders. Bondholders in turn suffer a loss of the amount by which the \$1000 owed to them exceeds the value of the firm's assets. But if the assets are worth more than \$1000, Limited's bondholders will receive only \$1000; the firm can and will pay the debt, so stockholders will retain the sole right to the residual value. In contrast, Ace Unlimited's bondholders *always* recover \$1000, either from the firm or from its stockholders. If Unlimited's assets are worth less than \$1000, stockholders must pay any deficiency from their own funds. If the firm's assets are worth more than \$1000, the firm will pay off the \$1000 debt, with stockholders again receiving the residual value.

Ace Limited's stock, which has unlimited upside benefit and a downside exposure limited to the amount of the stockholders' investment, is more valuable than Unlimited's stock. The reason is that although Unlimited's stock has unlimited upside potential, it has an additional \$1000 downside exposure. As a corollary, Limited's bonds are less valuable than Unlimited's. Although none of the bonds have any upside, Limited's bonds have a \$1000 downside risk while Unlimited's do not (assuming Unlimited's stockholders have sufficient personal assets to pay the bonds). Finally, notice that regardless of asset values, the *combined* bondholder/stockholder payoffs are always the same for each of Ace Limited and Ace Unlimited, regardless of firm value.

Bankruptcy Costs

Clarifying what the term *bankruptcy costs* does *not* mean aids our analysis of the distress costs assumed away by MM theory. In relevant part, MM is concerned with one category of losses: those due to the decline in value

---

*An uncovered (or naked) put has a payoff profile identical to that of a covered call. In an uncovered put, the put writer does not own the underlying asset. The writer, then, loses money if the value of the underlying asset falls below the exercise price; because it does not own the asset, it gains nothing (other than its original premium) if the asset's price rises above the exercise price. In a covered call, the call writer owns the underlying asset. Yet its gain will be capped at the exercise price if the underlying asset's price rises above the exercise price— a rational option holder will exercise its call option. The call writer, because it owns the underlying assets, remains completely exposed to downside risk—it will be stuck holding the underlying asset if the asset's price stays below the exercise price (in which case a rational option holder will not exercise its call right).

of a firm's assets. But those losses are the cause of bankruptcy, not a result.[6] Even in MM's frictionless market, asset values are expected to fluctuate. Neither MM nor corporate finance considers declining asset values not caused by bankruptcy to be a cost *of* bankruptcy. Nor do they consider the losses suffered by claimants because of those declining values to be bankruptcy costs. Those losses would have occurred with or without bankruptcy.

Figure 15.2 shows how bankruptcy costs reduce the combined payoffs of the debt and equity holders from the preceding Ace Limited and Ace Unlimited example. (The illustration assumes that bankruptcy costs are a constant $200, regardless of asset values. The assumption of constant bankruptcy costs is unnecessary, and it is modified in Figure 15.3.) The diagonal line along the upper border of Figure 15.2's shaded area represents the decline in an asset's value that occurs independently of any bankruptcy proceeding. The shaded area under that line represents additional losses due solely to bankruptcy costs. What, then, are those costs?

The literature of corporate finance describes bankruptcy as any of several *recontracting* processes under which holders of claims against (or interests in) an insolvent firm *renegotiate* those claims under bankruptcy

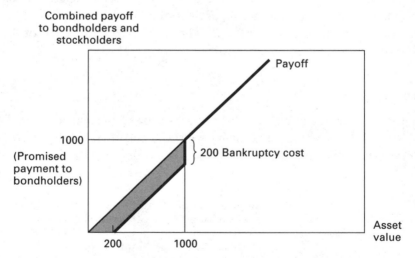

Total payment to Ace Limited security holders. There is a $200 bankruptcy cost in the event of default (shaded area).

Figure 15.2   Ace Limited bankruptcy costs. (*Source: Richard A. Brealey and Stewart C. Myers,* Principles of Corporate Finance. *Copyright© 1996; reproduced with permission of The McGraw-Hill Companies.*)

court supervision.[7] Renegotiation involves the insolvent firm and all interested stakeholders. An important aspect of the renegotiation process is fact finding and mediation to establish several points, including (1) the value of claims, (2) the value of the firm's assets, and (3) how to maximize asset values for the benefit of all interested parties, consistent with their legal rights. A threshold issue is whether assets are worth more if the firm continues to operate in some reorganized form or is instead liquidated.[8]

Direct transaction costs of bankruptcy

Bankruptcy has many costs. Among the most obvious are direct administrative and other transaction costs of formal proceedings. These include (1) court costs; (2) the costs of legal, financial advisory, accounting, and other professional fees and expenses incurred by creditors, stockholders, bankrupt firms, and other interested parties; (3) the cost and administrative burden upon bankruptcy courts of conducting what "is really a mediation and fact finding service provided by society at large;"[9] (4) the cost and administrative burden on all parties of often extensive and rancorous negotiations and litigation; and (5) discounts on asset sales. Often a substantial cost to any claimholder, even if its claim is ultimately paid, is (6) the lost time value of money implicit in a delayed recovery.

Recoveries can vary anywhere from cash payments of a claim's full economic value (e.g., when a creditor's claim, together with interest during bankruptcy, is fully secured), to new securities issued by a reorganized entity (e.g., new common stock in substitution for old unsecured debt), to a complete loss (a typical fate of stockholders in liquidation cases). The reasons for inadequate recoveries are myriad. In Chapter 1, for example, we examined the extraordinary rash of railroad bankruptcies in the late 1800s studied by Tufano. To reorganize firms, bankruptcy judges often "changed the rules of the game" governing the rights and obligations of private parties and "emasculated prior debt contracts." In any bankruptcy case, a danger exists that parties will use their legal rights for the sole purpose of delaying proceedings and creating confusion and uncertainty as to the outcome. The objective may be to salvage some value from otherwise economically worthless claims by using legal rights in a way that enables a claimant to extract valuable concessions from other parties. Often, those other parties, and courts, do yield. When companies end up in Chapter 11, for example, "often creditors' absolute priority over stockholders is sacrificed in the search for a reorganization plan that can be accepted by all parties."[10]

Indirect costs of bankruptcy

In addition to direct administrative and transaction costs, bankruptcy entails "potentially larger 'indirect' costs. Companies that wind up in Chapter 11 face considerable interference from the bankruptcy court with their investment and operating decisions. And such interference has the potential to cause significant reductions in the ongoing operating value of the firm."[11] Although bankruptcy judges and lawyers may be experts in protecting parties' legal rights, there is little reason to consider them expert managers of a debtor's business. To the extent that judges and contesting parties exert control over management's investment and operating decisions, they may, in an effort to protect legal rights, inadvertently harm the debtor economically, to the detriment of all parties.

Indirect costs of bankruptcy court supervision and legal contests include the competitive harm from an inability to fund needed maintenance and technological upgrading of existing facilities and equipment. They also include the loss of strategic positioning when inadequate or delayed funding precludes a firm from taking timely action to protect its market share. Most indirect costs result from conflicts of interests among claimholders. These conflicts can adversely affect all major investment and operating decisions. For example, senior claimants with valuable claims may resist debtors' attempts to improve their businesses. If a debtor's estate is sufficiently valuable to satisfy the claims of senior unsecured creditors, those creditors may strongly resist investments that create new business risks. They may resist even if the investments are positive NPV investments likely to enhance the chances of a successful reorganization. If a debtor's estate is sufficiently valuable to satisfy a given claim, the claimholder might rationally oppose NPV investments that increase the debtor's business risk. Although an investment might increase the value of other claims, the holder of an otherwise fully satisfied claim has the most to lose if the investment turns out badly.

Difficulties raised by claimants' conflicting interests may be exacerbated by the natural reluctance of bankruptcy judges to authorize nonroutine expenditures. If an expenditure enhances the value of the estate and the debtor successfully emerges from bankruptcy, the bankruptcy judge is unlikely to receive the credit. If, instead, the expenditure diminishes the estate, further impairing creditors' claims, the judge may be criticized. "Thus, firms undergoing reorganizations are likely to pass up positive net-present-value projects systematically because of the nature of oversight by the bankruptcy court."[12]

Costs of international insolvencies

All costs, direct and indirect, can reach lofty heights when a debtor has international operations. One reason is a lack of "uniform bankruptcy and insolvency laws or international treaties."[13] Absent an agreed-upon protocol for resolving disputes, operating efficiencies that promote profitability in good times can destroy a firm in bad times. In good times management can efficiently make and implement strategic decisions. Upon insolvency, everything can change. Firm management may become decentralized, with decisions as to foreign operations subject to local bankruptcy court supervision. Serious potential for conflicting localized proceedings exists, as "different sets of creditors assert different sets of claims to different assets under different rules. Transfers of assets between geographical jurisdictions become severely impeded or, at worst, come to an end entirely. Deprived of the ability to rely on the multinational interdependence that enhanced and facilitated its growth and success, a multinational enterprise in financial difficulty is likely to starve or implode."[14]

Using derivatives to reduce bankruptcy costs

Figures 15.3 and 15.4 illustrate how risk management using derivatives can reduce bankruptcy costs. They show the relationship between firm value and bankruptcy costs for firm X. Figure 15.3 depicts this relationship for X in an MM world of costless bankruptcy. (In that world, X could be either an all-equity firm or an issuer of both debt and equity securities. Figure 15.3 shows it as an issuer of both debt and equity.) The diagonal

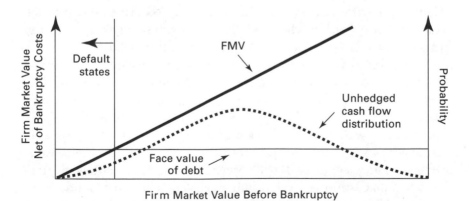

Figure 15.3   Firm market value, costless bankruptcy.

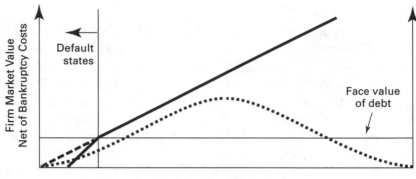

Figure 15.4   Firm market value, costly bankruptcy.

line depicts the MM relationship that firm value is a direct function of operating cashflows. As cashflows go (increase or decrease), so does firm value. Of interest is the region labeled "default states," in which the market value of X's assets is less than the face amount of its debt. By definition, the firm is insolvent and, we will assume, in bankruptcy. Let us also assume that cashflows have declined enough to push X's value into the default region and that X is bankrupt. If so, and bankruptcy were costless, bankruptcy itself would not affect X's value. As shown, firm value is lower in default states than prior to default, but the reason is that X's business has declined, causing its cashflows to decline too.

Figure 15.4 shows conceptually how the introduction of bankruptcy costs alters the relationship between operating cashflows and firm market value. Again, firm X has both debt and equity securities outstanding. Again, assume that default has led to bankruptcy. If so, bankruptcy causes firm value suddenly to decline more precipitously than it did in Figure 15.3. The triangular area (analogous the shaded region in Figure 15.2) between the former (broken) and new (solid) firm value lines represents the loss of value in the default states that is attributable solely to bankruptcy costs.

To see how derivatives can be used to reduce bankruptcy costs, consider Figure 15.5. It depicts, again for firm X, two possible cashflow distributions. The wider (dotted) bell curve represents X's cashflow distribution when its cashflows are left unhedged. The narrower (solid) curve represents X's cashflows if financial risks are at least partially hedged. A comparison of the two curves reveals that hedging reduces the width of

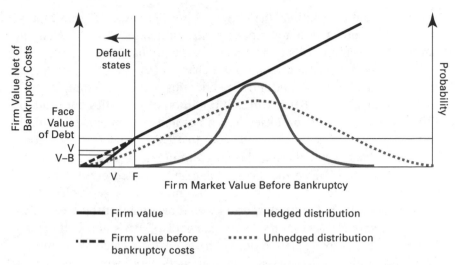

Figure 15.5   Debt equity and firm value with bankruptcy costs. (*Source: René Stulz,* "*Rethinking Risk Management,*" Journal of Applied Corporate Finance, *Fall 1996, materials reproduced with permission of Stern Stewart & Co.*)

X's cashflow distribution. Recall that the width of the distribution is one way of depicting the riskiness of a firm's cashflows—that is, risk increases as a distribution widens and flattens. That suggests, then, that hedging, by narrowing the distribution, can reduce X's cashflow risk, or variability.

So far, though, we have not given any reason why, in an efficient market, lowering cashflow variability will, alone, increase a firm's market value. CAPM holds that more is needed, because investors can manage the risks of variable cashflows on their own by holding diversified portfolios. The "more" becomes apparent upon inspection of the left sides of the two cashflow distributions in Figure 15.5. Assume that hedging enables X to narrow its distribution to that of the narrow, solid curve. If so, X will have rendered negligible the chances of experiencing a costly "lower tail" outcome in the default region. For practical purposes, none of X's hedged distribution lies in the default region. Thus, the chance of bankruptcy is remote (absent some other major market movement or event that changes X's distribution).

The point of Figure 15.5 is that hedging, by reducing the risk of bankruptcy, also reduces the *current* expected costs of bankruptcy. To find current expected costs, we multiply the costs of bankruptcy should it occur by the probability that it will occur. When stockholders believe bankruptcy is a real possibility, "the expected present value of [bankruptcy] costs will be reflected in a company's *current* market value."[15] Hedging can reduce the current negative impact of *potential* bankruptcy on X's current stock price, because it reduces the chances that the firm will default on its debt and become bankrupt. Consider this numerical example.

X is a U.S. firm, BBB, with $300 million of securities outstanding, $200 million of which are unsecured notes and the remainder, publicly traded common stock. Investors believe that BBB, operationally strong, has a 10% chance of bankruptcy because of fully hedgeable FX and interest rate exposures. Bankruptcy costs have an estimated present value of $20 million. Indirect costs prior to bankruptcy (discussed below) cost another $30 million. Bankruptcy costs would be greater still if a U.S. case were to precipitate foreign proceedings against BBB's non-U.S. assets. The risk of bankruptcy, then, reduces *current* market value by $4 million (10%×$40 million). BBB could, then, immediately increase the market value of its equity by up to $4 million by hedging its FX and interest rate exposures. Furthermore, "if cashflow and value should decline sharply from current levels [materially increasing the odds of bankruptcy], the value added by risk management increases in absolute dollars, and even more on a percentage-of-value basis."[16]

Figure 15.6 shows conceptually how risk management can enhance BBB's value prior to bankruptcy. The upper diagonal (dashed) line again depicts firm value in a perfect MM world of costless bankruptcy. The shaded region below that line in the default region depicts bankruptcy

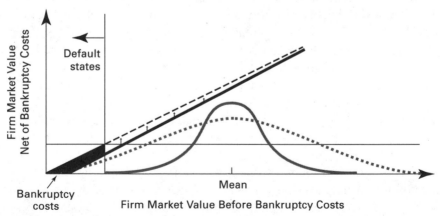

Figure 15.6   Reducing distress costs prior to bankruptcy.

costs once the firm is in bankruptcy. Finally, the slightly curved (solid) line just below the upper diagonal (dashed) line indicates actual firm value, net of bankruptcy costs. Given that the chances of bankruptcy decrease as firm value increases, other things equal, the lower line gradually converges upward toward the upper line, the farther the distribution of firm value moves away from the default region. Figure 15.6 shows that risk management, by causing the two lines to converge more quickly, can increase BBB's market value even prior to bankruptcy.

Costs of Financial Distress; "Trade-off" Theory[17]

The costs of financial distress short of bankruptcy have two principal components: (1) the costs of suboptimal investment decisions and (2) direct and indirect transaction costs. The source of both costs is the same: potential conflicts of interests among investors in a levered firm that can distort management's investment incentives. Lenders anticipate before lending that management of a levered firm approaching insolvency will have a powerful incentive to abandon its normal, sound decision rule in making discretionary investment decisions. Investment spending is crucial, because "the ultimate payoff of almost all assets depends on future discretionary investment by the firm. The discretionary investment may be maintenance of plant and equipment. It may be advertising or other marketing expenses, or expenditures on raw materials, labor, research and development, etc. All variable costs are discretionary investments."[18]

Corporate finance apparently presumes that, at least prior to distress, management authorizes only those expenditures intended to enhance or protect firm value. The law generally presumes that, prior to financial distress, the interests of the firm are the same as those of its stockholders.* In distress, however, economic incentives change. The interests of lenders, stockholders, management, and the firm can begin to diverge radically. Management acting, for instance, strictly in the interests of stockholders may "pass up valuable investment opportunities which would make a positive contribution to the market value of the firm."[19]† Alternatively, such management may accept costly investments that decrease firm value, thereby harming creditors yet benefiting stockholders.

---

*We examine the legal implications of this issue in Chapter 16.
†Importantly, management's fiduciary duties, at least under Delaware law, change once the firm is
    "operating in the vicinity of insolvency."

Transaction costs

Lenders foresee the prospect that management of a distressed firm will face distorted incentives. Lenders view that prospect as an additional risk, one that they must be compensated to carry or that must otherwise be controlled. As compensation for the additional risk, lenders at a minimum charge higher pricing in the form of interest rates. However, price increases alone seldom are the best or most efficient solution. High interest rates, for example, will offer little comfort to a lender lacking essential legal and contractual protections necessary to ensure that it can collect amounts owed to it. Thus, to enhance their legal rights, lenders demand additional contractual protections. For present purposes, the important protections are those designed to reduce the risks of suboptimal investment decisions. Although those protections benefit lenders, they can be costly to borrowers. As discussed in detail in Chapter 14, higher interest rates and loan fees, and tougher contract terms, are the primary agency costs of borrowing. Both have an immediate adverse impact upon firm value, even prior to the appearance of any signs of actual distress. "When debt is issued, the costs' present value is reflected in the market value of the firm and absorbed by stockholders, who have the residual claim on firm value."[20]

Despite the explicit costs of contractual restrictions, they are advantageous because they reduce the rates that lenders would otherwise have to charge for the agency risks they bear. As to the content of the restrictions, lenders attempt to specify, among other things, appropriate decision rules that borrowers must follow in accepting or rejecting investment opportunities. However, the effort to specify a meaningful decision rule can be complicated and costly, especially for weaker borrowers. The parties confront unavoidable tension between the lender's need for meaningful contractual assurances and the borrower's need for flexibility in taking risks essential to its business. Contracts require negotiation, drafting, monitoring, and enforcement.

More important, any attempt to specify in advance a decision rule is inherently imperfect. Contractual terms intended to protect the lender often commit firms to decision rules that are suboptimal from the perspective of a borrower and its stockholders. An overly restrictive rule may prevent management from making investments that increase the firm's market value for the benefit of all parties. Loan documents may inadvertently deprive management of its ability to exercise its fundamental business investment and operating expertise, jeopardizing the firm's business and the lender's chances of repayment. Still, for most borrowers and stockholders the acceptance of potentially burdensome contractual restraints is rational.[21] One can logically assume that, absent those restrictions, borrowing costs would be much higher; perhaps for many firms they would even be prohibitively expensive, assuming credit were even available to them in the first place.

Suboptimal investments

To see how management incentives to make suboptimal investment decisions may arise, we begin our analysis with the basic proposition that, legally, stockholders are the firm's owners. "The most basic principle of corporate law is that a corporation is to be primarily run for the benefit of its shareholders."[22] Moreover, the traditional legal concept holds that the corporation should be managed to maximize stockholders' economic value, subject to limited legal and contractual constraints. Managers owe statutory and common law fiduciary duties to stockholders, particularly duties of care and loyalty. The traditional concept also presumes that, absent special circumstances, the interests of the corporation and its stockholders are for practical purposes indistinct. In practice, managers are normally free in discharging their fiduciary duties to pursue the interests of the firm without separately asking whether the firm's interests conflict with those of its stockholders.

In stark contrast to stockholders, creditors are not owners of the firm. Prior to financial distress, creditors' rights are essentially contractual in nature; management generally owes no fiduciary duties to creditors, whose rights are set forth in their contracts and in statutes governing debtor-creditor relationships.[23] As discussed in Chapter 17, bankruptcy, insolvency, or even "*near* insolvency" can trigger a profound "shift" in the duties owed by management from stockholders to creditors.

For healthy firms, differences in the duties owed to stockholders and creditors have little bearing on the decision rule that management follows in making investment, financing, and operating decisions. Management can freely pursue opportunities and make expenditures that are in the best interest of the firm, confident that whatever benefits the firm ought to benefit all its investors. That logic leads naturally to discretionary spending that enhances firm value. Specifically, management's decision rule is to accept investment opportunities (construed broadly) with the greatest positive NPV* and reject any with a negative NPV.

---

*The NPV calculation factors in firm-specific details such as the extent to which a proposed investment strategically fits with the rest of the firm's business and operations.

Yet in distress, not all decisions that affect firm value benefit both creditors and stockholders alike—stockholders and creditors can at times have divergent, even seriously conflicting interests. Management and different investors may reach opposite conclusions as to the desirability of any particular investment or expenditure. In times of financial distress, conflicts of interests can distort management's incentives (at least from the view of the firm and its lenders). Creditors must be concerned that, unless otherwise constrained, management will be tempted to reject positive NPV investments that would increase firm value, if those investments would also reduce the value of the firm's common stock. Likewise, management may accept a negative NPV investment that reduces firm value, if it increases equity values. Option pricing theory and CCA again help explain why.

CCA and option pricing theory

CCA treats the total value of the firm as a "'basic' security…[T]he individual securities within the capital structure (e.g. debt, convertible bonds, common stock, etc.) can be viewed as 'options' or 'contingent claims' on the firm and priced accordingly."[24] Common stock, as noted earlier, is in essence a call option on the residual value of a firm's assets after all senior claims have been satisfied. "For firms approaching financial distress, the option-like character of common stock becomes more pronounced."[25] Option pricing theory teaches that a key determinant of option values is uncertainty (i.e., variance or volatility) as to the price of the underlying security—here, that means uncertainty as to firm market value. Other things being equal, an option's value increases as volatility increases.

Recall also that the speed at which an option's price is changing is its *delta.* Because option risk is "curved," not "linear" (as are forwards), an option's delta is always changing. Another Greek letter is used, *gamma,* to denote the acceleration of an option's price change. Gamma is greatest when an option is at the money. (It is extremely low when an option is deeply in the money or out of the money.) Critical here is that when a stock is near or at the money—that is, when the firm has just barely enough to pay off its outstanding debt—even a small increase in volatility of the firm's underlying assets, regardless of whether the value of those assets changes, can cause the option's value to increase. As with any other option, then, the value of common stock, especially when the firm is near insolvency, "rises as the variance in the returns to the underlying asset increases."[26] The critical implication is that the value of common stock increases, other things being equal, simply by increasing the amount of business risk, or volatility, to which a nearly insolvent firm is exposed.

Management acting in stockholders' interests is tempted, precisely when creditors most want management to act conservatively to preserve the value of the firm, to engage in risky transactions. "If shareholders switch from low-variance investment projects to high-variance projects, they could transfer wealth from the bondholders to themselves."* Moreover, the transfer is greatest as the value of the firm approaches the face amount of the outstanding debt (in which case the common equity is approaching its at-the-money price).

Ace Limited illustration

Let us return to the Ace Limited example, again assuming that $1000 of unmatured bonds is the only debt outstanding. Assume that the firm's value has, since the bonds were issued, declined from $2000 to $1025. If so, the firm is worth slightly more than the bondholders' claims. If firm value remains steady until the bonds mature, Ace will have just enough value to satisfy bondholders' claims, with only $25 left over for stockholders. Under those conditions, bondholders will want the firm prior to maturity to avoid large risks, even though, for example, a risky investment might have a very high NPV. Any increase in business risk will jeopardize bondholders' full recovery, which, although not certain, looks likely. Furthermore, bondholders will not benefit little from large gains, because no matter what happens, their claims are limited to $1000. Yet bondholders must absorb almost the entire amount of any large losses. They will clearly want Ace to undertake a conservative investment strategy that generates steady, low-risk returns. But such a strategy is unlikely to satisfy the firm's stockholders, the value of whose equity has dwindled.

At a value of $1025, Ace's stock is in effect a slightly in-the-money call option: it has time value, but comparatively little ($25) intrinsic value. The stock would be out of the money if Ace's assets were worth less than $1000. The assets could not then even satisfy bondholders' senior claims. When a firm's stock is at the money, out of the money, or slightly in the money, the firm is in financial distress. One way to increase the value of the common stock is to make safe, positive NPV investments, because firm asset values would likely continue to exceed $1000, although not by

---

*As with any other option, a gain to one party means an equal and offsetting loss to the other.

much. Any increase above $1025 will accrue to the stockholders, because bondholders' claims are capped at $1000. However, any decrease in value below $1000 will reduce the value of the bonds but only lower the intrinsic value of the equity by at least $25. As mentioned earlier, though, option pricing theory tells us that another way exists to increase the value of the common stock: namely, by increasing the riskiness of the firm's investments, even if some of those investments have a negative NPV. With only $25 at stake, stockholders have little to lose and much to gain if Ace uses its entire $1025 of remaining capital to make high-risk investments.

Prior to the bond maturity date, any increase in the volatility of Ace's underlying asset values will automatically increase the common stock's time value. Likewise, given that bondholders and stockholders are claimants to the same limited pot of assets, any action that increases the stock's value necessarily decreases that of the bonds. As discussed earlier, the bonds, from their holders' perspective, are economically equivalent to a risk-free asset plus a short put against the firm's assets. The greater the value of the option to the option holders—the stockholders—the more the option costs the option writers—the bondholders.

We know from earlier discussions that, other things being equal, increased volatility of the security underlying an option increases the option's value, especially when the option is at the money. Here, the higher volatility of Ace's asset values will increase the potential for "upper tail" outcomes that can save the firm from financial distress and push the value of the common stock into the money. Unfortunately for bondholders, higher volatility also increases the risk of a "lower tail" outcome that can force the firm into bankruptcy, jeopardizing the bondholders' recoveries. Because of its optionality, common stock under distress conditions, in direct contrast to and at the expense of senior debt, increases in value when business risk increases.*

The foregoing point is illustrated by Figure 15.7. The firm called S&L in the diagram is clearly in deep financial distress. Its cashflow (dotted) distribution lies almost entirely in the region labeled "default states."

---

*Actually, because of its optionality, common stock of a levered firm always increases in value, other things being equal, as business risk increases. However, when common stock is deeply in the money, it has very little gamma risk. In contrast, a stock at the money has the highest gamma. Other things being equal, if a stock is deeply in the money (e.g., if there is little debt in the capital structure) or out of the money (the company is insolvent), only a dramatic increase in volatility will affect its value. Yet, when a stock is near or at the money, even a small increase in volatility can increase the option's value.

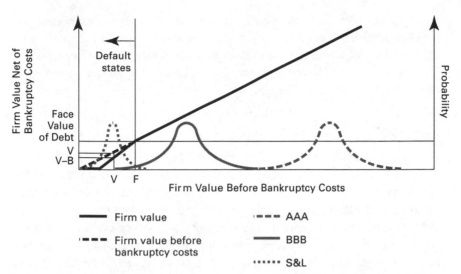

Figure 15.7   Optimal hedging for firms AAA, BBB, S&L. (*Source: Reneé Stulz,* "*Rethinking Risk Management,*" Journal of Applied Corporate Finance, *Fall 1996, materials reproduced with permission of Stern Stewart & Co.*)

Other things being equal, S&L's owners would probably happily bet on a stroke of luck to save the firm, since otherwise it appears that they will most certainly lose it. "In these circumstances, a management intent on maximizing shareholder value will not only accept bets that present themselves, but will *seek out* new ones....Such managers will take bets even if they believe markets are efficient, because introducing *new sources of volatility* raises the probability of the 'upper-tail' outcomes that are capable of rescuing the firm from financial distress."[27] Managers become risk seekers. In dramatic contrast, management interested only in maximizing total recoveries to all parties would continue only to make investments with positive NPVs.

The incentive to engage in risky transactions increases only as asset values fall and equity drops further out of the money. Under such conditions, safe investments offer meager help to common stockholders, because they hold little potential to generate enough value to propel the common stock back in the money. Before the common regains any intrinsic value, all losses on senior claims must be recovered. Highly risky investments, even if unlikely to succeed, are often the best, perhaps only, chance stockholders have of realizing any value. Moreover, what economic (as opposed to legal) incentive do stockholders have not to make risky investments? If a risky investment fails, they are no worse off than before; because of limited liability, they assume no additional downside exposure. Stockholders of a deeply distressed firm, and management acting strictly in stockholders' interests, would likely welcome the opportunity to gamble with money that will almost certainly be allocated to bondholders.

Illustration

Assume that the assets of S&L in Figure 15.7 are worth $5 million less than the face amount of its liabilities. The firm is, of course, in distress and its equity, all of which is common stock, is $5 million out of the money. Assume that management, under severe pressure from creditors, is considering one last investment before filing a voluntary petition for bankruptcy. The firm has two investment opportunities costing $5 million each and lasting the same length of time. It can accept either or neither, but the firm cannot accept both. The first investment has a 90% chance of success: if it succeeds, it will produce a net gain of $3 million; if it fails, it will lose up to $1 million. Its NPV is $2.6 million $[(.9 \times 3) + (.1 \times - 1) = 2.6]$. The second investment has a 25% chance of success: if it succeeds, it will produce a net gain of $13 million; if it fails, however, it will result in a total loss of the $5 million investment. Its NPV is negative $0.5 million $[(.25 \times 13) + (.75 \times - 5) = -0.5]$.

To the common stockholders, the first investment is worthless—at best, it makes up $3 million of the $5 million of losses the firm must recover before the common stock has any intrinsic value. Yet the other investment is quite attractive: although it has a 3-to-1 chance of failure, what do holders of common stock have to lose? If it is lucky and the investment succeeds, the firm will recover its $5 million investment, earn back the $5 million preexisting deficiency, *plus* gain an additional $8 million—that gain will accrue directly to the common stock. Success could also enable management* to stave off bankruptcy. If the investment fails,

---

*Similar to the potential for conflicts of interests between stockholders and creditors is the potential for conflicts between management and all external investors, whether debt or equity. Managers' interests do not always coincide with those of stockholders. On the problems of managerial risk aversion, see Tufano, *Who Manages Risk?, supra,* Chapter 10, note 8. See also Denis et al., *Agency Problems, Equity Ownership, and Corporate Diversification, supra,* Chapter 14, note 25 (arguing that "managers may maintain a diversification strategy even if doing so reduces shareholder wealth").

the common stock was worthless anyway. To common stockholders, it pays to take a long shot.

Using derivatives to reduce costs of financial distress

The same logic, depicted in Figure 15.7, that led to a reduction in BBB's bankruptcy costs through derivatives interest rate and FX risk management also leads to a reduction in BBB's distress costs short of bankruptcy. Hedging reduces the variability of the firm's cashflows. It thus narrows the underlying distribution of firm value, perhaps reducing dramatically the chances that BBB may encounter financial distress. By implication, that reduces management's incentive to make suboptimal investment decisions. In terms of Figure 15.7, hedging shifts BBB's distribution to the right, in the direction of AAA.* Thus, BBB can use derivatives to reduce its risk of experiencing a costly lower-tail outcome that might lead to default and bankruptcy. The exact distance of the shift and the precise measure of cost savings attributable to the avoidance of suboptimal investment incentives may be difficult to quantify. Yet available evidence suggests that for firms exposed to significant currency, interest rate, and commodity price risks, the shift and costs savings can be significant.

By reducing the variability of BBB's cashflows, derivatives can, as Stulz explains, strengthen the firm's capital structure. This point has several important positive implications. First, by using derivatives to strengthen its capital structure, BBB can become a stronger borrower, able to borrow more cheaply and on better terms. Derivatives reduce the firm's agency costs of borrowing, thus directly increasing its firm value and the value of stockholders' equity. Second, by strengthening BBB's capital structure, derivatives serve as a direct substitute for new equity capital. Should the firm choose also to borrow, derivatives should, then, increase its debt capacity. Third, although debt has trade-offs, the firm may decide that it could use additional financing, perhaps "to strengthen management incentives to improve efficiency and add value."[28] Additional debt reduces overinvestment by forcing management to return excess capital to investors through interest payments.

---

*Recall also Equation 14.1: $V_L = V_U + PV(tax\ shield) - PV(COFD)$. Thus, hedging reduces $PV(COFD)$, directly increasing V_L, the value of the levered firm.

BOARD POLICY ISSUE: RISK MANAGEMENT AND THE FORM OF MANAGERIAL EQUITY

Agency costs are endemic to all external financings, whether debt or equity.[29] Besides the agency costs of borrowing, other agency costs can arise from the potentially divergent risk-taking and risk management objectives of management and stockholders. Firms try to reduce those costs partly by aligning the two groups' risk preferences through properly structured management compensation packages. A critical component of most management compensation is incentive equity.

Recent evidence appears to confirm finance theory that the extent and form of management equity are integral to firms' risk management practices. By implication, the evidence also suggests that the failure of compensation plans properly to align management's risk preferences with a firm's business objectives may frustrate the achievement of those objectives. CCA and option pricing theory offer important insights into the incentives created by different types of equity compensation. By so doing, they aid managers, stockholders, and other interested parties in designing effective risk-taking and risk management incentives.

Aligning Risk Preferences

Risk preferences are misaligned, in the sense used here, whenever management causes a firm to assume or hedge different amounts or types of risk than stockholders would otherwise prefer. For example, well-diversified public stockholders might invest in an oil and gas firm specifically because of its oil and gas price exposures. If so, they will want the firm not to hedge its oil and gas price risks. In contrast, other stockholders might invest in a different commodity firm not because of its price risk but because the firm is an efficient, low-cost producer. If so, those investors might want the firm hedging as much price risk as practicable to enable management to focus on operating efficiency, the source of the firm's competitive advantage. Hedging furthers corporate strategy by "removing the 'noise' introduced by a major performance variable—the [commodity] price."[30]

Finally, perhaps management of the efficient, low-cost producer has begun believing that it does after all enjoy a comparative advantage in predicting commodity prices. If so, management might want to scale back the firm's "full cover" hedging program and replace it with "selective," or partial hedging. Under selective hedging, management would allow the firm's view of future commodity prices to affect that portion of projected commodity price risk it hedges. Stockholders, however, may consider such a change of focus unnecessary if not dangerous. It could, particularly if short-run failures distract senior managers, jeopardize the operating efficiency that has until now made the firm an attractive investment. Lacking any track record, management may have a hard time convincing investors that, as currently configured, the firm has any comparative advantage in which others should invest.

Conflicting Risk Preferences: Managers Versus Stockholders

To realize the benefits of diversification while taking advantage of limited liability, most stockholders want the firms represented in their portfolios to accept significant business risks. For stockholders, business risk is an essential raw material in the manufacture of portfolio profits. After all, an investor that wishes to avoid business risk and is satisfied earning risk-free returns can easily do so by investing in Treasury securities. In contrast to outside stockholders, most managers are naturally risk-averse, at least with respect to the firms they manage.

Managers often have much of their wealth and "human capital"— their knowledge, skill, experience, and career opportunities—invested in their firms. They also bear reputational risks and potential legal liability for difficult business decisions. Legal and reputational risks are often unavoidable, because even sound decisions can turn out badly. And almost any business decision that turns out badly can, with hindsight, be characterized by some critic as having been imprudent when made. Knowing that, a risk-averse manager's natural inclination is to avoid difficult business decisions and their accompanying risks. Daniel Fischel of the University of Chicago Law School explains the resulting problem for stockholders as follows: "If managers can be sued whenever decisions, even if desirable when made, turn out poorly, they will respond by avoiding risk in a number of different ways....This result—reinforcement of managers' tendency to avoid risk—is precisely the opposite of how shareholders, the superior risk bearers, want their managers to act."[31]

As large stakeholders and bearers of legal and reputational risk, managers have limited ability to diversify their substantial and numerous firm-specific risks. The combination of nondiversifiable risks and managerial risk aversion can, as Smith and Stulz predicted in 1985 and Tufano confirmed in 1996 (at least as to the North American gold mining industry), markedly affect a firm's risk management practices.[32] Stockholders' objective, then, in designing a management incentive package, is to provide adequate incentives to counteract managers' natural risk aversion. However, they must be careful not to create inadvertently incentives for managers to become seekers of risks that are contrary to stockholders' interests.

Expected Utility

Smith and Stulz assert unambiguously that, "unless faced with proper incentives, managers will not maximize shareholder wealth."[33] To work, management incentives "must be designed so that when managers increase the value of the firm, they also increase their expected utility"— that is, their expected personal, subjective welfare or benefit. Modern finance, particularly CCA and option pricing theory, shows why properly designing incentive packages can be challenging.

Theory

Figure 15.8 shows that a risk-averse manager's expected utility is a concave function of her or his total wealth.* Two implications are relevant

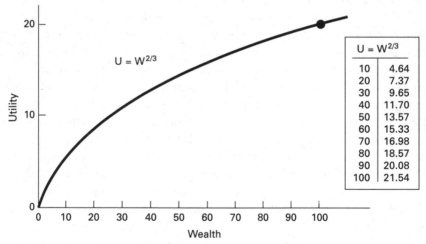

Figure 15.8   Utility function of a risk-averse manager.

---

*Because utility is subjective, utility functions are customarily scaled along the vertical axis in terms of nebulous "units" of utility. The functions can be expressed as equations, such as $U = W^{1/2}$ or, as in Figure 15.8, $U = W^{2/3}$, where U is utility and W is wealth. Later illustrations substitute stock price for wealth. See, generally, *MIT Dictionary, supra,* Chapter 12, note 13 ("to say that someone derives utility from a good…is to say that they prefer the good to exist rather than not to exist"): 445; Tufano, *Who Manages Risk?, supra,* Chapter 10, note 8 (explaining, with accompanying diagram, methodology for analyzing managerial risk aversion in the context of the gold mining industry): 1109–1111.

here. First, the utility functions imply that one always wants more wealth, as suggested by the constantly upward-sloping curve in Figure 15.8. Second, they also imply that as total wealth increases, each extra unit of wealth brings less and less additional satisfaction. So, although risk-averse managers always derive more satisfaction from additional income, the wealthier they become, the less satisfaction they derive from each extra unit of income. Put differently, the wealthier risk-averse managers become, the greater each extra amount of income they will demand to induce them to assume an additional unit of risk.

For example, at given odds (i.e., risk), someone might be willing to bet $10 for a chance to quadruple his or her money. Yet the same person might be unwilling, with the same or better odds, to bet $1000 for a chance to win $4000. To bet $1000, people might (if willing to bet at all), demand either a much higher payoff—say, $10,000—or much better odds for the same payoff. Risk aversion explains such phenomena as people's willingness to place manifestly poor bets (i.e., those with highly negative NPVs) on state lottery tickets. Ticket prices are set low enough so that the risk assumed seems negligible. At substantially higher ticket prices, fewer lottery tickets would likely be sold.*

HLCo illustration

HLCo's board is trying to decide which of two forms of incentive equity packages to offer its managers. The first would consist solely of no-dividend HLCo common stock; the second would consist solely of options to purchase common stock at an exercise price of mean. The board wants to motivate managers to improve the firm's financial performance, but without causing the firm to assume imprudent risks. A critical factor that the board is considering is the likely effect each form of compensation will

---

*Consider what would happen if ticket prices were raised and the odds of winning improved enormously. Note that a state lottery ticket always has a negative expected payoff, or NPV. Assume that the odds of winning a prize with a present value of $1 million are 1 in 10 million, or 0.00001%. Each $1 ticket, then, has a pretax NPV of *negative* 90 cents (.0000001 × $1,000,000 = $0.10; and $0.10 − $1.00 = −$.90). A bettor should expect to *lose* 90 cents on (or get back only 10 cents of) every dollar spent on lottery tickets. But what if ticket prices were increased to, say, $1000 and the odds of winning improved tremendously to, say, 1 in 2000 (0.05%)? The pretax NPV per dollar invested would improve dramatically, to a loss rate of *only* 50 cents per $1 invested(.0005 × $1,000,000 = $500; and $500 − $1000 = −$500). A bettor would, then, expect over the long run to lose *only* $500 on every $1000 ticket purchase (that's better than losing $900 at the former odds). Doubtless, states would sell few lottery tickets with those "improved" odds.

have on a typical manager's risk management incentives. Not only are the firm's managers risk-averse; they also bear substantial nondiversifiable HLCo risk. Assume also that in managing financial risks, HLCo enjoys economies of scale and comparative advantages over individual managers. "In other words, it should not pay for the manager to hedge his…wealth on his personal account."[34] Rather, managers can hedge their personal financial risks more effectively by doing so indirectly by causing the firm to hedge its financial risks.

To assist the board in comparing the two forms of equity incentives, treasury has prepared Figure 15.9. It shows the value of a share of common stock, and the intrinsic value of a call option on one such share at a strike price of mean, each as a function of the stock's trading price. Figure 15.9 assumes that stock prices are derived directly from HLCo's cashflows, which are based on the simple high-low distribution used in earlier examples. The firm expects that 50% of the time its cashflows and stock price will be low and that the other 50% they will be high. One important point quickly emerges from the diagram: although the common stock will always have value (if HLCo is solvent), a call option on the common stock will have no intrinsic value until the stock price trades above mean. At a common stock price of mean, the option is at the money; at a price below mean, it is out of the money. Given our high-low cashflow assumption, an option should have intrinsic value 50% of the time, whenever the stock price is high.

Treasury has also prepared Figure 15.10 to help explain the very different hedging incentives created by the two equity packages. Figure 15.10

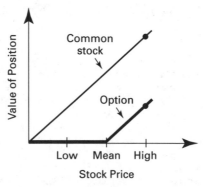

Figure 15.9   Value of HLCo stock and call operations.

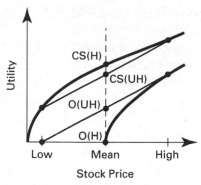

Figure 15.10   Risk management incentives.

illustrates the utility of each form of equity to a typical manager. Notice first that the two curves have identical shapes, but start at different points along the horizontal axis. Notice also that the expected stock price is always mean, which is the average of high and low. Finally, diagonal lines have been drawn from the point on each curve of utility at a low stock price to the corresponding point of utility at a high price. The midpoint of each diagonal line indicates respective average utilities when cashflows are unhedged and the stock price fluctuates between low and high. As explained below, Figure 15.10 suggests that a manager holding common stock should prefer that the firm fully hedge, while a manager holding options should prefer that the firm not hedge at all.

In Figure 15.10, when cashflows are fully hedged, the stock price is always mean. The utility of common stock when the firm is fully hedged is designated CS(H), and when unhedged, CS(UH). CS(H) plots above CS(UH), so CS(H) has a higher utility than CS(UH). A manager who receives common stock should prefer that the firm hedge fully, because hedging increases the utility, or satisfaction, the manager derives from the stock. It follows that awarding common stock should induce the manager to cause HLCo to hedge fully. Now compare that result to the incentives created by an option package.

In Figure 15.10, the utility of an option when HLCo is fully hedged is O(H); it is O(UH) when the firm is unhedged. Hedging again locks in a stock price of mean, which is the exercise price of the option. But at that price, the option is by definition at the money and has *no* intrinsic value. Thus, O(H) plots along the horizontal axis. In contrast, when the firm is unhedged, the intrinsic value of the option, O(UH), plots at the mean stock price, but above the horizontal axis. That means that although the option will be in the money only half the time, variability of stock prices will cause the option to have a higher average utility to a manager when the firm is unhedged. Solely on the basis of intrinsic value, the utility of O(UH) is higher than that of O(H), so the manager holding options should prefer that the firm not hedge. One more step remains.

We know from earlier discussions that prior to expiration, options have time value as well as intrinsic value. Might the time value of an option alter the preference against hedging of a manager receiving options? It is doubtful. A major determinant of time value is the volatility of the price of the underlying stock. Yet we assumed that fully hedging HLCo's cashflows would remove all the stock's price variation, or volatility. Lacking volatility, options with a mean strike price have no intrinsic value and no chance of becoming in the money. Therefore, those options should have no time value if the firm is fully hedged. Figure 15.10 suggests that, when the firm is fully hedged, the time value of the options at a strike price of mean is negligible and would have no effect on a manager's preference. Thus, options with a mean strike price should encourage HLCo's management to avoid hedging, because hedging would render the options worthless.

General incentive effects of options

Options and option-like incentives can, depending on how they are structured, moderate or even overwhelm a manager's natural risk aversion, converting the manager into a risk seeker. Stulz uses Figure 15.11 to illustrate this point. His illustration is based on the firm value distributions of Figure 13.1.* Notice that managerial options have a strike price that for practical purposes lies outside the hedged distribution; the options are clearly out of the money. Notice also that a portion of the upper tail of the unhedged distribution lies in the region where the options are in the money. Assume a hedging firm that displays the solid distribution has issued the Figure 15.11 options.

Stockholders of an underperforming firm, for example, may have

---

*One distinction between Figure 15.11 and Figures 15.9 and 15.10 is that the variable along the horizontal axis now is firm value rather than stock price. For present purposes, the distinction is irrelevant.

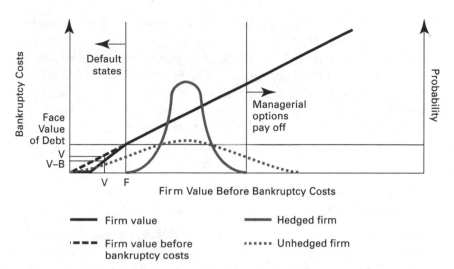

Figure 15.11   Impact of options in managerial compensation contracts. (*Source: Reneé Stulz, "Rethinking Risk Management,"* Journal of Applied Corporate Finance, *Fall 1996, materials reproduced with permission of Stern Stewart & Co.*)

designed the options to induce management to increase firm value enough to shift the distribution to the right. Perhaps these were options granted to new managers of S&L in Figure 15.7 upon its emergence from bankruptcy to motivate them to get S&L out of financial distress. Obviously, management must turn the firm around considerably to shift the distribution enough to move the options into the money. Of course, there might be other, easier ways for management to make its options valuable.

For one thing, management might simply discontinue the existing hedging program. It would then be possible, though unlikely, to realize an upper-tail outcome of the unhedged distribution, which lies in the in-the-money region of the option payoff profiles. Or management might cause the firm to increase its volatility, or its general level of business risk. It might, for example, accept a series of highly risky investments, perhaps even some with negative NPVs. If so, existing managers might be the only ones reasonably capable of truly assessing the value of the investments' NPVs to the firm. If the investments fail and the firm slips into insolvency, outside investors may have difficulty establishing, without management's cooperation, that the NPVs were negative.[35] Clearly here, the "one-sided payoff from stock options effectively rewards management for taking bets and so increasing volatility."[36]

The preceding analysis explains how in theory the form of incentive equity may not only affect but *determine* a manager's incentive to manage risk. Common stock encourages managers to hedge fully, whereas options induce them to avoid hedging entirely. The impact of option packages is particularly striking when one considers that without them, managers would naturally be risk-averse. A powerful implication is that option-like incentives, which besides true options include performance bonuses, can easily overwhelm a manager's natural risk aversion. By receiving options, a naturally risk-averse manager may become a risk seeker.

Gold Mining Industry

Tufano recently tested to see if, among other things, the preceding theory explains how equity compensation in fact affects managers' incentives to manage risk. He found that managerial risk aversion explains, or at least strongly predicts, much of the risk management practices of firms in the North American gold mining industry. Tufano concluded that "the data bear out Smith and Stulz's [1985] prediction that firms whose managers own more stock options manage less gold price risk, and those whose managers have more wealth invested in common stock manage more gold price risk."[37] His finding and conclusion are based on two important positive associations.*

First, there is an association between the form of managerial equity incentive and the level of a firm's risk management. This association supports the view that firms whose managers receive options manage less gold risk than do firms whose managers receive common stock. As the Ace Limited and HLCo examples and Figure 15.10 illustrate, option pricing theory teaches that other things being equal, holders of stock options benefit from increased stock price volatility. "The global convexity of the option contract may induce managers to take on *greater* risk because lower risk would reduce the volatility and hence the value of the expected utility of their option contracts."[38]

Second, management's ownership of common stock is associated with the level of the firm's risk management. Firms whose managers have

---

*Logically, a positive association means only that an increase (decrease) in one variable corresponds, or occurs together with, an increase (decrease) in the other. It does *not* mean that the change in either variable *causes* the corresponding change in the other. The changes in both variables could be caused, for example, by a third factor.

a large percentage of their wealth invested in the firms' common stock manage more gold risk than comparable firms. This again comports with the principles of modern finance. Those principles generally state that risk-averse stockholders prefer lower price risk, or volatility. The logic of Tufano's findings is plain. "The evidence suggests that risk management policies may be set as if to satisfy the needs of poorly diversified, risk-adverse managers."[39]

Board Policy Implications

Ultimately, Tufano is unable to conclude that the form of equity incentive determines firms' risk management practices. For example, he states that "one cannot distinguish whether management teams with more options are less likely to manage price risk, or whether managers of firms with greater risk management are less likely to seek and receive option-based compensation." Moreover, he is careful to stress that the results of his single-industry study, particularly given the industry's unique characteristics, must not be overinterpreted.

Nevertheless, the strength of the association between risk management practices and managerial equity compensation alone is enough to convey "important message[s] for corporate policy."[40] The importance of those messages is heightened by the strong theoretical support for Tufano's findings, findings that have to some extent been replicated in other industries.[41] The immediate message is that "[m]anagement incentives may have a lot to do with why some firms take bets and others do not." It follows, then, that the determination of managerial compensation packages must also be coordinated at the board level with firm derivatives risk management policy. In addition, boards should understand and senior management should coordinate with firm policy the compensation incentives of those who make and implement derivatives risk management decisions.

ENDNOTES: CHAPTER 15

1. Contingent claims analysis is introduced in Chapter 11. See, generally, Mason et al., *Financial Engineering, supra,* Chapter 1, note 2: 353–375.
2. Smith and Stulz, *Determinants of Firms' Hedging Policies, supra,* Chapter 13, note 17: 399.
3. Merton, *Continuous-Time Finance, supra,* Chapter 1, note 26 (citations omitted): 422.

4. See, generally, Mason et al., *Financial Engineering, supra,* Chapter 1, note 2: 355–362.

5. See, generally, Brealey and Myers, *Principles of Corporate Finance, supra,* Chapter 11, note 10 (the source of the Ace Limited and Ace Unlimited illustration used in the text *infra*): 485–487; Miller, *MM Theory After Thirty Years, supra,* Chapter 11, note 16: 109–111.

6. Brealey and Myers, *Principles of Corporate Finance, supra,* Chapter 11, note 10: 487; Myers, *The Search for Optimal Capital Structure, supra,* Chapter 11, note 43: 147–148.

7. Miller, *MM Theory After Thirty Years, supra,* Chapter 11, note 16: 113; see also Brealey and Myers, *Principles of Corporate Finance, supra,* Chapter 11, note 10 (describing bankruptcy as "merely a legal mechanism for allowing creditors to take over" the firm when a decline in asset values puts a firm in a default state): 487.

8. For firms whose bankruptcies are governed by Chapter 11 of the U.S. Bankruptcy Code, see 11 U.S.C. § 1129(a)(11) (1994) (confirmation of a plan of reorganization is conditioned on a "feasibility" finding, that "[c]onfirmation of the plan is not likely to be followed by the liquidation, or the need for further financial reorganization, of the debtor"). See, generally, Peter V. Panteleo and Barry W. Ridings, "Reorganization Value," *Business Lawyer,* 51 (February 1996) (discussing the "surprising" failure of case law in the United States to explain the appropriate valuation methodology to be applied in a reorganization proceeding—particularly, whether or under what circumstances it is to be based on either a "comparable company" or a "discounted cashflow" analysis) [hereafter, *Reorganization Value*]: 419–442. A bankruptcy case is ordinarily categorized on the basis of whether its goal is reorganization or liquidation.

9. Myers, *Determinants of Corporate Borrowing, supra,* Chapter 14, note 10: 159.

10. Myers, *Determinants of Corporate Borrowing, supra,* Chapter 14, note 10: 159; see, generally, Michael C. Jensen, "Corporate Control and the Politics of Finance," *Journal of Applied Corporate Finance,* 4(2) (Summer 1991) (characterizing Chapter 11 as "fundamentally flawed. It is expensive, it exacerbates conflicts of interest among different classes of creditors, and it often takes years to resolve individual cases"): 13–33. But see Richard F. Broude, "Chapter 11 and Its Critics," *International Business Lawyer,* 24(5) (May 1996) (arguing that, in light of its underlying policy decision favoring rehabilitation of debtors, "for the most part, [Chapter 11] functions well"): 241–245.

11. Stulz, *Rethinking Risk Management, supra,* Chapter 10, note 8: 12.

12. See Smithson et al., *Managing Financial Risk, supra,* Chapter 11, note 13: 106; see also Brealey and Myers, *Principles of Corporate Finance, supra,*

Chapter 11, note 10 (detailing many important indirect costs of Penn Central Railroad and discussing the market impact of Texaco's Chapter 11 case): 488–490.

13. J. M. Farley, "A Judicial Perspective on Cross-Border Insolvencies and Restructurings," *International Business Lawyer,* 24(5) (May 1996) (Judge Farley is Chief Judge of the Commercial Division of the Ontario Court of Justice): 221.

14. E. Bruce Leonard, "Internationalisation of Insolvency and Reorganisations," *International Business Lawyer,* 24(5) (May 1996) [hereafter, *Internationalisation of Insolvency*]: 203–206.

15. Stulz, *Rethinking Risk Management, supra,* Chapter 10, note 8 (emphasis in original): 12.

16. See Stulz, *Rethinking Risk Management, supra,* Chapter 10, note 8: 13.

17. See, generally, Brealey and Myers, *Principles of Corporate Finance, supra,* Chapter 11, note 10: 490–498; Myers, *Determinants of Corporate Borrowing, supra,* Chapter 14, note 10.

18. Myers, *Determinants of Corporate Borrowing, supra,* Chapter 14, note 10: 155.

19. See Myers, *Determinants of Corporate Borrowing, supra,* Chapter 14, note 10: 149.

20. Myers, *Determinants of Corporate Borrowing, supra,* Chapter 14, note 10 (noting also that "Where covenants exist, we must conclude that managers and shareholders have found that it pays to accept them"): 161; see also Brealey and Myers, *Principles of Corporate Finance, supra,* Chapter 11, note 10: 494.

21. Myers, *Determinants of Corporate Borrowing, supra,* Chapter 14, note 10: 161.

22. Hu, *The Puzzle of Shareholder Welfare, supra,* Chapter 13, note 20: 1278. This article, together with *Behind the Corporate Hedge, supra,* Chapter 10, note 9; *Hedging Expectations, supra,* Chapter 2, note 36; and other articles authored by Hu and referred to in the foregoing articles, explores in detail the potentially jarring impact of derivatives and financial innovation on traditional fiduciary duties. More fundamentally, these articles explore traditional conceptions of the corporation itself, deeply embedded in corporate law. They suggest for many reasons that the traditional conceptions, which prevail in most states, are based on outdated financial theories. As such, they are inadequate and in need of modernization to accommodate the now widely accepted principles of modern finance.

23. Corinne Ball and Robert L. Messineo, "Fiduciary Duties of Officers and Directors of the Financially Troubled Company: A Primer," in *Mergers and Acquisitions in the 90s,* Richard A. Goldberg, Chair (Practising Law Institute, 1996) [hereafter, *Fiduciary Duties of Officers and Directors of the Financially Troubled Company*]: 127–150, 133-134; see, generally, Hu,

Hedging Expectations, supra, Chapter 2, note 36 (discussing the Delaware law shift in directors' duties when a firm is "in the vicinity of insolvency"): 1027–1030; Brent Nicholson, "Recent Delaware Case Law Regarding Directors' Duties to Bondholders," *Delaware Journal of Corporate Law,* 19 (1994) ("it is settled Delaware law that directors do not owe bondholders any duty other than compliance with the terms of the bond indenture"): 573; Hu, *The Puzzle of Shareholder Welfare, supra,* Chapter 13, note 20 (noting that the firms must also comply with statutes governing the payment of dividends and other distributions, fraudulent conveyances laws, and other laws protecting creditors' rights): 1289.

24. Merton, *Continuous-Time Finance, supra,* Chapter 1, note 17: 306. See, generally, *Id.* (discussing, with cross-references, problem of managers with heavy debt loads in their capital structures assuming negative NPV projects that benefit common stock prices at the expense of overall firm market value): 419–427.

25. Tufano, *Who Manages Risk?, supra,* Chapter 10, note 8: 1126.

26. This and the following quotation are from Smithson et al., *Managing Financial Risk, supra,* Chapter 11, note 13: 108.

27. Stulz, *Rethinking Risk Management, supra,* Chapter 10, note 8 (emphasis modified): 17.

28. See Stulz, *Rethinking Risk Management, supra,* Chapter 10, note 8: 16–17.

29. For discussions of agency problems as they relate to external equity, see Michael C. Jensen and W. H. Meckling, "Theory of the Firm: Managerial Behavior, Agency Costs and Capital Structure," *Journal of Financial Economics,* 3 (1976): 305–360, and Denis et al., *Agency Problems, Equity Ownership, and Corporate Diversification, supra,* Chapter 14, note 25. For a discussion of agency conflicts as they relate directly to the use of derivatives to manage financial risks, see Tufano, *Who Manages Risk?, supra,* Chapter 10, note 8 (discussing the "agency conflict" that extant theory posits may induce risk-averse managers to manage risk through their firms indirectly rather than directly for their own account, because indirectly they bear proportionately less costs): 1122.

30. Stulz, *Rethinking Risk Management, supra,* Chapter 10, note 8: 19.

31. Fischel, *The Trans Union Case, supra,* Chapter 14, note 13 [noting also that it is "always possible to argue that a bad outcome could have been avoided (or a good outcome would have been better)"]: 1442; see also Mark A. Sargent, "Two Cheers for the Maryland Director and Officer Liability Statute," *Baltimore Law Review,* 18 (1989) (noting that liability rules holding directors responsible for bad outcomes and awarding to stockholders gains from good outcomes (1) are against stockholders' interests and (2) transfer risk "from more efficient to less efficient risk-bearers") [hereafter, *Two Cheers for the Maryland Statute*]: 278–309, 288.

32. See Smith and Stulz, *Determinants of Firms' Hedging Policies, supra,* Chapter 13, note 17; Tufano, *Who Manages Risk?, supra,* Chapter 10, note 8.

33. The quotations in this paragraph are from Smith and Stulz, *Determinants of Firms' Hedging Policies, supra,* Chapter 13, note 15: 399; see, generally, Denis et al., *Agency Problems, Equity Ownership, and Corporate Diversification, supra,* Chapter 14, note 25.

34. *Id.:* 402.

35. See, generally, Myers, *Determinants of Corporate Borrowing, supra,* Chapter 14, note 10 (noting that outsiders cannot "intelligently" determine the NPV of projects without management's estimates): 158–159.

36. This and the following quotation are from Stulz, *Rethinking Risk Management, supra,* Chapter 10, note 8: 18–19.

37. Tufano, *Who Manages Risk?, supra,* Chapter 10, note 8 (citation omitted): 1099.

38. Tufano, *Who Manages Risk?, supra,* Chapter 10, note 8 (emphasis in original): 1109; see also Smith and Stulz, *Determinants of Firms' Hedging Policies, supra,* Chapter 13, note 15 ("If the manager's expected utility is a convex function of the value of the firm, the manager will behave like a risk seeker even though his expected utility function is a concave function"): 401.

39. This and the quotation in the following paragraph are from *Id.:* 1120. Tufano notes that his findings are generally consistent with those of other comparable studies of different industries. One set of studies explored the relationship between managerial risk aversion and corporate diversification through mergers and acquisitions. See Don O. May, "Do Managerial Motives Influence Firm Risk Reduction Strategies?" *Journal of Finance,* 50 (1995): 1275–1290; Yakov Ahimud and Baruch Lev, "Risk Reduction as a Managerial Motive for Conglomerate Mergers," *Bell Journal of Economics,* 12 (1981): 605–617. The other set of studies examined the equity ownership and risk management practices of managers of thrift institutions. See C. M. Schrand and H. Unal, "Coordinated Risk Management: On- and Off-Balance Sheet Hedging and Thrift Conversion," unpublished working paper (1995), Wharton School, University of Pennsylvania.

40. This and the following quotation are from Stulz, *Rethinking Risk Management, supra,* Chapter 10, note 8: 17–20.

41. In a footnote Tufano discusses the findings of two studies. One, a study of thrift institutions, found that those institutions whose managers hold more common stock hedge more while those who managers hold options hedge less. The other, however, found no such association. Tufano, *Who Manages Risk?, supra,* Chapter 10, note 8 (citations omitted): 1118, note 25.

Derivatives-Related Fiduciary Duties: A Functional Analysis

> But there may be a deeper reason for caution. Examination of the activities of fiduciaries involves, above all, an inquiry into the propriety of profit-making. What is at stake is whether the court should sanction or stigmatize a particular act performed by a businessman in a commercial context.
>
> *Ernest Weinrib*
> *"The Fiduciary Obligation," 1975*

> It is striking to see contemporary courts, citing the Restatement, [Professor Scott's] Treatise, or authority derived from those two sources, haul professional trustees over the coals for investment policies that few financial economists would find exceptional.
>
> *Jeffrey Gordon*
> *"The Puzzling Persistence of the*
> *Prudent Man Rule,"* NYU Law Review,
> *1987*

The fiduciary concept in American law is a direct descendent of the English law of trusts. However, its use continues to expand far beyond the confines of trust law, both through common law and through state and federal statutes and regulations. Unfortunately, expansion has created doctrinal confusion and legal uncertainty. Courts, legislatures, and regulators routinely apply the concept to so many disparate commercial relationships that many commentators view it as lacking legal coherence. Others find coherence, but they do so by dismissing the distinctive function and history of the fiduciary concept. These scholars treat fiduciary law as nothing more than an aspect of contract law, as a peculiarly intense version of the contractual obligation of good faith.

Legal uncertainty, always problematic, is more so when the topic shifts to derivatives. Many derivatives losses have been spectacular, newsworthy events. Recent history shows that when losses are reported, the initial public shock can quickly degenerate into indignation and moral outrage. In such cases, the moral element and elusive nature of fiduciary duties seemingly make charges and countercharges of fiduciary violations all but inevitable. If a loss has occurred, surely someone must be to blame, someone must be held accountable!

Not surprisingly, many observers and market participants worry that the complexity and opacity of derivatives heighten their legal risks, particularly in the morally and emotionally charged realm of fiduciary duties. The current paucity of judicial and statutory authority specifically addressing the fiduciary implications of modern financial derivatives use exacerbates tensions. It even seems to have led one former CFTC chairman to muse that there might one day "evolve a concept of *per se,* or automatic, liability whenever unwanted risks that can be avoided are not properly hedged."[1] Although the former chairman expressly limited his comments to institutional investors "having sobering fiduciary duties," the limitation is meaningless. The essence of all fiduciary duties is that they are ethical and hence sobering matters.

Earlier chapters have shown how familiarity with derivatives' economic functions enhances the ability to control the products' financial risks. Likewise, familiarity with the functions of fiduciary law offers a firm foundation for managing risks that trustees, directors, and other senior managers might violate derivatives-related fiduciary duties. However, managing those risks does not guarantee that a business or portfolio will never incur losses. Derivatives may be powerful risk management tools, but they are neither panaceas nor the proverbial free lunch. Their use implies direct transaction and infrastructure costs and indirect strategic trade-offs. Little support exists for the theory that directors, trustees, or other fiduciaries have a general duty to hedge, the violation of which is a "fundamental management flaw." Much support exists for the notion that management of a firm that does hedge must understand its hedging operations well enough to supervise them properly.

In this chapter, we begin analyzing derivatives-related fiduciary duties using the tools of functional analysis. We rely largely on traditional fiduciary analyses, such as those articulated by Professor Tamar Frankel of Boston University School of Law and Victor Brudney, Professor of Law Emeritus of the Harvard Law School and Visiting Professor of Boston College Law School.[2] Our analysis incorporates important insights from modern finance and those aspects of the "contractarian" approach to fiduciary duties that enrich a traditional analysis.

FUNCTION OF FIDUCIARY LAW

Structure of Fiduciary Relationships

Fiduciary law applies to diverse types of consensual relationships established for the provision of services by one party, a fiduciary, for the benefit of another, the entrustor.* The fiduciary acts as a substitute for the entrustor in performing those services. The entrustor, for any number of reasons, either is incapable of performing or chooses not to perform the services itself.

To perform its services, the fiduciary receives delegated discretionary power over the entrustor's property from the entrustor or a third party. That power, the nature and scope of which varies depending on the contemplated services, enables the fiduciary to alter the entrustor's legal rights in the entrusted property. Of critical importance is that the power is "delegated to the fiduciary not for his own use, but solely for the purpose of facilitating the performance of his [services]."[3] The fiduciary has no right or entitlement to the property or powers, but instead receives them as a necessary condition to enable it to perform its services.

Structural Dependence

To the extent of the delegation, an entrustor becomes dependent on the fiduciary to perform the contemplated services; delegation implies not only a grant of power to the fiduciary, but also a relinquishing of power by the entrustor. Private attempts to limit or control the fiduciary's ability to exercise its delegated power are either impracticable or so costly that they defeat the purposes of the relationship. Thus, the dependency results not

---

*Frankel coined the term *entrustor* and uses it for want of a better alternative. Entrustor is sufficiently descriptive to connote the two "unifying features of all fiduciary relations": first, the
root "trust" identifies the "substitution function" that a fiduciary performs, standing in the
entrustor's place as to entrusted matters; second, "entrust" suggests the delegation of powers
to the fiduciary to perform contemplated services. Frankel readily acknowledges the imperfections of the term. For example, the settlor of a trust, not the beneficiary, does the delegating. Yet all things considered, the imperfections are minor. *Entrustor* is less confusing than
other terms such as *beneficiary,* an odd term for describing such diverse entrustors as, general partners, joint venturers, patients of physicians or psychiatrists, clients of lawyers, union
members, stockholders, and, at times, bondholders and institutional lenders. See Frankel,
Fiduciary Law, supra, note 2: 800 n. 17.

from the relative sophistication of the parties, but rather from the nature and structure of the relationship. (Among other things, this structural dependency party explains the strange phenomenon of otherwise sophisticated parties to derivatives transactions suing their dealers for alleged breaches of fiduciary duties.)[4]

Often, for example, investors seek to benefit from the expertise of professional money managers. Doing so, however, requires them to delegate to the managers significant discretionary power over their investment funds. As discussed shortly, such relationships are often fiduciary.

> Ideally, for the beneficiary [i.e., the entrustor], this relationship would be governed by specific rules that dictate how the fiduciary should manage the asset in the beneficiary's interest. In fact, however, the fiduciary's obligation's are open-ended. Because asset management necessarily involves risk and uncertainty, the specific behavior of the fiduciary cannot be dictated in advance.[5]

Attempts to dictate that behavior or determine a decision rule with any specificity could undermine the benefits of the relationship.

For example, a fiduciary's investment responsibilities might require it to monitor a constantly changing mix of potential risk-return trade-offs. Consider a perfectly balanced portfolio that is to be invested half in stocks, half in cash. It will likely soon fall out of balance absent active intervention. Changing FX and interest rates, changing fortunes of portfolio companies, and other fluid factors should over time alter the proportionate values of stock and cash investments. The fiduciary will need to actively rebalance the portfolio to maintain the 50-50 ratio.

Similarly, corporations operate in highly competitive and uncertain business environments. Consider the difficulty of attempting, say, to forecast a firm's and its competitors' product demand, FX and interest rates, and changing costs of machinery, labor, and raw materials. Attempts to document and prespecify a detailed decision rule to cover all combinations and permutations of circumstances that might foreseeably arise in the life of a firm would be futile. Corporations face a vast array of possible variations in fortune, all of which come and go in highly charged, competitive environments. Opportunities and risks arise constantly and in combinations, most of which will become clear only in hindsight, not when they first appear and demand a manager's attention.

To overcome the problem, the fiduciary might volunteer to craft, or it might offer advice or suggestions as to, restrictions that might benefit the entrustor while preserving adequate discretion for the fiduciary to exercise its expertise and perform its services properly. But how useful would the fiduciary's contribution here be, given the entrustor's lack of expertise in evaluating whether the contribution is self-serving or disinterested? How will the entrustor confirm that restrictions suggested by the fiduciary are appropriate? One way might be to seek confirmation by retaining the services of a second expert, but that will likely dramatically increase costs without necessarily solving the problem. On what basis would the entrustor rely on the second fiduciary? The problem becomes circular, because "[w]hen one party hires the other's knowledge and expertise, there is not much they can write down."[6]

Many other reasons may explain the parties' inability to specify in writing the services to be provided and thus detail the content of the fiduciary's obligations. Perhaps the task is too complex or open-ended. Or it may depend on too many presently unforeseeable contingencies for the parties to specify in advance what must be done under any given set of circumstances. Consider also the case of a public company in which many stockholders invest. Doing so enables them to pool their capital to undertake large-scale operations, and otherwise to obtain the benefits of centralized and specialized management. Attempts by investors to limit management's ability to exercise its discretion to some extent undermine the benefits of separation of ownership and management. As investors independently try to restrict management's discretionary power, they begin to defeat the purposes of centralized management. In sum, "if the entrustor lessens his exposure to loss by reducing the delegated power, he may also reduce the benefit expected from the relation."[7]

Difficulty Monitoring or Controlling

Efforts by the entrustor to monitor and control the fiduciary's performance are of limited utility and may undermine the benefits of the relationship. The same expertise required to perform a professional service may be needed to evaluate the content and quality of that service. Again, an entrustor who lacks that expertise might monitor performance by, for example, hiring a second professional. But doing so increases the entrustor's costs and may entail the same fiduciary problems as the original relationship. It may also create conflicts of interest, especially if the second fiduciary stands to benefit by capturing the first's business.

Alternatively, even if the entrustor has the relevant expertise, constantly monitoring the fiduciary's performance may defeat the purpose of the relationship. It would deprive the entrustor of the ability to rely on someone else to perform the contemplated services. Consider also that neither the fiduciary nor anyone else may, regardless of expertise, be capable of evaluating performance on the basis of outcomes. Perhaps outcomes are independent of the quality or intensity of the fiduciary's effort; even skilled and hardworking litigators can lose cases, and highly talented and diligent investment professionals can incur losses. Maybe outcomes will be unknowable for a long while, as is often the case with portfolio managers who pursue long-term growth strategies.

Central Problem: Abuse of Delegated Power[8]

All fiduciary relationships pose the same fundamental problem: the delegation of discretionary powers exposes entrustors to risks of loss that far exceed any potential gains they might expect from their fiduciaries' services. To permit fiduciaries' to exercise the discretion at the core of the relationship, entrustors must delegate broad and to varying degrees open-ended powers. Those powers are capable of general but not specific limitations, because they must convey adequate discretion to permit the fiduciary to perform its services. Fiduciaries' powers are, then, intrinsically overly broad. They enable fiduciaries to use the entrustors' property for unauthorized purposes outside the scope of the parties' relationship. Entrustors are exposed to risks arising from their fiduciaries' misappropriation or neglect of the entrusted property.

Often, however, an abuse of delegated powers is exceptionally difficult to detect, because the fiduciary maintains legitimate possession of the property entrusted to it. Likewise, the entrustor, having relinquished possession and control, may be unable to monitor the fiduciary's activities: the "'beneficiary being on the outside, cannot know everything that is going on. Moreover, the beneficiary is off his guard.'"[9] The problem is not the fiduciary's control or possession of the property, but its use of the property for a purpose other than that contemplated by the relationship.

For example, an investor might entrust a large sum of money to a professional money manager to invest on the investor's behalf. Often such relationships enable investors to earn higher expected returns on their funds than they would otherwise expect to earn investing on their own. Depending on its risk-return preferences, an investor might be prepared to accept significant investment risk in the hope of generating significant returns. If so, the investor would be willing to delegate significant discretionary investment authority to its professional. Certainly, however, the investor does not contemplate that the professional might freely appropriate those funds for its own investment or other use. Nor does the investor intend to permit the professional to invest the funds on the investor's behalf carelessly or irresponsibly.

Function of Fiduciary Law

The fiduciary law's function derives from the unique nature and structure of the fiduciary relationship and the "extraordinary risks" to which an entrustor is exposed.[10] That function is to protect the entrustor from the risk of loss resulting from its fiduciary's potential misappropriation, often likened to embezzlement, or neglect of the entrusted property. Absent such protection, few entrustors would enter into fiduciary relationships, because the risks of the relationships would be unacceptably high. To see why, consider the plight of the typical entrustor in a commercial relationship absent fiduciary protections.

By parting with and delegating to the fiduciary the power to alter its legal rights, the entrustor accepts risks of loss that far exceed its potential gain from the relationship. In particular, the entrustor runs the risk that its fiduciary will misappropriate or negligently manage the entrusted property. Moreover, as we have seen, the entrustor parts with power over its property under conditions that preclude it from effectively monitoring and controlling the fiduciary's behavior. As discussed, contractual solutions and alternative mechanisms to protect the entrustor and minimize its risks are either unavailable or inadequate.

To encourage entrustors to enter into fiduciary relationships, society must intervene in those relationships to mitigate entrustors' exposure: "entrustors must be induced to enter the relationships by assurances that overcome their concern for the safety of their assets. They must be convinced that the relationship is likely to bring them net economic benefits."[11] One of the important mechanisms by which society provides entrustors with those assurances is through fiduciary law. Backed by the coercive power of the state, fiduciary law imposes on fiduciaries paramount duties to their entrustors of *loyalty* and *care* in the management of the entrusted property. Those duties are considered the "two *building blocks* of fiduciary law...[that] constitute 'reliance rules.'"[12] They entitle entrustors to trust and rely on their fiduciaries' honesty. Depending on the circumstances, fiduciary law also imposes ancillary duties designed to implement the duties of loyalty and care.

Functional Distinction Between Fiduciary Law and Contract Law

An important scholarly dispute regarding the distinction between fiduciary law and contract law helps better illuminate fiduciary law's distinctive function. Moreover, the dispute has begun to influence decided cases. Still, "U.S. courts have thus far refused to sweep fiduciary duties under the contract rug, although some courts have tended to limit the reach of fiduciary duties."[13]

Fiduciary law

As discussed earlier, the primary function of fiduciary law is to mitigate the extraordinary risks to which entrustors would otherwise be subject. Hence, fiduciary law is, in this respect, one-sided. Its concern is solely directed to the protection of the entrustor. When legal obligations, such as the reimbursement of fiduciaries' expenses, are imposed on entrustors, those obligations are fundamentally intended to reinforce the entrustors' protections. Without such reimbursement, for example, fiduciaries would be less likely to take steps to protect entrusted property that require them to expend their own funds.

Moreover, fiduciary law is not concerned with the process by which parties establish fiduciary relationships. Instead, the law looks merely to the terms of the relationship to decide whether those terms meet the appropriate criteria warranting the intervention of fiduciary law. Thus, the "relationship may arise as an incidence of contract, trust, will, statute, charter, election, or without any legally binding agreement. Fiduciary law is triggered merely by the fiduciary's consent to provide services, coupled with entrustment."[14]

Finally, fiduciary law does not, absent an agreement between the parties to the contrary, entitle the fiduciary to compensation for its services:

> To be sure, the trustee [or other commercial fiduciary] does not function as an altruist who foregoes all concern with advancing self-interest. With rare exceptions the fiduciary expects, and receives, compensation for performing his or her function. That compensation is provided by the express terms of the arrangement, or by the courts in the absence of such a provision. But apart from such compensation, the exclusive benefit principle precludes rewards to the fiduciary.[15]

All that is needed to incur fiduciary obligations is entrustment plus consent: unlike a contract, the fiduciary relationship requires no mutual exchange of bargained-for consideration. The purpose of fiduciary law is to protect entrustors, not fiduciaries. Entrustors are at risk once they part with power over their property. So that is when fiduciary law's protections kick in, giving the entrustor the legal right to rely on the fiduciary's honesty and care.

Contract law

Fiduciary and contract law display many similarities, perhaps the most obvious being the process by which the two types of relationships are often established. The primary reason contractarians cite for concluding that fiduciary obligations are contractual is the high degree of correlation between fiduciary obligations and formal contracts. In the words of two leading contractarians: "Nothing illustrates the contractual character of fiduciary law better than one of the cornerstones of trust law: an express provision in the trust instrument governs over the duty of loyalty in the event of conflict."[16]

However, the process orientation of the contractarians, at least in the traditionalists' view, is misplaced. Although many, perhaps most, fiduciary relationships are established through a formal contract,* as both Frankel and Brudney have shown, no formal or even enforceable contract is needed. Nor must there be mutual exchange of consideration. Also, the contractarians find that the "fiduciary relation is a contractual one characterized by unusually high costs of specification and monitoring. The duty of loyalty replaces detailed contractual terms."

Two important points of disagreement between the contractarian and fiduciary view relate to the rights, if any, of the fiduciary to compensation and the ability of the entrustor to rely on the fiduciary. As to the former,

---

*Even this assumption is dubious. Scholars argue, for example, that the consent of public entrustors to the actions of corporate fiduciaries is illusory, especially given problems of inadequate disclosure, investor "rational apathy," and problematic consent solicitation procedures that inherently favor management. If so, given the sheer size of public equities markets, the vast majority of fiduciary relations are likely established by means of transactions that do fall short of formal agreements. See Frankel, *Fiduciary Duties, supra,* note 2 (arguing that notions of "apparent consent," much like the philosophers' construct of "social contract," "represent a theoretical model, not reality"): 1251–1276; Brudney, *Contract and Fiduciary Duty in Corporate Law, supra,* note 2 (characterizing as a de facto rejection of the fiduciary duty of loyalty protections corporate law's tendency with "ease" to find stockholder consent to management "self-aggrandizing behavior"; "the restrictions on self-aggrandizement are not simply looser... but they tend to become invisible"): 613.

traditional fiduciary notions clearly contemplate that fiduciaries have no compensation rights at all, other than those designed to enable them to perform their obligations and potential claims for recovery on theories such as unjust enrichment. Contractarians, however, assert that both the fiduciary and the entrustor enter into the fiduciary relationship for gain. Therefore, "the details [of the duty of loyalty] should be those that maximize that gain, which the contracting parties can divide." Under the contractarian view, then, the fiduciary has a right, a legitimate interest, to share in some portion of that gain.

As to reliance rights, a fundamental tenet of the traditionalist view is that the entrustor has the right to rely on the fiduciary to act in the entrustor's best interest. Although the intensity of this duty varies depending on the circumstances, inherent in the substitution function is that the fiduciary will act as the entrustor's "alter ego." As one federal circuit court held: "The essence of a fiduciary relationship is that the fiduciary agrees to act as his principal's alter ego rather than to assume the standard arm's-length stance of traders in a market. Hence the principal is not armed with the usual wariness that one has in dealing with strangers; he trusts the fiduciary."[17] Put differently, the fiduciary must identify with the entrustor's interests, acting in pursuit of those interests only as the entrustor would act for itself.

"Thickness" and "thinness"

Brudney offers a useful way to characterize the differences between the fiduciary and contract views. He compares the traditional and contractarian approaches on the basis of how each views the role of the state in the parties' relationship. The two groups see the state as, within limits, using its coercive power to give effect to the terms of the parties' arrangements and also, within limits, restricting the arrangements' permissible content. The contractarians view the first role of the state as enforcing the parties' agreement by giving effect to the agreement's express terms and any implied terms reasonably inferred. In this capacity, the state merely completes the parties' agreement.

The state also, however, has a limited role in deciding the content of those agreements. By and large, the parties are free to ignore the state's restrictions, treating them merely as "default" rules that apply unless the parties exclude them. Contract restrictions are, in Brudney's terminology, only "thinly textured." Tto contractarians: "Loyalty and prudence, the norms of trust fiduciary law, embody the default regime that the parties to the trust deal would choose as the criteria for regulating the trustee's behavior in these setting in which it is impractical to foresee precise circumstances and to specify more exact terms."[18] They are like standardized form contracts; "the fiduciary duty is a standby or off-the-rack guess about what parties would agree to if they dickered about the subject explicitly."[19]

In contrast, Brudney finds that "fiduciaries start with thick restrictions that substantially hamper their freedom to act with respect to, or to alter their state-imposed obligations to, their beneficiaries."[20] The restrictions do not apply only to the fiduciary; the state has an interest in protecting entrustors, so it also imposes limitations and rigorous conditions or their ability to waive restrictions on their fiduciaries.

To see the radical departure from current law that would be affected by the contract view, Frankel concludes that the contract view reverses traditional default rules. Traditionally, the default rule is that fiduciaries are prohibited from acting negligently or in conflict of interest. Generally, the parties are free within limits expressly to alter that default rule to permit, narrowly and subject to compelling procedural conditions, waivers of the duty of loyalty and limitations on the care requirement. Under the contract view, however, the traditional default rule would be reversed. Fiduciaries would be free to act negligently or in conflict with their entrustors' interests unless expressly or impliedly prohibited.[21]

Public Policy Implications

The function of mitigating the risks to entrustors in commercial relationships is imbued with public policy implications. To see why, we need only consider the increasing interdependence of modern society. Modern economies depend on specialization of labor to increase the productivity of capital, and essential to that specialization is the separation of ownership and control. To achieve the economies of scale needed to undertake large-scale indivisible enterprises, typically many investors must pool resources and entrust them to a "professional managerial class."[22] Those managers perform for investors the centralized management function essential to the day-to-day operations of large-scale enterprises. Centralized, specialized management is efficient only if investors delegate to management the power to control the use of their capital.

Specialization and pooling also serve other vital economic functions. Specialization "increases the total amount of available expert services," with each expert acting as the substitute for all others in society who entrust their property to that expert.[23] In addition to providing entrepreneurs with the risk capital needed to undertake large-scale ventures, pooling enables investors to engage in risk pooling and risk sharing. Those functions are, of course, essential to modern investment theory and practice. The vast majority of individual investors typically engage in diversification strategies. Even when they do not, they seldom have sufficient capital invested in any given public company to have, individually, an effective say in its management.

Essential to efficient capital markets is trust in the financial system. "The price of mistrust is high"; available evidence suggests that if investors' trust in the financial system fails, they will withdraw their capital from the system, rendering that capital unproductive.[24] Mitchell starkly poses the central question for investors: "Would you entrust your money to people who you were told had the power, practical ability, and legal right to take some of it for themselves? Of course, not. You might, however, if you were told they had to treat you fairly."[25] Well, perhaps you would if you also knew they had to manage that money in your best interest, subject only to their limited rights to compensation for services rendered.

Judicial Classification

Given the public policy implications of fiduciary law, classification of a relationship as fiduciary or not is too important a matter to be left to private ordering.[26] Otherwise, parties could defeat the underlying public policy of the fiduciary law merely by calling a fiduciary relationship something else, and perhaps disclaiming fiduciary responsibilities. Presently, courts decide the classification of various relationships as fiduciary or otherwise, and also whether to accord entrustors the protections of fiduciary laws. Although the parties' stated intentions are relevant, in the words of New York's highest court, "[m]ere words will not blind us to realities."[27]

Imposition of fiduciary duties depends only on the nature and terms of the relationship arranged by the parties: it does not require express or implied an agreement by the fiduciary specifically to assume obligations that are fiduciary in character. Within limits, the parties can set the terms of their relationship, but courts ultimately decide whether those terms create a fiduciary relationship. Courts also decide the nature and extent of the correlative fiduciary duties.

In deciding upon a classification, courts begin from the parties' private arrangements. They also weigh factors such as equity, public policy, mandatory legal obligations, and state-imposed limitations on the parties' freedom privately to structure their dealings. Once a court has classified a relationship as fiduciary, it must decide the content and intensity of the fiduciary duties. That decision is again a task requiring the court to weigh factors besides the parties' private arrangements. Both the classification and the decision regarding the nature of any duties can be complicated. Circumstances implicating fiduciary duties and affecting the content and intensity of any duties found vary over time and across different types of relationships. Those same circumstances also vary among relationships of the same type and can have over time varying effects on individual relationships.

Given its concern with and deference to extracontractual factors, fiduciary law sets substantial limitations on fiduciaries' "freedom to act with respect to, or to alter their state-imposed obligations to, their [entrustors]."[28] Likewise, it imposes substantial procedural and substantive limitations on entrustors' freedom to consent to restrictions on their fiduciary protections. Both sets of limitations apply regardless of any express desire of the parties to waive, alter, or "bargain around" them. Viewed functionally, then, fiduciary duties automatically, without regard to the parties' intentions or private arrangements, entitle entrustors to varying degrees of mandatory, nonwaivable legal protections. Even in the case of those protections that are waivable, fiduciary law imposes significant requirements designed to ensure that any waiver is fully informed and volitional.

When Fiduciary Law Does Not Apply, or Is Relaxed

Scholars have shown that much of the confusion surrounding the fiduciary concept is due to the many and varied conditions that implicate fiduciary law. In a commercial context, the starting point for analysis is that discussed earlier: namely, one party delegates to another certain power over property, and that other party agrees or consents to provide services relating to the property for the benefit of the delegator or a third party. Yet some service relationships, such as bailments, involving delegations of power over property have been held not fiduciary. The question, then, is: What distinguishes service relationships that are fiduciary from those that are not?

Frankel and Brudney find that the answer to the classification question lies in the central problem of all fiduciary relationships: the abuse of delegated powers. By implication, that problem is not sufficient to invoke the protections of fiduciary law under a variety of circumstances. For example: "If the entrustor is able to protect himself from abuse of power, there is no need for the intervention of fiduciary law."[29] Similarly, if the application of fiduciary law would undermine a competing public policy or cause great doctrinal confusion, courts are unlikely to apply it. To date, courts have resisted applying fiduciary law, or at least softened its restrictions, under circumstances such as those discussed below.

Contract law; respect for individual autonomy

A foundation of Anglo-American law is respect for individual autonomy, out of which the law, in classifying relationships, favors individual private ordering. "In our society…personal freedom is cherished."[30] It is so cherished that ordinarily the state uses its coercive powers to protect private ordering rather than interfere with it, even when private ordering permits opportunistic behavior. Generally, the law presumes that contracting parties can protect themselves from each other's opportunism, even that in the form of negligence or conflict of interest.

In this sense, contract law safeguards private ordering by enabling individuals to invoke the state's coercive powers to enforce their private bargains. Above all, enforcement gives effect to the express terms of a bargain and to any other terms that can reasonably be implied from or read into those express terms. Under classic contract doctrine, then, "autonomous human beings are deemed to negotiate with one another volitionally and more or less knowledgeably as adversaries who seek some level of cooperation."[31] The parties enter into bargained-for exchanges in which each expects the other to be acting opportunistically and so is on its guard to protect itself. To be sure, the state may at times limit the scope of the parties' contractual freedom. Yet the limitations are mainly designed to reinforce freedom of contract, not limit it. For example, a court might interfere with a contract that it finds to be the product of duress, adhesion, or bad faith, or the terms of which are unconscionable. But it does so to ensure that each party acted autonomously and that it freely and knowingly agreed to the contract's terms. The presence of any such defect suggests a lack of requisite autonomy.

Generally, protecting the ability of autonomous individuals to contract freely requires that the state tolerate some degree of opportunistic behavior. Clearly, at the margins the opportunistic behavior tolerated under contract law may "rub shoulders" with that which fiduciary law prohibits, but conceptually the two are different.[32] Still, contract law holds that autonomous, wary actors who want protection from their counterparties' negligence and disloyalty must bargain for it. In contrast, fiduciary law protects entrustors even in the absence of bargaining.

Important, however, is that federal law has in recent years begun to play a more prominent role in the formulation of fiduciary law. Certain countervailing federal public policies argue in favor of statutory interference with private ordering. Traditionally, state common law, much of which has now been codified in state statutes, has determined the content of fiduciary duties. Yet as the massive amount of retirement savings entrusted by employees to private institutions continues to grow, likewise does the importance to individuals and society of the fiduciary standards imposed under the Employee Retirement Income Security Act of 1974 (ERISA).[33] ERISA effectively intervenes in private ordering to establish comprehensive standards governing the conduct of plan fiduciaries. Also important, though as discussed immediately below less far-reaching, has been the role of the SEC in attempting to impose fiduciary duties on securities market intermediaries.

Competing public policies

A direct conflict of public policies arose in recent decades over efforts by the SEC to protect the "paramount importance of the integrity of our capital markets."[34] The SEC has, since the 1970s and with mixed results, taken active interest in matters of corporate governance traditionally left to state corporate law under the "internal affairs" doctrine. The SEC's goal has been to foster market integrity through its doctrine of "corporate accountability." That goal can easily conflict with states' recognized interests in regulating the internal affairs of their domestic corporations.

SEC concerns in this regard focus on precisely the same issues as state fiduciary law: namely, the potential for corporate management to abuse its power and position by engaging in self-interested transactions contrary to stockholders' interests. The SEC has been successful in establishing the importance of outside directors, acting on behalf of outside investors, in functioning as independent monitors and providing management oversight. Yet significant questions remain regarding the effectiveness of that and other mechanisms as tools for management oversight.[35] Still, the SEC's perceived and judicially sanctioned role is confined to policing corporate governance solely to ensure accurate, timely, and complete disclosure of material information. State law continues to define officers' and directors' fiduciary duties.

Overall, then, the latitude allowed to the SEC to intervene in matters traditionally left to state law and private ordering is limited. In contrast, courts have permitted the SEC to expand its reach, using fiduciary doctrine to protect the integrity of securities markets where such expansion does not encroach on states' interests. For example, the U.S. Supreme Court recently upheld the SEC's effort to combat insider trading through fiduciary principals.[36]

Potential overprohibition; the "business judgment rule"[37]

Often, the potential costs to society and individuals of prohibiting conduct that would technically be prohibited under a strict fiduciary regime lead courts and legislatures to relax fiduciary requirements. Consider, for example, the "business judgment rule" (discussed below) of corporate law. The rule is a presumption that precludes the vast majority of management's business decisions from second-guessing by stockholders under charges that the decisions were made in violation of management's duty of care. The reasons for the rule are twofold. First, without its protections, the risks of potential liability might make it exceedingly difficult for many corporations to attract qualified candidates, especially for board positions.

Second, enabling stockholders easily to commence actions attacking management decisions will undermine management's willingness to cause firms to take the business risks that are in the stockholders' best interests. Corporations are enterprises undertaken to maximize stockholder wealth, and business risk is needed to generate profits. Few investors can expect risk-free activities to generate more than risk-free returns. As residual risk bearers whose interest is wealth maximization and who can diversify, stockholders have strong incentives to encourage management to assume business risk. Those incentives often conflict with management's natural risk aversion. Most managers are, after all, stakeholders who are overinvested in their firms and inclined to avoid business risk. Threats of lawsuits increase managerial risk aversion, risking overprohibiting risky business activities.

On the other hand, courts and legislators are more resistant to efforts to relax the exclusive benefit principle that precludes fiduciaries from acting in their self-interest. The principle is strictly enforced in most areas of fiduciary law. Under corporate law, the principle is sufficiently powerful to overcome initially the protections of the business judgment rule. If sufficient evidence is adduced to suggest that a decision was motivated by managerial self-interest, the burden of proving a proper motive shifts back to management. If, however, management is then able to demonstrate a proper business motive, the presumption of the business judgment rule shifts back, protecting management's decisions.

Legal and market mechanisms protecting entrustors

A variety of legal and market mechanisms for protecting entrustors are relied on by courts to justify relaxing or not applying fiduciary law. One that is straightforward is the ability of entrustors to control or terminate the services of their fiduciaries. Compare, for example, agency relationships to private trusts. The feasibility of monitoring and controlling any particular agent varies among agency relationships. Still, as a general proposition, principals have much less difficulty terminating their agents than beneficiaries under private trusts have in removing trustees. Thus, fiduciary protections created under trust law are ordinarily stronger than those created under the law of agency.

One area in which the ability to terminate relationships has generated controversy involves "public fiduciary relationships—i.e., mass-produced relationships with numerous entrustors such as shareholders of [public] corporations."[38] A common economic argument for relaxing fiduciary restrictions on public fiduciaries is that stockholders, for example, can always terminate or "exit" the relationship simply by selling their interests. The argument is particularly compelling when the interests at issue consists of stock of large public companies having active trading markets. However, the economic argument raises a number of important concerns. One is the question of fairness to exiting stockholders who are unlikely to recover the full value they could otherwice expect for their stock, if they are selling as a result of some careless or self-interested transaction by a fiduciary.

Alternatively, many potential fiduciary relationships are governed by alternative regulatory regimes that render the protections of fiduciary law superfluous. A good example is the comprehensive regulation of stockbrokers that has led to a relaxation of some fiduciary protections.[39]

ELUSIVE FIDUCIARY CONCEPT

Before we examine in Chapter 17 the function of fiduciary law and its application to derivatives, it helps to consider why fiduciary law has generated so much uncertainty. Legal uncertainty, actual or perceived, may predispose fiduciaries and their legal advisers to be overly cautious, avoiding entirely products and activities that could plausibly raise fiduciary duty questions. But not every question is a problem. In a global economy, few businesses and portfolios can afford categorically to rule out products that are as commercially and competitively significant as derivatives. If we show that actual uncertainty as to fiduciary duties is less than commonly believed, then it follows that much of the concern over derivatives' legal risks is unwarranted.

Here, an understanding of the defects of traditional methods of developing fiduciary law and of the paucity of judicial decisions offering definitive derivatives guidance is instructive. It fosters receptivity to the idea that fiduciary duties need not be more problematic in their application to derivatives than to most other business activities.

Trust Law Origins; Equitable Principles

Historically, the fiduciary concept traces its origins to trust law. Transplanted in the United States from England, trust law is rooted in ancient principles of equity.[40] Equitable principles empower courts and administrative bodies to apply abstract notions of justice and fairness to concrete situations without rigid adherence to legal rules. Consequently, decision makers are free to act "pragmatically rather than logically."[41] Trust concepts are flexible and elastic, and courts exercising equitable powers readily apply them with wide latitude to many relationships other than formal trusts. Courts often use those powers and concepts to remedy past wrongs or prevent perceived injustice.

Much of the popularity of the fiduciary concept is due to the flexibility that it, like all equitable powers, affords courts and agencies in fashioning remedies where none might otherwise exist. "A court or agency faced with an ethical breach, or a sharp practice or lapse in judgment that falls short of violating statutory or common law standards can use the fiduciary concept to fill the gap in the law and protect those who are disadvantaged."[42] Alternatively, courts and agencies can use that flexibility to avoid imposing sanctions for technical legal violations under circumstances where sanctions would be unfair. Finally, the same flexibility allows judges to exercise discretion in deciding difficult cases involving newly appearing forms of economic relationships or unforeseen changes in existing relationships. Equitable powers, however, have their drawbacks.

Flexibility or Subjectivity?

Despite the impressive heritage and expansive application of the fiduciary concept, a unified, consistent definition of it remains elusive. Consider Professor Scott's attempt at a definition. He defines a fiduciary relation as one involving "a duty on the part of the fiduciary to act for the benefit of the other party as to matters within the scope of the relation."[43] Yet the definition is circular.* Before deciding that a relation is fiduciary, one must find a fiduciary with a predicate duty. Yet a fiduciary is defined as someone with a fiduciary duty to act for the benefit of another in the performance of matters contemplated by their relation.[44]

Scott, aware of the circularity, downplays its significance. He suggests that practical defects are common to all legal definitions. "Even if it were possible to frame an exact definition of a legal concept, the definition would not be of great practical value....All that one can properly attempt to do is to give such a description of a legal concept that others will know in a general way what one is talking about." Yet, given the myriad possible fiduciary relations, knowing only "in a general way" what courts are talking about can lead, and has led, to confusing case law; and decided cases, for good or ill, establish standards of conduct for fiduciaries "in the mass of cases that never will be litigated."[45]

Much criticism of and difficulty with the fiduciary concept is due to its elusive nature. The concept's flexibility and circularity, undoubtedly useful in many cases, are susceptible of confusing and seemingly unprincipled decision making. They also give activist judges power to impose their own subjective moral views in ways that, although perhaps useful at times, can create doctrinal confusion and legal uncertainty. The most vocal critics of judicial activism in fiduciary cases are the contractarians. A contract approach to analyzing fiduciary duties would considerably constrain judges in exercising their discretion. The leeway given to discretion constrained only by imprecise notions of fairness, justice, and equity is extremely broad. In contrast, contract-based duties would force judges to exercise self-restraint in creating or "finding" duties, because those duties would have to be somehow rooted in the express or implied terms of the parties' contract.[46]

---

*Easterbrook and Fischel also find circularity in other noneconomic explanations for fiduciary doctrine. *Contract and Fiduciary Duty, supra,* note 6: 435–436.

Mere Rhetoric?

A growing body of legal scholarship has emerged in recent decades attempting to identify and elaborate upon the nature of the fiduciary concept. Much of it is in response to concerns about the increasing importance of fiduciary law and the unsatisfactory way in which that law has historically developed. For present purposes, most of the relevant scholarship falls into either of two previously mentioned camps.

The traditionalists, consistent with the vast majority of decided fiduciary duty cases (and certainly with the cases' rhetoric), accept the importance of a distinct fiduciary concept with avowedly moral underpinnings. Traditionalists exhibit many doctrinal differences in their various views and often take issue with the results and reasoning of decided cases. Generally, however, they begin with a descriptive approach to fiduciary law, first inferring its values and principles from actual cases. They then seek "an elucidation of the purposes that these rules [derived from cases] serve, the values they promote, and the processes they seek to protect."[47] Based on an understanding of those purposes, values, and processes, traditionalists theorize about fiduciary law, criticize its application in particular instances, and may take various stances on issues of public policy.

In contrast, the contractarians purport to take a "value neutral" approach to fiduciary law, one derived from economic theory. They reject the commonly perceived moral content of the fiduciary concept, conceiving of fiduciary law as indistinct from contract law. All fiduciary relationships are, then, private contracts. The contractarians see the proper role of fiduciary law as providing private parties with "efficient" contract terms. Efficient terms are those "prescribing the outcomes the parties themselves would have reached had information been plentiful and negotiation costless."[48] Thus, they hold that any legal rule that alters outcomes that private contracting parties would otherwise have reached on their own is inefficient and will be "self-defeating." For example, "[a]cting on moral belief that agents [i.e., fiduciaries] ought to be selfless will not make principals [i.e., entrustors] better off; it will instead lead to fewer agents, or higher costs of hiring agents."*

---

*The contractarians claim that "efficiency" is morally neutral is dubious. Inevitably, their arguments
    depend on "oughts" or "shoulds," both value-laden terms. Consider, for example,
    Easterbrook and Fischel's basic principle that the fiduciary contract's "details *should* be
    those that maximize that gain, which the contracting parties can divide." *Contract and
    Fiduciary Duty, supra,* note 7 (emphasis added). 426. For a detailed criticism of the "supposedly neutral principle of economic efficiency," see Hazen, *Corporate Persona, supra,* note 2.

Given the "default" nature of fiduciary obligations, contractarians find that the objective of fiduciary law calls merely for "filling gaps in fiduciary relations in the same way courts fill gaps in other contracts." Contractarians are undaunted by the notion that few judges view their roles in fiduciary cases as that of merely filling gaps. Nor are they bothered by the ubiquitous moralistic language of fiduciary decisions. In their view, that language is rhetorical, and contractarians are not interested in a "theory of rhetoric." Whether judges properly understand and can explain what they are doing is irrelevant, for the contractarians seek "a theory of what judges *do,* not of explanations they give."

Disconcerting Moral Overtones

Potential violations of fiduciary duties regarding any economic activity can be alarming, partly because they may result in personal monetary liability. Often, however, they raise more troubling moral concerns and can result in significant reputational costs. In the famous words of Chief Judge Cardozo, speaking in 1928 on behalf of New York's highest court, fiduciaries are "held to something stricter than the morals of the market place. Not honesty alone, but the punctilio of an honor the most sensitive, is then the standard of behavior."[49] Unlike breach of contract, often viewed as morally neutral, breach of fiduciary duty implies dishonorable, at least irresponsible, conduct. "Therefore, a serious moral stigma attaches to those fiduciaries who breach their duties."[50]

The prospect that fiduciary law might be used to stigmatize complex financial decisions that merely happen to turn out badly is disturbing, particularly in derivatives cases: one *expects* even perfectly designed and executed risk management programs employing derivatives from time to time to incur derivatives losses. Moral concerns are exacerbated by the indeterminacy of the fiduciary standard and what conduct it requires. For example, although many scholars believe Cardozo's famous statement "stands as a sublime exposition of the fiduciary standard," the decision was rendered by a sharply divided court.[51] Three of the seven judges dissented.

The case, *Meinhard v. Salmon,* involved a hotel venture between two individuals, whom the court classified as "coadventurers," not partners. They agreed to share the costs of renovating and operating, and all net profits from, the hotel. The precise subject of the venture was a 20-year lease between Salmon, as lessee, and a third-party lessor, who did not know of Meinhard's involvement. Salmon was the property manager;

Meinhard, a passive investor. Months before the lease's expiration, an entity owned by Salmon concluded a new lease with the same lessor. The new lease contemplated the development of a far larger building, at great expense to Salmon, on land including that underlying the original hotel. The new rental payment exceeded 10 times that of the original lease. During the negotiations Salmon never informed Meinhard of the new transaction or offered him an opportunity to participate in it.

The question presented to the court was whether Meinhard had any interest in the new lease. To give an answer, the court first had to decide whether Salmon owed Meinhard any obligations beyond a duty to deal fairly and honesty. The entire court agreed "[t]here was nothing unfair in Mr. Salmon's conduct." Thus, absent a higher duty, Meinhard had no claim. The duty question depended entirely on the court's classification of the original relationship. Cardozo's majority opinion found "duties akin to those of partners." The majority agreed that the new lease was not strictly a renewal. And though Salmon had not acted dishonestly, they found that his failure to inform Meinhard of the new negotiation deprived Meinhard of a commercial opportunity in which he had a legitimate interest. That opportunity was "an incident of the enterprise, [which] Salmon appropriated to himself in secrecy and silence." The court imposed a constructive trust on Salmon's interest, to be held for his and Meinhard's benefit.

In contrast, the dissent objected vigorously that the majority's decision turned on the "mere label of a transaction." The dissent concluded that a coadventure "does not call for the strict rule that applies to general partners." "[F]air dealing and a scrupulous regard for honesty is required. But nothing more." The dissent found the venture, which did not squarely fit any prototypical fiduciary relationship, to be "governed by less drastic [fiduciary] principles" applicable only within the temporally limited scope of the relationship. Absent an ongoing partnership or finding of dishonesty, and given an express 20-year limit to the venture, the dissent was "of the opinion that the issue [was] quite simple." It thus applied rules of contract interpretation to analyze the terms of the parties' relationship. "No fraud, no deceit, no calculated secrecy [was] found." So the dissent rejected the claim of broad fiduciary duties.

The case's harsh moral tone, evident whenever vidations are found and at times even when they are merch, alleged, complicates complex business and investment decisions. Experience suggests that trustees, directors, and other senior managers take their fiduciary duties seriously, regardless of the risks of monetary liability. Such is the teaching of Justice Holmes's "bad man/good man" maxim—that is, the conduct of the "bad man" is guided by its "material consequences," while that of the "good man" by "the vaguer sanctions of conscience."[52] As Coffee maintains, the duties have a "socializing and exhortative impact."

Certainly, fiduciary duties in commercial cases play a limited role in compensation and loss allocation. Empirically, the number of cases imposing monetary liability for breaches of the two main fiduciary duties—care and loyalty—is too small to account satisfactorily for the influence of the duties on fiduciaries' conduct. For example, under corporate law, liability for breach of the duty of care "is, quite simply, very rare."[53] Although potential liability for breach of the corporate law duty of loyalty has become more problematic, the duty's substance has been diluted; the loyalty standard now "offers murky and permeable limits on management's self-aggrandizing behavior and serves more as an admonitory ghost that hovers than a substantive proscription."[54] Likewise, liability under modern trust law is uncommon. That law exhibits a "remarkable…paucity of modern cases raising the question of investment prudence."[55]

Common Law Evolution; Prototype Development[56]

An important reason for uncertainty in fiduciary law is that the fiduciary concept is a fragmented by-product of the common law. The concept evolved over many centuries, through cases in which courts applied it as needed to resolve concrete disputes arising under discrete fields of substantive law. Given the concept's equitable origins, courts were not constrained to construct a unified fiduciary concept spanning all areas of substantive law. Rather, they were free to develop the concept and corresponding rules piecemeal, or as needed to decide actual cases.

Historically, courts have applied the concept in a compartmentalized fashion, interpreting it consistently only within the confines of each discrete field of substantive law. Seldom have courts viewed fiduciary law as an independent substantive field governed by its own rules, policies, and principles. Legal theorists, then, are left to ponder whether "anything other than the word `fiduciary' and an appeal to duty of loyalty…unite these situations? Principles of ethics? Is the fiduciary morally bound to act in a particular way, perhaps? Or are the different situations wholly distinct?"[57]

To answer those questions, one must recognize that, instead of a unified fiduciary concept, the ad hoc common law process produced several distinct prototype fiduciary relationships. The development of a prototype began once a court decided that a given disputed relationship was fiduciary and designed rules to resolve the instant dispute. Later courts called on to decide cases involving similar relationships would typically add to and refine the original rules. Eventually, the process yielded a comprehensive set of rules and subrules for that clearly identified prototype, and the rules would dictate the fiduciary's corresponding duties and powers. Important, however, is that within a given body of substantive law, the rules for a given prototype relationship were and remain consistent.

Over the centuries, courts recognized and established rules for a small number of readily identifiable prototypes. Those prototypes and rules sufficed for the mass of fiduciary cases. Yet occasionally new relationships would appear that courts would deem fiduciary even though they did not conform neatly to any existing prototype. Still, to decide disputes, courts could reason by analogy to recognized prototypes, applying some existing rules and creating other new rules as needed to settle novel questions. Then, the process of developing a new prototype complete with associated fiduciary rules would begin anew.

Historically, few prototypical fiduciary relationships were recognized, and new types of relationships arose infrequently. The law first applied the fiduciary concept to trustees in ancient Roman times, and later to bailees and administrators. In recent centuries, courts applied it to agents, partners, and corporate officers and directors. Only in the twentieth century did the law begin imposing fiduciary duties on majority and controlling stockholders. Generally, however, difficulties with the pace of the common law process were manageable. New rules seldom effected massive doctrinal shifts; at most they affected discrete substantive areas. Radical departures from established rules in any given substantive area seldom immediately impacted prototype fiduciary relationships governed by other areas of law.

Expanding Diversity of Fiduciary Relations

Many scholars question the ongoing viability of ad hoc prototype development. For derivatives markets, given their dependence on legal certainty, it is peculiarly inadequate. Although the specter of public censure for sound derivatives decisions that turn out badly exacerbates tensions, new types of commercial relationships proliferate. Over time, derivatives activities judicially permissible for one type of relationship may be found impermissible for another, similar relationship. Here, a sampling of the diversity of possible fiduciary relationships and their potential for nettlesome derivatives issues is informative.

Private trusts; common funds

The oldest, simplest fiduciary relationship is the private trust through which a settlor devotes property to the use of designated beneficiaries. Complexity is introduced first by the remarkable flexibility that trusts afford settlors.[58] A trust creator is free to use a trust to dispose of property for about any purpose neither illegal nor contrary to public policy. "[N]o technical rules" restrict the creation of private trusts. Further, the nature and identity of a trustee, the duties imposed on it, and the interests of the beneficiaries can be whatever the creator chooses.

A trustee might be an individual or a bank trust department, and the array of potential investments and investment strategies is theoretically unlimited. "The modern trust has become a management regime for a portfolio of financial assets."[59] These assets typically require continuous administration, placing "growing pressure on amateur trustees to yield to professionals." Individual trustees often delegate investment responsibilities to professionals, which might be corporations, professional trustees, or institutional investors. The products held in trust today include foreign and domestic stocks, government securities, index funds, venture capital interests, real estate investments, precious metals, collectible assets, American depository receipts, index options and options on individual stocks and commodities, and futures on domestic and foreign indices. Given the variety of possible trust relationships and investment opportunities, even simple private trusts can generate complex legal questions.

Consider a trust formed to invest in trust investments such as participations in loans secured by mortgages: "the question arises whether it is improper if in making the investments the trustee combines the trust funds with his own funds, or the funds of another trust, or funds of a third person."[60] Such arrangements facilitate the pooling of funds essential to raising capital for large-scale commercial enterprises.[61] Moreover, they enable investors to share investment risks, an economic function essential to diversification. Without risk pooling and diversification, many investors would have little meaningful access to most investment opportunities. Pooling arrangements also enable trustees and other fiduciaries to reduce investment costs through economies of scale in account management.

Another important device for many trustees is the "common trust fund," through which trustees combine the assets of many trusts to make otherwise permissible investments in groups of securities. Each trust receives a fractional interest in an undivided group of securities.

Generally, such investments would be impermissible, if most states had not enacted statutes expressly permitting trustees to invest through common funds.

Charitable institutions

Greater complexity is often introduced when trust property is devoted to charitable purposes through express trusts or other vehicles of less certain legal status.* Colleges, universities, hospitals, religious organizations, and other eleemosynary institutions are often funded through endowments dedicated to narrowly defined purposes. Foundations, endowment funds, and similar organizations often "regard themselves as somewhat less confined" by trust rules than private trusts. Most prefer to analogize their legal status to that of corporations and the more flexible standards of corporate fiduciaries.[62]

Investment companies; investment advisers; broker-dealers

Other arrangements present additional complications and uncertainties. For example, "investment advisers and money managers present a bewildering variety of old and new services."[63] Depending on the circumstances, fiduciary duties may be owed by mutual funds, investment companies, and pension funds. They can also be created by other investment and money management vehicles such as public cash pools, municipal treasuries, and insurance companies. Investment companies and similar arrangements offer additional means for investors to pool funds and share risks, thus facilitating diversification and the financing of large-scale enterprises.

Broker-dealers may have any of a number of different types of fiduciary responsibilities to their customers imposed on them under state common law and the federal securities laws. Typically, the content of any duty depends largely on whether the broker-dealer exercises discretionary

---

*Consider how Scott, after an extensive review of case law, wavers over the status of charitable corporations. "The truth is that it cannot be stated dogmatically that a charitable corporation is or is not a trustee....Ordinarily the rules that are applicable to charitable trusts are applicable to charitable corporations, as we have seen, although some are not. It is probably more misleading to say that a charitable corporation is not a trustee than to say that it is, but the statement that it is a trustee must be taken with some qualifications." Scott and Fratcher, *Scott on Trusts,* 4th ed., *supra,* note 3: § 348.1.

authority over accounts and funds entrusted to it or merely executes trades. Absent discretion, those fiduciary duties imposed are ordinarily limited to ensuring proper execution of trades and otherwise conforming to the principal's instructions. Significant fiduciary duties are also imposed under federal law on investment advisers.

Different types of investment arrangements present complex fiduciary duty questions. When many fiduciaries invest, they may, depending on understandings with their customers, do so directly or delegate investment and management functions to third parties, or external managers. The modern "prudent" investor rule encorages trustees to consider investments in mutual funds rather than directly in the underlying securities held by the funds. One objection to indirect investment strategies using such vehicles as investment companies or investment trusts is that they deprive fiduciaries of direct control over the ultimate disposition of a beneficiary's assets. The use of such vehicles, unless expressly permitted by statutes or governing instruments, may be an improper delegation of discretionary authority.

It should be noted that when indirect investment techniques are permitted, the primary fiduciary ordinarily remains fully subject to its fiduciary obligations. Basic hornbook law holds that fiduciaries cannot delegate their ultimate supervisory responsibility, although they can delegate responsibility for a host of administrative functions and other acts. Thus, a primary fiduciary that engages an external manager must exercise prudence and care in selecting a manager and carefully monitor the manager's performance. The external manager's obligations arc often mainly contractual. Still, those managers often have common law or statutory fiduciary obligations, regardless of their contractual terms. Contractual terms purporting to release external managers from fiduciary duty claims may be void as against public policy.

Corporations; partnerships; and more

Fiduciary duties arise in numerous other business relations, including partnerships, limited liability companies, and private and publicly held corporations. These entities are, in economic jargon, the ultimate users of capital who invest in real, productive assets as opposed to financial instruments. Fiduciary relations within such entities include the relations among partners in a partnership, between majority and minority stockholders in closely held corporations, and between management and investors in limited liability companies. They also include the complex nexus of bilateral relations within public companies, the most important of which are those that directors and officers each have with their firms, and the fiduciary responsibilities that majority stockholders owe to the minority.

ENDNOTES: CHAPTER 16

1. This and the following two quotation are from Philip McBride Johnson, "Is Failing to Hedge a Legal Virus?" *Futures* (November 1993) [hereafter, *A Legal Virus?*]: 18. For more balanced appraisals, see George Crawford, "A Fiduciary Duty to Use Derivatives?" *Stanford Journal of Law, Business, and Finance,* 1 (1995) [hereafter, *A Fiduciary Duty to Use Derivatives?*]: 307–332; Gregory J. Millman, "The Risk Not Taken: American Corporations Hesitate at a Fork in the Financial Road," *Barron's* (May 1, 1995) (arguing that "imprudent companies are the ones that don't use derivatives. They are, on the whole, much riskier than companies that do.") [hereafter, *The Risk Not Taken*]: 46.

2. See, generally, Victor Brudney, "Contract and Fiduciary Duty in Corporate Law," *Boston College Law Review,* 38 (July 1997) (rejecting the contractarian account of fiduciary duties, though arguing for the application in some contexts of "richer notions that might be developed in contract law—e.g., the concepts of duress, adhesion and the evolving concepts of unconscionability and good faith") [hereafter, *Contract and Fiduciary Duty in Corporate Law*]: 595–665, 601; Tamar Frankel, "Fiduciary Law," *California Law Review,* 71(3) (May 1983) (articulating the distinct rules, principles, and policies of fiduciary law) [hereafter, *Fiduciary Law*]: 795–836; Tamar Frankel, "Fiduciary Duties as Default Rules," *Oregon Law Review,* 74 (Winter 1995) (expanding upon and updating *Fiduciary Law*) [hereafter, *Fiduciary Duties*]: 1209–1277; see also; Tamar Frankel, "Fiduciary Duties," in *The New Palgrave Dictionary of Economics and the Law,* Peter Newman, ed. (forthcoming) [hereafter, *New Palgrave*]; Thomas Lee Hazen, "The Corporate Persona, Contract (and Market) Failure, and Moral Values, *North Carolina Law Review,* 69 (1991) [hereafter, *The Corporate Persona*]: 273–318; Ernest J. Weinrib, "The Fiduciary Obligation," *University of Toronto Law Journal,* 25 (1975) [hereafter, *The Fiduciary Obligation*]: 1–22.

3. Frankel, *Fiduciary Law, supra,* note 2: 808; see, generally, Frankel, *Fiduciary Duties, supra,* note 2 ("Entrustors must entrust power or property to the fiduciaries because the fiduciaries could not perform their services effectively otherwise"): 1212; Weinrib, *The Fiduciary Obligations supra,* note 2 (describing the two "core elements" of the fiduciary relationship as, "[f]irst, the fiduciary must have scope for the exercise of discretion, and, second, this discretion must be capable of affecting the legal position of the principal"): 4.

4. Frankel, *Fiduciary Duties, supra,* note 2: 1216; see Robert Cooter and Bradley J. Freedman, "The Fiduciary Relationship: Its Economic Character and Legal Consequences," *NYU Law Review,* 66 (1991) [hereafter, *The Fiduciary Relationship*]: 1045, 1048; *cf.* Henry T. C. Hu, "Illiteracy and Intervention: Wholesale Derivatives, Retail Mutual Funds, and the Matter of Asset Class," *Georgetown Law Journal,* 84(7) (July 1996) (finding "especially interesting" the nature of plaintiffs claiming to be illiterate with respect to OTC derivatives, because these are typically institutions that would otherwise "be instantly considered sophisticated and capable of fending for themselves") [hereafter, *Asset Class Illiteracy*]: 2319–2379, 2324.

5. Cooter and Freedman, *The Fiduciary Relationship, supra,* note 4: 1046; *cf.* Lawrence E. Mitchell, "Fairness and Trust in Corporate Law," *Duke Law Journal,* 43(3) (December 1993) ("trust might be unimportant in its functional capacity if it were possible in advance to detail the corporate contract. In that case, the ideal contract would itself eliminate the complexity and indeterminacy of corporate life") [hereafter, *Fairness and Trust*]: 425–491, 447.

6. Frank H. Easterbrook and Daniel R. Fischel, "Contract and Fiduciary Duty," *Journal of Law and Economics,* 36 (1993) [hereafter, *Contract and Fiduciary Duty*]: 425–446, 426.

7. Frankel, *Fiduciary Law, supra,* note 2: 809.

8. See, generally, Frankel, *Fiduciary Duties, supra,* note 2 (discussing the risk of misappropriation from broad discretion and difficulties of detecting abuse): 1215–1219; Frankel, *Fiduciary Law, supra,* note 2 (discussing the overly broad nature of discretion): 810; John H. Langbein, "The Contractarian Basis of the Law of Trusts," *Yale Law Journal,* 25 (December 1995) ("Discretion entails the risk of harm as well as the opportunity to enhance the trust assets.") [hereafter, *The Contractarian Basis of the Law of Trusts*]: 625–675, 642.

9. Cooter and Freedman, *The Fiduciary Relationship, supra,* note 4 (citation omitted): 1049 n. 9.

10. See Frankel, *Fiduciary Duties, supra,* note 2: 1211–1213.

11. *Id.*: 1223.

12. *Id.* (emphasis added): 1226.

13. Frankel, *New Palgrave, supra,* note 2; see also John H. Langbien, "The Contractarian Basis of the Law of Trusts," *Yale Law Journal,* 105 (December 1995) ("The theme that the fiduciary law is prevailingly contractarian has not been much appreciated in trust or other fiduciary law."): 625–675, 658.

14. *Id.*: 1224.

15. Brudney, *Contract and Fiduciary Duty in Corporate Law, supra,* note 2: 602; see also Langbien, *The Contractarian Basis of the Law of Trusts, supra,* note 13 ("prototypical modern trustee is a fee-paid professional") [hereafter, *The Contractarian Basis of the Law of Trusts*]: 638.

16. This and the following two quotations are from Easterbrook and Fischel, *Contract and Fiduciary Duty, supra,* note 6: 426–429. See also Langbien, *The Contractarian Basis of the Law of Trusts, supra,* note 13: 657–658.

17. *U.S. v. Dial,* 757 F.2d 163, 168 (7th Cir. 1985); see also Brudney, *Contract and Fiduciary Duty in Corporate Law, supra,* note 2: 601; Frankel, *Fiduciary Law, supra,* note 2: 23–24.

18. Langbien, *The Contractarian Basis of the Law of Trusts, supra, note 13: 658.*

19. Jordan v. Duff and Phelps, Inc., 815 F.2d 429 (7th Cir. 1987) (Easterbrook, J.): 436, *cert. dismissed,* 485 U.S. 901 (1988).

20. Brudney, *Contract and Fiduciary Duty in Corporate Law, supra, note 2: 598.*

21. *Frankel,* Fiduciary Duties, supra, note 2: 1211.

22. See Hamilton et al., *Responsibilities of Officers and Directors Under Federal Securities Laws, supra,* Chapter 14, note 24: ¶ 104; see also Mason et al., *Financial Engineering, supra,* Chapter 1, note 2: 11; Samuelson and Nordhaus, *Economics, supra,* Chapter 1, note 9: 27–28.

23. Frankel, *Fiduciary Law, supra,* note 2: 803.

24. Frankel, *Fiduciary Duties, supra,* note 2 (citing congressional testimony in which a managing director of T. Rowe Price Associates, Inc. asserted that mutual funds "are the success story of the financial services industry because... [they] have garnered investor confidence"): 1260 n. 133, 1265 n. 148.

25. Mitchell, *Fairness and Trust, supra,* note 5: 491. Combining Mitchell's concerns about trust with concerns expressed by Hu regarding individual investors' sophistication as to their retirement funds is troubling. *Cf.* Hu, *Asset Class Illiteracy, supra,* note 4 (discussing democratization of securities markets, systematic investor error due *inter alia* to lack of knowledge of statistics and importance of asset allocation, and the possibility of investor panic): 2363–2370. See also Jonathan Clements, "A 93.6% Solution? No, Asset Allocation Isn't Everything, but It Has an Impact," *Wall Street Journal* (October 7, 1997) (discussing the scholarly debate over the importance of asset allocation—critics refer to the "asset allocation hoax"—and specifically a study noted in *Asset Class Illiteracy, supra*): C1.

26. See, generally, Frankel, *Fiduciary Duties, supra,* note 2 (discussing at length with citations the classification issue): 1214, 1233, 1246–1251; Weinrib, *The Fiduciary Obligation, supra,* note 2 ("More astoundingly, this development [of fiduciary doctrine] has proceeded without regard for, and indeed in the face of, the prevalent individualistic notions of consensual private ordering."): 21. For an interesting comment on the Procter & Gamble and Bankers Trust litigation, see Hu, *Asset Class Illiteracy, supra,* note 4: 2351–2352. Hu questions whether anything short of a written agreement expressing an intention to establish a fiduciary relationship might have led Judge Feikens to find such a relationship. Given that courts, especially New York courts (see note 17, *infra*), retain power to decide the classification issue, the question is intriguing.

27. *Martin v. Peyton,* 246 N.Y. 213, 217–218, 158 N.E. 77, 78 (N.Y. 1927).

28. Brudney, *Contract and Fiduciary Duty in Corporate Law, supra,* note 2: 598; see, generally, Frankel, *Fiduciary Duties, supra,* note 2 (discussing the importance of fiduciary protections and the conditions under which parties can legitimately waive or alter those protections).

29. Frankel, *Fiduciary Law, supra,* note 2: 811.

30. Frankel, *Fiduciary Law, supra,* note 2: 802; see also Mitchell, *Paradox of Preferred Stock, supra,* Chapter 14, note 25: 457.

31. Brudney, *Contract and Fiduciary Duty in Corporate Law, supra,* note 2: 625 n. 77.

32. Frankel, *Fiduciary Duties, supra,* note 2: 1229 n. 54; *cf. HB Korenvaes Inv., L.P. v. Marriott Corp.,* No. 12922, 1993 WL 257422 (Del. Ch. July 1, 1993) ("Indeed the contract doctrine of an implied covenant of good faith and fair dealing may be thought in some ways to function analogously to the fiduciary concept").

33. Pub. L. No. 93-406, 88 Stat. 1 (codified as amended at 29 U.S.C. §§ 1001–1461 (1988)); see, generally, Keith P. Ambachtsheer and D. Don Ezra, *Pension Fund Excelence: Creating Value for Stakeholders* (John Wiley&Sons Inc., 1998) [hereafter, *Pension Fund Excelence*]. By early 1995, "[o]ver one-third of the common stock of American companies [was] owned by pension fund fiduciaries on behalf of those who depend on it for their retirement." Crawford, *A Fiduciary Duty to Use Derivatives?, supra,* note 1: 327; see also Marla J. Kreindler, and Perry J. Shwachman, "Derivatives Offer Unique Opportunities for Employee Benefit Plan Counterparties," *Derivatives,* 1(6) (Warren, Gorham & Lamont, July–August 1996): 252–260; *Understanding ERISA: An Introduction to Employee Retirement Benefits,* Joseph R. Simone, chair (Practising Law Institute, 1995).

34. See, generally, Hamilton et al., *Responsibilities of Officers and Directors Under Federal Securities Laws, supra,* Chapter 14, note 24 (discussing, among other things, *Cooper Companies, supra,* Chapter 10, note 5): ¶ 104.

35. See Frankel, *Fiduciary Duties, supra,* note 2: 1251–1276.

36. See, e.g., *U.S. v. O'Hagan,* 117 S.Ct. 2199, 1997 U.S. LEXIS 4033, 138 L.Ed.2d 724 (June 25, 1997) ("A person who trades in securities for personal profit, using confidential information misappropriated in breach of a fiduciary duty to the source of the information, may be held liable for violating § 10(b) [of the Securities Exchange Act of 1934] and Rule 10b-5").

37. See, generally, Brudney, *Contract and Fiduciary Duty in Corporate Law, supra,* note 2 (discussing, among other things, risks of both over- and underprohibiting via the "exclusive benefit principle" and its "prophylactic

prohibition on self-dealing"): 601–607; Cooter and Freedman, *The Fiduciary Relationship, supra,* note 4 (arguing that it is appropriate to infer disloyalty and misappropriation from their appearance and impose punitive sanctions, yet it is inappropriate to so infer lack of care or award more than compensatory damages).

38. See Frankel, *Fiduciary Duties, supra,* note 2: 1215, 1251–1276; Brudney, *Contract and Fiduciary Duty in Corporate Law, supra,* note 2; Mitchell, *Fairness and Trust, supra,* note 5.

39. See Brudney, *Contract and Fiduciary Duty in Corporate Law, supra,* note 2: 605–607 and accompanying notes; Easterbrook and Fischel, *Contract and Fiduciary Duty, supra,* note 6: 430–431.

40. See Frankel, *Fiduciary Law, supra,* note 2: 804–808; *Black's Law Dictionary,* 6th ed. (West Publishing Co., 1990) ("The term [fiduciary] is derived from the Roman law, and means [as a noun] a person holding the character of a trustee, or a character analogous to that of a trustee"): 625.

41. Austin W. Scott and William F. Fratcher, *The Law of Trusts,* 4th ed., 1 (Little, Brown and Company, 1989) [hereafter, *Scott on Trusts*]: § 1; see, e.g., *Cinerama, Inc. v. Technicolor, Inc.,* 663 A.2d 1156 (Del.Supr. 1995) (discussing the power of the Delaware Court of Chancery to "fashion any form of equitable and monetary relief as may be appropriate"): 1166.

42. See, generally, Jerry W. Markham, "Fiduciary Duties Under the Commodity Exchange Act," *Notre Dame Law Review,* 68 (1992) (commenting in detail on the benefits and economic risks of judicial and regulatory activism and passivity in effecting or changing social or economic policy through fiduciary duty analysis) [hereafter, *Fiduciary Duties Under the Commodity Exchange Act*]: 199–270, 256–258; see, e.g., *Schnell v. Chris-Craft Industries, Inc.,* 285 A.2d 437 (Del.Supr. 1971) (where management used proper corporate procedures but for improper entrenchment purposes, the court held that "inequitable action does not become permissible simply because it is legally possible"): 437.

43. This and the following quotation are from Scott and Fratcher, *Scott on Trusts,* 4th, *supra,* note 4: §§ 2.5 and 2.3.

44. See e.g., *Black's Law Dictionary,* 6th ed. (West Publishing Co., 1990): 625.

45. Mitchell, *Fairness and Trust, supra,* note 5: 445.

46. See Frankel, *New Palgrave, supra,* note 2.

47. Weinrib, *The Fiduciary Obligation, supra,* note 2: 2.

48. This and the remaining quotations in this and the following paragraph are from Easterbrook and Fischel, *Contract and Fiduciary Duty, supra,* note 6 ("Fiduciary duties are not special duties: they have no moral footing") (emphasis in original); see also Henry N. Butler and Larry E. Ribstein, "Opting Out of Fiduciary Duties: A Response to Anti-Contractarians," *Washington Law Review,* 65 (1990): 1–72; R. H. Coase, "The Problem of Social Cost," *Journal of Law and Economics,* 3 (1960): 1.

49. *Meinhard v. Salmon,* 249 N.Y. 458 (1928): 464. For a criticism, see Langbien, *The Contractarian Basis of the Law of Trusts, supra,* note 13 ("Cardozo's incessantly cited opinion" exemplifies "the rhetorical excesses of fiduciary law"): 658.

50. Tamar Frankel, "Fiduciary Relationship in the United States Today," in *Equity, Fiduciaries, and Trusts,* Donovan W. M. Waters, ed. (Carswell, 1993) [hereafter, *Equity, Fiduciaries, and Trusts*]: 173–194, 175; see Weinrib, *The Fiduciary Obligation, supra,* note 2: 2; Frankel, *Fiduciary Duties, supra,* note 2: 1250; Langbien, *The Contractarian Basis for the Law of Trusts, supra,* note 13 (acknowledging that fiduciary duties "embody deep moral precepts about the behavior appropriate for a trustee or other fiduciary"): 658.

51. Weinrib, *The Fiduciary Obligation, supra,* note 2: 17; see also Jerry W. Markham, "Fiduciary Duties Under the Commodity Exchange Act," *Notre Dame Law Review,* 68 (1992) [hereafter, *Fiduciary Duties Under the Commodity Exchange Act*]: 199–270, 220–221; Cooter and Freedman, *The Fiduciary Relationship, supra,* note 4 (noting that "the precise nature of the fiduciary relationship remains a source of confusion and dispute"): 1045.

52. Oliver Wendall Holmes, "The Path of the Law," in *Collected Legal Papers* (1920): 171, quoted in John C. Coffee, Jr., "Litigation and Corporate Governance: An Essay on Steering Between Scylla and Charybdis," *George Washington Law Review,* 52 (1984) [hereafter, *Scylla and Charybdis*]: 789–828, 796 n. 18.

53. Mark A. Sargent, *An Overview of D&O Liability* (Clark Boardman Callaghan, 1997 edition) [hereafter, *An Overview of D&O Liability*]: I-4; Mark A. Sargent, "Two Cheers for the Maryland Director and Officer Liability Statute," *University of Baltimore Law Review,* 18 (1989) [hereafter, *Two Cheers*]: 278–309, 283.

54. See Brudney, *Contract and Fiduciary Duty in Corporate Law, supra,* note 2: 615.

55. Jeffrey N. Gordon, "The Puzzling Persistence of the Constrained Prudent Man Rule," *NYU Law Review,* 62 (April 1987) [hereafter, *Constrained Prudent Man Rule*]: 62–114.

56. See, generally, Frankel, *Fiduciary Law, supra,* note 2 (outlining the historical prototype development and discussing the expansion of fiduciary law): 796, 804–808; Markham, *Fiduciary Duties Under the Commodity Exchange Act, supra,* note 5 (same): 207–256; Weinrib, *The Fiduciary Obligation, supra,* note 2 (describing the "doctrinal evolution" of fiduciary law through the "case-law system").

57. Easterbrook and Fischel: 425.

58. See, generally, Scott and Fratcher, *Scott on Trusts,* 4th ed., *supra,* note 3 ("The purposes for which a trust can be created are as unlimited as the imagination of lawyers."): §§ 1, 348.

59. This and the following quotation are from Langbien, *The Contractarian Basis for the Law of Trusts, supra,* note 13: 629, 640.

60. This and the following quotation are from Scott and Fratcher, *Scott on Trusts,* 4th ed., *supra,* note 3: § 227.9. See, generally, *Id.* (discussing mortgage participations, common trust funds, and investment trusts): §§ 227.9 and 227.9A.

61. See Merton, *Financial Innovation, supra,* Chapter 1, note 7: 21; Mason et al., *Financial Engineering, supra,* Chapter 1, note 2: 11–12.

62. Gordon, *Constrained Prudent Man Rule, supra,* note 55: 80, n. 116. Gordon also cites W. Cary and C. Bright, *The Law and the Lore of Endowment Funds* (1969): 19–27, for the proposition that corporate fiduciary standards rather than trust standards ought to govern the investment activities of charitable corporations. *Id.*

63. Tamar Frankel, *The Regulation of Money Managers,* 1 (Little, Brown and Company, 1978 and 1996 Supp.) [hereafter, *The Regulation of Money Managers*]: 3.

CHAPTER 17

Derivatives-Related Fiduciary Duties: Trust Investment and Corporate Law

[T]he directors breached their duties by retaining a manager inexperienced in hedging; failing to maintain reasonable supervision over him; and failing to attain knowledge of the basic fundamentals of hedging to be able to direct the hedging activities and supervise the manager properly.

> Brane v. Roth
> *Court of Appeals of Indiana, First District (1992)*

Given the scale of operation of modern public corporations, this stupefying disjunction between risk and reward for corporate directors threatens undesirable effects....The law protects shareholder investment interests against the uneconomic consequences that the presence of...second-guessing would have on director action and shareholder wealth.

> Galgiardi v. Trifoods International, Inc.
> *Delaware Court of Chancery, 1996*
> *(emphasis in original)*

In Chapter 16 we discussed the deficiencies of the traditional methods by which fiduciary law develops. We also noted the paucity of cases specifically addressing derivatives-related issues of fiduciary duty.* We concluded the chapter by examining the rich diversity of prototypical commercial relationships potentially raising questions of such fiduciary duties. Given the foregoing factors and the need for legal certainty in derivatives markets, the following practical question arises: How might one analyze questions about derivatives-related fiduciary duties given the apparent lack of specific and authoritative legal guidance?

---

*Consider how striking in the aggregate is the dearth of derivatives litigation, given the size of the markets and potential complexity of the transactions. More remarkable still is the paucity of litigated cases, even though, as Miller notes, every derivative is essentially a zero-sum transaction. Therefore, every transaction has a "winner" and a "loser." Put differently, "a loser and hence potential plaintiff is present in every one of the thousands and thousands of derivatives deals." Miller, "Keynote Address to Seventh Annual Pacific Basic Capital Market Research Conference, July 7, 1995," *Pacific-Basin Finance Journal,* 2 (1996), reprinted in *Merton Miller on Derivatives, supra,* note 53: 20.

This chapter addresses that question using the functional analysis of fiduciary duties introduced in Chapter 16. A functional approach will help cut through much of the current confusion to get to the likely content and intensity of derivatives-related fiduciary duties.

OVERVIEW OF DERIVATIVES-RELATED DUTIES

Properly understood, the risks of violations of derivatives-related fiduciary duties need not be disconcerting. Compelling reasons exist to believe that the duties apply to derivatives activities no differently than they apply to any other commercial activity. The major cause for concern so far has been the apparent magnitude of many derivatives losses. Yet all told, those losses are modest compared with losses routinely incurred by businesses in other commercially significant areas. Merton Miller, among others, has emphasized that aggregate derivatives losses to date pale in comparison with losses suffered by the world's banks on bad real estate loans.

Alan Greenspan notes that improper use of derivatives undoubtedly poses hazards to individual institutions. Yet he also emphasizes that little if any evidence exists to believe that derivatives are more likely to cause broad systemic collapse than any other important economic activity. Maintaining appropriate credit standards for institutional lending, for example, is realistically a greater concern. Although our focus here is mainly an institutional risk management rather than public policy, knowing that no consensus against derivatives exists is important. And if anything, the typical government and regulatory attitude toward the products is now favorable. After due consideration of the losses suffered by and potential harm to individual institutions, most lawmakers and regulators agree that derivatives are key to reducing financial risk in a global economy. The importance of derivatives to the international competitiveness of domestic industries is widely recognized.

Further, courts, lawmakers, and regulators know the societal costs of stigmatizing conduct that is morally ambiguous. Apart from unfairness to individuals, such stigmatizing can have a seriously adverse impact, if the underlying activity is socially or economically significant. Overdeterrence may keep qualified individuals from engaging in important businesses. Abundant empirical evidence shows derivatives are integral to many firms' efforts to manage unwanted financial risks incidental to their core businesses.

Moreover, when doubts as to the legitimacy of derivatives-related activities arise, it is usually because the two main bodies of fiduciary law—

state corporate law and state law of trust investments—offer little specific guidance as to how the duties they establish apply to derivatives; neither body of law has yet adequately and consistently integrated widely accepted principles of modern finance. However, things are rapidly changing.

Trust investment law is undergoing sweeping and profound modernization, while corporate law recently began revisiting and clarifying seemingly dormant issues of management oversight responsibility. Furthermore, cases in corporate law and related legislative trends evidence a deepening awareness of the need to protect sound business decisions that happen to turn out badly. A growing body of financial theory and empirical data explains and supports many important derivatives uses. Complementing that trend is the proliferation of instructional materials designed to guide users in properly applying the products to achieve sound business goals.

Still, until efforts to clarify the law are farther along and beneficial uses of derivatives better understood, doubts about the application of fiduciary law to derivatives will persist. Perhaps the greatest legal risk to market participants is that those called on to determine the legality of legitimate derivatives uses will misapprehend the relevant economics. Trustees, business executives, and legal counsel contemplating derivatives use must recognize and manage the resulting legal uncertainty. A functional approach is particularly useful in helping fiduciaries and their counsel avoid potential legal pitfalls.

In Chapter 16 we began considering the circumstances under which fiduciary duties are ordinarily imposed and the nature and intensity of the actual duties. Here we explore decided cases demonstrating the standards against which fiduciaries' conduct has been judged in derivatives decisions and, equally important, other commercial areas. Decisions from other areas of law suggest that judicial reasoning in derivatives cases ought not to be especially difficult to predict. In retrospect, perhaps this is not surprising. Regulators and market participants alike believe that derivatives do not pose financial risks of a different kind or greater scale than those already present in the financial system. Analytically, we might logically start by assuming then that derivatives likewise do not present any different or greater legal risks.

A FUNCTIONAL APPROACH

Given the dearth of reported derivatives decisions, an important decision must be made at the outset of any analysis of derivatives-related fiduciary duties. In particular, what are the sources from which authority regarding those duties is likely to be drawn by judges and regulators in deciding derivatives cases? So viewed, a functional approach to fiduciary duties offers guidance, because it points to the criteria likely to determine the content and intensity of duties in a range of cases. Above all, a functional approach directs the inquiry to the central problem of all fiduciary relationships: the abuse of delegated power. The implication is that courts will likely hold fiduciaries to more exacting standards, based not on the riskiness of an underlying activity, but on the *risk* posed by the *delegation*. Although those risks may vary in degree and intensity among relationships, they are always of two types: misappropriation and neglect.

We begin by analyzing the delegation risks to entrustors to see whether those risks vary among different relationships in a legally significant way. As discussed in Chapter 16, a key determinant of when courts tighten or relax fiduciary duties is the presence of alternative monitoring and control mechanisms over fiduciaries.[1] Important precedent exists suggesting that state law relaxes the fiduciary duties of officers and directors of public companies and tightens those of trustees of private trusts. Further, the divergence between the duties of public company managers and those of private trustees offers a useful dichotomy for evaluating fiduciary duties, which lie somewhere between the two.

Corporate Fiduciaries

As holders of residual economic interests in a corporation, stockholders have an economic interest in encouraging the corporation to assume significant business risk.* Their equity is equivalent to a call option on the firm's assets. Any increase in the value of those assets beyond that needed to satisfy fixed claims and cover operating expenses accrues directly to the stockholders. For stockholders, of course, the downside is that they are also the residual risk bearers and thus holders of the riskiest direct claims on the value of the firm. However, modern portfolio theory teaches that stockholders have an efficient means of controlling their economic risk without unduly sacrificing opportunities for reward. By holding a well-diversified efficient portfolio of liquid assets, stockholders can minimize the level of risk they must assume to generate a given expected return. In

---

*Recall that the tax-adjusted MM theory states that the stockholder's interests in having the corporation assume significant financial risk—namely, leverage—is a more complex matter.

addition, a stockholder's risk is limited through corporate limited liability to the amount of its investment. What about management?

Management's interest in the corporation is highly concentrated. Officers have little meaningful opportunity to diversify their employment risk. They are typically required to devote substantially all their business efforts to their primary employer. Even if they were not, doing otherwise would entail holding a "portfolio" of jobs. Directors, particularly outside or nonmanagement directors, are in a similar situation, though with one important caveat. The position of an outside director is usually more precarious than that of an officer. Outside directors are thought to sit on corporate boards for purposes other than obtaining direct pecuniary gain. "Corporate directors of public companies typically have a very small proportionate ownership interest in their corporations and little or no incentive compensation."[2] Thus, management's participation in the firm's upside is limited. Yet if an individual manager can be held personally liable for corporate losses, the manager's potential downside is enormous. According to Chancellor Allen, corporate directors face a "stupefying disjunction between risk and reward," that "threatens undesirable effects" for stockholders. The same reasoning applies to officers.

To redress the disjunction and better align management's interests with those of stockholders—especially to overcome managerial risk-aversion and encourage prudent risk-taking—corporate law uses two principal devices, both of which we discussed below. First, the law frames the standard of officer and director liability in fairly lenient terms. An executive who satisfies minimum statutory or common law requirements of care has no legal liability. Second, and more important, corporate law extends to management the procedural and substantive protections of the so-called business judgment rule. The rule shields the vast majority of managerial decisions from judicial review, no matter how badly they may turn out.

Many commentators argue that the business judgment rule is overly protective of management, shielding managerial behavior to an extent that permits violations of stockholders' reasonable expectations. Others counter that the protections of the rule are offset by market-based controls that ensure effective management.[3] Of course, the basic monitoring device is the market price of a firm's stock. In economic theory, disgruntled stockholders will sell their stock, lowering demand and reducing market prices, which in turns signals management's inadequate performance. In response, others argue that the information conveyed by market prices is too opaque and inexact to permit anyone to draw such direct and meaningful inferences. As noted earlier, modern portfolio theory suggests that as much as two-third's of a stock's price is dictated by systemic rather than firm-specific factors.

Whichever side in the debate is right, two points are clear: both the standard of liability and the business judgment rule are profoundly protective of management, greatly narrowing the potential grounds on which managers might incur personal liability; and the express rationale of both the standard and the rule, rooted in modern portfolio theory, is a public policy of protecting stockholders. According to one prominent judge, an allegation of a violation of oversight responsibilities, absent suspect managerial motives, amounts to a claimed violation of the manager's "duty of attention"; that claim, in turn, relies on "possibly the most difficult theory in corporation law upon which a plaintiff might hope to win a judgment."[4]

Trustees[5]

Beneficiaries have an obvious economic interest in trust property. And, to the extent that a beneficiary's wealth is represented by its interest in the trust, the beneficiary has an undiversified exposure to the trust. Of course, adequate diversification of trust property by the trustee achieves the beneficiary's diversification objective. Yet a beneficiary usually does not, on its own, have significant power to control the investment of trust assets. It usually does not select the trustee or have the power easily to remove it. Likewise, the beneficiary seldom has the power to decide the trustee's investment strategy. Beneficiaries often encounter problems of "founder's stock," or stock left by a founder of a business to be held in trust for the benefit of family members. Usually, the founder has specified in the trust instrument that the stock is not to be sold.

In addition, individual beneficiaries commonly are not the only people with interests in a trust. Frequently trusts are established for the benefit of many people, such as several income beneficiaries and various "remaindermen." If the interests of the different beneficiaries diverge, any single beneficiary seeking to influence the trustee faces obvious "collective action" problems: taking action, through legal process or otherwise, to cause the trustee to alter its strategy will pit the beneficiary against other beneficiaries. Moreover, an unsuccessful beneficiary has no right to reimbursement of legal and other expenses incurred in attempting to influence the trustee. The real up-front costs of those expenses can easily exceed any additional benefit the beneficiary is likely to achieve through independent legal action, especially if the trustee is entitled to reimbursement from trust assets. Thus, the beneficiary remains highly dependent on the trustee to invest trust assets properly. What about the trustee?

Trust investment law imposes on trustees substantial duties to exercise caution or to preserve trust assets. The law usually expects the trustee to invest on behalf of not only those beneficiaries entitled to current distributions but also those entitled to future distributions. In addition, the law imposes on trustees duties to avoid speculation, creating an incentive to avoid any risky investments. Necessarily, the trustee encounters conflicts, because what might increase the payout to some beneficiaries might decrease the payout to others. The trustee thus faces substantial distributional concerns. When founder's stock is involved, a trustee often sells or distributes that stock at its own peril. Finally, market mechanisms controlling the trustee's behavior are often unhelpful to beneficiaries. Once the trust is created and funded, the trust assets are virtually immobilized with that trustee. The beneficiary's ability to transfer those funds for management by new trustees is limited.

Functionally Opposite Prototypes

"A comparison of the parties to be protected—shareholders and trust beneficiaries—shows that the two are situated quite differently."[6] For present purposes, trust relationships and corporate fiduciary relationships can be viewed as two opposite prototype fiduciary relationships. One, the trust, inclines toward a high degree of risk aversion, while the other, the public company, favors substantial business risks. In trust law, the risks of delegation are high, because the difficulty of remarry a trustee practically immobilizes entrusted funds. Even if the trustee does not economically diversify those funds, the trustee's performance, assuming no losses, will be difficult for beneficiaries to control. In corporate law, the risks of delegation are, in theory, muted by the mobility of funds and ability of investors to diversify. In addition, market realities, such as easy price discovery, suggest active alternative monitoring and control mechanisms of management's performance. Accordingly, the traditional approaches to trust investment law and corporate law can be viewed as polar opposites in the same sense, with the two lying at opposite ends of a spectrum.

Both trust investment law and corporate law influence other bodies of law that look to them for guidance and that may include elements of each in their legal structures. For example, pension funds and mutual funds, which are investment trusts, both display some but not all elements of private trusts and may have other important elements of public corporations. Pension funds, for example, can afford to assume greater risks, because they are structured to provide for the retiree and not her or his remaindermen. Mutual funds, although structured as trusts, are like public companies in that investors have substantial rights to withdraw and transfer their investment funds.

Close corporations and partnerships present other examples. Partners have historically (recall Cardozo's rhetoric) been imbued with a high degree of fiduciary duty to their partners, but the dominant goal of their ventures is wealth maximization. In contrast, although closely held corporations are corporations, the obligations of stockholders to each other are normally closer to those of partners than to those of public stockholders.

The purpose of the spectrum is to show that trust investment law and corporate law define polar opposite approaches that the law may take regarding derivatives-related fiduciary duties. One set of rules, those of trust law, is highly conservative; the other, corporate law, actively encourages risk taking. Given that helpful though limited derivatives guidance exists under both trust law and corporate law, the two serve as useful bases of comparison. They help us understand, or at least serve as useful analytical starting points for understanding, relevant fiduciary duties across the entire spectrum.

EVOLUTION OF FIDUCIARY DUTIES

Law of Trusts: "Prudent Man" Rule[7]

Original "timeless" formula

In the United States, the fiduciary duties of trustees trace their origins to the early 1800s. Early case law tried to give trustees guidance without imposing rigid and detailed codes of conduct. Generally, those cases evinced an awareness of the limitations on a court's ability to make investment decisions superior to those of professional trustees. Courts also realized that judicially mandated standards could not eliminate investment risks or the economic risks of holding idle assets. As Justice Putnam remarked[8] in the landmark 1830 case of *Harvard College v. Amory*,[8] "Do what you will; the capital is at hazard."

Justice Putnam was the first to enunciate the traditional "prudent man" formulation of a trustee's legal duties:

All that can be required of a trustee to invest, is, that he shall conduct himself faithfully and exercise a sound discretion. He is to observe how men of prudence, discretion and intelligence manage their own affairs, not in regard to speculation, but in regard to the permanent disposition of their funds, considering the probable income, as well as the probable safety of the capital to be invested.*

Although Justice Putnam intended to guard against speculation and to encourage the conservation of trust assets, he eschewed any attempt to establish rigid investment standards. He intended his rule, through its dependence on contemporary conduct of people of "prudence, discretion and intelligence," to remain responsive to evolving best practices.

Legal lists and other modifications

Justice Putnam's approach eventually lost most of its original generality and adaptability as courts elaborated on it:

[T]two problems developed in applying the standard of prudence to trust investments. First, when an investment was held improper in one case, courts often treated the question of fact in that case as a question of law, and the case became precedent holding that no investment of that type was proper. Second, courts often treated the rules they established as universal rules, even though prudence is dependent on the time and place of an investment.[9]

State statutes exacerbated those problems by codifying case results. The prudent man rule thus degenerated into a variety of forms that, although clear and easy to apply, made little lasting economic sense. "As the common law rigidified, two different approaches developed: a legal list rule and a modified prudent man rule."

Under those two approaches, many categories of investments and investment techniques were rendered "*imprudent per se*. Accordingly, *the exercise of care, skill, and caution would be no defense* if the property acquired or retained by a trustee, or the strategy pursued for a trust, was characterized as impermissible."[10] By 1990, some form of the prudent man rule had "been adopted by decision or legislation in most American jurisdictions."

---

*This rule is reflected in the current restatement of the law of trusts, in effect in most states: *Restatement of the Law Second, Trusts* (1959): § 227. The *Restatement Second* directs trustees "to make such investments and only such investments as a prudent man would make of his own property having in view the preservation of the estate and the amount and regularity of the income to be derived."

Dominant philosophy: avoidance of loss

The dominant concern of the current prudent man rule is the risk of loss, which has two components: first, "the probability that the capital value of each investment will be less at some future date than when bought,"[11] and second, the risk of loss of income available for distribution to income beneficiaries.[12] Moreover, in evaluating the risk of loss, the prudent man rule treats each investment separately; it does not consider overall effects on the portfolio. As one court declared, "losses in one investment can not be set off against other investments, and...each investment must stand or fall by itself."[13] So stated, the prudent man rule precludes the application of modern finance's explicit balancing of risk against expected return. It also precludes the making of an "otherwise dubious, volatile investment that can make a major contribution to risk management if the shifts in its returns tend not to correlate with the movements of other investments in the portfolio."[14]

"Incomplete" product range

Historical circumstances largely explain the traditional legal emphasis on risk of loss. Until the twentieth century, income taxes had only modest effects on portfolio returns. In addition, the absence of easily accessible and liquid investment vehicles formerly limited the investment alternatives reasonably available to most trustees. Until recent decades, capital markets were highly "incomplete," at least compared with the range of products now offered.

As early as 1869, in the celebrated case of *King v. Talbot,* the influential New York Court of Appeals held that "a prudent man would never invest in railroad, bank, or insurance stock, and [the court] strongly intimated that he would hold no common stock at all. Subsequently, state statutory legal lists were enacted limiting eligible investment to government and municipal obligations and high-quality bonds and notes. Common stocks were 'emphatically taboo.'"[15]

Until the 1950s, courts, legislatures, "the academic world and the general public...perceived the stock market as little more than a playground for speculators."[16] As such, investment in stock was thought inappropriate for trustees. However, by the 1980s as the markets became more "complete," trustees could be held liable for failing to include well-diversified stocks in their trust portfolios.[17]

Law of Trusts: "Prudent Investor" Rule

The avoidance of loss is unquestionably an important investment objective of any trustee. Nevertheless, the restrictions of traditional trust investment law can make it difficult to invest trust assets to generate adequate real returns. In an inflationary, high-tax environment, portfolios that earn nominally positive returns may nevertheless suffer real economic losses. The failure to compensate for the adverse effects of inflation and taxes can quickly erode a portfolio's value and purchasing power just as surely as actual losses can. Under the traditional prudent man rule, however, many types of investments and investment techniques available in capital markets to help investors avoid real losses were (and still are) impermissible for trustees.

Recently, however, there has been a "major national trend in the law of fiduciary investment, in response to changing economic conditions, new investment vehicles and strategies, modern investment theory and an evolving regulatory environment for fiduciaries."[18] The trend, embodied in the *Restatement of the Law Third, Trusts* (*Prudent Investor Rule*) (*Restatement Third*), seeks to modernize trust investment law by explicitly incorporating certain basic principles of modern finance. It replaces the traditional prudent man rule with a more flexible "prudent investor" standard. "Several bodies of state and federal legislation dealing with various types of charitable, pension, or public funds have incorporated rules more or less similar to the prudent investor rule."[19] New York's statute is the most detailed version of the new rule enacted thus far.

The prudent investor approach attempts to restore the "generality and flexibility of the original doctrine" articulated by Justice Putnam. It frees trustees from rigid and arbitrary constraints read into the original rule by courts and exacerbated by legislatures. The new rule purports to "liberate" sophisticated trustees by expressly sanctioning their use of "widely accepted" theories and practices of investment management. Nontraditional strategies, such as derivatives strategies, arguably prohibited by the old rule are expressly permitted and at times required under the new rule "when appropriate to the particular trust."

The drafters of the *Restatement Third* were sensitive to the danger of repeating the mistakes made by courts and legislators in interpreting Justice Putnam's original formulation. They were also aware, as many commentators have observed, that financial economic theory is still in its "formative stages."[20] So, believing that market practices and financial theory would continue to evolve, the drafters of the *Restatement Third* attempted to refrain from "freezing" into the law any specific set of investments or strategies. The new rule is expressly intended to "preserve the law's adaptability" as financial theory and market practices continue to evolve.

Endorsement of principles of modern finance

The most significant aspect of the new *Restatement Third* is how it reconsiders the meaning of risk, explicitly balances risk and return, and reinterprets the objectives of diversification. The new rule refocuses trust investment law away from a singular pursuit of minimizing "risk of loss." "[Prudent] risk management is concerned with more than the failure of collection and the loss of dollar value. It takes account of all hazards that may follow from inflation, volatility of price and yield, lack of liquidity, and the like."[21] Risk management under the new rule is concerned with the preservation of the real value of entire portfolios after adjusting for the effects of inflation and taxes, meeting the needs of income beneficiaries, and other factors.[22]

Diversification

Perhaps the clearest contrast between the prudent man and prudent investor rules is found in a comparison of the diversification requirements of the *Restatements Second* and *Third*. Section 227(a) of the *Restatement Third* includes a diversification requirement couched in the language of modern portfolio theory. A trustee must consider "investments not in isolation but in the context of the trust portfolio and as part of an overall investment strategy, which should incorporate risk and return objectives suitable to the trust."

In stark contrast, the comparable provision of the *Restatement Second* is devoid of references to portfolio returns or risk-return trade-offs:

> § 228. *Distribution of Risk of Loss.*   Except as otherwise provided by the terms of the trust, the trustee is under a duty to the beneficiary to *distribute the risk of loss* by a reasonable *diversification* of investments, unless under the circumstances it is prudent not to do so.[23]

As the Reporter's Notes to the *Restatement Second* state unambiguously, the sole reason for § 228's diversification requirement is to "minimize the risk of large losses"—to diversify against losses due to adverse business conditions, misappropriation, or negligent management. The Reporter's Notes also discuss seven factors to be considered in deciding on a diversification strategy—none of them mentions expected return.

Modern diversification is called one of the "two pillars" of modern finance expressly mandated by the *Restatement Third*'s prudent investor rule. The rule also expressly eliminates categoric restrictions on and requirements of particular types of investments and investment strategies. It recognizes that investments and techniques that in isolation are highly risky can, because of their marginal effects on overall portfolio risks, help minimize portfolio risk.

The prudent investor rule abstains from classifying any investment or technique as imprudent—or prudent, for that matter—in the abstract.[24] Rather, the *Restatement Third* reinterprets prudence. Now, a "continuous, long-term strategy of investing the trust estate in short-term bank and federal obligations...is improper."[25] "Although in a sense cautious, this investment program would ordinarily be viewed as failing to take adequate account of the fiduciary duty of caution as it applies to safeguarding the real value of capital."[26] The General Comments to the *Restatement Third* further note that certain types of derivatives—namely, options and futures—are

> often characterized as risky or "speculative."...[Yet, t]he rule recognizes that what may be...risky—or even characterized as speculative—in isolation, or in a different context, may play a role in an investment strategy that contributes to the trustee's compliance with the requirement of caution.

Diversifiable versus compensated risk

The new prudent investor rule is concerned with real economic loss, including the loss of expected return through inadequate diversification. Modern finance holds that efficient markets compensate investors only for bearing "market" or "nondiversifiable" risks. Inadequate diversification results in the assumption of "specific" or "nonmarket" risks that investors are not compensated for bearing. Therefore, the new rule asserts that "[o]pportunities for gain...normally bear a direct relationship to the degree of compensated risk....For purposes of understanding and applying the fiduciary duty of prudent investing, it is essential to recognize that compensated risk is not inherently bad....Beneficiaries can be disserved by undue conservatism as well as by excessive risk-taking."[27]

Modulating portfolio risk through leverage

Relying on "separation theorem" and CAPM, the General Comments and Reporter's Notes to the new prudent investor rule also discuss at length how a trustee can modulate portfolio risk. One way is by altering the composition of risky assets held in the trust portfolio. Yet often more "efficient" means of doing so involve *lending* and *leverage*. Without lending, the only way to reduce portfolio risk is to alter the composition of risky securities in a portfolio. However, as indicated in Figure 11.5, the optimal result in that case is an efficient portfolio that lies on the risky-asset efficient frontier, but not along the capital market line. Theoretically, higher returns can be achieved for the same low risk by maintaining an optimal risky-asset portfolio and lending at the risk-free rate.

Conversely, leverage, or borrowing, "may play an inverse role to that of lending and is permissible for trustees provided that the tactic is employed selectively and cautiously....The objective of such strategies is to achieve the desired result with a more modest or efficient increase in risk than might result from raising the risk level of the investment [i.e., risky-asset] portfolio."[28] Determinations of how much risk is appropriate in any case depends on many factors. Those factors include the needs of income beneficiaries and remaindermen and ultimately involve "subjective judgments that are essentially unavoidable." Furthermore, "no objective, general standard can be set for a degree of risk that is or is not prudent."

Higher Standards?

Concern has been expressed that the prudent investor rule imposes more exacting standards on trustees because it raises the law's expectations as to a trustee's investment skill and sophistication,[29] as well as to its knowledge of the needs and resources of beneficiaries. In addition, compliance with the new rule does require familiarity with evolving best investment practices. A trustee failing to meet and maintain those standards will be vulnerable to criticism and potential liability. Therefore, some commentators have concluded that "[f]iduciaries will be acting in a realm of uncertainty for some time to come."[30] Nevertheless, for a number of reasons, the rule reduces the legal uncertainty facing commercial trustees, although it may become unduly onerous for many individual trustees.

Greater trustee protections

Fundamentally, at least with respect to the use of derivatives, the new rule evinces an intent to provide greater flexibility and protection to trustees than the prudent man rule. For example, the Introduction to the *Restatement Third* provides: "Thus, the objectives of the 'prudent investor rule' of this Restatement Third range from that of liberating expert trustees to pursue challenging, rewarding, non-traditional strategies when appropriate to the particular trust, to that of providing other trustees with reasonably clear guidance to *safe harbors that are practical, adaptable, readily identifiable, and expectedly rewarding.*" Moreover, various comments to the *Restatement Third* repeatedly endorse the use of futures, options, leverage, and other "abstractly high-risk investments and techniques," when appropriate under the circumstances.*

Process, not results

As noted above, the new rule provides "safe harbors" for trustees, expert or otherwise. Perhaps most important is the explicit recognition that the "trustee's compliance with these fiduciary standards is to be judged...not with the benefit of hindsight or by taking account of developments that occurred after the time of a decision to make, retain, or sell an investment. The question of whether a breach of trust has occurred turns on the prudence of the trustee's conduct, not on the eventual results of investment decisions."[31] Put differently, "lack of clairvoyance is not negligence. 'The executive is not chargeable with the gift of prescience or prophecy.'"[32] Similarly, the New York statute provides that the "prudent investor rule requires a standard of conduct, not outcome or performance....A trustee is not liable to a beneficiary to the extent that the trustee acted in substantial compliance with the prudent investor standard or in reasonable reliance on the express terms and provisions of the governing instrument."[33]

---

*Under the traditional prudent man rule, those investments and techniques "have been potential sources of unjustified liability for trustees generally and, more particularly, of inhibitions limiting the exercise of sound judgment by skilled trustees....These criticisms of the prudent man rule are supported by a large and growing body of literature that is in turn supported by empirical research, well documented and essentially compelling....In addition, the need for revision is evident from conflicts between the prudent-man rule and modern asset management practices." See *Introduction, Rest. 3rd, Trusts (Prudent Investor Rule), supra,* Chapter 10, note 13: 4.

Delegation

The *Restatement Third* affords nonexpert and expert trustees alike substantial protection in delegating investment responsibilities, if the terms and conduct of the delegation are prudent. The prudent investor rule "views delegation from a positive perspective."[34] Among other things, it permits investments in mutual funds and allows expressly trustees who are unfamiliar with modern finance to seek outside guidance. "[D]elegation is...likely to be important to non-expert investors who nevertheless may be well situated and qualified to serve as trustees, as will often be the case with family members or friends." Yet even after the delegation the original delegator retains responsibility for monitoring the delegatee's performance.

Prudence in the context of delegation requires, as detailed in New York's Prudent Investor Act of 1995, that the trustee "exercise care, skill and caution in...(A) selecting a delegee suitable to exercise the delegated function...; (B) establishing the scope and terms of the delegation...; (C) periodically reviewing the delegee's exercise of the delegated function and compliance with the scope and terms of the delegation; and (D) controlling the overall cost by reason of the delegation." Equally important is that, under the act, the delegee is also expressly subject to *its own* fiduciary duty to the trustee and the trust, and that duty cannot be waived. "An attempted exoneration of the delegee from liability for failure to meet such duty is contrary to public policy and void."

Use of derivatives to reduce administrative expenses

Financial economists repeatedly emphasize that a primary virtue of derivatives is that they enable investors to take positions in underlying assets and markets at transaction costs that "can be a tenth to a twentieth of the cost of using the underlying cash-market."[35] This benefit should prove particularly important to trustees, who have a fiduciary duty to avoid excessive administrative expenses. New York's Prudent Investor Act, for example, expressly provides that trustees are authorized "to incur costs only to the extent they are appropriate and reasonable in relation to the purposes of the governing instrument, the assets held by the trustee and the skills of the trustee."

A promising benefit of this approach relates to the use of equity derivatives, such as index options or futures, to achieve broad diversification. An alternative, more conservative strategy, might involve investing in mutual funds. However, expert trustees may find anticipated mutual fund returns unsatisfactory compared with the expected returns to be generated through derivatives strategies. Equity derivatives are often particularly effective diversification tools; when properly structured, they offer many opportunities to reduce nonsystemic, diversifiable risk without triggering undesirable tax consequences.

Corporate Law: "Prudent Man" Rule and Management Oversight[36]

Prior to the takeover era of the 1970s and 1980s, lawyers advising corporate managers customarily began by describing the two pillars of directors' fiduciary duties: the duties of care and loyalty. Lawyers would also inform their clients of the availability of the "business judgment rule [discussed below] as a judicial test to shield directors from liability in actual litigation." The takeover era altered the customary legal advice. A heavy volume of litigation during the takeover era inquired into the standards governing the propriety of management decisions to institute defenses against unwanted takeovers. That litigation focused primarily on the business judgment rule. Until recently, the presence or absence of that rule's protections was thought to be outcome-determinative.

In determining derivatives-related oversight responsibilities, one must be aware that takeover cases offer potentially confusing precedent. Every takeover case, whether involving an actual takeover or merely establishing defenses in the normal course of business, exposes management to duty of loyalty attacks. Logically, management's motives in defending or failing adequately to defend a target company are always suspect. A decision to institute defenses renders management vulnerable to claims of improper entrenchment motive; yet the failure to rebuff a takeover or institute defenses is challengeable as a management failure to protect a company's independence or obtain an adequate price for its stock.

Managers and legal advisers should take comfort, though, in one undeniable legal conclusion drawn from takeover precedent: namely, once management successfully invokes the business judgment rule, a court's focus shifts entirely to the process by which management reached whatever decision it made. Distinctions between the business judgment rule and management's duties of care and loyalty have been "blurred." Courts have elevated the status of the rule, treating it not only as a procedural protection but also as a rule of substance, a conclusive presumption that management acted properly. Thus, judicially, the duties are "ignored apart from their incorporation into the business judgment rule."

Briggs v. Spaulding

A legal matter that has received little attention (but that is potentially important to derivatives users) is that well-settled fiduciary duties of directors established in the "predawn" of the takeover era include a prudent man rule. Those cases remain good law. The most authoritative early statement of the corporate law rule is from the U.S. Supreme Court's 1891 ruling in *Briggs v. Spaulding*[37]

> In any view the degree of care to which these defendants [corporate directors] were bound is that which *ordinarily prudent and diligent men* would exercise under similar circumstances, and in determining that [degree of care]...the usages of business should be taken into account. What may be negligence in one case may not be want of ordinary care in another, and the question of negligence is, therefore, ultimately a question of fact, to be determined under all the circumstances.

The language of the *Briggs* prudent man rule is on its face similar in many respects to that of the prudent man rule enunciated in *Harvard College*. However, the standard applicable to corporate officers* and directors is in both language and application far less onerous than the standard applicable to trustees. Corporate law's objective, as noted earlier, is to overcome managers' natural risk aversion. Thus, if anything it is designed to encourage risk taking rather than impose requirements that managers avoid speculation or that they conserve corporate assets. The basic corporate law requirements are due care and loyalty, requirements that over the years have afforded directors considerable latitude.

Allis-Chalmers

The content of the prudent man rule governing the conduct of corporate managers was restated in 1962 by the Delaware Supreme Court in *Graham v. Allis-Chalmers*—that case summarizes the basic duties of directors with respect to matters of internal corporate control immediately prior to the dawn of the takeover era:

---

*Case law construing the duties of officers apart from those of directors is sparse. Nevertheless, several important points are generally recognized: (1) executive officers are fiduciaries, (2) their duties as officers are limited to the scope of their office, and (3) as to matters within that scope, officers' duties are strong, because officers presumptively have greater information as to and control and responsibility over the relevant activities. See, e.g., Corrine Ball and Robert L. Messineo, "Fiduciary Duties of Officers and Directors of the Financially Troubled Company: A Primer," in *Mergers and Acquisitions in the 90s,* Richard A. Goldberg, Chair (Practising Law Institute, 1996): 127–150, 133.

> [D]irectors of a corporation in managing the corporate affairs are bound to
> use that amount of care which ordinarily careful and *prudent men* would use
> in similar circumstances. Their duties are those of *control,* and whether or
> not by *neglect* they have made themselves *liable for failure to exercise*
> *proper control* depends upon the circumstances of and facts of the particu-
> lar case.[38]

The corporate law prudent man rule in a derivatives context applies
to monitoring and oversight responsibilities that might *not* involve managerial action or decisions. Absent management's conscious decision, the
rule focuses on oversight issues or what are becoming known more generally as "practice standards." The absence of director action is significant, and upon cursory inspection may appear outcome-determinative.
Judicial opinions state clearly thatinformed, deliberate inaction is protected, but a mere uninformed, unconsidered failure to act vitiates the liability shield (discussed below) of the business judgment rule.

The language of judicial opinions evinces great concern about not
only managerial decisions but also oversight responsibilities that are more
difficult to evaluate. Although the duty of care applies to decisions and
oversight, the legal analyzes underlying the two responsibilities are different. Although decisions ordinarily are entitled to the protections of the
business judgment rule, mere inaction is not. Empirically, adequate data as
to the legal significance of the difference between the two contexts is
sparse—few courts have undertaken to consider the difficult question of
whether a manager has met her or his "duty of attention."

However, as Chancellor Allen recently pointed out, even in an oversight context a manager's duty is essentially one of process. The reason is
that satisfaction of the duty of care "can never appropriately be judicially
determined by reference to the content of the...decision that leads to a
loss, apart from the consideration of the good faith or rationality of the
process involved."[39] Even absent the shield of the business judgment rule,
courts are disinclined to second-guess managerial decisions:

> That is, whether a judge or jury considering the matter after the fact, believes
> a decision substantively wrong, or degrees of wrong extending through "stu-
> pid" to "egregious" or "irrational," provides no ground for director liability,
> so long as the court determines that the *process* employed was either ratio-
> nal or employed in a good faith effort to advance corporate interests.

The importance of process regardless of whether the business judgment
rule applies is as a legal matter central to the analysis. Thus, the process
orientation should be considered in cases discussing derivatives-related

fiduciary duties. As *Brane* shows, if the shield of the business judgment rule is unavailable because of a failure of *process,* courts will second-guess managers' actions or inaction.

Managerial Decision Making and the Business Judgment Rule[40]

The application of the business judgment rule provides directors with a typically impenetrable shield against liability.[41] The rule has been expressed in many different ways. Its best-known formulation is that of *Aronson v. Lewis*[42]: "It is a [rebuttable] presumption that in making a business decision the directors of a corporation acted on an informed basis, in good faith, and in the honest belief that the action taken was in the best interests of the company." In 1971, the Delaware Supreme Court articulated the rule's rationale:

> [A] court will not interfere with the judgment of a board of directors unless there is a showing of gross and palpable overreaching. A board of directors enjoys a presumption of sound business judgment, and its decisions will not be disturbed if they can be attributed to any rational business purpose. A court under such circumstances will not substitute its own notions of what is or is not sound business judgment.[43]

Over the years, the basic elements of the business judgment rule, particularly as applied in the takeover context, have often been difficult to reconcile. As a result, the precise results of the rule's application have often been difficult to predict. Still, important observations can be made as to the rule's likely application to derivatives activities.

First, a precondition to the rule's application is a showing that a *business judgment* was made. Absent a showing by the defendants that an action was taken or decision consciously made (not merely neglected), courts are reluctant to find a predicate business judgment. According to *Aronson v. Lewis* (a Delaware case expressly relied on in *Brane*): "the business judgment rule operates only in the context of director action. Technically speaking, it has no role where directors have either abdicated their functions, or absent a conscious decision, failed to act."[44]

Second, Delaware courts have held that the business judgment rule is more than a mere procedural presumption that directors have acted with the requisite care and loyalty; it is an outcome-determinative substantive rule of law. "Thus, where independent director action is challenged and the presumption is not overcome, the substantive aspects of the rule mandates the outcome of litigation."[45] In other words, if those who challenge a board's action are unable to rebut, or overcome, the presumption of the rule's applicability, the challenged director action will be upheld.

Third, the protections of the rule will be available only if certain additional elements are present. In particular, (1) the directors who acted must have been disinterested and independent; (2) they must have exercised due care, meaning that they must have been *reasonably informed* about the subject matter of the decision; (3) they must have acted in good faith; and (4) they must not have abused their discretion. Of these additional elements, that of greatest practical significance to derivatives activities is the requirement of due care and informed decision making. In a derivatives context, as in *Brane,* the business judgment rule analysis will likely turn on the due care requirement—a plaintiff attacking a board decision must meet the burden of demonstrating that board action was *not* taken on a reasonably informed basis. "Cases holding directors liable for a breach of the duty of attention or care, uncomplicated by self-dealing or conflict of interest are rare."[46]

Fourth, courts may substitute their judgments for those of a board, if those seeking to attack director conduct can show by a preponderance of the evidence that a breach of fiduciary duty occurred. Overcoming the procedural presumption of the business judgment rule shifts the burden to the defendants to justify their action (or inaction):

> Under [normal] circumstances the board's action is entitled to be measured by the standards of the business judgment rule. Thus, unless it is shown by a preponderance of the evidence that the directors' decisions were primarily based on perpetuating themselves in office, or some other breach of fiduciary duty [or care or loyalty] such as fraud, overreaching, lack of good faith, or being uninformed, a Court will not substitute its judgment for that of the board.[47]

Rebutting the presumption of the rule does not result in automatic, or per se, officer or director liability; rather, it shifts the burden to the defendants to prove that the challenged action (or inaction) was "entirely fair." To date, the entire fairness standard has been applied exclusively in takeover contests. In those cases, "the entire standard requires the board of directors to establish 'to the *court's* satisfaction that the transaction was the product of both fair dealing *and* fair price.'…Thus, an initial judicial determination that a given breach of a board's fiduciary duties has rebutted the presumption of the business judgment rule does not preclude a subsequent judicial review that the board action was entirely fair, and is, therefore, not outcome determinative *per se*."[48]

Although the exact manner in which the entire fairness test will be applied in a derivatives context is not easily predictable, clearly the test should apply when a court has found a violation of a fiduciary duty of care or loyalty. The *Brane* court apparently followed that logical reasoning. Once it found a violation of the duty of care, the court looked to the merits of the challenged hedging activities. Given that those activities were entirely inadequate, the court can easily be viewed as having reached a conclusion that the hedging activities did not survive an "entire fairness" or comparable substantive review.

Finally, the net effect of the business judgment rule is that, so long as there is no proven breach of a fiduciary duty other than the duty of care, a court's due care examination will focus entirely on the process by which the directors (or presumably corporate officers) reached their decision. "In the corporate law duty of care cases, the central inquiry always has been process rather than result. If corporate directors [and officers] have utilized thorough methods, competent advisors, and other safeguards, those elements of process are earmarks of due care. Directors acting with due care never have been held liable for adverse outcomes or bad results. Both the duty of care and its corollary, the business judgment rule, incorporate the view that corporate directors are neither insurers nor guarantors of the success of the enterprise."[49]

Awareness of Derivatives Strategies and Risks

A fiduciary with derivatives supervisory responsibilities must understand the fundamentals of derivatives strategies and risks well enough to decide upon and supervise the products' use. Although there is little authoritative guidance on the point specifically mentioning derivatives, as a matter of prudence, fiduciaries should at a minimum understand (1) the risk management strategies that derivatives serve and how derivatives further those strategies, (2) the major categories of new risks introduced by derivatives, and (3) the available risk management alternatives to derivatives.

Law of trusts

For example, General Comment *d* to § 227 of the *Restatement Third* states notes that "a person who serves as trustee should be capable of reasonably understanding the basic duties of prudent trusteeship." This language suggests that, in appropriate circumstances, trustees may need a basic familiarity with the types of derivatives strategies reasonably available. At least one commentator has argued—although no case has so held—that the law may be moving in the direction of a specific duty to use derivatives (or at a minimum to understand their risk management function), at least for skilled investment advisers. "Fiduciaries may even be required to use derivatives to hedge against risk in cases where the best result for the beneficiaries can be achieved in no other way."[50]

A trustee that employs derivatives must be familiar with the main types of derivatives risks: (1) market or price, (2) liquidity, (3) credit, (4) legal, and (5) operations. Market risks are best understood through a knowledge of the principles of modern finance and the functional characteristics of forward- and option-based instruments. Liquidity risks, which many consider a subcategory of market risks, have two components: first, the ability to liquidate assets on short notice; second, the ability to meet cashflow requirements of derivatives that include funding obligations—for example, premiums must be paid for option-based products, and ongoing payments, depending on market movements, may need to be made for forward-based products. Culp and Miller, analyzing the failure of certain Metallgesellschaft subsidiaries associated with a "synthetic storage" program, explain a benign view of the true cause of the firms' losses. That cause, which they dub "hedger's ruin," is that management failed to understand the long-term funding commitments needed to make the program work. Those long-term commitments were obligations to meet margin calls while the relevant futures positions were out of the money, a classic liquidity problem.[51] According to Culp and Miller, the benign view is that management failed to "understand the essential logic behind their firms' marketing and hedging strategies." Thus, management prematurely liquidated the entire operation, not realizing the temporary liquidity drains would eventually be offset by gains either on the long-term delivery contracts or on recovery of the futures positions.

Derivatives' credit risks are not necessarily greater than those of any other type of asset, but unlike, for example, loan transactions, derivatives' risks are often two-sided and uncertain. Users who may be frequent borrowers are often unfamiliar with the practices and procedures that constitute an adequate credit review for a swap transaction. Depending on market movements after commencement of the swap, a user may be a net lender to its dealer counterparty. If so, it will want to monitor the dealer's financial condition. Yet dealers often publicly report their financial statements, either because they are public companies or to meet other regulatory requirements. If so, a counterparty will almost certainly encounter resistance in requesting dealer credit information not otherwise publicly available.

Also, a fundamental difference between loan transactions and two-sided swap contracts is that in most loans the lender knows what its potential credit risk is—it is the principal amount of the loan plus accrued and unpaid interest. In a swap contract, potential exposure is often theoretically unlimited. A user party to a currency swap, for example, may be expecting upon termination to receive from its dealer a repayment of a hard currency such as U.S. dollars, deutschmarks, or pounds sterling. Perhaps at the same time its obligations are denominated in a currency of an emerging-market nation. If, prior to termination, the emerging-market currency devalues significantly, the dealer may have a difficult time meeting its swap obligations. The emerging-market currency in which it is active may have lost far too much of its value.

Legal risks affect transaction structuring and documentation, as well as the permissible investments a fiduciary may make or authorize. But a primary message of this book is that legal risk must be understood much more broadly than is commonly discussed. Issues of fiduciary duty can be thought of as fundamental legal risks. In this regard, however, professional trustees are likely to take comfort in the new prudent investor rule, which some commentators liken to a business judgment rule for trustees. Certainly the rule treats derivatives far more favorably than the customary prudent man rule. Nevertheless, as Jeffrey Gordon emphasizes, nothing in the prudent investor rule relieves trustees of their duty of caution; nor is the rule a presumption in favor of trustees' prudence. Furthermore, some reported cases decided under the old prudent man rule suggest that even under that rule the emphasis may have been more on process than on substance. Detailed and accurate record keeping has defeated beneficiary challenges to trustee investment strategies that might otherwise have appeared improper.

Operations risk span a range of systems and personnel risks. This category covers critical risk management issues such as the separation of trading and booking functions. The Barings collapse is the most vivid example to date of a failure to segregate the trading and reporting functions. It is widely recognized to have resulted from the ability of a single trader, Nick Leeson, to both trade and report his transactions, without meaningful independent oversight. Misreporting enabled what otherwise appeared to be a modest, nearly risk-free arbitrage operation between two futures markets to balloon into losses that equaled "more than two and a half times…Barings' capital."[52] Whether or not senior management is aware of misreporting is likely in any event to be irrelevant. In this sense satisfying one's fiduciary duties is beneficial, not merely from a liability perspective but also from an employment point of view. As Merton Miller observes, new management that took over after the Barings collapse "recognized that [former] top management didn't know what Nick Leeson was up to. But they *should* have known. And because they didn't know or try to find out, they're gone."[53]

Corporate law

Each of the foregoing information requirements is also entailed by applicable case law setting forth the requirements for the application of the protections of the business judgment rule. For example, *Aronson v. Lewis* held that directors "have a duty to inform themselves, prior to making a business decision, of all information reasonably available to them. So informed, they must *then* act with requisite care in the discharge of their duties.[54]

Generally

Most observers agree that derivatives by their nature do not introduce fundamentally new or greater economic risks to capital markets. Thus, in principle, fiduciary duties should apply to derivatives activities just as they apply to any other business or investment activity. In general, that appears to be the case. For example, in its March 21, 1996 letter (*ERISA Letter*) to the Comptroller of the Currency (OCC), the Department of Labor (DOL)[55] stated its view on investments in derivatives by plans subject to the Employee Retirement Income Security Act of 1974: "ERISA establishes comprehensive standards to govern fiduciary conduct....Investments in derivatives are subject to the fiduciary responsibility rules in the same manner as are any other plan investments."[56]

However, uncertainty exists as to how courts and regulators will view fiduciary conduct in actual derivatives cases. Little definitive legal authority is available to which fiduciaries might turn for guidance in determining appropriate derivatives uses. Various regulators, such as the DOL, the OCC, and state insurance departments, have issued guidelines concerning "investments" in derivatives.[57] Yet, with the exception of some state insurance regulations specifying limits on certain investment categories, most of the guidelines are in the nature of general cautionary advice.[58]

Although many derivatives lawsuits and enforcement actions have been filed in recent years, most now either have been settled or continue to work their way through the judicial system. To date, the only significant judicial guidance specifically addressing the objectives of derivatives use is the 1992 Indiana appellate case *Brane v. Roth.*

Brane v. Roth [59]

Much of the language of *Brane* can be, and arguably has been, construed to stand for the proposition that managers and directors, perhaps even trustees, at times have a "duty to hedge." Properly understood, neither the holding nor the language of the case stands for that proposition. First, however, the facts.

Brane involved "a shareholders' action against the directors of a rural grain elevator cooperative for losses Co-op suffered in 1980 due to the directors' failure to protect [Co-op's] position by adequately hedging in the grain market." Ninety percent of Co-op's business was buying and selling grain, and its profits had fallen continuously from 1977. "After a substantial loss in 1979, Co-op's CPA, Michael Matchette, recommended that the directors hedge Co-op's grain position to protect itself from future losses. The directors authorized the manager [, Eldon Richison,] to hedge for Co-op. Only a minimal amount was hedged, specifically $20,050 in hedging contracts were made, whereas Co-op had $7,300,000 in grain sales." Co-op suffered 1980 losses of $424,038.

The trial court held that the losses were due to the inadequate hedging program. It further held that "the directors breached their duty by their failure to supervise the manager and become aware of the essentials of hedging to be able to monitor the business[,] which was a proximate cause of Co-op's losses." In reviewing and upholding the trial court's findings and rulings, the *Brane* court reached three notable and controversial conclusions.

Decision

The appellate court held, using unfortunately overly broad language, that the trial record contained "probative evidence that Co-op's losses were due to a failure to hedge." The only evidence the court mentioned is the testimony of two witnesses: one was an "expert in the grain elevator business and hedging"; the other was an accountant consulted by Co-op to evaluate its financial condition after the 1980 losses first surfaced. The first witness testified that "co-ops should not speculate and that Co-op's losses stemmed from the failure to hedge." Likewise, the accountant testified that "grain elevators should engage in hedging to protect the co-op from losses from price swings." He also "opined that the primary cause of the gross loss was the failure to hedge."

The reliance solely on that testimony to establish "proximate cause" at first blush appears to imply that a failure to hedge is, without more, speculation. Is that what the case stands for, though? Equating a mere failure to hedge with speculation leads to unsupportable conclusions. It would mean, for instance, that a business that does not hedge all its price (and other) risks is speculating as to the unhedged risks. Yet no business hedges all its risks. According to what some commentators have viewed as the court's reasoning, every business is speculative. If so, the term *speculation* (and likewise, a failure to hedge) is meaningless.

Brane simply does not address the potentially significant legal distinction between failing to prevent, and causing, a loss. Nor does it raise any questions about such matters as transaction costs and new risks introduced by the use of futures.* Regarding the lower court's legal reasoning, all the appellate court was called upon to decide, apart from evidentiary matters, was whether the lower court correctly stated the law in holding that (1) prior to authorizing a hedging program, management must understand the fundamentals of hedging and (2) once a *decision* to hedge has been made, management must supervise the hedging to make sure it is being handled correctly. The appellate court found the lower court to have correctly construed and applied the law on both issues.

Confusion and controversy

One commentator relies partly on *Brane* to conclude that trustees "may now have a duty to understand the uses of derivatives to achieve the most appropriate mix of risk and return for their beneficiaries, and to use derivatives when they offer the best means of achieving that mix.[60] That conclusion is sound. Other commentators, however, seem confused by *Brane*. For example, a former CFTC chairman wonders partly because of *Brane* whether "we are moving to a time when failing to hedge may become a

---

*The liquidity risks of recent "hedge-to-arrive" contracts are discussed in Chapter 18. The issues raised by these contracts demonstrate how remarkably difficult it is for anyone to hedge safely, and hence why judicial reluctance to find a duty to hedge is sensible.

fundamental management flaw and if there might eventually evolve a concept of per se (or automatic) liability whenever unwanted risks that can be avoided are not properly hedged."[61]

Also surprising is ISDA's outside counsel's* reading of the *Brane* opinion.[†] He observes: "The Indiana Court of Appeals held that the failure to hedge constituted a breach of the fiduciary duty of care owed by the directors to the cooperative's shareholders."[62] Shortly thereafter, he concludes:

> In *Brane,* the grain cooperative derived 90 percent of its income from grain sales, so the court *simply assumed* that *hedging was a necessary activity* to reduce the risk of a decline in grain prices....Given these problems, *Brane* may stand alone as an anomalous departure from the mandate of the business judgment rule.

But the court made no such assumption and the decision is entirely consistent with a traditional business judgment rule analysis. The court found merely that the rule did not apply given the facts of the case, because the directors, who authorized hedging, failed to become informed of how to supervise it. The court looked to see whether the evidence developed below supported a finding that the directors failed to satisfy their duty of care. *Brane* carefully notes that the court relied on the *fact* that the directors made a *decision* to authorize hedging and that they failed to gain the requisite knowledge to supervise the program. Nothing in the opinion expresses any view as to whether the directors had a duty to hedge. ISDA's counsel suggests that *Brane* "could be interpreted to introduce a 'duty to hedge' against business risks through the use of financial derivatives." With all due respect, no, it could not.

Other commentators[63] criticize the implications of any so-called duty to hedge, finding that duty deeply flawed for two reasons. *First,* modern finance questions "entity level" hedging when stockholders have the ability to manage risks on their own. Theoretically, stockholders can diversify away unsystematic risks, those unique to individual companies;

---

*As discussed in Chapter 18, however, the conclusions criticized here may not have been surprising when offered, given contemporaneous events. They may just appear so in light of more recent events and judicial pronouncements: in hindsight, in other words.

†ISDA's counsel also misconstrues the posture of another derivatives litigation, a class action suit, *In re Compaq Securities Litigation,* No. H-91-9191 (S.D. Tex. May 16, 1991). Perhaps his argument is simply misstated. It accompanies his discussion of *Brane* referred to in the text and accompanying endnote.

markets do not compensate for bearing diversifiable risks, but only systematic, or market, risk.

However, to question entity-level hedging is not to reject it. We saw in earlier chapters that a number of economically sound reasons exist to justify such hedging even by corporations whose stockholders are presumptively well diversified. Moreover, the presumption of such diversification relies heavily on the efficiency market hypothesis and modern portfolio theory. Judicial endorsement of both theories, while in process, is by no means complete. Courts wisely act with circumspection before fully mandating any economic theory.

Second, Brane's causation discussion was *dicta*—that is, a superfluous, nonbinding discussion of the judges' individual views. Viewed properly, *Brane* is not a "duty to hedge" case, just a "duty of care" case that happened to involve careless hedging. Whether the directors should have authorized hedging was not an issue in dispute. The only question was whether, once having authorized hedging, the directors properly supervised the hedging program. The court noted that the standard of care applicable to oversight responsibilities is that the directors must have acted "as ordinarily prudent persons in like positions in similar circumstances would have acted." The court found that the directors breached that duty "by their failure to supervise the manager and become aware of the essentials of hedging to be able to monitor the business."

Once a breach was found, the next question before the court was whether the directors were protected from liability by the business judgment rule. Relying on a long line of Delaware and Indiana cases, *Brane* held that the business judgment rule did not "shield the directors from liability," because they had "made no meaningful attempts to be informed of the hedging activities and their effects upon Co-op's financial condition." "[The] rule protects directors from liability only if their decisions were informed ones."[64] *Brane*, if truly a "derivatives" case, stands merely for the proposition that a board's duty of care in supervising a hedging program is no different from its duty concerning any other important business activity.

Current State of the Law

Beyond *Brane,* little direct authority considers the legally appropriate uses of derivatives and other risk management strategies. Most experts agree that the absence of legal analysis is surprising. Some conclude that most of the current legal attention concerning the "corporate use of derivatives has dealt not with the question of what is to be achieved through their use, but instead with ancillary, second-order questions."[65]

However, *Gagliardi* and *Caremark*[66] may throw light on first-order questions, suggesting a new and different twist on the typical *Brane* analysis. The broad and possibly difficult questions of whether and when a fiduciary duty to use derivatives might arise, and how derivatives should be used, apparently have not produced any reported decisions. But read carefully, *Gagliardi* and *Caremark* suggest that the absence of reported cases is indicative of the judiciary's attitude toward directorial decisions and oversight activities that meet appropriate process standards. No reported cases have been found standing for the proposition that directors or trustees have a duty to use or avoid derivatives.

Only two clear rules emerge: first, before a decision to use the products is made, management must understand the fundamentals, though not necessarily the mechanics, of the intended use; second, management must supervise and monitor the actual use to ensure that the products are used as intended. It helps here to reconsider a former CFTC chairman's observation that "we may be heading toward a future where hedging risk is more than just a sound policy, it's the law." Although his remark may someday prove to be accurate, nothing in current case law stands for that proposition. Indeed, recent fiascos involving overhedging via hedge-to-arrive futures contracts* suggest that courts and legislatures ought to be and are cautious about any intervention into questions of financial risk management. These are business matters. Of course, speculation is another matter entirely. Courts, lawmakers, and regulators all at times find compelling justification for interfering with activities that they consider to be speculative. As we will see in Chapter 18, speculation may be far more difficult to define than most people would ordinarily expect.

ENDNOTES: CHAPTER 17

1. See Frankel, *Fiduciary Duties, supra,* Chapter 16, note 2: 1212; Frankel, *Equity, Fiduciaries and Trusts, supra,* Chapter 16, note 50: 178.
2. This and the following quotation are from *Gagliardi v. Trifoods International, Inc.,* 683 A.2d 1049 (Del.Ch. July 19, 1996) [hereafter, *Gagliardi*]: 1052.

---

*See Chapter 18.

3. For a discussion of the criticism, the market-based response, and the problems of both, see Frankel, *Fiduciary Duties, supra,* Chapter 16, note 2 (citing many sources).

4. See, e..g., *Gagliardi, supra,* note 2 (noting also the "good policy reasons" underlying the rule); see also *In re Caremark International Inc. Derivative Litigation,* No. 13670 (Del.Ch. Sept. 25, 1996) [hereafter, *Caremark*].

5. See Gordon, *Constrained Prudent Man Rule, supra,* Chapter 16, note 55.

6. Gordon, *Constrained Prudent Man Rule, supra,* Chapter 16, note 55: 95.

7. See *Risky Investments, supra,* Chapter 1, note 15 (emphasis added): 616; see, generally, *Rest. 3rd, Trusts (Prudent Investor Rule), supra,* Chapter 10, note 13.

8. 26 Mass. (9 Pick.) 446.

9. This and the following quotation are from *Risky Investments, supra,* Chapter 1, note 15: 613.

10. The quotations in this paragraph are from Introduction, *Rest. 3rd, Trusts (Prudent Investor Rule), supra,* Chapter 10, note 9: 3–4; see also *Risky Investments, supra,* Chapter 1, note 15: 613.

11. *Risky Investments, supra,* Chapter 1, note 15: 616.

12. See e.g., *In re Estate of Janes,* 630 N.Y.S.2d 472 (Sur. 1995) (decided under the prudent man rule formerly in effect).

13. *McKechnie v. Springfield,* 311 Mass. 406, 414, 414 N.E.2d 557, 561 (1942).

14. See Introduction, *Rest. 3rd, Trusts (Prudent Investor Rule), supra,* Chapter 10, note 13: 9.

15. *Risky Investments, supra,* Chapter 1, note 15 (citations omitted): 613–614; scc *King v. Talbot,* 40 N.Y. 76 (1869).

16. Bernstein, *Capital Ideas, supra,* Chapter 4, note 24: 42; see, e.g., In *re Westfield Trust,* 172 A. 212 (N.J. Prerog. Ct. 1934) ("The stock market is not a playground for trustees. The ethics of trusteeship is not to be found in the code of the speculator. An executor's function is to conserve, not to venture. It is no less a breach of trust to speculate with securities of an estate than to gamble with its money, though the motive be to advance its interests."): 214.

17. See, e.g., *Boyer National Bank v. Garver,* 719 P.2d 583 (Wash. Ct. App. 1986), noted in *Rest. 3rd, Trusts (Prudent Investor Rule), supra,* Chapter 10, note 13: § 211; *Robertson v. Central Jersey Bank & Trust Company,* 47 F.3d 1268 (3rd Cir. 1995) [hereafter, *Robertson*].

18. See, generally, New York State Assembly, "Memorandum in Support of Legislation" [hereafter, *New York Supporting Memorandum*], regarding State of New York A.B. 11683-B, dated May 19, 1994. New York's Prudent Investor Act [hereafter, *New York Act* or *New York Prudent Investor Act*], EPTL § 11.2–3, became effective January 1, 1995; it applies to any investment made or held on or after that date.

19. General Comment *a, Rest. 3rd, Trusts* (*Prudent Investor Rule*), *supra,*
Chapter 10, note 13: 9.

20. See, e.g., William J. Carney, "Signaling and Causation in Insider Trading,"
Catholic University Law Review, 863 (1987): 865, n. 5; Glaser, *Capital
Asset Pricing Model, supra,* Chapter 11, note 10.

21. See General Comment *e, Rest. 3rd, Trusts* (*Prudent Investor Rule*), *supra,*
Chapter 10, note 13: 18; see also Aalberts and Poon, *New Prudent Investor
Rule, supra,* Chapter 16, note 5 (using historical return data compiled by
John Clements of *The Wall Street Journal* to show the deleterious effects
that inflation would have had on preservation of capital over three time
periods, each ending in 1993, given investments in 30-day Treasuries, long-
term Treasuries, and S&P 500 Index): 62–63

22. New York, for example, expressly requires (absent a contrary provision in
the governing instrument or a court order) that a trustee consider the risk
and return features of the entire portfolio rather than those of each asset in
isolation:

A trustee shall exercise reasonable care, skill and caution to make and
implement investment and management decisions as a prudent investor
would for the entire portfolio....The prudent investor standard requires a
trustee...to pursue an overall investment strategy to enable the trustee to
make appropriate present and future distributions to or for the benefit of the
beneficiaries under the governing instrument, in accordance with risk and
return objectives reasonably suited to the entire portfolio.

New York also requires that trustees consider factors other than risk and
return. Included are: "liquidity and distribution requirements of the
governing instrument, general economic conditions, the possible effect of
inflation or deflation, the expected tax consequences of investment
decisions or strategies and of distributions of income and principal...and
the needs of beneficiaries (to the extent reasonably known to the trustee) for
present and future distributions." *New York Act, supra,* note 14: § 11-2.3.

23. *Restatement of the Law Second, Trusts* (1959) (emphasis modified)
[hereafter, *Restatement Second* or *Rest. 2d, Trusts*]: § 228. Note, however,
that some states specifically reject the diversification requirement. See
Gordon, *Constrained Prudent Man Rule, supra,* Chapter 16, note 2: 98.

24. Loosely tracking the language of the General Comments to the *Restatement
Third,* New York's statute provides that "no particular investment is
inherently prudent or imprudent for purposes of the prudent investor
standard." *New York Act, supra,* note 14: § 11-2.3(b)(3)(D)(4)(A). The
related *Memorandum in Support of Legislation* states that New York's rule
is "influenced by modern investment theory...[and] recognizes that new
and seemingly risky investment vehicles and strategies can actually be
conservative, singularly or in combination." *New York Supporting
Memorandum, supra,* note 16: item 10.

25. Except as otherwise noted, the quotations in this paragraph are from General Comment *e, Rest. 3rd, Trusts (Prudent Investor Rule), supra,* Chapter 10, note 13: 21–22.

26. Likewise, the *New York Supporting Memorandum, supra,* note 16, states that "long term investment of fiduciary funds entirely in fixed income securities with no possibility of growth may be an inappropriate investment strategy for certain fiduciary accounts because inflation may in effect deplete principal."

27. General Comment *e, Rest. 3rd, Trusts (Prudent Investor Rule), supra,* Chapter 10, note 13: 19–20.

28. This and the following quotation are from Comments *e* and *h, Rest. 3rd, Trusts (Prudent Investor Rule), supra,* Chapter 10, note 13: 19–20, 29; see also *Id.:* 74–79.

29. It is difficult to see how the new rule would increase the responsibilities of trustees who hold themselves out as experts. New York's Prudent Investor Act, for example, provides that a bank, trust company, or other paid professional adviser who "represents that such trustee has special investment skills" must "exercise such diligence in investing and managing assets as would customarily be exercised by prudent investors of discretion and intelligence having special investment skills." Yet this is *not* a change from prior law. The *New York Supporting Memorandum* states that the "bill *continues the present law* requiring the use of special investment skills by a bank or paid professional investment advisor…and also by any other fiduciary representing that such fiduciary has special investment skills." (emphasis added)

30. See, e.g., Bernard Karol and M. Antoinette Thomas, "Prudent-Investor Rule Demands New Strategies," *American Banker* (March 19, 1996): 6.

31. General Comment *b, Rest. 3rd, Trusts (Prudent Investor Rule), supra,* Chapter 10, note 13: 11; see Ambachtsheer and Ezra, *Pension Fund Excellence, supra,* Chapter 16, note 33 ("Prudence is Process"): 33.

32. *Hamilton v. Nielsen,* 678 F.2d 709 (7th Cir. 1982) (citation omitted): 713.

33. *New York Act, supra,* note 14: § 11-2.3(b)(1).

34. The quotations in this paragraph are from Introduction, *Rest. 3rd, Trusts (Prudent Investor Rule), supra,* Chapter 10, note 13: 7; see also *New York Supporting Memorandum, supra,* note 16. Directors and trustees may rely on information, reports, and opinions of employees and agents, such as outside investment managers or consultants. They may also delegate investment and risk management functions. All such acts of reliance and delegation are judged according to the requirements of prudence and loyalty, and therefore against the core duties of due care, skill, caution, and diligence. See, e.g., *Rest. 3rd Trusts (Prudent Investor Rule), supra,* Chapter 10, note 13: § 227(c)(2); *Principles of Corporate Governance: Analysis and Recommendations,* 1 (American Law Institute, 1994): § 4.01(b); Model Business Corporation Act: § 8.30. *Cf. Restatement of the*

Law Second, Trusts (1959) ("The trustee is under a duty to the beneficiary not to delegate to others the doing of acts which the trustee can reasonably be required to perform"): § 171. Under the *Restatement Third,* "trustees may have a duty as well as the authority to delegate as prudent investors would." See Introduction, *Rest. 3rd, Trusts (Prudent Investor Rule), supra,* Chapter 10, note 13: 6.

35. Chew, *Leverage, supra,* Chapter 1, note 1: xiii.

36. See, generally, *Unitrin, Inc. v. American General Corp.,* 651 A.2d 1361 (Del.Supr. 1995) (discussing standards of judicial review in a takeover context under three circumstances: (1) the traditional business judgment rule, (2) the so-called *Unocal* standard applicable once a decision has been made to sell the company, and (3) the "entire fairness" test applicable when the business judgment rule is unavailable); Tobin, *The Squeeze on Directors, supra,* note 9. The quotations in this section, unless otherwise noted, are Tobin's.

37. *Briggs v. Spaulding,* 141 U.S. 132 (1891): 152; see, generally, Block, Barton, and Radin, *The Business Judgment Rule: Fiduciary Duties of Corporate Directors, 4th ed., (Prentice Hall Law and Business, 1993 and 1995 Supplement) [hereafter,* The Business Judgment Rule]; Mark A. Sargent, *D&O Liability Handbook: Law—Sample Documents—Forms, 1997 ed. (Clark Boardman Callaghan, 1996) [hereafter,* D&O Liability].

38. *Graham v. Allis-Chalmers Mfg. Co.,* 188 A.2d 125 (Del.Supr. 1963): 130.

39. This and the following quotation are from *Caremark, supra,* note 4 (emphasis added). *Cf.* Hansen, *Business Judgment Rule, supra,* note 2 (noting that when the business judgment rule is inapplicable, courts apply "some form of results-oriented due care standard that measures the merits of the directors' supervisory performance"): 1356.

40. This and the following quotation are from James E. Spiotto, "Director and Officer Liability: Who Watches the Watchmen?" in *Derivatives 1996: Avoiding the Risk and Managing the Litigation,* 1, Denis M. Forster, chair (Practicing Law Institute 1996) (emphasis added) [citing *Rabkin v. Phillip A. Hunt Chemical Corp.,* 547 A.2d 963 (Del. Ch. 1986)] [hereafter, *Director and Officer Liability*]: 373–374; see, generally, Welch and Turezyn, *Folk on the Delaware General Corporation Law: Fundamentals,* 1997 ed. (Little, Brown and Company, 1997) [hereafter, *Folk*]: § 141.2.

41. Courts have held that when the business judgment rule is *in*applicable, negligence is the standard of liability against which director conduct or inaction will be judged. The business judgment rule protects directors by raising the standard of care against which their actions or inaction will be judged. Instead of an ordinary, or simple, negligence standard, the requirement for challenging shielded director actions is a much harder to satisfy "gross negligence" standard. See, e.g., *Citron v. Fairchild Camera &*

Instrument Corp., 569 A.2d 53 (Del 1989): 53; see, generally Spiotto, *Director and Officer Liability, supra,* note 39.

42. 473 A.2d 805 (Del.Supr. 1984) (emphasis added): 812.

43. *Sinclair Oil Corp. v. Levien,* 280 A.2d 717 (Del.Supr. 1971) (citation omitted): 720.

44. 473 A.2d 805 (Del.Supr. 1984) (emphasis added): 812–813; see also *Kaplan v. Centex Corp.,* 284 A.2d 119 (Del. Ch. 1971) (directors were found to have breached the duty of care, and the court held that the business judgment rule "of necessity depends upon a showing that informed directors did, in fact, make a business judgment"): 124; Spiotto, *Director and Officer Liability, supra,* note 17: 373–374.

45. Welch and Turezyn, *Folk, supra,* note 69 (citations omitted): 97; see *Cinerama, Inc. v. Technicolor, Inc.,* 663 A.2d 1156 (Del.Supr. 1995) ("The business judgment rule 'operates as *both* a procedural guide for litigants and a substantive rule of law'" (emphasis in original)): 1162; *Mills Acquisition Co. v. Macmillan, Inc.,* 559 A.2d 1261 (Del.Supr. 1989) ("'Because the effect of the proper invocation of the business judgment rule is so powerful and the standard of entire fairness so exacting, the determination of the appropriate standard of judicial review frequently is determinative of the outcome of [the] litigation'"): 1279. However, in one case, *Van de Walle v. Unimation, Inc.,* [1990–1991 Transfer Binder] Fed. Sec. L. Rep. (CCH) ¶94,834 (Del. Ch. 1991) (holding that a merger survived an inquiry into its merits, because it was found to have been intrinsically fair): ¶99,031, the Delaware Court of Chancery expressly skipped the business judgment rule analysis and proceeded directly to examine the merits of the decision: "I have done that because in my view a determination of the merits ought not to turn upon the standard of review or burden of proof, except where that standard or burden is truly outcome determinative."

46. *Cinerama, Inc. v. Technicolor, Inc.,* 663 A.2d 1134 (Del. Ch. 1994), *aff'd,* 663 A.2d 1156 (Del.Supr. 1995).

47. *Unocal Corp. v. Mesa Petroleum Co.,* 493 A.2d 946 (Del.Supr. 1985): 958.

48. *Cinerama, Inc. v. Technicolor, Inc.,* 663 A.2d 1156 (Del.Supr. 1995) (emphasis in original) (citations omitted): 1163.

49. Branson, *Intracorporate Process, supra,* note 8: 97.

50. The argument for a potential duty to use derivatives states that "the colossal scale and widespread use of derivatives requires 'observation' of their potential uses by fiduciaries….The newest restatements of the Prudent Investor Rule…make it clear that every category of investment is permitted, including derivatives, so long as it plays an appropriate part in a diversified portfolio whose potential returns are balanced against a level of risk suitable for the beneficiaries." Equity derivatives such as index futures, for example,

can often be legitimately used to lock in capital gains, and reduce price risk, without triggering adverse tax events. Index futures and options can be used "as proxies for the underlying investments from which they are derived. As long as the [trust] has allocated to its position cash equal to that which would be required to buy the stocks represented by the futures contract, this use of derivatives is unleveraged and no more or less speculative than buying the stocks themselves." One other purpose suggested by the *Restatement Third* is the use of derivatives for "defensive" purposes. Specifically, General Comment *f* to § 227 of the *Restatement Third* discusses the use of options "to reduce the risk of an investment strategy and to do so at a lower 'price' in terms of program goals than might be exacted by converting to a more conservative portfolio of assets." Crawford, *A Fiduciary Duty to Use Derivatives?, supra,* Chapter 16, note 1: 331–332.

51. See Christopher L. Culp and Merton H. Miller, "Metallgesellschaft and the Economics of Synthetic Storage," *Journal of Applied Corporate Finance,* 7(4) (Winter 1995) (also referring tongue in cheek to hedger's ruin as "an insidious new phenomenon of the derivatives age") [hereafter, *The Economics of Synthetic Storage*]: 62–75, 75; see also, by the same authors, "Hedging in the Theory of Corporate Finance: A Reply to Our Critics," *Journal of Applied Corporate Finance,* 8(1) (Spring 1995) [hereafter, *A Reply to Our Critics*]: 121–127. But see Antonio S. Mello and John E. Parsons, "Maturity Structure of a Hedge Matters: Lessons from the Metallgesellschaft Debacle," *Journal of Applied Corporate Finance,* 8(1) (Spring 1995) (criticizing *The Economics of Synthetic Storage, supra*) [hereafter, *Maturity Structure of a Hedge Matters*]: 106–120.

52. Chew, *Leverage, supra,* Chapter 1, note 1: 224.

53. Merton H. Miller, *Merton Miller on Derivatives* (John Wiley & Sons, 1997) (emphasis in original): 129–130.

54. 473 A.2d at 812 (emphasis in original).

55. The DOL administers Title I (commonly called the Labor Title) of ERISA. Title I sets forth general standards of conduct for plan fiduciaries.

56. Letter dated March 21, 1996 from Olena Berg, U.S. Department of Labor, addressed to Hon. Eugene A. Ludwig, Comptroller of the Currency [hereafter, *ERISA Letter*]; see, generally, "Department of Labor Releases Letter Regarding Investment in Derivatives by Employee Benefit Plans Subject to ERISA," *Derivatives,* 2(2) (Warren, Gorham & Lamont, November–December 1996): 88–89; see also *Moench v. Robertson,* 62 F.3d 553 (3rd Cir. 1995) (addressing potential conflicts of interests confronting fiduciaries of employee stock ownership plans (ESOPs); although not involving derivatives, the case is instructive in its application of the prudent investor rule, particularly given the *ERISA Letter*).

57. See, e.g., *ERISA Letter*; OCC Bulletin 96-25, *Fiduciary Risk Management*

of Derivatives and Mortgage-Backed Securities (April 30, 1996); OCC
Advisory Letter, *Structured Notes,* CCH Fed. Banking L. Rep. ¶58,719
(July 21, 1994); OCC Banking Circular 277, *Risk Management of Financial
Derivatives* (October 27, 1993); see, generally, Michael P. Goldman and
Michael J. Pinsel, "A Regulatory Overview of the Insurance Industry's Use
of Over-the-Counter Derivatives," *Derivatives,* 1(5) (Warren, Gorham &
Lamont, May-June 1996): 202–216.

58. For example, the OCC warns that "banks should recognize that when they
purchase structured notes, in most instances they are taking a market view
that interest rates will not rise as fast as predicted by the current yield
curve." OCC Advisory Letter 94-2, *Structured Notes,* CCH Fed. Banking L.
Rep. ¶58,719 (July 21, 1994).

59. 590 N.E.2d 587 (Ind.App. 1 Dist. 1992). The quotations in this discussion
of the case, except as otherwise noted, are from 590 N.E.2d 589–593.

60. Crawford, *A Fiduciary Duty to Use Derivatives?, supra,* Chapter 16, note 1:
307.

61. See Hu, *Hedging Expectations, supra,* Chapter 2, note 37 (discussing the
argument of former CFTC commissioner Philip McBride Johnson) (citation
omitted): 1015–1016.

62. This and the following two quotations are from Daniel P. Cunningham, "Do
Corporations Have a Duty to Hedge? *Brane v. Roth* and *In re Compaq,*" in
Smithson et al., *Managing Financial Risk, supra,* Chapter 11, note 28
(emphasis added): 67–70.

63. According to Hu, shareholders of public companies can diversify on their
own. Thus:

> [T]he chances are somewhat higher that corporate-level hedging activities
> [at public companies] are wasteful. The closely held corporation and the
> rural co-op, on the other hand, may have a large number of poorly diversi-
> fied stockholders who will be well served by hedging and diversification.
> This distinction has not become manifest. Of the lawyer comments on
> *Brane*... I was unable to find any that suggested any reason not to apply a
> hedging precedent involving a rural co-operative to the publicly held cor-
> poration.

See Hu, *Hedging Expectations, supra,* Chapter 2, note 37.

64. Since *Brane v. Roth* was decided, shareholder lawsuits against directors for
derivatives losses have routinely emphasized, and will surely continue to
emphasize, directors' oversight responsibilities. Concerns about oversight
have been heightened by the recent Delaware *Caremark* decision. *See*
Chapter 10, note 20.

65. Hu, *Hedging Expectations, supra,* Chapter 2, note 37: 1014. For general
discussions of the types of second-order questions referred to by Hu, see,
generally, William J. McSherry et al., "Litigation Involving Derivatives," in

Klein and Lederman, eds., *Derivatives Risk and Responsibility, supra,* Chapter 2, note 20: 659–695; *Derivatives 1996: Avoiding the Risk and Managing the Litigation,* Denis M. Forster, chair (Practising Law Institute, 1996) [hereafter, *PLI Derivatives Litigation*].

   Among the most frequently raised second-order questions are those involving traditional claims of violations of securities law disclosure requirements, or Rule 10b-5; charges of fraudulent sales practices, misrepresentations, or breaches of fiduciary duties to customers or clients; suitability issues; *ultra vires* and lack of capacity or individual authority defenses to payment; and other regulatory matters. See, e.g., *In re Hyperion Securities Litigation,* No. 93 Civ. 7179 (S.D.N.Y. October 18, 1993); *In re Piper Funds, Inc. Institutional Government Income Portfolio Litigation,* No. 3-94-587 (D.Minn. May 5, 1994) (disclosure case: class action by mutual fund shareholders against Piper Jaffray entities, claiming that impermissible exotic derivatives, purchased in violation of the prospectus, caused a 30% decline in the value of the fund; Piper Jaffray agreed to a $70 million settlement); *Lehman Bros. v. Minmetals International Non-Ferrous Metals Trading Co., et al.,* No. 94 Civ. 8301, 1995 WL 380119 (S.D.N.Y. 1995) (Rule 10b-5 case). For cases involving alleged fraudulent sales practices, misrepresentations, or breaches of fiduciary duties to clients, see, e.g., *Proctor & Gamble*; *Vazquez. Dharmala* is a suitability case. For cases involving *ultra vires* and lack of capacity or individual authority defenses to payment, see, e.g., *Hammersmith v. Fulham*; *In re County of Orange, et al. v. Merrill Lynch & Co., Inc., et al.,* Adv. SA 95-0-1045-JR, 1995 WL 331412 (Bankr. C.D. Cal. 1995). Finally, *Dunn v. CFTC* falls into the "other regulatory matters" category.

66. See Committee or corporate Laws, "Changes in the Modal Business Corporation Act—Amendments Pertaining to Electronic Filings/Standards of Conduct and Standards of Liability for Directors," *The Busines Lawer,* 53 (November 1997): 157–191.

CHAPTER 18

Disclosure and Strategic Focus: Reducing, Increasing, or Transforming Risk?

In order that speculation should contribute to economically desirable price formation, speculators must keep well informed concerning the pertinent economic facts, and must be able to appraise those facts properly....Such speculation deserves to command a wage, and that fact is ignored when the returns from speculation are viewed solely as a reward for risk-bearing.

Holbrook Working
"New Concepts Concerning Futures
Markets and Prices," Economic Review,
June 1962

The young kids coming up today will look back 30 years from now and say, "Do you realize that in 1996, most corporate honchos did not know the difference between an option and a future?" and everybody will laugh and say, "You're kidding."

Nobel Laureate Merton H. Miller,
Derivatives Strategy, *August 1996*

Aside from the term *derivative,* arguably the two most imprecise terms used in derivatives markets are *hedging* and *speculation.* Given the importance of the underlying concepts that the terms connote, the imprecision can lead to unfortunate confusion, even among experts. At so basic a conceptual level, confusion creates risks, both business and legal. Equally important, in a competitive economy, it can lead management to misperceive risk, needlessly foregoing prudent derivatives uses; likewise it can frighten investors who misunderstand derivatives into needlessly shunning investments in firms that prudently use derivatives for strategic advantages in their core businesses and in funds that use derivatives to minimize the transaction costs of constructing efficient portfolios.

Certainly, in recent years many business executives—commercial fiduciaries who put other people's money to work in the "real economy"—had a litigation incentive to avoid derivatives. Likewise, many trustees and other fiduciaries who invest other people's money had a litigation incentive to avoid using derivatives and purchasing investments in firms that use derivatives. Now, things are changing. As Crawford suggests, such fiduciaries, caught in what might be called a "fiduciary's dilemma," may be at risk for *not* using derivatives, or for investing in firms that avoid derivatives.[1] As a business matter, we can easily see how summarily dismissing derivatives implies competitive risks.

Thinking of derivatives in terms of the three "pure" risk management strategies central to functional analysis leads to a precise and informative understanding of derivatives' risks. That precision is particularly helpful to trustees, directors, business and fund managers, and legal advisers who might not be intimately acquainted with derivatives trading and its consequences. It also enables practitioners and academics alike to accept Henry Hu's challenge to begin developing for derivatives "a richly textured body of supporting legal and financial analysis."[2] As Hu aptly observes, "If the hedging question is framed in functional terms, one would expect both ends and means to be clear." Robert Merton has given us the necessary functional tools for a financial analysis. Frankel, Brudney, ISDA, EUDA, and others have supplied many of the functional tools for a legal analysis.

This chapter suggests a formal means-ends approach to thinking strategically about the hedging or, more precisely, risk management question. It shows that aside from being an interesting academic or intellectual puzzle, properly defining derivatives strategies is essential to any sound risk management system. This chapter also explores a number of related disclosure, documentation, and other business and legal issues.

THINKING STRATEGICALLY: A FORMAL ENDS-MEANS ANALYSIS

Henry Kissinger wrote recently in a political context that "Strategy must define what we are trying to accomplish and whether our means are relevant to our ends."[3] That advice applies equally to the use of derivatives for business and investment purposes. Thus, an appropriately structured formal analysis looks first to the objectives, or ends, of a business or portfolio. Once the ends have been clarified, one can better evaluate how effective derivatives and other alternative strategies might be for achieving those ends. The analysis then considers the alternative means, which may or may not include derivatives. Finally, one must evaluate the relationships between various ends and means and compare alternative strategies on the basis of those relationships. A formal ends-means analysis isolates, and helps one reason clearly about, three distinct sources of potential derivatives-related confusion:

1. The goals, or alternative *ends* served by the products
2. The *means,* or economic behavior of the products themselves
3. The *relation* between ends and means, or whether products are properly chosen and tailored to fit the desired objectives

Reasoning clearly about those three items is the essence of strategic thinking.

From a business and legal risk management perspective, separate consideration and documentation of each logical step in the process is invaluable. Those steps help fiduciaries and legal advisers demonstrate the rationality of the decision-making process leading to a given use, or nonuse, of derivatives. Most reporting entities with market risk exposure arising from derivatives or certain other financial instruments either now are or soon will be required by the SEC to disclose their risk management strategies. SEC rules define market risk broadly to include risks from charges in interest rates, FX rates, commodity prices, and other market factors.

Although the disclosure rules use different terminology, essentially the primary qualitative market risk disclosures the SEC requires is a discussion of a firm's objectives (ends), instruments (means), and strategies. In any event an inability to define one's strategy, whether or not it involves derivatives, is likely to be read as a sign of weak or troubled management. Further, as discussed in Chapter 17, the main concern of courts is the care and deliberation that goes into a decision or general oversight; as a legal matter, process is far more important than results. Whether viewed from a business or legal perspective, attempts to analyze all three logical steps simultaneously usually falter. Ignoring clear deliberation of any of the three sources is risky.

Regardless of the level of formality or specific analysis used, the decision-making approach should address the "logically prior" questions of risk management strategy: What sorts of risks should be managed? Should they be managed partially or fully? What kinds of instruments will best accomplish the risk management objectives? Should we shed, diversify, or insure risks?[4] These are all ultimate trustee, board of directors, or other senior management issues. A functional analysis suggests that we not rely on imprecise terminology, but focus instead on increasing, decreasing, or transforming risk.

Schematic Structure of Ends-Means Analysis

The analytical scheme adopted here is shown in Figure 18.1, which illustrates simply that a chosen means must be related to the desired end. It would be illogical, for example, to fault means 3 in panel (b) for failing to produce end A, because means 3 is related to end B, not A. If, however, means 1 or 2 were selected and failed to produce end A, the cause of the failure might indeed be the selected means.

Assume that the selected means was a dollar/deutschmark currency swap. Also, assume that DMs were used as a proxy for another less liquid currency, fluctuations in the dollar value of which historically have been highly correlated with the DM. Such "proxy hedging" strategies (in futures parlance, "cross hedging") are sometimes used by market participants who consider pricing in a desired currency unfavorable. If the dollar/deutschmark swap in our example failed to give the desired currency protection, two potential reasons immediately recommend themselves. First, the strategy may have failed because it was improperly implemented. Maybe the swap covered only half the needed principal amount or it matured while the user still had significant FX exposure. Alternatively, the swap might have had a design defect—perhaps the desired currency broke away from its historically high DM ties, rising in dollar value even though the DM did not.*

Figure 18.1 also illustrates why ends must be clarified. Any judgment as to the effectiveness of a chosen means is dubious if the related end is vague or ambiguous. Figure 18.1(b) shows that means 1 achieves end A or C. The user who wants to achieve end A needs to know that a strategy using means 1 may produce C, an undesirable result. Put differently, C can occur even if means 1 performs as expected. If C, not A occurs, then absent design defects and faulty implementation, the problem is *not* means 1—it performed as expected. The problem is the *selection* of a means with an ambiguous end. Means 2 would likely have been a better choice, because it leads only to end A.[†]

---

*Recent examples of such "breaking away" are provided by the currency market turmoil in Southeast Asia. Apparently, many companies doing business in Indonesia and Thailand had long grown accustomed to central bank activities pegging local currency values to the U.S. dollar. Many companies borrowed in dollars, then a relatively cheaper currency, and left their exposures unhedged. Reportedly, other companies viewed this as an opportunity for a "free lunch"; they used a variety of derivatives to increase their domestic currency exposures [i.e., speculate] by agreeing "to receive their domestic currency and pay US dollars." When the currency controls fell apart, the dollar-denominated obligations instantly became onerous. See Louise Lucas, "Turmoil Prompts Currency Rethink," *Financial Times* (October 31, 1997).

[†]We have not, of course, discussed the comparative costs or probabilities of the various alternative strategies. For example, means 1 might not be dangerous, because the odds of C happening are remote, while means 2 might be considerably more expensive than means 1. Surely, costs and probabilities will weigh heavily in any strategy decision.

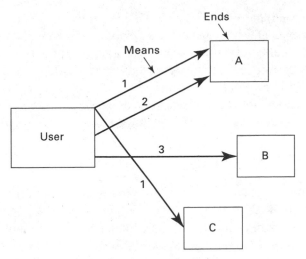

Figure 18.1   Formal ends-means analysis.

To judge a strategy's effectiveness, we need to ensure that the strategy's ends and means are related. Confusion over ends, means, or relationships between the two will bias any assessment of a strategy's performance, and that is dangerous whether the bias is for or against. If, for example, we assume that derivatives are used only for speculation, that assumption undermines any discussion of the effectiveness of a hedging strategy. If we are concerned about speculation or, more accurately, increasing risk beyond that naturally present—here, an end to be avoided—the logic of focusing exclusively on derivatives (i.e., a means) is suspect. A more fruitful exercise is one that begins by clarifying both the desired end, risk reduction, and the undesired end, increasing risk. A useful analysis is one that tailors a strategy to achieve the former and avoid the latter.*

FX Illustration

Assume that A and B are alternative FX objectives. A is the elimination of exchange rate risk through complete hedging; B is the opposite, the retention of full FX exposure. Management of a closely held exporting company whose owners' are poorly diversified might choose goal A. Given their con-

---

*Clearly defining what is meant by speculation or increasing risk is an often surprisingly complex subject. We look at some of the complexities later in the chapter.

centrated wealth, those owners may wish to protect their firm and, therefore, their personal wealth against the risk of a weakening home currency. In contrast, goal B might be suitable for a large, publicly held importer whose investors are presumptively well diversified. Those investors might hold the importer's stock for its protection against a strengthening home currency. Consider the possible reactions of the two firms' respective stockholders to a sudden weakening of the home currency.

Isolating Issues

The declining home currency should increase the home currency denominated costs, or prices, of imported goods, depressing the importer's earnings. Still, the public should not fault management for maintaining full currency exposure, given that the stock was bought precisely for that exposure. The importer's (1) objective was to increase firm value (2) by leaving its FX risk unmanaged, and (3) the strategy performed as expected. Judged ahead of time, or *ex ante,* the firm's action was presumably rewarded by the market's bidding up the price of its stock specifically because the firm left its FX exposure unmanaged. By the same reasoning, the market would have punished, or bid down, the stock price if the firm had hedged.*

Meanwhile, the private exporter, having fully hedged its FX risk, could not profit, at least directly, from the weakened currency. Had the exporter remained unhedged, the weakening currency should have improved earnings by decreasing the firm's costs of goods and increasing its revenues, each as measured in the home currency. Yet the exporter's owners, too, would have little reason to fault their risk management program for the missed profit opportunity. The owners' (1) objective was to preserve their wealth (2) through FX hedging, and (3) the strategy worked: the program performed as expected. Presumably those owners knew that complete hedging would eliminate not only downside but also upside "exposure."

---

*Brealey and Meyers emphasize that under Fisher's view of the firm, the view that underlies MM theory, managers can simply focus on share price, treating stockholders' personal tastes (and their own) as irrelevant. Management's task is quite simple: maximize the firm's net present value. See Brealey and Myers, *Principles of Corporate Finance, supra,* Chapter 11, note 10: 24. *Cf.* Hu, *Hedging Expectations, supra,* Chapter 2, note 37 (concluding that corporate managers should "adhere to the 'hedging expectations' of their shareholders").

HEDGING VERSUS SPECULATION

An important point of formal reasoning is that it helps us understand more clearly what is commonly intended, or not meant, by hedging and speculation. Certainly, most people use the term *hedging* to indicate some form of risk reduction and *speculation* to mean some sort of risk increase. But are the concepts really so straightforward? After all, a failed proxy hedging strategy might be regarded as speculative; it depended on a presumed correlation between two currencies that in fact did not persist. Was the hedger, then, speculating on the strength of the correlation? In our example, we assumed that the hedger knowingly took on the currency correlation risk in the hope of avoiding "unfavorable pricing" through direct hedging. In retrospect, the pricing might not have been unfavorable.

Alternatively, consider the common case of a lender who extends a fixed-rate loan and simultaneously hedges its interest rate risk through a fixed-for-floating interest rate swap. If the borrower prepays while the swap is outstanding and the lender does not liquidate the swap or put it to another hedging use, it will have a swap on its books that serves no hedging purpose. If so, the U.S. Supreme Court would likely consider that lender, to the extent of the swap, to be speculating. Consider footnote 10 to its *Curran* decision: "Of course, when a hedger takes a long or a short position that is greater than its interest in the commodity itself, it is to that extent no longer a hedger, but a speculator."[5]

Moreover, many hedging strategies involve some form of correlation, or basis, risk. Basis risk arises whenever the hedging vehicle does not have properties that perfectly offset those of the hedge asset, liability, or exposure. Should the inability to find a "perfect hedge" automatically render the hedging decision speculative? It depends. As a statistician would likely ask, quoting Tufte again, "The deep, fundamental question...is *Compared with what?*" Was the basis risk introduced by the hedging transaction greater in magnitude than that of the unhedged transaction? If not, logically the hedging transaction did not increase risk so should not be thought of as speculation.

Brane v. Roth: Redux

A major concern expressed at the end of Chapter 17 was the inadequacy of those legal analyzes of the *Brane* decision that find a purported "duty to hedge." To see why such a duty would be surprising (at least for anyone other than a trustee obligated to act prudently in conserving trust property), consider the ongoing unfortunate saga involving "hedge to arrive" contracts (HTAs).* Reportedly hundreds of lawsuits have been filed and are making their way through the court system.

Failed HTA programs are having enormously destructive effects on many U.S. farming communities. The immediate cause of the failure could hardly be more ironic: by the summer of 1996, grain prices had risen too high. Many farmers had been hurt badly in the 1980s by a deep recession in the farming industry. Apparently, many then "got into a bind thinking *low* [grain] prices were endless."[6] The assumption that prices would remain low apparently induced many farmers in the early 1990s to try to look in a supposedly temporary surge in grain prices.

About the same time, HTAs became widely available. HTAs are private fixed-price contracts typically entered into by farmers with their local grain elevator cooperatives. Most of the contracts provide for the sale of a fixed quantity of grain for deferred delivery. For present purposes, the key determinant of the fixed price would be a specified futures contract price from the Chicago Board of Trade for the month in which delivery was anticipated. It appears that the contracts required (or contemplated) the cooperative, upon commencement of the HTA, to enter into an offsetting futures contract. In theory, the structure was effectively hedged, though subject to basis risk mainly because local delivery points were at different locations than those provided for in futures contracts. Yet any hedging program involving futures contracts implies liquidity risk.

Grain elevators customarily use futures to protect against price declines while a commodity is either held in storage or being produced. Assume for discussion purposes that an elevator, or coop, is obligated to buy grain from a farmer when it is harvested: thus, the elevator is "long" a grain forward contract, while the farmer is "short." To offset the coop's risk of a subsequent spot price decline, it promptly "sells" a futures contract under which it agrees to sell a set quantity and type of grain at a set price on the settlement date. The short position directly offsets the risk of the elevator's agreement to buy grain from its farmer. Price swings prior to settlement of the offsetting short and long positions can, however, have serious cashflow consequences that sooner or later must be passed on to the farmer.

The unusual feature of many HTAs is that they enable farmers to roll

---

*HTAs are OTC contracts subject to a wide range of negotiated terms. The following discussion, then, is a simplification based on the author's assessment of a typical HTA contract.

over their delivery obligations indefinitely, for a small fee payable upon each rollover. Thus, a farmer who believes that current spot prices are high and who has an outstanding delivery obligation under an HTA might elect to defer delivery until the next crop. Meanwhile, the farmer can sell the current crop into the spot market at the today's "high" price. A farmer using this strategy expects that by the next harvest, prices will have retreated. If so, the farmer can then satisfy the deferred delivery obligation and receive the "high" fixed-price previously agreed upon under the HTA. As long as prices go back to their low levels, the HTA price will be higher than spot prices upon delivery.

For most farmers and coops, this seemed like an all-around win-win situation. Thus, when grain prices rose unexpectedly in 1995 many farmers eagerly entered into HTAs to lock in the high prices. Some "hedged" as many as five years' worth of their forward production.

The structure had one drawback. Once the cooperative entered into its offsetting futures contract, it had to post initial margin and, if prices moved against it, "variation margin" on its futures contracts. In turn, the elevator maintained the right to call upon farmers if necessary to make good on those payments. Margin payments here protect the buyer of the futures contract— the long—from the cooperatives' failure to make delivery. Cooperatives could continue rolling over short futures positions, but as prices rose their futures positions would move progressively farther out of the money. Margin calls became harder and harder to meet.

Until receiving delivery from the farmer, the cooperative would not have grain on hand to deliver under the futures contracts or to post as collateral to finance margin calls. As long as the futures contracts remained "open" and prices climbed, the cooperative's cost of satisfying margin calls mounted. Many coops were forced in the summer of 1996 to simply close out their futures positions, effectively locking in massive losses. The cooperatives charged those losses back to the farmers, usually as an offset to the fixed price payable at the time of the deferred delivery. Farmers, realizing that the offset would wipe out most of their fixed HTA price, then began refusing to make deliveries, leaving the cooperatives with staggering losses. Many hundreds of cases are now being litigated: some on the (to date losing) theory that the HTA contracts are illegal off-exchange futures contracts that are thus unenforceable, others on the theory that the elevators failed to disclose to the farmers the true risks of the HTAs.[7]

Although the regulatory implications of the litigation are important, for present purposes the important point is that the immediate cause of the disastrous losses was the futures hedging program essential to the HTA structure. In other words, in dramatic contrast to *Brane,* the hedging program itself was the direct source of the losses—even though it was properly executed. "When physical delivery ultimately results, the argument goes, the overriding effect of the entire HTA will not have been to give the former up front assurance of a price, but to allow the former the option to indirectly win (or loss) in speculative transactions".[9] The hedging decision, it seems, is not as straightforward or simple as it might normally seem.

Meanings Begin to Break Down; Working's Remarkable Insights[8]

Culp and Miller, in their commentary on the Metallgesellschaft problems noted in Chapter 1, rely heavily on important theoretical work done by Holbrook Working decades ago. Working was first and foremost a statistician, drawn to market research by an interest in empirical data. He made observations and tried to explain them, and he did so in an incisive manner. Even a cursory review of his findings and theories reveals powerful insights. And these insights are gained from a study of some of the most ordinary of markets, like those for agricultural commodities such as wheat and corn.

Of critical importance when following his studies is that Working focused on physical markets, those that involve commodities such as metals and grains. Financial futures did not yet exist. Arguably, the relevance of many of his thoughts has been overlooked because they do not translate into direct applications in derivatives markets involving stocks, bonds, currencies, and other financial instruments. Certainly, though, their relevance is clear for industries dealing in physical commodities, such as oil, metals, minerals, and chocolate.

Working's numerous findings, and the terminology he used, today might seem startling. For example, he demonstrated how little understood the word hedging is, particularly noting that the use of hedging to reduce risk—the standard "variance minimization model of corporate finance"—is misapplied in physical futures markets. The problem is that, for those not intimately acquainted with such markets, the reason that those models fail to apply is not immediately apparent.

Working's analyzes contain remarkable observations. For example, he notes in his discussion of selective hedging, or avoidance of loss, that "[e]fforts on the part of…small firms to gain profits from appraisal of price prospects, as is implied by selectivity in hedging, appear ordinarily ill-advised." His reasoning is that the purpose of selective hedging is to avoid losses, not earn profits. Judging by the available evidence to date, the HTA cases are replete with instances of farmers and "small firms" attempting to profit from selective hedging rather than from loss avoidance. Furthermore, he states that pure risk-avoidance hedging is "unimportant or virtually nonexistent in modern business practice."

Perhaps the three most startling comments of all are the following. First, Working suggests that the practice which he identifies as selective hedging and anticipatory hedging, and which occurs all the time in physical commodity markets today, "requires either regarding hedging as sometimes closely akin to speculation, or defining speculation otherwise than has been usual in economics texts." Second, he notes that hedge selling (such as the HTA grain elevators) can depress futures market prices to the point where a "many dealers and processors are attracted by the possibilities of profit through *speculative holding* of the commodity. Even among handlers of commodities which attract broad public participation to their futures markets, such as wheat, *discretionary hedging* is not uncommon." Third, Working notes that someone who holds the underlying fidget and does not hedge has made a decision effectively to go long the underlying "by merely refraining from hedging."

Another way of thinking about speculative holding is to consider what happens when the price of a commodity is, for whatever reason, temporarily depressed. Low prices are recognized as such by experts familiar with market behavior. Those experts are willing to buy the commodity—not the futures, but the commodity itself—and hold it in the expectation of selling it later at a profit. Farmers might choose not to sell a crop immediately after harvest, because they might consider the market flooded and prices unacceptably low. If so, they hold back their stock, waiting to sell when prices rebound—in some sense, they are speculating. The implications of Working's conclusions are striking.

Current Implications:
Taking a "Market View"

Working's analysis remains vital today. This may seem surprising, given that he studied what seem today to be the ancient markets of the 1930s, 1940s, and 1950s. Yet abundant examples can be found of how concepts about which he wrote directly apply to much of today's finance theory and practice. For example, the different hedging practices that Working wrote about are now prevalent throughout the modern economy. They may go by different names, however, as in the now commonly used expression that a firm alters its derivatives positions on the basis of a "market view."[10] That expression is normally associated with speculation, because it suggests that investors can outguess an efficient market. According to Working, properly understood, most speculation is based on comparative advantages in market information, not guessing.

René Stulz applies the principle of comparative advantage to risk management practices of two hypothetical firms.[11] One is a producer of consumer durables that uses large amounts of copper in the manufacturing of its goods. The other is a foreign currency trading operation in a large commercial bank. Assume that when the producer has no definitive expectation or view of future copper prices, management will hedge 50% of anticipated future copper needs. Yet the firm, through its operations, has access to specialized knowledge* of copper market conditions that are unlikely to be generally known or understood. If so, the firm might want to allow its views of future copper prices to affect its hedge ratio. Stulz suggests that if the firm expects a significant price increase, it might hedge 100% of anticipated needs; if a decrease, perhaps 20%, maybe zero.† By tailoring its hedge ratio, the firm will be exploiting its comparative advantage—the source of which is its specialized knowledge of copper prices. As Stulz notes, the strategy is not foolproof, but "it seems quite plausible that companies could have such informational advantages."

Indeed, this is precisely what Working was writing about when he stated that the speculator ought to command a wage. A knowledgeable speculator brings specialized and reliable information essential to proper price formation. But notice that the "speculators" we are talking about, and that Working and Stulz write about, are not speculators in the commonly understood sense of the term. They are market participants who merely use specialized knowledge to determine appropriate hedge ratios. As long as a

---

*Not to be confused with "inside information."

†For example, concerning its currency exposures, Union Carbide "will hedge as much [as] 100% in
   some cases or we will hedge zero or somewhere in between, depending on what we feel is
   the trend in the U.S. dollar." Similarly, R. J. Reynolds Nabisco, in managing its currency
   exposures, considers its policy as "best described as one of 'selective' hedging. In managing
   our various currency exposures, we can be hedged anywhere from zero to 100%. Normally,
   it's not on either end of this spectrum but somewhere in the middle....In our view, hedging
   either 0% or 100% of an exposure amounts to taking a very strong view on the market."
   Derivatives and Corporate Risk Management, supra, note 7 (comments of vice president
   and treasurer of Union Carbide, and vice president and treasurer of R. J. Reynolds Tobacco).

firm's hedge ratio ranges between 0% and 100%, hedging does not increase the firm's risk above what it would have been had the firm not hedged at all.

According to the Supreme Court's sense of the term *hedging,* as stated in *Curran,* such speculation is hedging. The Court does say that to hedge more than 100% is "to that extent" speculation. Empirical and anecdotal evidence suggests that although many firms allow their "views" or market expectations to influence their hedge ratios, they do not exceed their maximum commercial needs. This is what Tufano found in his study of the North American gold mining industry: "There are no firms that used these financial transactions to increase gold price exposure; thus, it appears that the financial risk management programs produce risk reduction, rather than risk enhancement (or speculation)."[12] The results are consistent with other hedging practices we discussed in earlier chapters.

Consider, however, how easily comparative advantage can be misunderstood. Stulz explains that banks should expect to profit from position taking in foreign exchange markets only "if they have access to information before most other firms. In the case of FX, this is likely to happen only if the bank's trading operation is very large—large enough so that its deal flow is likely to reflect general shifts in demand for foreign currencies." Stulz doubts that many firms are in such a position, and explains that most firms' "FX trading profits come from market-making, not position-taking." If a bank misjudges the source of its comparative advantage, thinking it is good at predicting currency movements rather than making a market for its customers, it is likely to make serious strategic errors. Hiring ace traders lacking customer relations skills will likely jeopardize the firm's market-making capabilities. At the same time, it will likely encourage the type of speculative position taking from which the firm has no legitimate expectation of profiting.

One derivatives expert summed up nicely the general, often unspoken reaction of most market participants and observers to the imprecision of market terminology; he also added some valuable advice:

> I've always had problems with the imprecision, even confusion, that surround the terms in this business of risk management. "Hedging," "speculation," "trading," "risk-taking," "risk avoidance"—we all seem to be using these words somewhat differently. So, when someone begins by saying that their treasury is not a profit center, but they add value by taking views on a selective basis, that statement raises questions about the objective of the risk management program. And because this kind of confusion is so widespread, I would argue unquestionably the most important step in risk management is figuring out exactly what you're trying to accomplish.[13]

Working's persuasive explanation of the problems with market terminology suggests that that imprecision is not likely to be clarified soon. Working talked about needing intimate knowledge of markets, not definitions.

DISCLOSURE

Currently, much uncertainty surrounds the issue of derivatives disclosure. Alarms have been sounded as to the purportedly harsh effect of recently instituted SEC guidelines,[14] and even louder alarms concerning recently adopted accounting regulations. Regardless of current disclosure requirements, one thing is certain: continuing experimentation with these rules by the SEC, the Federal Reserve, the OCC, the FASB, and other domestic and international regulatory and quasi-regulatory bodies. Clearly, the perfect disclosure regime has not yet been found. Does it exist? It is doubtful. The intention in this section is not try to find that regime, but to point out some of the most important issues that are otherwise seldom fully or clearly addressed.

Few if any commentators question the legitimacy of investors' interest in ready access to abundant derivatives information that gives better insight into a firm's risk-return features and those of its securities. Similarly, few question the legitimate competitive and strategic interests of companies in *not* disclosing that information. Rather, arguments concern more the proper balancing of interests: Is the investor's economic interest best served by disclosures that might be used by a reporting firm's competitors to compete with that firm? Are individual investors realistically capable of properly evaluating the information, especially when portfolio theory counsels them to avoid focusing on the risks of isolated investments? What about securities analysts, when they act as the investors' surrogates? Do the benefits of additional disclosure justify the costs? Will detailed and costly disclosure requirements drive some companies away from public securities markets? From U.S. public securities markets? Will they have the opposite effect of causing many firms simply to steer clear of derivatives? What is a derivative? How difficult will it be for financial innovators to innovate around the disclosure rules, especially since their financial incentives for doing so are likely to be high?

A conceptual framework is needed for thinking about various disclosure issues. Most disclosure objections from issuers and academics fall into three main categories: (1) excessive regulatory burden and cost, (2) creation of an appearance of undue emphasis on derivatives risks as opposed to other business risks, and (3) forced disclosures of competitively sensitive information. On the other side of the issue are the legitimate needs of investors. To formulate sound investment strategies, investors need information about (1) the business and financial risks of specific issuers, (2) the risks of particular classes of securities, such as common stock, preferred stock, and junk bonds, (3) the risks of a particular issuer's securities, and (4) how to interpret the data.

Preliminary Issue:
Function of Disclosure?

Investors, creditors, economists, and financial analysts read financial statements with one overriding objective in mind: to determine the market value of firm's future net cashflows. As we saw in Chapter 13 and 14, that depends initially on the risk-adjusted present value of the firms overall expected *future* cashflows.Investors, creditors, and analysts are, of course, further concerned about the respective values of specific securities. According to Equation 13.1, the value of any given security within a firm's capital structure can theoretically be derived straightforwardly from overall firm value. In contrast, Accounting numbers traditionally have served a quite different, more modest function.

Rather than attempt to estimate economic value—an inherently subjective exercise—"[l]ong ago, accountants and financial statement users came to the realization that, although measurements and reports of economic market values would be very useful, this was not a task for which accountants had a comparative advantage."[20] Hence, accountants attempt to measure what can perhaps best be described as accounting or book value, not economic market value. Traditionally, book value has been measured from historical asset and liability prices, recorded on a balance sheet and modified over time, when an objective measurement event is determined, to reflect the realization of losses or gains in value. One immediate divergence of accounting principles from economic valuation is that accounting does not attempt to measure future values—it looks at historical costs and changes in values over past periods. While that information is helpful to investors, it is not ultimately what they seek.

Historical costs and hence recorded book values do not necessarily bear any direct relation to market values. Quite simply, "the balance sheet is not intended to and does not provide a statement of economic values. Rather,...with some exceptions it is a report of account balances not yet charged or credited to an income statement account." To the extent that financial statements measure economic value, they do so through the income statement.

Derivatives accounting presents a future problem. To begin, the historical cost of forward-based transactions, as we have shown, is on balance zero. Similarly, the historical cost of an option-based transaction is the premium, which often quickly bears little relation to the option's economic value. Thus, most derivatives would, absent special rules, escape in large part measurement by accounting systems prior to their actual close out or termination Those special rules, which has varied considerably over the past twenty years, generally attempt to book changes in derivatives "fair value." Hence, fair value accounting for derivatives, when applicable, operates as an exception to traditional accounting practices. Unfortunately, the fair market valuation of a host of derivatives is, in many respects and despite the availability of rigorous analytical tools, an art and not a science.

To alleviate potential distorting impressions investors might draw from cursory inspection of these hybrid "historical cost/fair value" financial statements, accounting rules enable firms, subject to strict guidelines, to apply "hedge accounting" to certain derivatives transactions. Under hedge accounting, firms may defer booking changes in the values of specified derivatives positions that closely offset various other exposures. Much of the debate over derivatives accounting principles is focused on the appropriateness of the offset principles behind hedge accounting rules. For instance, under what circumstances should firm's who hedge net portfolio exposures be allowed to apply hedge accounting? Under what circumstances are hedges put in place for unticipated, but not firm committed exposures be permitted hedge accounting treatment?

A further distorting wrinkle is added by SEC disclosure requirements. SEC rules try to provide financial statement users with a sense of derivatives' market risks, an inherently future-oriented concept that future strays from traditional accounting principles. To measure however bluntly future exposures, the SEC requires most derivative users to provide statements of either projected future cashflow requirements, sensitivity analyzes, or values at risk (VAR) from derivatives and other market sensitive instruments. The fundamental debate over derivatives disclosure and accounting requirements concerns the reliability of information that, while reported in numbers that suggest objectivity, are inherently derived from such divers sets of valuation principles that fundamentally serve distinct functions.

Issuer Concerns

Regulatory burden

Regulatory burdens are important issues for direct and indirect reasons. Miller has demonstrated that the "pearls" of financial innovation are largely unintended consequences of government regulation. Once a perceived burden or problem is created, innovators seek a way around it. Three immediate concerns arise as to the regulatory burden. First, excessive costs are toughest for those firms that arguably are most in need of derivatives—the small firms that cannot self-insure. For example, Walter Dolde reported in 1993 that "among firms that have surmounted the initial investment barrier, more complete hedgers tend to be smaller, perhaps reflecting their higher expected costs of financial distress."[15] If small firms are the ones that benefit most from derivatives use, and if large firms can afford to self-insure or absorb many risks because of their large capital bases, public policy concerns argue toward reducing the regulatory burden on small issuers, not increasing it.

Second, excessive costs will cause some issuers to avoid either disclosure or derivatives. Avoiding disclosure is not a viable option for most issuers, because they are in a sense captive reporting companies. Naturally, many actual or potential users that perceive substantial compliance costs may simply forgo using products that trigger the disclosure requirements. Third, litigation risks are increased by greater disclosure. Despite safe harbors (not available for footnote disclosures), a firm must always concern itself with allegations of improper derivatives use or nonuse.

Undue derivatives emphasis

Don Chance cogently summarizes a basic problem with derivatives disclosure as follows: "Financial Risks [of derivatives] are only one of the risks companies face—and pale in comparison to the fundamental business risks they assume in their line of business....Yet has anyone at the SEC or anywhere else suggested that firms be required to disclose that their planes might crash, their factories might blow up or their drugs might kill?"[16] This problem is one of emphasis. It is a problem with which derivatives users are well familiar.

Competitive disadvantage

For firms that enjoy a comparative advantage as to the conditions and movements of various markets, quite possibly any detailed disclosure will undermine that advantage. One concern, than, is basic fairness. If a firm works hard and is expert and knowledgeable at predicting future trends, why should it not be compensated for that work and knowledge? The second is that undermining a firm's comparative advantage may discourage it and other firms from continuing to invest in and exploit their existing information advantages. If the disincentive is great, and if the information derivative users bring to the market is significant to price formation, the loss of such information could be costly. As the quality of information brought to bear on prices deteriorates, market prices will become less informative and markets less efficient.

Investor Concerns

Issuer-specific risk

Investors have a legitimate interest in evaluating the risk profiles of their portfolio companies. As Hu has emphasized and as Tufano's studies of the gold mining industry have confirmed, sophisticated investors care greatly about risk management details.[17] The degree to which investors care about different industries and the extent to which individual investors have the capacity to analyze all information meaningfully is another question. But market efficiency suggests that the information will be priced. The real issue is whether investors will be able to tell how derivatives affect the interaction of specific companies' securities with other assets in portfolios. The diversity of reporting formats available suggests real difficulties in making cross-company comparisons.

Asset class information[18]

Hu correctly perceives the importance of asset class information to a diversified investor. An investor that is incapable of comparing high-risk bonds with equity securities will have trouble constructing a well-diversified portfolio. The question pertains most importantly to asset allocation decisions.

Issuer-specific securities

Rather than broad asset class information, this category looks at specific individual securities of an issuer. The analysis of the issuer's overall profitability and revenues, for example, is only the first step in determining how the issuer's individual liabilities are carved up.

Is the data meaningful?

Investors need to be able to understand the different methodologies behind various reporting methods. The current rules allow issuers to report cash-flow requirements, sensitivity analysis, or value at risk. Serious questions exist as to whether this information is meaningful. VAR's simplicity, and for that matter the simplicity of all three methodologies, is seductive.[19]

ENDNOTES: CHAPTER 18

1. See Crawford, *A Fiduciary Duty to Use Derivatives?, supra,* Chapter 16, note 1. Crawford's exact expression is "trustee's dilemma."

2. Hu, *Hedging Expectations, supra,* Chapter 2, note 36: 1014.

3. Henry A. Kissinger, "Why Clinton Lost to Saddam—Again," *New York Post* (March 22, 1998): 53.

4. See Froot et al., *Risk Management: Coordinating Corporate Investment and Financing Policies, supra,* note 18: 1629–1630.

5. *Merrill Lynch, Pierce, Fenner & Smith v. Curran,* 456 U.S. 353, 72 L.Ed. 2d 182, 102 S.Ct. 1825 (1982).

6. Scott Kilman, "Hedge Row: As Corn Prices Soar, a Futures Tactic Brings Rancor to Rural Towns," *Wall Street Journal* (July 2, 1996) (an excellent introduction to the disturbing economic and social impact of failed HTA programs) (emphasis in original) [hereafter, *Hedge Row*]: A1; see *In re Grain Land Coop Cases,* No. 3-96-1209, *CCH Commodity Futures Law Reports,* No. 562, ¶ 27,164 (U.S.D.C., Minn., September 25, 1997) [hereafter, *Grain Land Coop*]; *Eby, et al. v. Producers Co-op, Inc.,* Case No. 1:96-CV-567, *CCH Commodity Futures Law Reports,* ¶ 27,051 (U.S.D.C., West. Mich., February 11, 1997).

7. See, e.g., *In re Grain Land Coop,* 978 F.Supp. 1267, Comm. Fut. L. Rep. ¶ 27,164 (D. Minn. 1997); *Eby v. Producers Co-op, Inc.,* 959 F.Supp. 428, Comm. Fut. L. Rep. ¶ 37,062 (W.D. Mich. S.D. 1997); see generally Paul J. Pantano, Jr., "Courts Decline to Use Hindsight to Find a Future," *Futures & Derivatives Law Report,* 17(8) (November 1997); Nicholas P. Iavarone, "Understanding the Hedge-to-Arrive Controversy," 2 Drake Agricultural Law Journal 371 (Winter 1997).

8. Donald B. Pedersen, "Headge-to- Arrive Contracts in the Courts-Part II," *Agricultural Law Update* (September 1997): 4,6.

9. Working, *Economic Functions of Futures Markets, supra,* Chapter 1, note 4: 285.

10. See, e.g., Walter Dolde, "The Trajectory of Corporate Financial Risk Management," *Journal of Applied Corporate Finance,* 6(3) (Fall 1993) (using the findings of one of the earliest and most informative market surveys of derivatives users conducted to shed light on a number of important risk management issues; among other things, of the 244 Fortune 500 firms that responded to the survey, "almost 90%" said they sometimes used derivatives because "they had a 'view' on future market movements") [hereafter, *The Trajectory of Risk Management*]: 33–41.

11. The discussions of Stulz's examples are from Stulz, *Rethinking Risk Management, supra,* Chapter 10, note 8: 14–16; see also "Bank of America Roundtable on Derivatives and Corporate Risk Management," *Journal of Applied Corporate Finance,* 8(3) (Fall 1995) [hereafter, *Derivatives and Corporate Risk Management*]: 58–74.

12. Tufano, *Who Manages Risk?, supra,* Chapter 10, note 8: 1105.

13. *Derivatives and Corporate Risk Management, supra,* note 7 (statement of Robert McKnew, an executive vice president at Bank of America): 71.

14. See *supra,* Chapter 1, note 45.

15. Dolde, *The Trajectory of Risk Management, supra,* note 7: 35.

16. Don M. Chance, "[Title]," *Derivatives Quarterly,* 3(1) (Fall 1996).

17. Tufano, *Who Manages Risk?, supra,* Chapter 10, note 8; Hu, *Behind the Corporate Hedge, supra,* Chapter 10, note 9.

18. See Hu, *Asset Class Illiteracy, supra,* Chapter 16, note 4.

19. *Cf.* Tanya Styblo Beder, "VAR: Seductive but Dangerous," *Financial Analysts Journal* (September–October 1995): 12–24.>

20. This and the following quotation are from George J. Benston, "Accounting for Derivatives: Back to basics," *Journal of Applied Corporate Finance,* 10(3) (Fall 1997) [hereafter, *Back to Basics*]: 46–58, 52, 55; see also Thomas J. O'Brien, "Accounting Versus Economic Exposure to Currency Risk," *Journal of Financial Statement Analysis* (Summer 1997) [hereafter, *Accounting Versus Economic Exposure*]: 21–29.

INDEX

Accounting (*see* FASB)
Agency costs, 350–360
   external debt and, 355–360
   external equity and, 352–355
   pecking order theory and, 349–350, 360–361
American Law Institute (ALI), 250–253, 301–302
American options, 81–82
Anticipatory hedging, 2, 491
Arbitrage:
   in MM model, 262–264
   regulatory, 196–197
   in risk management, 3, 100–102, 116–117
Aronson v. Lewis, 462, 467
Availability effect, 274

Back-to-back loans, 38–39, 159–160
Bank for International Settlements (BIS), 61
Bankers Trust Company, 22, 26, 179
   Dharmala case, 206–212
   Procter & Gamble Company case, 183, 203–224
Bankruptcy (*see* Insolvency or bankruptcy)
Barings Bank, 466–467
Barrick Gold Corporation, 234–235
Beta, 306, 308–309
Bilateral netting, 136–137, 160–161
Black-Scholes option pricing model, 86, 266, 337, 371
Bond Market Association, 136–137

Brane v. Roth, 462–464, 468–471, 487–490
Brent oil market, 195
Bretton Woods monetary system, 1, 39, 40–41
Briggs v. Spaulding, 460
Broker-dealers, 434–435
Bucket shop laws, 141
Business judgment rule, 424–425, 447, 459, 462–464, 467

Call, 77–81
California Public Employees' Retirement System (Calpers), 238
Capacity issues, 133–134
Capital asset pricing model (CAPM), 298, 299, 302–309, 313–316, 317, 383, 456
Capital Market Risk Advisors (CMRA), 278–279, 280
Capital structure:
   CCA and, 266–268
   Modigliani-Miller (MM) model and, 252, 261–265, 313–326, 335–337
Caps, 88–89, 90
Carrying charge hedging, 3
Cash equivalents, 346–347
Cashflow variability, 323–325, 332–333, 347–348, 361–362, 393
CCA (*see* Contingent claims analysis)
Center for Study of Futures and Options Markets, 26

About the Author

Robert M. McLaughlin is a partner with the New York, NY, law firm of Eaton & Van Winkle, specializing in derivatives transactions and sophisticated international financings. Mr. McLaughlin a graduate of Dartmouth College, and NYU School of Law represents foreign and domestic banks and leading public companies. He has represented some of the world's largest hedge funds in a wide range of currency, interest rate, and equity derivatives transactions. Mr. McLaughlin writes frequently on the legal and financial implications of derivatives and other subjects, and his articles have appeared in journals and magazines including *The American Banker, Risk Management, Derivatives Strategy, Directorship,* and *Corporate Times.* He is frequently quoted in leading financial and legal publications.